Treasures of Love & Inspiration

Compiled by
Marjorie Barrows

Galahad Books   New York City

Published in 1985 by
Galahad Books, Inc.
149 Madison Avenue
New York, New York 10016
By arrangement with Lexicon Publications, Inc.

Library of Congress Catalog Card Number: 85-070378

ISBN: 0-88365-698-1

Printed in the United States of America

Contents

Publisher's Foreword

THE GREAT GERMAN POET, GOETHE, was once asked by a friend what he would suggest as a daily exercise for spiritual betterment. He said:

"I would like to read a noble poem.

I would like to see a beautiful picture.

I would like to hear a bit of inspiring music.

I would like to meet a great soul.

And for my fellow men I would like to say a few sensible words."

Because we recommend this wish of the great poet to you, we offer an anthology resplendent with beautiful things to enrich your daily life.

Not all of us see beauty in the same painting, in the same poem, in the same music. We each bring to any form of the fine arts our own feeling, our own past experience, our own appreciation. That is why seven editors compiled this book from seven different points of view. That is why this book should have a wider appeal than the ordinary anthology.

The basis of selection required that each piece chosen should stand by itself as a thing of beauty. Special stories, plays, poems, essays in this book will have great emotional and great inspirational appeal to some. Others will find noble ideas, sheer magic of style, exalted mood in other selections. Nearly all of these pages hold favorite, inspiring passages of significant poetry and prose; and most of us will find this book a doorway to the whole world of beauty.

Whether one opens the book at the first page or the last, for amusement or instruction, the reader will find *some* beautiful selection which will capture his fancy and provoke him to read further.

GOD'S WORLD
EDNA ST. VINCENT MILLAY

O world, I cannot hold thee close enough!
   Thy winds, thy wide gray skies!
   Thy mists, that roll and rise!
Thy woods, this autumn day, that ache and sag
And all but cry with color! That gaunt crag
To crush! To lift the lean of that black bluff!
World, world! I cannot get thee close enough!

Long have I known a glory in it all
   But never knew I this,
   Here such a passion is
As stretcheth me apart. Lord, I do fear
Thou'st made the world too beautiful this year.
My soul is all but out of me—let fall
No burning leaf; prithee, let no bird call.

1

DAYS
Karle Wilson Baker

Some days my thoughts are just cocoons—all cold, and
    dull, and blind,
They hang from dripping branches in the grey woods of my
    mind;

And other days they drift and shine—such free and flying
    things!
I find the gold-dust in my hair, left by their brushing wings.

BEAUTIFUL SUNDAY
Jake Falstaff

It was such a bright morning
That the cows, coming out of the cool dark barns
    feeling a good deal better,
Stood for a while and blinked,
And the young heifers said to each other,
"Oh my!
I never saw such a pretty day!
Let's jump over fences!
Let's go running up and down lanes with our tails in the air."
And the old sisterly Jerseys
Thought to themselves, "That patch of white clover
Over in the corner where the woodchucks are
Ought to be about ready for a good going over."

Well, you never saw anything in your life like the way
    the young ducks were acting.
They were tearing in and out of the water
Making enough noise to be heard all over the township;
Even the robins were scandalized
And sat around in the trees looking sideways and one-eyed at them.
All the crawdads in that part of the creek
Picked up and moved, and the sober old snake
Slipped off his rock and went for a walk in the briars.

The ghosts of dead spiders
Had been busy all night, and every few feet along the road
There was a rope of gossamer.
The old white horse taking two gray people to meeting

2

Held up his head and said to himself,
"Look at those ropes!
Watch me bust them!
Whammy, there goes another one!
Doggone, I'll bet there isn't another horse in 42 counties
Can run along a road pulling a buggy and busting ropes and cables."
And all of a sudden he felt so good
That he threw up his hindquarters and gave a big two-legged kick.
And the old gray woman said, "Well, I swan to gracious,"
And the old gray man got all tangled up in the lines
And nearly fell out of the buggy reaching for the whip.
"Whoa, there," he said. "Whoa, there, Roosevelt!
Hold on now! What in the Sam Hill is into you?"

About fourteen hundred Mayapple stems,
With their parasols up, marched down the hill
And all the spring beauties turned up their pale, peaked noses
And said, "Don't them Mayapples
Think they're somebody
With their bumbershoots up!"

Oh, it was a grand day, a specially grand day,
And all the flowers were so sweet
That the butterflies sneezed,
And the young goats and the lambs
Couldn't think of anything special enough
In the way of capers and didoes,
So they just stood still and looked wise.

GOOD COMPANY
Karle Wilson Baker

Today I have grown taller from walking with the trees,
　　The seven sister-poplars that go softly in a line;
And I think my heart is whiter for its parley with a star
　　That trembled out at nightfall and hung above the pine.

The call-note of a redbird from the cedars in the dusk
　　Woke his happy mate within me to an answer free and fine;
And a sudden angel beckoned from a column of blue smoke—
　　..Lord, who am I that they should stoop—these holy folk of Thine?

3

ANN RUTLEDGE
EDGAR LEE MASTERS

Out of me unworthy and unknown
The vibrations of deathless music:
"With malice toward none, with charity
    for all."
Out of me the forgiveness of millions
    toward millions,
And the beneficent face of a nation
Shining with justice and truth.

I am Ann Rutledge who sleep beneath
    these weeds,
Beloved in life of Abraham Lincoln,
Wedded to him, not through union,
But through separation.
Bloom forever, O Republic,
From the dust of my bosom!

THIS MAN LINCOLN
By T. V. SMITH

No MAN made great by death offers more hope to lowly pride than does Abraham Lincoln; for while living he was himself so simple as often to be dubbed a fool. Foolish he was, they said, in losing his youthful heart to a grave and living his life on married patience; foolish in pitting his homely ignorance against Douglas, brilliant, courtly, and urbane; foolish in setting himself to do the right in a world where the day goes mostly to the strong; foolish in dreaming of freedom for a long-suffering folk whom the North was as anxious to keep out as the South was to keep down; foolish in choosing the silent Grant to lead to victory the hesitant armies of the North; foolish, finally, in presuming that government for the people must be government of and by the people.

Foolish many said; foolish many, many believed.

This Lincoln whom so many living friends and foes alike deemed foolish, hid his bitterness in laughter; fed his sympathy on solitude; and met recurring disaster with whimsicality to muffle the murmur of a bleeding heart. Out of the tragic sense of life he pitied where others blamed; bowed his own shoulders with the woes of the weak; endured humanely his little day of chance power; and won through death what life disdains to bestow upon such simple souls —lasting peace and everlasting glory.

How prudently we proud men compete for nameless graves, while now and then some starveling of Fate forgets himself into immortality.

* * *

4

THE MASTER
[Lincoln]
EDWIN ARLINGTON ROBINSON

A flying word from here and there
Had sown the name at which we
     sneered,
But soon the name was everywhere,
To be reviled and then revered:
A presence to be loved and feared,
We cannot hide it, or deny
That we, the gentlemen who jeered,
May be forgotten by and by.

He came when days were perilous
And hearts of men were sore beguiled;
And having made his note of us,
He pondered and was reconciled.
Was ever master yet so mild
As he, and so untamable?
We doubted, even when he smiled,
Not knowing what he knew so well.

He knew that undeceiving fate
Would shame us whom he served
     unsought;
He knew that he must wince and wait—
The jest of those for whom he fought;
He knew devoutly what he thought
Of us and of our ridicule;
He knew that we must all be taught
Like little children in a school.

We gave a glamor to the task
That he encountered and saw through,
But little of us did he ask,
And little did we ever do.
And what appears if we review
The season when we railed and chaffed?
It is the face of one who knew
That we were learning while we
     laughed.

The face that in our vision feels
Again the venom that we flung,
Transfigured to the world reveals
The vigilance to which we clung.
Shrewd, hallowed, harassed,
     and among
The mysteries that are untold,
The face we see was never young
Nor could it wholly have been old.

For he, to whom we had applied
Our shopman's test of age and worth,
Was elemental when he died,
As he was ancient at his birth:
The saddest among kings of earth,
Bowed with a galling crown,
     this man
Met rancour with a cryptic mirth,
Laconic—and Olympian.

The love, the grandeur, and the fame
Are bounded by the world alone;
The calm, the smouldering, and the
     flame
Of awful patience were his own:
With him they are forever flown
Past all our fond self-shadowings,
Wherewith we cumber the Unknown
As with inept, Icarian wings.

For we were not as other men:
'Twas ours to soar and his to see;
But we are coming down again,
And we shall come down pleasantly;
Nor shall we longer disagree
On what it is to be sublime,
But flourish in our perigee
And have one Titan at a time.

* * *

When I look back on the processes of history, when I survey the genesis
of America, I see this written over every page: that the nations are renewed
from the bottom, not from the top; that the genius which springs up from
the ranks of unknown men is the genius which renews the youth and energy
of the people.
                                                                    —*Woodrow Wilson*

5

LITTLE THINGS
ORRICK JOHNS

There's nothing very beautiful and nothing very gay
About the rush of faces in the town by day;
But a light tan cow in a pale green mead,
That is very beautiful, beautiful indeed.
And the soft March wind, and the low March mist
Are better than kisses in a dark street kissed.
The fragrance of the forest when it wakes at dawn,
The fragrance of a trim green village lawn,
The hearing of the murmur of the rain at play—
These things are beautiful, beautiful as day!
And I shan't stand waiting for love or scorn
When the feast is laid for a day new-born . . .
Oh, better let the little things I loved when little
Return when the heart finds the great things brittle;
And better is a temple made of bark and thong
Than a tall stone temple that may stand too long.

From *LIFE ON THE MISSISSIPPI*
By MARK TWAIN

THE MAJESTIC bluffs that overlook the river, along through this region, charm one with the grace and variety of their forms, and the soft beauty of their adornment. The steep, verdant slope, whose base is at the water's edge, is topped by a lofty rampart of broken, turreted rocks, which are exquisitely rich and mellow in color—mainly dark browns and dull greens, but splashed with other tints. And then you have the shining river, winding here and there and yonder, its sweep interrupted at intervals by clusters of wooded islands threaded by silver channels; and you have glimpses of distant villages, asleep upon capes; and of stealthy rafts slipping along in the shade of the forest walls; and of white steamers vanishing around remote points. And it is all as tranquil and reposeful as dreamland, and has nothing this-worldly about it—nothing to hang a fret or a worry upon.

* * *

❧ IF THE DAY and the night are such that you greet them with joy, and life emits a fragrance like flowers and sweet-scented herbs, is more elastic, more starry, more immortal,—that is your success.　　　　　—*Thoreau*

❧ ONE HOUR OF LIFE, crowded to the full with glorious action, and filled with noble risks, is worth whole years of those mean observances of paltry decorum, in which men steal through existence, like sluggish waters through a marsh, without either honour or observation.　　　　　—*Sir Walter Scott*

6

BARTER

Sara Teasdale

Life has loveliness to sell,
  All beautiful and splendid things,
Blue waves whitened on a cliff,
  Soaring fire that sways and sings
'And children's faces looking up
Holding wonder like a cup.

Life has loveliness to sell,
  Music like a curve of gold,
Scent of pine trees in the rain,
  Eyes that love you, arms that hold,
'And for your spirit's still delight,
Holy thoughts that star the night.

Spend all you have for loveliness,
  Buy it and never count the cost;
For one white singing hour of peace
  Count many a year of strife well lost,
'And for a breath of ecstasy
Give all you have been, or could be.

AMERICAN HERO

By Mary West Jorgensen

Our history is studded with heroic names. These names compose a world roster from which almost every nation may choose one and say: He is ours! We produced the clan from which he sprung. See how he spells his name! That is how his family spelled their name years ago, here, in this land.

The tale of heroism runs true from Valley Forge to Gettysburg, from the Argonne to Guadalcanal. How is it possible to select one and say of him: He is the bravest of all?

Therefore, I choose one who lies in Arlington beneath the inscription: "Here rests in honored glory, an American soldier, known but to God."

Of him we know three things: he was an American, he died for freedom, he sleeps in the comfortable keeping of the Lord of Hosts.

He is a symbol of heroic qualities, of the vision of Washington, of the humanity of Lincoln, of the courage of MacArthur, of the faith of Rickenbacker, of the sacrifice of Kelly. He is, moreover, a symbol of the common man who dies daily in order that freedom may not perish from the earth.

* * *

Beauty is in the eye of the beholder.—*Old Proverb*

WAVES*
By Dorothy Easton

I LAY under the low yellow cliff, on a bank of shingle facing the sea.

It was October. All night a new unfriendly gale had rattled our windows; in the morning trees looked harassed, and leaves, speckled, as though they had the plague, whirled distractedly at street corners.

The sea had a far, wide look; brown and grey shadows lay across it from the wave's edge to the horizon.

One had seen the tide slip in and out, gently running up and down the sands all through September, but suddenly I made the discovery that the body of the sea moved. There was a thin silver flash on the far edge—a line of indigo—that rose up into a dazzle of light with each fresh wave; the whole energy of that mass of water was drawn up into a long wall that curved and brimmed and rolled over flat wastes of foam; that was pushed on irresistibly.

When it broke in thunder, my heart leaped. Happy the sun-sparkles that can play like reflections of a white furnace upon it.

I watched lather, like soap-suds, dashed on to dead-looking, sea-weed banks, that came to life in the contact, with wet brown shadows, and blowing ribbons of amber. One felt that disease must perish, if all the sick could be laid at the edge of the waves, with this salt, fresh gale in their faces.

Baby was with me, her little red cloak peaked like a hobgoblin's. With quite fearless, unspeculative eyes she looked at the water, her attention absorbed in finding "Mermaid's purses."

She felt, without thinking, that the sea had its bounds; and the angry colour, that to me was indicative of its spirit, was sand stirred up and lights from the storm clouds. The waves were "white horses," and the fact of the great sea, fresh and thundering forever, lay in her quiet child's balance as something infinitely less than herself. So she stooped with her back to it—searching for "mermaid's purses" in the sea weed.

But the wonder of waves had gone over me; the force of attraction which drew them to rise out of the level sea, and shatter themselves on stones; which caused that little after-ripple, and compelled the next wave.

The edge of the sea was black with weed, that floated on the oily swell stretching between, and was thrown up dark and heavy in the foam.

From far out one could watch the seventh wave, undulating along the top of the water; growing, rising, a line of darkness towering to a thin edge; then it sweeps the shadows before it; rolls, as though it were the depth of the sea risen up to the clouds.

One held one's breath; suddenly hollowed and curving, with yellow sunlight through its arching crest, unspeakable blackness in its trough, it topples forward, pulled by the force that had drawn it up—breaking, a foaming waterfall, thunder, wild horses plunging, and its wet reflection in the sea before it. A white waste of driven foam boiling over the black weed. Silence, but for its death-sigh effervescing into fresh life on the wind. And then the long wash back, with the rolling stones—to the sea.

* * *

❧ KNOW YOU THE LAND where the lemon-trees bloom? In the dark foliage the gold oranges glow, a soft wind hovers from the sky, the myrtle is still and the laurel stands tall—do you know it well? There, there, I would go, O my beloved, with thee!
—*Goethe*

OLD SHIPS
DAVID MORTON

There is a memory stays upon old ships,
  A weightless cargo in the musty hold,—
Of bright lagoons and prow-caressing lips,
  Of stormy midnights,—and a tale untold.
They have remembered islands in the dawn,
  And windy capes that tried their slender spars,
And tortuous channels where their keels have gone,
  And calm blue nights of stillness and the stars.
Oh, never think that ships forget a shore,
  Or bitter seas, or winds that made them wise;
There is a dream upon them, evermore;
  And there be some who say that sunk ships rise
To seek familiar harbors in the night,
  Blowing in mists, their spectral sails like light.

THE WANDERER'S SONG
JOHN MASEFIELD

A wind's in the heart of me, a fire's in my heels,
I am tired of brick and stone and rumbling wagon-wheels,
I am hungry for the sea's edge, the limits of the land,
Where the wild old Atlantic is shouting on the sand.

Oh I'll be going, leaving the noises of the street,
To where a lifting foresail-foot is yanking at the sheet;
To a windy, tossing anchorage where yawls and ketches ride,
Oh I'll be going, going, until I meet the tide.

And first I'll hear the sea-wind, the mewing of the gulls,
The clucking, sucking of the sea about the rusty hulls,
The songs at the capstan in the hooker warping out.
And then the heart of me'll know I'm there or thereabout.

Oh I am tired of brick and stone, the heart of me is sick,
For windy green, unquiet sea, the realm of Moby Dick;
And I'll be going, going, from the roaring of the wheels,
For a wind's in the heart of me, a fire's in my heels.

9

A White Heron

By Sarah Orne Jewett

*T*HE WOODS were already filled with shadows one June evening, just before eight o'clock, though a bright sunset still glimmered faintly among the trunks of the trees. A little girl was driving home her cow, a plodding, dilatory, provoking creature in her behavior, but a valued companion for all that. They were going away from the western light, and striking deep into the dark woods, but their feet were familiar with the path, and it was no matter whether their eyes could see it or not.

There was hardly a night the summer through when the old cow could be found waiting at the pasture bars; on the contrary, it was her greatest pleasure to hide herself away among the high huckleberry bushes, and though she wore a loud bell she had made the discovery that if one stood perfectly still it would not ring. So Sylvia had to hunt for her until she found her, and call Co'! Co'! with never an answering Moo, until her childish patience was quite spent. If the creature had not given good milk and plenty of it, the case would have seemed very different to her owners. Besides, Sylvia had all the time there was, and very little use to make of it. Sometimes in pleasant weather it was a consolation to look upon the cow's pranks as an intelligent attempt to play hide and seek, and as the child had no playmates she lent herself to this amusement with a good deal of zest. Though this chase had been so long that the wary animal herself had given an unusual signal of her whereabouts, Sylvia had only laughed when she came upon Mistress Moolly at the swampside, and urged her affectionately homeward with a twig of birch leaves. The old cow was not inclined to wander farther, she even turned in the right direction for once as they left the pasture, and stepped along the road at a good pace. She was quite ready to be milked now, and seldom stopped to browse. Sylvia wondered what her grandmother would say because they were so late. It was a great while since she had left home at half past five o'clock, but everybody knew the difficulty of making this errand a short one. Mrs. Tilley had chased the hornéd torment too many summer evenings herself to blame any one else for lingering, and was only thankful as she waited that she had Sylvia, nowadays, to give such valuable assistance. The good woman suspected that Sylvia loitered occasionally on her own account; there never was such a child for straying about out-of-doors since the world was made! Everybody said that it was a good change for a little maid who had tried to grow for eight years in a crowded manufacturing town, but, as for Sylvia herself, it seemed as if she never had been alive at all before she came to live at the farm. She thought often with wistful compassion of a wretched dry geranium that belonged to a town neighbor.

" 'Afraid of folks,' " old Mrs. Tilley said to herself, with a smile, after she had made the unlikely choice of Sylvia from her daughter's houseful of children, and was returning to the farm. " 'Afraid of folks,' they said! I guess she won't be troubled no great with 'em up to the old place!" When they reached the door of the lonely house and stopped to unlock it, and the cat came to purr loudly, and rub against them, a deserted pussy, indeed, but fat with young robins, Sylvia whispered that this was a beautiful place to live in, and she never should wish to go home.

The companions followed the shady wood-road, the cow taking slow steps, and the child very fast ones. The cow stopped long at the brook to drink, as if the pasture were not half a swamp, and Sylvia stood still and waited, letting her bare feet cool themselves in the shoal water, while the great twilight moths stuck softly against her. She waded on through the brook as the cow moved away, and listened to the thrushes with a heart that beat fast with pleasure. There was a stirring in the great boughs overhead. They were full of little birds and beasts that seemed to be wide-awake, and going about their world, or else saying good-night to each other in sleepy twitters. Sylvia herself felt sleepy as she walked along. However, it was not much farther to the house, and the air was soft and sweet. She was not often in the woods so late as this, and it made her feel as if she were a part of the gray shadows and the moving leaves. She was just thinking how long it seemed since she first came to the farm a year ago, and wondering if everything went on in the noisy town just the same as when she was there; the thought of the great red-faced boy who used to chase and frighten her made her hurry along the path to escape from the shadow of the trees.

Suddenly this little woods-girl is horror-stricken to hear a clear whistle not very far away. Not a bird's whistle, which would have a sort of friendliness, but a boy's whistle, determined, and somewhat aggressive. Sylvia left the cow to whatever sad fate might await her, and stepped discreetly aside into the bushes, but she was just too late. The enemy had discovered her, and called out in a very cheerful and persuasive tone, "Halloa, little girl, how far is it to the road?" and trembling Sylvia answered almost inaudibly, "A good ways."

She did not dare to look boldly at the tall young man, who carried a gun over his shoulder, but she came out of her bush and again followed the cow, while he walked alongside.

"I have been hunting for some birds," the stranger said kindly, "and I have lost my way, and need a friend very much. Don't be afraid," he added gallantly. "Speak up and tell me what your name is, and whether you think I can spend the night at your house, and go out gunning early in the morning."

Sylvia was more alarmed than before. Would not her grandmother consider her much to blame? But who could have foreseen such an accident as this? It did not appear to be her fault, and she hung her head as if the stem of it were broken, but managed to answer "Sylvy," with much effort when her companion again asked her name.

Mrs. Tilley was standing in the doorway when the trio came into view. The cow gave a loud moo by way of explanation.

"Yes, you'd better speak up for yourself, you old trial! Where'd she tucked herself away this time, Sylvy?" Sylvia kept an awed silence; she knew by instinct that her grandmother did not comprehend the gravity of the situation. She must be mistaking the stranger for one of the farmer-lads of the region.

The young man stood his gun beside the door, and dropped a heavy game-bag beside it; then he bade Mrs. Tilley good-evening, and repeated his wayfarer's story, and asked if he could have a night's lodging.

"Put me anywhere you like," he said. "I must be off early in the morning, before day; but I am very hungry, indeed. You can give me some milk at any rate, that's plain."

"Dear sakes, yes," responded the hostess, whose long slumbering hospitality seemed to be easily awakened. "You might fare better if you went out on the main road a mile or so, but you're welcome to what we've got. I'll milk right off, and you make yourself at home. You can sleep on husks or feathers," she proffered graciously. "I raised them all myself. There's good pasturing for geese just below here towards the ma'sh. Now step round and set a plate for the gentleman, Sylvy!" And Sylvia promptly stepped. She was glad to have something to do, and she was hungry herself.

It was a surprise to find so clean and comfortable a little dwelling in this New England wilderness. The young man had known the horrors of its most primitive housekeeping, and the dreary squalor of that level of society which does not rebel at the companionship of hens. This was the best thrift of an old-fashioned farmstead, though on such a small scale that it seemed like a hermitage. He listened eagerly to the old woman's quaint talk, he watched Sylvia's pale face and shining gray eyes with ever growing enthusiasm, and insisted that this was the best supper he had eaten for a month; then, afterward, the newmade friends sat down in the doorway together while the moon came up.

Soon it would be berry-time, and Sylvia was a great help at picking. The cow was a good milker, though a plaguy thing to keep track of, the hostess gossiped frankly, adding presently that she had buried four children, so that Sylvia's mother, and a son (who might be dead) in California were all the children she had left. "Dan, my boy, was a great hand to go gunning," she explained sadly. "I never wanted for pa'-tridges or gray squer'ls while he was to home. He's been a great wand'rer, I expect, and he's no hand to write letters. There, I don't blame him. I'd ha' seen the world myself if it had been so I could.

"Sylvia takes after him," the grandmother continued affectionately, after a minute's pause. "There ain't a foot o' ground she don't know her way over, and the wild creatur's counts her one o' themselves. Squer'ls she'll tame to come an' feed right out o' her hands, and all sorts o' birds. Last winter she got the jay-birds to bangeing here, and I believe she'd 'a' scanted herself of her own meals to have plenty to throw out amongst 'em, if I hadn't kep' watch. Anything but crows, I tell her, I'm willin' to help support,—though Dan he went an' tamed one o' them that did seem to have reason same as folks. It was round here a good spell after he went away. Dan an' his father they didn't hitch,—but he never held up his head ag'in after Dan had dared him an' gone off."

The guest did not notice this hint of family sorrows in his eager interest in something else.

"So Sylvy knows all about birds, does she?" he exclaimed, as he looked round at the little girl who sat, very demure but increasingly sleepy, in the moonlight. "I am making a collection of birds myself. I have been at it ever since I was a boy." (Mrs. Tilley smiled.) "There are two or three very rare ones I have been hunting for these five years. I mean to get them on my own ground if they can be found."

"Do you cage 'em up?" asked Mrs. Tilley doubtfully, in response to this enthusiastic announcement.

"Oh, no, they're stuffed and preserved, dozens and dozens of them," said the ornithologist, "and I have shot or snared every one myself. I caught a glimpse of a white heron three miles from here on Saturday, and I have followed it in this direction. They have never been found in this district at all. The little white heron, it is," and he turned again to look at Sylvia with the hope of discovering that the rare bird was one of her acquaintances.

But Sylvia was watching a hop-toad in the narrow footpath.

12

"You would know the heron if you saw it," the stranger continued eagerly. "A queer tall white bird with soft feathers and long thin legs. And it would have a nest perhaps in the top of a high tree, made of sticks, something like a hawk's nest."

Sylvia's heart gave a wild beat; she knew that strange white bird, and had once stolen softly near where it stood in some bright green swamp grass, away over at the other side of the woods. There was an open place where the sunshine always seemed strangely yellow and hot, where tall, nodding rushes grew, and her grandmother had warned her that she might sink in the soft black mud underneath and never be heard of more. Not far beyond were the salt marshes and beyond those was the sea, the sea which Sylvia wondered and dreamed about, but never had looked upon, though its great voice could often be heard above the noise of the woods on stormy nights.

"I can't think of anything I should like so much as to find that heron's nest," the handsome stranger was saying. "I would give ten dollars to anybody who could show it to me," he added desperately, "and I mean to spend my whole vacation hunting for it if need be. Perhaps it was only migrating, or had been chased out of its own region by some bird of prey."

Mrs. Tilley gave amazed attention to all this, but Sylvia still watched the toad, not divining, as she might have done at some calmer time, that the creature wished to get to its hole under the doorstep, and was much hindered by the unusual spectators at that hour of the evening. No amount of thought, that night, could decide how many wished-for treasures the ten dollars, so lightly spoken of, would buy.

The next day the young sportsman hovered about the woods, and Sylvia kept him company, having lost her first fear of the friendly lad, who proved to be most kind and sympathetic. He told her many things about the birds and what they knew and where they lived and what they did with themselves. And he gave her a jack-knife, which she thought as great a treasure as if she were a desert-islander. All day long he did not once make her troubled or afraid except when he brought down some unsuspecting singing creature from its bough. Sylvia would have liked him vastly better without his gun; she could not understand why he killed the very birds he seemed to like so much. But as the day waned, Sylvia still watched the young man with loving admiration. She had never seen anybody so charming and delightful; the woman's heart, asleep in the child, was vaguely thrilled by a dream of love. Some premonition of that great power stirred and swayed these young foresters who traversed the solemn woodlands with soft-footed silent care. They stopped to listen to a bird's song; they pressed forward again eagerly, parting the branches,—speaking to each other rarely and in whispers; the young man going first and Sylvia following, fascinated, a few steps behind, with her gray eyes dark with excitement.

She grieved because the longed-for white heron was elusive, but she did not lead the guest, she only followed, and there was no such thing as speaking first. The sound of her own unquestioned voice would have terrified her,—it was hard enough to answer yes or no when there was need of that. At last evening began to fall, and they drove the .cow home together, and Sylvia smiled with pleasure when they came to the place where she heard the whistle and was afraid only the night before.

Half a mile from home, at the farther edge of the woods, where the land was highest, a great pine-tree stood, the last of its generation. Whether it was left for a boundary mark, or for what

13

reason, no one could say; the wood-choppers who had felled its mates were dead and gone long ago, and a whole forest of sturdy trees, pines and oaks and maples, had grown again. But the stately head of this old pine towered above them all and made a landmark for sea and shore miles and miles away. Sylvia knew it well. She had always believed that whoever climbed to the top of it could see the ocean; and the little girl had often laid her hand on the great rough trunk and looked up wistfully at those dark boughs that the wind always stirred, no matter how hot and still the air might be below. Now she thought of the tree with a new excitement, for why, if one climbed it at break of day, could not one see all the world, and easily discover whence the white heron flew, and mark the place, and find the hidden nest?

What a spirit of adventure, what wild ambition! What fancied triumph and delight and glory for the later morning when she could make known the secret! It was almost too real and too great for the childish heart to bear.

All night the door of the little house stood open, and the whippoorwills came and sang upon the very step. The young sportsman and his old hostess were sound asleep, but Sylvia's great design kept her broad awake and watching. She forgot to think of sleep. The short summer night seemed as long as the winter darkness, and at last when the whippoorwills ceased, and she was afraid the morning would after all come too soon, she stole out of the house and followed the pasture path through the woods, hastening toward the open ground beyond, listening with a sense of comfort and companionship to the drowsy twitter of a half-awakened bird, whose perch she had jarred in passing. Alas, if the great wave of human interest which flooded for the first time this dull little life should sweep away the satisfactions of an existence heart to heart with nature and the dumb life of the forest!

There was the huge tree asleep yet in the paling moonlight, and small and hopeful Sylvia began with utmost bravery to mount to the top of it, with tingling, eager blood coursing the channels of her whole frame, with her bare feet and fingers, that pinched and held like bird's claws to the monstrous ladder reaching up, up, almost to the sky itself. First she must mount the white oak tree that grew alongside, where she was almost lost among the dark branches and the green leaves heavy and wet with dew; a bird fluttered off its nest, and a red squirrel ran to and fro and scolded pettishly at the harmless housebreaker. Sylvia felt her way easily. She had often climbed there, and knew that higher still one of the oak's upper branches chafed against the pine trunk, just where its lower boughs were set close together. There, when she made the dangerous pass from one tree to the other, the great enterprise would really begin.

She crept out along the swaying oak limb at last, and took the daring step across into the old pine-tree. The way was harder than she thought; she must reach far and hold fast, the sharp dry twigs caught and held her and scratched her like angry talons, the pitch made her thin little fingers clumsy and stiff as she went round and round the tree's great stem, higher and higher upward. The sparrows and robins in the woods below were beginning to wake and twitter to the dawn, yet it seemed much lighter there aloft in the pine-tree, and the child knew that she must hurry if her project were to be of any use.

The tree seemed to lengthen itself out as she went up, and reach farther and farther upward. It was like a great main-mast to the voyaging earth; it must truly have been amazed that morning through all its ponderous frame as it felt this determined spark of human

14

spirit creeping and climbing from higher branch to branch. Who knows how steadily the least twigs held themselves to advantage this light, weak creature on her way! The old pine must have loved his new dependent. More than all the hawks, and bats, and moths, and even the sweet-voiced thrushes, was the brave, beating heart of the solitary gray-eyed child. And the tree stood still and held away the winds that June morning while the dawn grew bright in the east.

Sylvia's face was like a pale star, if one had seen it from the ground, when the last thorny bough was past, and she stood trembling and tired but wholly triumphant, high in the tree-top. Yes, there was the sea with the dawning sun making a golden dazzle over it, and toward that glorious east flew two hawks with slow-moving pinions. How low they looked in the air from that height when before one had only seen them far up, and dark against the blue sky. Their gray feathers were as soft as moths; they seemed only a little way from the tree, and Sylvia felt as if she too could go flying away among the clouds. Westward, the woodlands and farms reached miles and miles into the distance; here and there were church steeples, and white villages; truly it was a vast and awesome world.

The birds sang louder and louder. At last the sun came up bewilderingly bright. Sylvia could see the white sails of ships out at sea, and the clouds that were purple and rose-colored and yellow at first began to fade away. Where was the white heron's nest in the sea of green branches, and was this wonderful sight and pageant of the world the only reward for having climbed to such a giddy height? Now look down again, Sylvia, where the green marsh is set among the shining birches and dark hemlocks; there where you saw the white heron once you will see him again; look, look! a white spot of him

like a single floating feather comes up from the dead hemlock and grows larger, and rises, and comes close at last, and goes by the landmark pine with steady sweep of wing and outstretched slender neck and crested head. And wait! wait! do not move a foot or a finger, little girl, do not send an arrow of light and consciousness from your two eager eyes, for the heron has perched on a pine bough not far beyond yours, and cries back to his mate on the nest, and plumes his feathers for the new day!

The child gives a long sigh a minute later when a company of shouting catbirds comes also to the tree, and vexed by their fluttering and lawlessness the solemn heron goes away. She knows his secret now, the wild, light, slender bird that floats and wavers, and goes back like an arrow presently to his home in the green world beneath. Then Sylvia, well satisfied, makes her perilous way down again, not daring to look far below the branch she stands on, ready to cry sometimes because her fingers ache and her lamed feet slip. Wondering over and over again what the stranger would say to her, and what he would think when she told him how to find his way straight to the heron's nest.

"Sylvy, Sylvy!" called the busy old grandmother again and again, but nobody answered, and the small husk bed was empty, and Sylvia had disappeared.

The guest waked from a dream, and remembering his day's pleasure hurried to dress himself that it might sooner begin. He was sure from the way the shy little girl looked once or twice yesterday that she had at least seen the white heron, and now she must really be persuaded to tell. Here she comes now, paler than ever, and her worn old frock is torn and tattered, and smeared with pine pitch. The grandmother and the sportsman stand in the door together and question her, and the splendid moment has come to speak of the dead hemlock-tree by the green marsh.

But Sylvia does not speak after all, though the old grandmother fretfully rebukes her, and the young man's kind appealing eyes are looking straight into her own. He can make them rich with money; he has promised it, and they are poor now. He is so well worth making happy, and he waits to hear the story she can tell.

No, she must keep silence! What is it that suddenly forbids her and makes her dumb? Has she been nine years growing, and now, when the great world for the first time puts out a hand to her, must she thrust it aside for a bird's sake? The murmur of the pine's green branches is in her ears, she remembers how the white heron came flying through the golden air and how they watched the sea and the morning together, and Sylvia cannot speak; she cannot tell the heron's secret and give its life away.

Dear loyalty, that suffered a sharp pang as the guest went away disappointed later in the day, that could have served and followed him and loved him as a dog loves! Many a night Sylvia heard the echo of his whistle haunting the pasture path as she came home with the loitering cow. She forgot even her sorrow at the sharp report of his gun and the piteous sight of thrushes and sparrows dropping silent to the ground, their songs hushed and their pretty feathers stained and wet with blood. Were the birds better friends than their hunter might have been,—who can tell? Whatever treasures were lost to her, woodlands and summer-time, remember! Bring your gifts and graces and tell your secrets to this lonely country child!

❧ ❧ ❧

FOR TRANSIENT THINGS
JAMES A. S. McPEEK

Let us thank God for unfulfilled desire,
For beauty that escapes our clutch and flies;
Let us thank God for loveliness that dies,
For violet leapings of a dying fire,
For ebbing lives and seas, the fading choir
Of quiet stars, the momentary guise
That love assumes within a lover's eyes
Before it fades with other things that tire.
Better that beauty wear into the night
An inky garment of uncandled hours
Than stay forever robed in festal white,
And so, familiar grown, like flowers
One counts as common weeds, begin to pall—
Better that beauty should not be at all.

* * *

❧ IT IS ONLY through the morning gate of the beautiful that you can penetrate into the realm of knowledge. That which we feel here as beauty we shall one day know as truth.
—Schiller

16

IN ALL RANKS OF LIFE the human heart yearns for the beautiful; and the beautiful things that God makes are his gift to all alike.

—*Harriet Beecher Stowe*

* * *

THESE I'VE LOVED
ELIZABETH-ELLEN LONG

These I've loved since I was little:
Wood to build with or to whittle,
Wind in the grass and falling rain,
First leaves along an April lane,
Yellow flowers, cloudy weather,
River-bottom smell, old leather,
Fields newly plowed, young corn in
    rows,

Back-country roads and cawing crows,
Stone walls with stiles going over,
Daisies, Queen Anne's lace, and clover,
Night tunes of crickets, frog songs, too,
Starched cotton cloth, the color blue,
Bells that ring from white church
    steeple,
Friendly dogs and friendly people.

I HOPE
MILDRED BOWERS ARMSTRONG

I hope that I shall never tire
Of watching colors in the fire.
I hope I shall not be too old
To see the lilac-stars unfold,
Or find the pear tree wearing white
When spring is summer over-night.
When I am tired of rapture,
Let me die then.
Let me never see the frost
Or a fern again.
When songs do not delight,
When waves that lip the pier,
Or driftwood fires,
Or faces,
Are no longer dear—
Let me die quickly;
Let me not know
The eyes of friends,
Candlelight, silence, or snow.

EVERY CHILD
EDNA CASLER JOLL

Every child should know a hill,
And the clean joy of running down its
    long slope
With the wind in his hair.
He should know a tree—
The comfort of its cool lap of shade,
And the supple strength of its arms
Balancing him between earth and sky
So he is the creature of both.
He should know bits of singing water—
The strange mysteries of its depths,
And the long sweet grasses that
    border it.
Every child should know some scrap
Of uninterrupted sky, to shout against;
And have one star, dependable
    and bright,
For wishing on.

* * *

SOMETIMES, looking deep into the eyes of a child, you are conscious of meeting a glance full of wisdom. The child has known nothing yet but love and beauty—all this piled-up world knowledge you have acquired is unguessed at by him. And yet you meet this wonderful look that tells you in a moment more than all the years of experience have seemed to teach.

—*Hildegarde Hawthorne*

17

YOUNG TREES
Frances M. Frost

A young tree standing
Slim and still
Is a tall green flower
On a quiet hill.

A young tree bending
Along a lane
Is a green flame blowing
In wind and rain.

A young tree growing
In any weather
By a silver barn
Is an emerald feather.

My heart grows breathless
When I pass by
A young tree reaching
Toward a golden sky,

Or stretching upward,
Brave and proud,
To toss its branches
Against a cloud.

RECIPROCITY
John Drinkwater

I do not think that skies and meadows are
Moral, or that the fixture of a star
Comes of a quiet spirit, or that trees
Have wisdom in their windless silences.
Yet these are things invested in my mood
With constancy, and peace, and fortitude;
That in my troubled season I can cry
Upon the wide composure of the sky,
And envy fields, and wish that I might be
As little daunted as a star or tree.

SWIFT THINGS ARE BEAUTIFUL
Elizabeth Coatsworth

Swift things are beautiful:
Swallows and deer,
And lightning that falls
Bright-veined and clear,
Rivers and meteors,
Wind in the wheat,
The strong-withered horse,
The runners sure feet.

And slow things are beautiful:
The closing of day,
The pause of the wave
That curves downward to spray,
The ember that crumbles,
The opening flower,
And the ox that moves on
In the quiet of power.

THE LITTLE SPRING FLOWS CLEAR AGAIN
Glenn Ward Dresbach

The little spring flows clear again
  While I stand watching close to see
What clouded it. If wings were here
  To splash the silver merrily
They flew before I came too near.

And if a fawn had rubbed its nose,
  Thrust deep in silver running cool,
Upon the bottom of the spring,
  It heard me wading in the pool
Of shadow where the thrushes sing.

The little spring flows clear again,
  But now is clouded in my mind
The flight of wings that went away—
  And something that I came to find
Was loveliness afraid to stay.

* * *

A HOUSE without a woman and firelight is like a body without soul or spirit.
                                                —*Franklin*

18

AUTUMN CHANT
EDNA ST. VINCENT MILLAY

Now the autumn shudders
  In the rose's root.
Far and wide the ladders
  Lean among the fruit.

Now the autumn clambers
  Up the trellised frame,
And the rose remembers
  The dust from which it came.

Brighter than the blossom
  On the rose's bough
Sits the wizened orange,
  Bitter berry now;

Beauty never slumbers;
  All is in her name;
But the rose remembers
  The dust from which it came.

WHITE FIELDS
JAMES STEPHENS

In the winter time we go
Walking in the fields of snow;
Where there is no grass at all;
Where the top of every wall,
Every fence, and every tree,
Is as white as white can be.

Pointing out the way we came,
—Every one of them the same—
All across the fields there be
Prints in silver filigree;
And our mothers always know,
By the footprints in the snow,
Where it is the children go.

THE LINNET
WALTER DE LA MARE

Upon this leafy bush
  With thorns and roses in it,
Flutters a thing of light,
  A twittering linnet.
And all the throbbing world
  Of dew and sun and air
By this small parcel of life
  Is made more fair;
As if each bramble-spray
And mounded gold-wreathed furze,
  Harebell and little thyme,
  Were only hers;
As if this beauty and grace
  Did to one bird belong,
And, at a flutter of wing,
  Might vanish in song.

DREAM-SONG
WALTER DE LA MARE

Sunlight, moonlight,
  Twilight, starlight—
Gloaming at the close of day,
  And an owl calling,
  Cool dews falling
In a wood of oak and may.
  Lantern-light, taper-light,
  Torchlight, no-light:
Darkness at the shut of day,
  And lions roaring,
  Their wrath pouring
In wild waste places far away.
  Elf-light, bat-light,
  Touchwood-light and toad-light,
And the sea a shimmering gloom of grey,
  And a small face smiling
  In a dream's beguiling
In a world of wonders far away.

*   *   *

⌀ ON THE BANKS of the James River, a husband erected a tombstone in memory of his wife, one of those 100 maidens who had come to Virginia in 1619 to marry the lonely settlers. The stone bore this legend: "She touched the soil of Virginia with her little foot and the wilderness became a home."

—*Eudora Ramsay Richardson*

19

TO A SKYLARK
PERCY BYSSHE SHELLEY

Hail to thee, blithe spirit!—bird thou never wert,—
That from heaven, or near it, pourest thy full heart
In profuse strains of unpremeditated art.

Higher still, and higher, from the earth thou springest
Like a cloud of fire; the blue deep thou wingest,
And singing still dost soar, and soaring, ever singest.

In the golden lightening of the sunken sun,
O'er which clouds are brightening, thou dost float and run,
Like an unbodied joy whose race is just begun.

The pale purple even melts around thy flight:
Like a star of heaven in the broad daylight,
Thou art unseen, but yet I hear thy shrill delight.

Keen as are the arrows of that silver sphere,
Whose intense lamp narrows in the white dawn clear
Until we hardly see, we feel that it is there.

All the earth and air with thy voice is loud,
As, when night is bare, from one lonely cloud
The moon rains out her beams, and heaven is overflowed.

What thou art we know not: what is most like thee?
From rainbow clouds there flow not drops so bright to see,
As from thy presence showers a rain of melody.

Like a poet hidden in the light of thought,
Singing hymns unbidden, till the world is wrought
To sympathy with hopes and fears it heeded not.

Like a high-born maiden in a palace tower,
Soothing her love-laden soul in secret hour
With music sweet as love, which overflows her bower.

Like a glow-worm golden in a dell of dew,
Scattering unbeholden its aërial hue
Among the flowers and grass, which screen it from the view.

Like a rose embowered in its own green leaves,
By warm winds deflowered, till the scent it gives
Makes faint with too much sweet these heavy-winged thieves.

Sound of vernal showers on the twinkling grass,
Rain-awakened flowers, all that ever was
Joyous, and clear, and fresh, thy music doth surpass.

Teach us, sprite or bird, what sweet thoughts are thine:
I have never heard praise of love or wine
That panted forth a flood of rapture so divine.

Chorus hymeneal, or triumphal chant,
Matched with thine would be all but an empty vaunt—
A thing wherein we feel there is some hidden want.

What objects are the fountains of thy happy strain?
What fields, or waves, or mountains? what shapes of sky or plain?
What love of thine own kind? what ignorance of pain?

With thy clear keen joyance, languor cannot be:
Shadow of annoyance never came near thee:
Thou lovest; but ne'er knew love's sad satiety.

Waking or asleep, thou of death must deem
Things more true and deep than we mortals dream,
Or how could thy notes flow in such a crystal stream?

We look before and after, and pine for what is not:
Our sincerest laughter with some pain is fraught:
Our sweetest songs are those that tell of saddest thought.

Yet if we could scorn hate, and pride, and fear;
If we were things born not to shed a tear,
I know not how thy joy we ever could come near.

Better than all measures of delight and sound,
Better than all treasures that in books are found,
Thy skill to poet were, thou scorner of the ground!

Teach me half the gladness that thy brain must know,
Such harmonious madness from my lips would flow,
The world should listen then, as I am listening now.

WHEN I HAVE FEARS
THAT I MAY CEASE TO BE
JOHN KEATS

When I have fears that I may cease to be
Before my pen has glean'd my teeming brain,
Before high piléd books, in charactery,
Hold like rich garners the full-ripened grain;
When I behold, upon the night's starred face,
Huge cloudy symbols of a high romance,
And think that I may never live to trace
Their shadows, with the magic hand of chance;
And when I feel, fair creature of an hour!
That I shall never look upon thee more,
Never have relish in the faery power
Of unreflecting love!—then on the shore
Of the wide world I stand alone, and think
Till Love and Fame to nothingness do sink.

HIGH FLIGHT
JOHN GILLESPIE MAGEE, JR.

Oh, I have slipped the surly bonds of earth,
And danced the skies on laughter-silvered wings;
Sunward I've climbed and joined the tumbling mirth
Of sun-split clouds—and done a hundred things
You have not dreamed of—wheeled and soared and swung
High in the sunlit silence. Hovering there,
I've chased the shouting wind along and flung
My eager craft through footless halls of air.
Up, up the long delirious, burning blue
I've topped the wind-swept heights with easy grace,
Where never lark, or even eagle, flew;
And, while with silent, lifting mind I've trod
The high untrespassed sanctity of space,
Put out my hand, and touched the face of God.

* * *

❦ THOUGH MY SOUL may set in darkness, it will rise in perfect light; I have
loved the stars too fondly to be fearful of the night.
                                        —*An Old Astronomer To His Pupil*

SO LONG!

By Howard Vincent O'Brien

This famous writer speaks here for all fathers whose sons go off to war.

THERE was no band, no flags, no ceremonial. It wasn't even dramatic. A car honked outside and he said: "Well, I guess that's for me." He picked up his little bag, and his mother said: "You haven't forgotten your gloves?"

He kissed his mother and held out his hand to me. "Well, so long," he said. I took his hand but all I could say was "Good luck."

The door slammed and that was that —another boy gone to war.

I had advised waiting for the draft— waiting at least until he was required to register. I had pointed out that he was not yet of age. He had smiled at that, and assured me that his mind was made up. He wanted peace, he said. Without peace, what good was living?

There was finality in the way he said this—a finality at once grim and gentle. I said no more about waiting.

After the door closed behind him I went upstairs. I went to what had been his room. It was in worse chaos than usual. His bureau was littered—an incredible collection of things, letters, keys, invitations to parties he would not attend.

Clothing was scattered about—dancing pumps, a tennis racket, his precious collection of phonograph records, his trumpet, gleaming in its case.

I went then to my room. On the wall was a picture of a little boy, his toothless grin framed in tawny curls—the same boy who had just taken my hand and said: "Well, so long."

Not much time, I thought, between the making of that picture and the slamming of the front door. Not much more than a decade.

Suddenly, a queer thing happened. Objects came alive—whispered to me. The house was full of soft voices. They led me up to the attic—to a box of toy soldiers, a broken music rack, a football helmet, a homemade guitar, school books, class pictures, a stamp album, a penny bank with the lid pried off . . . ancient history, long hidden under dust.

The voices led me on to a filing case and a folder stuffed with papers—report cards, letters—among them the wail of an exasperated teacher: "Though he looks like an angel. . ."—telegrams, passports, a baptismal certificate, a ribbon won in a track meet, faded photographs —one taken on the memorable first day of long pants—a bit of golden hair.

I sat down and thought how time had flown. Why, it was only yesterday when I had held him in my arms! That, somehow, made me remember all the scoldings I had given him, the preachments, the exhortation to a virtue and wisdom I did not myself possess. . . .

I thought, too, of that last inarticulate "good luck," that last perfunctory handclasp; and I wished that I had somehow been able to tell him how much I really loved him. Had he perhaps penetrated my brusque reserve? Had he perhaps guessed what was in my heart?

And then I thought: what fools we are with our children—always plotting what we shall make of them, always planning for a future that never comes, always intent on what they may be, never accepting what they are.

Well, curly-head—you're a man now, bearing your bright new shield and spear. I hated to see you go out of my house and close the door behind you; but I think I would not have halted you if I could. I salute you, sir. I cannot pretend that I am not sad; but I am proud, too. So long.

LETTER TO SAINT PETER
ELMA DEAN

Let them in, Peter, they are very tired;
Give them the couches where the angels sleep.
Let them wake whole again to new dawns fired
With sun, not war. And may their peace be deep.
Remember where the broken bodies lie. . .
And give them things they like. Let them have noise.
God knows how young they were to have to die!
Give swing bands, not gold harps, to these our boys.
Let them love, Peter—they have had no time—
Girls sweet as meadow wind, with flowering hair. . .
They should have trees and bird song, hills to climb—
The taste of summer in a ripened pear.
Tell them how they are missed. Say not to fear;
It's going to be all right with us down here.

VICTORY
OWEN SEAMAN

Ye that have faith to look with fearless eyes
   Beyond the tragedy of a world at strife,
And know that out of death and night shall rise
   The dawn of ampler life:
Rejoice, whatever anguish rend the heart,
   That God has given you the priceless dower
To live in these great times and have your part
   In Freedom's crowning hour,
That ye may tell your sons who see the light
   High in the heavens—their heritage to take—
"I saw the powers of darkness take their flight;
   I saw the morning break."

* * *

❧ LET OUR OBJECT be our country, our whole country, and nothing but our country. And, by the blessing of God, may that country itself become a vast and splendid monument, not of oppression and terror, but of wisdom, of peace and of liberty, upon which the world may gaze with admiration forever.   —*Webster*

❧ HAPPY HE who dares courageously to defend what he loves.—*Ovid*

FOR THE FALLEN

LAURENCE BINYON

With proud thanksgiving, a mother for her children,
England mourns for her dead across the sea.
Flesh of her flesh they were, spirit of her spirit,
  Fallen in the cause of the free.

Solemn the drums thrill: Death august and royal
Sings sorrow up into immortal spheres.
There is music in the midst of desolation
  And a glory that shines upon our tears.

They went with songs to the battle, they were young,
Straight of limb, true of eye, steady and aglow.
They were stanch to the end against odds uncounted,
  They fell with their faces to the foe.

They shall grow not old, as we that are left grow old:
Age shall not weary them, nor the years contemn.
At the going down of the sun and in the morning
  We will remember them.

They mingle not with their laughing comrades again;
They sit no more at familiar tables of home;
They have no lot in our labor of the daytime;
  They sleep beyond England's foam.

But where our desires are and our hopes profound,
Felt as a well-spring that is hidden from sight,
To the innermost heart of their own land they are known
  As the stars are known to the Night;

As the stars that shall be bright when we are dust,
Moving in marches upon the heavenly plain;
As the stars that are starry in the time of our darkness,
  To the end, to the end, they remain.

* * *

❧ HEROISM is the brilliant triumph of the soul over the flesh, that is to say over fear: fear of poverty, of suffering, of calumny, of illness, of loneliness and of death. There is no real piety without heroism. It is the glorious concentration of courage.   —*Amiel*

INVENTORY AT DAWN

Eleanor Saltzman

I have gathered violets in April
And watched the silent falling of a star.
The wind has touched my hair, and I have laid
My ear against the earth to hear the grasses
Whisper. I have shocked the new-bound oats
In summer and walked bareheaded in the rain,
Thrilling with the thunder. I have baked
A ham and sat with friends at supper. We talked
Of ghosts and Bach and vegetables, and filled
Our coffee cups again. I have kissed
My heart goodby at nightfall, and I have loved,
But deeply.

And still to sit in the sun, to know
The breadth of tenderness deep as the earth.
And bread. And sleep. And waking after pain,
To eat my breakfast at Walden. To feel the hush
Of snow against my lips. And still to love,
But deeply.

BEAUTY

By A. C. Benson

I WAS VISITED, as I sat in my room today, by one of those sudden impressions of rare beauty that come and go like flashes, and which leave one desiring a similar experience. The materials of the impression were simple and familiar enough. My room looks out into a little court; there is a plot of grass, and to the right of it an old stone-built wall, close against which stands a row of aged lime-trees. Straight opposite, at right angles to the wall, is the east side of the Hall, with its big plain traceried window enlivened with a few heraldic shields of stained glass. While I was looking out today there came a flying burst of sun, and the little corner became a sudden feast of delicate colour; the rich green of the grass, the foliage of the lime-trees, their brown wrinkled stems, the pale moss on the walls, the bright points of colour in the emblazonries of the window, made a sudden delicate harmony of tints. I had seen the place a hundred times before without ever guessing what a perfect picture it made.

What a strange power the perception of beauty is! It seems to ebb and flow like some secret tide, independent alike of health or disease, of joy or sorrow. There are times in our lives when we seem to go singing on our way, and when the beauty of the world sets itself like a quiet harmony to the song we uplift.

—From *From A College Window*

26

L'ENVOI
RUDYARD KIPLING

When Earth's last picture is painted, and the tubes are twisted and dried,
When the oldest colors have faded, and the youngest critic has died,
We shall rest, and, faith, we shall need it—lie down for an eon or two,
Till the Master of All Good Workmen shall set us to work anew!

And those that were good shall be happy: they shall sit in a golden chair;
They shall splash at a ten-league canvas with brushes of comet's hair;
They shall find real saints to draw from—Magdalene, Peter, and Paul;
They shall work for an age at a sitting and never be tired at all!

And only the Master shall praise us, and only the Master shall blame;
And no one shall work for money, and no one shall work for fame;
But each for the joy of the working, and each, in his separate star
Shall draw the Thing as he sees It for the God of Things as They are!

LAUGH AND BE MERRY
JOHN MASEFIELD

Laugh and be merry, remember, better the world with a song,
Better the world with a blow in the teeth of a wrong.
Laugh, for the time is brief, a thread the length of a span.
Laugh and be proud to belong to the old proud pageant of man.

Laugh and be merry: remembering, in older time,
God made Heaven and Earth for joy He took in a rhyme,
Made them, and filled them full with the strong red wine of His mirth,
The splendid joy of the stars: the joy of the earth.

So we must laugh and drink from the deep blue cup of the sky,
Join the jubilant song of the great stars sweeping by,
Laugh, and battle, and work, and drink of the wine outpoured
In the dear green earth, the sign of the joy of the Lord.

Laugh and be merry together, like brothers akin,
Guesting awhile in the rooms of a beautiful inn,
Glad till the dancing stops, and the lilt of the music ends.
Laugh till the game is played; and be you merry, my friends.

27

From *WIND, SAND AND STARS*

By Antoine de Saint Exupery

THE FACE OF THE SEA is as variable as that of the earth. To passengers, the storm is invisible. Seen from a great height, the waves have no relief and the packets of fog have no movement. The surface of the sea appears to be covered with great white motionless palm-trees, palms marked with ribs and seams stiff in a sort of frost. The sea is like a splintered mirror. But the hydroplane pilot knows there is no landing here.

The hours during which a man flies over this mirror are hours in which there is no assurance of the possession of anything in the world. These palms beneath the plane are so many poisoned flowers. And even when the flight is an easy one, made under a shining sun, the pilot navigating at some point on the line is not gazing upon a scene. These colors of earth and sky, these traces of wind over the face of the sea, these clouds golden in the afterglow, are not objects of the pilot's admiration, but of his cogitation. He looks to them to tell him the direction of the wind or the progress of the storm, and the quality of the night to come.

Even as the peasant strolling about his domain is able to foresee in a thousand signs the coming of the spring, the threat of frost, a promise of rain, so all that happens in the sky signals to the pilot the oncoming snow, the expectancy of fog, or the peace of a blessed night. The machine which at first blush seems a means of isolating man from the great problems of nature, actually plunges him more deeply into them. As for the peasant so for the pilot, dawn and twilight become events of consequence. His essential problems are set him by the mountain, the sea, the wind. Alone before the vast tribunal of the tempestuous sky, the pilot defends his mails and debates on terms of equality with those three elemental divinities.

The mail pouches for which he is responsible are stowed away in the after hold. They constitute the dogma of the religion of his craft, the torch which, in this aerial race, is passed from runner to runner. What matter though they hold but the scribblings of tradesmen and nondescript lovers? The interests which dictated them may very well not be worth the embrace of man and storm; but I know what they become once they have been entrusted to the crew, taken over, as the phrase is. The crew care not a rap for banker or tradesman. If, some day, the crew are hooked by a cliff it will not have been in the interest of tradespeople that they will have died, but in obedience to orders which ennoble the sacks of mail once they are on board ship.

What concerns us is not even the orders—it is the men they cast in their mould.

* * *

❧ IT IS A GLORIOUS privilege to live, to know, to act, to listen, to behold, to love. To look up at the blue summer sky; to see the sun sink slowly beyond the line of the horizon; to watch the worlds come twinkling into view, first one by one, and the myriads that no man can count, and lo! the universe is white with them; and you and I are here. —*Marco Morrow*

❧ SO LONG AS we love, we serve. So long as we are loved by others I would almost say we are indispensable; and no man is useless while he has a friend.
—*Stevenson*

A TROPICAL MORNING AT SEA
EDWARD ROWLAND SILL

Sky in its lucent splendor lifted
  Higher than cloud can be;
Air with no breath of earth to stain it,
  Pure on the perfect sea.

Crests that touch and tilt each other,
  Jostling as they comb;
Delicate crash of tinkling water,
  Broken in pearling foam.

Plashings—or is it the pinewood's
    whispers,
  Babble of brooks unseen,
Laughter of winds when they find the
    blossoms,
  Brushing aside the green?

Waves that dip, and dash, and sparkle;
  Foam-wreaths slipping by,
Soft as a snow of broken roses
  Afloat over mirrored sky.

Off to the East the steady sun-track
  Golden meshes fill—
Webs of fire, that lace and tangle,
  Never a moment still.

Liquid palms that clap together,
  Fountains, flower-like, grow—
Limpid bells on stems of silver—
  Out of a slope of snow.

Sea-depths, blue as the blue of violets—
  Blue as a summer sky,
When you blink at its arch sprung over
  Where in the grass you lie.

Dimly an orange bit of rainbow
  Burns where the low west clears,
Broken in air, like a passionate promise
  Born of a moment's tears.

Thinned to amber, rimmed with silver,
  Clouds in the distance dwell,
Clouds that are cool, for all their color,
  Pure as a rose-lipped shell.

Fleets of wool in the upper heavens
  Gossamer wings unfurl;
Sailing so high they seem but sleeping
  Over yon bar of pearl.

What would the great world lose, I
    wonder—
  Would it be missed or no—
If we stayed in the opal morning,
  Floating forever so?

Swung to sleep by the swaying water,
  Only to dream all day—
Blow, salt wind from the north up-
    starting,
  Scatter such dreams away!

TWILIGHT AT SEA
AMELIA B. WELBY

The twilight hours, like birds, flew by,
  As lightly and as free,
Ten thousand stars were in the sky,
  Ten thousand on the sea;

For every wave, with dimpled face,
  That leaped upon the air,
Had caught a star in its embrace
  And held it trembling there.

* * *

❦ THE SEA never tells what it means to do. There is everything in this abyss, even chicanery. One might almost say that the sea had designs; it advances and retreats, it proposes and retracts, it prepares a squall and then gives up its plan, it promises destruction and does not keep its word.

—*Hugo*

29

AMERICAN LANDSCAPE
By THOMAS WOLFE

AMERICA has a thousand lights and weathers and we walk the streets, we walk the streets forever, we walk the streets of life alone.

It is the place of the howling winds, the hurrying of the leaves in old October, the hard clean falling to the earth of acorns. The place of the storm-tossed moaning of the wintry mountainside, where the young men cry out in their throats and feel the savage vigor, the rude strong energies; the place also where the trains cross rivers.

It is a fabulous country, the only fabulous country; it is the one place where miracles not only happen, but where they happen all the time.

It is the place of exultancy and strong joy, the place of the darkened brooding air, the smell of snow; it is the place of all the fierce, the bitten colors in October, when all of the wild, sweet woods flame up; it is also the place of the cider press and the last brown oozings of the York Imperials. . . .

It is the place where great boats are baying at the harbor's mouth, where great ships are putting out to sea; it is the place where great boats are blowing in the gulf of night, and where the river, the dark and secret river, full of strange time, is forever flowing by us to the sea. . . .

It is the place of autumnal moons hung low and orange at the frosty edges of the pines; it is the place of frost and silence; of the clean dry shocks and the opulence of enormous pumpkins that yellow on hard clotted earth; it is the place of the stir and feathery stumble of the hens upon their roost, the frosty, broken barking of the dogs, the great barn-shapes and solid shadows in the running sweep of the moon-whited countryside, the wailing whistle of the fast express. It is the place of flares and steamings on the tracks, and the swing and bob and tottering dance of lanterns in the yards; it is the place of dings and knellings and the sudden glare of mighty engines over sleeping faces in the night; it is the place of the terrific web and spread and smouldering, the distant glare of Philadelphia and the solid rumble of the sleepers; it is also the place where the Transcontinental Limited is stroking eighty miles an hour across the continent and the small dark towns whip by like bullets, and there is only the fanlike stroke of the secret, immense and lonely earth again. . . .

It is the place of the wild and exultant winter's morning and the wind, with the powdery snow, that has been howling all night long; it is the place of solitude and the branches of the spruce and hemlock piled with snow; it is the place where the Fall River boats are tethered to the wharf, and the wild gray snow of furious, secret, and storm-whited morning whips across them. It is the place of the lodge by the frozen lake and the sweet breath and amorous flesh of sinful woman; it is the place of the tragic and lonely beauty of New England; it is the place of the red barn and the sound of the stabled hooves and of bright tatters of old circus posters; it is the place of the immense and pungent smell of breakfast, the country sausages and the ham and eggs, the smoking wheat cakes and the fragrant coffee, and of lonely hunters in the frosty thickets who whistle to their lop-eared hounds. . . .

It is the place of the crack athletes and of the runners who limber up in March; it is the place of the ten-second men and the great jumpers and vaulters; it is the place where spring comes, and the young birch trees have white and tender barks, of the thaw of the earth, and the feathery smoke of the trees; it is the place of the burst of grass and bud, the wild and sudden tenderness of the wilderness, and of the crews out on the river and the coaches coming down behind them in the motor-boats, the surges rolling out behind when they are gone with heavy sudden wash. . . .

It is the place where they like to win always, and boast about their victories; it is the place of quick money and sudden loss; it is the place of the mile-long freights with their strong, solid, clanking, heavy loneliness at night, and of the silent freight of cars that curve away among raw piney desolations with their promise of new lands and unknown distances—the huge attentive gape of emptiness. It is the place where the bums come singly from the woods at sunset, the huge stillness of the water-tower, the fading light, the rails, secret and alive, and trembling with the oncoming train; it is the place of the great tramps, Oklahoma Red, Fargo Pete, and the Jersey Dutchman, who grab fast rattlers for the Western shore; it is the place of old blown bums who come up in October skirls of dust and wind and crumpled newspapers and beg, with canned heat on their breaths: "Help Old McGuire: McGuire's a good guy, kid. You're not so tough, kid: McGuire's your pal, kid: How about McGuire, McGuire—?"

. . .It is the place of the immense and lonely earth, the place of fat ears and abundance where they grow cotton, corn, and wheat, the wine-red apples of October, and the good tobacco. . . .

It is the place where you come up through Virginia on the great trains in the night-time, and rumble slowly across the wide Potomac and see the morning sunlight on the nation's dome at Washington, and where the fat man shaving in the Pullman washroom grunts, "What's this? What's this we're coming to—Washington?"—And the thin man glancing out the window says, "Yep, this is Washington. That's what it is, all right. You gettin' off here?"—And where the fat man grunts, "Who—me? Naw—I'm goin' on to Baltimore." It is the place where you get off at Baltimore and find your brother waiting. . . .

It is the place of the fast approach, the hot blind smoky passage, the tragic lonely beauty of New England, and the web of Boston; the place of the mighty station there, and engines passive as great cats, the straight dense plumes of engine smoke, the acrid and exciting smell of trains and stations, and of the man-swarm passing ever in its million-footed weft, the smell of the sea in harbors and the thought of voyages—and the place of the goat-cry, the strong joy of our youth, the magic city, when we knew the most fortunate life on earth would certainly be ours, that we were twenty and could never die.

And always America is the place of the deathless and enraptured moments, the eye that looked, the mouth that smiled and vanished, and the word; the stone, the leaf, the door we never found and never have forgotten. And these are the things that we remember of America, for we have known all her thousand lights and weathers, and we walk the streets, we walk the streets forever, we walk the streets of life alone.

* * *

⌘ I WISH MY COUNTRYMEN to consider, that whatever the human law may be, neither an individual nor a nation can ever commit the least act of injustice against the obscurest individual without having to pay the penalty for it. A government which deliberately enacts injustice, and persists in it, will at length even become the laughingstock of the world.   —*Thoreau*

⌘ THOUGH WE TRAVEL the world over to find the beautiful, we must carry it with us or we find it not.   —*Emerson*

No LEGACY is so rich as honesty.—*Shakespeare*

You HAVE greatly ventured, but all must do so, who
would greatly win.—*Byron*

A TASK without a vision is drudgery; a vision without a task is a
dream; a task with a vision is victory.—*Anonymous*

A TEACHER who can arouse a feeling for one single good action, for one single
good poem, accomplishes more than he who fills our memory with rows on
rows of natural objects, classified with name and form.—*Goethe*

BOOKS, like friends, should be few and well chosen.—*Samuel Paterson*

ABOVE ALL, let us never forget that an act of goodness is in itself an act of
happiness. It is the flower of a long inner life of joy and contentment; it
tells of peaceful hours and days on the sunniest heights of our soul.
—*Maeterlinck*

A good book is the best of friends, the same today and forever.—*Tupper*

WE WILL BE HAPPY if we can get around to the idea that art is not an outside
and extra thing; that it is a natural outcome of a state of being; that the state
of being is the important thing; that a man can be a carpenter and be a great
man.—*Robert Henri*

IT IS AS impossible for a man to be cheated by any one but himself, as for a
thing to be, and not to be, at the same time.—*Emerson*

GIVE ME the making of the songs of a nation, and I care not who
makes its laws.—*Andrew Fletcher of Saltoun*

I DISAPPROVE of what you say, but I will defend to the death
your right to say it.—*Voltaire*

LOVE is friendship set to music.—*Pollock*

FRIENDS . . . AND LIFE

HELP THYSELF, and God will help thee.—*La Fontaine*

WHAT I GAVE, I have; what I spent, I had; what
I kept, I lost.—*An Old Epitaph*

WE ARE ALL travellers in the wilderness of this world, and the
best that we find in our travels is an honest friend.—*Stevenson*

NOTHING CAN SUPPLY the place of books. They are cheering or soothing companions in solitude, illness, affliction. The wealth of both continents would
not compensate for the good they impart.—*Channing*

A PLEASANT POSSESSION is useless without a friend.—*Seneca*

WHAT IS TIME?—the shadow on the dial,—the striking of the clock,—the running of the sand,—day and night,—summer and winter,—months, years, centuries? These are but arbitrary and outward signs,—the measure of time, not
time itself. Time is the life of the soul. If not this,—then tell me, what is
time?—*Anonymous*

IN SMALL PROPORTIONS we just beauties see; and in short measures life may
perfect be.—*Jonson*

IT IS CHIEFLY through books that we enjoy intercourse with superior minds,
and these invaluable means of communication are in the reach of all. In the
best books, great men talk to us, give us their most precious thoughts, and
pour their souls into ours.—*Channing*

THE GREATER the obstacle the more glory in overcoming it.—*Molière*

EVERYTHING has been thought of before, but the difficulty is to think
of it again.—*Goethe*

CHILDREN need models more than they need critics.—*Joseph Joubert*

TRUE FRIENDS have no solitary joy or sorrow.—*Channing*

SUMMUM BONUM
ROBERT BROWNING

All the breath and the bloom of the year in the bag of one bee:
  All the wonder and wealth of the mine in the heart of one gem:
In the core of one pearl all the shade and the shine of the sea:
  Breath and bloom, shade and shine,—wonder, wealth, and—how
    far above them—
        Truth, that's brighter than gem,
        Trust, that's purer than pearl,—
  Brightest truth, purest trust in the universe—all were for me
    In the kiss of one girl.

THE GARDEN
NOEL LANE

My heart was once a garden
  By dim, enchanted trees,
With hint of untouched violets
  And shy anemones.

I showed my love the garden
  Where April dreams I'd hide,
But heedlessly he lost the key
  And now—we're both inside!

SONG
RICHARD WATSON GILDER

Not from the whole wide world I chose
    thee,
  Sweetheart, light of the land and the
    sea!
The wide, wide world could not inclose
    thee,
  For thou art the whole wide world
    to me.

ONE GIRL
DANTE GABRIEL ROSSETTI

Like the sweet apple which reddens upon the topmost bough,
A-top on the topmost twig,—which the pluckers forgot, somehow,—
Forgot it not, nay, but got it not, for none could get it till now.

Like the wild hyacinth flower which on the hills is found,
Which the passing feet of the shepherds forever tear and wound,
Until the purple blossom is trodden into the ground.

[A Combination from *Sappho*]

* * *

FOR LOVE and beauty and delight, there is no death nor change.—*Shelley*

ABSENCE is to love what wind is to fire; it extinguishes the small, it
enkindles the great.   —*Comte de Bussy-Rabutin*

34

DOWN IN A GARDEN SAT MY DEAREST LOVE
HERBERT HORNE

Down in a garden sat my dearest love;
   Gay saffron flowers grew all around her;
The bluest sky shone in the heavens above:
   Nay! had, but thus, the bright-limbed Cynthius found her,
He would have loved her, so that she had been
His Daphne, and his laurels green.

DOWN BY THE SALLEY GARDENS
WILLIAM BUTLER YEATS

Down by the salley gardens my love and I did meet;
She passed the salley gardens with little snow-white feet.
She bid me take love easy, as the leaves grow on the tree;
But I, being young and foolish, with her would not agree.

In a field by the river my love and I did stand,
And on my leaning shoulder she laid her snow-white hand.
She bid me take life easy, as the grass grows on the weirs;
But I was young and foolish, and now am full of tears.

ON AN OLD SUN DIAL

Time flies,
Suns rise
And shadows fall.
Let time go by.
Love is forever over all.

A KISS
EDMOND ROSTAND

And what is a kiss, when all is done?
A promise given under seal—a vow
A signature acknowledged—a rosy dot
Over the i of Loving—a secret whispered
To listening lips apart—a moment made
Immortal, with a rush of wings unseen—
A sacrament of blossoms, a new song
Sung by two hearts to an old simple tune—
The ring of one horizon around two souls
Together, all alone!

—From *Cyrano de Bergerac*

ROXANNE
EDMOND ROSTAND

Mortally without meaning; exquisite
Without imagining. Nature's own snare
To allure manhood. A white rose wherein
Love lies in ambush for his natural prey.
Who knows her smile has known a perfect thing.
She creates grace in her own image, brings
Heaven to earth in one movement of her hand—
Nor thou, O Venus! balancing thy shell
Over the Mediterranean blue, nor thou,
Diana! marching through broad, blossoming woods,
Art so divine as when she mounts her chair,
And goes abroad through Paris!

—From *Cyrano de Bergerac*

THE HIGHWAYMAN*
ALFRED NOYES
I

The wind was a torrent of darkness among the gusty trees,
The moon was a ghostly galleon tossed upon cloudy seas,
The road was a ribbon of moonlight over the purple moor,
And the highwayman came riding,
Riding, riding,
The highwayman came riding, up to the old inn-door.

He'd a French cocked-hat on his forehead, a bunch of lace at his chin,
A coat of the claret velvet, and breeches of brown doe-skin;
They fitted with never a wrinkle; his boots were up to the thigh!
And he rode with a jeweled twinkle,
His pistol butts a-twinkle,
His rapier hilt a-twinkle, under the jeweled sky.

Over the cobbles he clattered and clashed in the dark inn-yard,
And he tapped with his whip on the shutters, but all was locked and
barred;
He whistled a tune to the window, and who should be waiting there
But the landlord's black-eyed daughter,
Bess, the landlord's daughter,
Plaiting a dark red love-knot into her long black hair.

And dark in the dark old inn-yard a stable-wicket creaked
Where Tim the ostler listened; his face was white and peaked;
His eyes were hollows of madness, his hair like mouldy hay,
But he loved the landlord's daughter,
The landlord's red-lipped daughter
Dumb as a dog he listened, and he heard the robber say:

"One kiss, my bonny sweetheart, I'm after a prize tonight,
But I shall be back with the yellow gold before the morning light;
Yet, if they press me sharply, and harry me through the day,
Then look for me by moonlight,
Watch for me by moonlight,
I'll come to thee by moonlight, though hell should bar the way."

He rose upright in the stirrups; he scarce could reach her hand,
But she loosened her hair i' the casement! His face burnt like a brand
As the black cascade of perfume came tumbling over his breast;

And he kissed its waves in the moonlight,
  (Oh, sweet black waves in the moonlight!).
Then he tugged at his rein in the moonlight, and galloped away
  to the West.

II

He did not come in the dawning: he did not come at noon;
And out o' the tawny sunset, before the rise o' the moon,
When the road was a gypsy's ribbon, looping the purple moor,
  A red-coat troop came marching,
  Marching, marching,
King George's men came marching, up to the old inn-door.

They said no word to the landlord, they drank his ale instead,
But they gagged his daughter and bound her to the foot of her
  narrow bed;
Two of them knelt at her casement, with muskets at their side!
  There was death at every window;
  And hell at one dark window;
For Bess could see, through her casement, the road that *he* would ride.

They had tied her up to attention, with many a sniggering jest;
They had bound a musket beside her, with the barrel beneath her breast!
"Now keep good watch!" and they kissed her.
She heard the dead man say—
  Look for me by moonlight;
  Watch for me by moonlight;
I'll come to thee by moonlight, though hell should bar the way!

She twisted her hands behind her; but all the knots held good!
She writhed her hands till her fingers were wet with sweat or blood!
They stretched and strained in the darkness, and the hours
  crawled by like years,
  Till, now, on the stroke of midnight,
  Cold, on the stroke of midnight,
The tip of one finger touched it! The trigger at least was hers!

The tip of one finger touched it; she strove no more for the rest!
Up, she stood up to attention, with the barrel beneath her breast.
She would not risk their hearing! she would not strive again;
  For the road lay bare in the moonlight,
  Blank and bare in the moonlight;

And the blood of her veins in the moonlight throbbed to her
    love's refrain.

Tlot-tlot, tlot-tlot! Had they heard it? The horse-hoofs ringing clear;
Tlot-tlot, tlot,-tlot, in the distance? Were they deaf that they did not hear?
Down the ribbon of moonlight, over the brow of the hill,
        The highwayman came riding,
        Riding, riding!
The red-coats looked to their priming! She stood up, straight and still!

Tlot-tlot, in the frosty silence! *Tlot-tlot,* in the echoing night!
Nearer he came and nearer! Her face was like a light!
Her eyes grew wide for a moment! she drew one last deep breath,
        Then her finger moved in the moonlight,
        Her musket shattered the moonlight,
Shattered her breast in the moonlight and warned him—with her death.

He turned; he spurred to the West; he did not know she stood
Bowed, with her head o'er the musket, drenched with her own red blood!
Not till the dawn he heard it; his face grew grey to hear
        How Bess, the landlord's daughter,
        The landlord's black-eyed daughter,
Had watched for her love in the moonlight, and died in the
    darkness there.

Back, he spurred like a madman, shrieking a curse to the sky,
With the white road smoking behind him and his rapier brandished
    high!
Blood-red were his spurs i' the golden noon; wine-red was
    his velvet coat,
        When they shot him down on the highway,
        Down like a dog on the highway,
And he lay in his blood on the highway, with the bunch of
    lace at his throat.

And still of a winter's night, they say, when the wind is in the trees,
When the moon is a ghostly galleon tossed upon cloudy seas,
When the road is a ribbon of moonlight over the purple moor,
        A highwayman comes riding,
        Riding, riding,
A highwayman comes riding, up to the old inn-door.

Over the cobbles he clatters and clangs in the dark inn-yard;
He taps with his whip on the shutters, but all is locked and barred;
He whistles a tune to the window, and who should be waiting there
　　But the landlord's black-eyed daughter,
　　Bess, the landlord's daughter,
Plaiting a dark red love-knot into her long black hair.

EPILOGUE TO ASOLANDO
ROBERT BROWNING

At the midnight in the silence of the sleep-time,
　When you set your fancies free,
Will they pass to where—by death, fools think, imprisoned—
Low he lies who once so loved you, whom you loved so,
　　—Pity me?

Oh to love so, be so loved, yet so mistaken!
　What had I on earth to do
With the slothful, with the mawkish, the unmanly?
Like the aimless, helpless, hopeless, did I drivel
　　—Being—who?

One who never turned his back but marched breast forward,
　Never doubted clouds would break,
Never dreamed, though right were worsted, wrong would triumph,
Held we fall to rise, are baffled to fight better,
　　Sleep to wake.

No, at noonday in the bustle of man's work-time
　Greet the unseen with a cheer!
Bid him forward, breast and back as either should be,
"Strive and thrive!" cry "Speed,—fight on, fare ever
　　There as here!"

* * *

❧ BUT THIS MYSTERIOUS universe, through which, half veiled in its own shadow, our dim little planet is wheeling, with its star worlds and thought-wearying spaces, remains.　　　　　　　　　　　　　　*—Whittier*

❧ GO CONFIDENTLY in the direction of your dreams! Live the life you've imagined! As you simplify your life, the laws of the universe will be simpler, solitude will not be solitude, poverty will not be poverty, nor weakness weakness.　　　　　　　　　　　　　　　　　　　*—Thoreau*

39

The Master of the Inn

By ROBERT HERRICK

*I*T WAS A PLAIN BRICK HOUSE, three full stories, with four broad chimneys, and overhanging eaves. The tradition was that it had been a colonial tavern—a dot among the fir-covered northern hills on the climbing post-road into Canada. The village scattered along the road below the inn was called Albany—and soon forgotten when the railroad sought an opening through a valley less rugged, eight miles to the west.

Rather more than thirty years ago the Doctor had arrived, one summer day, and opened all the doors and windows of the neglected old house, which he had bought from scattered heirs. He was a quiet man, the Doctor, in middle life then or nearly so; and he sank almost without remark into the world of Albany, where they raise hay and potatoes and still cut good white pine off the hills. Gradually the old brick tavern resumed the functions of life: many buildings were added to it as well as many acres of farm and forest to the Doctor's original purchase of intervale land. The new Master did not open his house to the public, yet he, too, kept a sort of Inn, where men came and stayed a long time. Although no sign now hung from the old elm tree in front of the house, nevertheless an ever-widening stream of humanity mounted the winding road from White River and passed through the doors of the Inn, seeking life. . . .

That first summer the Doctor brought with him Sam, the Chinaman, whom we all came to know and love, and also a young man, who loafed much while the Doctor worked, and occasionally fished. This was John Herring—now a famous architect—and it was from his designs, sketched those first idle summer days, that were built all the additions to the simple old house—the two low wings in the rear for the "cells,"

with the Italian garden between them; the marble seat curving around the pool that joined the wings on the west; also the substantial wall that hid the Inn, its terraced gardens and orchards, from Albanian curiosity. Herring found a store of red brick in some crumbling buildings in the neighborhood, and he discovered the quarry whence came those thick slabs of purple slate. The blue-veined marble was had from a fissure in the hills, and the Doctor's School made the tiles.

I think Herring never did better work than in the making over of this old tavern: he divined that subtle affinity which exists between north Italy, with all its art, and our bare New England; and he dared to graft boldly one to the other, having the rear of the Inn altogether Italian with its portico, its dainty colonnades, the garden and the fountain and the pool. From all this one looked down on the waving grass of the Intervale, which fell away gently to the turbulent White River, then rose again to the wooded hills that folded one upon another, with ever deepening blue, always upward and beyond.

Not all this building at once, to be sure, as the millionaire builds; but a gradual growth over a couple of decades; and all built lovingly by the "Brothers," stone on stone, brick and beam and tile—many a hand taking part in it that came weak to the task and left it sturdy. There was also the terraced arrangement of gardens and orchards on either side of the Inn, reaching to the farm buildings on the one side and to the village on the other. For a time Herring respected the quaint old tavern with its small rooms and pine wainscot; then he made a stately two-storied hall out of one half where we dined in bad weather, and a pleasant study for the Doctor from the rest. The doors east and west always stood open in the summer, giving the rare passer-by a glimpse of that radiant blue heaven among the hills, with the silver flash of the river in the middle distance, and a little square of peaceful garden close at hand. . . . The tough northern grasses rustled in the breezes that always played about Albany; and the scent of spruce drawn by the hot sun—the strong resinous breath of the north—was borne from the woods.

Thus it started, that household of men in the old Inn at the far end of Albany village among the northern hills, with the Doctor and Sam and Herring, who had been flung aside after his first skirmish with life and was picked up in pure kindness by the Doctor, as a bit of the broken waste of our modern world, and carried off with him out of the city. The young architect returning in due time to the fight—sing-ing—naturally venerated the Doctor as a father; and when a dear friend stumbled and fell in the *via dura* of this life, he whispered to him word of the Inn and its Master—of the life up there among the hills where Man is little and God looks down on his earth. . . . "Oh, you'll understand when you put your eyes on White Face some morning! The Doctor? He heals both body and soul." And this one having heeded spoke the word in turn to others in need—"to the right sort, who would understand." Thus the custom grew like a faith, and a kind of brotherhood was formed, of those who had found more than health at the Inn—who had found themselves. The Doctor, ever busy about his farms and his woods, his building, and above

all his School, soon had on his hands a dozen or more patients or guests, as you might call them, and he set them to work speedily. There was little medi-cine to be found in the Inn: the sick labored as they could and thus grew strong. \ . . .

And so, as one was added to another, they began to call themselves in joke "Brothers," and the Doctor "Father." The older "Brothers" would return to the Inn from all parts of the land, for a few days or a few weeks, to grasp the Doctor's hand, to have a dip in the pool, to try the little brooks among the hills. Young men and middle-aged, and even the old, they came from the cities where the heat of living had scorched them, where they had faltered and doubted the goodness of life. In some way word of the Master had reached them, with this compelling advice—"Go! And tell him I sent you." So from the clinic or the lecture-room, from the office or the mill—wherever men labor with tighten-ing nerves—the needy one started on his long journey. Toward evening he was set down before the plain red face of the Inn. And as the Stranger entered the old hall, a voice was sure to greet him from within somewhere, the deep voice of a hearty man, and presently the Master appeared to welcome the new-comer, resting one hand on his guest's shoulder perhaps, with a yearning af-fection that ran before knowledge.

"So you've come, my boy," he said. "Herring [or some one] wrote me to look for you."

And after a few more words of greet-ing, the Doctor beckoned to Sam, and gave the guest over to his hands. There-upon the Chinaman slippered through tiled passageways to the court, where the Stranger, caught by the beauty and peace so well hidden, lingered a while. The little space within the wings was filled with flowers as far as the yellow water of the pool and the marble bench. In the centre of the court was an old gray fountain—sent from Verona by a Brother—from which the water dropped and ran away among the flower beds to the pool. A stately elm tree shaded this place, flecking the water below. The sun shot long rays beneath its branches into the court, and over all there was an odor of blossoming flowers and the murmur of bees.

"Bath!" Sam explained, grinning toward the pool.

With the trickle of the fountain in his ears the Stranger looked out across the ripening fields of the Intervale to the noble sky-line of the Stowe hills. Those little mountains of the north! Mere hills to all who know the giants of the earth—not mountains in the brotherhood of ice and snow and rock! But in form and color, in the lesser things that create the love of men for places, they rise nobly toward heaven, those little hills! On a summer day like this their broad breasts flutter with waving tree-tops, and at evening depth on depth of purple mist gathers over them, dropping into those soft curves where the little brooks flow, and mounting even to the sky-line. When the sun has fallen, there rests a band of pure saffron, and in the calm and perfect peace of evening there is a hint of coming moonlight. Ah, they are of the fellowship of mountains, those little hills of Stowe! And when in winter their flanks are jewelled with ice and snow, then they raise their heads proudly to the stars, calling across the frozen valleys to their greater brethren in the midriff of the continent—"Behold, we also are hills, in the sight of the Lord!" . . .

Meantime Sam, with Oriental ease, goes slipping along the arcade until he comes to a certain oak door, where he drops your bag, and disappears, having saluted. It is an ample and lofty room, and on the outer side of it hangs a little balcony above the orchard, from which there is a view of the valley and the woods beyond, and from somewhere in the fields the note of the thrush rises. The room itself is cool, of a gray tone, with a broad fireplace, a heavy table, and many books. Otherwise there are bed and chairs and dressing-table, the necessities of life austerely provided. And Peace! God, what Peace to him who has escaped from the furnace men make! It is as if he had come all the way to the end of the world, and found there a great still room of peace.

Soon a bell sounds—with a strange vibration as though in distant lands it had summoned many a body of men together—and the household assembles under the arcade. If it is fair and not cold, Sam and his helpers bring out the long narrow table and place it, as Veronese places his feasters, lengthwise beneath the colonnade, and thus the evening meal is served. A fresh, coarse napkin is laid on the bare board before each man, no more than enough for all those present, and the Doctor sits in the middle, serving all. There are few dishes, and for the most part such as may be got at home there in the hills. There is a pitcher of cider at one end and a pitcher of mild white wine at the other, and the men eat and drink, with jokes and talk—the laughter of the day. (The novice might feel only the harmony of it all, but later he will learn how many considered elements go to the making of Peace.) Afterward, when Sam has brought pipes and tobacco, the Master leads the way to the sweeping semicircle of marble seat around the pool with the leafy tree overhead; and there they sit into the soft night, talking of all things with the glow of pipes, until one after another slips away to sleep. For as the Master said, "Talk among men in common softens the muscles of the mind and quickens the heart." Yet he loved most to hear the talk of others.

Thus insensibly for the Novice there begins the life of the place, opening in a gentle and persistent routine that takes him in its flow and carries him on with it. He finds Tradition and Habit all about him, in the ordered, unconscious life of the Inn, to which he yields without question. . . . Shortly after dawn the bell sounds, and then the men meet at the pool, where the Doctor is always first. A plunge into the yellow water which is flecked with the fallen leaves, and afterward to each man's room there is brought a large bowl of coffee and hot milk, with bread and eggs and fruit. What more he craves may be found in the hall.

Soon there is a tap on the newcomer's door, and a neighborly voice calls out —"We all go into the fields every morning, you know. You must earn your dinner, the Doctor says, or borrow it!" So the Novice goes forth to earn his first dinner with his hands. Beyond the gardens and the orchards are the barns and sheds, and a vista of level acres of hay and potatoes and rye, the bearing acres of the farm, and beyond these the woods on the hills. "Nearly a thousand acres, fields and woods," the neighbor explains. "Oh, there's plenty to do all times!" Meantime the Doctor strides ahead through the wet grass, his eyes roaming here and there, inquiring the state of his land. And watching him the newcomer believes that there is always much to be done wherever the Doctor leads.

It may be July and hay time—all the intervale grass land is mowed by hand—there is a sweat-breaking task! Or it may be potatoes to hoe. Or later in the season the apples have to be gathered—a pleasant pungent job, filling the baskets and pouring them into the fat-bellied barrels. But whatever the work may be the Doctor keeps the Novice in his mind, and as the sun climbs high over the Stowe hills, he taps the new one on the shoulder—" Better stop here to-day, my boy! You'll find a good tree over there by the brook for a nap. . . ."

Under that particular tree in the tall timothy, there is the coolest spot, and the Novice drowses, thinking of those wonderful mowers in *Anna,* as he gazes at the marching files eating their way through the meadow until his eyelids fall and he sleeps, the ripple of waving timothy in his ears. At noon the bell sounds again from the Inn, and the men come striding homeward wiping the sweat from their faces. They gather at the swimming pool, and still panting from their labor strip off their wet garments, then plunge one after another, like happy boys. From bath to room, and a few minutes for fresh clothes, and all troop into the hall, which is dark and cool. The old brick walls of the tavern never held a gayer lot of guests.

From this time on each one is his own master; there is no common toil. The farmer and his men take up the care of the farm, and the Master usually goes down to his School, in company with some of the Brothers. Each one finds his own way of spending the hours till sunset—some fishing or shooting, according to the season; others, in tennis or games with the boys of the School; and some reading or loafing—until the shadows begin to fall across the pool into the court, and Sam brings out the long table for dinner.

The seasons shading imperceptibly into one another vary the course of the day. Early in Steptember the men begin to sit long about the hall-fire of an evening, and when the snow packs hard on the hills there is wood-cutting to be done, and in early spring it is the carpenter's shop. So the form alters, but the substance remains—work and play and rest. . . .

To each one a time will come when the Doctor speaks to him alone. At some hour, before many days have passed, the Novice will find himself with those large eyes resting on his face, searchingly. It may be in the study after the others have scattered, or at the pool where the Master loved to sit beneath the great tree and hear his "confessions," as the men called these talks. At such times, when the man came to remember it afterward, the Doctor asked few questions, said little, but listened. He had the confessing ear! And as if by chance his hand would rest on the man's arm or shoulder. For he said—"Touch speaks: soul flows through flesh into soul."

Thus he sat and confessed his patients one after another, and his dark eyes seemed familiar with all man's woes, as if he had listened always. Men said to him what they had never before let pass their lips to a man or woman, what they themselves scarce looked at in the gloom of their souls. Unawares it slipped from them, the reason within the reason for their ill, the ultimate cause of sorrow. From the moment they had revealed to him this hidden thing—had slipped the leash on their tongues—it seemed no longer to be feared. "Trouble evaporates, being properly aired," said the Doctor. And already in the troubled one's mind the sense of the confused snarl of life began to lessen and veils began to descend between him and it. . . . "For you must learn to forget," counselled the Doctor, "forget day by day until the recording soul beneath your mind is clean. Therefore—work, forget, be new!" . . .

A self-important young man, much concerned with himself, once asked the Master:

"Doctor, what is the regimen that you would recommend to me?"

And we all heard him say in reply—

"The potatoes need hilling, and then you'll feel like having a dip in the pool."

The young man, it seems, wrote back to the friend in the city who had sent him—"This Doctor cannot understand my case: he tells me to dig potatoes and bathe in a swimming pool. That is all! All!" But the friend, who was an old member of the Brotherhood, tele-

graphed back—"Dig and swim, you fool!" Sam took the message at the telephone while we were dining, and repeated it faithfully to the young man within the hearing of all. A laugh rose that was hard in dying, and I think the Doctor's lips wreathed in smile. . . . In the old days they say the Master gave medicine like other doctors. That was when he spent part of the year in the city and had an office there and believed in drugs. But as he gave up going to the city, the stock of drugs in the cabinet at the end of the study became exhausted, and was never renewed. All who needed medicine were sent to an old Brother, who had settled down the valley at Stowe. "He knows more about pills than I do," the Doctor said. "At least he can give you the stuff with confidence." Few of the inmates of the Inn ever went to Stowe, though Dr. Williams was an excellent physician. And it was from about this time that we began to drop the title of doctor, calling him instead the Master; and the younger men sometimes, Father. He seemed to like these new terms, as denoting affection and respect for his authority.

By the time that we called him Master, the Inn had come to its maturity. Altogether it could hold eighteen guests, and if more came, as in midsummer or autumn, they lived in tents in the orchard or in the hill camps. The Master was still adding to the forest land—fish and game preserve the village people called it; for the Master was a hunter and a fisherman. But up among those curving hills, when he looked out through the waving trees, measuring by eye a fir or a pine, he would say, nodding his head—"Boys, behold my heirs—from generation to generation!"

He was now fifty and had ceased altogether to go to the city. There were ripe men in the great hospitals that still remembered him as a young man in the medical school; but he had dropped out, they said—why? He might have answered that, instead of following the beaten path, he had spoken his word to the world through men—and spoken widely. For there was no break in the stream of life that flowed upward to the old Inn. The "cells" were always full, winter and summer. Now there were coming children of the older Brothers, and these, having learned the ways of the place from their fathers, were already house-broken, as we said, when they came. They knew that no door was locked about the Inn, but that if they returned after ten it behooved them to come in by the pool and make no noise. They knew that when the first ice formed on the pool, then they were not expected to get out of bed for the morning plunge. They knew that there was an old custom which no one ever forgot, and that was to put money in the house-box behind the hall door on leaving, at least something for each day of the time spent, and as much more as one cared to give. For, as every one knew, all in the box beyond the daily expense went to maintain the School on the road below the village. So the books of the Inn were easy to keep—there was never a word about money in the place—but I know that many a large sum of money was found in this box, and the School never wanted means.

That I might tell more of what took place in the Inn, and what the Master said, and the sort of men one found there, and the talk we all had summer evenings beside the pool and winter nights in the hall! Winter, I think, was the best time of all the year, the greatest beauty and the greatest joy, from the first fall of the snow to the yellow brook water and the floating ice in White River. Then the broad velvety shadows lay on the hills between the stiff spruces, then came rosy mornings out of darkness when you knew that some good thing was waiting for you in the world. After you had drunk your bowl of coffee, you got your axe and followed the procession of choppers, who were carefully foresting the Doctor's woods. In the spring, when the little brooks had begun to run down the slopes, there was road making and mending; for the Master kept in repair most of the roads about Albany, grinding the rock in his pit, saying that—"a good road is one sure blessing."

And the dusks I shall never forget—those gold and violet moments with the light of immortal heavens behind the rampart of hills; and the nights, so still, so still like everlasting death, each star set jewel-wise in a black sky above a white earth. How splendid it was to turn out of the warm hall where we had been reading and talking into the frosty court, with the thermometer at twenty below and still falling, and look down across the broad white valley, marked by the streak of bushy alders where the dumb river flowed, up to the little frozen water courses among the hills, up above where the stars glittered! You took your way to your room in the silence, rejoicing that it was all so, that somewhere in this tumultuous world of ours there was hidden all this beauty and the secret of living and that you were of the brotherhood of those who had found it. . . .

Thus was the Inn and its Master in the year when he touched sixty, and his hair and beard were more white than gray.

II

THEN there came to the Inn one day in the early part of the summer a new guest—a man about fifty, with an aging, worldly face. Bill, the Albany stage man, had brought him from Island Junction, and on the way had answered all his questions, discreetly, reckoning in his wisdom that his passenger was "one of those queer folks that went up to the old Doctor's place." For there was something smart and fashionable about the stranger's appearance that made Bill uncomfortable.

"There," he said, as he pulled up outside the red brick house and pointed over the wall into the garden, "mos' likely you'll find the old man fussin' 'round somewheres inside there, if he hain't down to the School," and he drove off with the people's mail.

The stranger looked back through the village street, which was as silent as a village street should be at four o'clock on a summer day. Then he muttered to himself, whimsically, "Mos' likely you'll find the old man fussin' 'round somewheres inside!" Well, *what next?* And he glanced at the homely red brick building with the cold eye of one who has made many goings out and comings in, and to whom novelty offers little entertainment. As he stood there (thinking possibly of that early train from the junction on the morrow) the hall door opened wide, and an oldish man with white eye-brows and black eyes appeared. He was dressed in a linen suit that deepened the dark tan of his face and hands. He said:

"You are Dr. Augustus Norton?"

"And you," the Stranger replied with a graceful smile, "are the Master—and this is the Inn!"

He had forgotten what Percival called the old boy—forgot everything these days—had tried to remember the name all the way up—nevertheless, he had turned it off well! So the two looked at each other—one a little younger as years go, but with lined face and shaking fingers; the other solid and self-contained, with less of that ready language which comes from always jostling with nimble wits. But as they stood there, each saw a Man and an Equal.

"The great surgeon of St. Jerome's," said our Master in further welcome.

"Honored by praise from your lips!" Thus the man of the city lightly turned the compliment and extended his hand,

which the Master took slowly, gazing meanwhile steadily at his guest.

"Pray come into my house," said the Master of the Inn, with more stateliness of manner than he usually had with a new Brother. But, it may be said, Dr. Augustus Norton had the most distinguished name of that day in his profession. He followed the Master to his study, with uncertain steps, and sinking into a deep chair before the smouldering ashes looked at his host with a sad grin—"Perhaps you'll give me something—the journey, you know? . . ."

Two years before the head surgeon of St. Jerome's had come to the hospital of a morning to perform some operation —one of those affairs for which he was known from coast to coast. As he entered the officers' room that day, with the arrogant eye of the commander-in-chief, one of his aides looked at him suspiciously, then glanced again—and the great surgeon felt those eyes upon him when he turned his back. And he knew why! Something was wrong with him. Nevertheless in glum silence he made ready to operate. But when the moment came, and he was about to take the part of God toward the piece of flesh lying in the ether sleep before him, he hesitated. Then, in the terrible recoil of Fear, he turned back.

"Macroe!" he cried to his assistant, "you will have to operate. I cannot— I am not well!"

There was almost panic, but Macroe was a man, too, and proceeded to do his work without a word. The great surgeon, his hands now trembling beyond disguise, went back to the officers' room, took off his white robes, and returned to his home. There he wrote his resignation to the directors of St. Jerome's, and his resignation from other offices of honor and responsibility. Then he sent for a medical man, an old friend, and held out his shaking hand to him:

"The damn thing won't go," he said, pointing also to his head.

46

"Too much work," the doctor replied, of course.

But the great surgeon, who was a man of clear views, added impersonally, "Too much everything, I guess!"

There followed the usual prescription, making the sick man a wanderer and pariah—first to Europe, "to get rid of me," the surgeon growled; then to Georgia for golf, to Montana for elk, to Canada for salmon, and so forth. Each time the sick man returned with a thin coat of tan that peeled off in a few days, and with those shaking hands that suggested immediately another journey to another climate. Until it happened finally that the men of St. Jerome's who had first talked of the date of their chief's return merely raised their eyebrows at the mention of his name.

"Done for, poor old boy!" and the great surgeon read it with his lynx eyes, in the faces of the men he met at his clubs. His mouth drew together sourly and his back sloped. "Fifty-two," he muttered. "God, that is too early—something ought to pull me together." So he went on trying this and that, while his friends said he was "resting," until he had slipped from men's thoughts.

One day Percival of St. Jerome's, one of those boys he had growled at and cursed in former times, met him crawling down the avenue to his quietest club, and the old surgeon took him by the arm—he was gray in face and his neck was wasting away—and told the story of his troubles—as he would to anyone these days. The young man listened respectfully. Then he spoke of the old Inn, of the Brotherhood, of the Master and what he had done for miserable men, who had despaired. The famous surgeon, shaking his head as one who has heard of these miracles many times and found them naught, was drinking it all in, nevertheless.

"He takes a man," said the young surgeon, "who doesn't want to live and makes him fall in love with life."

Dr. Augustus Norton sniffed.

"In love with life! That's good! If your Wonder of the Ages can make a man of fifty fall in love with anything, I must try him." He laughed a sneering laugh, the feeble merriment of doubt.

"Ah, Doctor!" cried the young man, "you must go and live with the Master. And then come back to us at St. Jerome's: for we need you!"

And the great surgeon, touched to the heart by these last words, said:

"Well, what's the name of your miracle-worker, and where is he to be found? . . . I might as well try all the cures—write a book on 'em one of these days!" . . .

So he came by the stage to the gate of the old Inn, and the Master, who had been warned by a telegram from the young doctor only that morning, stood at his door to welcome his celebrated guest.

He put him in the room of state above the study, a great square room at the southwest, overlooking the wings and the flower-scented garden, the pool, and the waving grass fields beyond, dotted with tall elms—all freshly green.

"Not a bad sort of place," murmured the weary man, "and there must be trout in those brooks up yonder. Well, it will do for a week or two, if there's fishing." . . . Then the bell sounded for dinner which was served for the first time that season out of doors in the soft twilight. The Brothers had gathered in the court beside the fountain, young men and middle-aged—all having bent under some burden, which they were now learning to carry easily. They stood about the hall door until the distinguished Stranger appeared, and he walked between them to the place of honor at the Master's side. Every one at the long table was named to the great surgeon, and then with the coming of the soup he was promptly forgotten, while the talk of the day's work and

47

the morrow's rose vigorously from all sides. It was a question of the old mill, which had given way. An engineer among the company described what would have to be done to get at the foundations. And a young man who happened to sit next to the surgeon explained that the Master had reopened an old mill above the Inn in the Intervale, where he ground corn and wheat and rye with the old water-wheel; for the country people, who had always got their grain ground there, complained when the mill had been closed. It seemed to the Stranger that the dark coarse bread which was served was extraordinarily good, and he wondered if the ancient process had anything to do with it and he resolved to see the old mill. Then the young man said something about bass: there was a cool lake up the valley, which had been stocked. The surgeon's eye gleamed. Did he know how to fish for bass! Why, before this boy—yes, he would go at five in the morning, sharp. . . . After the meal, while the blue wreaths of smoke floated across the flowers and the talk rose and fell in the court, the Master and his new guest were seated alone beneath the great elm. The surgeon could trace the Master's face in the still waters of the pool at their feet, and it seemed to him like a finely cut cameo, with gentle lines about the mouth and eyes that relieved the thick nose. Nevertheless he knew by certain instinct that they were not of the same kind. The Master was very silent this night, and his guest felt that some mystery, some vacuum existed between them, as he gazed on the face in the water. It was as if the old man were holding him off at arm's length while he looked into him. But the great surgeon, who was used to the amenities of city life, resolved to make his host talk:

"Extraordinary sort of place you have here! I don't know that I have seen anything just like it. And what is your System?"

"What is my System?" repeated the Master wonderingly.

"Yes! Your method of building these fellows up—electricity, diet, massage, baths—what is your line?" An urbane smile removed the offence of the banter.

"I have no System!" the Master replied thoughtfully. "I live my life here with my work, and those you see come and live with me as my friends."

"Ah, but you have ideas . . . extraordinary success . . . so many cases," the great man muttered, confused by the Master's steady gaze.

"You will learn more about us after you have been here a little time. You will see, and the others will help you to understand. To-morrow we work at the mill, and the next day we shall be in the gardens—but you may be too tired to join us. And we bathe here, morning and noon. Harvey will tell you all our customs."

The celebrated surgeon of St. Jerome's wrote that night to an old friend: "And the learned doctor's prescription seems to be to dig in the garden and bathe in a great pool! A daffy sort of place—but I am going bass fishing to-morrow at five with a young man, who is just the right age for a son! So to bed, but I suspect that I shall see you soon—novelties wear out quickly at my years."

Just here there entered that lovely night wind, rising far away beyond the low lakes to the south—it soughed through the room, swaying the draperies, sighing, sighing, and it blew out the candle. The sick man looked down on the court below, white in the moonlight, and his eyes roved farther to the dark orchard, and the great barns and the huddled cattle.

"Quite a bit of country here!" the surgeon murmured. As he stood there looking into the misty light which covered the Intervale, up to the great hills above which floated luminous cloud banks, the chorus of an old song rose from below where the pipes gleamed in the dark about the pool. He leaned out into the air, filled with all the wild scent of green fields, and added under a sort of compulsion—"And a good place, enough!"

He went to bed to a deep sleep, and over his tired, worldly face the night wind passed gently, stripping leaf by leaf from his weary mind that heavy coating of care which he had wrapped about him in the course of many years.

Dr. Augustus Norton did not return at the end of one week, nor of two. The city saw him, indeed, no more that year. It was said that a frisky, rosy ghost of the great surgeon had slipped into St. Jerome's near Christmas—had skipped through a club or two and shaken hands about pretty generally — and disappeared. Sometimes letters came from him with an out-of-the-way postmark on them, saying in a jesting tone that he was studying the methods of an extraordinary country doctor, who seemed to cure men by touch. "He lives up here among the hills in forty degrees of frost, and if I am not mistaken he is nearer the Secret than all of you pill slingers" — (for he was writing a mere doctor of medicine!). "Anyhow I shall stay on until I learn the Secret—or my host turns me out; for life up here seems as good to me as ice-cream and kisses to a girl of sixteen. . . . Why should I go back mucking about with you fellows— just yet? I caught a five-pounder yesterday, and *ate* him!"

There are many stories of the great surgeon that have come to me from those days. He was much liked, especially by the younger men, after the first gloom had worn off, and he began to feel the blood run once more. He had a joking way with him that made him a good table companion, and the Brothers pretending that he would become the historian of the order taught him all the traditions of the place. "But the Secret, the Secret! Where is it?" he would demand jestingly. One night —it was at table and all were there— Harvey asked him:

"Has the Master confessed you?"

" 'Confessed me'?" repeated the surgeon. "What's that?"

A sudden silence fell on all, because this was the one thing never spoken of, at least in public. Then the Master, who had been silent all that evening, turned the talk to other matters.

The Master, to be sure, gave this distinguished guest all liberties, and they often talked together as men of the same profession. And the surgeon witnessed all—the mending of the mill, the planting and the hoeing and the harvesting, the preparations for the long winter, the chopping and the road-making—all, and he tested it with his hands. "Not bad sport," he would say, "with so many sick-well young men about to help!"

But meanwhile the "secret" escaped the keen mind, though he sought for it daily.

"You give no drugs, Doctor," he complained. "You're a scab on the profession!"

"The drugs gave out," the Master explained, "and I neglected to order more. . . . There's always Bert Williams at Stowe, who can give you anything you might want—shall I send for him, Doctor?"

There was laughter all about, and when it died down the great surgeon returned to the attack.

"Well, come, tell us now what you do believe in? Magic, the laying on of hands? Come, there are four doctors here, and we have the right to know— or we'll report you!"

"I believe," said the Master solemnly, in reply to the banter, "I believe in Man and in God." And there followed such talk as had never been in the old hall; for the surgeon was, after his kind, a materialist and pushed the Master for definition. The Master believed, as I recall it, that Disease could not be cured, for the most part. No chemistry

49

would ever solve the mystery of pain! But Disease could be ignored, and the best way to forget pain was through labor. Not labor merely for oneself; but also something for others. Wherefore the School, around which the Inn and the farm and all had grown. For he told us then that he had bought the Inn as a home for his boys, the waste product of the city. Finding the old tavern too small for his purpose and seeing how he should need helpers, he had encouraged ailing men to come to live with him and to cure themselves by curing others. Without that School below in the valley, with its workshops and cottages, there would have been no Inn!

As for God—that night he would go no further, and the surgeon said rather flippantly, we all thought, that the Master had left little room in his world for God, anyhow—he had made man so large. It was a stormy August evening, I remember, when we had been forced to dine within on account of the gusty rain that had come after a still, hot day. The valley seemed filled with murk, which was momentarily torn by fire, revealing the trembling leaves upon the trees. When we passed through the arcade to reach our rooms, the surgeon pointed out into this sea of fire and darkness, and muttered with a touch of irony—

"HE seems to be talking for himself this evening!"

Just then a bolt shot downward, revealing with large exaggeration the hills, the folded valleys—the descents.

"It's like standing on a thin plank in a turbulent sea!" the surgeon remarked wryly. "Ah, my boy, Life's like that!" and he disappeared into his room.

Nevertheless, it was that night he wrote to his friend: "I am getting nearer this Mystery, which I take to be, the inner heart of it, a mixture of the Holy Ghost and Sweat—with a good bath afterward! But the old boy is the mixer of the Pills, mind you, and he *is* a Master! Most likely I shall never get hold of the heart of it; for somehow, yet with all courtesy he keeps me at a distance. I have never been 'confessed,' whatever that may be—an experience that comes to the youngest boy among them! Perhaps the Doctor thinks that old fellows like you and me have only dead sins to confess, which would crumble to dust if exposed. But there is a sting in very old sins, I think—for instance—oh! if you were here tonight, I should be as foolish as a woman. . . ."

The storm that night struck one of the school buildings and killed a lad. In the morning the Master and the surgeon set out for the School Village, which was lower in the valley beyond Albany. It was warm and clear at the Inn; but thick mist wreaths still lay heavily over the Intervale. The hills all about glittered as in October, and there was in the air that laughing peace, that breath of sweet plenty which comes the morning after a storm. The two men followed the foot-path, which wound downward from the Inn across the Intervale. The sun filled the windless air, sucking up the spicy odors of the tangled path—fern and balsam and the mother scent of earth and rain and sun. The new green rioted over the dead leaves. . . . The Master closely observing his guest, remarked:

"You seem quite well, Doctor. I suppose you will be leaving us soon?"

"Leaving?" the surgeon questioned slowly, as if a secret dread had risen at the Master's hint of departure.

"Yes," he admitted, after a time, "I suppose I am what you would call well —well enough. But something still clogs within me. It may be the memory of Fear. I am afraid of myself!"

"Afraid? You need some test, perhaps. That will come sooner or later; we need not hurry it!"

"No, we need not hurry!"

Yet he knew well enough that the Inn never sheltered drones, and that many special indulgences had been granted him: he had borrowed freely from the younger Brothers—of their time and strength. He thought complacently of the large cheque which he should drop into the house-box on his departure. With it the Master would be able to build a new cottage or a small hospital for the School.

"Some of them," mused the Master, "never go back to the machine that once broke them. They stay about here and help me—buy a farm and revert! But for the most part they are keen to get back to the fight, as is right and best. Sometimes when they loiter too long, I shove them out of the nest!"

"And I am near the shoving point?" his companion retorted quickly. "So I must leave all your dear boys and Peace and Fishing and *you!* Suppose so, suppose so! . . . Doctor, you've saved my life—oh, hang it, that doesn't tell the story. But even *I* can feel what it is to live at the Inn!"

Instinctively he grasped his host by the arm—he was an impulsive man. But the Master's arm did not respond to the clasp; indeed, a slight shiver seemed to shake it, so that the surgeon's hand fell away while the Master said:

"I am glad to have been of service—to you—yes, especially to *you*. . . ."

They came into the school village, a tiny place of old white houses, very clean and trim, with a number of sweeping elms along the narrow road. A mountain brook turned an old water-wheel, supplying power for the work-shops where the boys were trained. The great surgeon had visited the place many times in company with the Master, and though he admired the order and economy of the institution, and respected its purpose—that is, to create men out of the refuse of society—to tell the truth, the place bored him a trifle. This morning they went directly to the little cottage that served as infirmary, where the dead boy had been brought. He was a black-haired Italian, and his lips curved upward pleasantly. The Master putting his hand on the dead boy's brow as he might have done in life stood looking at the face.

"I've got a case in the next room, I'd like to have your opinion on, Doctor," the young physician said in a low tone to the surgeon, and the two crossed the passage into the neighboring room. The surgeon fastened his eyes on the sick lad's body; here was a case he understood, a problem with a solution. The old Master coming in from the dead stood behind the two.

"Williams," the surgeon said, "it's so, sure enough—you must operate—at once!"

"I was afraid it was that," the younger man replied. "But how can I operate here?"

The surgeon shrugged his shoulders— "He would never reach the city!"

"Then I must, you think——"

The shrewd surgeon recognized Fear in the young man's voice. Quick the thrill shot through his nerves, and he cried, "I will operate, *now.*"

In half an hour it was over, and the Master and the surgeon were leaving the village, climbing up by the steep path under the blazing noon sun. The Master glanced at the man by his side, who strode along confidently, a trifle of a swagger in his buoyant steps. The Master remarked:

"The test came, and you took it—splendidly."

"Yes," the great surgeon replied, smiling happily, "it's all there, Doctor, the old power. I believe I am about ready to get into harness again!" After they had walked more of the way without speaking, the surgeon added, as to himself—"But there are other things to be feared!"

Though the Master looked at him closely he invited no explanation, and they finished their homeward walk without remark.

It soon got about among the inmates of the Inn what a wonderful operation the surgeon of St. Jerome's had performed, and it was rumored that at the beginning of autumn he would go back to his old position. Meantime the great surgeon enjoyed the homage that men always pay to power, the consideration of his fellows. He had been much liked; but now that the Brothers knew how soon he was to leave them, they surrounded him with those attentions that men most love, elevating him almost to the rank of the Master—and they feared him less. His fame spread, so that from some mill beyond Stowe they brought to the Inn a desperate case, and the surgeon operated again successfully, demonstrating that he was once more master of his art, and master of himself. So he stayed on merely to enjoy his triumph and escape the dull season in the city.

It was a wonderful summer, that! The fitful temper of the north played in all its moods. There were days when the sun shone tropically down into the valleys, without a breath of air, when the earthy, woodsy smells were strong—and the nights—perfect stillness and peace, as if some spirit of the air were listening for love words on the earth. The great elms along Albany road hung their branches motionless, and when the moon came over behind the house the great hills began to swim ghostly, vague —beyond, always beyond! . . . And then there were the fierce storms that swept up the valley and hung growling along the hills for days, and afterward, sky-washed and clear, the westerly breeze would come tearing down the Intervale, drying the earth before it. . . . But each day there was a change in the sound and the smell of the fields and the woods—in the quick race of the northern summer—a change that the surgeon, fishing up the tiny streams, felt and

noted. Each day, so radiant with its abundant life, sounded some undernote of fulfilment and change—speaking beforehand of death to come.

Toward the end of August a snap of cold drove us in-doors for the night meal. Then around the fire there was great talk between the Master and the surgeon, a sort of battle of the soul, to which we others paid silent attention. For wherever those nights the talk might rise, in the little rills of accidental words, it always flowed down to the deep underlying thoughts of men. And in those depths, as I said, these two wrestled with each other. The Master, who had grown silent of late years, woke once more with fire. The light, keen thrusts of the surgeon, who argued like a fencer, roused his whole being; and as day by day it went on we who watched saw that in a way the talk of these two men set forth the great conflict of conflicts, that deepest fissure of life and belief anent the Soul and the Body. And the Master, who had lived his faiths by his life before our eyes, was being worsted in the argument! The great surgeon had the better mind, and he had seen all of life that one may see with eyes. . . .

They were talking of the day of departure for the distinguished guest, and arranging for some kind of triumphal procession to escort him to White River. But he would not set the time, shrinking from this act, as if all were not yet done. There came a warm, glowing day early in September, and at night after the pipes were lighted the surgeon and the Master strolled off in the direction of the pool, arm in arm. There had been no talk that day, the surgeon apparently shrinking from coming to the last grapple with one whose faiths were so important to him as the Master's.

"The flowers are dying: they tell me it's time to move on," said the surgeon. "And yet, my dear host, I go without the Secret, without understanding All!"

"Perhaps there is no inner Secret," the Master smiled. "It is all here before you."

"I know that—you have been very good to me, shared everything. If I have not learned the Secret, it is my fault, my incapacity. But—" and the gay tone dropped quickly and a flash of bitterness succeeded—"I at least know that there *is* a Secret!"

They sat down on the marble bench and looked into the water, each thinking his thoughts. Suddenly the surgeon began to speak, hesitantly, as if there had long been something in his mind that he was compelled to say.

"My friend," he said, "I too have something to tell—the cause within the cause, the reason of the reason—at least, sometimes I think it is! The root reason for all—unhappiness, defeat, for the shaking hand and the jesting voice. And I want you to hear it—if you will."

The Master raised his face from the pool but said never a word. The surgeon continued, his voice trembling at times, though he spoke slowly evidently trying to banish all feeling.

"It is a common enough story at the start, at least among men of our kind. You know that I was trained largely in Europe. My father had the means to give me the best, and time to take it in. So I was over there, before I came back to St. Jerome's, three, four years at Paris, Munich, Vienna, all about. . . . While I was away I lived as the others, for the most part—you know our profession—and youth. The rascals are pretty much the same to-day, I judge from what my friends say of their sons! Well, at least I worked like the devil, and was decent. . . . Oh, it isn't for that I'm telling the tale! I was ambitious, then. And the time came to go back, as it does in the end, and I took a few weeks' run through Italy as a final taste of the lovely European thing, and came down to Naples to get the boat for New York. I've never been back to Naples since,

and that was twenty-six years ago this autumn. But I can see the city always as it was then! The seething human hive—the fellows piling in the freight to the music of their songs—the fiery mouth of Vesuvius up above. And the soft, dark night with just a splash of waves on the quay!"

The Master listened, his eyes again buried in the water at their feet.

"Well, *she* was there on board, of course—looking out also into that warm dark night and sighing for all that was to be lost so soon. There were few passengers in those days. . . . She was my countrywoman, and beautiful, and there was something—at least so I thought then—of especial sweetness in her eyes, something strong in her heart. She was engaged to a man living somewhere in the States, and she was going back to marry him. Why she was over there then I forget, and it is of no importance. I think that the man was a doctor, too—in some small city. . . . I loved her!"

The Master raised his eyes from the pool and leaning on his folded arms looked into the surgeon's face.

"I am afraid I never thought much about that other fellow—never have to this day! That was part of the brute I am—to see only what is before my eyes. And I knew by the time we had swung into the Atlantic that I wanted that woman as I had never wanted things before. She stirred me, mind and all, Of course it might have been some one else—any one you will say—and if she had been an ordinary young girl, it might have gone differently? It is one of the things we can't tell in this life. There was something in that woman that was big all through and roused the spirit in me. I never knew man or woman who thirsted more for greatness, for accomplishment. Perhaps the man she was to marry gave her little to hope for—probably it was some raw boy-and-girl affair such as we have in America. . . . The days went by, and it was clearer to both of us what must be. But we didn't speak of it. She found in me, I suppose, the power, the sort of thing she had missed in the other. I was to do all those grand things she was so hot after. I have done some of them too. But that was when she had gone and I no longer needed her. . . . I needed her then, and I took her—that is all.

"The detail is old and dim—and what do you care to hear of a young man's loves! Before we reached port it was understood between us. I told her I wanted her to leave the other chap—he was never altogether clear to me—and to marry me as soon as she could. We did not stumble or slide into it, not in the least: we looked it through and through —that was her kind and mine. How she loved to look life in the face! I have found few women who like that. . . . In the end she asked me not to come near her the last day. She would write me the day after we had landed, either yes or no. So she kissed me, and we parted still out at sea."

All the Brothers had left the court and the arcades, where they had been strolling, and old Sam was putting out the Inn lights. But the two men beside the pool made no movement. The west wind still drew in down the valley with summer warmth and ruffled the water at their feet.

"My father met me at the dock—you know he was the first surgeon at St. Jerome's before me. My mother was with him. . . . But as she kissed me I was thinking of that letter. . . . I knew it would come. Some things must! Well, it came."

The silent listener bent his head, and the surgeon mused on his passionate memory. At last the Master whispered in a low voice that hardly reached into the night:

"Did you make her happy?"

The surgeon did not answer the question at once.

"Did you make her happy?" the old man demanded again, and his voice trembled this time with such intensity that his companion looked at him wonderingly. And in those dark eyes of the Master's he read something that made him shrink away. Then for the third time the old man demanded sternly:

"Tell me—did you make her happy?"

It was the voice of one who had a right to know, and the surgeon whispered back slowly:

"Happy? No, my God! Perhaps at first, in the struggle, a little. But afterward there was too much—too many things. It went, the inspiration and the love. I broke her heart—she left me! That—that is *my* Reason!"

"It *is* the Reason! For you took all, all—you let her give all, and you gave her—what?"

"Nothing—she died."

"I know—she died."

The Master had risen, and with folded arms faced his guest, a pitying look in his eyes. The surgeon covered his face with his hands, and after a long time said:

"So you knew this?"

"Yes, I knew!"

"And knowing you let me come here. You took me into your house, you healed me, you gave me back my life!"

And the Master replied with a firm voice:

"I knew, and I gave you back your life." In a little while he explained more softly: "You and I are no longer young men who feel hotly and settle such a matter with hate. We cannot quarrel now for the possession of a woman. . . . She chose: remember that! . . . It was twenty-six years this September. We have lived our lives, you and I; we have lived out our lives, the good and the evil. Why should we now for the second time add passion to sorrow?"

"And yet knowing all you took me in!"

"Yes!" the old man cried almost proudly. "And I have made you again

54

what you once were. . . . What *she* loved as you," he added to himself, "a man full of Power."

Then they were speechless in face of the fact: the one had taken all and the sweet love turned to acid in his heart, and the other had lost and the bitter turned to sweet! When a long time had passed the surgeon spoke timidly:

"It might have been so different for her with you! You loved her—more."

There was the light of a compassionate smile on the Master's lips as he replied:

"Yes, I loved her, too."

"And it changed things—for you!"

"It changed things. There might have been my St. Jerome's—my fame also. Instead, I came here with my boys. And here I shall die, please God."

The old Master then became silent, his face set in a dream of life, as it was, as it would have been; while the great surgeon of St. Jerome's thought such thoughts as had never passed before into his mind. The night wind had died at this late hour, and in its place there was a coldness of the turning season. The stars shone near the earth and all was silent with the peace of mysteries. The Master looked at the man beside him and said calmly:

"It is well as it is—all well!"

At last the surgeon rose and stood before the Master.

"I have learned the Secret," he said, "and now it is time for me to go."

He went up to the house through the little court and disappeared within the Inn, while the Master sat by the pool, his face graven like the face of an old man, who has seen the circle of life and understands. . . . The next morning there was much talk about Dr. Norton's disappearance, until some one ex-plained that the surgeon had been suddenly called back to the city.

The news spread through the Brotherhood one winter that the old Inn had been burned to the ground, a bitter December night when all the water-taps were frozen. And the Master, who had grown deaf of late, had been caught in his remote chamber, and burned or rather suffocated. There were few men in the Inn at the time, it being the holiday season, and when they had fought their way to the old man's room, they found him lying on the lounge by the window, the lids fallen over the dark eyes and his face placid with sleep or contemplation. . . . They sought in vain for the reason of the fire—but why search for causes?

All those beautiful hills that we loved to watch as the evening haze gathered, the Master left in trust for the people of the State—many acres of waving forests. And the School continued in its old place, the Brothers looking after its wants and supplying it with means to continue its work. But the Inn was never rebuilt. The blackened ruins of buildings were removed and the garden in the court extended so that it covered the whole space where the Inn had stood. This was enclosed with a thick plantation of firs on all sides but that one which looked westward across the Intervale. The spot can be seen for miles around on the Albany hill side.

And when it was ready—all fragrant and radiant with flowers—they placed the Master there beside the pool, where he had loved to sit, surrounded by men. On the sunken slab his title was engraved—

THE MASTER OF THE INN

* * *

❧ O LORD GOD, we pray that we may be inspired to nobleness of life in the least things. May we dignify all our daily life. May we set such a sacredness upon every part of our life, that nothing shall be trivial, nothing unimportant, and nothing dull, in the daily round. Amen. *—Beecher*

SWEET ARE THE USES OF ADVERSITY
WILLIAM SHAKESPEARE

Sweet are the uses of adversity,
Which, like the toad, ugly and venomous,
Wears yet a precious jewel in his head;
And this our life exempt from public haunt
Finds tongues in trees, books in the running brooks,
Sermons in stones and good in everything.

—From As You Like It

THE MAN THAT HATH NO MUSIC IN HIMSELF
WILLIAM SHAKESPEARE

The man that hath no music in himself,
Nor is not moved with concord of sweet sounds,
Is fit for treasons, stratagems, and spoils;
The motions of his spirit are dull as night,
And his affections dark as Erebus.
Let no such man be trusted.

—From The Merchant of Venice

HOW SWEET THE MOONLIGHT
WILLIAM SHAKESPEARE

How sweet the moonlight sleeps upon this bank!
Here we will sit and let the sounds of music
Creep in our ears: soft stillness and the night
Become the touches of sweet harmony.
Sit, Jessica. Look how the floor of heaven
Is thick inlaid with patines of bright gold:
There's not the smallest orb which thou behold'st
But in his motion like an angel sings,
Still quiring to the young-eyed cherubins.
Such harmony is in immortal souls;
But whilst this muddy vesture of decay
Doth grossly close it in, we cannot hear it.

—From The Merchant of Ven.

56

WHO STEALS MY PURSE
WILLIAM SHAKESPEARE

Who steals my purse steals trash; 'tis something, nothing;
'Twas mine, 'tis his, and has been slave to thousands;
But he that filches from me my good name
Robs me of that which not enriches him,
And makes me poor indeed.

—From *Othello*

From *ROMEO AND JULIET*,
WILLIAM SHAKESPEARE

Capulet's orchard.
Enter ROMEO and JULIET above, at the window

JULIET. Wilt thou be gone? it is not yet near day:
It was the nightingale, and not the lark,
That pierced the fearful hollow of thine ear;
Nightly she sings on yon pomegranate-tree:
Believe me, love, it was the nightingale.

ROMEO. It was the lark, the herald of the morn
No nightingale: look, love, what envious streaks
Do lace the severing clouds in yonder east:
Nights candles are burnt out, and jocund day
Stands tiptoe on the misty mountain tops.

OVER HILL, OVER DALE
WILLIAM SHAKESPEARE

Over hill, over dale,
　Thorough bush, thorough brier,
Over park, over pale,
　Thorough flood, thorough fire,
I do wander everywhere,
Swifter than the moon's sphere;
And I serve the fairy queen,
To dew her orbs upon the green:
The cowslips tall her pensioners be;
In their gold coats spots you see;
Those be rubies, fairy favors,
In those freckles live their savors:
must go seek some dew-drops here,
nd hang a pearl in every cowslip's ear.

O MISTRESS MINE,
WHERE ARE YOU ROAMING?
WILLIAM SHAKESPEARE

O Mistress mine, where are you roam-
　ing?
Oh, stay and hear; your true love's
　coming,
　That can sing both high and low.
Trip no further, pretty sweeting,
Journeys end in lovers meeting,
　Every wise man's son doth know.

What is love? 'tis not hereafter;
Present mirth hath present laughter;
　What's to come is still unsure.
In delay there lies no plenty;
Then come kiss me, sweet and twenty;
　Youth's a stuff will not endure.

57

FOUR LITTLE FOXES
LEW SARETT

Speak gently, Spring, and make no sudden sound;
For in my windy valley, yesterday I found
New-born foxes squirming on the ground—
    Speak gently.

Walk softly, March, forbear the bitter blow;
Her feet within a trap, her blood upon the snow,
The four little foxes saw their mother go—
    Walk softly.

Go lightly, Spring, oh, give them no alarm;
When I covered them with boughs to shelter them from harm,
The thin blue foxes suckled at my arm—
    Go lightly.

Step softly, March, with your rampant hurricane;
Nuzzling one another, and whimpering with pain,
The new little foxes are shivering in the rain—
    Step softly.

OH, THE WILD JOYS OF LIVING!
ROBERT BROWNING

Oh, the wild joys of living! the leaping from rock up to rock,
The strong rending of boughs from the fir-tree, the cool silver shock
Of the plunge in the pool's living water, the hunt of the bear,
And the sultriness showing the lion is couched in his lair.
And the meal, the rich dates yellowed over the gold dust divine,
And the locust-flesh steeped in the pitcher, the full draft of wine,
And the sleep in the dried river-channel where bulrushes tell
That the water was wont to go warbling so softly and well.
How good is man's life, the mere living! how fit to employ
All the heart and the soul and the senses forever in joy!

—From *Saul*

* * *

WE ARE LIVING in a world of beauty but how few of us open our eyes to see it! What a different place this would be if our senses were trained to see and hear! We are the heirs of wonderful treasures from the past: treasures of literature and of the arts. The are ours for the asking—all our own to have and to enjoy, if only we desire them enough. —*Lorado Taft*

58

SYMBOL
DAVID MORTON

My faith is all a doubtful thing,
  Wove on a doubtful loom,—
Until there comes, each showery spring,
  A cherry tree in bloom;

And Christ who died upon a tree
  That death had stricken bare,
Comes beautifully back to me,
  In blossoms, everywhere.

From *ENDYMION*
HENRY WADSWORTH LONGFELLOW

The rising moon has hid the stars;
Her level rays, like golden bars,
  Lie on the landscape green,
  With shadows brown between.

And silver white the river gleams,
As if Diana, in her dreams,
  Had dropt her silver bow
  Upon the meadows low.

THE DOLPHIN*
By VAN CAMPEN HEILNER

... THE MOST beautiful (fish) of all, to me, has been the dolphin.

Nature, with all her masterpieces, outdid herself in the creation of this lovely creature. The blue of every sea in the world, the purple of distant mountain peaks, the gold of every sunrise and sunset since Time began, the lush green of tropical mountains rising from a cobalt sea; these and a thousand other colors all were blended to make the dolphin.

As if his color was not enough, he is endowed with speed, leaping abilities. ... Many's the time I've watched a dolphin chasing flying fish. Just behind and just beneath the surface the dolphin with incredible speed would keep pace with his prospective prey and the moment the hapless winged quarry hit the water, the dolphin had him. I timed over a hundred flying fish in the South Atlantic with a stop watch and their average time in the air was between four and five seconds. Some stayed up as long as seven. With the speed at which a flying fish travels, seven seconds is a long time, and for a dolphin, handicapped as he is by the resistance of the water, to keep pace with one of these bird-like creatures and to capture it is an amazing thing.

It was way down the keys in the early days right after the railroad had first come to Key West. The sun was just setting on its "pedestal" across the Bay of Florida and the trestle was a dim line of arches on the horizon as we turned homeward. Then I had the last strike of the day and into the air shot a *dorado* which in the lovely language of Castile means "golden." Leaping, twisting, shaking his head like a bull terrier I brought him in closer until, lifting him over the side, he lay quivering in the cockpit.

Then occurred that unforgettable sight, the death of a dolphin. Like fields of wheat rippling in the summer wind, the waves of color washed across his body. First gold, then blue, then gold and blue, amethyst, cerulean and jade kept beat with his dying heart. And then the last gasp, and like the quick descent of a tropic night the colors were gone and with it the sunset.

—From *The Delight Makers*

★ ★ ★

❧ THE TWO MOST BEAUTIFUL things in the universe are the starry heavens above our heads, and the feeling of duty in our hearts.   —*Bossuet*

*Reprinted from *Salt Water Fishing*, by Van Campen Heilner, by permission of ALFRED A. KNOPF, INC. Copyright 1937 by Alfred A. Knopf, Inc.

THE TWO LEAVES

By Felix Salten

THE LEAVES WERE FALLING from the great oak at the meadow's edge. They were falling from all the trees.

One branch of the oak reached high above the others and stretched far out over the meadow. Two leaves clung to its very tip.

"It isn't the way it used to be," said one leaf to the other.

"No," the other leaf answered. "So many of us have fallen off to-night, we're almost the only ones left on our branch."

"You never know who's going to go next," said the first leaf. "Even when it was warm and the sun shone, a storm or a cloudburst would come sometimes, and many leaves were torn off, though they were still young. You never know who's going to go next."

"The sun seldom shines now," sighed the second leaf, "and when it does it gives no warmth. We must have warmth again."

"Can it be true," said the first leaf, "can it really be true, that others come to take our places when we're gone and after them still others, and more and more?"

"It is really true," whispered the second leaf. "We can't even begin to imagine it, it's beyond our powers."

"It makes me very sad," added the first leaf.

They were silent a while. Then the first leaf said quietly to herself, "Why must we fall . . . ?"

The second leaf asked, "What happens to us when we have fallen?"

"We sink down. . . ."

"What is under us?"

The first leaf answered, "I don't know, some say one thing, some another, but nobody knows."

The second leaf asked, "Do we feel anything, do we know anything about ourselves when we're down there?"

The first leaf answered, "Who knows? Not one of all those down there has ever come back to tell us about it."

They were silent again. Then the first leaf said tenderly to the other, "Don't worry so much about it, you're trembling."

"That's nothing," the second leaf answered, "I tremble at the least thing now. I don't feel so sure of my hold as I used to."

"Let's not talk any more about such things," said the first leaf.

The other replied, "No, we'll let be. But,—what else shall we talk about?" She was silent and went on after a little while, "Which of us will go first?"

"There's still plenty of time to worry about that," the other leaf assured her. "Let's remember how beautiful it was, how wonderful, when the sun came out and shone so warmly that we thought we'd burst with life. Do you remember? And the morning dew, and the mild and splendid nights. . . ."

"Now the nights are dreadful," the second leaf complained, "and there is no end to them."

"We shouldn't complain," said the first leaf gently. "We've outlived many, many others."

"Have I changed much?" asked the second leaf shyly but determinedly.

"Not in the least," the first leaf assured her. "You only think so because I've got to be so yellow and ugly. But it's different in your case."

"You're fooling me," the second leaf said.

"No, really," the first leaf exclaimed eagerly, "believe me, you're as lovely as the day you were born. Here and there may be a little yellow spot but it's hardly noticeable and only makes you handsomer, believe me."

"Thanks," whispered the second leaf,

quite touched. "I don't believe you, not altogether, but I thank you because you're so kind, you've always been so kind to me. I'm just beginning to understand how kind you are."

"Hush," said the other leaf, and kept silent herself for she was too troubled to talk any more.

Then they were both silent. Hours passed.

A moist wind blew, cold and hostile, through the tree tops.

"Ah, now," said the second leaf, "I . . ." Then her voice broke off. She was torn from her place and spun down.

Winter had come.   —From *Bambi*

TEWKESBURY ROAD
John Masefield

It is good to be out on the road, and going one knows not where,
   Going through meadow and village, one knows not whither nor why;
Through the grey light drift of the dust, in the keen, cool rush of the air,
   Under the flying white clouds, and the broad blue lift of the sky.

And to halt at the chattering brook, in the tall green fern at the brink
   Where the harebell grows, and the gorse, and the fox-gloves purple and white;
Where the shy-eyed delicate deer troop down to the brook to drink
   When the stars are mellow and large at the coming on of the night.

O, to feel the beat of the rain, and the homely smell of the earth,
   Is a tune for the blood to jig to, a joy past power of words;
And the blessed green comely meadows are all a-ripple with mirth
   At the noise of the lambs at play and the dear wild cry of the birds.

AUTUMN SUNSET
By Henry David Thoreau

The sun sets on some retired meadow, where no house is visible, with all the glory and splendour that it lavished on cities, and, perchance, as it has never set before—where there is but a solitary marsh-hawk to have his wings gilded by it, or only a musquash looks out from his cabin, and there is some little black-veined brook in the midst of the marsh, just beginning to meander, winding slowly round a decaying stump. We walked in so pure and bright a light, gilding the withered grass and leaves, so softly and serenely bright, I thought I had never bathed in such a golden flood, without a ripple or a murmur to it. The west side of every wood and rising ground gleamed like a boundary of Elysium, and the sun on our backs seemed like a gentle herdsman driving us home at evening.

So we saunter toward the Holy Land, till one day the sun shall shine more brightly than ever he has done, shall perchance shine into our minds and hearts, and light up our whole lives with a great awakening light, as warm and serene and golden as on a bank-side in autumn.

61

THE FLOWER'S NAME

ROBERT BROWNING

Here's the garden she walked across,
  Arm in my arm, such a short while since:
Hark! now I push its wicket, the moss
  Hinders the hinges, and makes them wince.
She must have reached this shrub ere she turned,
  As back with that murmur the wicket swung;
For she laid the poor snail my chance foot spurned,
  To feed and forget it the leaves among.

Down this side of the gravel walk
  She went while her robe's edge brushed the box;
And here she paused in her gracious talk
  To point me a moth on the milk-white phlox.
Roses, ranged in valiant row,
  I will never think that she passed you by!
She loves you, noble roses, I know;
  But yonder see where the rock-plants lie!

This flower she stopped at, finger on lip,—
  Stooped over, in doubt, as settling its claim;
Till she gave me, with pride to make no slip,
  Its soft meandering Spanish name.
What a name! Was it love or praise?
  Speech half asleep, or song half awake?
I must learn Spanish one of these days,
  Only for that slow sweet name's sake.

Roses, if I live and do well,
  I may bring her one of these days,
To fix you fast with as fine a spell,—
  Fit you each with his Spanish phrase.
But do not detain me now, for she lingers
  There, like sunshine over the ground;
And ever I see her soft white fingers
  Searching after the bud she found.

Flower, you Spaniard! look that you grow not,—
  Stay as you are, and be loved forever.
Bud, if I kiss you, 'tis that you blow not,—
  Mind! the shut pink mouth opens never!

For while thus it pouts, her fingers wrestle,
  Twinkling the audacious leaves between,
Till round they turn, and down they nestle:
  Is not the dear mark still to be seen?

Where I find her not, beauties vanish;
  Whither I follow her, beauties flee.
Is there no method to tell her in Spanish
  June's twice June since she breathed it with me?
Come, bud! show me the least of her traces.
  Treasure my lady's lightest footfall:
Ah! you may flout and turn up your faces,—
  Roses, you are not so fair after all!

I HAVE ALWAYS SAID I WOULD GO
Glenn Ward Dresbach

I have always said I would go sometime in the autumn
  Away from the bare boughs and the fallen leaves,
Away from the lonely sounds and the faded colors,
  And all the ancient sorrow, and change that grieves.

I have always said I would go—and now it's autumn—
  To an island where the wild hibiscus grows
And parakeets flock to the groves at twilight
  And fragrance drifts from bays where moonlight glows.

But there would be the vasty sound of breakers
  Come in to toss their pearls upon the sand.
All through the night—a longing of great waters
  Trying to make the vastness understand.

I have always said I would go sometime in the autumn
  Away from the lonely sounds and change that grieves—
But here in my heart is the sound of a distant ocean
  And here in my heart is the sound of these falling leaves.

* * *

❧ THE HAPPINESS of life is made up of minute fractions—the little soon-forgotten charities of a kiss or smile, a kind look, a heartfelt compliment, and the countless infinitesimals of pleasurable and genial feeling.
—Coleridge

AMERICAN LAUGHTER
KENNETH ALLAN ROBINSON

Oh the men who laughed the American laughter
Whittled their jokes from the fresh tree-pines;
They were tall men, sharpened before and after;
They studied the sky for the weather-signs;
They tilted their hats and they smoked long-nines.

Their laughter was ladled in Western flagons
And poured down throats that were parched for more;
This was the laughter of democrat-wagons
And homely men at the crossroads store
—It tickled the shawl that a lawyer wore!

It hurt the ears of the dainty and pretty
But they laughed the louder and laughed their fill,
A laughter made for Virginia City,
Springfield, and Natchez-under-the-Hill,
And the river that flows past Hannibal still!

American laughter was lucky laughter,
A coonskin tune by a homespun bard;
It tasted of hams from the smokehouse rafter
And locust trees in the courthouse yard,
And Petroleum Nasby and Artemus Ward!

They laughed at the Mormons and Mike Fink's daughter
And the corncob tale of Sut Lovingood's dog,
Till the ague fled from the fever-water
And the damps deserted the tree-stump bog,
—They laughed at the tale of the jumping frog!

They laughed at the British, they laughed at the Shakers,
At Horace Greeley and stovepipe hats;
They split their fences and plowed their acres,
And treed their troubles like mountain cats;
—They laughed calamity out of the flats!

Now the Boston man, according to rumor,
Said, as he turned in his high-backed bed,
"This doesn't conform to my rules for humor,"
And he settled his night cap over his head,
—But it shook the earth like the buffalo tread!

And the corn grew tall and the fields grew wider,
And the land grew sleek with the mirth they sowed;
They laughed the fat meat into the spider,
They laughed the blues from the Wilderness Road,
—They crossed hard times to the Comstock Lode!

I SHALL NOT CARE
SARA TEASDALE

When I am dead and over me bright April
    Shakes out her rain-drenched hair,
Though you should lean above me broken-hearted,
    I shall not care.

I shall have peace, as leafy trees are peaceful
    When rain bends down the bough;
And I shall be more silent and cold-hearted
    Than you are now.

ALL MEN ARE PIONEERS
LIONEL WIGGAM

All men are pioneers inside their hearts.
They are forever seeking wilderness.
Behind strong teams they ride in hooded carts,
Avid for life, and masterless.

They would take their women west or north,
They would invade a country terrible with peril,
They would eternally be riding forth
Out of the cities they have found so sterile.

In their hearts they are forever cutting clover,
They are forever drawing water from a well.
In their dreams they are observing, over and over,
The ground they would clear, the forests they would fell.

They are dreaming of lands uncivilized that sprawl
Unfound, or unimagined or forgot. . . .
Knowing they will not leave the town at all,
As like as not.

MAKE a joyful noise unto the Lord, all ye lands.

Serve the Lord with gladness: come before his presence with singing.

Know ye that the Lord he is God: it is he that hath made us, and not we ourselves; we are his people, and the sheep of his pasture.

Enter into his gates with thanksgiving, and into his courts with praise: be thankful unto him, and bless his name.

For the Lord is good; his mercy is everlasting; and his truth endureth to all generations.

THE PRODIGAL
LOUISE AYRES GARNETT

God has such a splendid way
Of launching his unchallenged yea:

Of giving sphery grapes their sheen;
Of painting trees and grasses green;

Of sharing April rains that we
May wash us in simplicity;

Of swinging little smiling moons
Beyond the reach of noisy noons;

Or storing in the honey bee
The whole of life's epitome.

God has such a splendid way
Of tempting beauty out of clay,

And from the scattered dust that sleep
Summoning men who laugh and weep,

And by and by of letting death
Draw into space our thread of breath.

HE THAT dwelleth in the secret place of the most High shall abide under the shadow of the Almighty.

I will say of the Lord, He is my refuge and my fortress: my God; in him will I trust.

Surely he shall deliver thee from the snare of the fowler, and from the noisome pestilence.

He shall cover thee with his feathers, and under his wings shalt thou trust: his truth shall be thy shield and buckler.

Thou shalt not be afraid for the terror by night; *nor* for the arrow that flieth by day;

Nor for the pestilence that walketh in darkness; *nor* for the destruction that wasteth at noonday.

A thousand shall fall at thy side, and ten thousand at thy right hand; but it shall not come nigh thee.

Only with thine eyes shalt thou behold and see the reward of the wicked.

Because thou hast made the Lord, which is my refuge, even the most High, thy habitation;

There shall no evil befall thee, neither shall any plague come nigh thy dwelling.

For he shall give his angels charge over thee, to keep thee in all thy ways.

They shall bear thee up in their hands, lest thou dash thy foot against a stone.

Thou shalt tread upon the lion and adder: the young lion and the dragon shalt thou trample under foot.

Because he hath set his love upon me, therefore will I deliver him: I will set him on high, because he hath known my name.

He shall call upon me, and I will answer him: I will be with him in trouble; I will deliver him, and honour him.

With long life will I satisfy him, and show him my salvation.

THIS IS MY PRAYER
Rabindranath Tagore

This is my prayer to thee, my lord—strike,
Strike at the root of penury in my heart.
Give me the strength lightly to bear my joys and sorrows.
Give me the strength to make my love fruitful in service.
Give me the strength never to disown the poor or
    bend my knees before insolent might.
Give me the strength to raise my mind high above daily trifles.
And give me the strength to surrender my strength
    to thy will with love.

MOTHERHOOD
Agnes Lee

Mary, the Christ long slain, passed silently,
Following the children joyously astir
Under the cedrus and the olive-tree,
Pausing to let their laughter float to her.
Each voice an echo of a voice more dear,
She saw a little Christ in every face.

Then came another woman gliding near
To watch the tender life that filled the place.
And Mary sought the woman's hand, and spoke:
"I know thee not, yet know thy memory tossed
With all a thousand dreams their eyes evoke
Who bring to thee a child beloved and lost.

"I, too, have rocked my Little One.
And he was fair!
Oh, fairer than the fairest sun,
And like its rays through amber spun
His sun-bright hair!

Still I can see it shine and shine."
"Even so," the woman said, "was mine."

"His ways were ever darling ways"—
And Mary smiled—
"So soft, so clinging! Glad relays
Of love were all his precious days.
My Little Child!
My vanished star! My music fled!"
"Even so was mine," the woman said.

And Mary whispered: "Tell me, thou,
Of thine." And she:
"Oh, mine was rosy as a bough
Blooming with roses, sent, somehow,
To bloom for me!
His balmy fingers left a thrill
Deep in my breast that warms me still."

Then she gazed down some wilder, darker hour,
And said—when Mary questioned, knowing not:
"Who art thou, mother of so sweet a flower?"—
"I am the mother of Iscariot."

* * *

❧ It is in vain to gather virtues without humility, for the spirit of God delighteth to dwell in the hearts of the humble.   —*Erasmus*

NOTHING WILL ever be attempted if all possible objections must be first overcome.—*Johnson*

NOTHING GREAT was ever achieved without enthusiasm.—*Emerson*

A NOBLE AIM, faithfully kept, is as a noble deed.—*Wordsworth*

KEEP A BRAVE SPIRIT, and never despair; Hope brings you messages through the keen air—Good is victorious—God everywhere.—*Anonymous*

THE ONLY CONQUESTS which are permanent, and leave no regrets, are our conquests over ourselves.—*Napoleon*

AND HAVING THUS chosen our course without guile and with pure purpose, let us renew our trust in God and go forward without fear and with manly hearts.—*Lincoln*

LIBERTY is one of the most valuable blessings that Heaven has bestowed upon mankind.—*Cervantes*

AND BECAUSE right is right, to follow right were wisdom in the scorn of consequence.—*Tennyson*

THE PURE, the beautiful . . . the impulse to a wordless prayer, . . . these things can never die.—*Doudney*

MOTHER is the name for God in the lips and hearts of little children.
—*Thackeray*

GOLDEN HOURS of vision come to us in this present life when we are at our best.—*Dole*

TRUTH . . . is the highest summit of art and of life.—*Amiel*

THE GREATER the difficulty, the greater the glory.—*Cicero*

BETTER LIFE

FORTIFY YOURSELF with contentment, for this is an
impregnable fortress.—*Epictetus*

IT TAKES a wise man to discover a wise man.—*Diogenes*

GOOD WILL is the mightiest practical force in the universe.—*Dole*

MAKE THY STUDY a regular thing; say little and do much; and
meet every man with friendliness.—*The Talmud*

WHEN MEN are rightly occupied their amusement grows out of their work as
the color-petals out of a fruitful flower.—*Ruskin*

THE REAL USE of all knowledge is this: that we should dedicate that
reason which was given us by God for the use and advantage of man.
—*Bacon*

CHARACTER is nurtured midst the tempests of the world.—*Goethe*

LIBERTY is not in any form of government. It is in the heart of free man; he
carries it with him everywhere.—*Rousseau*

IN CONTEMPLATION of created things by steps we may
ascend to God.—*Milton*

A GOOD BOOK is the precious lifeblood of a master-spirit embalmed and
treasured up on purpose to a life beyond life.—*Milton*

GOD GRANTS LIBERTY only to those who love it, and are always ready
to guard and defend it.—*Webster*

IN THE MOUNTAINS of truth you never climb in vain.—*Nietzche*

No SEED shall perish which the soul hath sown.—*Symonds*

The Princess Marries the Page

By EDNA ST. VINCENT MILLAY

SCENE

A room in the top of a tower. Half the room is to be seen, bounded by a grey wall which curves away from the audience. In the centre of the wall is a large open window, framed by reddening ivy and flooded with sunlight. On the outer ledge of the window, in the sunshine, sits a slim and handsome Page, playing on a pipe. Inside the room, in a very big chair, reading a very big book, sits the most beautiful Princess you have ever seen.

PRINCESS

I came up here to read! . . . Go down!
Play in the court—there is a fountain
  there;
Or in the garden, where are coloured
  roses;
Go to the cook, who's making cakes
  today,
And say I said you were to have your
  fill;
Only, disturb me not; I came up here
To read.

PAGE

    I came up here to play.
Go down! Read in the garden—where
  are wasps,
Or in the court—where there are col-
  oured lizards;
Go to the King, who's making search
  today,
And say that I have climbed unto a
  ledge
Of air, and play a pipe, and will not
  come;
Only, disturb me not—I came up here
To play.
[*Plays*]
    Tu-luri-lu! Tu-luri-la!

PRINCESS

This is my father's tower—you just go
  down now!
I have to read this reading, and I can't
Read while you play—you ought to
  know I cannot!

Besides, you throw a shadow on the
  book.

PAGE

I have to play this tune; 'tis in my head
And clamours to be out! Who knows?
  It may be
The last that I shall play!—there is a
  thought
Should comfort you.
[*Plays*]

PRINCESS

[*Reading aloud*]
        "So then the maiden came
Clothed all in delicate colours, like a
  garden,
And very sweet to smell; her little hands
Were like white moths i' the dusk,—
  long afterwards
In dreams he saw their drowsy flutter-
  ing—;
Her soft, infrequent phrases, hurriedly
Articulate against his lips, her eyes,
Like drowned stars i' the pool of her
  dark hair;
Her breath upon his neck,—all these he
  knew,
Long afterwards, in dreams; when she
  was gone
He stood beside the honeysuckle bush
Alone, more than an hour, and thought
  of her."
[*The Page, who has been playing a sad and lovely melody, has gradually ceased playing, charmed by the Prin-*

cess' story; in the same way the Prin-*
cess, enraptured by the Page's piping,
has been reading more and more slow-
ly, softly, and abstractedly, until she
has ceased altogether. They now turn
to each other simultaneously]
Don't stop!

PAGE

That's beautiful!

PRINCESS

Go on!

PAGE

Go on!

[They gaze at one another for a mo-
ment, then the Page laughs amusedly.
The Princess turns from him in anger]

PRINCESS

I hate you!

PAGE

By my soul I do not blame you!
A piper that will dumb his pipe with
  myrtle,
And pipe no more;—almost I hate myself.

PRINCESS

I would I had the grace my fathers
  wore,
So I might pry you off the ledge, or tear
The ivy from beneath you, that you
  might
Find your way down without it!

PAGE

And I would
Your hair were longer,—I would seize
  you by it,
And my grey ladder not descend alone.

PRINCESS

My hair is very long! It is too long!
It is too heavy! It weighs down my
  head!
Oh, how I hate you! How I hate you!
  Oh!

[There is a sound of some one coming
up the stairs]
Hark! Is that some one coming here?
  —I'll wager
A hawk against a tennis-ball my father
Wants you and comes in search of you!
  Climb down
A little way, and cling to the ivy!
  Quick!
[The Page climbs out of sight below
the window; the Princess goes back to
her book.]
[Enter the Lord High Chancellor]

CHANCELLOR

I crave Your Highness' grace for this
intrusion.

PRINCESS

I know your errand, sir.

CHANCELLOR

Madam, you know it?

PRINCESS

Aye, sir, my father—

CHANCELLOR

Madam, the King, your father—

PRINCESS

Has tried to feed my goldfish once
  again,
And Blue-Fin will not eat! You tell him
Blue-Fin does not like oat-cakes! And
  besides
He dropped his crown i' the bowl one
  day, and scared them!
Tell him I say to leave my fish alone!

CHANCELLOR

[Very solemnly]
Madam, it is not fish.

PRINCESS

Oh, never tell me
He has found my journal! Oh, he has
  not the right
To read my journal, e'en though he be

71

a King!
Snatch it away!

CHANCELLOR

   Madam, your royal father
Sends me to ask if you perchance have
 seen
A wretched page, in russet hose and
 doublet,
About the tower; 'tis said he turned
 this way.

PRINCESS

A page. A page? H'm, let me see, page
 —page—
There's been no page i' the tower—that
 I can swear to;
Indeed, I've sat here all the afternoon,
And not a soul, until yourself made
 entrance,
Has come into this room. Nor have I
 heard—
Assure 'm of this—a single sound below
 me;
I have not heard one step upon the
 stairs.
Page—page—huh-uh!
[*The Chancellor starts to go; as the
Princess begins to speak again, he turns
and listens. She is leaning against the
window, speaking loud enough to be
heard by the Page*]

   I know the man you mean!
A piping fellow, and discourteous,
New to the court, I know! You'll come
 upon him
Asleep somewhere i' the sun, mayhap,
 or else
Flat on his back beneath a hawthorn-
 bush,
Love-piping to some freckled shep-
 herdess!
As for the tower—nay, sir, he is not in it.

CHANCELLOR

I thank Your Highness, Madam, and
 crave grace
For this intrusion.

PRINCESS

   Nay, sir, I am glad
If I have been of ne'er so slight assist-
 ance
To one in need.
[*Curtseys*]
   My reverence to the King.
[*Exit the Chancellor*]
     [*With amusement*]
"There's been no page i' the tower—
 you'll come upon him
Asleep somewhere i' the sun, mayhap"
 —mayhap
You will, and then again mayhap you
 will not!
Mayhap most anything! How do I know
But he has fallen asleep, or found a
 tree
To flute beneath—mayhap if I could see
Through a wall—to make no mention
 of the ivy!—
I then might tell what's going on with-
 out;
As 'tis—troth's me! I know not!
[*The Page leaps into the room*]
     Shrive my soul!
Who told you to come in?

PAGE

   Madam—his pages
Are passing by beneath in search of me!
I sue for pardon—in a moment more
They will be gone. I would ha'e gi'en
 me up
Rather than plague you further, only
 that
I feared if they should take me on the
 wall
[*He goes on bravely, but with embar-
rassment, not looking at her*]
'Twould spread a tale that you had hid
 me here
For love, and lied to cover my escape.

PRINCESS

For love? For love of you? Lied—out
 of love
For you? Heav'n's blessing on me! Do

72

I look
As if I loved you?

PAGE

[*Distressed*]
Nay, I said not so,
Your Highness—

PRINCESS

Do I look as I would lie
To shield you from a beating?

PAGE

[*With emotion*]
Nay, indeed,
I do not think so! Since in all the
world
Is not one tongue so fond would lie to
shield me
From death.

PRINCESS

[*After a pause*]
Why, boy! Why, nay, then, you
are wrong;
For that would I. In all the world not
one?
What of your sweetheart? Is there not
some maiden,
Some golden-headed herder of white
geese,
Some shepherdess, some dark-eyed vio-
let-vendor
That holds you dear? Some fisher-girl,
that daily,
Swinging her basket, barefoot, crosses
the court
And turns to smile at you?

PAGE

Madam, there is not.

PRINCESS

[*Aside*]
'Tis difficult to explain: where are
their eyes?
I' faith, he is not ill to look upon!
Clothed like a gentleman, myself
should find
Him perilous,—aye, and even as he

stands,
I' faith, he is not ill to look upon!
[*To the Page*]
Where is your mother?

PAGE

An it please Your Highness,
I think she be in Heaven, with your
own.

PRINCESS

Have you no father?

PAGE

Aye, I have a father,
Such as he is.

PRINCESS

Poor boy,—in all the world
Not one! Come here!
[*She holds out her arms to him. As he
starts forward toward her she drops her
arms with shame and some confusion*]
There is a bit of cobweb
Caught in your hair. So!
[*She removes the cobweb, an imaginary
speck, from his hair, then kisses him
suddenly on the cheek, and turns away,
appalled at herself*]
Prithee to forgive me!
[*She begins to weep*]
I could not bear to see thee so dis-
tressed,
And no one caring!

PAGE

[*Deeply stirred*]
Lady, do not weep!
I am no longer sad, save for your
grieving.
Melt not my tears for you, that for
myself
Lie like a frozen pool i' the breast,—
I pray you,
Weep not, sweet soul,—I am not worth
your tears.

PRINCESS

Nay, that may be;—there's many a
worthless thing

73

Wept over!
[*Turns to him in instant deprecation
of her rudeness, and takes him into her
confidence, her voice rising into sobs
and finally coming out into a wail at
the end of her speech*]
        I am not quite sure for what
I do weep; but I have not wept in
days,—
And it is time I did—now that I'm at
it—
I might as well keep on—and weep it
ou-u-ut. . .

PAGE

[*Deeply distressed and entirely
at a loss*]
Please do not cry so! Listen, wouldn't
you like
My silver pipe to play on?

PRINCESS

[*Still weeping*]
        No—no, thank you!

PAGE

[*Hastily searching the big pocket-bag
he wears at his side*]
I have a golden string long as a lance.

PRINCESS

I have a golden train longer than that.
[*Sobs*]

PAGE

I have a peacock's feather

PRINCESS

[*Unpleasantly, looking up*]
        Aye, no doubt!
Plucked from the tail of my most fa-
vourite fowl!
You may retain it.
[*Crosses away from him*]

PAGE

[*Uncertainly*]
        Well, I have—I have, then—
[*Finds an apple in his pocket*]
Do you like apples?

PRINCESS

[*Very eager*]
Apples? What about them?

PAGE

Why—do you like them?

PRINCESS

[*Humiliated but desirous*]
        No! That is—no, no!
At least—
[*She turns and surrenders to him with
an appreciative smile*]
Have you an apple?
[*Sees it*]
        Give it to me!

PAGE

[*Holding it out of her reach*]
Ah, but so easily won? And such an
apple?
So ruddy and incomparable a fruit?
[*He looks quietly into her face, which
is very near him, and speaks playfully
but intensely*]
What have you in your pockets for
exchange?

PRINCESS

[*She is held by his gaze for a full mo-
ment, then drops her eyes*]
Pockets? Exchange?
[*She looks at him, but again drops her
eyes*]
        Nay, I have nothing, then.
[*She remembers the apple*]
Oh, but please give it to me—please!
—I love
Apples!
[*Suddenly becoming very sweet and im-
perious*]
I want it so, I have to have it!
[*The Page, amused, after a slight pause
gives it to her*]

PAGE

Against such reasoning is no debate.
[*She seizes the apple and scurries with
it to the seat in the window, where she
begins to eat it, with both hands, like*

a squirrel. He goes up to her little throne and sits insolently in her chair, one leg over the arm of it]

PRINCESS

[With a deep sigh of satisfaction]
Ah-h-h!
[Looking up and catching his amused and almost paternal smile, she holds out her hand to him with an instant access of tremendous, but mock, dignity]
You may kiss my hand.
[The Page drops to his knees before her, and seizing her hand in both his, bows his head over it. He does not move for some time, and the Princess becomes very uneasy. She wriggles her hand a bit to free it; but he does not release it. She looks about the room nervously, and then back at him; she scowls, and wriggles her hand again. Then she laughs in a fit of terror. Finally she has a thought, and proffers him her apple]
[Very hospitably]
Bite?
[The Page looks up at her, and seizes her other hand, apple and all. His face is tragically sad]
What's the matter? Why, you look so sad!

PAGE

And so I am . . . the saddest man, mayhap,
That e'er your eyes beheld.

PRINCESS

[Deeply touched by his grief, but considering]
The saddest man
I ever saw? Ah, no—that cannot be!
For I have looked upon that wretched King
Who rules the wide dominions to the west—
The "Sullen King" men call him—but I know
That he is only sad; he was so sad

The day I saw him, that I needs must pat
His cloak to comfort him! At least they say so;
I have forgotten,—I was very small.
[The Page has risen at the mention of the Sullen King, and turned from her; at the close of her speech, however, he comes back, and stands looking down at the top of her head, which she has hung in pretty embarrassment, like a child]

PAGE

It is a sovereign remedy, this patting
Of gentlemen's cloaks by ladies,—be they small
Or not so small;—I would I wore a cloak.

PRINCESS

[Very brightly, grateful that they are playing once more]
Yet, surely in your pocket still remains
Some certain cure for sorrow! Let me look!
[She makes room for him on the window ledge; he jumps up beside her]
Give all you have, and I will choose among them!
Oh, what is that?

PAGE

That is a stripèd stone
To keep away the fairies.

PRINCESS

[Examining it]
But who wants
To keep away the fairies?

PAGE

[After a delighted pause]
Well, I have, then,
A fluted shell to conjure them about.

PRINCESS

[Reaching for it greedily]
Give it to me!

Ah, but I need it more!
You've but to call them, and they all
    will come;
Whilst I—ah, many's the night I've
    waited for them,
Thirsting, and fasting, and adrip with
    dew,
I' the depths of some dark bosk—until
    they should
Appear and dance about me in the
    clearing;
But never once beheld them, never
    once
Even so much as caught the fragile
    clangour,
Incredibly, of their clear bugles and
    bells,
And high, sweet, rollicking shouts—
    until I found
This.

PRINCESS

[*Awed*]
And they come now?

PAGE

Aye, on any night
When the moon is white and the woods
    are black, and scarves
Of silver mist are drawn, and then
    withdrawn
About the trunks of the trees—ah,
[*Closes his eyes*]
    aye, they come.
[*They have both been looking ahead
of them with wide eyes, as if seeing the
same thing, while the Page has been
speaking. When the Page sighs "Ah,"
and closes his eyes, the Princess echoes
the sigh, and closes her eyes, too. At
the close of the speech, however, she
suddenly becomes very alert, and leans
toward him beseechingly*]

PRINCESS

Oh, sometime take me with you! I have
    never
Beheld a fairy!—Oh, I *say* I have,
Because I *may* have.

[*Considering, with a frown*]
    And it seems I *must* have,
So that I'm *sure* I *have*—but all the
    while
[*Rapidly, and in a lower voice*]
Down in my heart I know I *never* have.
You understand.

PAGE

[*Elaborately*]
    Aye—or at least, that is,
I may, so that it seems to me I must,
And I am sure I do—though all the
    while
Down in my heart of hearts, I am con-
    vinced
I do not understand you. Women are
Superior to men in every way,
But chiefly in the intellect.

PRINCESS

[*Joyfully*]
    'Tis so!
And so I will protest until I prove it
To all who doubt.
[*Aside, to the Page comically*]
    Albeit I know 'tis false.
[*They both laugh. She takes another
bite of her apple, and comes back to
the treasures scattered on the window
ledge*]
Well, is that all you have? There's little
    here
To balm a wound.

PAGE

[*Stuffing the things back into his
pocket*]
    Aye, it is all I have.

PRINCESS

Nay, but I heard a crackling under
    your hand!
What may that be? Out with it! Give
    it to me!

PAGE

[*He has leapt from the window, at her
words, and crossed away from her*]
No, no! Oh, no, no, no! You must not

ask me!
It is—
[*He does not continue, but turns his face from her*]

PRINCESS

It is a letter from a girl,
That's what it is!

PAGE

Well, then, what if it is?

PRINCESS

[*Mortified, extravagantly protestant*]
Why, nothing! Why-why, nothing! Less than nothing
To me! What do I care about your letters?
You speak as if you thought perhaps I cared,
Was jealous, maybe, of your paltry letters!
Why, what is it to me who writes you letters?
Or how many letters she writes? I'm only glad
It's not *my* letters that you bear about
To flaunt before my face—I mean, her face—
I mean I'm glad I am indifferent to you,
And wish that you had died e'er ever we met!

PAGE

Lady, be comforted, for I shall die
Full soon. But as for this, it is my grief
Itself, and should be pleasant to your touch.
[*He gives her the paper which he had in his pocket. It is heavily official-looking, and bears a large seal*]
Ah, for a little while I had forgotten,
But now I do recall. Lady, I thank you
For this sweet play.
[*He looks at her with intense tenderness, then turns abruptly, and goes to the window*]
⠀⠀⠀⠀The sun is off the ivy
Now, and the darling world is growing dark.

[*He turns to her and speaks very gently, as to a child*]
Tonight I think the fairies will come forth.
Here: you may have my shell if you would go
Tonight and watch them dance,—for it may be
They could not hear you calling, through their clatter.
Be there at moonrise.

PRINCESS

[*Fearfully, not taking the proffered shell*]
⠀⠀⠀⠀Aye, but where will you be?

PAGE

[*As if struck by the thought for the first time*]
Where shall I be? But where shall I be? Why,
'Tis strange to think upon.—I do not know
Where I shall be.

PRINCESS

[*After a terrified pause*]
⠀⠀⠀⠀What is this dreadful paper?
It frightens me! Oh, I am terrified!
[*Drops the paper on the floor*]
What is the matter?—Tell me! Everything
Is strange about you and the things you say!
Ah, what is that!
[*She gives a little nervous scream and goes to the window*]
[*After a slight pause, reassuring herself*]
⠀⠀⠀⠀Nay, it is nothing. Nay!
There's some one on the bridge!
[*Stiffening with horror, she turns slowly, and looks at the Page*]
⠀⠀⠀⠀It is the guard!
Is't you they seek?
[*Rapidly, but pitifully, without assurance*]
⠀⠀⠀⠀A heavier punishment

Belike, for this long absence?

PAGE

Nay, indeed,
A heavier punishment,—the heaviest
Of all; but not for absence,—rather for
My presence at the court. I am a spy,
Madam, and map your father's ruin!—
  My father,
Such as he is!—is king unto your bor-
ders.

PRINCESS

Oh, no, no, no! You are not! No, you
are not!

PAGE

Dear child Oh, my heart, you lovely,
lovely child!
[*He starts toward the door*]

PRINCESS

Where are you going?

PAGE

Down to meet them.

PRINCESS

Ah,
No, no! And yet—oh, this is terrible!
I came up here to read! Why did you
come here?
I was so happy till you—

PAGE

Why did I come here?
Why does a man who is doomed to Hell
for ever
Climb into Heaven for a day? I came
up here
To look into your lovely, angry eyes!
To listen to your sweet, inclement
voice!
I came up here to laugh! I came up
here
To play!
[*He lifts the pipe to his lips*]

PRINCESS

[*Reaching out for it*]

Oh, no! They are in the tower!
The window!
It is your only chance!

PAGE

[*Wearily*]
Nay, I am weary
Of chances. Grant me the grace to bide
with you
Until they come.
[*He lifts the pipe again*]

PRINCESS

[*In anguish*]
Oh, don't! Out of the window!
[*With sudden exasperation*]
'Twill save your silly life! Do as I bid
you,
Fellow!
[*Remembering his rank*]
Oh, sir, if they take you in this
room
'Twill spread a tale that I have held
you here
For love—will it not please you to be
gone?

PAGE

I am your servant ever, and God forbid
That they should say you loved me!—
As for my life,
'Tis but of small account without your
love.
[*He bows very low, and lowers himself
out of sight beneath the window. The
Princess picks up the paper. Going
back to her chair, she thrusts the paper
into her book, and searches feverishly
for something suitable for reading
aloud when the soldiers shall come in.
Finding nothing, she begins to extem-
porize, speaking in a high voice to rep-
resent the lady, and then in a very low
voice to show the knight*]

PRINCESS

[*Pretending to read aloud*]
Whereat the youth replied, "Madam,
my life
Is but of small account without your

78

love.
Say if you love me." "Nay," replied the
    lady,
"But rather hate—or would hate if I
    could;
And since I cannot, do so all the more!
Art satisfied?" "Nay, then," replied the
    youth,
"That am I not, nor see I any logic
In what you say."
[*To the Soldiers, who have entered
some time since, and whom she has pre-
tended not to see before*]
                Shrive me! Good afternoon!
Chains and mischances! Now what
    have I done?

FIRST SOLDIER

We crave Your Highness' grace, we
    thought we heard
Two voices in the tower.

PRINCESS

[*As if delighted*]
                Nay, not really?
Two voices! Nay, but hear me then
    again!
Where was I—Oh! "Look not in me for
    logic,
Nor in no lady," quo' she, "nor on oaks
For quinces—you'll not find them—fare
    you well."
"Madam," replied the youth, "Madam,
    b'r Lady,
And by my halidome, and by my troth,
And by my knightly spurs—" "Oath me
    no oaths,"
Quo' she. . . . Nay, is it not well done?
—Two voices!

FIRST SOLDIER

The book is upside down.

PRINCESS

[*After a slight pause, brightly*]
                Aye, and why not?
That is the way 'tis written. Look and
    see.
[*She holds out the book to them in
turn, so that they see it, upside down*]

FIRST SOLDIER

'Tis so.

SECOND SOLDIER

Aye, so it is.

THIRD SOLDIER

Why, so it is.

FIRST SOLDIER

It is a foreign book.

SECOND SOLDIER

Aye, true.

THIRD SOLDIER

'Tis so.

FIRST SOLDIER

I crave Your Highness' grace. This
    fellow here
Vowed that he heard two voices in the
    tower.
And so I thought—

SECOND SOLDIER

Nay, then, not I—I said—
I *thought* I heard two voices!

FIRST SOLDIER

                Then 'twas you!

THIRD SOLDIER

Nay, sir, not I! Indeed it was not I!
I only said it *sounded* like two voices—
And so it did.

FIRST SOLDIER

Aye, that it did.

SECOND SOLDIER

It did that.

FIRST SOLDIER

Your Highness, pardon us.

PRINCESS

                With all my heart,
Good sirs—it was a natural mistake.
[*The Princess takes up her book again,*

79

and begins to read. The Soldiers go toward the exit, and there meet the King and Chancellor, who are just entering. The Soldiers fall back against the wall as the King enters the room. The Princess does not know what has occurred]

KING

My dear, I came to ask you—

PRINCESS

[*Jumping up, startled, in such a way that her book falls to the floor, and the paper falls out of it*]
Why, Papa!
[*Curtseys hurriedly, and speaks very rapidly, without inflection*]
Your-Majesty's-health-and-may-Your-Majesty
For-ever-reign. . . . Papa! What do you mean,
Climbing about the tower with a foot
Like yours? . . . When will you learn to be discreet?
Your crown's on crooked—Father, is that your best crown
You're wearing every day? Oh, dear!
Here! . . . There!
[*She straightens his crown*]

KING

My dear, I came to ask you, have you seen—

PRINCESS

Now, Father, have I seen! What should I see,
Shut up in a tower and bending over a book
All afternoon? What could I see? Instruct me!
And now you're here—answer without evasion!
You're so evasive, sometimes!—Have you been
Experimenting with my goldfish, Father? . . . Father!
You have, you know you have!

KING

My dear, I came—

PRINCESS

Quite right—to make confession of your fault!
But I shall not forgive you. . . . I have spoiled you,
Forgiving you so often—and this time,
I assure you, I am grievously annoyed!
Henceforth you will be spared the ignominy
Of losing to me hoplessly at chess
Five evenings in the week. . . . In solitude
I'll walk abroad, and take my goldfish with me
Wherever I go.

KING

[*Troubled*]
My dear, I beg that you
Will consider this so rash decision.
Think of my loneliness, I beg of you.
[*Slowly*]
Five evenings in the week.

PRINCESS

Well, I will think.

KING

Moreover, you exaggerate, and grossly,
To say I constantly am beaten by you
At chess! 'Tis at the best a matter of chance,
Even if it were the case, which I will not
Admit it to be,—and as the matter stands,
I say that you exaggerate!

PRINCESS

[*With intensity*]
Natheless
I'll wager I can weary you ere dinner!

KING

Accomplished!—Now! My sack four times a day,

80

Openly, and no comments, Miss,
  against—
That necklace that you covet.

PRINCESS

Oh, I grieve
To think how long you will sit thirsty.
  Father,
And blink before my jade magnifi-
  cence!

KING

That is as shall be seen. Out with you
  now!
Yet stay—it seems to me—I have for-
  gotten—
Precisely what it was—and yet it seems
To me, I have forgotten—

PRINCESS

[With pretended lightness]
You will remember
Later, belike.

KING

Belike,—and yet—it seems—

CHANCELLOR

Your Majesty, if I may make so bold,
You were about to—

PRINCESS

[Hastily]
Very true. You were
About to—lose to me at chess! Oh,
  Father,
Come along, will you?
[She is dragging him with her toward
the door, when the Chancellor spies her
book on the floor, and goes to get it
for her]

CHANCELLOR

Highness, Your Highness' book.

PRINCESS

[Seizing it]
I thank you.
[She looks feverishly through it for the
paper. The Chancellor picks up the
paper from the floor, and is about to

give it to her when the King, made suspicious by her anxiety, intercepts it,
and takes it]
Oh, I thank you!
[About to take it]

KING

[Taking it and motioning her away]
What is this,
My dear?

PRINCESS

It is a private matter, Father,
It is—it is a testament of love
To me, and not intended for your eyes!
[Trying to snatch it]
I beg you to return it, sir!

KING

Soft! Soft!
[Examining the document]
I can believe it was not meant for me,
And will return it later; but your lover,
Having had the inadvertence to adorn
  his prayers
With sketches of the drawbridge and
  the moat
And one fine silver-point o' the secret
  passage
Under the chapel,
[Turning to her]
small wonder if I do
Remember now the thing I had forgot!
Madam, give heed: we seek a fugitive
From the court, a thankless boy, lately
  our page
And playmate, now our enemy, the son
And spying servant of our sullen neigh-
  bour;
His life, when he is found, answers his
  crime.
'Tis said he turned this way. Now, have
  you seen him?

PRINCESS

In sooth, how should I know if I have
  or have not
Seen him? Doubloons! Is he the only
  page i' the court?

81

How goes he clad?—I saw a scarlet page,
Fair, and immoderate fat—so that I laughed,
[*Laughing*]
A-fishing in the moat, if it is he
You seek—oh, the fat fellow!—let him escape!

The man goes not in scarlet that we seek.
Thou knowest the scarlet page is a fond fellow
Born at the court, and for his father's sake
Retained. Where didst thou come upon—?
[*Points to the paper*]

PRINCESS

[*With exaggerated protest. She is gradually losing her steady nerve, and is becoming peevish and hysterical*]
"Thou knowest!
Thou knowest!" sayst thou! Is it a gentle thing
To say, "thou knowest"? "Knowest thou not?" were gentler.
[*Flaring up and turning upon him with reproachful accusation*]
When well *thou* knowest how easily I forget
Who passes in and out, and toward, and thence,
And up, and down, and round about, and over!
"Thou knowest!"

KING

[*Angrily*]
And so thou dost, and I'll be bound so!
Whence comes this paper?

PRINCESS

[*Subsiding*]
Sir—it was on the floor—
And I thrust it in my book—the ribbon is lost

That marked the place—I had **not** looked within it,
Nor knew what it contained.

KING

"A testament
Of love," I think you said.

CHANCELLOR

Your Majesty,
If I may make so bold—

PRINCESS

[*Furiously*]
Aye, but you may not!
So bold is too bold, sir! I do not like you!
Be silent in my presence!

KING

And thou in mine
Be silent!
[*With repressed wrath, very rapidly*]
I wish to know if you have seen—
Or, failing that, if you have heard, touched, tasted,
A russet page, or got the scent of him
On any wind—and if so, in what quarter!
[*The Princess, who has been told to be silent, stands like a silly child, pressing her lips together, her finger on them*]
Well, well, can you not speak?

PRINCESS

[*With mock humility*]
Aye, sir, when bidden—
"If I may make so bold—"
[*Suddenly losing her temper altogether*]
I came up here
To read. "Page—page—page—page"—! I have neither smelled
Nor tasted your page!
[*More softly*]
And if I had seen or heard
Or—
[*Slowly*]
touched him with my hand—I should remember.

[*Loudly again*]
There is no spy i' the tower—unless
he be—
[*To the Chancellor*]
Among *your* retinue!

KING

Enough of this!
I sought straightforward speech, and
you evade me
At every turn. "There is no spy i' the
tower?"
Is there a page?

PRINCESS

[*Thoroughly frightened, and now thoroughly confused*]
No, sir, there is no page *in* the—
I mean to say—there is no *page* in the—

KING

[*Tripping her at once*]
"No page *in*
The tower!" So! 'Tis a game!—and we
shall find him
Under the tower, perchance, or on it?

PRINCESS

[*Wearily*]
Nay,
I beg of you, I will no longer jest,
But answer straight. I know the man
you mean:
A stranger, different from the rest—
who goes
In russet, playing on a silver pipe.
Father, unless it is the truth I say,
May dogs run out and bark at me, and
children
Flee from me in the street! May my
warm body
Be buried in lime, and my soul sit in
Hell!
I swear to you, by my dead mother's
tears,
And by my hope
[*Staring straight ahead of her*]
to look on her in Heaven,
I have not—

PAGE

[*Who has for a moment been listening
from the window ledge, expecting to
be delivered up, now, understanding
what she is doing, and horrified at her
terrible perjury and consequent damnation, leaping into the room*]
Lied—to shelter such a man!
[*Turning to the King. He does not
once look at the Princess*]
Your Majesty, in terror of your chase
I climbed into this tower and begged
for hiding;
Whereat Her Highness, out of her
sweet pity,
But knowing not my sin, lodged me
without.

PRINCESS

Oh, think what you have done! Now
they will take you
And shut you in a cellar, with mouldy
walls—
And rats—and standing water—and
tomorrow—
If you survive the night—you will be
hanged!
I care not for my soul—I never knew it!
It is a stranger lodging in my house!
I care not when it leaves! But as for
you,
I'd set my heart upon your being
saved.—
[*Weeping*]
I think you might have let me.

KING

[*Watching her*]
Sir, my daughter
Seems to be fond of you.

PAGE

Your Majesty,
It is but pity, it will soon be spent.

PRINCESS

[*Making up her mind to her course of
action*]
Nay then, it is not pity, and I care not

Who calls it what it is. Do as you will,
Father—I will not live without this
man.

PAGE

Your Highness—!

PRINCESS

Silence, fellow! Father—

PAGE

Nay,
I will not have my life so purchased!—
When well I know—

PRINCESS

When well you know! In sooth,
What know you—save to scramble
walls, and blow
Indifferently along a silver stick?
Be silent whilst I speak, that am in-
formed
Upon this matter! Father, from the
hour
Wherein yon
[*Turning to Page*]
        scurvy mountebank sees death,
Shall you sit childless.

KING

[*Distressed*]
But, my dear—my dear—

PRINCESS

I know what you would say: "Affairs
of court
Cannot be so conducted, that the man
Is after all a spy, and as a spy
Convicted, and so punishable—
[*She delivers this in a singsong, per-
functory court-room voice*]
                All of which
Is true.
[*Turning to the Page*]
        And more is true! But this as well
Is true, sir—that I may not live without
him.
[*After a tense moment, during which
no one has spoken, she turns furiously
on the Page*]

Be silent!

PAGE

Nay, I said no word, Your High-
ness.
[*Softly*]
I had no word to say.

KING

By my crown and sceptre,
A difficult affair, and one requiring
Most delicate government.
[*To soldiers*]
                Await without.
[*To the Chancellor, who thinks to re-
main*]
                You, too.
[*Exeunt Chancellor and Soldiers*]
Now, sir, you may defend yourself.
If your defense shall merit your release,
I will not hold you further. You may
speak

PAGE

I offer no defense, Your Majesty.

KING

So? 'Tis a bitter thing for you to be
Defenseless now—have you no word to
say?

PAGE

[*Gently*]
None, sir. I am sorry.

KING

Well—

PRINCESS

                Remember, Father,
What I said!

KING

[*Anguished*]
My child!

PAGE

[*To Princess*]
        Your Highness!

PRINCESS

                    Oh, be still!
Think you you are the only living
    thing
May die tomorrow? If I set my hour
At the same stroke with yours—what
    is't to you?
None goes so lonely to his death but
    thousands
Pass through the door with him. Be
    not offended;
I shall not crowd your grave. Nor need
    you feel
'Tis that I loved you!—'Tis but that
    when you
Are dead, I shall be amorous of death.

PAGE

[After a long pause, speaking with difficulty, as if the words were very hard
to pronounce]

Your Majesty, there is upon my per-
    son,
Thrust through the inner lining of the
    doublet,
Above the breast—a—letter, that I
    would
Your men might take from me.

KING

                    What ho! Without!
[To the Soldiers, who enter]
Make search upon this gentleman, and
    take
From him, with courteous fingers,
    what he hath
Concealed on his breast—i' the inner
    doublet.

FIRST SOLDIER

Aye, sire.
[Goes to the Page and takes a paper,
which he gives to the King]

KING

Your pardon, sir, that I read it forth.
[Reads]
"Undutiful and disobedient sir,
My son, that for a woman's hair and
    hands

And arbitrary favour, have abandoned
My side, to bear aloft the tail of a
    gown,
And serve sweet suppers, kneeling,—
    once again,
And not again hereafter, I command
    you:
Deliver up your lord into my power.
Upon that chart which heretofore I
    sent you,
A map I long have cherished, you will
    find,
By a scarlet rood made manifest, a door
Leading from out the chapel crypt into
A long and narrow passage under-
    ground;
On Saturday, which is the seventeenth,
At twilight, when the King and all his
    court
Are at their common prayers i' the
    chapel slumbering,
Do you await my men at the end of the
    passage
And open to them. Not again here-
    after
Shall I command you thus. Fulfil me
    now
Herein, or from my living presence be
For ever banished." The seventeenth
Is when?

CHANCELLOR

[Consulting tablets]
Your Majesty, the seventeenth
Was yesterday.

KING

[To Page]
                    Sir, your defence is more
Than adequate, being noble. You are
    free.
But ere you go, somewhat I have to
    tell you:
Your father—

PAGE

[Who has turned and gone to the window at the beginning of the letter, now
coming swiftly to the King and kneel-

85

ing, with great emotion]
    Oh, gracious Majesty, forgive him!
He is an old, old man. No harm can
   come
To you through him—there is the only
   paper
[*Pointing to the chart*]
He held that might betray you: he but
   sits
And broods all day—it is a sickness with
   him.
He is too sad, sir, since my mother
   died:
He hates me for her death, and hates
   all men
Because they live—and all men hate my
   father!
I pity him—his life is one big hate
Ingrowing on itself! Oh, sire, bear with
   him
A little while! He will not live long!

KING

[*Very gently*]
                    Boy,
You have outlived your father by a day.

PAGE

[*Rising slowly*]
Nay—is it so?—Oh, sir, I would that I
Had been beside him in the final hour!
They say that oft in death a gracious
   softness
Comes over the most hard—and the old
   days
Return to them!—I would that I had
   been there!

KING

[*Very gently, pausing*]
My boy, you are a King.

PAGE

[*Without interest*]
              Aye, so I am—
Oh, sir, I would with all my heart,
   that I
Had been beside my father when he
   died!

KING

Girl, when thy father, who hath been
   to thee
Gentler than some, 'twould seem, bows
   him in state
For the last coronation, see that thou
As nobly mourn. Sir, I would call thee
   Son,
But that the name might grieve thee.
[*With assumed playfulness and light-
ness, pointing to the Princess, who
turns her back to him as though re-
pudiating his suggestion*]
              When thou hast
Accomplished thy quarrel with my
   daughter,
Come in to dinner! And yet—ah, yes,
   I am told
That lovers never eat!
[*To the Chancellor*]
              Attend us hence!
[*To the Soldiers*]
Conduct me to my chamber!
[*Exeunt the King, Chancellor, and
Soldiers*]
[*The Princess has gone back to her
chair, and is pretending to read from
the book; but she is humming, to show
her indifference. Unfortunately, she is
humming the very tune the Page has
played from time to time, during the
action of the play. Finally her humming dwindles into a half sob, and she
looks up at the Page, who is standing
beside her*]

PRINCESS

I am sorry
About your father—I am very sorry—
[*In sudden panic*]
Go—go eat your dinner!

PAGE

[*Boyishly*]
I am not hungry!

PRINCESS

[*Quite simply*]

Neither
Am I.
[*Simultaneously they remember the King's words, and laugh. The Page comes close to her, and would take her in his arms, but she shrinks from him*]
No, no! Sweet cousin-prince! Majesty!
I do beseech you!
[*After a moment of silence, during which neither stirs, the Princess turns to him and stretches out her hand. He drops to his knees and presses his lips to it*]
When didst thou love me first?

PAGE
[*Gazing at her*]
When first I did behold thee!
[*Still playfully looking into her eyes*]

PRINCESS
Aye, to be sure.
But when was that?

PAGE
[*Gravely*]
'Twas once upon a time.
You came into my father's council room
And stood beside his chair, and needs must pat
His cloak to—
[*Dropping his head on her knee*]
comfort him!

[*Looking up almost instantly, and speaking in a tone of worshipful indulgence, as to a very small child*]
"At least they say so—
You have forgotten—you were very small."

PRINCESS
My love, my love! Can love endure so long?

PAGE
Longer than life!

PRINCESS
And we shall live alway!
[*Looking down at the book*]
I came up here to read!

PAGE
Aye, so you did!
I fear me you have lost the place, sweetheart!

PRINCESS
Belike—but then, it does not greatly matter;
The more I think on it, the more I feel
I've read the book before, or if not that,
[*Laying her cheek to his*]
That I have somewhere heard the end of the story!
[*They are both looking out straight ahead of them as—*]

The Curtain Falls

🐦 🐦 🐦

UNDER THE GREENWOOD TREE
WILLIAM SHAKESPEARE

Under the greenwood tree
Who loves to lie with me,
And turn his merry note
Unto the sweet bird's throat,
Come hither! come hither! come hither!
Here shall he see
No enemy
But winter and rough weather.

Who doth ambition shun
And loves to live i' the sun,
Seeking the food he eats
And pleased with what he gets,
Come hither! come hither! come hither!
Here shall he see
No enemy
But winter and rough weather.

COLUMBUS

Vachel Lindsay

Would that we had the fortunes of Columbus,

Sailing his caravels a trackless way,

He found a Universe—he sought Cathay.

God give such dawns, as when, his venture o'er,

The Sailor looked upon San Salvador.

God lead us past the setting of the sun

To wizard islands, of august surprise;

God make our blunders wise.

From *THE HAIRY APE*
By Eugene O'Neill

PADDY.... "Oh, to be back in the fine days of my youth, ochone! Oh, there was fine beautiful ships them days—clippers wid tall masts touching the sky—fine strong men in them—men that was sons of the sea as if 'twas the mother that bore them. Oh, the clean skins of them, and the clear eyes, the straight backs and full chests of them! Brave men they was, and bold men surely! We'd be sailing out, bound down round the Horn maybe. We'd be making sail in the dawn, with a fair breeze, singing a chanty song wid no care to it. And astern the land would be sinking low and dying out, but we'd give it no heed but a laugh, and never a look behind. For the day that was, was enough, for we was free men—and I'm thinking 'tis only slaves do be giving heed to the day that's gone or the day to come—until they're old like me. (*With a sort of religious exaltation*) Oh, to be scudding south again wid the power of the Trade Wind driving her on steady through the nights and the days! Full sail on her! Nights and days! Nights when the foam of the wake would be flaming wid fire, when the sky'd be blazing and winking wid stars. Or the full of the moon maybe. Then you'd see her driving through the gray night, her sails stretching aloft all silver and white, not a sound on the deck, the lot of us dreaming dreams, till you'd believe 'twas no real ship at all you was on but a ghost ship like the *Flying Dutchman* they say does be roaming the seas forevermore widout touching a port. And there was the days, too. A warm sun on the clean decks. Sun warming the blood of you, and wind over the miles of shiny green ocean like strong drink to your lungs. Work—aye, hard work—but who'd mind that at all? Sure, you worked under the sky and 'twas work wid skill and daring to it. And wid the day done, in the dog watch, smoking me pipe at ease, the lookout would be raising land maybe, and we'd see the mountains of South Americy wid the red fire of the setting sun painting their white tops and the clouds floating by them! (*His tone of exaltation ceases. He goes on mournfully*) Yerra, what's the use of talking? 'Tis a dead man's whisper. (*To* YANK *resentfully*) 'Twas them days men belonged to ships, not now. 'Twas them days a ship was part of the sea, and a man was part of a ship, and the sea joined all together and made it one.

A LAND THAT MAN HAS NEWLY TROD

JOAQUIN MILLER

A land that man has newly trod,
A land that only God has known,
Through all the soundless cycles
flown.
Yet perfect blossoms bless the sod,
And perfect birds illume the trees
And perfect unheard harmonies
Pour out eternally to God.

A thousand miles of mighty wood
Where thunder-storms stride fireshod;
A thousand flowers every rod,
A stately tree on every rood;
Ten thousand leaves on every tree,
And each a miracle to me;
And yet there be men who question
God!

THE NEW COLOSSUS

EMMA LAZARUS

Not like the brazen giant of Greek fame,
With conquering limbs astride from
land to land,
Here at our sea-washed, sunset gates
shall stand
A mighty woman with a torch, whose
flame
Is the imprisoned lightning, and her
name
Mother of Exiles. From her beacon-
hand
Glows world-wide welcome; her mild
eyes command

The air-bridged harbor that twin cities
frame.
"Keep, ancient lands, your storied
pomp!" cries she
With silent lips. "Give me your tired,
your poor,
Your huddled masses yearning to
breathe free,
The wretched refuse of your teeming
shore.
Send these, the homeless, tempest-
tossed to me,
I lift my lamp beside the golden door!"

ELDORADO

EDGAR ALLAN POE

Gaily bedight,
A gallant knight,
In sunshine and in shadow;
Had journeyed long,
Singing a song,
In search of Eldorado.

But he grew old—
This knight so bold—
And o'er his heart a shadow
Fell as he found
No spot of ground
That looked like Eldorado.

And, as his strength
Failed him at length,
He met a pilgrim shadow—
"Shadow," said he,
"Where can it be—
This land of Eldorado?"

"Over the Mountains
Of the Moon,
Down the Valley of the Shadow,
Ride, boldly ride,"
The shade replied,—
"If you seek for Eldorado!"

SPRING

ALFRED, LORD TENNYSON

Now fades the last long streak of snow,
Now burgeons every maze of quick
About the flowering squares, and thick
By ashen roots the violets blow.

Now rings the woodland loud and long,
The distance takes a lovelier hue,
And drowned in yonder living blue
The lark becomes a sightless song.

Now dance the lights on lawn and lea,
The flocks are whiter down the vale,
And milkier every milky sail,
On winding stream or distant sea;

Where now the seamew pipes, or dives
In yonder greening gleam, and fly
The happy birds, that change their sky
To build and brood, that live their lives.

From land to land; and in my breast
Spring wakens too; and my regret
Becomes an April violet,
And buds and blossoms like the rest.

EARTH IS ENOUGH

EDWIN MARKHAM

We men of Earth have here the stuff
Of Paradise—we have enough!
We need no other thing to build
The stairs into the Unfulfilled—
No other ivory for the doors—
No other marble for the floors—
No other cedar for the beam
And dome of man's immortal dream.
Here on the paths of everyday—
Here on the common human way
Is all the stuff the Gods would take
To build a Heaven, to mold and make
New Edens. Ours the stuff sublime
To build Eternity in Time!

TAKE, O, TAKE THOSE LIPS AWAY

WILLIAM SHAKESPEARE

Take, O, take those lips away,
That so sweetly were forsworn;
And those eyes, the break of day,
Lights that do mislead the morn;
But my kisses bring again,
Seals of love, but sealed in vain.

APRIL

[Written in 1626]

BY NICHOLAS BRETON

IT IS NOW April, and the Nightingale begins to tune her throat against May: the Sunny showers perfume the aire, and the Bees begin to goe abroad for honey: the Dewe, as is Pearles, hangs upon the tops of the grasse, while the turtles sit billing upon the little green boughes: the Trowt begins to play in the Brookes, and the Sammon leaves the Sea, to play in the freshe waters. The Garden bankes are full of gay flowers, and the Thorne and the Plumme send forth their faire Blossomes: the March Colt begins to play; and the Cosset Lamb is learned to butt. The Poets now make their studies in the woods, and the Youth of the Country make ready for the Morris-dance; the little Fishes lye nibbling at a bait, and the Porpus playes and the healthfull Souldier hath a pleasant march. The Larke and the Lambe looke up at the Sun, and the labourer is abroad by the dawning of the day: Sheepes eyes in Lambs heads tell kind hearts strange tales, while faith and troth make the true Lovers knot; the aged haires find a fresh life, and the youthfull cheeks are as red as a cherry. It was a world to set down the worth of this moneth.

But in summe, I thus conclude, I hold it the heavens blessing, and the Earths Comfort. Farewell.

THE LENT LILY

A. E. HOUSMAN

'T is spring; come out to ramble
  The hilly brakes around,
For under thorn and bramble
  About the hollow ground
  The primroses are found.

And there's the windflower chilly
  With all the winds at play,
And there's the Lenten lily
  That has not long to stay
  And dies on Easter day.

And since till girls go maying
  You find the primrose still,
And find the windflower playing
  With every wind at will,
  But not the daffodil.

Bring baskets now, and sally
  Upon the spring's array,
And bear from hill and valley
  The daffodil away
  That dies on Easter day.

AT DAWN

IF EVERY day is a repetition of life, every dawn signs as it were a new contract with existence. At dawn everything is fresh, light, simple, as it is for children. At dawn spiritual truth, like the atmosphere, is more transparent, and our organs, like the young leaves, drink in the light more eagerly, breathe in more ether, and less of things earthly. If night and the starry sky speak to the meditative soul of God, of eternity and the infinite, the dawn is the time for projects, for resolutions, for the birth of action. While the silence and the 'sad serenity of the azure vault' incline the soul to self-recollection, the vigour and gaiety of nature spread into the heart and make it eager for life and living.—Spring is upon us. Primroses and violets have already hailed her coming. Rash blooms are showing on the peach trees; the swollen buds of the pear trees and the lilacs point to the blossoming that is to be; the honeysuckles are already green.

—Amiel

MARCH

WILLIAM WORDSWORTH

The cock is crowing,
The stream is flowing,
The small birds twitter,
The lake doth glitter,
The green field sleeps in the sun;
  The oldest and youngest
  Are at work with the strongest;
The cattle are grazing,
Their heads never raising;
There are forty feeding like one!

Like an army defeated
The snow hath retreated,
And now doth fare ill
On the top of the bare hill;
The Plowboy is whooping—anon—anon:
  There's joy in the mountains;
  There's life in the fountains;
Small clouds are sailing,
Blue sky prevailing;
The rain is over and gone!

* * *

WHEN WE ARE collecting books, we are collecting happiness.
—Vincent Starrett

91

The Other Wise Man

By HENRY VAN DYKE

*Y*OU KNOW THE STORY of the Three Wise Men of the East, and how they travelled from far away to offer their gifts at the manger-cradle in Bethlehem. But have you ever heard the story of the Other Wise Men, who also saw the star in its rising, and set out to follow it, yet did not arrive with his brethren in the presence of the young child Jesus? Of the great desire of this fourth pilgrim, and how it was denied, yet accomplished in the denial; of his many wanderings and the probations of his soul; of the long way of his seeking and the strange way of his finding the One whom he sought—I would tell the tale as I have heard fragments of it in the Hall of Dreams, in the palace of the Heart of Man.

I

IN the days when Augustus Caesar was master of many k i n g s a n d Herod reigned in Jerusalem, there lived in the city of Ecbatana, among the mountains of Persia, a certain man named Artaban. His house stood close to the outermost of the walls which encircled the royal treasury. From his roof he could look over the seven-fold battlements of black and white and crimson and blue and red and silver and gold, to the hill where the summer palace of the Parthian emperors glittered like a jewel in a crown.

Around the dwelling of Artaban spread a fair garden, a tangle of flowers and fruit-trees, watered by a score of streams descending from the slopes of Mount Orontes, and made musical by innumerable birds. But all colour was lost in the soft and odorous darkness of the late September night, and all sounds were hushed in the deep charm of its silence, save the plashing of the water, like a voice half-sobbing and half-laughing under the shadows. High above the trees a dim glow of light shone through the curtained arches of the upper chamber, where the master of the house was holding council with his friends.

He stood by the doorway to greet his guests—a tall, dark man of about forty years, with brilliant eyes set near together under his broad brow, and firm lines graven around his fine, thin lips; the brow of a dreamer and the mouth of a soldier, a man of sensitive feeling but inflexible will—one of those who, in whatever age they may live, are born of inward conflict and a life of quest.

His robe was of pure white wool, thrown over a tunic of silk; and a white, pointed cap, with long lapels at the sides, rested on his flowing black hair. It was the dress of the ancient priesthood of the Magi, called the fire-worshippers.

"Welcome!" he said, in his low, pleasant voice, as one after another entered the room—"welcome, Abdus; peace be with you, Rhodaspes and Tigranes, and with you my father, Abgarus. You are all welcome. This house grows bright with the joy of your presence."

There were nine of the men, differing widely in age, but alike in the richness of their dress of many-coloured silks, and in the massive golden collars around their necks, marking them as Parthian nobles, and in the winged circles of gold resting upon their breasts, the sign of the followers of Zoroaster.

They took their places around a small black altar at the end of the room, where a tiny flame was burning. Arta-ban, standing beside it, and waving a barsom of thin tamarisk branches above the fire, fed it with dry sticks of pine and fragrant oils. Then he began the ancient chant of the Yasna, and the voices of his companions joined in the hymn to Ahura-Mazda:

We worship the Spirit Divine,
      all wisdom and goodness possessing.
Surrounded by Holy Immortals,
      the givers of bounty and blessing;
We joy in the work of His hands,
      His truth and His power confessing.

We praise all the things that are pure,
      for these are His only Creation;
The thoughts that are true, and the words
      and the deeds that have won approbation;
These are supported by Him,
      and for these we make adoration.

Hear us, O Mazda! Thou livest
      in truth and in heavenly gladness;
Cleanse us from falsehood, and keep us
      from evil and bondage to badness;
Pour out the light and the joy of Thy life
      on our darkness and sadness.

Shine on our gardens and fields,
      shine on our working and weaving;
Shine on the whole race of man,
      believing and unbelieving;
Shine on us now through the night,
Shine on us now in Thy might,
The flame of our holy love
      and the song of our worship receiving.

The fire rose with the chant, throb-bing as if the flame responded to the music, until it cast a bright illumina-tion through the whole apartment, re-vealing its simplicity and splendour.

The floor was laid with tiles of dark blue veined with white; pilasters of twisted silver stood out against the blue walls; the clear-story of round-arched windows above them was hung with azure silk; the vaulted ceiling was a pavement of blue stones, like the body of heaven in its clearness, sown with silver stars. From the four corners of the roof hung four golden magic-wheels, called the tongues of the gods. At the eastern end, behind the altar, there were two dark-red pillars of porphyry;

above them a lintel of the same stone, on which was carved the figure of a winged archer, with his arrow set to the string and his bow drawn.

The doorway between the pillars, which opened upon the terrace of the roof, was covered with a heavy curtain of the colour of a ripe pomegranate, embroidered with innumerable golden rays shooting upward from the floor. In effect the room was like a quiet, starry night, all azure and silver, flushed in the east with rosy promise of the dawn. It was, as the house of a man should be, an expression of the char-acter and spirit of the master.

He turned to his friends when the song was ended, and invited them to be seated on the divan at the western end of the room.

"You have come tonight," said he, looking around the circle, "at my call, as the faithful scholars of Zoroaster, to renew your worship and rekindle your faith in the God of Purity, even as this fire has been rekindled on the altar. We worship not the fire, but Him of whom it is the chosen symbol, because it is the purest of all created things. It speaks to us of one who is Light and Truth. Is it not so, my father?"

"It is well said, my son," answered the venerable Abgarus. "The enlight-ened are never idolaters. They lift the veil of form and go in to the shrine of reality, and new light and truth are coming to them continually through the old symbols."

"Hear me, then, my father and my friends," said Artaban, "while I tell you of the new light and truth that have come to me through the most ancient of all signs. We have searched the secrets of Nature together, and studied the healing virtues of water and fire and the plants. We have read also the books of prophecy in which the future is dim-ly foretold in words that are hard to understand. But the highest of all learning is the knowledge of the stars.

To trace their course is to untangle the threads of the mystery of life from the beginning to the end. If we could follow them perfectly, nothing would be hidden from us. But is not our knowledge of them still incomplete? Are there not many stars still beyond our horizon—lights that are known only to the dwellers in the far south-land, among the spice-trees of Punt and the gold mines of Ophir?"

There was a murmur of assent among the listeners.

"The stars," said Tigranes, "are the thoughts of the Eternal. They are numberless. But the thoughts of man can be counted, like the years of his life. The wisdom of the Magi is the greatest of all wisdoms on earth, because it knows its own ignorance. And that is the secret of power. We keep men always looking and waiting for a new sunrise. But we ourselves understand that the darkness is equal to the light, and that the conflict between them will never be ended."

"That does not satisfy me," answered Artaban, "for, if the waiting must be endless, if there could be no fulfilment of it, then it would not be wisdom to look and wait. We should become like those new teachers of the Greeks, who say that there is no truth, and that the only wise men are those who spend their lives in discovering and exposing the lies that have been believed in the world. But the new sunrise will certainly appear in the appointed time. Do not our own books tell us that this will come to pass, and that men will see the brightness of a great light?"

"That is true," said the voice of Abgarus; "every faithful disciple of Zoroaster knows the prophecy of the Avesta, and carries the word in his heart. 'In that day Sosiosh the Victorious shall arise out of the number of the prophets in the east country. Around him shall shine a mighty brightness, and he shall make life everlasting, incorruptible, and immortal, and the dead shall rise again.'"

"This is a dark saying," said Tigranes, "and it may be that we shall never understand it. It is better to consider the things that are near at hand, and to increase the influence of the Magi in their own country, rather than to look for one who may be a stranger, and to whom we must resign our power."

The others seemed to approve these words. There was a silent feeling of agreement manifest among them; their looks responded with that indefinable expression which always follows when a speaker has uttered the thought that has been slumbering in the hearts of his listeners. But Artaban turned to Abgarus with a glow on his face, and said:

"My father, I have kept this prophecy in the secret place of my soul. Religion without a great hope would be like an altar without a living fire. And now the flame has burned more brightly, and by the light of it I have read other words which also have come from the fountain of Truth, and speak yet more clearly of the rising of the Victorious One in his brightness."

He drew from the breast of his tunic two small rolls of fine parchment, with writing upon them, and unfolded them carefully upon his knee.

"In the years that are lost in the past, long before our fathers came into the land of Babylon, there were wise men in Chaldea, from whom the first of the Magi learned the secret of the heavens. And of these Balaam the son of Beor was one of the mightiest. Hear the words of his prophecy: 'There shall come a star out of Jacob, and a sceptre shall arise out of Israel.'"

The lips of Tigranes drew downward with contempt, as he said:

"Judah was a captive by the waters of Babylon, and the sons of Jacob were in bondage to our kings. The tribes of

Israel are scattered through the mountains like lost sheep, and from the remnant that dwells in Judea under the yoke of Rome neither star nor sceptre shall arise."

"And yet," answered Artaban, "it was the Hebrew Daniel, the mighty searcher of dreams, the counsellor of kings, the wise Belteshazzar, who was most honoured and beloved of our great King Cyrus. A prophet of sure things and a reader of the thoughts of the Eternal, Daniel proved himself to our people. And these are the words that he wrote." (Artaban read from the second roll:) " 'Know, therefore, and understand that from the going forth of the commandment to restore Jerusalem, unto the Anointed One, the Prince, the time shall be seven and threescore and two weeks.' "

"But, my son," said Abgarus, doubtfully, "these are mystical numbers. Who can interpret them, or who can find the key that shall unlock their meaning?"

Artaban answered: "It has been shown to me and to my three companions among the Magi—Caspar, Melchior, and Balthazar. We have searched the ancient tablets of Chaldea and computed the time. It falls in this year. We have studied the sky, and in the spring of the year we saw two of the greatest planets draw near together in the sign of the Fish, which is the house of the Hebrews. We also saw a new star there, which shone for one night and then vanished. Now again the two great planets are meeting. This night is their conjunction. My three brothers are watching by the ancient Temple of the Seven Spheres, at Borsippa, in Babylonia, and I am watching here. If the star shines again, they will wait ten days for me at the temple, and then we will set out together for Jerusalem, to see and worship the promised one who shall be born King of Israel. I believe the sign will come. I have made ready

for the journey. I have sold my possessions, and bought these three jewels—a sapphire, a ruby, and a pearl—to carry them as tribute to the King. And I ask you to go with me on the pilgrimage, that we may have joy together in finding the Prince who is worthy to be served."

While he was speaking he thrust his hand into the inmost fold of his girdle and drew out three great gems—one blue as a fragment of the night sky, one redder than a ray of sunrise, and one as pure as the peak of a snow-mountain at twilight—and laid them on the outspread scrolls before him.

But his friends looked on with strange and alien eyes. A veil of doubt and mistrust came over their faces, like a fog creeping up from the marshes to hide the hills. They glanced at each other with looks of wonder and pity, as those who have listened to incredible sayings, the story of a wild vision, or the proposal of an impossible enterprise.

At last Tigranes said: "Artaban, this is a vain dream. It comes from too much looking upon the stars and the cherishing of lofty thoughts. It would be wiser to spend the time in gathering money for the new fire-temple at Chala. No king will ever rise from the broken race of Israel, and no end will ever come to the eternal strife of light and darkness. He who looks for it is a chaser of shadows. Farewell."

And another said: "Artaban, I have no knowledge of these things, and my office as guardian of the royal treasure binds me here. The quest is not for me. But if thou must follow it, fare thee well."

And another said: "In my house there sleeps a new bride, and I cannot leave her nor take her with me on this strange journey. This quest is not for me. But may thy steps be prospered wherever thou goest. So, farewell."

And another said: "I am ill and unfit for hardship, but there is a man among my servants whom I will send with thee when thou goest, to bring me word how thou farest."

So, one by one, they left the house of Artaban. But Abgarus, the oldest and the one who loved him the best, lingered after the others had gone, and said, gravely: "My son, it may be that the light of truth is in this sign that has appeared in the skies, and then it will surely lead to the Prince and the mighty brightness. Or it may be that it is only a shadow of the light, as Tigranes has said, and then he who follows it will have a long pilgrimage and a fruitless search. But it is better to follow even the shadow of the best than to remain content with the worst. And those who would see wonderful things must often be ready to travel alone. I am too old for this journey, but my heart shall be a companion of thy pilgrimage day and night, and I shall know the end of thy quest. Go in peace."

Then Abgarus went out of the azure chamber with its silver stars, and Artaban was left in solitude.

He gathered up the jewels and replaced them in his girdle. For a long time he stood and watched the flame that flickered and sank upon the altar. Then he crossed the hall, lifted the heavy curtain, and passed out between the pillars of porphyry to the terrace on the roof.

The shiver that runs through the earth ere she rouses from her night-sleep had already begun, and the cool wind that heralds the daybreak was drawing downward from the lofty snow-traced ravines of Mount Orontes. Birds, half-awakened, crept and chirped among the rustling leaves, and the smell of ripened grapes came in brief wafts from the arbours.

Far over the eastern plain a white mist stretched like a lake. But where the distant peaks of Zagros serrated the western horizon the sky was clear. Jupi-ter and Saturn rolled together like drops of lambent flame about to blend in one.

As Artaban watched them, a steel-blue spark was born out of the darkness beneath, rounding itself with purple splendours to a crimson sphere, and spiring upward through rays of saffron and orange into a point of white radiance. Tiny and infinitely remote, yet perfect in every part, it pulsated in the enormous vault as if the three jewels in the Magian's girdle had mingled and been transformed into a living heart of light.

He bowed his head. He covered his brow with his hands.

"It is the sign," he said. "The King is coming, and I will go to meet him."

II

ALL night long, Vasda, the swiftest of Artaban's horses, had been waiting, saddled and bridled, in her stall, pawing the ground impatiently, and shaking her bit as if she shared the eagerness of her master's purpose, though she knew not its meaning.

Before the birds had fully roused to their strong, high, joyful chant of morning song, before the white mist had begun to lift lazily from the plain, the Other Wise Man was in the saddle, riding swiftly along the high-road, which skirted the base of Mount Orontes, westward.

How close, how intimate is the comradeship between a man and his favourite horse on a long journey! It is a silent, comprehensive friendship, an intercourse beyond the need of words.

They drink at the same way-side springs, and sleep under the same guardian stars. They are conscious together of the subduing spell of nightfall and the quickening joy of daybreak. The master shares his evening meal with his hungry companion, and feels the soft, moist lips caressing the palm of his hand as they close over the morsel of bread. In the gray dawn he is roused from his bivouac by the gentle stir of a warm, sweet breath over his sleeping face, and looks up into the eyes of his faithful fellow-traveller, ready and waiting for the toil of the day. Surely, unless he is a pagan and an unbeliever, by whatever name he calls upon his God, he will thank Him for this voiceless sympathy, this dumb affection, and his morning prayer will embrace a double blessing—God bless us both, the horse and the rider, and keep our feet from falling and our souls from death!

Then, through the keen morning air, the swift hoofs beat their tattoo along the road, keeping time to the pulsing of two hearts that are moved with the same eager desire—to conquer space, to devour the distance, to attain the goal of the journey.

Artaban must indeed ride wisely and well if he would keep the appointed hour with the other Magi; for the route was a hundred and fifty parasangs, and fifteen was the utmost that he could travel in a day. But he knew Vasda's strength, and pushed forward without anxiety, making the fixed distance every day, though he must travel late into the night, and in the morning long before sunrise.

He passed along the brown slopes of Mount Orontes, furrowed by the rocky courses of a hundred torrents.

He crossed the level plains of the Nisæans, where the famous herds of horses, feeding in the wide pastures, tossed their heads at Vasda's approach, and galloped away with a thunder of many hoofs, and flocks of wild birds rose suddenly from the swampy meadows, wheeling in great circles with a shining flutter of innumerable wings and shrill cries of surprise.

He traversed the fertile fields of Concabar, where the dust from the threshing-floors filled the air with a golden mist, half hiding the huge temple of Astarte with its four hundred pillars.

At Baghistan, among the rich gardens watered by fountains from the rock, he looked up at the mountain thrusting its immense rugged brow out over the road, and saw the figure of King Darius trampling upon his fallen foes, and the proud list of his wars and conquests graven high upon the face of the eternal cliff.

Over many a cold and desolate pass, crawling painfully across the wind-swept shoulders of the hills; down many a black mountain-gorge, where the river roared and raced before him like a savage guide; across many a smiling vale, with terraces of yellow limestone full of vines and fruit-trees; through the oak-groves of Carine and the dark Gates of Zagros, walled in by precipices; into the ancient city of Chala, where the people of Samaria had been kept in captivity long ago; and out again by the mighty portal, riven through the encircling hills, where he saw the image of the High Priest of the Magi sculptured on the wall of rock, with hand uplifted as if to bless the centuries of pilgrims; past the entrance of the narrow defile, filled from end to end with orchards of peaches and figs, through which the river Gyndes foamed down to meet him; over the broad rice-fields, where the autumnal vapours spread their deadly mists; following along the course of the river, under tremulous shadows of poplar and tamarind, among the lower hills; and out upon the flat plain, where the road ran straight as an arrow through the stubble-fields and parched meadows; past the city of Ctesiphon, where the Parthian emperors reigned, and the vast metropolis of Seleucia which Alexander built; across the swirling floods of Tigris and the many channels of Euphrates, flowing yellow through the corn-lands—Artaban pressed onward until he arrived, at nightfall on the tenth day, beneath the shattered walls of populous Babylon.

Vasda was almost spent, and Artaban would gladly have turned into the city to find rest and refreshment for himself and for her. But he knew that it was three hours' journey yet to the Temple of the Seven Spheres, and he must reach the place by midnight if he would find his comrades waiting. So he did not halt, but rode steadily across the stubble-fields.

A grove of date-palms made an island of gloom in the pale yellow sea. As she passed into the shadow Vasda slackened her pace, and began to pick her way more carefully.

Near the farther end of the darkness an access of caution seemed to fall upon her. She scented some danger or difficulty; it was not in her heart to fly from it—only to be prepared for it, and to meet it wisely, as a good horse should do. The grove was close and silent as the tomb; not a leaf rustled, not a bird sang.

She felt her steps before her delicately, carrying her head low, and sighing now and then with apprehension. At last she gave a quick breath of anxiety and dismay, and stood stock-still, quivering in every muscle, before a dark object in the shadow of the last palm-tree.

Artaban dismounted. The dim starlight revealed the form of a man lying across the road. His humble dress and the outline of his haggard face showed that he was probably one of the Hebrews who still dwelt in great numbers around the city. His pallid skin, dry and yellow as parchment, bore the mark of the deadly fever which ravaged the marsh-lands in autumn. The chill of death was in his lean hand, and, as Artaban released it, the arm fell back inertly upon the motionless breast.

He turned away with a thought of pity, leaving the body to that strange burial which the Magians deemed most fitting—the funeral of the desert, from which the kites and vultures rise on dark wings, and the beasts of prey slink furtively away. When they are gone there is only a heap of white bones on the sand.

But, as he turned, a long, faint, ghostly sigh came from the man's lips. The bony fingers gripped the hem of the Magian's robe and held him fast.

Artaban's heart leaped to his throat, not with fear, but with a dumb resentment at the importunity of this blind delay.

How could he stay here in the darkness to minister to a dying stranger? What claim had this unknown fragment of human life upon his compassion or his service? If he lingered but for an hour he could hardly reach Borsippa at the appointed time. His companions would think he had given up the journey. They would go without him. He would lose his quest.

But if he went on now, the man would surely die. If Artaban stayed, life might be restored. His spirit throbbed and fluttered with the urgency of the crisis. Should he risk the great reward of his faith for the sake of a single deed of charity? Should he turn aside, if only for a moment, from the following of the star, to give a cup of cold water to a poor, perishing Hebrew?

"God of truth and purity," he prayed, "direct me in the holy path, the way of wisdom which Thou only knowest."

Then he turned back to the sick man. Loosening the grasp of his hand, he carried him to a little mound at the foot of the palm-tree.

He unbound the thick folds of the turban and opened the garment above the sunken breast. He brought water from one of the small canals near by, and moistened the sufferer's brow and mouth. He mingled a draught of one of those simple but potent remedies which he carried always in his girdle—for the Magians were physicians as well as astrologers—and poured it slowly between the colourless lips. Hour after hour he laboured as only a skilful healer of disease can do. At last the man's strength returned; he sat up and looked about him.

"Who art thou?" he said, in the rude dialect of the country, "and why hast thou sought me here to bring back my life?"

"I am Artaban the Magian, of the city of Ecbatana, and I am going to Jerusalem in search of one who is to be born King of the Jews, a great Prince and Deliverer of all men. I dare not delay any longer upon my journey, for the caravan that has waited for me may depart without me. But see, here is all that I have left of bread and wine, and here is a potion of healing herbs. When thy strength is restored thou canst find the dwellings of the Hebrews among the houses of Babylon."

The Jew raised his trembling hand solemnly to heaven.

"Now may the God of Abraham and Isaac and Jacob bless and prosper the journey of the merciful, and bring him in peace to his desired haven. Stay! I have nothing to give thee in return—only this: that I can tell thee where the Messiah must be sought. For our prophets have said that he should be born not in Jerusalem, but in Bethlehem of Judah. May the Lord bring thee in safety to that place, because thou hast had pity upon the sick."

It was already long past midnight. Artaban rode in haste, and Vasda, restored by the brief rest, ran eagerly through the silent plain and swam the channels of the river. She put forth the remnant of her strength, and fled over the ground like a gazelle.

But the first beam of the rising sun sent a long shadow before her as she entered upon the final stadium of the journey, and the eyes of Artaban, anxiously scanning the great mound of Nimrod and the Temple of the Seven Spheres, could discern no trace of his friends.

The many-coloured terraces of black and orange and red and yellow and green and blue and white, shattered by the convulsions of nature, and crumbling under the repeated blows of human violence, still glittered like a ruined rainbow in the morning light.

Artaban rode swiftly around the hill. He dismounted and climbed to the highest terrace, looking out toward the west.

The huge desolation of the marshes stretched away to the horizon and the border of the desert. Bitterns stood by the stagnant pools and jackals skulked through the low bushes; but there was no sign of the caravan of the Wise Men, far or near.

At the edge of the terrace he saw a little cairn of broken bricks, and under them a piece of papyrus. He caught it up and read: "We have waited past the midnight, and can delay no longer. We go to find the King. Follow us across the desert."

Artaban sat down upon the ground and covered his head in despair.

"How can I cross the desert," said he, "with no food and with a spent horse? I must return to Babylon, sell my sapphire, and buy a train of camels, and provision for the journey. I may never overtake my friends. Only God the merciful knows whether I shall not lose the sight of the King because I tarried to show mercy."

III

THERE was a silence in the Hall of Dreams, where I was listening to the story of the Other Wise Man. Through this silence I saw, but very dimly, his figure passing over the dreary undulations of the desert, high upon the back of his camel, rocking steadily onward like a ship over the waves.

The land of death spread its cruel net around him. The stony waste bore

99

no fruit but briers and thorns. The dark ledges of rock thrust themselves above the surface here and there, like the bones of perished monsters. Arid and inhospitable mountain-ranges rose before him, furrowed with dry channels of ancient torrents, white and ghastly as scars on the face of nature. Shifting hills of treacherous sand were heaped like tombs along the horizon. By day, the fierce heat pressed its intolerable burden on the quivering air. No living creature moved on the dumb, swooning earth, but tiny jerboas scuttling through the parched bushes, or lizards vanishing in the clefts of the rock. By night the jackals prowled and barked in the distance, and the lion made the black ravines echo with his hollow roaring, while a bitter, blighting chill followed the fever of the day. Through heat and cold, the Magian moved steadily onward.

Then I saw the gardens and orchards of Damascus, watered by the streams of Abana and Pharpar, with their sloping swards inlaid with bloom, and their thickets of myrrh and roses. I saw the long, snowy-ridge of Hermon, and the dark groves of cedars, and the valley of the Jordan, and the blue waters of the Lake of Galilee, and the fertile plain of Esdraelon, and the hills of Ephraim, and the highlands of Judah. Through all these I followed the figure of Artaban moving steadily onward, until he arrived at Bethlehem. And it was the third day after the three Wise Men had come to that place and had found Mary and Joseph, with the young child, Jesus, and had laid their gifts of gold and frankincense and myrrh at his feet.

Then the Other Wise Man drew near, weary, but full of hope, bearing his ruby and his pearl to offer to the King. "For now at last," he said, "I shall surely find him, though I be alone, and later than my brethren. This is the place of which the Hebrew exile told me that the prophets had spoken, and

here I shall behold the rising of the great light. But I must inquire about the visit of my brethren, and to what house the star directed them, and to whom they presented their tribute."

The streets of the village seemed to be deserted, and Artaban wondered whether the men had all gone up to the hill-pastures to bring down their sheep. From the open door of a cottage he heard the sound of a woman's voice singing softly. He entered and found a young mother hushing her baby to rest. She told him of the strangers from the far East who had appeared in the village three days ago, and how they said that a star had guided them to the place where Joseph of Nazareth was lodging with his wife and her new-born child, and how they had paid reverence to the child and given him many rich gifts.

"But the travellers disappeared again," she continued, "as suddenly as they had come. We were afraid at the strangeness of their visit. We could not understand it. The man of Nazareth took the child and his mother, and fled away that same night secretly, and it was whispered that they were going to Egypt. Ever since, there has been a spell upon the village; something evil hangs over it. They say that the Roman soldiers are coming from Jerusalem to force a new tax from us, and the men have driven the flocks and herds far back among the hills, and hidden themselves to escape it."

Artaban listened to her gentle, timid speech, and the child in her arms looked up in his face and smiled, stretching out its rosy hands to grasp at the winged circle of gold on his breast. His heart warmed to the touch. It seemed like a greeting of love and trust to one who had journeyed long in loneliness and perplexity, fighting with his own doubts and fears, and following a light that was veiled in clouds.

"Why might not this child have been the promised Prince?" he asked within himself, as he touched its soft cheek. "Kings have been born ere now in lowlier houses than this, and the favourite of the stars may rise even from a cottage. But it has not seemed good to the God of wisdom to reward my search so soon and so easily. The one whom I seek has gone before me; and now I must follow the King to Egypt."

The young mother laid the baby in its cradle, and rose to minister to the wants of the strange guest that fate had brought into her house. She set food before him, the plain fare of peasants, but willingly offered, and therefore full of refreshment for the soul as well as for the body. Artaban accepted it gratefully; and, as he ate, the child fell into a happy slumber, and murmured sweetly in its dreams, and a great peace filled the room.

But suddenly there came the noise of a wild confusion in the streets of the village, a shrieking and wailing of women's voices, a clangour of brazen trumpets and a clashing of swords, and a desperate cry: "The soldiers! the soldiers of Herod! They are killing our children."

The young mother's face grew white with terror. She clasped her child to her bosom, and crouched motionless in the darkest corner of the room, covering him with the folds of her robe, lest he should wake and cry.

But Artaban went quickly and stood in the doorway of the house. His broad shoulders filled the portal from side to side, and the peak of his white cap all but touched the lintel.

The soldiers came hurrying down the street with bloody hands and dripping swords. At the sight of the stranger in his imposing dress they hesitated with surprise. The captain of the band approached the threshold to thrust him aside. But Artaban did not stir. His face was as calm as though he were watching the stars, and in his eyes there burned that steady radiance before which even the half-tamed hunting leopard shrinks, and the bloodhound pauses in his leap. He held the soldier silently for an instant, and then said in a low voice:

"I am all alone in this place, and I am waiting to give this jewel to the prudent captain who will leave me in peace."

He showed the ruby, glistening in the hollow of his hand like a great drop of blood.

The captain was amazed at the splendour of the gem. The pupils of his eyes expanded with desire, and the hard lines of greed wrinkled around his lips. He stretched out his hand and took the ruby.

"March on!" he cried to his men, "there is no child here. The house is empty."

The clamour and the clang of arms passed down the street as the headlong fury of the chase sweeps by the secret covert where the trembling deer is hidden. Artaban re-entered the cottage. He turned his face to the east and prayed:

"God of truth, forgive my sin! I have said the thing that is not, to save the life of a child. And two of my gifts are gone. I have spent for man that which was meant for God. Shall I ever be worthy to see the face of the King?"

But the voice of the woman, weeping for joy in the shadow behind him, said very gently:

"Because thou hast saved the life of my little one, may the Lord bless thee and keep thee; the Lord make His face to shine upon thee and be gracious unto thee; the Lord lift up His countenance upon thee and give thee peace."

IV

AGAIN there was a silence in the Hall of Dreams, deeper and more mysterious than the first interval, and I understood that the years of Artaban were flowing

101

very swiftly under the stillness, and I caught only a glimpse, here and there, of the river of his life shining through the mist that concealed its course.

I saw him moving among the throngs of men in the populous Egypt, seeking everywhere for traces of the household that had come down from Bethlehem, and finding them under the spreading sycamore-trees of Heliopolis, and beneath the walls of the Roman fortress of New Babylon beside the Nile—traces so faint and dim that they vanished before him continually, as footprints on the wet river-sand glisten for a moment with moisture and then disappear.

I saw him again at the foot of the pyramids, which lifted their sharp points into the intense saffron glow of the sunset sky, changeless monuments of the perishable glory and the imperishable hope of man. He looked up into the face of the crouching Sphinx and vainly tried to read the meaning of the calm eyes and smiling mouth. Was it, indeed, the mockery of all effort and all aspiration, as Tigranes had said—the cruel jest of a riddle that has no answer, a search that never can succeed? Or was there a touch of pity and encouragement in that inscrutable smile —a promise that even the defeated should attain a victory, and the disappointed should discover a prize, and the ignorant should be made wise, and the blind should see, and the wandering should come into the haven at last?

I saw him again in an obscure house of Alexandria, taking counsel with a Hebrew rabbi. The venerable man, bending over the rolls of parchment on which the prophecies of Israel were written, read aloud the pathetic words which foretold the sufferings of the promised Messiah—the despised and rejected of men, the man of sorrows and acquainted with grief.

"And remember, my son," said he, fixing his eyes upon the face of Artaban, "the King whom thou seekest is not to be found in a palace, nor among the rich and powerful. If the light of the world and the glory of Israel had been appointed to come with the greatness of earthly splendour, it must have appeared long ago. For no son of Abraham will ever again rival the power which Joseph had in the palaces of Egypt, or the magnificence of Solomon throned between the lions in Jerusalem. But the light for which the world is waiting is a new light, the glory that shall rise out of patient and triumphant suffering. And the kingdom which is to be established forever is a new kingdom, the royalty of unconquerable love.

"I do not know how this shall come to pass, nor how the turbulent kings and peoples of earth shall be brought to acknowledge the Messiah and pay homage to him. But this I know. Those who seek him will do well to look among the poor and the lowly, the sorrowful and the oppressed."

So I saw the Other Wise Man again and again, travelling from place to place, and searching among the people of the dispersion, with whom the little family from Bethlehem might, perhaps, have found a refuge. He passed through countries where famine lay heavy upon the land, and the poor were crying for bread. He made his dwelling in plague-stricken cities where the sick were languishing in the bitter companionship of helpless misery. He visited the oppressed and the afflicted in the gloom of subterranean prisons, and the crowded wretchedness of slave-markets, and the weary toil of galley-ships. In all this populous and intricate world of anguish, though he found none to worship, he found many to help. He fed the hungry, and clothed the naked, and healed the sick, and comforted the captive; and his years passed more swiftly than the weaver's shuttle that flashes back and forth through the loom while the web grows and the pattern is completed.

It seemed almost as if he had forgotten his quest. But once I saw him for a moment as he stood alone at sunrise, waiting at the gate of a Roman prison. He had taken from a secret resting-place in his bosom the pearl, the last of his jewels. As he looked at it, a mellower lustre, a soft and iridescent light, full of shifting gleams of azure and rose, trembled upon its surface. It seemed to have absorbed some reflection of the lost sapphire and ruby. So the secret purpose of a noble life draws into itself the memories of past joy and past sorrow. All that has helped it, all that has hindered it, is transfused by a subtle magic into its very essence. It becomes more luminous and precious the longer it is carried close to the warmth of the beating heart.

Then, at last, while I was thinking of this pearl, and of its meaning, I heard the end of the story of the Other Wise Man.

V

THREE-AND-THIRTY years of the life of Artaban had passed away, and he was still a pilgrim and a seeker after light. His hair, once darker than the cliffs of Zagros, was now white as the wintry snow that covered them. His eyes, that once flashed like flames of fire, were dull as embers smouldering among the ashes.

Worn and weary and ready to die, but still looking for the King, he had come for the last time to Jerusalem. He had often visited the holy city before, and had searched all its lanes and crowded hovels and black prisons without finding any trace of the family of Nazarenes who had fled from Bethlehem long ago. But now it seemed as if he must make one more effort, and something whispered in his heart that, at last, he might succeed.

It was the season of the Passover. The city was thronged with strangers. The children of Israel, scattered in far lands, had returned to the Temple for the great feast, and there had been a confusion of tongues in the narrow streets for many days.

But on this day a singular agitation was visible in the multitude. The sky was veiled with a portentous gloom. Currents of excitement seemed to flash through the crowd. A secret tide was sweeping them all one way. The clatter of sandals and the soft, thick sound of thousands of bare feet shuffling over the stones, flowed unceasingly along the street that leads to the Damascus gate.

Artaban joined a group of people from his own country, Parathian Jews who had come up to keep the Passover, and inquired of them the cause of the tumult, and where they were going.

"We are going," they answered, "to the place called Golgotha, outside the city walls, where there is to be an execution. Have you not heard what has happened? Two famous robbers are to be crucified, and with them another, called Jesus of Nazareth, a man who has done many wonderful works among the people, so that they love him greatly. But the priests and elders have said that he must die, because he gave himself out to be the Son of God. And Pilate has sent him to the cross because he said that he was the 'King of the Jews.'"

How strangely these familiar words fell upon the tired heart of Artaban! They had led him for a lifetime over land and sea. And now they came to him mysteriously, like a message of despair. The King had arisen, but he had been denied and cast out. He was about to perish. Perhaps he was already dying. Could it be the same who had been born in Bethlehem thirty-three years ago, at whose birth the star had appeared in heaven, and of whose coming the prophets had spoken?

Artaban's heart beat unsteadily with that troubled, doubtful apprehension which is the excitement of old age. But he said within himself: "The ways of God are stranger than the thoughts of men, and it may be that I shall find the King, at last, in the hands of his enemies, and shall come in time to offer my pearl for his ransom before he dies."

So the old man followed the multitude with slow and painful steps toward the Damascus gate of the city. Just beyond the entrance of the guardhouse a troop of Macedonian soldiers came down the street, dragging a young girl with torn dress and dishevelled hair. As the Magian paused to look at her with compassion, she broke suddenly from the hands of her tormentors, and threw herself at his feet, clasping him around the knees. She had seen his white cap and the winged circle on his breast.

"Have pity on me," she cried, "and save me, for the sake of the God of Purity! I also am a daughter of the true religion which is taught by the Magi. My father was a merchant of Parthia, but he is dead, and I am seized for his debts to be sold as a slave. Save me from worse than death!"

Artaban trembled.

It was the old conflict in his soul, which had come to him in the palm-grove of Babylon and in the cottage at Bethlehem—the conflict between the expectation of faith and the impulse of love. Twice the gift which he had consecrated to the worship of religion had been drawn to the service of humanity. This was the third trial, the ultimate probation, the final and irrevocable choice.

Was it his great opportunity, or his last temptation? He could not tell. One thing only was clear in the darkness of his mind—it was inevitable. And does not the inevitable come from God?

One thing only was sure to his divided heart—to rescue this helpless girl would be a true deed of love. And is not love the light of the soul?

He took the pearl from his bosom. Never had it seemed so luminous, so radiant, so full of tender, living lustre. He laid it in the hand of the slave.

"This is thy ransom, daughter! It is the last of my treasures which I kept for the King."

While he spoke, the darkness of the sky deepened, and shuddering tremors ran through the earth heaving convulsively like the breast of one who struggles with mighty grief.

The walls of the houses rocked to and fro. Stones were loosened and crashed into the street. Dust clouds filled the air. The soldiers fled in terror, reeling like drunken men. But Artaban and the girl whom he had ransomed crouched helpless beneath the wall of the Praetorium.

What had he to fear? What had he to hope? He had given away the last remnant of his tribute for the King. He had parted with the last hope of finding him. The quest was over, and it had failed. But, even in that thought, accepted and embraced, there was peace. It was not resignation. It was not submission. It was something more profound and searching. He knew that all was well, because he had done the best that he could from day to day. He had been true to the light that had been given to him. He had looked for more. And if he had not found it, if a failure was all that came out of his life, doubtless that was the best that was possible. He had not seen the revelation of "life everlasting, incorruptible and immortal." But he knew that even if he could live his earthly life over again, it could not be otherwise than it had been.

One more lingering pulsation of the earthquake quivered through the ground. A heavy tile, shaken from the roof, fell and struck the old man on the temple. He lay breathless and pale, with his gray head resting on the young girl's shoulder, and the blood trickling from the wound. As she bent over him, fearing that he was dead, there came a voice through the twilight, very small and still, like music sounding from a distance, in which the notes are clear but the words are lost. The girl turned to see if some one had spoken from the window above them, but she saw no one.

Then the old man's lips began to move, as if in answer, and she heard him say in the Parthian tongue:

"Not so, my Lord! For when saw I thee hungered and fed thee? Or thirsty, and gave thee drink? When saw I thee a stranger, and took thee in? Or naked, and clothed thee? When saw I thee sick or in prison, and came unto thee? Three-and-thirty years have I looked for thee; but I have never seen thy face, nor ministered to thee, my King."

He ceased, and the sweet voice came again. And again the maid heard it, very faint and far away. But now it seemed as though she understood the words:

"Verily I say unto thee, Inasmuch as thou hast done it unto one of the least of these my brethren, thou has done it unto me."

A calm radiance of wonder and joy lighted the pale face of Artaban like the first ray of dawn on a snowy mountain-peak. A long breath of relief exhaled gently from his lips.

His journey was ended. His treasures were accepted. The Other Wise Man had found the King.

❧ ❧ ❧

PSALM 113—THE BIBLE

PRAISE ye the Lord. Praise, O ye servants of the Lord, praise the name of the Lord.

Blessed be the name of the Lord from this time forth and for evermore.

From the rising of the sun unto the going down of the same the Lord's name is to be praised.

The Lord is high above all nations, and his glory above the heavens.

Who is like unto the Lord our God, who dwelleth on high.

Who humbleth himself to behold the things that are in heaven, and in the earth!

He raiseth up the poor out of the dust, and lifteth the needy out of the dunghill.

That he may set him with princes, even with the princes of his people.

He maketh the barren woman to keep house, and to be a joyful mother of children. Praise ye the Lord.

THE HEAVENS DECLARE THY GLORY, LORD!

[*Psalm XIX*]
ISAAC WATTS

The heavens declare thy glory, Lord!
  In every star thy wisdom shines;
But when our eyes behold thy word,
  We read thy name in fairer lines.

The rolling sun, the changing light,
  And nights and days thy power confess;
But the blest volume thou has writ
  Reveals thy justice and thy grace.

PRAYER

JOHN GREENLEAF WHITTIER

Dear Lord and Father of mankind,
  Forgive our foolish ways!
Reclothe us in our rightful mind,
In purer lives Thy service find,
  In deeper reverence, praise.

Drop Thy still dews of quietness,
  Till all our strivings cease;
Take from our souls the strain and stress,
And let our ordered lives confess
  The beauty of Thy peace.

105

HOPE is the dream of a waking man.—*Diogenes*

POETRY is vocal painting, as painting is silent poetry.
—*Simonides of Ceos*

LOVE is the enchanted dawn of every heart.—*Lamartine*

THE PLEASANTEST THINGS in the world are pleasant thoughts: and the great art of life is to have as many of them as possible.—*Montaigne*

TRUTH is the highest thing that man may keep.—*Chaucer*

THE WORLD is a looking glass, and gives back to every man the reflection of his own face.—*Thackeray*

KINDNESS is the golden chain by which society is bound together.—*Goethe*

KNOWLEDGE, IN TRUTH, is the great sun in the firmament. Life and power are scattered with all its beams.—*Webster*

FINE ART is that in which the hand, the head, and the heart of man go together.—*Ruskin*

ARCHITECTURE is frozen music.—*Madame de Staël*

LIFE IS LIKE MUSIC; it must be composed by ear, feeling, and instinct, not by rule.—*Samuel Butler*

ART is a shadow of Divine perfection.—*Michelangelo*

JOY is the mainspring in the whole of endless Nature's calm rotation.—*Schiller*

MUSIC is well said to be the speech of angels.—*Carlyle*

106

OF WISE MEN

NATURE is the art of God.—*Dante*

SILENCE is a great peacemaker.—*Longfellow*

A PICTURE is a poem without words.—*Latin Proverb*

THE DAY is always his who works in it with serenity
and great aims.—*Emerson*

LIFE is music if one be rightly in tune and in time.—*Anonymous*

THE MEASURE of a man's life is the well spending of it,
and not the length.—*Plutarch*

ENTHUSIASM is the genius of sincerity, and truth accomplishes no victories
without it.—*Bulwer-Lytton*

KNOWLEDGE is proud that he has learned so much; wisdom is humble that he
knows no more.—*Cowper*

SOLITUDE is as needful to the imagination as society is wholesome for the character.—*Lowell*

CHEERFULNESS AND CONTENT are great beautifiers, and are famous preservers of
youthful looks.—*Dickens*

THE TRUE TEST of a man's worth is not his theology
but his life.—*The Talmud*

LOVE IS A FAITH, and one faith leads to another.—*Amiel*

POETRY is emotion recollected in tranquillity.—*Wordsworth*

THE TRUTH is always the strongest argument.—*Sophocles*

I MEANT TO DO MY WORK TODAY
RICHARD LE GALLIENNE

I meant to do my work today
But a brown bird sang in the apple-
tree,
And a butterfly flitted across the field,
And all the leaves were calling me.

And the wind went sighing over the
land,
Tossing the grasses to and fro,
And a rainbow held out its shining
hand—
So what could I do but laugh and go?

ARISTOCRACY
EMILY DICKINSON

The pedigree of honey
    Does not concern the bee;
A clover, any time, to him
    Is aristocracy.

ADVENTURE*
ADELAIDE CRAPSEY

Sun and moon and beat of sea—
Great lands stretching endlessly.
Where be bonds to bind the free?
All the world was made for me!

THE GREAT DIVIDE
LEW SARETT

When I drift out on the Silver Sea,
O may it be
A blue night
With a white moon
And a sprinkling of stars in the cedar
tree;
And the silence of God,
And the low call
Of a lone bird,—
When I drift out on the Silver Sea.

*Reprinted from *Verse* by Adelaide Crapsey, by permission of ALFRED A. KNOPF, INC. Copyright 1915, 1922, by Algernon S. Crapsey.

TO ARCTURUS RETURNING
SARA TEASDALE

Arcturus, with the spring returning,
    I love you best; I cannot tell
Why, save that your recurrent burning
    Is spring's most punctual miracle.

You bring with you all longed-for
    things,
    Birds with their song, leaves with
    their stir,
And you, beyond all other stars,
    Have been man's comforter.

THE WIND FROM THE WEST
ELLA YOUNG

Blow high, blow low,
O wind from the West:
You come from the country
I love the best.

O say have the lilies
Yet lifted their heads
Above the lake-water
That ripples and spreads?

Do the little sedges
Still shake with delight,
And whisper together
All through the night?

Have the mountains the purple
I used to love,
And peace about them
Around and above?

O wind from the West,
· Blow high, blow low,
You come from the country
I loved long ago.

THE GENEROUS THOUGHT

God blesses still the generous thought
    And still the fitting word He speeds
And Truth, at his requiring taught,
    He quickens into deeds.
                —Whittier

LOVELIEST OF TREES
A. E. HOUSMAN

Loveliest of trees, the cherry now
Is hung with bloom along the bough,
And stands about the woodland ride
Wearing white for Eastertide.

Now, of my threescore years and ten,
Twenty will not come again,
And take from seventy springs a score,
It only leaves me fifty more.

And since to look at things in bloom
Fifty springs are little room,
About the woodlands I will go
To see the cherry hung with snow.

WORDS
DOROTHY ALDIS

Now she is gone
Like a flight of wild birds,
And things that were words before
And more than words.

Courage and Loyalty,
Humor and Pride—
These are the weapons
She used till she died.

Love gives life meaning
In a look, in a breath,
But never so truly
Or deeply as death.

LEISURE
W. H. DAVIES

What is this life, if, full of care,
We have no time to stand and stare,

No time to stand beneath the boughs
And stare as long as sheep or cows.

No time to see, when woods we pass,
Where squirrels hide their nuts in grass.

No time to see, in broad daylight,
Streams full of stars, like skies at night.

No time to turn at Beauty's glance,
And watch her feet, how they can dance.

No time to wait till her mouth can
Enrich that smile her eyes began.

A poor life this if, full of care,
We have no time to stand and stare.

FOUR-LEAF CLOVERS
ELLA HIGGINSON

I know a place where the sun is like
    gold,
    And the cherry blooms burst with
    snow;
And down underneath is the loveliest
    nook,
    Where the four-leaf clovers grow.

One leaf is for hope, and one for faith,
    And one is for love, you know;
But God put another in for luck—
    If you search, you will find where
    they grow.

But you must have hope, and you must
    have faith;
    You must love and be strong; and so,
If you work, if you wait, you will find
    the place
    Where the four-leaf clovers grow.

* * *

You MAY PADDLE all day long, but it is when you come back at nightfall,
and look in at the familiar room, that you find Love or Death awaiting you
beside the stove; and the most beautiful adventures are not those we go
to seek.
                                                            —*Stevenson*

109

From *LORD JIM*
By Joseph Conrad

THE *Patna* was a local steamer as old as the hills, lean like a greyhound, and eaten up with rust worse than a condemned water-tank. . . . After she had been painted outside and whitewashed inside, eight hundred pilgrims (more or less) were driven on board of her as she lay with steam up alongside a wooden jetty.

They streamed aboard over three gangways, they streamed in urged by faith and the hope of paradise, they streamed in with a continuous tramp and shuffle of bare feet, without a word, a murmur, or a look back; and when clear of confining rails spread on all sides over the deck, flowed forward and aft, overflowed down the yawning hatchways, filled the inner recesses of the ship—like water filling a cistern, like water flowing into crevices and crannies, like water rising silently even with the rim. Eight hundred men and women with faith and hopes, with affections and memories, they had collected there, coming from north and south and from the outskirts of the East, after treading the jungle paths, descending the rivers, coasting in praus along the shallows, crossing in small canoes from island to island, passing through suffering, meeting strange sights, beset by strange fears, upheld by one desire. They came from solitary huts in the wilderness, from populous campongs, from villages by the sea. At the call of an idea they had left their forests, their clearings, the protection of their rulers, their prosperity, their poverty, the surroundings of their youth and the graves of their fathers. They came covered with dust, with sweat, with grime, with rags—the strong men at the head of family parties, the lean old men pressing forward without hope of return; young boys with fearless eyes glancing curiously, shy little girls with tumbled long hair; the timid women muffled up and clasping to their breasts, wrapped in loose ends of soiled head-cloths, their sleeping babies, the unconscious pilgrims of an exacting belief. . . .

An Arab, the leader of that pious voyage, came last. He walked slowly aboard, handsome and grave in his white gown and large turban. A string of servants followed, loaded with his luggage; the *Patna* cast off and backed away from the wharf.

She was headed between two small islets, crossed obliquely the anchoring-ground of sailing-ships, swung through half a circle on the shadow of a hill, then ranged close to a ledge of foaming reefs. The Arab, standing up aft, recited aloud the prayer of travellers by sea. He invoked the favour of the Most High upon that journey, implored His blessing on men's toil and on the secret purposes of their hearts; the steamer pounded in the dusk the calm water of the Strait; and far astern of the pilgrim ship a screw-pile lighthouse, planted by unbelievers on a treacherous shoal, seemed to wink at her its eye of flame, as if in derision of her errand of faith.

She cleared the Straits, crossed the bay, continued on her way through the "One-degree" passage. She held on straight for the Red Sea under a serene sky, under a sky scorching and unclouded, enveloped in a fulgor of sunshine that killed all thought, oppressed the heart, withered all impulses of strength and energy. And under the sinister splendour of that sky the sea, blue and profound, remained still, without a stir, without a ripple, without a wrinkle—viscous, stagnant, dead. The *Patna*, with a slight hiss, passed over that plain luminous and smooth, unrolled a black ribbon of smoke across the sky, left behind her on the water a white ribbon of foam that vanished at once, like the phantom of a track drawn upon a lifeless sea by the phantom of a steamer.

Every morning the sun, as if keeping pace in his revolutions with the progress of the pilgrimage, emerged with a silent burst of light exactly at the same distance astern of the ship, caught up with her at noon, pouring the concentrated fire of his rays on the pious purposes of the men, glided past on his descent, and sank mysteriously into the sea evening after evening, preserving the same distance ahead of her advancing bows. The five whites on board lived amidships, isolated from the human cargo. The awnings covered the deck with a white roof from stem to stern, and a faint hum, a low murmur of sad voices, alone revealed the presence of a crowd of people upon the great blaze of hte ocean. Such were the days, still, hot, heavy, disappearing one by one into the past, as if falling into an abyss for ever open in the wake of the ship; and the ship, lonely under a wisp of smoke, held on her steadfast way black and smouldering in a luminous immensity, as if scorched with a flame flicked at her from a heaven without pity.

The nights descended on her like a benediction.

THE SEA GIPSY
Richard Hovey

I am fevered with the sunset,
  I am fretful with the bay,
For the wander-thirst is on me
  And my soul is in Cathay.

There's a schooner in the offing
  With her topsails shot with fire,
And my heart has gone aboard her
  For the Islands of Desire.

I must forth again tomorrow,
  With the sunset I must be,
Hull down on the trail of rapture
  In the wonder of the sea

THERE IS A TIDE
William Shakespeare

There is a tide in the affairs of men,
Which, taken at the flood, leads on to
  fortune;
Omitted, all the voyage of their life
Is bound in shallows and in miseries.
On such a full sea are we now affoat;
And we must take the current when it
  serves,
Or lose our ventures.

—From *Julius Caesar*

* * *

A VISIT FROM THE SEA
Robert Louis Stevenson

Far from the loud sea beaches
  Where he goes fishing and crying,
Here in the inland garden
  Why is the seagull flying?

Here are no fish to dive for;
  Here is the corn and lea;
Here are the green trees rustling.
  Hie away home to sea!

Fresh is the river water
  And quiet among the rushes;

This is no home for the seagull
  But for the rooks and thrushes.

Pity the bird that has wandered!
  Pity the sailor ashore!
Hurry him home to the ocean,
  Let him come here no more!

High on the seacliff ledges
  The white gulls are trooping and
    crying,
Here among rooks and roses,
  Why is the seagull flying?

111

POLO PONIES

ELEANOR BALDWIN

Has Pegasus, then, visited the earth,
Borne on great pinions lyrical with thunder,
And these his foals,—this breed of racing wonder,
Fearless and free, and sensible of worth?
With flash of eye and silver gleam of girth,
They charge, now neck to neck, now wheeled asunder,
With shining sides, small feet that scorn to blunder,
Dark nostrils trembling in their pride of birth.
Sired from the skies, they eddy down the plain,
Chestnut and black and the fast-flying dun,
And swift and strong they crowd, and tense and fain,
Eager as fire though the last goal is won,
These wilding creatures gentled to the rein,
These little brothers of the wind and sun!

THE MUSTANG

GRACE NOLL CROWELL

A darkened hill, and a crimson West,
  And silhouetted against the light
A black mustang on a tawny crest
  Rears aloft in a sudden fright.

Startled perhaps by a coyote's cry,
  Or a scent on the wind; a moment
    there
He is a marble chiseled on the sky;
  He is motion captured on the air.

Sinewed power and strength and grace,
  And wild, wild beauty, and the hill
Is only a canvas on whose face
  An upreared muscled form stands
    still.

A moment only, and then a hand
  Has swept the canvas clean, to leave
A lonely barren space, a hush—
  And something lost for which I
    grieve.

WILD GEESE

ROBERT P. TRISTRAM COFFIN

Beauty is coming north again
Slanting eager as the rain;
  With necks like arrows on a bow
  Across the sky the wild geese go.

Beauty is coming moulded by
High winds of the upper sky
  Into shapes that burn to be
  In a patterned symmetry.

Loveliness comes like a host
Of lean ships headed for a coast,
  Every sail and every keel
  Pointed at a common weal.

Comeliness in company,
Every wing where it should be,
  Their feathers are communal
    things,
  They help each other with their
    wings.

* * *

❧ IN THOSE VERNAL seasons of the year, when the air is calm and pleasant,
it were an injury and sullenness against Nature not to go out and see her
riches, and partake in her rejoicing with heaven and earth.   —*Milton*

SONG OF THE RABBITS
OUTSIDE THE TAVERN
Elizabeth Coatsworth

We who play under the pines,
We who dance in the snow
That shines blue in the light of the
        moon
Sometimes halt as we go,
Stand with our ears erect,
Our noses testing the air,
To gaze at the golden world
Behind the windows there.

Suns they have in a cave,
And stars each on a tall white stem
And the thought of fox or of owl
Seems never to bother them.
They laugh and eat and are warm,
Their food is ready at hand
While hungry out in the cold
We little rabbits stand.

But they never dance as we dance
They have not the speed nor the grace,
We scorn both the cat and the dog
Who lie by their fireplace,
We scorn them, licking their paws
Their eyes on an upraised spoon—
We who dance hungry and wild
Under a winter's moon!

THE EAGLE
Alfred, Lord Tennyson

He clasps the crag with crooked hands;
Close to the sun in lonely lands,
Ringed with the azure world, he stands.

The wrinkled sea beneath him crawls;
He watches from his mountain walls,
And like a thunderbolt he falls.

EYES ARE LIT UP
Robert P. Tristram Coffin

Someone whom no man can see
Is lighting candles in the tree.

Star by star, on every bough
There is a taper burning now.

Quietly, the forest through,
Eyes are lit up, two by two.

The silky moles and velvet mice
Have eyes as sharp as cracks of ice.

Dark-lanterns of the owls begin
To burn like emeralds and sin.

The racoon built of hidden wire
Prowls by the glow of his brain-fire.

Herons stand as still as years
And see the fish swim through their
        tears.

All the creatures of the night
Are busy being their own light.

MUSIC

There's music in the sighing of a reed;
There's music in the gushing of a rill;
There's music in all things, if men had
        ears;
The earth is but the music of the
        spheres.
                            —*Byron*

WHEN DAISIES PIED

When daisies pied, and violets blue,
    And lady-smocks all silver white,
And cuckoo-buds of yellow hue
    Do paint the meadows with delight.
                        —*Shakespeare*

* * *

Life is always flowing on like a river, sometimes with murmurs, sometimes without bending this way and that, we do not exactly see why; now in beautiful picturesque places, now through barren and uninteresting scenes, but always flowing with a look of treachery about it; it is so swift, so voiceless, yet so continuous.
                                            —*Faber*

113

NAVAJO CHANT

The voice that beautifies the soil!
The voice on high,
The voice of the rolling thunder,
Above the darkening clouds
Again and again it is heard,
The voice that beautifies the soil!

The voice that beautifies the soil!
The voice on earth,
The voice of the grasshopper,
Among the flowers and grasses
Again and again it is heard,
The voice that beautifies the soil!

AMERICA FOR ME
Henry van Dyke

It's fine to see the Old World, and travel up and down
Among the famous palaces and cities of renown,
To admire the crumbly castles and the statues of the kings,—
But now I think I've had enough of antiquated things.

So it's home again, and home again, America for me!
My heart is turning home again, and there I long to be,
In the land of youth and freedom beyond the ocean bars,
Where the air is full of sunlight and the flag is full of stars.

Oh, London is a man's town, there's power in the air;
And Paris is a woman's town, with flowers in her hair;
And it's sweet to dream in Venice, and it's great to study Rome;
But when it comes to living there is no place like home.

I like the German fir-woods, in green battalions drilled;
I like the gardens of Versailles with flashing fountains filled;
But, oh, to take your hand, my dear, and ramble for a day
In the friendly western woodland where Nature has her way!

I know that Europe's wonderful, yet something seems to lack:
The Past is too much with her, and the people looking back.
But the glory of the Present is to make the Future free,—
We love our land for what she is and what she is to be.

Oh, it's home again, and home again, America for me!
I want a ship that's westward bound to plough the rolling sea,
To the blessed Land of Room Enough beyond the ocean bars,
Where the air is full of sunlight and the flag is full of stars.

114

TO NIGHT
ARTHUR SYMONS

I have loved wind and light,
  And the bright sea,
But, holy and most secret Night,
  Not as I love and have loved thee.

God, like all highest things,
  Hides light in shade,
And in the night his visitings
  To sleep and dreams are clearliest
  made.

Love, that knows all things well,
  Loves the night best;
Joys whereof daylight dares not tell
Are his, and the diviner rest.

And Life, whom day shows plain
  Its prison-bars,
Feels the close wall and the hard chain
Fade when the darkness brings the
stars.

I AM AN AMERICAN
ELIAS LIEBERMAN

I am an American.
My father belongs to the Sons of the
  Revolution;
My mother, to the Colonial Dames.
One of my ancestors pitched tea over-
  board in Boston Harbor;
Another stood his ground with Warren;
Another hungered with Washington at
  Valley Forge.
My forefathers were America in the
  making:
They spoke in her council halls;
They died on her battle-fields;
They commanded her ships;
They cleared her forests.
Dawns reddened and paled.
Stanch hearts of mine beat fast at each
  new star
  In the nation's flag.
Keen eyes of mine foresaw her greater
  glory:
The sweep of her seas,
The plenty of her plains,
The man-hives in her billion-wired
  cities.
Every drop of blood in me holds a
  heritage of patriotism.
I am proud of my past.
I am an American.

I am an American.
My father was an atom of dust,

My mother a straw in the wind,
To His Serene Majesty.
One of my ancestors died in the mines
  of Siberia;
Another was crippled for life by twenty
  blows of the knout;
Another was killed, defending his home
  during the massacres.
The history of my ancestors is a trail of
  blood
To the palace-gate of the Great White
  Czar.
But then the dream came—
The dream of America.
In the light of the Liberty torch
The atom of dust became a man
And the straw in the wind became a
  woman
For the first time.
"See," said my father, pointing to the
  flag that fluttered near,
"That flag of stars and stripes is yours;
It is the emblem of the promised land.
It means, my son, the hope of humanity.
Live for it—die for it!"
Under the open sky of my new country
  I swore to do so;
And every drop of blood in me will
  keep that vow.
I am proud of my future.
I am an American.

He Knew Lincoln

By IDA M. TARBELL

*D*ID I KNOW LINCOLN? Well, I should say. See that chair there? Take it, set down. That's right. Comfortable, ain't it? Well, sir, Abraham Lincoln has set in that chair hours, him and Little Doug, and Logan and Judge Davis, all of 'em, all the big men in this State, set in that chair. See them marks? Whittlin'. Judge Logan did it, all-firedest man to whittle. Always cuttin' away at something. I just got that chair new, paid six dollars for it, and I be blamed if I didn't come in this store and find him slashin' right into that arm. I picked up a stick and said: 'Here, Judge, s'posin' you cut this.' He just looked at me and then flounced out, mad as a wet hen. Mr. Lincoln was here, and you ought to heard him tee-hee. He was always here. Come and set by the stove by the hour and tell stories and talk and argue. I'd ruther heard the debates them men had around this old stove than heard Webster and Clay and Calhoun and the whole United States Senate. There wa'n't never a United States Senate that could beat just what I've heard right here in this room with Lincoln settin' in that very chair where you are this minute.

"He traded here. I've got his accounts now. See here, 'quinine, quinine, quinine.' Greatest hand to buy quinine you ever see. Give it to his constituents. Oh, he knew how to be popular, Mr. Lincoln did. Cutest man in politics. I wa'n't a Whig. I was then and I am now a Democrat, a real old-fashioned Jackson Democrat, and my blood just would rise up sometimes hearin' him discuss. He was a dangerous man—a durned dangerous man to have agin you. He'd make you think a thing when you knew it wa'n't so, and cute! Why, he'd just slide in when you wa'n't expectin' it and do some unexpected thing that u'd make you laugh, and then he'd get your vote. You'd vote for him because you liked him—just because you liked him and because he was so all-fired smart, and do it when you knew he was wrong and it was agin the interest of the country.

"Tell stories? Nobody ever could beat him at that, and how he'd enjoy 'em, just slap his hands on his knees and jump up and turn around and then set down, laughin' to kill. Greatest man to git new yarns that ever lived, always askin', 'Heard any new stories, Billy?' And if I had I'd trot 'em out, and how he'd laugh. Often and often when I've told him something new and he'd kin' a forgit how it went, he'd come in and say, 'Billy, how about that story you'se tellin' me?' and then I'd tell it all over.

"He was away a lot, you know, ridin' the circuit along with some right smart lawyers. They had great doin's. Nuthin' to do evenings but to get around the tavern stove tellin' stories. That was enough when Lincoln was there. They was all lost without him. Old Judge Davis was boss of that lot, and he never would settle down till Lincoln got around. I've heard 'em laugh lots of times how the Judge would fuss around and keep askin', 'Where's Mr. Lincoln, why don't Mr. Lincoln come? Somebody go and find Lincoln,' and when Lincoln came he would just settle back and get him started to yarning, and there they'd set half the night.

"When he got home he'd come right in here first time he was downtown and tell me very blamed yarn he'd heard.

Whole crowd would get in here sometimes and talk over the trip, and I tell you it was something to hear 'em laugh. You could tell how Lincoln kept things stirred up. He was so blamed quick. Ever hear Judge Weldon tell that story about what Lincoln said one day up to Bloomington when they was takin' up a subscription to buy Jim Wheeler a new pair of pants? No? Well, perhaps I oughten to tell it to you, Ma says it ain't nice. It makes me mad to hear people objectin' to Mr. Lincoln's stories. Mebbe he did say words you wouldn't expect to hear at a church supper, but he never put no meanin' into 'em that wouldn't't'a' been fit for the minister to put into a sermon, and that's a blamed sight more'n you can say of a lot of stories I've heard some of the people tell who stick up their noses at Mr. Lincoln's yarns.

"Yes, sir, he used to keep things purty well stirred up on that circuit. That time I was a speakin' of he made Judge Davis real mad; it happened right in court and everybody got to gigglin' fit to kill. The Judge knew 'twas something Lincoln had said and he began to sputter.

"'I am not going to stand this any longer, Mr. Lincoln, you're always disturbin' this court with your tomfoolery. I'm goin' to fine you. The clerk will fine Mr. Lincoln five dollars for disorderly conduct.' The boys said Lincoln never said a word; he just set lookin' down with his hand over his mouth, tryin' not to laugh. About a minute later the Judge, who was always on pins and needles till he knew all the fun that was goin' on, called up Weldon and whispered to him, 'What was that Lincoln said?' Weldon told him, and I'll be blamed if the Judge didn't giggle right out loud there in court. The joke was on him then, and he knew it, and soon as he got his face straight he said, dignified like, 'The clerk may remit Mr. Lincoln's fine.'

"Yes, but he was a mighty cute story-teller, but he knew what he was about tellin' 'em. I tell you he got more arguments out of stories than he did out of law books, and the queer part was you couldn't answer 'em—they just made you see it and you couldn't get around it. I'm a Democrat, but I'll be blamed if I didn't have to vote for Mr. Lincoln as President, couldn't help it, and it was all on account of that snake story of his'n illustratin' the takin' of slavery into Kansas and Nebraska. Remember it? I heard him tell it in a speech once.

"'If I saw a pizen snake crawlin' in the road,' he says, 'I'd kill it with the first thing I could grab; but if I found it in bed with my children, I'd be mighty careful how I touched it fear I'd make it bite the children. If I found it in bed with somebody's else's children I'd let them take care of it; but if I found somebody puttin' a whole batch of young snakes into an empty bed where mine or anybody's children was going to sleep pretty soon, I'd stop him from doin' it if I had to fight him.' Perhaps he didn't say 'fight him,' but somehow I always tell that story that way because I know I would and so would he or you or anybody. That was what it was all about when you came down to it. They was tryin' to put a batch of snakes into an empty bed that folks was goin' to sleep in.

"Before I heard that story I'd heard Lincoln say a hundred times, settin' right there in that chair, where you are, 'Boys, we've got to stop slavery or it's goin' to spread all over this country,' but, somehow, I didn't see it before. Them snakes finished me. Then I knew he'd got it right and I'd got to vote for him. Pretty tough, though, for me to go back on Little Doug. You see he was our great man, so we thought. Been to the United States Senate and knew all the big bugs all over the country. Sort o' looked and talked great. Wa'n't no comparison between him and Lincoln in looks and talk. Of course, we all knew he wa'n't honest, like Lincoln, but blamed if I didn't think in them days Lincoln was too all-fired honest—kind of innocent honest. He couldn't stand it nohow to have things said that wa'n't so. He just felt plumb bad about lies. I remember once bein' in court over to Decatur when Mr. Lincoln was tryin' a case. There was a fellow agin him that didn't have no prejudices against lyin' in a lawsuit, and he was tellin' how Lincoln had said this an' that, tryin' to mix up the jury. It was snowin' bad outside, and Mr. Lincoln had wet his feet and he was tryin' to dry 'em at the stove. He had pulled off one shoe and was settin' there holdin' up his great big foot, his fore-head all puckered up, listenin' to that ornery lawyer's lies. All at onct he jumped up and hopped right out into the middle of the courtroom.

" 'Now, Judge,' he says, 'that ain't fair. I didn't say no sich thing, and he knows I didn't. I ain't goin' to have this jury all fuddled up.'

"You never seen anything so funny in a court-room as that big fellow standin' there in one stockin' foot, a shoe in his hand, talking so earnest. No, sir, he couldn't stand a lie.

" 'Think he was a big man, then?' Nope—never did. Just as I said, we all thought Douglas was *our* big man. You know I felt kind of sorry for Lincoln when they began to talk about him for President. It seemed almost as if some-body was makin' fun of him. He didn't look like a president. I never had seen one, but we had pictures of 'em, all of 'em from George Washington down, and they looked somehow as if they were different kind of timber from us. Leastwise that's always the way it struck me. Now Mr. Lincoln he was just like your own folks—no trouble to talk to him, no siree. Somehow you just settled down comfortable to visitin' the minute he come in. I couldn't imagine George

Washington or Thomas Jefferson set-tin' here in that chair you're in tee-heein' over some blamed yarn of mine. None of us around town took much stock in his bein' elected at first—that is, none of the men, the women was differ-ent. They always believed in him, and used to say, 'You mark my word, Mr. Lincoln will be president. He's just made for it, he's good, he's the best man ever lived and he ought to be presi-dent.' I didn't see no logic in that then, but I dunno but there was some after all.

"It seems all right now though. I reckon I learned somethin' watchin' him be President—learned a lot—not that it made any difference to *him*. Funniest thing to see him goin' around in this town—not a mite changed—and the whole United States a-watchin' him and the biggest men in the country runnin' after him and reporters hangin' around to talk to him and fellers makin' his pictures in ile and every other way. That didn't make no difference to him —only he didn't like bein' so busy he couldn't come in here much. He had a room over there in the Court House—room on that corner there. I never looked up that it wa'n't chuck full of people wantin' him. This old town was full of people all the time—delegations and committees and politicians and newspaper men. Only time I ever see Horace Greeley, he came in here to buy quinine. Mr. Lincoln sent him. Think of that, Horace Greely buyin' quinine of *me*.

"No end of other great men around. He saw 'em all. Sometimes I used to step over and watch him—didn't bother him a mite to see a big man—not a mite. He'd just shake hands and talk as easy and natural as if 'twas me—and he didn't do no struttin' either. Some of the fellers who come to see him looked as if *they* was goin' to be president, but Mr. Lincoln didn't put on any airs. No, sir, and he didn't cut any of his old

118

friends either. Tickled to death to see 'em every time, and they all come—blamed if every old man and woman in Sangamon County didn't trot up here to see him. They'd all knowed him when he was keepin' store down to New Salem and swingin' a chain—surveyed lots of their towns for 'em—he had—and then he'd electioneered all over that county, too, so they just come in droves to bid him good-by. I was over there one day when old Aunt Sally Lowdy came in the door. Aunt Sally lived down near New Salem, and I expect she'd mended Mr. Lincoln's pants many a time; for all them old women down there just doted on him and took care of him as if he was their own boy. Well, Aunt Sally stood lookin' kind of scared seein' so many strangers and not knowin' precisely what to do, when Mr. Lincoln spied her. Quick as a wink he said, 'Excuse me, gentlemen,' an' he just rushed over to that old woman and shook hands with both of his'n and says, 'Now, Aunt Sally, this is real kind of you to come and see me. How are you and how's Jake?' (Jake was her boy.) 'Come right over here,' and he led her over, as if she was the biggest lady in Illinois, and says, 'Gentlemen, this is a good old friend of mine. She can make the best flapjacks you ever tasted, and she's baked 'em for me many a time.' Aunt Sally was jest as pink as a rosy, she was so tickled. And she says, 'Abe'—all the old folks in Sangamon called him Abe. They knowed him as a boy, but don't you believe anybody ever did up here. No sir, we said Mr. Lincoln. He was like one of us, but he wa'n't no man to be over familiar with. 'Abe,' says Aunt Sally, 'I had to come and say good-by. They say down our way they're goin' to kill you if they get you down to Washington, but I don't believe it. I just tell 'em you're too smart to let 'em git ahead of you that way. I thought I'd come and bring you a present, knit 'em myself.' And I'll be blamed if that old lady didn't pull out a great big pair of yarn socks and hand 'em to Mr. Lincoln.

"Well, sir, it was the funniest thing to see Mr. Lincoln's face pucker up and his eyes twinkle and twinkle. He took them socks and held 'em up by the toes, one in each hand. They was the longest socks I ever see. 'The lady got my latitude and longitude 'bout right, didn't she, gentlemen?' he says, and then he laid 'em down, and he took Aunt Sally's hand and he says tenderlike, 'Aunt Sally, you couldn't 'a' done nothin' which would have pleased me better. I'll take 'em to Washington and wear 'em, and think of you when I do it.' And I declare he said it so first thing I knew I was blubberin' and I wa'n't the only one nuther, and I bet he did wear 'em in Washington. I can jest see him pullin' off his shoe and showin' them socks to Sumner or Seward or some other big bug that was botherin' him when he wanted to switch off on another subject and tellin' 'em the story about Aunt Sally and her flapjacks.

" 'Was there much talk about his bein' killed?' Well, there's an awful lot of fools in this world and when they don't git what they want they're always for killin' somebody. Mr. Lincoln never let on, but I reckon his mail was pretty lively readin' sometimes. He got pictures of gallows and pistols and other things and lots of threats, so they said. I don't think that worried him much. He was more bothered seein' old Buchanan givin' the game away. 'I wish I could have got down there before the horse was stole,' I heard him say onct in here, talkin' to some men. 'But I reckon I can find the tracks when I do git there.' It was his cabinet bothered him most, I always thought. He didn't know the men he'd got to take well enough. Didn't know how far he could count on 'em. He and Judge Gillespie and one or two others was in here one day sittin' by the stove talkin', and he says, 'Judge, I wisht I could take all you boys down to Washington with me, Democrats and all, and make a cabinet out of you. I'd know where every man would fit and we could git right down to work. Now, I've got to learn my men before I can do much.' 'Do you mean, Mr. Lincoln, you'd take a Democrat like Logan?' says the Judge, sort of shocked. 'Yes, sir, I would; I know Logan. He's agin me now and that's all right, but if we have trouble you can count on Logan to do the right thing by the country, and that's the kind of men I want —them as will do the right thing by the country. 'Tain't a question of Lincoln, or Democrat or Republican, Judge; it's a question of the country.'

"Of course he seemed pretty cheerful always. He wa'n't no man to show out all he felt. Lots of them little stuck-up chaps that came out here to talk to him said, solemn as owls, 'He don't realize the gravity of the situation.' Them's their words, 'gravity of the situation.' Think of that, Mr. Lincoln not realizing. They ought to heard him talk to us the night he went away. I'll never forget that speech—nor any man who heard it. I can see him now just how he looked, standin' there on the end of his car. He'd been shakin' hands with the crowd in the depot, laughin' and talkin', just like himself, but when he got onto that car he seemed suddint to be all changed. You never seen a face so sad in all the world. I tell you he had woe in his heart that minute, woe. He knew he was leavin' us for good, nuthin' else could explain the way he looked and what he said. It was rainin' hard, but when we saw him standin' there bare headed, his great big eyes lookin' at us so lovin' and mournful, every man of us took off his hat, just as if he'd been in church. You never heard him make a speech, of course? You missed a lot. Curious voice. You could hear it away off—kind of shrill, but went right to your heart—and that night it sounded

sadder than anything I ever heard. You know I always hear it to this day, nights when the wind howls around the house. Ma says it makes her nervous to hear me talk about him such nights, but I can't help it; just have to let out.

"He stood a minute lookin' at us, and then he began to talk. There ain't a man in this town that heard him that ever forgot what he said, but I don't believe there's a man that ever said it over out loud—he couldn't, without cryin'. He just talked to us that time out of his heart. Somehow we felt all of a suddint how we loved him and how he loved us. We hadn't taken any stock in all that talk about his bein' killed, but when he said he was goin' away not knowin' where or whether ever he would return I just got cold all over. I began to *see* that minute and everybody did. The women all fell to sobbin' and a kind of groan went up, and when he asked us to pray for him I don't believe that there was a man in the crowd, whether he ever went to church in his life, that didn't want to drop right down on his marrow bones and ask the Lord to take care of Abraham Lincoln and bring him back to us, where he belonged.

" 'Ever see him again?' Yes, onct down in Washington, summer of '64. Things was lookin' purty blue that summer. Didn't seem to be anybody who thought he'd git reelected. Greeley was abusin' him in the *Tribune* for not makin' peace, and you know there was about half the North that always let Greeley do their thinkin' fer 'em. The war wa'n't comin' on at all—seemed as if they never would do nuthin'. Grant was hangin' on to Petersburg like a dog to a root, but it didn't seem to do no good. Same with Sherman, who was tryin' to take Atlanta. The country was just petered out with the everlastin' taxes an' fightin' an' dyin'. It wa'n't human nature to be patient any longer, and they just spit it out on Mr. Lincoln, and then, right on top of all the grumblin' and abusin', he up and made another draft. Course he was right, but I tell you nobody but a brave man would 'a' done such a thing at that minute; but he did it. It was hard on us out here. I tell you there wa'nt many houses in this country where there wa'nt mournin' goin' on. It didn't seem as if we *could* stand any more blood lettin'. Some of the boys round the State went down to see him about it. They came back lookin' pretty sheepish, Joe Medill, up to Chicago, told me about it onct. He said, 'We just told Mr. Lincoln we couldn't stand another draft. We was through sendin' men down to Petersburg to be killed in trenches. He didn't say nuthin'; just stood still, lookin' down till we'd all talked ourselves out; and then, after a while, he lifted up his head, and looked around at us, slow-like; and I tell you, Billy, I never knew till that minute that Abraham Lincoln could get mad clean through. He was just white he was that mad. "Boys," he says, "you ought to be ashamed of yourselves. You're actin' like a lot of cowards. You've helped make this war, and you've got to help fight it. You go home and raise them men and don't you dare come down here again blubberin' about what I tell you to do. I won't stan' it." We was so scared we never said a word. We just took our hats and went out like a lot of schoolboys. Talk about Abraham Lincoln bein' easy! When it didn't matter mebbe he was easy, but when it did you couldn't stir him any more'n you could a mountain.'

"Well, I kept hearin' about the trouble he was havin' with everybody, and I just made up my mind I'd go down and see him and swap yarns and tell him how we was all countin' on his gettin' home. Thought maybe it would cheer him up to know we set such store on his comin' home if they didn't want him for president. So I jest picked up and went right off. Ma was real good

about my goin'. She says, 'I shouldn't wonder if 'twould do him good, William. And don't you ask him no questions about the war nor about politics. You just talk home to him and tell him some of them foolish stories of yourn.'

"Well, I had a brother in Washington, clerk in a department—awful set up 'cause he had an office—and when I got down there I told him I'd come to visit Mr. Lincoln. He says, 'William, be you a fool? Folks don't visit the President of the United States without an invitation, and he's too busy to see anybody but the very biggest people in this administration. Why, he don't even see me,' he says. Well, it made me huffy to hear him talk. 'Isaac,' I says, 'I don't wonder Mr. Lincoln don't see you. But it's different with me. Him and me is friends.'

" 'Well,' he says, 'you've got to have cards anyway.' 'Cards,' I says, 'what for! What kind?' 'Why,' he says, 'visitin' cards—with your name on.' 'Well,' I says, 'it's come to a pretty pass, if an old friend like me can't see Mr. Lincoln without sendin' him a piece of pasteboard. I'd be ashamed to do such a thing, Isaac Brown. Do you suppose he's forgotten me? Needs to see my name printed out to know who I am? You can't make me believe any such thing,' and I walked right out of the room, and that night I footed it up to the Soldier's Home where Mr. Lincoln was livin' then, right among the sick soldiers in their tents.

"There was lots of people settin' around in a little room, waitin' fer him, but there wa'nt anybody there I knowed, and I was feelin' a little funny when a door opened and out came little John Nicolay. He came from down this way, so I just went up and says, 'How'd you do, John; where's Mr. Lincoln?' Well, John didn't seem over glad to see me.

" 'Have you an appointment with Mr. Lincoln?' he says.

" 'No, sir,' I says; 'I ain't, and it ain't necessary. Mebbe it's all right and fittin' for them as wants post-offices to have appointments, but I reckon Mr. Lincoln's old friends don't need 'em so you just trot along, Johnnie, and tell him Billy Brown's here and see what he say.' Well, he kinda flushed up and set his lips together, but he knowed me, and so he went off. In about two minutes the door popped open and out came Mr. Lincoln, his face all lit up. He saw me first thing, and he laid holt of me and just shook my hands fit to kill. 'Billy,' he says, 'now I am glad to see you. Come right in. You're goin' to stay to supper with Mary and me.'

"Didn't I know it? Think bein' president would change him—not a mite. Well, he had a right smart lot of people to see, but soon as he was through we went out on the back stoop and set down and talked and talked. He asked me about pretty nigh everybody in Springfield. I just let loose and told him about the weddin's and births and the funerals and the buildin', and I guess there wa'nt a yarn I'd heard in the three years and a half he'd been away that I didn't spin for him. Laugh —you ought to a heard him laugh—just did my heart good, for I could see what they'd been doin' to him. Always a thin man, but, Lordy, he was thinner'n ever now, and his face was kind a drawn and gray—enough to make you cry.

"Well, we had supper and then talked some more, and about ten o'clock I started downtown. Wanted me to stay all night, but I says to myself, 'Billy, don't you overdo it. You've cheered him up, and you better light out and let him remember it when he's tired.' So I said, 'Nope, Mr. Lincoln, can't; goin' back to Springfield tomorrow. Ma don't like to have me away and my boy ain't no great shakes keepin' store.' 'Billy,' he says, 'what did you come down here for?' 'I come to see you, Mr. Lincoln.' 'But you ain't asked me for anything, Billy. What

is it? Out with it. Want a post-office?' he said, gigglin', for he knowed I didn't. 'No, Mr. Lincoln, just wanted to see *you* —felt kinda lonesome—been so long since I'd seen you, and I was afraid I'd forgit some of them yarns if I didn't unload soon.'

"Well, sir, you ought to seen his face as he looked at me.

" 'Billy Brown,' he says, slow-like, 'do you mean to tell me you came all the way from Springfield, Illinois, just to have a *visit* with me, that you don't want an office for anybody, nor a pardon for anybody, that you ain't got no complaints in your pocket, nor any advice up your sleeve?'

" 'Yes, sir,' I says, 'that's about it, and I'll be durned if I wouldn't go to *Europe* to see you, if I couldn't do it no other way, Mr. Lincoln.'

"Well, sir, I never was as astonished in my life. He just grabbed my hand and shook it nearly off, and the tears just poured down his face, and he says, 'Billy, you never'll know what good you've done me. I'm homesick, Billy, just plumb homesick, and it seems as if this war never would be over. Many a night I can see the boys a-dyin' on the fields and can hear their mothers cryin' for 'em at home, and I can't help 'em, Billy. I have to send them down there. We've got to save the Union, Billy, we've got to.'

" 'Course we have, Mr. Lincoln,' I says, cheerful as I could. 'Course we have. Don't you worry. It's most over. You're goin' to be reelected, and you and old Grant's goin' to finish this war mighty quick then. Just keep a stiff upper lip, Mr. Lincoln, and don't forget them yarns I told you.' And I started out. But seems as if he couldn't let me go. 'Wait a minute, Billy,' he says, 'till I get my hat and I'll walk a piece with you.' It was one of them still sweet-smellin' summer nights with no end of stars and you ain't no idee how pretty 'twas walkin' down the road. There was white tents showin' through the trees and every little way a tall soldier standin' stock still, a gun at his side. Made me feel mighty curious and solemn. By-and-by we come out of the trees to a sightly place where you could look all over Washington—see the Potomac and clean into Virginia. There was a bench there and we set down and after a while Mr. Lincoln he begun to talk. Well, sir, you or nobody ever heard anything like it. Blamed if he didn't tell me the whole thing—all about the war and the generals and Seward and Sumner and Congress and Greeley and the whole blamed lot. He just opened up his heart if I do say it. Seemed as if he'd come to a p'int where he must let out. I dunno how long we set there—must have been nigh morning, for the stars begun to go out before he got up to go. 'Good-by, Billy,' he says. 'You're the first person I ever unloaded onto, and I hope you won't think I'm a baby,' and then we shook hands again, and I walked down to town and next day I come home.

"Tell you what he said? Nope, I can't. Can't talk about it somehow. Fact is, I never told anybody what he said that night. Tried to tell Ma onct, but she cried, so I give it up.

"Yes, that's the last time I seen him—last time alive.

"Wa'n't long after that things began to look better. War began to move right smart, and, soon as it did, there wa'n't no use talkin' about anybody else for President. I see that plain enough, and, just as I told him, he was reelected, and him an' Grant finished up the war in a hurry. I tell you it was a great day out here when we heard Lee had surrendered. 'Twas just like getting converted to have the war over. Somehow the only thing I could think of was how glad Mr. Lincoln would be. Me and Ma reckoned he'd come right out and make us a visit and get rested, and we began right off to make plans about the recep-

tion we'd give him—brass band—parade —speeches—fireworks—everything. Seems as if I couldn't think about anything else. I was comin' down to open the store one mornin', and all the way down I was plannin' how I'd decorate the windows and how I'd tie a flag on that old chair, when I see Hiram Jones comin' toward me. He looked so old and all bent over I didn't know what had happened. 'Hiram,' I says, 'what's the matter? Be you sick?

" 'Billy,' he says, and he couldn't hardly say it, 'Billy, they've killed Mr. Lincoln.'

"Well, I just turned cold all over, and then I flared up. 'Hiram Jones,' I says, 'you're lyin', you're crazy. How dare you tell me that? It ain't so.'

" 'Don't, Billy,' he says, 'don't go on so. I ain't lyin'. It's so. He'll never come back, Billy. He's dead!' And he fell to sobbin' out loud right there in the street, and somehow I knew it was true.

"I come on down and opened the door. People must have paregoric and castor ile and liniment, no matter who dies; but I didn't put up the shades. I just sat here and thought and thought and groaned and groaned. It seemed that day as if the country was plumb ruined and I didn't care much. All I could think of was *him*. He wa'n't goin' to come back. He wouldn't never sit here in that chair again. He was dead.

"For days and days 'twas awful here. Waitin' and waitin'. Seemed as if that funeral never would end. I couldn't bear to think of him bein' dragged around the country and havin' all that fuss made over him. He always hated fussin' so. Still, I s'pose I'd been mad if they hadn't done it. Seemed awful, though. I kinda felt that he belonged to us now, that they ought to bring him back and let us have him now they'd killed him.

"Of course they got here at last, and I must say it was pretty grand. All sorts of big bugs, Senators and Congressmen, and officers in grand uniforms and music and flags and crape. They certainly didn't spare no pains givin' him a funeral. Only we didn't want 'em. We wanted to bury him ourselves, but they wouldn't let us. I went over onct where they'd laid him out for folks to see. I reckon I won't tell you about that. I ain't never goin' to get that out of my mind. I wisht a million times I'd never seen him lyin' there black and changed—that I could only see him as he looked sayin' 'good-by' to me up to the Soldiers' Home in Washington that night.

"Ma and me didn't get to the ceme-tery with 'em. I couldn't stan' it. Didn't seem right to have sich goin's on here at home where he belonged, for a man like him. But we go up often now, Ma and me does, and talk about him. Blamed if it don't seem sometimes as if he was right there—might step out any minute and say 'Hello, Billy, any new stories?'

"Yes. I knowed Abraham Lincoln; knowed him well; and I tell you there wa'n't never a better man made. Leastwise I don't want to know a better one. He just suited *me*—Abraham Lincoln did."

      ❧   ❧   ❧

ON ABRAHAM LINCOLN

JAMES RUSSELL LOWELL

Great captains, with their guns and drums,
Disturb our judgment for the hour,
But at last silence comes;
These all are gone, and, standing like a tower,
Our children shall behold his fame,
The kindly, earnest, brave, foreseeing man,
Sagacious, patient, dreading praise, not blame,
New birth of our new soil, the first American.

CHANT OF LOYALTY

ELIAS LIEBERMAN

Firm as the furnace heat
Rivets the bars of steel,
Thus to thy destiny,
  Flag, are we plighted;
One are the hearts that beat,
One is the throb we feel,
One in our loyalty,
  Stand we united.

Many a folk have brought
Sinew and brawn to thee;
Many an ancient wrong
  Well hast thou righted;
Here in the land we sought,
Stanchly, from sea to sea,
Here, where our hearts belong,
  Stand we united.

Ask us to pay the price,
All that we have to give,
Nothing shall be denied,
  All be requited;
Ready for sacrifice,
Ready for thee to live,
Over the country wide
  Stand we united.

One under palm and pine,
One in the prairie sun,
One on the rock-bound shore,
  Liberty-sighted;
All that we have is thine,
Thine, who hast made us one,
True to thee evermore,
  Stand we united.

THEY WILL LOOK FOR A FEW WORDS
Nancy Byrd Turner

The fast express for Gettysburg roared north
Among the hills one autumn day long gone,
At thirty miles an hour, from Washington
To the great Field; and beating along the ties,
Crying across the rivers, on it drew,
Echoing under bleak November skies.

The coaches rocked. One awkward traveler rode
Hunched in his seat, too tall for comfort there,
A gaunt, plain man with memorable air
Who talked at intervals with other men—
Companionable, keen of word—and then
Lapsed into silence, with his brooding look
Long on the changing scene, mile after mile—
A strange man, musing strangely, deeply, while
The rest talked on, or counted ties.

After a long, long time
Somebody reckoned the journey was half gone,
And all thoughts turned together to the town
Where soon the crowds would meet to praise their dead,
Their number less dead, living in memory.
The tall man's eyes grew darker. "They will look
For a few words from me," slowly he said,
And, searching clumsily for paper, spread
A crumpled scrap across his dusty knee.

Then while the long train on and upward beat,
His pencil slowly stumbled through the grime
On the smudged sheet. And as the breathless climb
Conquered the longest rise of all, and topped
A hill above a plain far-flung and broad,
The pencil wrote, "this nation under God . . ."
Then, shaken through phrase by phrase, after a time
Wrote, "shall not perish from the earth . . . . ." and stopped.

* * *

HERE IS MY CREED. I believe in one God, Creator of the Universe. That He governs it by His Providence. That He ought to be worshipped. That the most acceptable service we render Him is doing good to His other children. That the soul of man is immortal, and will be treated with justice in another life respecting its conduct in this. —*Franklin*

125

The Rubaiyat of Omar Khayyam

THE EDWARD FITZGERALD VERSION

I

Wake! For the Sun, who scatter'd into
flight
The Stars before him from the Field of
Night,
  Drives Night along with them from
Heav'n, and strikes
The Sultán's Turret with a Shaft of
Light.

II

Before the phantom of False morning
died,
Methought a Voice within the Tavern
cried,
  "When all the Temple is prepared
within,
"Why nods the drowsy Worshipper outside?"

III

And, as the Cock crew, those who stood
before
The Tavern shouted—"Open then the
Door!
  "You know how little while we have
to stay,
"And, once departed, may return no
more."

IV

Now the New Year reviving old Desires
The thoughtful Soul of Solitude retires,
  Where the WHITE HAND OF MOSES on
the Bough
Puts out, and Jesus from the Ground
suspires.

V

Iram indeed is gone with all his Rose,
And Jamshyd's Sev'n-ring'd Cup where
no one knows;
  But still a Ruby kindles in the Vine,
And many a Garden by the Water
blows.

VI

And David's lips are lockt; but in divine
High-piping Pehleví, with "Wine!
Wine! Wine!
  "Red Wine!"—the Nightingale cries
to the Rose
That sallow cheek of hers to' incarna-
dine.

VII

Come, fill the Cup, and in the fire of
Spring
Your Winter-garment of Repentance
fling:
  The Bird of Time has but a little way
To flutter—and the Bird is on the Wing.

VIII

Whether at Naishápúr or Babylon,
Whether the Cup with sweet or bitter
run,
  The Wine of Life keeps oozing drop
by drop,
The Leaves of Life keep falling one by
one.

IX

Each Morn a thousand Roses brings,
you say:
Yes, but where leaves the Rose of Yesterday?
  And this first Summer month that
brings the Rose
Shall take Jamshyd and Kaikobád away.

X

Well, let it take them! What have we to
do
With Kaikobád the Great, or Kaik-
hosrú?

Let Zál and Rustum bluster as they
will,
Or Hátim call to Supper—heed not you.

XI

With me along the strip of Herbage
strown
That just divides the desert from the
sown,
    Where name of Slave and Sultán is
forgot—
And Peace to Mahmúd on his golden
Throne!

XII

A Book of Verses underneath the
Bough,
A Jug of Wine, a Loaf of Bread—and
Thou
    Beside me singing in the Wilderness—
Oh, Wilderness were Paradise enow!

XIII

Some of the Glories of This World; and
some
Sigh for the Prophet's Paradise to come;
    Ah, take the Cash, and let the Credit
go,
Nor heed the rumble of a distant Drum!

XIV

Look to the blowing Rose about us—
"Lo,
"Laughing," she says, "into the world I
blow,
    "At once the silken tassel of my Purse
"Tear, and its Treasure on the Garden
throw."

XV

And those who husbanded the Golden
grain,
And those who flung it to the winds like
Rain,
    Alike to no such aureate Earth are
turn'd
As, buried once, Men want dug up
again.

XVI

The Worldly Hope men set their Hearts
upon
Turns Ashes—or it prospers; and anon,
    Like Snow upon the Desert's dusty
Face,
Lighting a little hour or two—is gone.

XVII

Think, in this batter'd Caravanserai
Whose Portals are alternate Night and
Day,
    How Sultán after Sultán with his
Pomp
Abode his destined Hour, and went his
way.

XVIII

They say the Lion and the Lizard keep
The Courts where Jamshyd gloried and
drank deep:
    And Bahrám, that great Hunter—the
Wild Ass
Stamps o'er his Head, but cannot break
his Sleep.

XIX

I sometimes think that never blows so
red
The Rose as where some buried Cæsar
bled;
    That every Hyacinth the Garden
wears
Dropt in her Lap from some once lovely Head.

XX

And this reviving Herb whose tender
Green
Fledges the River-Lip on which we
lean—
    Ah, lean upon it lightly! for who
knows
From what once lovely Lip it springs
unseen!

XXI

Ah, my Belovéd, fill the Cup that clears
To-DAY of past Regrets and future
Fears:

To-morrow!—Why, To-morrow I may be
Myself with Yesterday's Sev'n thousand Years.

XXII

For some we loved, the loveliest and the best
That from his Vintage rolling Time hath prest,
    Have drunk their Cup a Round or two before,
And one by one crept silently to rest.

XXIII

And we, that now make merry in the Room
The left, and Summer dresses in new bloom,
    Ourselves must we beneath the Couch of Earth
Descend—ourselves to make a Couch—for whom?

XXIV

Ah, make the most of what we yet may spend,
Before we too into the Dust descend;
    Dust into Dust, and under Dust to lie,
Sans Wine, sans Song, sans Singer, and sans End!

XXV

Alike for those who for TO-DAY prepare,
And those that after some TO-MORROW stare,
    A Muezzin from the Tower of Darkness cries,
"Fools! your Reward is neither Here nor There."

XXVI

Why, all the Saints and Sages who discuss'd
Of the Two Worlds so wisely—they are thrust
    Like foolish Prophets forth; their Words to Scorn
Are scatter'd, and their Mouths are stopt with Dust.

XXVII

Myself when young did eagerly frequent
Doctor and Saint, and heard great argument
    About it and about: but evermore
Came out by the same door where in I went.

XXVIII

With them the seed of Wisdom did I sow,
And with mine own hand wrought to make it grow;
    And this was all the Harvest that I reap'd—
"I came like Water, and like Wind I go."

XXIX

Into this Universe, and *Why* not knowing
Nor *Whence*, like Water willy-nilly flowing;
    And out of it, as Wind along the Waste,
I know not *Whither*, willy-nilly blowing.

XXX

What, without asking, hither hurried *Whence*?
And, without asking, *Whither* hurried hence!
    Oh, many a *Cup* of this forbidden Wine
Must drown the memory of that insolence!

XXXI

Up from Earth's Centre through the Seventh Gate
I rose, and on the Throne of Saturn sate,
    And many a Knot unravel'd by the Road;
But not the Master-knot of Human Fate.

XXXII

There was the Door to which I found
no Key;
There was the Veil through which I
might not see:
 Some little talk awhile of ME and
 THEE
There was—and then no more of THEE
and ME.

XXXIII

Earth could not answer; nor the Seas
that mourn
In flowing Purple, of their Lord for-
lorn;
 Nor rolling Heaven, with all his Signs
 reveal'd
And hidden by the sleeve of Night and
Morn.

XXXIV

Then of the THEE IN ME who works
behind
The Veil, I lifted up my hands to find
 A lamp amid the Darkness; and I
 heard,
As from Without—"THE ME WITHIN
THEE BLIND!"

XXXV

Then to the Lip of this poor earthen
Urn
I lean'd, the Secret of my Life to learn:
 And Lip to Lip it murmur'd—"While
 you live,
Drink!—for, once dead, you never shall
return."

XXXVI

I think the Vessel, that with fugitive
Articulation, answer'd, once did live,
 And drink; and Ah! the passive Lip
 I kiss'd,
How many Kisses might it take—and
give!

XXXVII

For I remember stopping by the way
To watch a Potter thumping his wet
Clay:

And with its all-obliterated Tongue
It murmur'd—"Gently, Brother, gently,
pray!"

XXXVIII

And has not such a Story from of Old
Down Man's successive generations
roll'd
 Of such a clod of saturated Earth
Cast by the Maker into Human mould?

XXXIX

And not a drop that from our Cups we
throw
For Earth to drink of, but may steal
below
 To quench the fire of Anguish in
 some Eye
There hidden—far beneath, and long
ago.

XL

As then the Tulip for her morning sup
Of Heav'nly Vintage from the soil looks
up,
 Do you devoutly do the like, till
 Heav'n
To Earth invert you—like an empty
Cup.

XLI

Perplext no more with Human or
Divine,
To-morrow's tangle to the winds resign,
 And lose your fingers in the tresses of
The Cypress-slender Minister of Wine·

XLII

And if the Wine you drink, the Lip you
press,
End in what All begins and ends in—
Yes;
 Think then you are TO-DAY what
 YESTERDAY
You were—TO-MORROW you shall not be
less.

XLIII

So when that Angel of the darker Drink
At last shall find you by the river-brink,

And, offering his Cup, invite your Soul
Forth to your Lips to quaff—you shall not shrink.

XLIV

Why, if the Soul can fling the Dust aside,
And naked on the Air of Heaven ride,
  Were't not a Shame—were't not a Shame for him
In this clay carcase crippled to abide?

XLV

'Tis but a Tent where takes his one day's rest
A Sultán to the realm of Death addrest;
  The Sultan rises, and the dark Ferrásh
Strikes, and prepares it for another Guest.

XLVI

And fear not lest Existence closing your
Account, and mine, should know the like no more;
  The Eternal Sáki from that Bowl has pour'd
Millions of Bubbles like us, and will pour.

XLVII

When You and I behind the Veil are past,
Oh, but the long, long while the World shall last,
  Which of our Coming and Departure heeds
As the Sea's self should heed a pebble-cast.

XLVIII

A Moment's Halt—a momentary taste
Of BEING from the Well amid the Waste—
  And Lo!—the phantom Caravan has reach'd
The NOTHING it set out from—Oh, make haste!

XLIX

Would you that spangle of Existence spend
About the SECRET—quick about it, Friend!
  A Hair perhaps divides the False and True—
And upon what, prithee, may life depend?

L

A Hair perhaps divides the False and True.
Yes; and a single Alif were the clue—
  Could you but find it—to the Treasure-house,
And peradventure to THE MASTER too;

LI

Whose secret Presence, through Creation's veins
Running Quicksilver-like eludes your pains;
  Taking all shapes from Máh to Máhi; and
They change and perish all—but He remains;

LII

A moment guess'd—then back behind the Fold
Immerst of Darkness round the Drama roll'd
  Which, for the Pastime of Eternity,
He doth Himself contrive, enact, behold.

LIII

But if in vain, down on the stubborn floor
Of Earth, and up to Heav'n's unopening Door,
  You gaze TO-DAY, while You are You—how then
TO-MORROW, when You shall be You no more?

LIV

Waste not your Hour, nor in the vain pursuit

Of This and That endeavour and dispute;
   Better be jocund with the fruitful Grape
Than sadden after none, or bitter, Fruit.

LV

You know, my Friends, with what a brave Carouse
I made a Second Marriage in my house;
   Divorced old barren Reason from my Bed,
And took the Daughter of the Vine to Spouse.

LVI

For "Is" and "Is-not" though with Rule and Line
And "Up-and-down" by Logic I define,
   Of all that one should care to fathom, I
Was never deep in anything but—Wine.

LVII

Ah, but my Computations, People say,
Reduced the Year to better reckoning?—Nay,
   'Twas only striking from the Calendar
Unborn To-morrow and dead Yesterday.

LVIII

And lately, by the Tavern Door agape,
Came shining through the Dusk an Angel Shape
   Bearing a Vessel on his Shoulder; and
He bid me taste of it; and 'twas—the Grape!

LIX

The Grape that can with Logic absolute
The Two-and-Seventy jarring Sects confute:
   The sovereign Alchemist that in a trice
Life's leaden metal into Gold transmute:

LX

The mighty Mahmúd, Allah-breathing Lord,
That all the misbelieving and black Horde
   Of Fears and Sorrows that infest the Soul
Scatters before him with his whirlwind Sword.

LXI

Why, be this Juice the growth of God, who dare
Blaspheme the twisted tendril as a Snare?
   A blessing, we should use it, should we not ?
And if a Curse—why, then, Who set it there?

LXII

I must abjure the Balm of Life, I must,
Scared by some After-reckoning ta'en on trust,
   Or lured with Hope of some Diviner Drink,
To fill the Cup—when crumbled into Dust!

LXIII

Oh threats of Hell and Hopes of Paradise!
One thing at least is certain—*This* Life flies;
   One thing is certain and the rest is Lies;
The Flower that once has blown for ever dies.

LXIV

Strange, is it not? that of the myriads who
Before us pass'd the door of Darkness through,
   Not one returns to tell us of the Road,
Which to discover we must travel too.

LXV

The Revelations of Devout and Learn'd
Who rose before us, and as Prophets burn'd,

Are all but Stories, which, awoke from Sleep
They told their comrades, and to Sleep return'd.

LXVI
I sent my Soul through the Invisible,
Some letter of that After-life to spell:
   And by and by my soul return'd to me,
And answer'd "I Myself am Heav'n and Hell:"

LXVII
Heav'n but the Vision of fulfill'd Desire,
And Hell the Shadow from a Soul on fire,
   Cast on the Darkness into which Ourselves,
So late emerged from, shall so soon expire.

LXVIII
We are no other than a moving row
Of Magic Shadow-shapes that come and go
   Round with the Sun-illumined Lantern held
In Midnight by the Master of the Show;

LXIX
But helpless Pieces of the Game He plays
Upon this Chequer-board of Nights and Days;
   Hither and thither moves, and checks, and slays,
And one by one back in the Closet lays.

LXX
The Ball no question makes of Ayes and Noes,
But Here or There as strikes the Player goes,
   And He that toss'd you down into the Field,
He knows about it all—HE knows—HE knows!

LXXI
The Moving Finger writes; and, having writ,
Moves on: nor all your Piety nor Wit
   Shall lure it back to cancel half a Line,
Nor all your Tears wash out a Word of it.

LXXII
And that inverted Bowl they call the Sky,
Whereunder crawling coop'd we live and die,
   Lift not your hands to *It* for help—for It
As impotently moves as you or I.

LXXIII
With Earth's first Clay They did the Last Man knead.
And there of the Last Harvest sow'd the Seed:
   And the first Morning of Creation wrote
What the Last Dawn of Reckoning shall read.

LXXIV
YESTERDAY *This* Day's Madness did prepare;
TO-MORROW's Silence, Triumph, or Despair:
   Drink! for you know not whence you came, nor why:
Drink! for you know not why you go, nor where.

LXXV
I tell you this—When, started from the Goal,
Over the flaming shoulders of the Foal
   Of Heav'n Parwin and Mushtari they flung,
In my predestined Plot of Dust and Soul.

LXXVI
The Vine had struck a fibre: which about

132

If clings my Being—let the Dervish
  flout;
  Of my Base metal may be filed a Key
That shall unlock the Door he howls
  without.

LXXVII

And this I know: whether the one True
  Light
Kindle to Love, or Wrath-consume me
  quite,
  One Flash of It within the Tavern
  caught
Better than in the Temple lost outright.

LXXVIII

What! out of senseless Nothing to pro-
  voke
A conscious Something to resent the
  yoke
  Of unpermitted Pleasure, under pain
Of Everlasting Penalties, if broke!

LXXIX

What! from his helpless Creature be
  repaid
Pure Gold for what he lent him dross-
  allay'd—
  Sue for a Debt he never did contract,
And cannot answer—Oh the sorry trade!

LXXX

Oh Thou, who didst with pitfall and
  with gin
Beset the Road I was to wander in,
  Thou wilt not with Predestined Evil
  round
Enmesh, and then impute my Fall to
  Sin!

LXXXI

Oh Thou, who Man of baser Earth
  didst make,
And ev'n with Paradise devise the
  Snake:
  For all the Sin wherewith the Face of
  Man
Is blacken'd—man's forgiveness give—
  and take!

LXXXII

As under cover of departing Day
Slunk hunger-stricken Ramazán away,
  Once more within the Potter's house
  alone
I stood, surrounded by the Shapes of
  Clay.

LXXXIII

Shapes of all Sorts and Sizes, great and
  small,
That stood along the floor and by the
  wall;
  And some loquacious Vessels were:
  and some
Listen'd perhaps, but never talk'd at all.

LXXXIV

Said one among them—"Surely not in
  vain
"My substance of the common Earth
  was ta'en
  "And to this Figure moulded, to be
  broke,
"Or trampled back to shapeless Earth
  again."

LXXXV

Then said a Second—"Ne'er a peevish
  Boy
"Would break the Bowl from which he
  drank in joy;
  "And He that with his hand the Ves-
  sel made
"Will surely not in after Wrath de-
  stroy."

LXXXVI

After a momentary silence spake
Some Vessel of a more ungainly Make;
  "They sneer at me for leaning all
  awry:
"What! did the Hand then of the Potter
  shake?"

LXXXVII

Whereat some one of the loquacious
  Lot—
I think a Súfi pipkin—waxing hot—

133

"All this of Pot and Potter—Tell me, then,
"Who is the Potter, pray, and who the Pot?"

LXXXVIII

"Why," said another, "Some there are who tell
"Of one who threatens he will toss to Hell
   "The luckless Pots he marr'd in making—Pish!
"He's a Good Fellow, and 'twill all be well."

LXXXIX

"Well," murmur'd one, "Let whoso make or buy,
"My Clay with long Oblivion is gone dry:
   "But fill me with the old familiar Juice
"Methinks I might recover by and by."

XC

So while the Vessels one by one were speaking,
The little Moon look'd in that all were seeking:
   And then they jogg'd each other, "Brother! Brother!
"Now for the Porter's shoulder-knot-a-creaking!"

XCI

Ah, with the Grape my fading life provide,
And wash the Body whence the Life has died.
   And lay me, shrouded in the living Leaf,
By some not unfrequented Garden-side.

XCII

That ev'n my buried Ashes such a snare
Of Vintage shall fling up into the Air
   As not a True-believer passing by
But shall be overtaken unaware.

XCIII

Indeed the Idols I have loved so long
Have done my credit in this World much wrong:
   Have drown'd my Glory in a shallow Cup,
And sold my Reputation for a Song.

XCIV

Indeed, indeed, Repentance oft before
I swore—but was I sober when I swore?
   And then and then came Spring, and Rose-in-hand
My thread-bare Penitence apieces tore.

XCV

And much as Wine has play'd the Infidel,
And robb'd me of my Robe of Honour Well,
   I wonder often what the Vintners buy
One half so precious as the stuff they sell.

XCVI

Yet Ah, that Spring should vanish with the Rose!
That Youth's sweet-scented manuscript should close!
   The Nightingale that in the branches sang,
Ah whence, and whither flown again, who knows!

XCVII

Would but the Desert of the Fountain yield
One glimpse—if dimly, yet indeed, reveal'd,
   To which the fainting Traveller might spring,
As springs the trampled herbage of the field!

XCVIII

Would but some wingéd Angel ere too late
Arrest the yet unfolded Roll of Fate,
   And make the stern Recorder otherwise

Enregister, or quite obliterate!

XCIX

Ah Love! could you and I with Him
  conspire
To grasp this sorry Scheme of Things
  entire,
  Would not we shatter it to bits—and
  then
Re-mould it nearer to the Heart's
  Desire!

C

Yon rising Moon that looks for us
  again—

How oft hereafter will she wax and
  wane;
How oft hereafter rising look for us
Through this same Garden—and for
  one in vain!

CI

And when like her, oh Sáki, you shall
  pass
Among the Guests Star-scatter'd on the
  Grass,
And in your joyous errand reach the
  spot
Where I made One—turn down an
  empty Glass!

TAMAM

❧ ❧ ❧

LETTER TO A FRIEND
[*Written in 1513 A.D.*]
By Fra Giovanni

I salute you. I am your friend and my love for you goes deep. There is nothing I can give you which you have not got; but there is much, very much, that, while I cannot give it, you can take.

No Heaven can come to us unless our hearts find rest in today. Take Heaven! No peace lies in the future which is not hidden in this present little instance. Take Peace! The gloom of the world is but a shadow. Behind it, yet within our reach, is Joy. There is radiance and glory in the darkness, could we but see —and to see we have only to look. I beseech you to look.

Life is so generous a giver, but we, judging its gifts by their covering, cast them away as ugly or heavy or hard. Remove the covering and you will find beneath it a living splendor, woven of love, by wisdom, with power.

Welcome it, grasp it, and you touch the Angel's hand that brings it to you. Everything we call a trial or a sorrow or a duty, believe me, that Angel's hand is there; the gift is there, and the wonder of an overshadowing presence. Our joys too: be not content with them as joys. They too conceal diviner gifts.

Life is so full of meaning and purpose, so full of beauty—beneath its covering—that you will find earth but cloaks your heaven. Courage then to claim it, that is all! But courage you have, and the knowledge that we are pilgrims together, wending through unknown country, home.

And so, at this Christmas time, I greet you. Not quite as the world sends greetings, but with profound esteem and with the prayer that for you, now and forever, the day breaks, and the shadows flee away.

* * *

❧ All the ancient philosophers and sages have held two things necessary safely and pleasantly to arrive at the knowledge of God and true wisdom; first, God's gracious guidance, then man's assistance. —*Rabelais*

From *THE MEANING OF CULTURE*
By John Cowper Powys

Loaves of bread . . . honey in the honeycomb . . . summer haystacks . . . the flames of candles . . . the flight of birds . . . the darting of shoals of fish . . . the shadows of clouds . . . the rising and sinking of the sun . . . old buildings, old rituals, old mythologies . . . the annual procession of the seasons . . . weeds and shells at the ocean's edge, wet pebbles and the thin black windrow . . . rain on roofs . . . thunder on horizons . . . murmuring of brooks, sweetness of grass . . . sadness of stirred leaves . . . the deep symbolic meaning of such objects as a plough, a sword, a grindstone, a windmill, a boat, a cradle, a coffin . . . the friendliness of wind-tossed smoke, arising from hearth or chimney . . . the forlornness of swaying reed-tops above lonely salt-marshes . . . the warmth of sun-scented leaf-mould . . . the horns of goats, the spouting of whales . . . frost marks in ditch-mud . . . vapour-circles round misty moons . . . rivers and highways that carry old legends, old memories, old tragic transactions into the unborn future—all these things, and the emanations proceeding from these things, possess some mysterious quality in common; and it would seem that this quality cannot be named by any other name than that of *the poetical element* in life.

THE ART SPIRIT
By Robert Henri

There are moments in our lives, there are moments in a day, when we seem to see beyond the usual. Such are the moments of our greatest happiness. Such are the moments of our greatest wisdom. . . . It was in this hope that the arts were invented. Sign-posts on the way to what may be. Sign-posts toward greater knowledge.

A PRAYER
By Max Ehrmann

Let me do my work each day; and if the darkened hours of despair overcome me, may I not forget the strength that comforted me in the desolation of other times.

May I still remember the bright hours that found me walking over the silent hills of my childhood, or dreaming on the margin of the quiet river, when a light glowed within me, and I promised my early God to have courage amid the tempests of the changing years. Spare me from bitterness and from the sharp passions of unguarded moments. May I not forget that poverty and riches are of the spirit. Though the world know me not, may my thoughts and actions be such as shall keep me friendly with myself.

Lift my eyes from the earth, and let me not forget the uses of the stars. Forbid that I should judge others lest I condemn myself. Let me not follow the clamor of the world, but walk calmly in my path.

Give me a few friends who will love me for what I am; and keep ever burning before my vagrant steps the kindly light of hope. And though age and infirmity overtake me, and I come not within sight of the castle of my dreams, teach me still to be thankful for life, and for time's olden memories that are good and sweet; and may the evening's twilight find me gentle still.

PEACE BE WITH YOU

I pray the prayer the Easterners do,
May the peace of Allah abide with you;
Wherever you stay, wherever you go,
May the beautiful palms of Allah grow;
Through days of labor and nights of rest,
The love of good Allah make you blest.

—*Anonymous*

HE WHOM A DREAM HATH POSSESSED
SHAEMUS O'SHEEL

He whom a dream hath possessed knoweth no more of doubting,
For mist and the blowing of winds and the mouthing of words he scorns;
Not the sinuous speech of schools he hears, but a knightly shouting,
And never comes darkness down, yet he greeteth a million morns.

He whom a dream hath possessed knoweth no more of roaming;
All roads and the flowing of waves and the speediest flight he knows,
But wherever his feet are set, his soul is forever homing,
And going, he comes, and coming he heareth a call and goes.

He whom a dream hath possessed knoweth no more of sorrow,
At death and the dropping of leaves and the fading of suns he smiles,
For a dream remembers no past and scorns the desire of a morrow,
And a dream in a sea of doom sets surely the ultimate isles.

He whom a dream hath possessed treads the impalpable marches,
From the dust of the day's long road he leaps to a laughing star,
And the ruin of worlds that fall he views from eternal arches,
And rides God's battlefield in a flashing and golden car.

From *BRAVE MEN*
By ERNIE PYLE

A HEAVY darkness had come inside the cabin. Passengers were indistinct shapes, kneeling at the windows—to absorb the spell of the hour. The remnants of the sun streaked the cloud banked horizon ahead, making it vividly red and savagely beautiful. We were high, and the motors throbbed in a timeless rhythm. Below us were the green peaks of the Atlas Mountains, lovely in the softening shroud of the dusk. Villages with red roofs nested on the peaktops. Down below lived sheep men—obscure mountain men who had never heard of a Nebelwerfer or a bazooka, men at home at the end of the day in the poor, narrow, beautiful security of their own walls.

And there high in the sky above us and yet a part of it all were plain Americans incongruously away from home. For a moment it seemed terribly dramatic that we should be there at all amid that darkening beauty so far away, so foreign, and so old.

It was one of those moments impossible to transmit to another mind. A moment of overpowering beauty, of the surge of a marching world, of the relentlessness of our own fate. It made me want to cry.

* * *

❧ THAT WHICH is striking and beautiful is not always good, but that which is good is always beautiful. —*Ninon de L'Enclos*

Prayer is Power

By ALEXIS CARREL, M. D.

*P*RAYER IS NOT ONLY WORSHIP; it is also an invisible emanation of man's worshiping spirit—the most powerful form of energy that one can generate. The influence of prayer on the human mind and body is as demonstrable as that of secreting glands. Its results can be measured in terms of increased physical buoyancy, greater intellectual vigor, moral stamina, and a deeper understanding of the realities underlying human relationships.

If you make a habit of sincere prayer, your life will be very noticeably and profoundly altered. Prayer stamps with its indelible mark our actions and demeanor. A tranquility of bearing, a facial and bodily repose, are observed in those whose inner lives are thus enriched. Within the depths of consciousness a flame kindles. And man sees himself. He discovers his selfishness, his silly pride, his fears, his greeds, his blunder. He develops a sense of moral obligation, intellectual humility. Thus begins a journey of the soul toward the realm of grace.

Prayer is a force as real as terrestrial gravity. As a physician, I have seen men, after all other therapy has failed, lifted out of disease and melancholy by the serene effort of prayer. It is the only power in the world that seems to overcome the so-called "laws of nature"; the occasions on which prayer has dramatically done this have been termed "miracles." But a constant, quieter miracle takes place hourly in the hearts of men and women who have discovered that prayer supplies them with a steady flow of sustaining power in their daily lives.

Too many people regard prayer as a formalized routine of words, a refuge for weaklings, or a childish petition for material things. We sadly undervalue prayer when we conceive it in these terms, just as we should underestimate rain by describing it as something that fills the birdbath in our garden. Properly understood, prayer is a mature activity indispensable to the fullest development of personality—the ultimate integration of man's highest faculties. Only in prayer do we achieve that complete and harmonious assembly of body, mind and spirit which gives the frail human reed its unshakable strength.

The words, "Ask and it shall be given to you," have been verified by the experience of humanity. True, prayer may not restore the dead child to life or bring relief from physical pain. But prayer, like radium, is a source of luminous, self-generating energy.

How does prayer fortify us with so much dynamic power? To answer this question (admittedly outside the jurisdiction of science) I must point out that all prayers have one thing in common. The triumphant hosannas of a great oratorio, or the humble supplication of an Iroquois hunter begging for luck in the chase, demonstrate the same truth: that human beings seek to augment their finite energy by addressing themselves to the Infinite source of all energy. When we pray, we link ourselves with the inexhaustible motive power that spins the universe. We ask that a part of this power be apportioned to our needs. Even in asking, our human deficiencies are filled and we arise strengthened and repaired.

138

But we must never summon God merely for the gratification of our whims. We derive most power from prayer when we use it, not as a petition, but as a supplication that we may become more like Him. Prayer should be regarded as practice of the Presence of God. An old peasant was seated alone in the last pew of the village church. "What are you waiting for?" he was asked; and he answered, "I am looking at Him and He is looking at me." Man prays not only that God should remember him, but also that he should remember God.

How can prayer be defined? Prayer is the effort of man to reach God, to commune with an invisible being, creator of all things, supreme wisdom, truth, beauty, and strength, father and redeemer of each man. This goal of prayer always remains hidden to intelligence. For both language and thought fail when we attempt to describe God.

We do know, however, that whenever we address God in fervent prayer we change both soul and body for the better. It could not happen that any man or woman could pray for a single moment without some good result. "No man ever prayed," said Emerson, "without learning something."

One can pray everywhere. In the streets, the subway, the office, the shop, the school, as well as in the solitude of one's own room or among the crowd in a church. There is no prescribed posture, time or place.

"Think of God more often than you breathe," said Epictetus the Stoic. In order really to mold personality, prayer must become a habit. It is meaningless to pray in the morning and to live like a barbarian the remainder of the day. True prayer is a way of life; the truest life is literally a way of prayer.

The best prayers are like the improvisations of gifted lovers, always about the same thing yet never twice the same. We cannot all be as creative in prayer as Saint Theresa or Bernard of Clairvaux, both of whom poured their adoration into words of mystical beauty. Fortunately, we do not need their eloquence; our slightest impulse to prayer is recognized by God. Even if we are pitifully dumb, or if our tongues are overlaid with vanity or deceit, our meager syllables of praise are acceptable to Him, and He showers us with strengthening manifestations of His love.

Today, as never before, prayer is a binding necessity in the lives of men and nations. The lack of emphasis on the religious sense has brought the world to the edge of destruction. Our deepest source of power and perfection has been left miserably undeveloped. Prayer, the basic exercise of the spirit, must be actively practiced in our private lives. The neglected soul of man must be made strong enough to assert itself once more. For if the power of prayer is again released and used in the lives of common men and women; if the spirit declares its aims clearly and boldly, there is yet hope that our prayers for a better world will be answered.

EPIGRAM

Sir William Watson

One music maketh its occult abode
  In all things scatter'd from great
    Beauty's hand;
And evermore the deepest words of
  God
Are yet the easiest to understand.

THE GREAT HEART OF GOD

James Russell Lowell

Nor is he far astray who deems
That every hope, which rises and grows
  broad
In the world's heart, by ordered impulse streams
From the great heart of God.

THE BEWITCHED TAILOR
By Ben Hecht

THERE USED to be a ludicrous and fantastic tailor on the sixth floor of the Roseland Building on 51st Street—an edifice in which all the plots you ever saw in the movies about the joys and sufferings of Broadway are continually going on.

This tailor's name was Boris Gordon. He was as fat as a deep-sea bass and he waddled, jiggled, grunted, and perspired through twenty years of insolvency like a half-collapsed balloon with a scissors dangling from its middle. This billowy little wizard of the needle wore a Windsor tie and a beret, for he loved beauty and was devoted to the arts.

When he was younger, Mr. Gordon had been an eminent designer of ladies' clothing, receiving from Bergdorf Goodman and other gaudy wardrobe peddlers a magnificent salary. But to the alarm of his family, money had palled on Mr. Gordon. The work of camouflaging the rumps and bosoms of dowagers with chic draperies left our tailor full of frustrations. And finally, turning a deaf ear to employers and dependents alike, the portly Boris spread his wings and landed on the sixth floor of the Roseland Building.

Here Boris, the tailor, served beauty. He designed costumes for dancers. Well, not exactly dancers, but dance aspirants. For Boris was unable to draw. Because of this cultural defect no dancers with enough money to go anywhere else ever came near Boris's emporium.

There came, however, dozens, then scores on scores, of hoofers, acrobats, and all manner of coryphees out of the attics of Bohemia. All the orphans of Broadway at whose dancing feet no roses or press notices ever bloomed, all the Pavlovas and Astaires who hovered futilely around the *No Casting Today* signs of the producing offices flocked to the Maison Gordon.

And Boris dressed them up as East Winds, Rose Buds, Leopards, Pierrettes, Sultanas, and Ballerinas. Daily, platoons of these undaunted votaries marched forth to give auditions in Boris's costumes, leaving behind their IOU's for our tailor to stuff into his cash drawer. And the joke was that not only did no one or hardly anyone ever pay Boris for his toil in behalf of beauty, but that if any of his protégés ever made good—and this also happened —they deserted the fat and ludicrous little tailor at once and took their patronage to a more professional atelier. The joke also was that frequently Boris's protégés returned after a fling in some road unit and sold him back the costumes for which they had never paid. On such occasions Boris was happy to purchase a wonderful Nymph costume for as little as $5.

As the years passed, Boris became quite a figure in the limbo art world of Broadway's step-children. Artists with palettes appeared and sat painting the fat and comical-looking tailor. His emporium filled up with portraits of a moon-faced and obese little man, not at all flattering. For Boris with all his philanthropies seemed to inspire in all who knew him and profited off him chiefly a sense of his ludicrousness. His soulful sighs for the beautiful, his fluttery fat man's love of all that was graceful spread laughter behind his back. Derision and ingratitude were in fact the chief rewards our tailor reaped. But in the twenty years the beam never quit his perspiring moon face.

"They are all children," he used to say, "and you got to understand them. I make a living making clothes for a few rich people who still come to me for suits. But I belong in the world of beauty."

140

And Boris's fat sides would jiggle and he would beam so soulfully that even a protégé without lunch money would be forced to titter.

Then Boris disappeared from the Roseland Building. The costume studio was closed, and word went out that the crazy tailor was sick. Four months later a girl from the ballet in need of a new Pierrette dress tried the door of the tailor shop just for good luck.

It opened. A strange man stood inside. He was a lean man with a pair of black eyes burning out of a taut and delicate face—and a wide mouth with pale lips smiling gently.

"I'm looking for Boris Gordon," said the ballet girl.

"I'm Boris Gordon," said this thin and radiant-looking man in a whisper. "I've been sick. I can't speak very loud. I got so thin. I lost ninety pounds in the hospital. What can I do for you? A Pierrette costume? Yes, yes—I know your measurements. I will make a beautiful thing for you."

Boris picked up his shears.

"Come back Monday," he said with a smile.

Monday Boris was dead, and the ballet girl who told me the story says:

"Nobody saw him this way except me. So when they talk about him sometimes and laugh at what a funny fat man he was and how crazy it was for him to be always talking about beauty, I tell them how he looked the last time he stood in his tailor shop—lean and with a face very gentle and beautiful—as if he was a dancer himself. Really, as if he had always been a dancer. But nobody believes me. Yet I saw him standing there a few days before he died just like somebody out of the *Arabian Nights* after the bad jinni has removed his evil spell."

STRANGE
MILDRED BOWERS ARMSTRONG

Strange—to grow up and not be different,
Not beautiful or even very wise . . .
No winging-out the way of butterflies,
No sudden blindfold-lifting from the eyes.

Strange—to grow up and still be wondering,
Reverent at petals and snow,
Still holding breath,
Still often tiptoe,
Questioning dew and stars,
Wanting to know!

THE ROAD AND THE END
CARL SANDBURG

I shall foot it
Down the roadway in the dusk,
Where shapes of hunger wander
And the fugitives of pain go by.

I shall foot it
In the silence of the morning,
See the night slur into dawn,
Hear the slow great winds arise
Where tall trees flank the way
And shoulder toward the sky.

The broken boulders by the road
Shall not commemorate my ruin.
Regret shall be the gravel under foot.
I shall watch for
Slim birds swift of wing
That go where wind and ranks of thunder
Drive the wild processionals of rain.

The dust of the traveled road
Shall touch my hands and face.

141

MEETING AT NIGHT
ROBERT BROWNING

The gray sea and the long black land;
And the yellow half-moon large and
    low;
And the startled little waves that leap
In fiery ringlets from their sleep,
As I gain the cove with pushing prow,
And quench its speed in the slushy
    sand.

Then a mile of warm sea-scented beach;
Three fields to cross till a farm appears;
A tap at the pane, the quick sharp
    scratch
And blue spurt of a lighted match,
And a voice less loud, through its joys
    and fears,
Than the two hearts beating each to
    each!

PARTING AT MORNING
ROBERT BROWNING

Round the cape of a sudden came the
    sea,
And the sun looked over the mountain's
    rim:
And straight was a path of gold for him,
And the need of a world of men for me.

TO SOPHIA
PERCY BYSSHE SHELLEY

Thou art fair, and few are fairer
    Of the Nymphs of earth or ocean;
They are robes that fit the wearer—
    Those soft limbs of thine, whose mo-
        tion
Ever falls and shifts and glances
As the life within them dances.
. . . .
As dew beneath the wind of morning,
    As the sea which whirlwinds waken,
As the birds at thunder's warning,
    As aught mute yet deeply shaken,
As one who feels an unseen spirit
Is my heart when thine is near it.

A BIRTHDAY
CHRISTINA GEORGINA ROSSETTI

My heart is like a singing bird
    Whose nest is in a watered shoot;
My heart is like an apple tree
    Whose boughs are bent with thickset
        fruit;
My heart is like a rainbow shell
    That paddles in a halcyon sea;
My heart is gladder than all these,
    Because my love is come to me.

Raise me a dais of silk and down;
    Hang it with vair and purple dyes;
Carve it in doves and pomegranates,
    And peacocks with a hundred eyes;
Work it in gold and silver grapes,
    In leaves and silver fleur-de-lys;
Because the birthday of my life
    Is come, my love is come to me.

HONESTY

For he who is honest is noble,
    Whatever his fortunes or birth.
                                    —*Cary*

From IDYLLS OF THE KING
ALFRED, LORD TENNYSON

O ye stars that shudder over me,
O earth that soundest hollow under me,
Vext with waste dreams? for saving I
    be join'd
To her that is the fairest under heaven,
I seem as nothing in the mighty world,
And cannot will my will nor work my
    work
Wholly, nor make myself in mine own
    realm
Victor and lord. But were I join'd with
    her,
Then might we live together as one life,
And reigning with one will in every-
    thing
Have power on this dark land to lighten
    it,
And power on this dead world to make
    it live.

ROSE AYLMER
WALTER SAVAGE LANDOR

Ah what avails the sceptred race,
  Ah what the form devine!
What every virtue, every grace!
  Rose Aylmer, all were thine.

Rose Aylmer, whom these wakeful eyes
  May weep, but never see,
A night of memories and of sighs
  I consecrate to thee.

OVER ALL

God is good and God is light,
In this faith I rest secure,
Evil can but serve the right,
Over all shall love endure.
          —*Whittier*

SERENADE
HENRY WADSWORTH LONGFELLOW

Stars of the summer night!
  Far in yon azure deeps,
Hide, hide your golden light!
  She sleeps!
My lady sleeps!
  Sleeps!

Moon of the summer night!
  Far down yon western steeps,
Sink, sink in silver light!
  She sleeps!
My lady sleeps!
  Sleeps!

Wind of the summer night!
  Where yonder woodbine creeps,
Fold, fold thy pinions light!
  She sleeps!
My lady sleeps!
  Sleeps!

Dreams of the summer night!
  Tell her, her lover keeps
Watch! while in slumbers light
  She sleeps!
My lady sleeps!
  Sleeps!

UNDER THE HARVEST MOON
CARL SANDBURG

Under the harvest moon,
When the soft silver
Drips shimmering
Over the garden nights,
Death, the gray mocker,
Comes and whispers to you
As a beautiful friend
Who remembers.
Under the summer roses,
When the flagrant crimson
Lurks in the dusk
Of the wild red leaves,
Love, with little hands,
Comes and touches you
With a thousand memories,
And asks you
Beautiful unanswerable questions.

NEEDS
CHARLES HANSON TOWNE

I want a little house
  Upon a little hill,
With lilacs laughing at the door
  When afternoons are still.

I want an apple tree
  Laden with drifts of bloom;
I want blue china all about
  In every little room.

I want a little path
  Bordered with brilliant phlox,
And on each windowsill I want
  A painted flower box.

And then—I want you there
  In sun, and frost, and rain,
To smile when I come trudging home
  Through a dim, scented lane.

For what's a little house
  Upon a little hill,
Unless you light the fire for me
  When nights are strangely still?

PUT trust in character.—*Greek Proverb*

HE THAT HAS patience may compass anything.—*Rabelais.*

WITHOUT COURAGE there cannot be truth, and without truth there can be no other virtue.—*Scott*

WHEN WEALTH is lost, nothing is lost; when health is lost, something is lost; when character is lost, all is lost.—*Anonymous*

THAT BEST PORTION of a good man's life,—his little, nameless, unremembered acts of kindness and of love.—*Wordsworth*

THE INTELLECTUAL attainments of a man who thinks for himself resemble a fine painting, where the light and shade are correct, the tone sustained, the colour perfectly harmonized; it is true to life.—*Schopenhauer*

ALL THE MEANS of action—the shapeless masses—the materials—lie everywhere about us.—What we need is the celestial fire to change the flint into the transparent crystal, bright and clear.—That fire is genius.—*Longfellow*

THEY are never alone that are accompanied with noble thoughts.—*Sidney*

TO LIVE in the presence of great truths and eternal laws—that is what keeps a man patient when the world ignores him and calm and unspoiled when the world praises him.—*Balzac*

MAN WHO man would be, must rule the empire of himself.—*Shelley*

RULE YOURSELF. Love your neighbor. Do the duty that lies nearest you.—*Alcott*

THE TONGUE—that is the pen of the heart.—*The Talmud*

WHAT IS LEFT when honour is lost?—*Syrus*

OF TRUTH

No BIRD soars too high, if he soars
with his own wings.—*Blake*

No ONE can work me injury but myself.—*Emerson*

OUR CHARACTER is our will, for what we will we are.—*Archbishop Manning*

No RACE can prosper till it learns that there is as much dignity in tilling a
field as in writing a poem.—*Booker T. Washington*

THERE ARE three marks of a superior man: being virtuous, he is free from
anxiety; being wise, he is free from perplexity; being brave, he is free from
fear.—*Confucius*

I CONSIDER an human soul without education like marble in the quarry, which
shows none of its inherent beauties till the skill of the polisher fetches out the
colours, makes the surface shine, and discovers every ornamental cloud, spot
and vein that runs through the body of it.—*Addison*

GOOD TEMPER, like a sunny day, sheds a brightness over everything; it is the
sweetener of toil and the soother of disquietude.—*Irving*

MAN KNOWS his littleness; his own mountains remind him; but the dreams of
man make up for our faults and failings; for the brevity of our lives, for
the narrowness of our scope; they leap over boundaries and are away and
away.—*Lord Dunsany*

IT MATTERS NOT what you are thought to be, but what you are.—*Syrus*

WE CAN never judge another soul above the high water mark
of our own.—*Maeterlinck*

HE WHO HAS truth need never fear the want of persuasion
on his Tongue.—*Ruskin*

THEY can conquer who believe they can.—*Virgil*

THE SONG OF THE SKI
WILSON MacDONALD

Norse am I when the first snow falls;
  Norse am I till the ice departs.
The fare for which my spirit calls
  Is blood from a hundred viking-
    hearts.
The curved wind wraps me like a cloak;
The pines blow out their ghostly smoke.
I'm high on the hill and ready to go—
A wingless bird in a world of snow:
    Yet I'll ride the air
    With a dauntless dare
That only a child of the North can
  know.

The bravest ski has a cautious heart
And moves like a tortoise at the start,
But when it tastes the tang of the air
It leaps away like a frightened hare.
The day is gloomy, the curtains half-
  drawn,
The light is stunted as at the dawn:
But my foot is sure and my arm is
  brawn.

I poise on the hill and I wave adieu
(My curving skis are firm and true):
The slim wood quickens, the air takes
  fire
And sings to me like a gipsy's lyre.
Swifter and swifter grows my flight:
The dark pines ease the unending
  white.
The lean, cold birches, as I go by,
Are like blurred etchings against the
  sky.

One am I for a moment's joy
  With the falling star and the plung-
    ing bird.
The world is swift as an Arab boy;
  The world is sweet as a woman's
    word.

Never came such a pure delight
To a bacchanal or a sybarite:
Swifter and swifter grows my flight,
And glad am I as I near the leap,
That the snow is fresh and the banks
  are deep.

Swifter and swifter on I fare,
And soon I'll float with the birds on air.
The speed is blinding; I'm over the
  ridge,
Spanning space on a phantom bridge.
The drift awaits me; I float, I fall:
  The world leaps up like a plunging
    carp.
I land erect and the tired winds drawl
A lazy rune on a broken harp.

Child of the roofless world am I;
  Not of those hibernating drones
Who fear the grey of a winter sky
  And the shrieking wind's ironic tones,
Who shuffle cards in a cloud of smoke
  Or crawl like frozen flies at chess,
Or gossip all day with meddling folk
  In collar of starch and a choking
    dress.
. . . .
Lord of the mountains dark with pine!
  Lord of the fields of the smoking
    snow!
Grant to this vagrant heart of mine
  A path of wood where my feet may go,
And a roofless world to my journey's
  end,
    And a cask of wind for my cup of
    wine,
And yellow gold of the sun to spend,
  And at night the stars in endless line,
And, after it all, the hand of a friend—
  The hand of a trusted friend in mine.

* * *

🪶 OLD AND NEW put their stamp to everything in Nature. The snowflake that
is now falling is marked by both; the present gives the motion and color to
the flakes; antiquity its form and properties. All things wear a lustre which
is the gift of the present and a tarnish of time.   —*Emerson*

146

THE CAMPER'S CREED

By Henry Wellington Wack

I SHALL HAVE joyous years of temperate and responsive life. For my heritage of the past, I shall strive to enrich the future. I know that God, the universe, and man are the immortal trinity upon which human progress depends. And I pledge myself to serve the Common Good in every wind and weather.

I love Nature and her loyal books. I will preserve a wholesome health and spirit—know and count the trees and stars my friends, the sun and shade my comforters afield.

I will never waste the natural resources of my native land; nor violate its laws nor a sportsman's honor; nor take of game from woods and waters beyond my need. If I light a fire in a grove, I will quench it. I will protect the forest and its shelter, its wild life and human boon, as a refuge for the weary follower on my trail. I will use a brother's camp as a sacred trust, with a loving care and conscience, and leave it inviolate and in order for the comfort of his late return.

Rambles shall inform my understanding, inspire my sympathies, and fit me to appraise the beauty of forest, stream, and sky. I shall explore the wilderness without fear, yet in its healing solitude feel humility in the benign presence of our common mother, the earth. I desire to be brave and just under every sting and test, bear a stout heart in a gentle manner, and stand erect on strong limbs to carry me through the verdant valley to the white glory of the mountain peak.

And then—when night has dimmed my trail with her sable robe, may I find a glowing hearth and a heartfelt welcome, in a brookside camp, under a smiling moon, in the Land o' Heart's Desire.

UNDER THE BROAD BEECH-TREE

By Isaak Walton

. . . LOOK! under that broad beech-tree I sat down, when I was last this way a-fishing; and the birds in the adjoining grove seemed to have a friendly contention with an echo, whose dead voice seemed to live in a hollow tree near to the brow of that primrose-hill. There I sat viewing the silver streams glide silently towards their centre, the tempestuous sea; yet sometimes opposed by rugged roots and pebblestones, which broke their waves, and turned them into foam; and sometimes I beguiled time by viewing the harmless lambs; some leaping securely in the cool shade, whilst others sported themselves in the cheerful sun; and saw others craving comfort from the swollen udders of their bleating dams. As I thus sat, these and other sights had so fully possest my soul with content, that I thought, as the poet has happily exprest it,

I was for that time lifted above earth;
And possest joys not promis'd in my
birth.

As I left this place, and entered into the next field, a second pleasure entertained me; 'twas a handsome milk-maid, that had not yet attained so much age and wisdom as to load her mind with any fears of many things that will never be, as too many men too often do; but she cast away all care, and sung like a nightingale. Her voice was good, and the ditty fitted for it; it was that smooth song which was made by Kit Marlow, now at least fifty years ago; and the milk-maid's mother sung an answer to it, which was made by Sir Walter Raleigh, in his younger days. They were old-fashioned poetry, but choicely good; I think much better than the strong lines that are now in fashion in this critical age.

147

THOU WHO DIDST THE STARS AND SUNBEAMS KNOW
[Matthew Arnold's Sonnet on Shakespeare]

Others abide our question. Thou art free.
We ask and ask—Thou smilest and art still,
Out-topping knowledge. For the loftiest hill
That to the stars uncrowns his majesty,
Planting his steadfast footsteps in the sea,
Making the heaven of heavens his dwelling-place,
Spares but the cloudy border of his base
To the foiled searching of mortality;
And thou, who didst the stars and sunbeams know,
Self-schooled, self-scanned, self-honoured, self-secure,
Didst tread on earth unguessed at. Better so!
All pains the immortal spirits must endure,
All weakness that impairs, all griefs that bow,
Find their sole voice in that victorious brow.

PLEASURE
By ALEXANDER SMITH

IN LIFE there is nothing more unexpected and surprising than the arrivals and departures of pleasure. If we find it in one place today, it is vain to seek it there tomorrow. You cannot lay a trap for it. It will fall into no ambuscade, concert it ever so cunningly. Pleasure has no logic; it never treads in its own footsteps. Into our commonplace existence it comes with a surprise, like a pure white swan from the airy void into the ordinary village lake; and just as the swan, for no reason that can be discovered, lifts itself on its wings and betakes itself to the void again, *it* leaves us, and our sole possession is its memory. And it is characteristic of pleasure that we can never recognize it to be pleasure till after it is gone. Happiness never lays its finger on its pulse. If we attempt to steal a glimpse of its features it disappears. It is a gleam of unreckoned gold. From the nature of the case, our happiness, such as in its degree it has been, lives in memory. We have not the voice itself; we have only its echo. We are never happy; we can only remember that we were so once. And while in the very heart and structure of the happy moment there lurked an obscure consciousness of death, the memory in which past happiness dwells is always a regretful memory. This is why the tritest utterance about the past, youth, early love, and the like, has always about it an indefinable flavour of poetry, which pleases and affects. In the wake of a ship there is always a melancholy splendour. The finest set of verses of our modern time described how the poet gazed on the "happy autumn fields," and remembered the "days that were no more." After all, man's real possession is his memory. In nothing else is he rich, in nothing else is he poor.

* * *

❧ CLIMB FAR, your goal the sky, your aim the star.—*Anonymous*

148

KEEN, FITFUL GUSTS ARE WHISPERING HERE AND THERE
JOHN KEATS

Keen, fitful gusts are whispering here and there
Among the bushes half leafless, and dry;
The stars look very cold about the sky,
And I have many miles on foot to fare.
Yet feel I little of the cool bleak air,
Or of the dead leaves rustling drearily,
Or of those silver lamps that burn on high,
Or of the distance from home's pleasant lair:
For I am brimful of the friendliness
That in a little cottage I have found;
Of fair-hair'd Milton's eloquent distress,
And all his love for gentle Lycid drowned;
Of lovely Laura in her light green dress,
And faithful Petrarch gloriously crowned.

TO CANCEL WRONG

To cancel wrong it ever was required
The wrong should be forgiven, and
    forgot:
Ah, see, how well have thou and I
    conspired,
Since I forgive, and thou rememberest
    not!   —Edith M. Thomas

THE STARS

IF A man would be alone, let him
look at the stars. The rays that come
from those heavenly worlds will separate between him and what he touches.

One might think the atmosphere was
made transparent with this design, to
give man, in the heavenly bodies, the
perpetual presence of the sublime.
Seen in the streets of cities, how great
they are!

If the stars should appear one night
in a thousand years, how would men
believe, and adore, and preserve for
many generations, the remembrance of
the city of God which had been shown?
But every night come out these envoys
of beauty, and light the universe with
their admonishing smile.   —Emerson

MOZART OR BEETHOVEN

WHICH IS the greater, Mozart or
Beethoven? Idle question! The one is
more perfect, the other more colossal.
The first gives you the peace of perfect
art, beauty at first sight. The second
gives you sublimity, terror, pity, a
beauty of second impression. The one
gives that for which the other rouses
a desire. Mozart has the classic purity
of light and the blue ocean; Beethoven
the romantic grandeur which belongs
to the storms of air and sea, and while
the soul of Mozart seems to dwell on
the ethereal peaks of Olympus, that of
Beethoven climbs shuddering the storm-
beaten sides of a Sinai. Blessed be
they both! Each represents a moment
of the ideal life, each does us good.
Our love is due to both.   —Amiel

WE THANK THEE
RALPH WALDO EMERSON

For flowers that bloom about our feet;
For tender grass so fresh and sweet;
For song of bird and hum of bee;
For all things fair we hear and see,
Father in Heaven, we thank Thee!

TO YOUR LITTLE HOUSE
MILDRED BOWERS ARMSTRONG

I shall remember candlelight
    And the low fire burning
When the only sound was a quiet word
    Or a book page turning.

I shall remember the song of the wind
    And the bias drive of rain
When cold days and dark days
    Beat at the windowpane.

Morning opened a golden fan
    In your elm tree
And evening spread her colors out
    For your little house to see.

I must follow a dark road,
    A road that has no turning—
But I shall remember candlelight
    And the low fire burning.

JUNE IN NEW ENGLAND
By GLADYS TABER

JUNE IN New England is like a lover's dream made tangible. Color and scent and sound; the hills indeed sing. Dawn comes so fresh and cool, and dusk flows like a still river into the deep sea of night. Noons are tranquil gold. There is nothing stern or sober about our Northern countryside now; even the gray rock ledges are gently blurred with silvery green lichens, and in the great cracks time has chipped out, a thousand tiny plants get a precarious hold.

Lilacs make their own purple dusk all day, or lift dreamy clusters pure as pearl. Their scent is cool and mysterious. It is surely one of the most romantic smells—it reminds one of old deserted gardens where long-vanished ladies come again to walk in the moonlight.

The white lilacs have a special delicacy, a purity. I always feel too solid when I pick them, and pick them I must! Their odor is even sweeter. I am sure in the dark of the moon my white unicorn comes on delicate little hoofs to find the place where the white lilacs grow and crop the flowers. Sometimes I can tell where he has moved, because the leaves are a little swayed aside. His horn is silver and his eyes dark amber. A white unicorn feeding on white lilacs would be a fine sight to see.

But there are the first roses too!

Also there are green peas to cook with a mint leaf, and crisp rosy radishes, and the asparagus bed still holds out. The early vegetables are a delight.

Then comes a day warm enough for the first swim, and Eight Mile is fresh and clean in June, before the water weeds get too thick. Nothing is more exciting than that first plunge, the breathless shock of clear water, the buoyant feeling of being held up in that special element again.

I think of what Van Gogh meant when he said, "But I always think that the best way to know God is to love many things."

* * *

❧ THE DAY RETURNS and brings us the petty round of irritating concerns and duties. Help us to play the man, help us to perform them with laughter and kind faces, let cheerfulness abound with industry. Give us to go blithely on our business all this day, bring us to our resting beds weary and content and undishonored, and grant us in the end the gift of sleep.

—*Robert Louis Stevenson*

THE ELFIN WIFE
JAKE FALSTAFF

Gravely she goes about her little duties:
    Smiling to show them she does not mind them:
Gravely she genuflects to small gnome beauties
    Wheresoever she may find them.

She pauses in her sweeping to make herself some wishes:
    She sits on her legs and thinks about the grate:
She feels a dear well-being when she does the dishes
    Because of the smoothness of a china plate.

Whether it is linens, clean-smelling, piled,
    Whether it is chairs or rugs or dresses,
She goes among them like a dreamy child
    Playing with the things she loves and possesses.

Can you not see her, cool eyes shady,
    Cool hands gentle, cool cheeks white?
Can you not see her, my love's lady,
    Doing the duties of her grave delight?

IRISH PEASANT SONG
LOUISE IMOGEN GUINEY

I tried to knead and spin, but my life is low the while.
Oh, I long to be alone, and walk abroad a mile;
Yet if I walk alone, and think of naught at all,
Why from me that's young should the wild tears fall?

The shower-sodden earth, the earth-coloured streams,
They breathe on me awake, and moan to me in dreams,
And yonder ivy fondling the broken castle-wall,
It pulls upon my heart till the wild tears fall.

The cabin-door looks down a furze-lighted hill,
And far as Leighlin Cross the fields are green and still;
But once I hear the blackbird in Leighlin hedges call,
The foolishness is on me, and the wild tears fall!

LONG AGO
EUGENE FIELD

I once knew all the birds that came
  And nested in our orchard trees;
For every flower I had a name—
  My friends were woodchucks, toads,
    and bees;
I knew where thrived in yonder glen
  What plants would soothe a stone-
    bruised toe—
Oh, I was very learned then;
  But that was long ago!

I knew the spot upon the hill
  Where checkerberries could be found,
I knew the rushes near the mill
  Where pickerel lay that weighed a
    pound!
I knew the wood,—the very tree
  Where lived the poaching, saucy
    crow,
And all the woods and crows knew me—
  But that was very long ago.

And pining for the joys of youth,
  I tread the old familiar spot
Only to learn this solemn truth:
  I have forgotten, am forgot.
Yet here's this youngster at my knee
  Knows all the things I used to know;
To think I once was wise as he—
  But that was very long ago.

I know it's folly to complain
  Of whatsoever the Fates decree;
Yet were not wishes all in vain,
  I tell you what my wish would be:
I'd wish to be a boy again,
  Back with the friends I used to know;
For I was, oh! so happy then—
  But that was very long ago!

THE ROCKER
ROBERT P. TRISTRAM COFFIN

When Tom Bailey wants to rest,
He finds the rocking-chair the best,
He leaves his weariness behind
And rocks the wrinkles from his mind.

He talks about his cows and bees
And makes a music with his knees,
East and west, his body bends,
And he becomes the best of friends.

His mind opens as he rocks,
He who was quiet talks and talks,
And his words take on the swing
Of a homing pigeon's wing.

He goes and comes, and as he goes
The man blossoms like the rose,
Gradually, as stars will slide,
He finds himself at the other side.

When he brings up at the wall,
He rises, rocking-chair and all,
And crosses back where he began,
Another and a fresher man.

SILENCE ALONE
ADELAIDE LOVE

There is no utterance for love or death;
Words cannot speak for grief or ecstasy;
They must stand by like impotent pale
  ghosts
When hearts are blest or stricken verily.

No eloquence is adequate to tell
Of beauty; man is mute as any clod
Of earth before an elemental truth;
He has no word that gives a hint of
  God.
Silence alone is great enough to hold
A thing so real it never can be told.

* * *

Sow A THOUGHT, and you reap an Act; sow an Act and you reap a Habit;
sow a Habit, and you reap a Character; sow a Character, and you reap a
Destiny.
                                       —*Anonymous*

COME WHERE MY LOVE LIES DREAMING
STEPHEN FOSTER

Come where my love lies dreaming,
Dreaming the happy hours away,
In visions bright redeeming
The fleeting joys of day;
Dreaming the happy hours,
Dreaming the happy hours away;
Come where my love lies dreaming,
Is sweetly dreaming the happy hours
    away.

Come where my love lies dreaming,
Is sweetly dreaming,
Her beauty beaming;
Come where my love lies dreaming,
Is sweetly dreaming the happy hours
    away.

Come with a lute, come with a lay,
My own love is sweetly dreaming,
Her beauty beaming;
Come where my love lies dreaming,
Is sweetly dreaming the happy hours
    away.

Soft is her slumber;
Thoughts bright and free
Dance through her dreams
Like gushing melody;
Light is her young heart,
Light may it be:
Come where my love lies dreaming.

ELLIS PARK
HELEN HOYT

Little park that I pass through,
I carry off a piece of you
Every morning hurrying down
To my work-day in the town;
Carry you for country there
To make the city ways more fair.
I take your trees,
And your breeze,
Your greenness,
Your cleanness,
Some of your shade, some of your sky,
Some of your calm as I go by;
Your flowers to trim
The pavements grim;
Your space for room in the jostled street
And grass for carpet to my feet.
Your fountains take and sweet bird calls
To sing me from my office walls.
All that I can see
I carry off with me.

But you never miss my theft,
So much treasure you have left.
As I find you, fresh at morning,
So I find you, home returning—
Nothing lacking from your grace.
All your riches wait in place
For me to borrow
On the morrow.

Do you hear this praise of you,
Little park that I pass through?

PLANTING A TREE
NANCY BYRD TURNER

Firm in the good brown earth
Set we our little tree.
Clear dews will freshen it,
Cool rain will feed it
Sun will be warming it
As warmth is needed.
Winds will blow round it free—
Take root, good tree!

Slowly, as days go on,
These boughs will stouter be,
Leaves will unfurl on them,
And when spring comes to them,
Blossoms uncurl on them,
Birds make their homes in them,
Shade outstretch, wide and free—
Grow well, good tree!

LOVE SCENE
By George Meredith

When nature has made us ripe for love, it seldom occurs that the Fates are behind hand in furnishing a temple for the flame.

Above green-flashing plunges of a weir, and shaken by the thunder below, lilies, golden and white, were swaying at anchor among the reeds. Meadow-sweet hung from the banks thick with weed and trailing bramble, and there also hung a daughter of earth. Her face was shaded by a broad straw hat with a flexible brim that left her lips and chin in the sun, and, sometimes nodding, sent forth a light of promising eyes. Across her shoulders, and behind, flowed large loose curls, brown in shadow, almost golden where the ray touched them. She was simply dressed, befitting decency and the season. On a closer inspection you might see that her lips were stained. This blooming young person was regaling on dewberries. They grew between the bank and the water. Apparently she found the fruit abundant, for her hand was making pretty progress to her mouth. Fastidious youth, which revolts at woman plumping her exquisite proportions on bread-and-butter, and would (we must suppose) joyfully have her scraggy to have her poetical, can hardly object to dewberries. Indeed the act of eating them is dainty and induces musing. The dewberry is a sister to the lotus, and an innocent sister. You eat: mouth, eye, and hand are occupied, and the undrugged mind free to roam. And so it was with the damsel who knelt there. The little skylark went up above her, all song, to the smooth southern cloud lying along the blue: from a dewy copse dark over her nodding hat the blackbird fluted, calling to her with thrice mellow note: the kingfisher flashed emerald out of green osiers: a bow-winged heron travelled aloft, seeking solitude: a boat slipped toward her, containing a dreamy youth; and still she plucked the fruit, and ate, and mused, as if no fairy prince were invading her territories, and as if she wished not for one, or knew not her wishes. Surrounded by the green shaven meadows, the pastoral summer buzz, the weir-fall's thundering white, amid the breath and beauty of wild flowers, she was a bit of lovely human life in a fair setting; a terrible attraction. The Magnetic Youth leaned round to note his proximity to the weir-piles, and beheld the sweet vision. Stiller and stiller grew nature, as at the meeting of two electric clouds. Her posture was so graceful, that though he was making straight for the weir, he dared not dip a scull. Just then one enticing dewberry caught her eyes. He was floating by unheeded, and saw that her hand stretched low, and could not gather what it sought. A stroke from his right brought him beside her. The damsel glanced up dismayed, and her whole shape trembled over the brink. Richard sprang from his boat into the water. Pressing a hand beneath her foot, which she had thrust against the crumbling wet sides of the bank to save herself, he enabled her to recover her balance, and gain safe earth, whither he followed her.

He had landed on an island of the still-vexed Bermoothes. The world lay wrecked behind him: Raynham hung in mists, remote, a phantom to the vivid reality of this white hand which had drawn him thither away thousands of leagues in an eye-twinkle. Hark, how Ariel sang overhead! What splendour in the heavens! What marvels of beauty about his enchanted brows! And, O you wonder! Fair Flame! by whose light the glories of being are now first seen ... Radiant Miranda! Prince Ferdinand is at your feet.

—From *The Ordeal of Richard Feverel*

154

CHURCH BELLS AT EVENING
ADELAIDE LOVE

Church bells at evening wafted far
To one who stands upon a hill
And gazes toward the sunset spire
Through distance luminous and still,

Are as a seal of peace upon
His heart, a laying of God's hand
Upon him in the evening glow
Above the quiet land.

THE BURIED CITY
By THOMAS DE QUINCEY

GOD smote Savannah-la-Mar, and in one night, by earthquake, removed her, with all her towers standing and population sleeping, from the steadfast foundations of the shore to the coral floors of ocean. And God said:—"Pompeii did I bury and conceal from men through seventeen centuries; this city I will bury, but not conceal. She shall be a monument to men of my mysterious anger, set in azure light through generations to come; for I will enshrine her in a crystal dome of my tropic seas." This city, therefore, like a mighty galleon with all her apparel mounted, streamers flying, and tackling perfect, seems floating along the noiseless depths of ocean; and oftentimes in glassy calms, through the translucid atmosphere of water that now stretches like an air-woven awning above the silent encampment, mariners from every clime look down into her courts and terraces, count her gates, and number the spires of her churches. She is one ample cemetery, and has been for many a year; but in the mighty calms that brood for weeks over tropic latitudes, she fascinates the eye with a *Fata Morgana* revelation, as of human life still subsisting in submarine asylums sacred from the storms that torment our upper air.

BEAUTY
By WILLIAM ELLERY CHANNING

BEAUTY is an all-pervading presence. It unfolds to the numberless flowers of the Spring; it waves in the branches of the trees and in the green blades of grass; it haunts the depths of the earth and the sea, and gleams out in the hues of the shell and the precious stone. And not only these minute objects, but the ocean, the mountains, the clouds, the heavens, the stars, the rising and the setting sun all overflow with beauty. The universe is its temple; and those men who are alive to it can not lift their eyes without feeling themselves encompassed with it on every side. Now, this beauty is so precious, the enjoyment it gives so refined and pure, so congenial without tenderest and noblest feelings, and so akin to worship, that it is painful to think of the multitude of men as living in the midst of it, and living almost as blind to it as if, instead of this fair earth and glorious sky, they were tenants of a dungeon. An infinite joy is lost to the world by the want of culture of this spiritual endowment. The greatest truths are wronged if not linked with beauty, and they win their way most surely and deeply into the soul when arrayed in this their natural and fit attire.

LOVE THE BEAUTIFUL
MOSES MENDELSSOHN

Love the beautiful,
Seek out the true,
Wish for the good,
And the best do.

THE HOUSE BEAUTIFUL

The Crown of the house is Godliness.
The Beauty of the house is Order.
The Glory of the house is Hospitality.
The Blessing of the house is Content-
ment.
—Old Inscription

155

THE CELESTIAL SURGEON
ROBERT LOUIS STEVENSON

If I have faltered more or less
In my great task of happiness;
If I have moved among my race
And shown no glorious morning face;
If beams from happy human eyes
Have moved me not; if morning skies,
Books and my food, and summer rain
Knocked on my sullen heart in vain:—
Lord, Thy most pointed pleasure take
And stab my spirit broad awake!
Or, Lord, if too obdurate I,
Choose Thou, before that spirit die,
A piercing pain, a killing sin
And to my dead heart run them in!

I HEAR AMERICA SINGING
WALT WHITMAN

I hear America singing, the varied carols I hear,
Those of mechanics, each one singing his as it should be, blithe and strong
The carpenter singing his as he measures his plank or beam,
The mason singing as he makes ready for work, or leaves off work,
The boatman singing what belongs to him in the boat, the deckhand singing
on the steamboat deck,
The shoemaker singing as he sits on his bench, the hatter singing as he stands,
The woodcutter's song, the ploughboy's on his way in the morning, or at noon
intermission, or at sundown,
The delicious singing of the mother, or of the young wife at work, or of the girl
singing or washing,
Each singing what belongs to him or her and to none else,
The day that belongs to the day—at night the party of young fellows,
robust, friendly,
Singing with open mouths their strong, melodious songs.

PSALM 8—THE BIBLE

O LORD our Lord, how excellent is thy name in all the earth! who hast set thy glory above the heavens.

Out of the mouth of babes and sucklings hast thou ordained strength because of thine enemies, that thou mightest still the enemy and the avenger.

When I consider thy heavens, the work of thy fingers, the moon and the stars, which thou hast ordained;

What is man, that thou art mindful of him? and the son of man, that thou visitest him?

For thou hast made him a little lower than the angels, and hast crowned him with glory and honour.

Thou madest him to have dominion over the works of thy hands; thou hast put all things under his feet:

All sheep and oxen, yea, and the beasts of the field;

The fowl of the air, and the fish of the sea, and whatsoever passeth through the paths of the seas.

O Lord our Lord, how excellent is thy name in all the earth!

ROAD SONG

W. G. TINCKOM-FERNANDEZ

Give me the clear blue sky overhead, and the long road to my feet,
And the winds of heaven to winnow me through, and a brother tramp to greet,
With an inn at the end of day for rest, and the world may keep its bays—
For these are the gifts of the wayside gods, and the gifts that I would praise.

Come from the murk of your city streets to the tent of all the world,
When your final word on Art is said, and your flag of Faith is furled,
When your heart no longer gives a throb at the first faint breath of Spring—
Ah, turn your feet to the ribbon-road with a chorus all may sing!

Where the sandalled Dawn like a Greek god takes the hurdles of the hills,
And the brooding earth rubs sleepy eyes at the song some lone bird trills,
Where a brook, like a silver scythe of the moon, awaits your warm caress—
Ah, these are the gifts that the High Gods fling to mortals in duress!

When the blood-red sun swings low in the west, and an end comes to Desire,
When the candle-gloom of the low-ceiled room is bared to a pine log fire,
And the tales of men are told anew till the Huntress leaves the sky—
Ah, these are the gifts for the sons of men to set their treasure by!

Then give me the clear blue sky overhead, and the long road to my feet,
And a dog to tell my secrets to, and a brother tramp to meet—
And the years may take their toll of me till I come to the weary West,
And I lodge for good in the world's own inn, a way-worn, waiting guest!

THE ANGLER'S COUNTRYSIDE

By CHARLES KINGSLEY

DEARER TO HIM than wild cataracts or Alpine glens are the still, hidden streams . . . the long, grassy shadow paved with yellow gravel, where he wades up between low walls of fern-fringed rock, between nut, and oak, and alder, to the low bar over which the stream comes swirling and dimpling, as the water-ousel flits piping before him, and the murmur of the ring-dove comes soft and sleepy through the wood. There, as he wades, he sees a hundred sights and hears a hundred tones, which are hidden from the traveller on the dusty highway above. The traveller fancies that he has seen the country. So he has; the outside of it at least. But the angler only sees the inside. The angler only is brought close, face to face with the flower, and bird, and insect life of the rich river banks, the only part of the landscape where the hand of man has never interfered, and the only part in general which never feels the drought of summer; the trees planted by the waterside, whose leaf shall not wither.

THE NIGHTINGALE AND THE ROSE
By Oscar Wilde

"She said that she would dance with me if I brought her red roses," cried the young Student; "but in all my garden there is no red rose."

From her nest in the holm-oak tree the Nightingale heard him, and she looked out through the leaves, and wondered.

"No red rose in all my garden!" he cried, and his beautiful eyes filled with tears. "Ah, on what little things does happiness depend! I have read all that the wise men have written, and all the secrets of philosophy are mine, yet for want of a red rose is my life made wretched."

"Here at last is a true lover," said the Nightingale. "Night after night have I sung of him, though I knew him not: night after night have I told his story to the stars, and now I see him. His hair is dark as the hyacinth-blossom, and his lips are red as the rose of his desire; but passion has made his face like pale ivory, and sorrow has set her seal upon his brow."

"The Prince gives a ball tomorrow night," murmured the young Student, "and my love will be of the company. If I bring her a red rose she will dance with me till dawn. If I bring her a red rose, I shall hold her in my arms, and she will lean her head upon my shoulder, and her hand will be clasped in mine. But there is no red rose in my garden, so I shall sit lonely, and she will pass me by. She will have no heed of me, and my heart will break."

"Here indeed is the true lover," said the Nightingale. "What I sing of, he suffers: what is joy to me, to him is pain. Surely Love is a wonderful thing. It is more precious than emeralds, and dearer than fine opals. Pearls and pomegranates cannot buy it, nor is it set forth in the market-place. It may not be purchased of the merchants, nor can it be weighed out in the balance for gold."

"The musicians will sit in their gallery," said the young Student, "and play upon their stringed instruments, and my love will dance to the sound of the harp and the violin. She will dance so lightly that her feet will not touch the floor, and the courtiers in their gay dresses will throng round her. But with me she will not dance, for I have no red rose to give her;" and he flung himself down on the grass, and buried his face in his hands, and wept.

"Why is he weeping?" asked a little Green Lizard, as he ran past him with his tail in the air.

"Why, indeed?" said a Butterfly, who was fluttering about after a sunbeam.

"Why, indeed?" whispered a Daisy to his neighbor, in a soft, low voice.

"He is weeping for a red rose," said the Nightingale.

"For a red rose!" they cried; "how very ridiculous!" and the little Lizard, who was something of a cynic, laughed outright.

But the Nightingale understood the secret of the Student's sorrow, and she sat silent in the oak-tree, and thought about the mystery of Love.

Suddenly she spread her brown wings for flight, and soared into the air. She passed through the grove like a shadow, and like a shadow she sailed across the garden.

In the centre of the grass-plot was standing a beautiful Rose-tree, and when she saw it she flew over to it, and lit upon a spray.

"Give me a red rose," she cried, "and I will sing you my sweetest song."

But the Tree shook its head.

"My roses are white," it answered; "as white as the foam of the sea, and whiter than the snow upon the mountain. But go to my brother who grows round the old sun-dial, and perhaps he will give you what you want."

So the Nightingale flew over to the Rose-tree that was growing round the old sun-dial.

"Give me a red rose," she cried, "and I will sing you my sweetest song."

But the Tree shook its head.

"My roses are yellow," it answered: "as yellow as the hair of the mermaiden who sits upon an amber throne, and yellower than the daffodil that blooms in the meadow before the mower comes with his scythe. But go to my brother who grows beneath the Student's window, and perhaps he will give you what you want."

So the Nightingale flew over to the Rose-tree that was growing beneath the Student's window.

"Give me a red rose," she cried, "and I will sing you my sweetest song."

But the Tree shook its head.

"My roses are red," it answered, "as red as the feet of the dove, and redder than the great fans of coral that wave and wave in the ocean-cavern. But the winter has chilled my veins, and the frost has nipped my buds, and the storm has broken my branches, and I shall have no roses at all this year."

"One red rose is all I want," cried the Nightingale, "only one red rose! Is there no way by which I can get it?"

"There is a way," answered the Tree; "but it is so terrible that I dare not tell it to you."

"Tell it to me," said the Nightingale, "I am not afraid."

"If you want a red rose," said the Tree, "you must build it out of music by moonlight, and stain it with your own heart's-blood. You must sing to me with your breast against a thorn. All night long you must sing to me, and the thorn must pierce your heart, and your life-blood must flow into my veins, and become mine."

"Death is a great price to pay for a red rose," cried the Nightingale, "and Life is very dear to all. It is pleasant to sit in the green wood, and to watch the Sun in his chariot of gold, and the Moon in her chariot of pearl. Sweet is the scent of the hawthorn, and sweet are the blue-bells that hide in the valley, and the heather that blows on the hill. Yet Love is better than Life, and what is the heart of a bird compared to the heart of a man?"

So she spread her brown wings for flight, and soared into the air. She swept over the garden like a shadow, and like a shadow she sailed through the grove.

The young Student was still lying on the grass, where she had left him, and the tears were not yet dry in his beautiful eyes.

"Be happy," cried the Nightingale, "be happy; you shall have your red rose. I will build it out of music by moonlight, and stain it with my own heart's-blood. All that I ask of you in return is that you will be a true lover, for Love is wiser than Philosophy, though she is wise, and mightier than Power, though he is mighty. Flame-coloured are his wings, and coloured like flame is his body. His lips are sweet as honey, and his breath is like frankincense."

The Student looked up from the grass, and listened, but he could not understand what the Nightingale was saying to him, for he only knew the things that are written down in books.

But the Oak-tree understood, and felt sad, for he was very fond of the little Nightingale who had built her nest in his branches.

"Sing me one last song," he whispered; "I will feel very lonely when you are gone."

So the Nightingale sang to the Oak-tree, and her voice was like water bubbling from a silver jar.

When she had finished her song the Student got up, and pulled a notebook and a lead-pencil out of his pocket.

"She has form," he said to himself, as

he walked away through the grove—"that cannot be denied to her; but has she got feeling? I am afraid not. In fact, she is like most artists; she is all style, without any sincerity. She would not sacrifice herself for others. She thinks merely of music, and everybody knows that the arts are selfish. Still, it must be admitted that she has some beautiful notes in her voice. What a pity it is that they do not mean anything, or do any practical good." And he went into his room, and lay down on his little pallet-bed, and began to think of his love; and, after a time, he fell asleep.

And when the Moon shone in the heavens the Nightingale flew to the Rose-tree, and set her breast against the thorn. All night long she sang with her breast against the thorn, and the cold crystal Moon leaned down and listened. All night long she sang, and the thorn went deeper and deeper into her breast, and her life-blood ebbed away from her.

She sang first of the birth of love in the heart of a boy and a girl. And on the topmost spray of the Rose-tree there blossomed a marvelous rose, petal following petal, as song followed song. Pale was it, at first, as the mist that hangs over the river—pale as the feet of the morning, and silver as the wings of the dawn.

As the shadow of a rose in a mirror of silver, as the shadow of a rose in a water-pool, so was the rose that blossomed on the topmost spray of the Tree.

But the Tree cried to the Nightingale to press closer against the thorn. "Press closer, little Nightingale," cried the Tree, "or the Day will come before the Rose is finished."

So the Nightingale pressed closer against the thorn, and louder and louder grew her song, for she sang of the birth of passion in the soul of a man and a maid.

And a delicate flush of pink came into the leaves of the rose, like the flush in the face of the bridegroom when he kisses the lips of the bride. But the thorn had not yet reached her heart, so the rose's heart remained white, for only a Nightingale's heart's-blood can crimson the heart of a rose.

And the Tree cried to the Nightingale to press closer against the thorn. "Press closer, little Nightingale," cried the Tree, "or the Day will come before the rose is finished."

So the Nightingale pressed closer against the thorn, and the thorn touched her heart, and a fierce pang of pain shot through her. Bitter, bitter was the pain, and wilder and wilder grew her song, for she sang of the Love that is perfected by Death, of the Love that dies not in the tomb.

And the marvellous rose became crimson, like the rose of the eastern sky. Crimson was the girdle of petals, and crimson as a ruby was the heart.

But the Nightingale's voice grew fainter, and her little wings began to beat, and a film came over her eyes. Fainter and fainter grew her song, and she felt something choking her in her throat.

Then she gave one last burst of music. The white Moon heard it, and she forgot the dawn, and lingered on in the sky. The red rose heard it, and it trembled all over with ecstasy, and opened its petals to the cold morning air. Echo bore it to her purple cavern in the hills, and woke the sleeping shepherds from their dreams. It floated through the reeds of the river, and they carried its message to the sea.

"Look, look!" cried the Tree, "the rose is finished now;" but the Nightingale made no answer, for she was lying dead in the long grass, with the thorn in her heart.

And at noon the Student opened his window and looked out.

"Why, what a wonderful piece of luck!" he cried; "here is a red rose! I have never seen any rose like it in all my life. It is so beautiful that I am sure it has a long Latin name;" and he leaned down and plucked it.

Then he put on his hat, and ran up to the Professor's house with the rose in his hand.

The daughter of the Professor was sitting in the doorway winding blue silk on a reel, and her little dog was lying at her feet.

"You said that you would dance with me if I brought you a red rose," cried the Student. "Here is the reddest rose in all the world. You will wear it to-night next your heart, and as we dance together it will tell you how I love you."

But the girl frowned.

"I am afraid it will not go with my dress," she answered; "and, besides, the Chamberlain's nephew has sent me some real jewels, and everybody knows that jewels cost far more than flowers."

"Well, upon my word, you are very ungrateful," said the Student angrily; and he threw the rose into the street, where it fell into the gutter, and a cartwheel went over it.

"Ungrateful!" said the girl. "I tell you what, you are very rude; and, after all, who are you? Only a Student. Why, I don't believe you have even got silver buckles to your shoes as the Chamberlain's nephew has;" and she got up from her chair and went into the house.

"What a silly thing Love is," said the Student as he walked away. "It is not half as useful as Logic, for it does not prove anything, and it is always telling one of things that are not going to happen, and making one believe things that are not true. In fact, it is quite unpractical, and, as in this age to be practical is everything, I shall go back to Philosophy and study Metaphysics."

So he returned to his room and pulled out a great dusty book, and began to read.

❧ ❧ ❧

AWAY

James Whitcomb Riley

I cannot say, and I will not say
That he is dead. He is just away!

With a cheery smile and a wave of the
      hand,
He has wandered into an unknown
      land,

And left us dreaming how very fair
It needs must be, since he lingers there.

And you—oh you, who the wildest yearn
For the old time step and the glad
      return—

Think of him faring on, as dear
In the love of There as the love of
      Here;

And loyal still, as he gave the blows
Of his warrior strength to his country's
      foes—

Mild and gentle, as he was brave,
When the sweetest love of his life he
      gave

To simple things; where the violets
      grew
Pure as the eyes they were likened to,

The touches of his hands have strayed
As reverently as his lips have prayed;

When the little brown thrush that
      harshly chirred
Was dear to him as the mocking-bird;

And he pitied as much as a man in pain
A writhing honey-bee wet with rain.

Think of him still as the same, I say;
He is not dead—he is just—away!

DEATH AND GENERAL PUTNAM
ARTHUR GUITERMAN

His iron arm had spent its force
No longer might he rein a horse;
Lone, beside the dying blaze
Dreaming dreams of younger days
Sat old Israel Putnam.

Twice he heard, then three times more
A knock upon the oaken door,
A knock he could not fail to know,
That old man in the ember-glow.
"Come," said General Putnam.

The door swung wide; in cloak and
    hood
Lean and tall the pilgrim stood
And spoke in tones none else might
    hear.
"Once more I come to bring you Fear!"
"Fear?" said General Putnam.

"You know not Fear? And yet this face
Your eyes have seen in many a place
Since first in stony Pomfret, when
You dragged the mad wolf from her
    den."
"Yes," said General Putnam.

"Was I not close, when, stripped and
    bound
With blazing fagots heaped around
You heard the Huron war cry shrill?
Was I not close at Bunker Hill?"
"Close," said General Putnam.

"Am I not that which strong men dread
On stricken field or fevered bed,
On gloomy trail and stormy sea,
And dare you name my name to me?"
"Death," said General Putnam.

"We have been comrades, you and I,
In chase and war beneath this sky;
And now, whatever Fate may send,
Old comrade, can you call me friend?"
"Friend!" said General Putnam.

Then up he rose, and forth they went
Away from battleground, fortress, tent,
Mountain, wilderness, field and farm,
Death and the General, arm-in-arm,
Death and General Putnam.

THESE ARE THE GIFTS I ASK
HENRY VAN DYKE

These are the gifts I ask
Of thee, Spirit serene:
Strength for the daily task,
Courage to face the road,
Good cheer to help me bear the travel-
    ler's load,
And, for the hours of rest that come
    between,
An inward joy in all things heard and
    seen.
These are the sins I fain
Would have thee take away:
Malice, and cold disdain,
Hot anger, sullen hate,
Scorn of the lowly, envy of the great,
And discontent that casts a shadow
    gray
On all the brightness of a common day.

From PROMETHEUS UNBOUND
PERCY BYSSHE SHELLEY

The point of one white star is quivering
    still
Deep in the orange light of widening
    morn
Beyond the purple mountains: thro' a
    chasm
Of wind-divided mist the darker lake
Reflects it: now it wanes: it gleams
    again
As the waves fade, and as the burning
    threads
Of woven cloud unravel in pale air:
'Tis lost! and thro' yon peaks of cloud-
    like snow
The roseate sunlight quivers: hear I not
The AEolian music of her sea-green
    plumes
Winnowing the crimson dawn?

EVELYN HOPE
ROBERT BROWNING

Beautiful Evelyn Hope is dead!
  Sit and watch by her side an hour.
That is her book-shelf, this her bed;
  She plucked that piece of geranium
    flower,
Beginning to die too, in the glass;
  Little has yet been changed, I think:
The shutters are shut, no light may pass
  Save two long rays through the
    hinge's chink.

Sixteen years old when she died!
  Perhaps she had scarcely heard my
    name;
It was not her time to love; beside,
  Her life had many a hope and aim,
Duties enough and little cares,
  And now was quiet, now astir,
Till God's hand beckoned unawares,—
  And the sweet white brow is all of
    her.

Is it too late then, Evelyn Hope?
  What, your soul was pure and true,
The good stars met in your horoscope,
  Made you of spirit, fire and dew—
And, just because I was thrice as old
  And our paths in the world diverged
    so wide,
Each was naught to each, must I be
    told?
  We were fellow mortals, naught
    beside?

No, indeed! for God above
  Is great to grant, as mighty to make,
And creates the love to reward the love:
  I claim you still, for my own love's
    sake!
Delayed it may be for more lives yet,
  Through worlds I shall traverse, not
    a few:

Much is to learn, much to forget
  Ere the time be come for taking you.

But the time will come—at last it will,
  When, Evelyn Hope, what meant
    (I shall say)
In the lower earth, in the years long
    still,
  That body and soul so pure and gay?
Why your hair was amber, I shall
    divine,
  And your mouth of your own
    geranium's red—
And what you would do with me, in
    fine,
  In the new life come in the old life's
    stead.

I have lived (I shall say) so much since
    then,
  Given up myself so many times,
Gained me the gains of various men,
  Ransacked the ages, spoiled the
    climes;
Yet one thing, one, in my soul's full
    scope,
  Either I missed or itself missed me:
And I want and find you, Evelyn Hope!
  What is the issue? Let us see!

I loved you, Evelyn all the while!
  My heart seemed full as it could hold;
There was place and to spare for the
    frank young smile,
  And the red young mouth, and the
    hair's young gold.
So, hush—I will give you this leaf to
    keep:
  See, I shut it inside the sweet cold
    hand!
There, that is our secret; go to sleep!
  You will wake, and remember, and
    understand.

* * *

❧ THE COMFORT of having a friend may be taken away, but not that of
having had one.
           —*Seneca*

LAST PRAYER
By Robert Louis Stevenson

When the day returns, call us up
with morning faces and with morning
hearts, eager to labor, happy if happiness
be our portion, and if the day be
marked for sorrow, strong to endure.

ALL'S BLUE
Robert Browning

I find earth not gray but rosy,
  Heaven not grim but fair of hue.
Do I stoop? I pluck a posy.
Do I stand and stare? All's blue.

ON A FINAL DAY
By Edwin Way Teale

If I were to choose the sights, the
sounds, the fragrances I most would
want to see and hear and smell—among
all the delights of the open world—on a
final day on earth, I think I would
choose these: the clear, ethereal song of
a white-throated sparrow singing at
dawn; the smell of pine trees in the
heat of noon; the lonely calling of Canada
geese; the sight of a dragon-fly glinting
in the sunshine; the voice of a hermit
thrush far in a darkening woods at
evening; and—most spiritual and moving
of sights—the white cathedral of a
cumulus cloud floating serenely in the
blue of the sky.

SILENCE
Charles Hanson Towne

I need not shout my faith. Thrice
    eloquent
  Are quiet trees and the green listening
    sod;
Hushed are the stars, whose power is
    never spent;
  The hills are mute: yet how they
    speak of God!

CLARION
Sir Walter Scott

Sound, sound the clarion, fill the fife!
To all the sensual world proclaim,
One crowded hour of glorious life
Is worth an age without a name.

TEN BEAUTIFUL WORDS

Wilfred J. Funk, poet, lexicographer
and president of Funk & Wagnalls, once
listed what he considered the ten most
beautiful words in the English language—"beautiful
in meaning and in
the musical arrangement of their letters."

His list, compiled after a "thorough
sifting of thousands of words," is—
*dawn, hush, lullaby, murmuring,
tranquil, mist, luminous, chimes, golden,*
and *melody.*

THE COMFORT OF FRIENDS
By William Penn

They that love beyond the world
cannot be separated by it.

Death cannot kill what never dies.

Nor can spirits ever be divided that
love and live in the same divine principle;
the root and record of their
friendship.

If absence be not death, neither is
theirs.

Death is but crossing the world, as
friends do the seas; they live in one
another still.

For they must needs be present, that
love and live in that which is Omnipresent.

In this divine glass they see face to
face; and their converse is free as well
as pure.

This is the comfort of friends, that
though they may be said to die, yet their
friendship and society are, in the best
sense, ever present, because immortal.

164

BUILDERS

By JOHN RUSKIN

WHEN we build, let us think that we build forever. Let it not be for present delight nor for present use alone. Let it be such work as our descendants will thank us for, and let us think, as we lay stone on stone, that a time is to come when those stones will be held sacred because our hands have touched them, and that men will say as they look upon the labor and wrought substance of them, "See! This our Fathers did for us."

From *DEDICATION OF THE CLOISTERS, New York*

By JOHN D. ROCKEFELLER, JR.

IF WHAT has been created here helps to interpret beauty as one of the great spiritual and inspirational forces of life having the power to transform drab duty into radiant living; if those who come under the influence of this place go out to face life with new courage and restored faith because of the peace, the calm, the loveliness they found here; if the many who thirst for beauty are refreshed and gladdened as they drink deep from this well of beauty, those who have builded here will not have built in vain.

ON JOHN BUNYAN

By JOHN GREENLEAF WHITTIER

THE BROAD and pleasant "river of the Water of Life" glided peacefully before him, fringed "on either side with green trees, with all manner of fruit," and leaves of healing, with "meadows beautified with lilies, and green all the year long"; he saw the Delectable Mountains, glorious with sunshine, overhung with gardens and orchards and vineyards; and beyond all, the Land of Beulah, with its eternal sunshine, its song of birds, its music of fountains, its purple clustered vines, and groves through which walked the Shining Ones, silver-winged and beautiful.

ON YOUTH

THE WHOLE secret of remaining young in spite of years, and even of gray hairs, is to cherish enthusiasm in oneself, by poetry, by contemplation, by charity, —that is, in fewer words, by the maintenance of harmony in the soul. When everything is in its right place within us, we ourselves are in equilibrium with the whole work of God. Deep and grave enthusiasm for the eternal beauty and the eternal order, reason touched with emotion and a serene tenderness of heart—these surely are the foundations of wisdom.   —*Amiel*

* * *

❧ THANK GOD every morning when you get up that you have something to do that day which must be done, whether you like it or not. Being forced to work and forced to do your best will breed in you temperance and self-control, diligence and strength of will, cheerfulness and content, and a hundred virtues which the idle never know.   —*Kingsley*

* * *

❧ THERE IS A TIME in every man's education when he arrives at the conviction that envy is ignorance; that imitation is suicide; that he must take himself, for better or for worse, as his portion; that, though the wide universe is full of good, no kernel of nourishing corn can come to him but through his toil bestowed on that plot of ground which is given him to till.
     —*Emerson*

From *THE GREATEST THING IN THE WORLD*
By Henry Drummond

EVERY ONE has asked himself the great question of antiquity as of the modern world: What is the *summum bonum*—the supreme good? You have life before you. Once only you can live it. What is the noblest object of desire, the supreme gift to covet?

We have been accustomed to be told that the greatest thing in the religious world is Faith. That great word has been the keynote for centuries of the popular religion; and we have easily learned to look upon it as the greatest thing in the world. Well, we are wrong. If we have been told that, we may miss the mark. . . . In Christianity at its source . . . we have seen, "The greatest of these is love." It is not an oversight. Paul was speaking of faith just a moment before. He says, "If I have all faith, so that I can remove mountains, and have not love, I am nothing." So far from forgetting he deliberately contrasts them, "Now abideth Faith, Hope, Love," and without a moment's hesitation the decision falls, "The greatest of these is Love."

And it is not prejudice. A man is apt to recommend to others his own strong point.

Love was not Paul's strong point. The observing student can detect a beautiful tenderness growing and ripening all through his character as Paul gets old; but the hand that wrote "The greatest of these is love," when we meet it first, is stained with blood.

Nor is his letter to the Corinthians peculiar in singling out love as the *summum bonum*. The masterpieces of Christianity are agreed about it. Peter says, "Above all things have fervent love among yourselves." *Above all things.* And John goes further, "God is love." And you remember the profound remark which Paul makes elsewhere, "Love is the fulfilling of the law." Did you ever think what he meant by that?

In those days men were working their passage to Heaven by keeping the Ten Commandments, and the hundred and ten other commandments which they had manufactured out of them. Christ said, "I will show you a more simple way." If you do one thing, you will do these hundred and ten things, without ever thinking about them. If you love, you will unconsciously fulfill the whole law. And you can readily see for yourselves how that must be so. Take any of the commandments: 'Thou shalt have no other gods before Me." If a man love God, you will not require to tell him that. Love is the fulfilling of that law. "Take not His name in vain." Would he ever dream of taking His name in vain if he loved Him? "Remember the Sabbath day to keep it holy." Would he not be too glad to have one day in seven to dedicate more exclusively to the object of his affection? Love would fulfill all these laws regarding God. And so, if he loved Man you would never think of telling him to honor his father and mother. He could not do anything else. It would be preposterous to tell him not to kill. You could only insult him if you suggested that he should not steal—how could he steal from those he loved. It would be superfluous to beg him not to bear false witness against his neighbor. If he loved him, it would be the last thing he would do.

And you would never dream of urging him not to covet what his neighbors had. He would rather they possessed it than himself. In this way "Love is the fulfilling of the law." It is the rule for fulfilling all rules, the new commandments for keeping all the old commandments, Christ's one secret of the Christian life.

Now Paul had learned that; and in this noble eulogy he has given us the most wonderful and original account

166

extant of the *summum bonum.* We may divide it into three parts. In the beginning of the short chapter, we have Love *contrasted;* in the heart of it, we have Love *analyzed;* toward the end, we have Love *defended* as the supreme gift.

❧ ❧ ❧

TWO LYRICS
James Thomson ("B.V.")

I

Let my voice ring out and over the
earth,
  Through all the grief and strife,
With a golden joy in a silver mirth:
    Thank God for Life!

Let my voice swell out through the
great abyss
  To the azure dome above,
With a chord of faith in the harp of
bliss:
    Thank God for Love!

Let my voice thrill out beneath and
above,
  The whole world through:
O my Love and Life, O my Life and
Love,
    Thank God for you!

II

As we rush, as we rush in the Train,
  The trees and the houses go wheeling
  back,
But the starry heavens above the plain
  Come flying on our track.

All the beautiful stars of the sky,
  The silver doves of the forest of
  Night,
Over the full earth swarm and fly,
  Companions of our flight.

We will rush ever on without fear;
  Let the goal be far, the flight be fleet!
For we carry the Heavens with us, Dear,
  While the Earth slips from our feet!

BEDOUIN LOVE-SONG
Bayard Taylor

From the Desert I come to thee,
  On a stallion shod with fire;
And the winds are left behind
  In the speed of my desire.
Under thy window I stand,
  And the midnight hears my cry:
I love thee, I love thee!
    With a love that shall not die
      Till the sun grows cold,
      And the stars are old,
      And the leaves of the Judgment
      Book unfold!

Look from thy window, and see
  My passion and my pain!
I lie on the sands below,
  And I faint in thy disdain.
Let the night-winds touch thy brow
  With the heat of my burning sigh,
And melt thee to hear the vow
    Of a love that shall not die
      Till the sun grows cold,
      And the stars are old,
      And the leaves of the Judgment
      Book unfold!

My steps are nightly driven,
  By the fever in my breast,
To hear from thy lattice breathed
  The word that shall give me rest.
Open the door of thy heart,
  And open thy chamber door,
And my kisses shall teach they lips
    The love that shall fade no more
      Till the sun grows cold,
      And the stars are old,
      And the leaves of the Judgment
      Book unfold!

* * *

❧ The whole worth of a kind deed lies in the love that inspires it.
          —*The Talmud*

DEAR LORD! KIND LORD!
James Whitcomb Riley

Dear Lord! Kind Lord!
  Gracious Lord! I pray
Thou wilt look on all I love
  Tenderly today!

Weed their hearts of weariness,
  Scatter every care
Down a wake of angel-wings
  Winnowing the air.

And with all the needy
  O divide, I pray,
This vast treasure of content
  That is mine today.

FAITH
Robert Browning

O never star
Was lost; here
We all aspire to heaven and there is
  heaven
Above us.
If I stoop
Into a dark tremendous sea of cloud,
It is but for a time; I press God's lamp
Close to my breast; its splendor soon or
  late
Will pierce the gloom. I shall emerge
  some day.

From THE SERVANT IN THE HOUSE
By Charles Rann Kennedy

Scene: Manson's Church
(The Bishop, a mercenary man of the world, has just said, "Now! Tell me about your church.")

MANSON. I am afraid you may not consider it an altogether substantial concern. It has to be seen in a certain way, under certain conditions. Some people never *see* it at all. You must understand, this is no dead pile of stones and unmeaning timber. *It is a living thing.*— When you enter it you hear a sound as of some mighty poem chanted. Listen long enough, and you will learn that it is made up of the beating of human hearts, of the nameless music of men's souls—that is, if you have ears. If you have eyes, you will presently see the church itself—a looming mystery of many shapes and shadows, leaping sheer from floor to dome. The work of no ordinary builder!

The pillars of it go up like the brawny trunks of heroes: the sweet human flesh of men and women is moulded about its bulwarks, strong impregnable: the faces of little children laugh out from every corner-stone; the terrible spans and arches of it are the joined hands of comrades; and up in the heights and spaces there are inscribed the numberless musings of all the dreamers of the world. It is yet building—building and built upon. Sometimes the work goes forward in deep darkness: sometimes in blinding light: now beneath the burden of unutterable anguish: now to the tune of a great laughter and heroic shoutings like the cry of thunder.

Sometimes, in the silence of the night-time, one may hear the tiny hammerings of the comrades at work up in the dome—the comrades who have climbed ahead.

* * *

❧ ALL THAT WE ARE is the result of what we have thought; it is founded on our thoughts, it is made up of our thoughts. If a man speaks or acts with a pure thought, happiness follows him, like a shadow that never leaves him.
—*Buddha*

THE BIBLE

We search the world for truth. We cull
The good, the true, the beautiful,
From graven stone and written scroll,
And all old flower-fields of the soul;
And, weary seekers of the best,
We come back laden from our quest,
To find that all the sages said
Is in the Book our mothers read.

—*John Greenleaf Whittier*

WORDS OF ST. FRANCIS

Lord, make me an instrument of Thy
  peace;
Where hate rules, let me bring love;
Where malice, forgiveness;
Where disputes, reconciliation;
Where error, truth;
Where despair, hope;
Where darkness, Thy light;
Where sorrow, joy.

ONLY THE WISE MAN

ONLY THE wise man draws from life, and from every stage of it, its true savour, because only he feels the beauty, the dignity, and the value of life. The flowers of youth may fade, but the summer, the autumn, and even the winter of human existence, have their majestic grandeur, which the wise man recognizes and glorifies. To see all things in God; to make of one's own life a journey towards the ideal; to live with gratitude, with devoutness, with gentleness and courage;—this was the splendid aim of Marcus Aurelius. And if you add to it the humility which kneels, and the charity which gives, you have the whole wisdom of the children of God, the immortal joy which is the heritage of the true Christian. —*Amiel*

I GOT A GLORY
By ARCHIBALD RUTLEDGE

ON A DAY memorable to me, I boarded a tiny tugboat that I used often in crossing a southern river and saw that we had a new Negro engineer. He sat in the doorway of the engine room reading the Bible; he was fat, squat and black, but immaculate, and in his eyes was the splendor of ancient wisdom and peace with the world. As I paused to talk with him I noticed that the characteristic odors that had always emanated from the engine room were no longer there. And the engine! It gleamed and shone; from beneath its seat all the bilge-water was gone. Instead of grime and filth and stench I found beauty and order. When I asked the engineer how in the world he had managed to clean up the old room and the old engine, he answered in words that would go far toward solving life's main problems for many people.

"Cap'n," he said, nodding fondly in the direction of the engine, "it's just this way: I got a glory."

Making that engine the best on the river was his glory in life, and having a glory he had everything. The only sure way out of suffering that I know is to find a glory, and to give to it the strength we might otherwise spend in despair.

* * *

❧ MY FRIEND is that one whom I can associate with my choicest thought.

—*Thoreau*

LET ME BE A STAR

Helen Hoyt

Let me be a star that shines over you,
Let me be a cloud that floats by you,
Let me be a mist that rests on the
    mountain's peak.
Do you feel the soft touch of the mist
As I lay my hair on your hair?

I have bent my head over,
I have leaned my head down over you,
As the moon leans on the mountain.
I have let fall the folds of my hair
To cover your head,
I have folded my hair about you
As the scarves of a cloud
Winding the brow of the mountain;

I have wrapped you about,
I have enwound you, I have leaned . . .

O mountain, my beautiful!
I am the follower you called to come,
I am the wanderer and you stayed my
    footsteps;
I saw you from far away, a blue horizon;
You called me from desert-spaces
To the cool of your shadow.
As a seed on the wind I was blown,
As a bird on spent wings I have come;
Now I rest in your sheltering rock.
Now as a flower, as a bird, I rest in your
    bosom.

BEAUTY

By J. M. T. [A College Student]

"Wherever snow falls, or water flows, or birds fly, wherever day and night meet in twilight, wherever the blue heaven is hung by clouds, or sown with stars, wherever are forms with transparent boundaries, wherever are outlets into celestial space, wherever is danger, and awe, and love, there is Beauty, plenteous as rain, shed for thee, and though thou shouldst walk the world over, thou shalt not be able to find a condition inopportune or ignoble."

Two years ago last summer I sat on the veranda of an Alpine hotel and was served luncheon by a pretty red-cheeked Swiss maid. The dining room was not especially attractive, but the scenery which enveloped it on all sides seemed like a magic curtain let down from heaven. Directly in front of me rose the snow-capped peaks of old Jungfrau towering like a giant above the other mountains. Half way down could be seen the grassy slopes of smaller mountains contrasting their bright green covering with the whiteness of the snow above them. Nestling in the valley be-

low was the little town of Interlaken with its squatty, red-roofed houses. On my right stretched another range of mountains. Lively streams came tumbling down the steep slopes looking like snow-white ribbons against the dark background. Tiny peasant cottages dotted the mountainside. A river flowed through the fertile valley below, forming an apple-green sash for its dark-green dress. Truly, my eyes were gazing on the handiwork of God!

Who has not at some period in his life gazed on a lovely landscape and marveled at the beauty of the scene? And yet the philosopher Emerson said: "The difference between landscape and landscape is small, but there is a great difference in the beholder." In other words, there are many things of great beauty in this world that the average individual never sees. Yet to the observant eye the world is full of hidden beauty.

There is beauty in courage, real, deep, self-sacrificing courage. I am thinking just now of a hot, dusty road that winds through a field in southern France. I well remember the day that I drove through the Argonne forest, along the trenches and dugouts, and finally arrived at the great memorial cemetery with its rows and rows of snow-white crosses. As I stooped to pluck a blood-red poppy that grew on one of the little graves, I could not help seeing that even in such barren waste there was great beauty. Those ugly heaps of dirt once sheltered hundreds of courageous young men who had left kith and kin to serve their country. That barren waste that stretches for miles around was once the scene of many daring drives, of long night marches, and of fearless assaults on the enemy. And as I held the crimson poppy in my hand, I could not help thinking of the red blood that flowed so freely over this same ground just ten years before. Suddenly, the ugly mounds of dirt and the muddy dugouts were transformed before my eyes into things of rare beauty; where courage is, there, too, is beauty.

There is something indescribably alluring and beautiful in falling water. Who could stand on the brink of Niagara Falls without being deeply stirred within him at the beauty of it all? The powerful current seems to carry everything before it; all one's cares and troubles, fears and doubts are swept away before it. Great sprays of foaming white water spring up into the air, and then subside into the depths below. One can hear the roar of the rapids as the water dashes upon the rocks below. It is one of those rare beauties that cannot be fitly expressed in mere words: it must be felt, and enjoyed in silence.

Not long ago we had as a visitor in our home a crusty old gentleman who feared neither God nor man. It is the custom in our home for little four-year-old Jimmie to lisp his evening prayer at mother's knee about nine o'clock each evening. Coming in one evening about this time, I found mother at the fireplace, and heard the familiar words in Jimmie's high treble: "Now I lay me down to sleep—." Tiptoeing softly across the room, I almost bumped into the old gentleman standing just outside the glass door. The hard lines of his face were relaxed, his stooped shoulders heaved slowly up and down, and he quickly brushed a tear from the corner of his eye as I looked up at him. Frankly, I was embarrassed, but the old gentleman whispered in my ear: "Oh, the simplicity and the beauty of that little fellow's faith." And with that word he bolted up the stairs to his room, and I was left standing in the middle of the floor thinking that even faith, pure, simple, childish faith is beautiful.

I shall never forget my first sight of a storm at sea. It was the third day out. About three o'clock in the afternoon the sky grew black and threatening. Great, dark clouds shut out the light of the sun. The ocean, so calm just a half an hour before, became turbulent with huge, choppy waves. The great ship lunged to and fro like a mere toy in the powerful grasp of some monster of the deep. Higher and yet higher rose the waves. Now and then a huge one washed across the deck of the ship leaving destruction in its wake. The thunder rolled above us, and the waters roared beneath. Streaks of lightning flashed across the blackened heavens. Then "down came the storm—." For two long hours my friend and I stood on the top inner deck and watched the wild waves dash. And in that sheltered nook, while the fierce winds blew and the storm raged, we stood awed by the splendor, the power, the grandeur—in short, the great beauty of a storm at sea.

I know a dear, little white-haired lady who guards, as one of her choicest treasures, an old patchwork quilt. The quilt itself is anything but beautiful. Its varied colors do not harmonize; some are faded, others are streaked, and many are worn and old. Yet to the old lady it is beautiful, yes, very beautiful, because of the memories it brings to her. The old, purple square was cut from her first long, party gown; the worn old bit of green is a piece of her mother's wedding dress; and the tiny little patch of faded white muslin is her son's first baby dress. And so the little lady cherishes the old, ugly quilt, and to her it is more beautiful than all the latest silk taffetas in the world. It is not the faded quilt that is so beautiful to my old friend, but it is the memories, the precious memories, that are beautiful to her.

There is beauty in a sunny smile. Many a person will look twice at a bright, cheery face with a happy smile, but a somber, though good-looking person, he will pass by with scarcely a thought. And who of us has not seen a very plain face made truly beautiful for its goodness' sake alone?

There is something beautiful in strength. Who has seen an athlete leap a hurdle, or a strong man lift a heavy weight, and not marveled at the beauty of great strength?

There is a certain solemn, silent beauty in the sable night. Those nights when the sky above looks like a carpet of black velvet inlaid with sparkling diamonds. The moon, like a great golden ball, floats across the heavens, and darkness reigns supreme. Who of us has not cast our eyes heavenward on such a night, and tried to peer through the vast celestial spaces into the beauties that lie beyond?

"Beauty is truth, truth beauty—that is all
Ye know on earth, and all ye need to know."

꙰ ꙰ ꙰

AMICO SUO
HERBERT HORNE

When on my country walks I go,
 I never am alone:
Though, whom 'twere pleasure then to
  know,
 Are gone, and you are gone;
From every side discourses flow.

There are rich counsels in the trees,
 And converse in the air;
All magic thoughts in those and these
 And what is sweet and rare;
And everything, that living is.

But most I love the meaner sort,
 For they have voices, too;
Yet speak with tongues, that never hurt,
 As ours are apt to do:
The weeds, the grass, the common wort.

From *EACH AND ALL*
RALPH WALDO EMERSON

Then I said, "I covet truth;
Beauty is unripe childhood's cheat;
I leave it behind with the games of
  youth."
As I spoke, beneath my feet
The ground-pine curled its pretty
  wreath,
Running over the club-moss burrs;
I inhaled the violets breath;
Around me stood the oaks and firs;
Pine cones and acorns lay on the
  ground;
Over me soared the eternal sky,
Full of light and of deity;
Again I saw, again I heard,
The rolling river, the morning bird;
Beauty through my sense stole;
I yielded myself to the perfect whole.

* * *

꙰ TIME IS infinitely long and each day is a vessel into which a great deal may be poured, if one will actually fill it up. —*Goethe*

172

A BALLAD OF DREAMLAND

ALGERNON CHARLES SWINBURNE

I hid my heart in a nest of roses,
  Out of the sun's way, hidden apart;
In a softer bed than the soft white snow's is,
  Under the roses I hid my heart.
Why would it sleep not? why should it start,
When never a leaf of the rose-tree stirred?
  What made sleep flutter his wings and part?
Only the song of a secret bird.

Lie still, I said, for the wind's wing closes,
  And mild leaves muffle the keen sun's dart;
Lie still, for the wind on the warm sea dozes,
  And the wind is unquieter yet than thou art.
Does a thought in thee still as a thorn's wound smart?
Does the fang still fret thee of hope deferred?
  What bids the lips of thy sleep dispart?
Only the song of a secret bird.

The green land's name that a charm encloses,
  It never was writ in the traveller's chart,
'And sweet on its trees as the fruit that grows is,
  It never was sold in the merchant's mart.
The swallows of dreams through its dim fields dart,
'And sleep's are the tunes in its tree-tops heard;
  No hound's note wakens the wildwood hart,
Only the song of a secret bird.

ENVOI

In the world of dreams I have chosen my part,
  To sleep for a season and hear no word
Of true loves' truth or of light love's art,
  Only the song of a secret bird.

THE HALF-PART OF A BLESSED MAN

WILLIAM SHAKESPEARE

He is the half-part of a blessed man,
Left to be finished by such as she;
And she a fair divided excellence,
Whose fulness of perfection lies in him.
—From *King John*

TIME IS

HENRY VAN DYKE

Too Slow for those who Wait,
Too Swift for those who Fear,
Too Long for those who Grieve,
Too Short for those who Rejoice;
  But for those who Love, Time is
eternity.

PATTERNS
AMY LOWELL

I walk down the garden paths,
And all the daffodils
Are blowing, and the bright blue squills.
I walk down the patterned garden paths
In my stiff, brocaded gown.
With my powdered hair and jewelled fan,
I, too, am a rare
Pattern.   As I wander down
The garden paths.

My dress is richly figured,
And the train
Makes a pink and silver stain
On the gravel, and the thrift
Of the borders.
Just a plate of current fashion,
Tripping by in high-heeled, ribboned shoes.
Not a softness anywhere about me,
Only whalebone and brocade.
And I sink on a seat in the shade
Of a lime tree. For my passion
Wars against the stiff brocade.
The daffodils and squills
Flutter in the breeze
As they please.
And I weep;
For the lime tree is in blossom
And one small flower has dropped upon my bosom.

And the plashing of waterdrops
In the marble fountain
Comes down the garden paths.
The dripping never stops.
Underneath my stiffened gown
Is the softness of a woman bathing in a marble basin,
A basin in the midst of hedges grown
So thick she cannot see her lover hiding,
But she guesses he is near,
And the sliding of the water
Seems the stroking of a dear
Hand upon her.
What is summer in a fine brocaded gown!

I should like to see it lying in a heap upon the ground,
All the pink and silver crumpled up on the ground.

I would be the pink and silver as I ran along the paths,
And he would stumble after,
Bewildered by my laughter.
I should see the sun flashing from his sword hilt and the buckles on his shoes.
I would choose
To lead him in a maze along the patterned paths,
A bright and laughing maze for my heavy-booted lover,
Till he caught me in the shade,
And the buttons of his waistcoat bruised my body as he clasped me,
Aching, melting, unafraid.
With the shadows of the leaves and the sundrops,
And the plopping of the waterdrops,
All about us in the open afternoon—
I am very like to swoon
With the weight of this brocade,
For the sun sifts through the shade.

Underneath the fallen blossom
In my bosom,
Is a letter I have hid.
It was brought to me this morning by a rider from the Duke.
"Madam, we regret to inform you that Lord Hartwell
Died in action Thursday se'n night."
As I read it in the white, morning sunlight,
The letters squirmed like snakes.
"Any answer, Madam?" said my footman.
"No," I told him.
"See that the messenger takes some refreshment.
No, no answer."
And I walked into the garden,

Up and down the patterned paths,
In my stiff, correct brocade.
The blue and yellow flowers stood up
    proudly in the sun,
Each one.
I stood upright, too,
Held rigid to the pattern
By the stiffness of my gown.
Up and down I walked,
Up and down.

In a month he would have been my
    husband.
In a month, here, underneath this lime,
We would have broke the pattern;
He for me, and I for him,
He as Colonel, I as Lady,
On this shady seat.
He had a whim
That sunlight carried blessing.
And I answered, "It shall be as you have
    said."

Now he is dead.

In summer and in winter I shall walk
Up and down
The patterned garden paths
In my stiff, brocaded gown.
The squills and daffodils
Will give place to pillard roses, and to
    asters, and to snow.
I shall go
Up and down,
In my gown.
Gorgeously arrayed,
Boned and stayed,
And the softness of my body will be
    guarded from embrace
By each button, hook, and lace.
For the man who should loose me is
    dead,
Fighting with the Duke in Flanders,
In a pattern called a war.
Christ! What are patterns for?

TAWNY LIONESS

By ELLA YOUNG

I THINK myself lucky that I have come to this country (America) in the Autumn. I say Autumn rather than Fall because I like the sound of the word, Autumn. It is a country that would be beautiful at any time, and I find myself wishing that I could see it in the Spring. If I can see it only once, I choose to see it now, as I do, in the Fall. It seems to me that Autumn is the really austere season. Everything burns into a glory of colour and disappears. The green splendour of Spring degenerates into lushness, the leaves are tarnished with dust, but the flaming reds and yellows, the pale gold, the rose colour, the splendid purple-red of these trees will swirl with the wind, will have one splendid moment of sailing in the blueness of the sky, one moment of motion beyond anything that a leaf could dream of. The forests will stand bare, beautiful in bareness, against the sky. They will not be dead, they will not be even asleep heavily. They will be dreaming of Springtime, furtively pushing buds into symmetry, steadying the sap in their veins for the riot of Spring. I have seen this country for the first time at an austere season. But it would always be austere because it is passionate. The earth burns with a colour of orange, with the colour of red, burns with a purple blackness, shows its ribs of stone, coloured, blanched, carved into fantasy. Its trees branch out with a delicate precision. Its cypress trees spring like the flame. I love those cypress trees. In them the very passion of the earth springs upward, lifting itself with a song.

This country is a lioness, tawny, alert, passionate, austere, a beautiful, splendid—perhaps terrible—thing!

—From *The Flowering Dusk*

LIFE IS not life at all without delight.—*Patmore*

REMEMBER THIS,—that very little is needed to make a happy life.—*Marcus Aurelius*

THE RATIONAL world is my friend, because I am a friend of its happiness. —*Paine*

THE OFFICE OF GOVERNMENT is not to confer happiness, but to give men opportunity to work out happiness for themselves.—*Channing*

TRUE HAPPINESS consists not in the multitude of friends, but in the worth and choice.—*Jonson*

HAPPINESS, eternal or temporal, is not the reward that mankind seeks. Happinesses are but his wayside companions. His soul is in the journey and in the struggle.—*Stevenson*

HAPPINESS comes from striving—doing—loving—achieving—conquering— always something positive and forceful.—*David Starr Jordan*

HAPPINESS ITSELF is sufficient excuse. Beautiful things are right and true; so beautiful actions are those pleasing to the gods. Wise men have an inward sense of what is beautiful, and the highest wisdom is to trust this intuition and be guided by it. The answer to the last appeal of what is right lies within a man's own breast. Trust thyself.—*Aristotle*

TO WORSHIP, to comprehend, to receive, to feel, to give, to act: this is our law, our duty, our happiness, our heaven.—*Amiel*

WITH A FEW FLOWERS in my garden, half a dozen pictures and some books, I live without envy.—*Lope de Vega*

NO ONE TRULY knows happiness who has not suffered, and the redeemed are happier than the elect.—*Amiel*

TIME ripens all things. No man is born wise.—*Cervantes*

TO HAPPINESS

To BE of use in the world is the only way to
be happy.—*Hans Christian Andersen*

SWEET are the thoughts that savour of content; the quiet
mind is richer than a crown.—*Robert Greene*

WE ARE HERE to help each other, to try to make each other happy.
—*Saying of the Polar Eskimos*

WE ARE ALL of us fellow-passengers on the same planet and we are all of us
equally responsible for the happiness and the well-being of the world in
which we happen to live.—*Hendrik Willem van Loon*

HAPPINESS in this world, when it comes, comes incidentally. Make it the
object of pursuit, and it leads us a wild-goose chase, and is never attained.
Follow some other object, and very possibly we may find that we have caught
happiness without dreaming of it.—*Hawthorne*

TRUTH is the beginning of every good thing, both in heaven and on earth;
and he who would be blessed and happy should be from the first a partaker
of the truth, that he may live a true man as long as possible, for then he can
be trusted.—*Plato*

IN ORDER THAT people may be happy in their work, these three things are
needed: They must be fit for it: They must not do too much of it: And they
must have a sense of success in it.—*Ruskin*

WHO is the happiest of men? He who values the merits of others, and in their
pleasure takes joy, even as though it were his own.—*Goethe*

HAPPINESS DEPENDS, as Nature shows, less on exterior things
than most suppose.—*Cowper*

ONE INCH OF JOY surmounts of grief a span,
Because to laugh is proper to the man.—*Rabelais*

PRAYER
LOUIS UNTERMEYER

God, though this life is but a wraith,
  Although we know not what we use,
Although we grope with little faith,
  Give me the heart to fight—and lose.

Ever insurgent let me be,
  Make me more daring than devout;
From sleek contentment keep me free,
  And fill me with a buoyant doubt.

Open my eyes to visions girt
  With beauty, and with wonder lit—
But let me always see the dirt,

And all that spawn and die in it.

Open my ears to music; let
  Me thrill with Spring's first flutes and
    drums—
But never let me dare forget
  The bitter ballads of the slums.

From compromise and things half-done
  Keep me, with stern and stubborn
    pride;
And when, at last, the fight is won,
  God, keep me still unsatisfied.

CALIBAN IN THE COAL MINES
LOUIS UNTERMEYER

God, we don't like to complain
  We know that the mine is no lark—
But—there's the pools from the rain;
  But—there's the cold and the dark.

God, You don't know what it is—
  You, in Your well-lighted sky—
Watching the meteors whizz;
  Warm, with the sun always by.

God, if You had but the moon
  Stuck in Your cap for a lamp,
Even You'd tire of it soon,
  Down in the dark and the damp.

Nothing but blackness above
  And nothing that moves but the
  cars . . .
God, if You wish for our love,
  Fling us a handful of stars!

From LINES WRITTEN A FEW MILES ABOVE TINTERN ABBEY
WILLIAM WORDSWORTH

       For I have learned
To look on nature, not as in the hour
Of thoughtless youth, but hearing often-
  times
The still, sad music of humanity,
Nor harsh nor grating, though of ample
  power
To chasten and subdue. And I have felt
A presence that disturbs me with the
  joy
Of elevated thoughts; a sense sublime
Of something far more deeply inter-
  fused,
Whose dwelling is the light of setting
  suns,
And the round ocean and the living air,
And the blue sky, and in the mind of
  man;
A motion and a spirit that impels
All thinking things, all objects of all
  thought,
And rolls through all things. Therefore
  am I still
A lover of the meadows and the woods
And mountains; and of all that we be-
  hold
From this green earth.

THIS MOUNTAIN IS MY PROPERTY ALONE
LIONEL WIGGAM

This mountain is my property alone:
A hard expanse of cocklebur and pines,
A lace of grass subsiding into stone,
And overhead a purple fret of vines.

These are my woods, and this my per-
    sonal scene:
Where fallen underfoot the balsam
    boughs
And partridge-feathers pattern each
    ravine,
And where the hornet plots his paper
    house.

For no man knows this place so well
    as I;
Not one has seen this roof of branches
    torn

By sun, or watched the overhanging sky
Scraped by a wing as sharply as a thorn.

This place is mine, where evening
    breeds alarm:
A thin disquiet sharpened with despair,
Where dusk approaches like a locust-
    swarm
Spreading its copper rumor down the
    air.

From here I came, and here I must
    return,
A rightful habitant to claim his own.
As any sharp-eyed creature's in the fern,
This mountain is my property alone.

TO A SKYLARK
WILLIAM WORDSWORTH

Ethereal minstrel! pilgrim of the sky!
Dost thou despise the earth where cares
    abound?
Or, while the wings aspire, are heart
    and eye
Both with thy nest upon the dewy
    ground?
Thy nest which thou canst drop into
    at will,
Those quivering wings composed, that
    music still!

Leave to the nightingale her shady
    wood;
A privacy of glorious light is thine;
Whence thou dost pour upon the world
    a flood
Of harmony, with instinct more divine;
Type of the wise who soar, but never
    roam;
True to the kindred points of Heaven
    and Home!

LAST SONNET
JOHN KEATS

Bright star! would I were steadfast as
    thou art—
Not in lone splendor hung aloft the
    night,
And watching, with eternal lids apart,
Like Nature's patient sleepless Eremite,
The moving waters at their priestlike
    task
Of pure ablution round Earth's human
    shores,
Or grazing on the new soft fallen mask
Of snow upon the mountains and the
    moors—
No—yet still steadfast, still unchange-
    able,
Pillowed upon my fair love's ripening
    breast,
To feel forever its soft fall and swell,
Awake forever in a sweet unrest,
Still, still to hear her tender-taken
    breath,
And so live ever—or else swoon to death.

The Night of the Storm

By ZONA GALE

*A*T ONE MINUTE the prairie had been empty and white under a low gray sky. At the next minute the air was filled with fine, pelting snow which drove with fury and whirled in a biting wind.

On the main road across the Lewiston Open, a man came riding. He was galloping with the wind, yet in all his haste he stopped at every one of the few scattered houses on the plain and pounded on the door. The women, already busy at supper, answered the summons wondering, or the men came running from stables and cowsheds, and to these the horseman cried his message, and was off before the gaping folk could stay him with questions.

"Stephen Mine's little girl's lost. She's been gone an hour. 'Nother searchin' party starts as soon's enough get to Stephen's. Take your lanterns and some rope."

With that he was off—Jake Mullet, on his way to Pillsbury's store in Lewiston to ring for the bucket brigade and to telephone to the few in the neighborhood who had telephones.

'Hannah Mine's girl,' said the women. 'Which one? Oh, not the baby. It can't be the baby!'

It went up like one cry, all over the Open, while the men made ready to leave and brought rope, and the women filled the lanterns. More than one woman girt her skirts about her and set forth with her man, certain that Hannah Mine needed comforting and, it might be, serving, and unable to wait at home in any case. But when they reached Mine's little house, they found that Hannah had gone with the first searching party, and their glances sweeping the three children huddled by the fire told the truth. The lost child was Hannah Mine's baby. Somewhere out in that storm, already for more than an hour, was Stephen and Hannah Mine's baby, three-year-old Lissa.

Meanwhile, Jake Mullet was riding. And when he had done what he could in Lewiston, he took the lower road back, and now he was facing the storm, and its fury was growing with the darkness. When the first farmhouse light showed through the thick white, Jake groaned. She was so little—if night came, or if in two hours they had not found her, who could hope that they would be in time?

He continued to call at the little houses and to shout his message to any whom he met lumbering through the snow. But when he came to one house, on the forty adjoining Stephen's forty, he did not stop.

'No use wastin' breath on Waldo Rowan,' he thought, and galloped on. He crossed the cut—a queer, ragged gap in the plain, shallow and rock-filled—and saw a figure fighting its way on foot.

'Turn back to Mine's!' Jake shouted. 'His little girl's lost. She's—'

Then he stopped. Here was Waldo Rowan himself, who had not spoken to Stephen and Hannah for ten years, as all the Open knew.

'They wouldn't have any help!' Waldo flung back.

Jake pounded on, carrying coils of rope for the searchers, who were now to spread in a great circle, threading the rope, and so come drawing in. He gave not another thought to the only one on the Open who had failed to answer his appeal. Everybody was used to this feud between Mine and Waldo. Stephen would have done the same if it had been Waldo whose child was lost. But Waldo had no children to lose. In the days when he and Stephen were friends they had loved the same woman, and Stephen had won her, Waldo said, through a lie. She and Stephen had raised their family and seemed happy. Waldo married a girl of the village who had died, with their two-year-old baby, only a year ago. Since then he lived alone, and he was dead to Stephen, as Stephen was to him.

At his own line fence Waldo Rowan left the road and plunged into a grove of dwarf oak and on into a denser stretch of wood. It was evident that this storm was to continue for at least twenty-four hours, and he wanted a look at his traps. He found some empty, one dragged away, and in one something pitiful and struggling helplessly, and moaning, which he dispatched and dropped in his bag. And as he did so he thought, as he had thought before: 'Blowed if I wouldn't druther live on corn bread than do it. Blowed if I never set another trap.'

He plunged down into the cut, which was the short way to his cabin. There was another reason for haste besides the weather. He had been out all day, and creeping in his veins came the giddiness and tremor which precede a chill; and with them, too, that curious lightness of head, of body, which presages a possible illness. He must get indoors, build a great fire, heat his kettle of soup, wrap up warmly, and sleep it off.

'I'd ought to had the doctor give me something when I met him this noon,' Waldo thought. 'What was't he said? He was going sixteen mile north. He won't be back to-night. I guess I can mope it out.'

The snow was of a deceiving softness and piled on the rocks of the cut as if billows of foam had rolled in, lapped, and now lay quiet. Here the wind roared through the northeast, catching the tops of the white pines and making a furious singing. And on that wind Waldo heard a cry.

He heard it for a little before he knew that he heard it—with that strange inner ear which catches sound too light to be less delicately measured. An animal, or a way of the wind, he might have called it and thought no more; but when he was deep in the cut, and before he began the rough ascent, abruptly this cry rose on a single, piercing note, and fell again to its quiet pulsing. He listened.

Still uncertain what he had heard, he turned north and kept along the cut, at every few steps stopping to turn his head to the wind. He was ready to face back, and then it came again. There was no mistaking now, and he broke into a run.

For all his running, he made slow progress, for there was no trail up the bottom of the cut, and the rocks were rough and huddled. He would have climbed the side and followed the trail on the west of the rim, but he had an instinct that whatever he sought cried from the bottom of the cut. He dared not halloo, for fear if this were, say, a child, he should frighten it. His impulse was to run back to the road and wait for the next passer to help him, but he dared not do that lest the faint cry be swallowed in a ruck of snow and darkness. He kept on, stumbling, scrambling over rocks waist-high. Once the faint voice ceased for so long that he told himself that he had imagined the whole. Then it came again; there was now no mistaking what it was. Then it was silent until he heard it as a deep, sobbing breath behind him, and he had passed it.

He turned, sought on his hands and knees, called softly, whistled, as might one to a little dog. A faint, wailing cry came from the slope just above him. He clambered toward it, his arms sweeping an arc; his hands brushed something yielding, and he was rewarded by a little scream of terror. He gathered the child into his arms.

She was very little and light. As soon as she felt herself on his breast, she yielded to him and snuggled weakly, like a spent puppy. This was an attitude that she knew, and she lay quiet, occasionally drawing a long, sobbing breath. She was cloaked and hooded, but Waldo, feeling for her hands, found them ice-cold, and one was bare. He unwound the scarf from his neck and wrapped her. All the time, the fact that it was Stephen Mine's child was barely in his consciousness. It was merely a child, terribly near freezing, terribly near death.

To retrace his steps over the rocks with her in his arms was another thing from forcing his own progress. Now he must move slowly and feel each step; he must go round the rock piles now, and not over them. He must get back to the point where the trail crossed the cut and ascended to his cabin. And now the darkness had almost fallen; the wind had its way with him, his neck was bared to the blowing snow, he was cutting his shoes on jagged points and edges of the rocks. When at last he found the up trail, made the ascent of the side, and traversed the distance to his cabin, he was shivering and chattering and hardly able to stand.

The cabin was cold, but he had left the fire ready to light. He laid the child on a quilt before the leaping blaze, untied her hood, and chafed her little hands. She was terribly cold and in a perilous drowsiness. Waldo brought in his kettle of soup, hung it on the crane, dipped a little in a tin cup, and held it in the blaze. When he had forced the warmed liquid between her lips, he undressed her feet and rubbed them with snow. Her cheeks and fingers were rosy, but he feared for the small white feet.

'How'll I get word to Stephen?' he thought, and in that area in which his sick brain was working there was no thought of anything wrong between Stephen and him. All that had dropped away.

'Hannah's little girl,' he thought once, and touched her hair wonderingly. He had never seen any of Hannah's children. As he sat there beside the child, hearing her soft breathing, talking to her a little in awkward repetitions, nothing was in his mind save deep thankfulness that he had found her. Occasionally he would rouse her, and she would give her sleepy smile and close her eyes again. Once or twice she yawned, and he was enchanted by the little tasting curl of her lips before she finally closed them.

His chill had now settled upon the man so that he was shaking. He drank a cupful of the soup, and said that it would have to be he who would go to tell Stephen that he had found her. But he could not leave her there alone, and he saw that when she was thoroughly warmed he must wrap her up and take her home. That half mile would not matter to him now—only he must make it soon, soon, before he grew worse. When the baby was warm and rested they would go.

He sat down in his chair before the hot fire; the strong soup ran in his blood, his weariness preyed upon him, his head sank upon his breast.

He was wakened by a sound which at first he thought came from without—a calling and a trampling. Abruptly this impression changed, and his eyes went to the child in terror. It was she—it was her breathing. That rough, rattling sound was in her little throat, and in a moment Waldo knew. His two years of fatherhood were there to serve him, and he sprang up in that terror which all watchers upon children know.

In the same instant the noise which he had fancied without was sharpened and defined. It was as he had thought

182

—a trampling of feet. He did not see the face outside the cabin window, but there was a leap of feet on to his threshold and Jake Mullet was there, looking like a snow man. And he whirled and shouted:

'Stephen! Here—she's here!'

There was a rush of cold air across the floor, and Waldo sprang before the child and lifted the quilt to cover her. At the same instant Stephen Mine leaped into the room.

'Here!' he cried out in a terrible voice. 'Here!'

He strode forward, tore the quilt from Waldo's hand, and looked. The door filled with faces with figures crusted with snow, and the cruel night air swept in and possessed the cabin. Waldo turned to the throng at the door and shook both fists in the air.

'Get in or get out!' he shouted. 'Don't leave the door open on her. She's sick!'

They crowded into the room, stamping and breathing loudly, and made way for a woman who came staggering in and threw herself beside the child. It was Hannah Mine, and she dared not touch the baby with her own stiff hands and in her wet garments. She only crouched beside her, and burst into terrible dry sobs. The cabin door was sharply shut, and then the thirty or more men and women who had crowded into the room became conscious of its fearful tension.

Stephen Mine stood with his child at his feet, and he lifted his head and looked at Waldo. Stephen was a huge man, black and thick. Waldo, small and shaken by his chill, began to tell how all this had come about.

'In the cut, Stephen,' he said, 'about a quarter mile down the cut, toward Rightsey's. I'd been to look at my traps, and I heard her cry. She was in the bottom of the cut. I found her. I've rubbed snow on her feet—but I'm afraid—'

Stephen Mine came close to Waldo and looked down at him.

'You expect I'm going to believe that?' he said.

The silence in the room was instant and terrifying.

Waldo lifted his face. The matted hair was low on his forehead; he brushed it aside and his clear eyes met Stephen's; but his shaking hands and his shaking voice gave doubt to his hearers.

'Stephen, I swear—' he began, and Stephen laughed.

'I seen you sneaking past my place twice to-day,' he said. 'I know you. You found a way to get even at last, and you took it, you dog.'

He stooped to the woman.

'Wrap her up, Hannah,' he said.

Waldo put out his trembling hands.

'Stephen!' he cried. 'The child's sick —she's done. You mustn't take her out. Stay here—you're all more than welcome—and keep care of her. I've got what she needs. Don't take her out into this.'

'How do I know,' said Stephen Mine, 'what it is you mean to give her? Hannah, wrap her up.'

The woman, still breathing heavily, put her hand on her husband's knee.

'No, no, Stephen,' she said. 'He's right. Can't you hear her breathe? Let her stay here—'

'So you and him can take care of her while I go for the doctor—is that it?' he sneered.

She seemed not to hear him.

'It's croup, Stephen,' she said. 'You can't take her out—' Stephen shook her off impatiently.

'I'll get out—I'll go for the doctor!' Waldo cried. 'And I'll keep away. But you and Hannah stay with her, here.'

'Wrap her up!' said Stephen Mine.

Two or three of the neighbor women came forward now, protesting, and Jake Mullet cried out:

'Look here, Mine. This ain't no time to remember old scores. You got the kid to think of.'

'Wrap her up!' said Stephen Mine.

'Well, wait till one of us gets some-wheres for a team,' cried one of the men.

'Stephen—leave her here! I can wring out the hot cloths till the doctor comes—'

'I've—I've got the stuff here that was my baby's,' Waldo chattered, but now they could hardly understand him.

'Wrap her up!' said Stephen Mine, and strode to the door.

The others gave way before him, and began to file out. Heavily Hannah Mine began drawing on the child's wraps, the sobs breaking through again. Some of the women gave of their own wraps, and, seeing that one little mitten was missing, they put two or three pairs on the still inert hands.

'You carry her.' said Jake Mullet to Stephen, 'and I'll go to Lewiston for the doctor.'

'I'll carry her—yes,' said Stephen Mine. 'And then I'll go up yonder and telephone for the doctor. I'll not trouble any of you that'd have me leave her here.'

He took the child from the mother and went out the door.

'He's beside himself,' they whispered, and they understood that it was the disease of anger, or he would never have let them go away from their task of that night without so much as a word of thanks. Some lingered for a word with Waldo and would have heard more of his adventure, but all that he could say was, 'In the cut,' and again and again, 'In the cut—all alone.' They saw that he was a sick man, and they left him with kindly words of advice, and even —though these folk are chary of expression—an outstretched hand or two. But there were some who went out muttering a half-acceptance of Stephen's implication.

Alone, Waldo began moving about the cabin, mechanically folding the quilt on which the child had lain, sweeping away the snow where the trampling feet had been, carrying the kettle back to its place in the lean-to. He felt sore and ill and weak. He felt stunned, as if he had been flung against some great impalpable thing which had struck back at him with living hands. He could no longer save a child from death and be believed. He had turned to evil in Stephen's eyes, so that what he did that was good seemed of evil. The black wall of the hate which he and Stephen had built was round them, and beyond lay now more hate and evil, born of this night.

Waldo began to think, 'If the child should die it would serve Stephen right' —but he could not finish that thought.

He pictured that slow fight through the snow, the child's breathing in the thick, cold air, the heart of the mother following, the neighbors falling off one by one at their own doors and their own waiting firesides. Then Stephen would leave the child with the mother while he went to the upper road for the doctor. Would he be in time? What if the doctor were out—and abruptly, through the blur of images in his mind, came the cheery face of the doctor, whom he had met on the road that noon, 'driving sixteen miles north.' When Waldo thought of that, it was as if his heart were a sword and smote him.

He ran to a little chest on a shelf and fumbled among its bottles. There it was, tightly corked, just as they had used it once when their baby had had such an illness; and they were alone with her, and had pulled her through. What if Hannah happened to have nothing?

He stood staring at the bottle. Then he began drawing on his mittens and his cap. His coat he had not had off the whole time. His scarf had been bundled up and carried away with the child. He let himself out into the storm.

His chill was passing and was succeeded by the lightheadedness and the imperfect correlation of the first stages of fever. To his fancy, wavering out and seizing upon any figment, it was as if, behind the invisible drive of the snow, there were a glow of pale light. Now right, now left it shone, as if at the back of his eyes; and he turned his head from side to side to find it. But there were only the cutting volleys of the snow in his face; and everywhere the siege of the wind. Then, as he fared on in the thick, impeding drifts, it was again as if he were beating toward and upon that great dark wall; and he kept saying to himself crazily that this was the wall that he and Stephen had raised, and that he must somehow get through it—beat it down, and get to the child to save her. Yet if he broke down the wall something would rush upon him—Stephen's hatred, Stephen's hatred! And his own hatred for Stephen, for there was rage in his heart when he remembered the man's look and the man's word. But of these he did not think—he thought only of the child, and he set his teeth and charged at the wall of darkness, and would not wonder what lay beyond.

He went throught the storm to Stephen's house, in a maze of darkness and light.

Toward eight o'clock Stephen came struggling back from the house on the upper road. He had heard what Waldo had already heard, of the doctor driving sixteen miles north. And when he called Oxnard, his heart sinking at the thought of the eighteen miles which lay between, there was a delay which snapped his courage—and then the word that the wires must be down, for Oxnard did not answer. He could only leave his message with Central, for to drive the distance on such a night would mean to return too late.

Stephen came down from the upper road, and his strength and his pride were gone. Abruptly now he was empty of anger, empty of malice, empty of all

save his terrible despair. It was strange to see the seat and the pride shrivel before the terrible fact that the baby might pay the price. 'If she dies,' he had heard Jake Mullet say, 'we'll all know who killed her.'

'O God! O God!' Stephen Mine said.

Abruptly, in the midst of the storm, he seemed to feel a lull, a silence. He went on.

It was before his gate that he stumbled over something yielding and mounded in the road. He stooped, touched the man, and with that which now at last is no decision, but merely the second nature of the race, he got him into his arms and to his own door.

At the sound Hannah flung the door open, and from the dark and wind and snow Stephen staggered across the threshold with Waldo in his arms.

Stephen looked down at him as he would have looked at any other man.

'How is she?' was all that his lips formed.

'Alive,' said Hannah Mine.

Waldo opened his eyes, and his snow-crusted mittens tried to find its way to his pocket.

'I brought something,' he said. 'We had it left; give it to her—'

At midnight, when the message having reached him at last, the doctor came, Stephen met him with a smile. 'She's safe,' he said. 'She's sleeping. But there's a man here—a friend of ours —sick and done for. We got him into bed. Come and have a look at him."

Up some measureless corridor Waldo at last struggled, when many days had passed. And at its far end it seemed to him that Stephen's face was waiting. That was queer, because it had been years since Stephen had waited for him. Yet there he was, only behind him was still that dead wall, which neither of them could pass, and beyond it lay that old hatred and bitterness, accumulated through the years. And then there was the child—he must find the child.

185

One day he opened his eyes on that corridor and saw it clear. A homely room, now his own, about which Stephen and Hannah were moving, and a neighbor in homely talk beside the stove.

'Honestly, you'll have to move out to make room for the truck they've brought him. The whole Open has lugged somethin' here.'

And Stephen's voice—surely Stephen's voice was saying:

'That's all right; he deserved it.'

And again the neighbor's voice:

'Well, I'll aways be proud it was my husband found Lissa's little red mitten down the cut.'

Then a child came to hang in the doorway, and to stare at the bed where Waldo was lying; and when she saw his eyes looking at her she smiled and ran away—Stephen's child, safe and well and smiling.

Waldo lay still. But in his heart there was a certain singing. And it was as if he had stood close to that dead wall of hatred which he had feared, but its door had swung open, and lo! there was nothing there.

❧ ❧ ❧

WHEN TO THE SESSIONS OF SWEET SILENT THOUGHT

WILLIAM SHAKESPEARE

When to the sessions of sweet silent thought
I summon up remembrance of things past,
I sigh the lack of many a thing I sought,
And with old woes new wail my dear time's waste.
Then can I drown an eye, unused to flow,
For precious friends hid in death's dateless night,
And weep afresh love's long since cancelled woe,
And moan the expense of many a vanished sight.
Then can I grieve at grievances foregone,
And heavily from woe to woe tell o'er
The sad account of fore-bemoanéd moan,
Which I now pay, as if not paid before;
But if the while I think on thee, dear friend,
All losses are restored and sorrows end.

* * *

❧ WHEN A HUMAN SOUL draws its first furrow straight, the rest will surely follow. Henceforth your existence becomes ceaseless activity. The universe belongs to him who wills, who knows, who prays, but he must will, he must know, he must pray. In a word, he must possess force, wisdom and faith. Be conquerors on earth, your convictions will be changed to certainties.—*Balzac*

❧ IF A MAN does not make new acquaintances as he advances through life, he will soon find himself alone. A man, sir, must keep his friendships in constant repair.

—*Johnson*

IF MUSIC BE THE FOOD OF LOVE
WILLIAM SHAKESPEARE

If music be the food of love, play on;
Give me excess of it, that, surfeiting,
The appetite may sicken, and so die.
That strain again! it had a dying fall:
O! it came o'er my ear like the sweet sound
That breathes upon a bank of violets,
Stealing and giving odour. Enough! no more:
'Tis not so sweet now as it was before.
O spirit of love! how quick and fresh art thou,
That, notwithstanding thy capacity
Receiveth as the sea, nought enters there,
Of what validity and pitch soe'er,
But falls into abatement and low price,
Even in a minute: so full of shapes is fancy,
That it alone is high fantastical.

—From *Twelfth Night*

FOR INSPIRATION
MICHELANGELO
[Translated By WILLIAM WORDSWORTH]

The prayers I make will then be sweet indeed,
  If Thou the spirit give by which I pray;
  My unassisted heart is barren clay,
Which of its native self can nothing feed;
Of good and pious works Thou art the seed
  Which quickens where Thou say'st it may;
  Unless Thou show us then Thine own true way,
No man can find it! Father, Thou must lead!
Do Thou, then, breathe those thoughts into my mind
  By which such virtue may in me be bred
  That in Thy holy footsteps I may tread:
The fetters of my tongue do Thou unbind,
  That I may have the power to sing of Thee
  And sound Thy praises everlastingly.

*   *   *

GIVE ME BEAUTY in the inward soul; and may the outward and inward
man be as one. May I reckon the wise to be the wealthy, and may I have
such a quantity of gold as none but the temperate can carry.   —*Socrates*

❧ THE CONTINUITY of life is never broken; the river flows onward and is lost to our sight; but under its new horizon it carries the same waters which it gathered under ours, and its unseen valleys are made glad by the offerings which are borne down to them from the past,—flowers, perchance, the germs of which its own waves had planted on the banks of Time.   —*Whittier*

* * *

A COUNTRY HOME
By HENRY W. GRADY

I VISITED a country home: a modest, quiet house sheltered by great trees and set in a circle of field and meadow, gracious with the promise of harvest. Barns and cribs were filled, and the old smokehouse odorous with treasure; the fragrance of pink and hollyhock mingling with the aroma of garden and orchard, and resonant with the hum of bees and the poultry's busy clucking; inside the house, thrift, comfort, and that cleanliness that is next to godliness; the restful beds, the open fireplace, the books and papers, and the old clock that had held its steadfast pace amid the frolic of weddings, that had welcomed in steady measure the new-born babes of the family, and kept company with the watchers of the sick-bed, and had ticked the solemn requiem of the dead; and the well-worn Bible that, thumbed by fingers long since stilled, and blurred with tears of eyes long since closed, held the simple annals of the family, and the heart and conscience of the home.

BOOKS
By RALPH WALDO EMERSON

CONSIDER what you have in the smallest chosen library. A company of the wisest and wittiest men that could be picked out of all civil countries, in a thousand years, have set in best order the results of their learning and wisdom. The men themselves were hid and inaccessible, solitary, impatient of interruption, fenced by etiquette; but the thought which they did not uncover to their bosom friend is here written out in transparent words to us, the strangers of another age.

BEAUTIFUL THOUGHTS

THE THOUGHT that is beautiful is the thought to cherish. The word that is beautiful is worthy to endure. The act that is beautiful is eternally and always true and right. Only beware that your appreciation of beauty is just and true; and to that end, I urge you to live intimately with beauty of the highest type, until it has become a part of you, until you have within you that fineness, that order, that calm, which puts you in tune with the finest things of the universe, and which links you with that spirit that is the enduring life of the world.   —*Bertha Bailey*

* * *

❧ IF YOU HAVE KNOWN how to compose your life, you have accomplished a great deal more than the man who knows how to compose a book. Have you been able to take your stride? You have done more than the man who has taken cities and empires. The great and glorious masterpiece of man is to live to the point. All other things—to reign, to hoard, to build—are, at most, but inconsiderate props and appendages.   —*Montaigne*

HILLS
Arthur Guiterman

I never loved your plains,
  Your gentle valleys,
Your drowsy country lanes
  And pleached alleys.

I want my hills—the trail
  That scorns the hollow—
Up, up the ragged shale
  Where few will follow.

Up, over wooded crest,
  And mossy boulder,
With strong thigh, heaving chest,
  And swinging shoulder.

So let me hold my way,
  By nothing halted,
Until, at close of day,
  I stand exalted.

High on my hills of dream—
  Dear hills that know me!
And then how fair will seem
  The land below me!

How pure, at vesper-time
  The far bells chiming!
God, give me hills to climb
  And strength for climbing!

VESTIGIA
Bliss Carman

I took a day to search for God,
And found Him not. But as I trod
By rocky ledge, through woods
    untamed,
I saw His footprint in the sod.

Then suddenly, all unaware,
Far off in the deep shadows, where
A solitary hermit thrush
Sang through the holy twilight hush—
I heard His voice upon the air.

And even as I marvelled how
God gives us Heaven here and now,
In a stir of wind that hardly shook
The poplar leaves beside the brook—
His hand was light upon my brow.

At last with evening as I turned
Homeward, and thought what I had
    learned
And all that there was still to probe—
I caught the glory of His robe
Where the last fires of sunset burned.

Back to the world with quickening start
I looked and longed for any part
In making saving Beauty be.
And from that kindling ecstasy
I knew God dwelt within my heart.

From *CROSS CREEK*
By Marjorie Kinnan Rawlings

Who owns Cross Creek? The red-birds, I think, more than I, for they will have their nests even in the face of delinquent mortgages. And after I am dead, who am childless, the human ownership of grove and field and hummock is hypothetical. But a long line of red-birds and whippoorwills and blue-jays and ground doves will descend from the present owners of nests in the orange trees, and their claim will be less subject to dispute than that of any human heirs. Houses are individual and can be owned, like nests, and fought for. But what of the land? It seems to me that the earth may be borrowed but not bought. It may be used, but not owned. It gives itself in response to love and tending, offers its seasonal flowering and fruiting. But we are tenants and not possessors, lovers and not masters. Cross Creek belongs to the wind and the rain, to the sun and the seasons, to the cosmic secrecy of seed, and beyond all, to time.

THE BIRD LET LOOSE
THOMAS MOORE

The bird let loose in eastern skies,
  When hastening fondly home,
Ne'er stoops to earth her wing, nor flies
  Where idle warblers roam;
But high she shoots through air and
    light,
  Above all low delay,
Where nothing earthly bounds her
    flight,
  Nor shadow dims her way.

So grant me, God, from every care
  And stain of passion free,
Aloft, through Virtue's purer air,
  To hold my course to thee!
No sin to cloud, no lure to stay
  My soul, as home she springs;—
Thy sunshine on her joyful way,
  Thy freedom in her wings!

IT IS A BEAUTEOUS EVENING, CALM AND FREE
WILLIAM WORDSWORTH

It is a beauteous evening, calm and free.
The holy time is quiet as a Nun
Breathless with adoration; the broad
    sun
Is sinking down in its tranquility;
The gentleness of heaven broods o'er
    the sea;
Listen! the mighty Being is awake,
And doth with his eternal motion make
A sound like thunder—everlastingly.

Dear Child! dear Girl! that walkest with
    me here,
If thou appear untouched by solemn
    thought,
Thy nature is not therefore less divine;
Thou liest in Abraham's bosom all the
    year,
And worship'st at the Temple's inner
    shrine,
God being with thee when we know it
    not.

THERE IS NO FRIEND LIKE AN OLD FRIEND
OLIVER WENDELL HOLMES

There is no friend like an old friend
  Who has shared our morning days,
No greeting like his welcome,
  No homage like his praise.

THE FUTURE LIFE
By VICTOR HUGO

I FEEL within me the future life. I am like a forest that has once been razed; the new shoots are stronger and brisker. I shall most certainly rise toward the heavens. The sun's rays bathe my head. The earth gives to me its generous sap, but the heavens illuminate me with the reflection of—of worlds unknown.

Some say the soul results merely from bodily powers. Why, then, does my soul become brighter when my bodily powers begin to waste away? Winter is above me, but eternal spring is within my heart. I inhale even now the fragrance of lilacs, violets, and roses just as I did when I was twenty.

The nearer my approach to the end, the plainer is the sound of immortal symphonies of worlds which invite me. It is wonderful, yet simple. It is a fairy tale; it is history.

For half a century I have been translating my thoughts into prose and verse; history, philosophy, drama, romance, tradition, satire, ode, and song; all of these have I tried. But I feel that I haven't given utterance to the thousandth part of what lies within me. When I go to the grave I can say as others have said, "My day's work is done." But I cannot say, "My life is done." My day's work will recommence the next morning. The tomb is not a blind alley; it is a thoroughfare. It closes upon the twilight, but opens upon the dawn.

BEAUTY

John Greenleaf Whittier

The Beauty which old Greece or Rome
Sung, painted, wrought, lies close at
    home;
  We need but eye and ear
In all our daily walks to trace
The outlines of incarnate grace,
  The hymns of gods to hear!

THE PROFESSION OF THE LAW

By Justice Oliver Wendell Holmes, Jr.

[From a lecture to Harvard students, 1886]

No MAN has earned the right to intellectual ambition until he has learned to lay his course by a star which he has never seen,—to dig by the divining rod for springs which he may never reach. In saying this, I point to that which will make your study heroic. For I say to you in all sadness of conviction, that to think great thoughts you must be heroes as well as idealists. Only when you have worked alone,—when you have felt around you a black gulf of solitude more isolating than that which surrounds a dying man, and in hope and in despair have trusted to your own unshaken will,—then only will you have achieved. Thus only can you gain the secret isolated joy of the thinker, who knows that, a hundred years after he is dead and forgotten, men who never heard of him will be moving to the measure of his thought,—the subtle rapture of a postponed power, which the world knows not because it has no external trappings, but which to its prophetic vision is more real than that which commands an army. And if this joy cannot be yours, still it is only thus that you can know that you have done what it lay in you to do,—can say that you have lived, and be ready for the end.

EPITAPH TO A DOG

Sir William Watson

His friends he loved. His fellest earthly
  foes—
  Cats—I believe he did but feign to
  hate.
My hand will miss the insinuated nose,
  Mine eyes that tail that wagged contempt at Fate.

MY SYMPHONY

By William Henry Channing

To LIVE CONTENT with small means; to seek elegance rather than luxury; and refinement rather than fashion; to be worthy, not respectable; and wealthy, not rich; to study hard, think quietly, talk gently, act frankly; to listen to stars and birds, to babes and sages, with open heart; to bear all cheerfully, do all bravely, await occasion, hurry never; in a word, to let the spiritual, unbidden and unconscious grow up through the common. This is to be my symphony.

LOUIS PASTEUR ADDRESSES THE FRENCH ACADEMY

You YOUNG MEN—doctors and scientists of the future—do not let yourselves be tainted by a barren skepticism, nor discouraged by the sadness of certain hours that creep over nations. Do not become angry at your opponents, for no scientific theory has ever been accepted without opposition. Live in the serene peace of libraries and laboratories. Say to yourself first: "What have I done for my instruction?" and as you gradually advance: "What am I accomplishing?" until the time comes when you may have the immense happiness of thinking that you have contributed in some way to the welfare and progress of mankind.

191

THE ROAD OF THE LOVING HEART

When Robert Louis Stevenson died, the following anonymous tribute was written:

"REMEMBERING the great love of his highness, Tusitala, and his loving care when we were in prison and sore distressed, we have prepared him an enduring present, this road which we have dug for ever."

In a far-off island, thousands of miles from the mainland, and unconnected with the world by cable, stands this inscription. It was set up at the corner of a new road, cut through a tropical jungle, and bears at its head the title of this article, signed by the names of ten prominent chiefs. This is the story of the road, and why it was built:

A number of years ago a Scotchman, broken in health and expecting an early death, sought out this lonely spot, because here the climate was favorable to the disease from which he suffered. He settled here for what remained to him of life.

He bought an estate of several hundred acres, and threw himself earnestly into the life of the natives of the island. There was great division among the many chiefs, and prolonged warfare. Very soon the chiefs found that this alien from a strange land was their best friend. They began coming to him for counsel, and invited him to their most important conferences.

Though he did not bear that name, he became a missionary to them. He was their hero, and they loved and trusted him because he tried to lead them aright. They had never had such a friend. And so it came about that when the wars ceased, the chiefs of both sides called him by a name of their own, and made him one of their own number, thus conferring upon him the highest honour within their power.

But many of the chiefs were still in prison, because of their political views or deeds, and in constant danger of be-ing put to death. Their sole friend was the Scotchman, whom they called Tusitala. He visited them, comforted them, repeated passages from the history of Christ to them, and busied himself incessantly to effect their release.

At length he obtained their freedom, and then, glowing with gratitude, in despite of age, decrepitude, and loss of strength, they started directly for the estate of their benefactor, and there, in the terrible heat, they laboured for weeks in building him a road which they knew he had long desired. Love conquered weakness, and they did not cease their toil until their handiwork, which they called "The Road of the Loving Heart," was finished.

Not long after this the white chief suddenly died. At the news the native chiefs flocked from all parts of the island to the house, and took charge of the body. They kissed his hand as they came in, and all night sat in silence about him. One of them, a feeble old man, threw himself on his knees beside the body of his benefactor, and cried out between his sobs:

"I am only a poor black man, and ignorant. Yet I am not afraid to come and take the last look of my dead friend's face. Behold, Tusitala is dead. We were in prison and he cared for us. The day was no longer than his kindness. Who is there so great as Tusitala? Who is there more loving-compassionate? What is your love to his love?"

So the chiefs took their friend to the top of a steep mountain which he had loved and there buried him. It was a mighty task.

The civilised world mourns the great author. The name of Robert Louis Stevenson is lastingly inwrought into English literature. But the Samoans mourn in his loss a brother, who outdid all others in loving-kindness, and so long as the far-off island in the Pacific exists, Tusitala will be gratefully remembered, not because he was so greatly gifted, but simply because he was a good man.

The phrase, "The Road of the Loving Heart," is a gospel in itself. "The day is not longer than his kindness" is a new beatitude. Fame dies, and honours perish, but "loving-kindness" is immortal.

*   *   *

ROMANCE
ROBERT LOUIS STEVENSON

I will make you brooches and toys for your delight
Of bird-song at morning and star-shine at night.
I will make a palace fit for you and me,
Of green days in forests and blue days at sea.

I will make my kitchen, and you shall keep your room,
Where white flows the river and bright blows the broom,
And you shall wash your linen and keep your body white
In rainfall at morning and dewfall at night.

And this shall be for music when no one else is near,
The fine song for singing, the rare song to hear!
That only I remember, that only you admire,
Of the broad road that stretches and the roadside fire.

WHERE THE MIND IS WITHOUT FEAR...
RABINDRANATH TAGORE

Where the mind is without fear and the head is held high;
Where knowledge is free;
Where the world has not been broken up into
    fragments of narrow domestic walls;
Where words come out from the depths of truth;
Where tireless striving stretches its arms towards perfection;
Where the clear stream of reason has not lost its way into
    the dreary desert sand of dead habit;
Where the mind is led forward by Thee into ever-widening
    thought and action—
Into that heaven of freedom, my Father, let my country awake.

*   *   *

❧ LET YOUR TASK be to render yourself worthy of love and this even more for your own happiness than for that of another.   —Maeterlinck

IN HEAVEN*
STEPHEN CRANE

In heaven,
Some little blades of grass
Stood before God.
"What did you do?"
Then all save one of the little blades
Began eagerly to relate
The merits of their lives.
This one stayed a small way behind,
Ashamed.
Presently, God said,
"And what did you do?"
The little blade answered, "O my lord,
Memory is bitter to me,
For, if I did good deeds,
I know not of them."
Then God, in all His splendour,
Arose from His throne.
"O best little blade of grass!" He said.

THE SALUTATION OF
THE DAWN

Listen to the exhortation of the dawn!
Look to this day! For it is life,
 The very life of life.
In its brief course lie all the varieties
And realities of your existence.
 The bliss of growth,
 The glory of action,
 The splendor of beauty,
For yesterday is but a dream,
And tomorrow is only a vision;
 But today well lived
Makes every yesterday a dream of hap-
 piness,
And every tomorrow a vision of hope.
Look well, therefore, to this day!
Such is the salutation of the dawn.
—From the Sanskrit

LONG, LONG AGO
ANONYMOUS

Winds through the olive trees
 Softly did blow,
Round little Bethlehem
 Long, long ago.

Sheep on the hillside lay
 Whiter than snow,
Shepherds were watching them,
 Long, long ago.

Then from the happy sky,
 Angels bent low
Singing their song of joy,
 Long, long ago.

For in a manger bed,
 Cradled we know,
Christ came to Bethlehem,
 Long, long ago.

THE UNKNOWN GOD
"A. E."
[George William Russell]

Far up the dim twilight fluttered
 Moth-wings of vapour and flame:
The lights danced over the mountains,
 Star after star they came.

The lights grew thicker unheeded,
 For silent and still were we;
Our hearts were drunk with a beauty
 Our eyes could never see.

GOD SCATTERS LOVE
JAMES RUSSELL LOWELL

God scatters love on every side
Freely among his children all,
And always hearts are lying open wide
Wherein some grains may fall.

* * *

♪ OUR CREATOR would never have made such lovely days, and have given us the deep hearts to enjoy them, above and beyond all thought, unless we were meant to be immortal.
—*Hawthorne*

THE CACTUS
LAURENCE HOPE

The scarlet flower, with never a sister leaf,
  Stemless, springs from the edge of the Cactus thorn:
Thus from the ragged wounds of desperate grief
  A beautiful Thought, perfect and pure, is born.

A LITTLE SONG OF LIFE
LIZETTE WOODWORTH REESE

Glad that I live am I;
That the sky is blue;
Glad for the country lanes,
And the fall of dew.

After the sun the rain,
After the rain the sun;
This is the way of life,
Till the work be done.

All that we need to do,
Be we low or high
Is to see that we grow
Nearer the sky.

PEACE
HENRY VAN DYKE

With eager heart and will on fire,
I fought to win my great desire
"Peace shall be mine," I said; but life
Grew bitter in the weary strife.

My soul was tired, and my pride
Was wounded deep: to Heaven I cried,
"God grant me peace or I must die;"
The dumb stars glittered no reply.

Broken at last, I bowed my head,
Forgetting all myself, and said,
"Whatever comes, His will be done;"
And in that moment peace was won.

THE UNKNOWABLE
By GEORGE SANTAYANA

I HAVE SOMETIMES wondered at the value ladies set upon jewels: as centres of light, jewels seem rather trivial and monotonous. And yet there is an unmistakable spell about these pebbles; they can be taken up and turned over; they can be kept; they are faithful possessions; the sparkle of them, shifting from moment to moment, is constant from age to age. They are substances. The same aspects of light and colour, if they were homeless in space, or could be spied only once, like fireworks, would have a less comfortable charm. In jewels there is the security, the mystery, the inexhaustible fixity proper to substance. The fascination they exercise over the ladies is the same that the eternal feminine exercises over us. Our contact with them is unmistakable, our contemplation of them gladly renewed, and pleasantly prolonged; yet in one sense they are unknowable; we cannot fathom the secret of their constancy, of their hardness, of that perpetual but uncertain brilliancy by which they dazzle us and hide themselves. These qualities of the jewel and of the eternal feminine are also the qualities of substance and of the world. The existence of this world is certain, or at least, it is unquestioningly to be assumed. Experience may explore it adventurously, and science may describe it with precision, but this same world, because it exists substantially, remains a foreign thing and a marvel to the spirit; unknowable as a drop of water is unknowable, or unknowable like a person loved.

THE TIME
CERVANTES

There is a time for some things,
And a time for all things;
A time for great things
And a time for small things.

TO THE CUCKOO
WILLIAM WORDSWORTH

O blithe new-comer! I have heard,
  I hear thee and rejoice:
O Cuckoo! shall I call thee Bird,
  Or but a wandering Voice?

While I am lying on the grass
  Thy twofold shout I hear;
From hill to hill it seems to pass,
  At once far off and near.

Though babbling only to the vale
  Of sunshine and of flowers,
Thou bringest unto me a tale
  Of visionary hours.

Thrice welcome, darling of the Spring!
  Even yet thou art to me
No bird, but an invisible thing,
  A voice, a mystery;

The same whom in my school-boy days
  I listened to: that Cry
Which made me look a thousand ways
  In bush and tree and sky.

To seek thee did I often rove
  Through woods and on the green;
And thou wert still a hope, a love;
  Still longed for, never seen.

And I can listen to thee yet;
  Can lie upon the plain
And listen, till I do beget
  That golden time again.

O blessed Bird! the earth we pace
  Again appears to be
An unsubstantial, fairy place,
  That is fit home for Thee!

MEMORY
THOMAS BAILEY ALDRICH

My mind lets go a thousand things,
Like dates of wars and deaths of kings,
And yet recalls the very hour—
One noon by yonder village tower,
And on the last blue noon in May—
The wind came briskly up this way,
Crisping the brook beside the road;
Then, pausing here, set down its load
Of pine-scents, and shook listlessly
Two petals from that wild-rose tree.

LINES WRITTEN IN EARLY SPRING
WILLIAM WORDSWORTH

I heard a thousand blended notes,
While in a grove I sate reclined,
In that sweet mood when pleasant
    thoughts
Bring sad thoughts to the mind.

To her fair works did Nature link
The human soul that through me ran;
And much it grieved my heart to think
What man has made of man.

Through primrose tufts, in that green
    bower,
The periwinkle trailed its wreaths;
And 'tis my faith that every flower
Enjoys the air it breathes.

The birds around me hopped and
    played,
Their thoughts I cannot measure:—
But the least motion which they made
It seemed a thrill of pleasure.

The budding twigs spread out their fan,
To catch the breezy air;
And I must think, do all I can,
That there was pleasure there.

If this belief from heaven be sent,
If such be Nature's holy plan,
Have I not reason to lament
What man has made of man?

WHERE THE BEE SUCKS, THERE SUCK I
WILLIAM SHAKESPEARE

Where the bee sucks, there suck I;
In a cowslip's bell I lie;
There I couch when owls do cry.
On the bat's back I do fly
After summer merrily.
Merrily, merrily, shall I live now
Under the blossom that hangs on the
bough.

SONG WITHOUT WORDS
ERNEST DOWSON

In the deep violet air,
    Not a leaf is stirred;
    There is no sound heard,
But afar, the rare
    Trilled voice of a bird.

Is the wood's dim heart,
    And the fragrant pine,
    Incense, and a shrine
Of her coming? Apart,
    I wait for a sign.

What the sudden hush said,
    She will hear, and forsake,
    Swift, for my sake,
Her green, grassy bed:
    She will hear and awake!

She will hearken and glide,
    From her place of deep rest,
    Dove-eyed, with the breast
Of a dove, to my side:
    The pines bow their crest.

I wait for a sign:
    The leaves to be waved,
.   The tall tree-tops laved
In a flood of sunshine,
    This world to be saved!

In the deep violet air,
    Not a leaf is stirred;
    There is no sound heard,
But afar, the rare
    Trilled voice of a bird.

EPIGRAM ON BEAUTY
SIR WILLIAM WATSON

I follow Beauty; of her train am I:
    Beauty whose voice is earth and sea
    and air;
Who serveth, and her hands for all
    things ply;
    Who reigneth, and her throne is
    everywhere.

THE GARDEN OF PROSERPINE
ALGERNON CHARLES SWINBURNE

We are not sure of sorrow,
    And joy was never sure;
Today will die tomorrow;
    Time stoops to no man's lure;
And love, grown faint and fretful
With lips but half regretful
Sighs, and with eyes forgetful
    Weeps that no loves endure.

From too much love of living,
    From hope and fear set free,
We thank with brief thanksgiving
    Whatever gods may be,
That no life lives forever;
That dead men rise up never;
That even the weariest river
    Winds somewhere safe to sea.

Here, where the world is quiet;
    Here, where all trouble seems
Dead winds' and spent waves' riot
    In doubtful dreams of dreams;
I watch the green field growing
For reaping folk and sowing,
For harvest-time and mowing,
    A sleepy world of streams.

I am tired of tears and laughter,
    And men that laugh and weep;
Of what may come hereafter
    For men that sow to reap.
I am weary of days and hours,
Blown buds of barren flowers,
Desires and dreams and powers
    And everything but sleep.

ST. MARK'S CATHEDRAL
By John Ruskin

... ALL THE great square seems to have opened from it (St. Mark's) in a kind of awe, that we may see it far away—a multitude of pillars and white domes, clustered into a long low pyramid of colored light; a treasure-heap, it seems, partly of gold, and partly of opal and mother-of-pearl, hollowed beneath into five great vaulted porches, ceiled with fair mosaic, and beset with sculpture of alabaster, clear as amber and delicate as ivory—sculpture fantastic and involved, of palm leaves and lilies, and grapes and pomegranates, and birds clinging and fluttering among the branches, all twined together into an endless net-work of buds and plumes; and, in the midst of it, the solemn forms of angels, sceptred, and robed to the feet, and leaning to each other across the gates, their figures indistinct among the gleaming of the golden ground through the leaves beside them, interrupted and dim, like the morning light as it faded back among the branches of Eden, when first its gates were angel-guarded long ago. And round the walls of the porches there are set pillars of variegated stones, jasper and porphyry, and deep-green serpentine spotted with flakes of snow, and marbles, that half refuse and half yield to the sunshine, Cleopatra-like, "their bluest veins to kiss"—the shadow, as it steals back from them, revealing line after line of azure undulation, as a receding tide leaves the waved sand; their capitals rich with interwoven tracery, rooted knots of herbage, and drifting leaves of acanthus and vine, and mystical signs, all beginning and ending in the Cross; and above them, in the broad archivolts, a continuous chain of language and of life-angels, and the signs of heaven, and the labours of men, each in its appointed season upon the earth; and above these, another range of glittering pinnacles, mixed with white arches edged with scarlet flowers—a confusion of delight, amidst which the breasts of the Greek horses are seen blazing in their breadth of golden strength, and the St. Marks's Lion, lifted on a blue field covered with stars, until at last, as if in ecstasy, the crests of the arches break into a marble foam, and toss themselves far into the blue sky in flashes and wreaths of sculptured spray, as if the breakers on the Lido shore had been frost-bound before they fell, and the sea-nymphs had inlaid them with coral and amethyst.

—From *The Stones of Venice*

THE COMING OF CHRISTIANITY TO ENGLAND, 627 A.D.
Words Spoken to Edwin, King of
Northumbria

THE PRESENT LIFE of men upon earth, O King, appears to me, in comparison with that time which is unknown to us, like to the swift flight of a sparrow through your hall, where you, with your caldormen and thanes, sit by the fire, at supper, in winter. The hall is warmed; without are storms of wind and rain and winter's snow. The sparrow passes swiftly in at one door and out at another, gaining awhile a short safety from the wintry blast; but soon after a little calm he flies once more into the unknown, passing from winter to winter again. So this life of ours appears for a moment, but whence or whither we are wending we know not. If, therefore, this new faith can teach us aught more sure, it seems truly to deserve to be followed.

THANKSGIVING
Ralph Waldo Emerson

For each new morning with its light,
  Father, we thank Thee,
For rest and shelter of the night,
  Father, we thank Thee,
For health and food, for love and
  friends,
For everything Thy goodness sends,
  Father, in heaven, we thank Thee.

From GRADATIM
Josiah Gilbert Holland

Heaven is not reached at a single
  bound;
  But we build the ladder by which we
    rise
From the lowly earth to the vaulted
  skies,
And we mount to its summit round by
  round.

IN JUDEA
Mildred Bowers Armstrong

The stars that looked on Joseph,
  The moon that Mary knew
Looked down on this Judean town
  The way they used to do.

And this old tree remembers
  The lad who used to play
Upon these very shadows
  Where I stand today.

ST. TERESA'S BOOK-MARK
Henry Wadsworth Longfellow

Let nothing disturb thee,
Nothing affright thee;
All things are passing;
God never changeth;
Patient endurance
Attaineth to all things;
Who God possesseth
In nothing is wanting;
Alone God sufficeth.

THROUGH LOVE TO LIGHT
Richard Watson Gilder

Through love to light! Oh wonderful
  the way
That leads from darkness to the perfect
  day!
From darkness and from sorrow of the
  night
To morning that comes singing over the
  sea,
Through love to light! Through light,
  O God to thee,
Who art the love of love, the eternal
  light of light.

FOLLOW THE GLEAM
Alfred, Lord Tennyson

Not of the sunlight,
Not of the moonlight,
Not of the starlight!
O young Mariner,
Down to the haven,
Call your companions,
Launch your vessel,
And crowd your canvas,
And, ere it vanishes
Over the margin,
After it, follow it,
Follow the Gleam.

* * *

O Lord, our God, under the shadow of Thy wings let us hope. Thou
wilt support us, both when little, and even to gray hairs. When our strength
is of Thee, it is strength; but, when our own, it is feebleness. We return
unto Thee, O Lord, that from their weariness our souls may rise towards
Thee; for with Thee is refreshment and true strength. Amen.

—*St. Augustine*

NIGHT
[*Written about 650 B.C.*]
ALCMAN

Over the drowsy earth still night pre-
vails;
Calm sleep the mountain tops and
shady vales,
The rugged cliffs and hollow glens,
The cattle on the hill. Deep in the sea
The countless finny race and monster
brood

Tranquil repose. Even the busy bee
Forgets her daily toil. The silent wood,
No more with noisy hum of insects
rings;
And all the feathered tribes, by gentle
sleep subdued,
Roost in the glade, and hang their
drooping wings.

From *LISTEN, THE WIND*
By ANNE MORROW LINDBERGH

TONIGHT or tomorrow we would fly across the Atlantic.

In the late afternon ("There's no wind in the harbor?" "No—no wind.") we went out to "Cape House" on a promontory overlooking the sea. We drove through gardens dripping with shade and tangled flowering vines, purple Bougainvillea, yellow Allamanda. We swam in a pool and sat, rested, on a terrace, looking over the water. Tea in thermos bottles, cushions to sit on, and the darkening world at our feet.

The cliff below us fell abruptly to the sea. The sea poured out, a great wide circle, to the sky. No bumps on the horizon, no islands broke that smooth expanse, rolled out like heavy corded silk to the edge of the world. Only one point of land down the coast —the plumed head of a palm, the jagged outline of a rock—reached out like a last articulately formed word against the great dark speechless stretch of ocean.

The sky was clear and limpid like some amber fluid, no wisps of cloud, no shreds of mist. The sun sank, a single globule of gold, through depths of liquid sky into a liquid sea. There were no dregs of day left behind, no untidy streaks of color, no blur of afterglow. It had been day; now it was night. Eyes, filled brimful of bright sky, turned to the land, startled to find it was dark; turned to the sea, surprised to find the waves, like the nap of velvet, brushed dark with a single stroke; turned to the sky again, to find pale silver pinpricks in its satin surface.

So imperceptibly night came, so peacefully. Here there was no struggle. Earth, sea, and sky—we had been in them this morning, fighting against them. Why, I wondered? Now, looking down on them, it all seemed incredible —now they were spread out in all their calm beauty below us.

The waves, no longer our opponents, on the rocks below, beat out an even rhythm, soothing to our ears. The sky, neither light nor dark, to be hoarded or spent, was only beautiful to our eyes. Nature was no longer the unjust opponent. She swept her gifts equally, on us sitting here on the terrace; on a boat, not visible before, now showing a tiny prick of light on the horizon; on that last point of land pushing out to sea; on the harbor around the corner at Bathurst. Beauty of earth and sky and water was here for us to take, lying peacefully at our feet.

The Earth, the Seas, the Light, the lofty Skies,

The Sun and Stars are mine; if these
I prize.   [—THOMAS TRAHERNE]

For gradually we were looking not at earth and sea but up at the stars. The pendulum of the mind swings first over land; then, wider, over the sea; and finally stretches to take in its compass the sky. Arcturus, Aldebaran, Alpheratz—the names sang in my mind like a half-remembered line of a poem. But I did not see any stars that I knew. I was not looking for navigating stars, only those bright points of light that shake out of the corners before the sky is fully clothed. Pale, at first, and shy —they disappear when you look right at them—gradually they bloom out of the dark; they dwarf the dark. They, and not the dark, are the sky. And, as you stare, they fasten upon you, draw you upward, until you feel no longer rooted in the earth. Arcturus, Aldebaran, Alpheratz—if only you could have your point of balance the sky! With such a pivot you could hold the world on your shoulders, another Atlas. In such an armor you could meet anything.

I turned and faced the dark sea. Suddenly I was aware that the feeling of cool strength flowing over me—against my face, past my ears, through my hair —was wind. And in the vast pattern of earth and sky and water, I was conscious only of that one element—wind. Like a familiar voice speaking to you through a light sleep, the wind roused us, and we woke, startled, shook off our dreams, stiffened to an old role. We put on our armor, half asleep still, but spurred to action.

"Look—there's a wind—a strong wind!"

We jumped up and leaned over the parapet.

"Can you see—down there—I think there are whitecaps—"

"Yes," said my husband. His words clipped out like heels on a stone pavement hurrying somewhere. "Yes—we'll leave at midnight."

NATURE
By HENRY DAVID THOREAU

NATURE is full of genius, full of the divinity, so that not a snowflake escapes its fashioning hand. Nothing is cheap and coarse, neither dewdrops nor snowflakes. . . . What a world we live in, where myriads of these little disks, so beautiful to the most prying eyes, are whirled down on every traveler's coat, the observant and the unobservant, on the restless squirrel's fur, on the far-stretching fields and forests, the wooded dells and the mountain tops. Far, far away from the haunts of men, they roll down some little slope, fall over and come to their bearings, and melt or lose their beauty in the mass, ready anon to swell some little rill with their contribution, and so, at last, the universal ocean from which they came. There they lie, like the wreck of chariot wheels after a battle in the skies. Meanwhile the meadow mouse shoves them aside in his gallery, the school-boy casts them in his snowball, or the woodsman's sled glides smoothly over them, these glorious spangles, the sweepings of heaven's floor. And they all sing, melting as they sing, of the mysteries of the number six; six, six, six. He takes up the waters of the sea in his hand, leaving the salt; he dispenses it in mist through the skies; he re-collects and sprinkles it like grain in six-rayed stars over the earth, there to lie till he dissolves its bonds again.

WELSH LULLABY

ANONYMOUS

Sleep, my babe, lie still and slumber,
  All through the night;
Guardian angels God will lend thee,
  All through the night;
Soft the drowsy hours are creeping,
Hill and vale in slumber sleeping,
Mother dear her watch is keeping,
  All through the night.

God is here, thou'lt not be lonely,
  All through the night;
'Tis not I who guards thee only,
  All through the night.
Night's dark shades will soon be over,
Still my watchful care shall hover,
God with me His watch is keeping,
  All through the night.

From *THE RENAISSANCE*
By WALTER PATER

LA GIOCONDA (Mona Lisa) is, in the truest sense, Leonardo's masterpiece, the thought and work. In suggestiveness, only the *Melancholia* of Durer is comparable to it; and no crude symbolism disturbs the effect of its subdued and graceful mystery. We all know the face and hands of the figure, set in its marble chair, in that circle of fantastic rocks, as in some faint light under sea. Perhaps of all ancient pictures time has chilled it least. As often happens with works in which invention seems to reach its limit, there is an element in it given to, not invented by, the master. In that inestimable folio of drawings, once in the possession of Vasari, were certain designs by Verrocchio, faces of such impressive beauty that Leonardo in his boyhood copied them many times. It is hard not to connect with these designs of the elder, by-past master, as with its germinal principle, the unfathomable smile, always with a touch of something sinister in it, which plays over all Leonardo's work. Besides, the picture is a portrait. From childhood we see this image defining itself on the fabric of his dreams; and but for express historical testimony, we might fancy that this was but his ideal lady, embodied and beheld at last.

What was the relationship of a living Florentine to this creature of his thought? By what strange affinities had the dream and the person grown up thus apart, and yet so closely together? Present from the first incorporeally in Leonardo's brain, dimly traced in the designs of Verrocchio, she is found present at last in *Il Giocondo's* house. That there is much of mere portraiture in the picture is attested by the legend that by artificial means, the presence of mimes and flute-players, that subtle expression was protracted on the face. Again, was it in four years and by renewed labour never really completed, or in four months and as by stroke of magic, that the image was projected?

The presence that rose thus so strangely beside the waters, is expressive of what in the ways of a thousand years men had come to desire. Hers is the head upon which all "the ends of the world are come," and the eyelids are a little weary. It is a beauty wrought out from within upon the flesh, the deposit, little cell by cell, of strange thoughts and fantastic reveries and exquisite passions. Set it for a moment beside one of those white Greek goddesses or beautiful women of antiquity, and how would they be troubled by this beauty, into which the soul with all its maladies has passed! All the thoughts and experience of the world have etched and moulded there, in that which they have of power to refine and make expressive the outward form, the animalism of Greece, the lust of Rome, the mysticism of the middle age with its spiritual ambition and imaginative loves, the return of the Pagan world, the sins of the Borgias. She is older than the rocks among which she sits; like the vampire, she has been dead many times, and learned the secrets of the grave; and has been a diver in deep seas, and keeps their fallen day about her; and trafficked for strange webs with Eastern merchants; and, as Leda, was the mother of Helen of Troy, and, as Saint Anne, the mother of Mary; and all this has been to her but as the sound of lyres and flutes, and lives only in the delicacy with which it has moulded the changing lineaments, and tinged the eyelids and the hands. The fancy of a perpetual life, sweeping together ten thousand experiences, is an old one; and modern philosophy has conceived the idea of humanity as wrought upon by, and summing up in itself, all modes of thought and life. Certainly Lady Lisa might stand as the embodiment of the old fancy, the symbol of the modern idea.

A GOLDEN SORROW

WILLIAM SHAKESPEARE

I swear 'tis better to be lowly born,
And range with humble livers in content,
Than to be perked up in a glistering grief,
And wear a golden sorrow.

THE INNER MAN

WE DO not know a nation until we know its pleasures of life, just as we do not know a man until we know how he spends his leisure. It is when a man ceases to do the things he has to do, and does the things he likes to do, that the character is revealed. It is when the repressions of society and business are gone and when the goads of money and fame and ambition are lifted, and man's spirit wanders where it listeth, that we see the inner man, his real self.

—*Lin Yutang*

RAINBOW TRAIL

WALK ON a rainbow trail; walk on a trail of song, and all about you will be beauty. There is a way out of every dark mist, over a rainbow trail.

—*Navajo Song*

THE RHODORA

RALPH WALDO EMERSON

In May, when sea-winds pierced our solitudes,
I found the fresh Rhodora in the woods,
Spreading its leafless blooms in a damp nook,
To please the desert and the sluggish brook.
The purple petals, fallen in the pool,
Made the black water with their beauty gay;
Here might the red-bird come his plumes to cool,
And court the flower that cheapens his array.
Rhodora! if the sages ask thee why
This charm is wasted on the earth and sky,
Tell them, dear, that if eyes were made for seeing,
Then Beauty is its own excuse for being:
Why thou were there, O rival of the rose!
I never thought to ask, I never knew:
But, in my simple ignorance, suppose
The self-same Power that brought me there brought you.

Ann Rutledge

By NORMAN CORWIN

Music: Introductory cue, andante trancuillo. This should have the quality of an American folksong and the flavor of the period.
After it has been established in the orchestra, cross-fade to voice of Ann, humming a variation on the tune. Humming sustains briefly, fading under:

NARRATOR. Let me tell you about the girl humming that tune. Her name is Ann Rutledge. A long time ago she lived with her mother and father and seven brothers and sisters in a tavern in New Salem, Illinois. Her name is familiar to you because a great man fell in love with her and never got over it. Otherwise you wouldn't have known about her, because she was an ordinary girl, a bit prettier than average, but still, very much like a lot of girls you know yourselves. Ann was not a phantom or a legend or a folk-tune. She was a girl—she was happy, she was sad, she was angry, she was coy, she was gentle, she was wise; she had fears . . . she had dreams. It is these things that she was that our story is about.

First of all, Ann Rutledge was a girl . . .

Humming continues aimlessly until:

ANN. Mother . . .

MOTHER (*busy with pots and pans*). Yes, Ann?

ANN. I have an important question to ask you.

MOTHER. Can it wait until we do the dishes?

ANN. Oh, yes, I guess it can wait, all right.

MOTHER (*curious*). Very well, what is it?

ANN. Don't laugh at me, now.

MOTHER. Come, do you want to ask me or don't you?

ANN. Mother . . . what's it like to be in love?

MOTHER. *What?* Why, Ann, now why should a thought like that be in your head at this hour of the morning?

ANN. Because I've been thinking about it all night.

MOTHER. You have?

ANN. Yes.

MOTHER. Well, er . . . what conclusion did you reach?

ANN. None. I just couldn't sleep. I kept listening to the crickets and the frogs, and the house creaking; and did you know there's a screech owl down in the glen somewhere?

MOTHER. No.

ANN. Well, there is, because I heard it. And I also heard Pa snoring.

MOTHER. I heard that myself.

ANN. Toward morning it got very still, and it seemed everything went to sleep, even the crickets and the frogs. All I could hear was leaves stirring faintly outside my window—very faintly . . . it's a beautiful sound, isn't it?

MOTHER. Yes.

ANN. And then I could hear my heart beating . . . slowly—like this: *bump*-bump . . . *bump*-bump . . . *bump*-bump—so slow I was afraid it would stop.

MOTHER. Maybe you shouldn't have eaten afore you went to bed, Ann.

ANN. Oh, no, I felt fine. Only I kept wondering how it must be to hear all those things when you're—well, when you're in love. I mean, when a man's in love with you, and . . .

MOTHER. See here, Ann, you're too

young to be bothering your head with thoughts the likes of that.

ANN. Too young? I'm seventeen, ain't I? How old were you when *you* fell in love?

MOTHER *(musing; after a pause)*. Sixteen.

ANN. Well, there! *(coaxingly)*. Mother . . . what's it like?

MOTHER. It—it's just what you suppose it's like . . . just what you imagine it's like.

ANN. If it's what I imagine—then it's like the way the leaves stirred all last night—and the little sounds kept coming from far away. Or it's like how the hay smelled down at Tuttle's farm just after they finished mowing last week—or the way the sky looks on those clear, clear nights in winter, all bright and glowing, and kind of pure—you know?

MOTHER. Yes, dear.

ANN. Like warm blankets and soft pillows when you're all snug in bed and it's blowing a blizzard outside and there are icicles on the window. *(a little laugh of delight)*. Is it—is it anything like that, Mother?

MOTHER. Yes, Ann . . . sometimes. When it's unspoiled. That's the *nice* part of love.

ANN. The nice part? But what can there be *bad* about being in love?

MOTHER. Oh . . . certain things . . . certain things I hope you'll never find out about. . . .

Music: Lyric theme sustaining under and fading after:

NARRATOR *(echoing his introductory narration)*. Ann Rutledge was not a phantom or a legend or a folktune. She was a girl—and she was happy.

Clop-clop of horse and buggy wheels.

McNEIL. Whoa. Whoa there.

Horse and buggy stop.

McNEIL. Do you mind my stopping?

ANN. Why should I mind?

McNEIL. Because I stopped just in order to look at you.

ANN. Then I *do* mind, John McNeil!

McNEIL. But it's so hard to see your eyes when I'm looking at the road . . . why, Ann, you're blushing!

ANN. Am I?

McNEIL. Yes. And it rather becomes you, too.

ANN. I'm not blushing. It's just the heat of the day. I'm very warm, that's all.

McNEIL. Whatever it is, you're very beautiful.

ANN. I—I'm glad you think so, John.

McNEIL *(after a pause)*. Ann—would you be offended if I kissed you?

ANN. *Kiss* me?

McNEIL. Yes.

ANN *(rather abruptly)*. No.

McNEIL. Oh—I'm sorry.

ANN *(shyly)*. I mean no, I wouldn't be offended.

McNEIL. I . . . *(a moment's silence)*. Why . . . thank you.

ANN. John, John . . . *(pause)*. Want to know something?

McNEIL. What?

ANN. That was the first time in my life I've ever been kissed.

McNEIL. Want to know something, Ann?

ANN. What?

McNEIL. This is the second.

Music: Sweeps up lushly and comes down for:

NARRATOR. Ann Rutledge was a girl . . . and she was happy . . . and she was sad.

VOICES *(cross-fading with music; ad-lib)*. Well, good night . . . good night, Mr. Rutledge . . . Mrs. Rutledge . . . good night, Ann . . . Night everybody . . .

ANN. Good night, Judge Green. Good night, Mr. Lincoln. Good night, Mr. Offut.

Footsteps going off; heavy door closing.

RUTLEDGE *(laughing)*. I must say Abe Lincoln is a funny man! I swear I never did hear anybody tell stories the way he tells 'em.

MOTHER. And he doesn't have to wet his tongue to do it, either. He's a fine Christian gentleman, Mr. Lincoln is.

RUTLEDGE *(laughing).* Did you hear the one he told about the . . . Land sakes, Ann, what're you looking so glum about?

ANN. Oh, I'm all right, Father.

RUTLEDGE. Do you mean to say you didn't think that bear story of Lincoln's was funny? Have you lost your sense of humor?

ANN. I didn't hear it, Father.

RUTLEDGE. But you were sitting right there listening.

MOTHER. Please leave her alone, Henry. She's tired. She's all worn out.

RUTLEDGE. Well, then—well, then why doesn't she go up to bed?

ANN. I'm all right now. Good night, Mother. Good night, Father.

ALL. *(ad-lib good nights.)*

Sounds of steps being climbed slowly. A few steps on the landing. Door opens, closes; more steps; then the creaking of a bedspring.

ANN. Dear God, please bless Mother and Father and the children and . . . John McNeil . . . and please make John change his mind and come back to New Salem as he promised he would . . . because I'm so lonely since he left. Dear God, make him not like the East; make him come back to me. . . . I love him so much. . . . *(The faintest suggestion of a sob. Then a very small whisper.)* So very much. . . .

Music: Appropriate mood music, fading under:

NARRATOR. Ann Rutledge was a girl . . . happy . . . and sad . . . and sometimes angry.

VOICES. *(ad-libs of low excitement, as though somebody had just been injured. Out of the general noise we can distinguish a few speeches, especially close to the mike.)*

MR. WINTHROP. Easy, there. He's bleedin' bad.

MOTHER. Give him air—give the poor man some air.

MR. WINTHROP. My! That's a nasty cut on his head, there.

RUTLEDGE. He's comin' to. He'll be all right.

ARMSTRONG *(bullying; quite drunk).* Well, now, is there anyone else cares to give an opinion about my drinkin' too much? If there is, just speak up—and I'll pile him in the corner with Mr. Williams and the rest of the wreckage. Mebbe that'll teach yer to let me an' the boys drink in peace without no preachin' as to how a gentleman should conduct hisself in a tavern.

RUTLEDGE *(sputtering).* Now listen here, Jack Armstrong. As proprietor of this tavern, I have a right to . . .

MR. WINTHROP. Take it easy, Mr. Rutledge. He's ugly.

ARMSTRONG. Rutledge, you see what I just done to Williams?

RUTLEDGE. Yes, and also what you've done to my good chair!

ARMSTRONG. Well, I'll break another one over *your* head if you don't shut up!

RUTLEDGE. Just because you can lick everybody in town you don't have to bully and strut all over the place. I wish I were younger, Armstrong—*I'd* take you on!

ARMSTRONG. Why, you bald-headed old coot, Rutledge, I'll take anybody on— young and old together! I'll take 'em in pairs, I will. Ain't a man in town's got guts enough to stand up to me. *(Shouting.)* Is there? *(There is no answer from the assemblage.)* Huh! That's the right answer. Hey, Ma Rutledge, some more o' this likker, an' quick—for I'm a pow'ful thirsty man.

MOTHER *(sighing).* Very well, Jack Armstrong. Drink yourself to death if you want to; sooner the better for us.

ARMSTRONG (goes into a gale of laughter, which stops suddenly). What you doin'?

ANN (coldly, determinedly). Taking this whisky away from you. You've made enough trouble for one night.

MOTHER (fearful). Ann—come away.

ARMSTRONG. Ju-u-ust a minute, Annie me gal, ju-u-ust a minute.

ANN. Let go of me, you filthy pig!
Terrific slap.

ARMSTRONG. Hey! That hurt!

ANN. I meant it to hurt.

ARMSTRONG. You did, eh? Well, look here, now.
Crashing of glass to floor, as of bottle wrested from Ann's grip; another terrific sock.

ANN. That hurt too, didn't it?

ARMSTRONG (after a moment; sullen and mad). You wouldn't of dared done that if you was a man!

ANN. I wouldn't have had to if you were a man.

ARMSTRONG. Oh, yes? Well . . . (Stopped. All he can do now is repeat himself.) No man'd dare stand up to me that-away.

ANN (archly). Oh, yes, there would.

ARMSTRONG. All right, who? Name him!

ANN. Have you tried Abe Lincoln?

ARMSTRONG (laughing). Lincoln? That long-legged, flop-eared donkey of a store clerk?

ANN. I'd like to see you call him that to his face.

ARMSTRONG. You would, would you? Well, come around tomorra by the store, say around the middle of the mornin'.

ANN. I'll be there—and it will be a great pleasure to see them carry you out.

Music: Transitional cue, fading as before under:

NARRATOR. Yes, Ann Rutledge was a girl—she could be happy . . . and sad . . . and angry . . . and gentle.

Music: Cross-fades to a low background of birds and outdoor sounds; river noises also, providing blend is not too muddy.

ANN. Aren't you getting too much sun on you, Mr. Lincoln?

ABE. Won't make much difference to a face like mine.

ANN. But the reflection of light from the water—that can burn, too.

ABE. Never heard of the Sangamon River burning anybody.

ANN (laughing). All right, but don't say I didn't warn you.

ABE. For anything concerning my looks, I'm afraid I'll have to take full responsibility.

ANN. You're—you're not bad-looking, Mr. Lincoln.

ABE. Light bother your eyes, Miss Rutledge?

ANN. No. I can see clearly. I like your looks.

ABE. Thank you. You're being very kind.

ANN. Aren't you—going to say anything about mine?

ABE. I'm not very good at—at expressing myself on things I feel very—er—deeply about.

ANN. You feel very deeply about my looks?

ABE (after a pause). About you.

ANN. Oh.

ABE (apologetically). I don't suppose I have any right to hope . . . but I do, nevertheless. I hope that some day I might perhaps be worthy of your—affection.

ANN. Oh.

ABE. (hurriedly). But in the meantime, though, I hope you'll just let me keep seeing you—that you'll let me take you for walks, and sit with me again like this, on the bank of the river, and . . .

ANN. Mr. Lincoln.

ABE (scared). Yes.

ANN. How is your memory?

ABE. Why—all right, I guess.

207

ANN. Do you remember how you threw Jack Armstrong the time he came down to the store looking for a fight?

ABE. Yes.

ANN. How you got your arms around him and spun him head over heels?

ABE. Yes.

ANN. Well—why don't you try putting your arms around me? . . . But leave out the spin.

Music: Romantic variation of the Narrator's theme, coming down for:

NARRATOR. Happy yes; and sad . . . and angry . . . and gentle . . . and wise . . .

PETER *(aged twelve)*. Sister?

ANN *(distracted; she is reading)*. Yes, Peter.

PETER. Which do you think is the best, a soldier or a sailor?

ANN. I'm sure I haven't the faintest idea.

PETER. That's been puzzling me.

ANN. Very well; now let me read, please.

PETER *(after a pause)*. Sister? *(No answer.)* Ann?

ANN. What?

PETER. Do sailors get seasick?

ANN *(annoyed)*. Can't you see I'm trying to read, Peter?

PETER *(hurt)*. I only wanted to know. I was only asking.

ANN *(repentantly)*. I'm sorry, Peter. . . . I was absorbed in what I was reading. What did you want to know?

PETER. Do sailors get seasick?

ANN. Well, I shouldn't think so. Not good sailors, anyway. Why do you ask?

PETER. I was just wondering what I'd be when I grow up, a soldier or a sailor. I think I'll be a soldier.

ANN. Why?

PETER. So I can carry a gun and be brave, an' all them nasty old Indians will run away when they see me coming.

ANN. Come over here, Peter. *(Pause.)* Have you been listening to old Dan Potter and his stories about what a

hero he was, fighting the Indians?

PETER. He killed twenty-one Indians with his bare fists after his powder ran dry, so the redskins wanted to make him chief on account of he was so brave; but he didn't let them, 'cause Indians aren't to be trusted, and they're no good nohow.

ANN. Dan Potter is a liar. The only Indians he ever saw are those old trappers who come to trade at Malcolm's store. Get the idea out of your head that Indians are nasty or no good nohow . . . and anyway "nohow" isn't a word anyhow.

PETER. Yes, but Dan Potter says . . .

ANN. As for carrying a gun and being brave and making Indians run away when they see you coming, better give that up, too. In the first place, only cowards need guns to make them brave, because bravery comes from your heart and not from anything you carry.

PETER *(not getting it at all; after a pause)*. But wouldn't the Indians run away if they saw a soldier coming with a gun? Loaded?

ANN. I doubt it. Ask Abe Lincoln sometime about his experiences in the Black Hawk War. He was a captain in the war, but he didn't see any Indians running away from white men—in fact, to the contrary.

PETER. Yes, but *white* men aren't afraid to die, are they?

ANN. Nobody likes to die—red or white or black or yellow. . . . It's just like Abe Lincoln says: the two most unpopular things in the world are not having any freedom and being dead.

PETER. Gosh, being dead's much worse than not having freedom, I should think.

ANN. I wouldn't be so sure. Everybody has to die sometime, and there's nothing they can do about it; but there's plenty a man can do about not being free.

PETER *(not interested)*. Do sailors

have to learn how to swim?

Music: Transitional motif, coming down behind:

The closing of a door. Slow footsteps.

DOCTOR. Mrs. Rutledge . . .

MOTHER. Yes, Doctor?

DOCTOR. You'll have to keep Ann as quiet as possible. Don't let her get up for anything.

MOTHER. Is it—serious, Doctor? *(There is no answer. Perhaps he is nodding his head affirmatively. Mrs. Rutledge tries to keep down her emotion.)* Will she be a long time getting well?

DOCTOR. Mrs. Rutledge . . . Ann isn't going to get well.

MOTHER. No! No!

DOCTOR. You might as well know now.

MOTHER. How long, Doctor?

DOCTOR. Don't know. Might be two days, might be two weeks.

MRS. RUTLEDGE. *(A little sob escapes her.)*

DOCTOR. I'm terribly . . . *(Gives up trying to commiserate even before he begins; he knows it will not help.)* I'm sorry.

MOTHER. I'm going in to her.

DOCTOR. I told you nothing, now.

MOTHER. There. *(Sniffs.)* Do I look all right?

DOCTOR. Yes, I'll wait here.

Foosteps. Door opens, closes.

MOTHER *(quietly).* Ann, dear . . .

ANN. Yes, Mother?

MOTHER. Are you comfortable? Is everything . . .

ANN *(weakly).* I feel wretched, Mother.

MOTHER. You're going to be all right. Doctor says so.

ANN. He says so?

MOTHER. Yes. You're going to be all right.

ANN. Do you believe him?

MOTHER. Why, of course, Ann! What a question!

ANN. Has Abe been here since yesterday?

MOTHER. He came last night, but you were asleep, and he didn't want to disturb you.

ANN. Even if I'm asleep, please wake me up when he comes, Mother.

MOTHER. No, not if you're asleep, dear. The doctor says you're asleep, dear.

ANN *(a little painfully; almost angrily).* Mother . . . I'll *get* enough rest! More than I need! . . . Please! I want to see Abe when he comes!

MOTHER. Yes, dear, of course.

ANN *(immediately repentant).* Oh, I'm sorry, Mother — I didn't mean to sound cross.

MOTHER. There, there, lie back. Here, this will cool your forehead.

ANN. You see, I've got to talk to Abe, because . . . well, you know how I feel about him.

MOTHER. We all feel the same way about him, Ann.

ANN. Yes, I love him. I love him. And I've got to see him now—or . . .

MOTHER *(after a pause; fearfully, quaveringly).* Or what?

ANN *(almost hysterically).* Or never, Mother, *never!*

Music: Tragic variation on transitional motif, fading under:

ABE. You mustn't talk so much, darling. Rest. Let me just look at you and wish hard.

ANN. Wish hard?

ABE. Wish so hard that nothing can stand up against me, like a—like a tornado blowin' the sky right off its hinges. Then I'd wish away your fever; I'd wish . . .

ANN. Abe—what are you going to do when I'm gone?

ABE *(trying to be cheerful).* When you're *gone!* What I do when I'm eighty is of no concern to me right now.

ANN. Do you love me, Abe?

ABE *(choking).* I—I—why, Ann—I—God in Heaven, Ann—I . . .

ANN. I know. You once told me you weren't very good at expressing yourself on things you feel deeply about.

ABE. Yes. That's it. *(A long pause.)* I do love you, Ann.

ANN. Then go on and be the big man I know you can be. Go on, because it's what I'd want you to be if I were with you.

ABE *(miserably)*. Be a big man, Ann? I'll never even be a little man without you. I'll be nothing.

ANN. Abraham Lincoln, I know you. I know you better than you know yourself. You'll grieve for me a bit—but you'll be all right after a while, when you find out that grieving doesn't help. . . . Abe, if it's at all possible for me to be near you after I'm gone—if in any way . . .

ABE *(agonized)*. Oh, God!

ANN. Then I will come to you, Abe. I will. And when your mind's at peace, you'll go back to your books, and you'll learn more and more, because you've always been hungry for learning . . . and you'll keep on being sweet and kind and honest and lovable . . . and you'll be great because you're just naturally *made* that way. . . .

ABE. Please, Ann—you're tiring yourself. . . . I don't want to be great. I just want you to be well again. Darling, never mind about me. You get some rest, now. You're going to be all right. I'll stay right here by your side.

ANN. Yes. . . . *(Sighs.)* I *am* a bit tired.

ABE. That's right. Just rest now.

ANN. You won't leave me, will you?

ABE. No, dear. I won't leave you. I'll never leave you.

ANN. Good . . . good.

Music: Sweeps up into finale, sustaining under:

NARRATOR. Yes . . . Ann Rutledge was a girl—an ordinary girl, a bit prettier than average, but still very much like a lot of girls you know. And when she died, all that was young and gay in Abe Lincoln died with her. And a sadness came into his eyes that never left them. There were many sorrows in his fitful life, and violence and tempest, and the terrible thunders of a nation torn apart; but never did those brooding eyes forget the little graveyard on the outskirts of New Salem, and the tavern girl who rested there . . . Ann Rutledge!

Music: Up and into maestoso finale.

AN OLD WOMAN OF THE ROADS
PADRAIC COLUM

O, to have a little house!
To own the hearth and stool and all!
The heaped up sods upon the fire,
The pile of turf against the wall!

To have a clock with weights and chains
And pendulum swinging up and down!
A dresser filled with shining delph,
Speckled and white and blue and brown!

I could be busy all the day
Clearing and sweeping hearth and floor,
And fixing on the shelf again
My white and blue and speckled store!

I could be quiet there at night

Beside the fire and by myself,
Sure of a bed and loth to leave
The ticking clock and the shining delph!

Och! but I'm weary of mist and dark,
And roads where there's never a house nor bush,
And tired I am of bog and road,
And the crying wind and the lonesome hush!

And I am praying to God on high,
And I am praying Him night and day,
For a little house—a house of my own—
Out of the wind's and the rain's way.

From *LOST HORIZON*

By James Hilton

This story, Lost Horizon, *is about a plane that has been mysteriously kidnaped. Its unwilling passengers have been flown to a beautiful mountain valley in remote Tibet. The valley is dominated by a lamasery, Shangri-La, where the travellers are treated well but are not allowed to return to the outside world. After a while, one of the plane's passengers, the Englishman Conway, is granted audience with the immensely old High Lama, who describes an ideal future life for Conway at Shangri-La and attempts to persuade him to remain. The High Lama is speaking:*

". . . IT IS . . . a prospect of much charm that I unfold for you—long tranquillities during which you will observe a sunset as men in the outer world hear the striking of a clock, and with far less care. The years will come and go, and you will pass from fleshly enjoyments into austerer but no less satisfying realms; you may lose the keenness of muscle and appetite, but there will be gain to match your loss; you will achieve calmness and profoundity, ripeness and wisdom, and the clear enchantment of memory. And, most precious of all, you will have Time—that rare and lovely gift that your Western countries have lost the more they have pursued it. Think for a moment. You will have time to read—never again will you skim pages to save minutes, or avoid some study lest it prove too engrossing. You have also a taste for music—here, then, are your scores and instruments, with Time, unruffled and unmeasured, to give you their richest savor. And you are also, we will say, a man of good fellowship—does it not charm you to think of wise and serene friendships, a long and kindly traffic of the mind from which death may not call you away with his customary hurry? Or, if it is solitude that you prefer, could you not employ our pavilions to enrich the gentleness of lonely thoughts?"

The voice made a pause which Conway did not seek to fill.

"You make no comment, my dear Conway. Forgive my eloquence—I belong to an age and a nation that never considered it bad form to be articulate . . . But perhaps you are thinking of wife, parents, children, left behind in the world? Or maybe ambitions to do this or that? Believe me, though the pang may be keen at first, in a decade from now even its ghost will not haunt you. Though in point of fact, if I read your mind correctly, you have no such griefs."

Conway was startled by the accuracy of the judgment. "That's so," he replied. "I'm unmarried; I have few close friends and no ambitions."

"No ambitions? And how have you contrived to escape those widespread maladies?"

For the first time Conway felt that he was actually taking part in a conversation. He said: "It always seemed to me in my profession that a good deal of what passed for success would be rather disagreeable, apart from needing more effort than I felt called upon to make. I was in the Consular Service—quite a subordinate post, but it suited me well enough."

"Yet your soul was not in it?"

"Neither my soul nor my heart nor more than half my energies. I'm naturally rather lazy."

The wrinkles deepened and twisted till Conway realized that the High Lama was very probably smiling. "Laziness in doing stupid things can be a great virtue," resumed the whisper. "In any case, you will scarcely find us exacting in such a matter. Chang, I believe, explained to you our principle of moderation, and one of the things in which we are always moderate is activity. I myself, for instance, have been able to learn ten languages; the ten might have been twenty had I worked immoderately. But I did not. And it is the same in other directions; you will find us neither profligate nor ascetic. Until we reach an age when care is advisable, we gladly accept the pleasure of the table, while—for the benefit of our younger colleagues—the women of the valley have happily applied the principle of moderation to their own chastity. All things considered, I feel sure you will get used to our ways without much effort. Chang, indeed, was very optimistic—and so, after this meeting, am I. But there is, I admit, an odd quality in you that I have never met in any of our visitors hitherto. It is not quite cynicism, still less bitterness; perhaps it is partly disillusionment, but it is also a clarity of mind that I should not have expected in any one younger than—say, a century or so. It is, if I had to put a single word to it, passionlessness."

Conway answered: "As good a word as most, no doubt. I don't know whether you classify the people who come here, but if so, you can label me '1914-1918.' That makes me, I should think, a unique specimen in your museum of antiquities—the other three who arrived along with me don't enter the category. I used up most of my passions and energies during the years I've mentioned, and though I don't talk much about it, the chief thing I've asked from the world since then is to leave me alone. I find in this place a certain charm and quietness that appeals to me, and no doubt, as you remark, I shall get used to things."

"Is that all, my son?"

"I hope I am keeping well to your own rule of moderation."

"You are clever—as Chang told me, you are very clever. But is there nothing in the prospect I have outlined that tempts you to any stronger feeling?"

Conway was silent for an interval and then replied: "I was deeply impressed by your story of the past, but to be candid, your sketch of the future interests me only in an abstract sense. I can't look so far ahead. I should certainly be sorry if I had to leave Shangri-La to-morrow or next week, or perhaps even next year; but how I shall feel about it if I live to be a hundred isn't a matter to prophesy. I can face it, like any other future, but in order to make me keen it must have a point. I've sometimes doubted whether life itself has any; and if not, long life must be even more pointless."

"My friend, the traditions of this building, both Buddhist and Christian, are very reassuring."

"Maybe. But I'm afraid I still hanker after some more definite reason for envying the centenarian."

"There *is* a reason, and a very definite one indeed. It is the whole reason for this colony of chance-sought strangers living beyond their years. We do not follow an idle experiment, a mere whimsy. We have a dream and a vision. It is a vision that first appeared to old Perault when he lay dying in this room in the year 1789. He looked back then on his long life, as I have already told you, and it seemed to him that all the loveliest things were transient and perishable, and that war, lust, and brutality might some day crush them until there were no more left in the world. He remembered sights he had seen with his own eyes, and with his mind he pictured others; he saw the nations strengthening, not in wisdom, but in vulgar passions and the will to destroy; he saw their machine power multiplying until a single-weaponed man might have matched a whole army of the Grand Monarque. And he perceived that when they had filled the land and sea with ruin, they would take to the air. . . . Can you say that his vision was untrue?"

"True indeed."

"But that was not all. He foresaw a time when men, exultant in the technique of homicide, would rage so hotly over the world that every precious thing would be in danger, every book and picture and harmony, every treasure garnered through two millenniums, the small, the delicate, the defenseless— all would be lost like the lost books of Livy, or wrecked as the English wrecked the Summer Palace in Pekin."

"I share your opinion of that."

"Of course. But what are the opinions of reasonable men against iron and steel? Believe me, that vision of old Perrault will come true. And that, my son, is why *I* am here, and why *you* are here, and why we may pray to outlive the doom that gathers around on every side."

"To outlive it?"

"There is a chance. It will all come to pass before you are as old as I am."

"And you think that Shangri-La will escape?"

"Perhaps. We may expect no mercy, but we may faintly hope for neglect. Here we shall stay with our books and our music and our meditations, conserving the frail elegancies of a dying age, and seeking such wisdom as men will need when their passions are all spent. We have a heritage to cherish and bequeath. Let us take what pleasure we may until that time comes."

"And then?"

"Then, my son, when the strong have devoured each other, the Christian ethic may at last be fulfilled, and the meek shall inherit the earth."

A shadow of emphasis had touched the whisper, and Conway surrendered to the beauty of it; again he felt the surge of darkness around, but now symbolically, as if the world outside were already brewing for the storm. And then he saw the High Lama of Shangri-La was actually astir, rising from his chair, standing upright like the half-embodiment of a ghost. In mere politeness Conway made to assist; but suddenly a deeper impulse seized him, and he did what he had never done to any man before; he knelt, and hardly knew why he did.

"I understand you, Father," he said.

He was not perfectly aware of how at last he took his leave; he was in a dream from which he did not emerge till long afterwards. He remembered the night air icy after the heat of those upper rooms, and Chang's presence, a silent serenity, as they crossed the starlit courtyards together. Never had Shangri-La offered more concentrated loveliness to his eyes; the valley lay imaged over the edge of the cliff, and the image was of a deep unrippled pool that matched the peace of his own thoughts. For Conway had passed beyond astonishments. The long talk, with its varying phases, had left him empty of all save a satisfaction that was as much of the mind as of the emotions, and as much of the spirit as of either; even his doubts were no longer harassing, but part of a subtle harmony. Chang did not speak, and neither did he. It was very late, and he was glad that all the others had gone to bed.

FOR EACH MAN

Let each man think himself an act of
    God,
His mind a thought, his life a breath of
    God.

          —Bailey

BY FAITH

He walked by faith and not by sight,
    By love and not by law;
The presence of the wrong or right
    He rather felt than saw.

          —Whittier

GREAT thoughts come from the heart.—*Vauvenargues*

GREATNESS and goodness are not means, but ends!—*Coleridge*

LET US make haste to live, since every day to a wise man is a new life.—*Seneca*

LIFE is really simple, but men insist on making it complicated.—*Confucius*

LOOK NOT MOURNFULLY into the Past. It comes not back again. Wisely improve the Present. It is thine. Go forth to meet the shadowy Future, without fear, and with a manly heart.—*Longfellow*

FINISH EVERY DAY and be done with it. You have done what you could. Some blunders and absurdities no doubt crept in; forget them as soon as you can. Tomorrow is a new day; begin it well and serenely and with too high a spirit to be cumbered with your old nonsense. This day is all that is good and fair. It is too dear, with its hopes and invitations, to waste a moment on the yesterdays.—*Emerson*

LET US BE of good cheer, remembering that the misfortunes hardest to bear are those that never come.—*Lowell*

STRIVE FOR the approval of your companions but do not be too easily moved by ridicule. When you know what you ought to do, permit not the laughter of others to deter you.—*Frederick Starr*

WHATEVER IS in any way beautiful hath its source of beauty in itself, and is complete in itself; praise forms no part of it. So it is none the worse nor the better for being praised.—*Marcus Aurelius*

THERE IS no such thing as a small country. The greatness of a people is no more affected by the number of its inhabitants than the greatness of an individual is measured by his height. Whoever presents a great example is great.—*Hugo*

PROBABLY he who never made a mistake never made a discovery.—*Smiles*

OF WISDOM

How shall I be able to rule over others, that have not full
power and command of myself?—*Rabelais*

THE JOURNEY of a thousand miles begins with one step.—*Lao-tse*

WHEN MERIT has been achieved, do not take it to yourself; for if you do not
take it to yourself, it shall never be taken from you.—*Lao-tse*

LET US HAVE FAITH that right makes might; and in that faith, let us, to the
end, dare to do our duty as we understand it.—*Lincoln*

I SHALL PASS through this world but once. If, therefore, there be any kindness
I can show, or any good thing I can do, let me do it now; let me not defer
it or neglect it, for I shall not pass this way again.—*De Grellet*

IT IS EASY in the world to live after the world's opinions; it is easy in solitude
to live after our own; but the Great Man is he who in the midst of the crowd
keeps with perfect sweetness the independence of solitude.—*Emerson*

THERE is no truer truth obtainable by man than comes of music.—*Browning*

ONE OUGHT every day at least to hear a little song, read a good poem,
see a fine picture, and, if it were possible, to speak a few reasonable
words.—*Goethe*

ALL that is beautiful shall abide, all that is base shall die.—*Buchanan*

THERE is no gathering the rose without being pricked by the
thorns.—*Pilpay*

TAKE from our hearts the love of the beautiful, and you take
away all the charm of life.—*Rousseau*

MUCH REMAINS to conquer still; peace hath her victories
no less renowned than war.—*Milton*

From *TREES*

By DONALD CULROSS PEATTIE

I SAW them first, the redwoods, at twilight, coming on them unexpectedly. Silent, awe-struck, I walked fearfully between their boles, greater than the shafts of any temple, and threw my head back to see the last sunset light sweeping through the dark, sempiternal fronds. My feet, on the deep humus carpet of centuries of needle-fall, made not a sound. Nowhere, in the mist rose-blurred with afterglow, was there a sound except the voice of a single bird, at his vespers, a disembodied voice in the clerestory of this sacred grove.

What a story a redwood stump could tell, with its 2000 rings of annual growth. One of the outermost rings carries us back to the landing of the Pilgrims. Count back from there: 1600, 1500, 1400, 1100—you are still only at the First Crusade. Keep on counting, year by year. Your eyes will be sore and strained before you get back to the year when Alaric was sacking a fallen humbled Rome. And yet this proud, this lusty American tree was already a strong young giant. When it was a sapling the Chinese were inventing paper. When it was a hopeful shoot, Pompeii, the pride of pagan pleasure cities, was buried under the ashes of Vesuvius. As the seed sprouted, Christ was born in Bethlehem.

EPIGRAM ON MORN

SIR WILLIAM WATSON

Once more a perfect morn! With feet
    that trod
  Earth's green, and sun-kissed hair
    that swept heaven's blue
Affable, smiling, aweless—I met God,
  Delighted with His work as when
    it was new.

SERENE WILL BE OUR DAYS . . .

WILLIAM WORDSWORTH

Serene will be our days and bright,
  And happy will our nature be,
When love is an unerring light,
  And joy its own security.

AMONG THE CLIMBING ROSES

By SELMA LAGERLÖF

I COULD WISH that the people with whom I have spent my summer would let their glance fall on these lines. Now when the cold, dark nights have come, I should like to carry their thoughts back to that bright, warm season.

Above all, I should like to remind them of the climbing-roses that enclosed the veranda, of the delicate, somewhat thin foliage of the clematis, which in the sunlight as well as in the moonlight was drawn in dark gray shadows on the light gray stone floor and threw a light lace-like veil over everything, and of its big, bright blossoms with their ragged edges.

Other summers remind me of fields of clover, or of birch-woods, or of apple-trees and berry bushes, but that summer took its character from the climbing-roses. The bright, delicate buds, that could resist neither wind nor rain, the light, waving, pale-green shoots, the soft, bending stems, the exuberant richness of blossoms, the gaily humming hosts of insects, all follow me and rise up before me in their glory, when I think of that summer, that rosy, delicate, dainty summer.

Now, when the time for work has come, people often ask me how I passed my summer. Then everything glides from my memory, and it seems to me as if I had sat day in and day out on the veranda behind the climbing-roses and breathed in fragrance and sunshine.

From *FREEDOM FROM FEAR*

By Stephen Vincent Benét

A hundred and sixty odd years ago, we, as a nation, asserted that all men were created equal, that all men were entitled to life, liberty and the pursuit of happiness. Those were large assertions, but we have tried to live up to them. We have not always succeeded, we have often failed. But our will and desire as a nation have been to live up to them.

Now, in concert with other free nations, we say that those children you see and other children like them all over the world shall grow to manhood and womanhood free from fear. We say that neither their minds nor their bodies shall be cramped or distorted or broken by tyranny and oppression. We say they shall have a chance, and an equal chance, to grow and develop and lead the lives they choose to lead, not lives mapped out for them by a master. And we say that freedom for ourselves involves freedom for others—that it is a universal right, neither lightly given by providence nor to be maintained by words alone, but by acts and deeds and living.

We who are alive today did not make our free institutions. We got them from the men of the past and we hold them in trust for the future. Should we put ease and selfishness above them, that trust will fail and we shall lose all, not a portion or a degree of liberty, but all that has been built for us and all that we hope to build. Real peace will not be won with one victory. It can be won only by long determination, firm resolve and a wish to share and work with other men, no matter what their race or creed or condition. And yet, we do have the choice. We can have freedom from fear.

THE MOUNTAINS ARE A LONELY FOLK

Hamlin Garland

The mountains they are silent folk,
They stand afar—alone;
And the clouds that kiss their brows
at night
Hear neither sigh or groan.
Each bears him in his ordered place
As soldiers do, and bold and high
They fold their forests round their
feet
And bolster up the sky.

From *ADDRESS TO THE OCEAN*

Barry Cornwall

O, lovely in repose! thy summer form
Is beautiful, and when thy silver waves
Make music in earth's dark and winding caves,
I love to wander on thy pebbled beach,
Marking the sunlight at the evening
hour,
And hearken to the thoughts thy waters
teach,—
Eternity—Eternity—and Power.

* * *

We ought all to be content with the time and portion assigned us. No man expects of any one actor in the theatre that he should perform all the parts of the piece himself: one role only is committed to him, and whatever that be, if he act it well, he is applauded. In the same way, it is not the part of a wise man to desire to be busy in these scenes to the last plaudit. A short term may be long enough to live it well and honourably.   —*Cicero*

217

Follow Your Nose!

By DAVID GRAYSON

*O*N A SPRING MORNING one has only to step out into the open country, lift his head to the sky—and follow his nose. . . .

It was a big and golden morning, and Sunday to boot, and I walked down the lane to the lower edge of the field, where the wood and the mash begin. The sun was just coming up over the hills and all the air was fresh and clear and cool. High in the heavens a few fleecy clouds were drifting, and the air was just enough astir to waken the hemlocks into faint and sleepy exchanges of confidence.

It seemed to me that morning that the world was never before so high, so airy, so golden. All filled to the brim with the essence of sunshine and spring morning—so that one's spirit dissolved in it, became a part of it. Such a morning! Such a morning!

From that place and just as I was I set off across the open land.

It was the time of all times for good odours—soon after sunrise—before the heat of the day had drawn off the rich distillations of the night.

In that keen moment I caught, drifting, a faint but wild fragrance upon the air, and veered northward full into the way of the wind. I could not at first tell what this particular odour was, nor separate it from the general good odour of the earth; but I followed it intently across the moor-like open land. Once I thought I had lost it entirely, or that the faint northern airs had shifted, but I soon caught it clearly again, and just as I was saying to myself, "I've got it, I've got it!"—for it is a great pleasure to identify a friendly odour in the fields—I saw, near the bank of the brook, among ferns and raspberry bushes, a thorn-apple tree in full bloom.

"So there you are!" I said.

I hastened toward it, now in the full current and glory of its fragrance. The sun, looking over the taller trees to the east, had crowned the top of it with gold, so that it was beautiful to see; and it was full of honey bees as excited as I.

A score of feet onward toward the wind, beyond the thorn-apple tree, I passed wholly out of the range of its fragrance into another world, and began trying for some new odour. After one or two false scents, for this pursuit has all the hazards known to the hunter, I caught an odour long known to me, not strong, nor yet very wonderful, but distinctive. It led me still a little distance northward to a sunny slope just beyond a bit of marsh, and, sure enough, I found an old friend, the wild sweet geranium, a world of it, in full bloom, and I sat down there for some time to enjoy it fully.

Beyond that, and across a field wild with tangles of huckleberry bushes and sheep laurel where the bluets and buttercups were blooming, and in shady spots the sky white violet, I searched for the odour of a certain clump of pine trees I discovered long ago. I knew that I must come upon it soon, but could not tell just when or where. I held up a moistened finger to make sure of the exact direction of the wind, and bearing, then, a little eastward, soon came full upon it—as a hunter might surprise a deer in the forest. I crossed the brook a second time and through a little marsh, making it the rule of the game never to lose for an instant the scent I was following—even though I stopped in a low spot to admire a mass of thrifty blue flags, now beginning to bloom—and came thus to the pines I was seeking. They are not great trees, nor noble, but gnarled and angular and stunted, for the soil in that place is poor and thin, and the winds in winter keen; but the brown blanket of needles they spread and the shade they offer the traveller are not less hospitable; nor the fragance they give off less enchanting. The odour of the pine is one I love.

I sat down there in a place I chose long ago—a place already as familiar with pleasing memories as a favourite room—so that I wonder that some of the notes I have written there do not of themselves exhale the very odour of the pines.

And all about was hung a fair tapestry of green, and the earthy floor was cleanly carpeted with brown, and the roof above was in arched mosaic, the deep, deep blue of the sky seen through the gnarled and knotted branches of the pines. Through a little opening among the trees, as through a window, I could see the cattle feeding in the wide meadows, all headed alike, and yellow butterflies drifted across the open spaces, and there were bumblebees and dragonflies. And presently I heard some one tapping, tapping, at the door of the wood and glancing up quickly I saw my early visitor. There he was, as neighbourly as you please, and not in the least awed by my intrusion; there he was, far out on the limb of a dead tree, stepping energetically up and down, like a sailor reefing a sail, and rapping and tapping as he worked—a downy woodpecker.

"Good morning, sir," I said.

He stopped for scarcely a second, cocked one eye at me, and went back to his work again. Who was I that I should interrupt his breakfast?

And I was glad I was there, and I began enumerating, as though I were the accredited reporter for the *Woodland Gazette,* all the good news of the day.

"The beech trees," I said aloud, "have come at last to full leafage. The wild blackberries are ready to bloom, the swamp roses are budded. Brown planted fields I see, and drooping elms, and the young crows cry from their nests on the knoll. . . . I know now that, whoever I am, whatever I do, I am welcome here; the meadows are as green this spring for Tom the drunkard, and for Jim the thief, as for Jonathan the parson, or for Walt the poet: the wild cherry blossoms as richly, and the odour of the pine is as sweet—"

At that moment, like a flame for clearness, I understood some of the deep and simple things of life, as that we are to be like the friendly pines, and the elm trees, and the open fields, and reject no man and judge no man. Once, a long time ago, I read a sober treatise by one who tried to prove with elaborate knowledge that, upon the whole, good was triumphant in this world, and that probably there was a God, and I remember going out dully afterward upon the hill, for I was weighed down with a strange depression, and the world seemed to me a hard, cold, narrow place where good must be heavily demonstrated in books. And as I sat there the evening fell, a star or two came out in the clear blue of the sky, and suddenly it became all simple to me, so that I laughed aloud at that laborious bigwig for spending so many futile years in seeking doubtful proof of what he might have learned in one rare hour upon my hill. And far more than he could prove—far more. . . .

As I came away from that place I knew I should never again be quite the same person I was before. . . .

Well, we cannot remain steadily upon the heights. At least I cannot, and would not if I could. After I have been out about so long on such an adventure as this, something lets go inside of me, and I come down out of the mountain—and yet know deeply that I have been where the bush was burning; and have

219

heard the Voice in the Fire.

So it was yesterday morning. I realized suddenly that I was hungry—commonly, coarsely hungry. My whole attention, I was going to say my whole soul, shifted to the thought of ham and eggs! This may seem a tremendous anti-climax, but it is, nevertheless, a sober report of what happened. At the first onset of this new mood, the ham-and-eggs mood, let us call it, I was a little ashamed or abashed at the remembrance of my wild flights, and had a laugh at the thought of myself floundering around in the marshes and fields a mile from home, when Harriet, no doubt, had breakfast waiting for me! What absurd, contradictory, inconsistent, cowardly creatures we are, anyway!

The house seemed an inconceivable distance away, and the only real thing in the world the gnawing emptiness under my belt. And I was wet to my knees, and the tangled huckleberry bushes and sheep laurel and hardhack I had passed through so joyously a short time before now clung heavily about my legs as I struggled through them. And the sun was hot and high—and there were innumerable small, black buzzing flies. . . .

To cap the climax, whom should I meet as I was crossing the fence into the lower land but my friend Horace. He had been out early looking for a cow that had dropped her calf in the woods, and was now driving them slowly up the lane, the cow a true pattern of solicitous motherhood, the calf a true pattern of youth, dashing about upon uncertain legs.

"Takin' the air, David?"

I amuse Horace. Horace in an important man in this community. He has big, solid barns, and money in the bank, and a reputation for hardheadedness. He is also known as a "driver"; and has had sore trouble with a favourite son. He believes in "goin' it slow" and "playin' safe," and he is convinced that "ye can't change human nature."

His question came to me with a kind of shock. I imagined with a vividness impossible to describe what Horace would think if I answered him squarely and honestly, if I were to say:

"I've been down in the marshes following my nose—enjoying the thorn apples and the wild geraniums, talking with a woodpecker and reporting the morning news of the woods for an imaginary newspaper."

I was hungry, and in a mood to smile at myself anyway (good-humoredly and forgivingly as we always smile at ourselves!) before I met Horace, and the flashing vision I had of Horace's dry, superior smile finished me. Was there really anything in this world but cows and calves, and great solid barns, and oat-crops, and cash in the bank?

"Been in the brook?" asked Horace, observing my wet legs.

Talk about the courage to face cannon and Cossacks! It is nothing to the courage required to speak aloud in broad daylight of the finest things we have in us! I was not equal to it.

"Oh, I've been down for a tramp in the marsh," I said, trying to put him off.

But Horace is a Yankee of the Yankees and loves nothing better than to chase his friends into corners with questions, and leave them ultimately with the impression that they are somehow less sound, sensible, practical, than he is—and he usually proves it, not because he is right, but because he is sure, and in a world of shadowy half-beliefs and half-believers he is without doubts.

"What ye find down there?" asked Horace.

"Oh, I was just looking around to see how the spring was coming on."

"Hm-m," said Horace, eloquently, and when I did not reply, he continued, "Often git out in the morning as early as this?"

"Yes," I said, "often."

"And do you find things any different

now from what they would be later in the day?"

At this the humour of the whole situation dawned on me and I began to revive. When things grow hopelessly complicated, and we can't laugh, we do either one of two things: we lie or we die. But if we can laugh, we can fight! And be honest!

"Horace," I said, "I know what you are thinking about."

Horace's face remained perfectly impassive, but there was a glint of curiosity in his eye.

"You've been thinking I've been wasting my time beating around down there in the swamp just to look at things and smell of things—which you wouldn't do. You think I'm a kind of impractical dreamer, now, don't you, Horace? I'll warrant you've told your wife just that more than once. Come, now!"

I think I made a rather shrewd hit, for Horace looked uncomfortable and a little foolish.

"Come now, honest!" I laughed and looked him in the eye.

"Waal, now, ye see—"

"Of course you do, and I don't mind it in the least."

A little dry gleam of humour came in his eye.

"Ain't ye?"

It's a fine thing to have it straight out with a friend.

"No," I said, "I'm the practical man and you're the dreamer. I've rarely known in all my life, Horace, such a confirmed dreamer as you are, nor a more impractical one."

Horace laughed.

"How do ye make that out?"

With this my spirit returned to me and I countered with a question as good as his. It is as valuable in argument as in war to secure the offensive.

"Horace, what are you working for, anyhow?"

This is always a devastating shot. Ninety-nine out of every hundred hu-

man beings are desperately at work grubbing, sweating, worrying, thinking, sorrowing, enjoying, without in the least knowing why.

"Why, to make a living—same as you," said Horace.

"Oh, come now, if I were to spread the report in town that a poor neighbour of mine—that's you, Horace—was just making his living, that he himself had told me so, what would you say? Horace, what are you working for? It's something more than a mere living."

"Waal, now, I'll tell ye, if ye want it straight, I'm layin' aside a little something for a rainy day."

"A little something!" this in the exact inflection of irony by which here in the country we express our opinion that a friend has really a good deal more laid aside than anybody knows about. Horace smiled also in the exact manner of one so complimented.

"Horace, what are you going to do with that thirty thousand dollars?"

"Thirty thousand!" Horace looks at me and smiles, and I look at Horace and smile.

"Honest now!"

"Waal, I'll tell ye—a little peace and comfort for me and Josie in our old age, and a little something to make the children remember us when we're gone. Isn't that worth working for?"

He said this with downright seriousness. I did not press him further, but if I had tried I could probably have got the even deeper admission of that faith that lies, like bedrock, in the thought of most men—that honesty and decency here will not be without its reward there, however they may define the "there." Some "prophet's paradise to come!"

"I knew it!" I said. "Horace, you're a dreamer, too. You are dreaming of peace and comfort in your old age, a little quiet house in town where you won't have to labour as hard as you do now, where you won't be worried by crops and weather, and where Mrs.

221

Horace will be able to rest after so many years of care and work and sorrow—a kind of earthly heaven! And you are dreaming of leaving a bit to your children and grandchildren, and dreaming of the gratitude they will express. All dreams, Horace!"

"Oh, waal—"

"The fact is, you are working for a dream, and living on dreams—isn't that true?"

"Waal. now, if you mean it that way—"

"I see I haven't got you beaten yet, Horace!"

He smiled broadly.

"We are all amiable enough with our own dreams. You think that you are working for—your dream—is somehow sounder and more practical than what I am working for."

Horace started to reply, but had scarcely debouched from his trenches when I opened on him with one of my twenty-fours.

"How do you know that you are ever going to be old?"

It hit.

"And if you do grow old, how do you know that thirty thousand dollars—oh, we'll call it that—is really enough, provided you don't lose it before, to buy peace and comfort for you, or that what you leave your children will make either you or them any happier? Peace and comfort and happiness are terribly expensive, Horace—and prices have been going up fast since this war began!"

Horace looked at me uncomfortably, as men do in the world when you shake the foundations of the tabernacle. I have thought since that I probably pressed him too far; but these things go deep with me.

"No, Horace," I said, "you are the dreamer—and the impractical dreamer at that!"

For a moment Horace answered nothing; and we both stood still there in the soft morning sunshine with the peaceful fields and woods all about us, two human atoms struggling hotly with questions too large for us. The cow and the new calf were long out of sight. Horace made a motion as if to follow them up the lane, but I held him with my glittering eye—as I think of it since, not without a kind of amusement at my own seriousness.

"I'm the practical man, Horace, for I want my peace now, and my happiness now, and my God now. I can't wait. My barns may burn or my cattle die, or the solid bank where I keep my deferred joy may fail, or I myself by tomorrow be no longer here."

So powerfully and vividly did this thought take possession of me that I cannot now remember to have said a decent good-bye to Horace (never mind, he knows me!) At least when I was halfway up the hill I found myself gesticulating with one clenched fist and saying to myself with a kind of passion: "Why wait to be peaceful? Why not be peaceful now? Why not be happy now? Why not be rich now?"

For I think it truth that a life uncommanded now is uncommanded; a life unenjoyed now is unenjoyed; a life not lived wisely now is not lived wisely: for the past is gone and no one knows the future.

As for Horace, is he convinced that he is an impractical dreamer? Not a bit of it! He was merely flurried for a moment in his mind, and probably thinks me now, more than ever before, just what I think him. Absurd place, isn't it, this world?

So I reached home at last. You have no idea, unless you have tried it yourself, how good breakfast tastes after a three-mile tramp in the sharp morning air. The odour of ham and eggs, and new muffins, and coffee, as you come up the hill—there is an odour for you! And it was good to see Harriet.

"Harriet," I said, "you are a sight for tired eyes." —From *Great Possessions*

222

THE FOOT-PATH TO PEACE
By HENRY VAN DYKE

TO BE GLAD of life because it gives you the chance to love and to work and to play and to look up at the stars—
to be satisfied with your possessions but not contented with yourself until you have made the best of them—
to despise nothing in the world except falsehood and meanness, and to fear nothing except cowardice—
to be governed by your admirations rather than by your disgusts; to covet nothing that is your neighbor's except his kindness of heart and gentleness of manners—
to think seldom of your enemies, often of your friends, and every day of Christ; and to spend as much time as you can, with body and with spirit, in God's out-of-doors—
these are little guide-posts on the foot-path to peace.

BECAUSE THERE IS A GOD
By LEO TOLSTOY

NOW HE HAD learnt to see the great, the eternal, and the infinite in everything; and naturally therefore, in order to see it, to revel in its contemplation, he flung aside the telescope through which he had hitherto been gazing over men's heads, and looked joyfully at the ever-changing, ever grand, unfathomable, and infinite life around him. And the closer he looked at it, the calmer and happier he was. The terrible question that had shattered all his intellectual edifices in old days, the question: What for? had no existenece for him now. To that question, What for? he had now always ready in his soul the simple answer: Because there is a God, that God without whom not one hair of a man's head falls.

LAST DAY'S CHORE
BERNARD RAYMUND

His hoe is where he left it in the shed,
His hat beside it on a harness-peg;
This was the last day's chore for him, he said,
Some other man could mow the hay and dig
The few potatoes that the drought might spare.
Wherefore a world of pea-vine chokes his corn,
Gates sag unlatched, fences are tangled wire,
Thistle and dock and hogweed go unshorn.

All is as if it waited his return
Who sometimes wakes at midnight in a sweat
(Bewildered by the town's electric stir)
Saying, Was that Pet whickered on the hill?
—When his worn hands grow smooth he may forget:
The fields that knew his labor never will.

A PRAYER
ADELAIDE LOVE

Not only in my summer let me sing
When Beauty storms my senses
       and my soul,
When mine is the mysterious and dark
Delight of one who feels the quivering
Tumultuous heart surrender utterly,
Idolatrous of that bright deity.
Let me not ever lose the moment when
I stand, transfigured, on the
       shining verge
Of dreams beyond all telling and
       I glimpse
The realm where earth and heaven
       subtly merge.
O God, when in my winter I shall walk
The quiet and the twilight ways along,
Let me feel still a breath upon my brow
And find in snow the silver seeds of song.

JULY TWENTY-THIRD
By Donald Culross Peattie

There are no truly wild spots hereabouts unless they may be the marshes —the marshes where no one ever goes, save a huntsman, sometimes, or an adventurous boy. Other topography and vegetation yield to man. The marshes are our tropical jungles; there the intense heat, the cutting edges of wild grass, the footing where one can neither walk nor swim but only sink, forbid intrusion. There grows the bulrush, as graceful as the brush-strokes in a Japanese painting. There the wild rice stands, like Indian corn growing in deep water; in the light breezes the reed grass bends like a forest under a great wind, and the great rosy blossoms of the swamp mallow rise in purity. It is perhaps the only habitat in which no foreign weed is found, nor animal inquilines. There I go to look for the blue pickerel weed, and for the leaf beetles that dwell upon it. There the strangest of all our birds are found—the pumping bittern, and the osprey, and on the surface of the water the striders skate as if on ice, and the male flowers of the eel grass drift in windrows and swirling sargassos amidst the female flowers held fast by thin spiral stalks. Everywhere, midsummer silence, save for the snapping flight of dragon flies, silence and a glory of shimmering heat.

—From *An Almanac for Moderns*

THE ALHAMBRA BY MOONLIGHT
By Washington Irving

The moon has gradually gained upon the nights, and now rolls in full splendor above the towers, pouring a flood of tempered light into every court and hall. The garden beneath my window is gently lighted up; the orange and citron trees are tipped with silver; the fountain sparkles in the moonbeams, and even the blush of the rose is faintly visible.

I have sat for hours at my window inhaling the sweetness of the garden, and musing on the checkered features of those whose history is dimly shadowed out in the elegant memorials around. Sometimes I have issued forth at midnight when every thing was quiet, and have wandered over the whole building. Who can do justice to a moonlight night in such a climate, and in such a place! The temperature of an Andalusian midnight, in summer, is perfectly ethereal. We seem lifted up into a purer atmosphere; there is a serenity of soul a buoyancy of spirits, and elasticity of frame, that render mere existence enjoyment. The effect of moonlight, too, on the Alhambra has something like enchantment. Every rent and chasm of time, every mouldering tint and weather stain disappears; the marble resumes its original whiteness; the long colonnades brighten in the moonbeams; the halls are illuminated with a softened radiance, until the whole edifice reminds one of the enchanted palace of an Arabian tale.

—From *The Alhambra*

* * *

To me it seems as if when God conceived the world, that was poetry; He formed it, and that was sculpture; He varied and colored it, and that was painting; and then, crowning all, He peopled it with living beings, and that was the grand divine, eternal drama. —*Charlotte Cushman*

From *MODERN PAINTERS*

By John Ruskin

Of all inorganic substances, acting in their own proper nature, and without assistance or combination, water is the most wonderful. If we think of it as the course of all the changefulness and beauty which we have seen in clouds; then as the instrument by which the earth we have contemplated was modeled into symmetry, and its crags chiseled into grace; then as, in the form of snow, it robes the mountains it has made with that transcendant light which we could not have conceived if we had not seen; then as it exists in the foam of the torrent—in the iris which spans it, in the morning mist which rises from it, in the deep crystalline pools which mirror its hanging shore, in the broad lake and glancing river; finally, in that which is to all human minds the best emblem of unwearied, unconquerable power, the wild, various, fantastic, tameless unity of the sea; what shall we compare to this mighty, this universal element, for glory and for beauty? or how shall we follow its eternal changefulness of feeling: It is like trying to paint a soul.

ENVOY

Robert Louis Stevenson

Go, little book, and wish to all
Flowers in the garden, meat in the hall,
A bin of wine, a spice of wit,
A house with lawns enclosing it,
A living river by the door,
A nightingale in the sycamore!

TRUTH

Arthur Hugh Clough

It fortifies my soul to know
That, though I perish, Truth is so;
That, howsoever I stray and range,
Whatever I do, Thou does not change.
I steadier step when I recall
That, if I slip, Thou dost not fall.

BEAUTY

By John Galsworthy

Beauty means this to one person, perhaps, and that to the other. And yet when any one of us has seen or heard or read that which to him is beautiful, he has known an emotion which is in every case the same in kind, if not in degree; an emotion precious and uplifting. A choirboy's voice, a ship in sail, an opening flower, a town at night, the song of the blackbird, a lovely poem, leaf shadows, a child's grace, the starry skies, a cathedral, apple trees in spring, a thorough-bred horse, sheep-bells on a hill, a rippling stream, a butterfly, the crescent moon—the thousand sights or sounds or words that evoke in us the thought of beauty—these are the drops of rain that keep the human spirit from death by drought. They are a stealing and a silent refreshment that we perhaps do not think about but which goes on all the time. The war brought a kind of revolt against beauty in art, literature, and music, a revolt that is already passing, and that I am sure will pass. It would surprise any of us if we realized how much store we unconsciously set by beauty, and how little savour there would be left in life if it were withdrawn. It is the smile on the earth's face, open to all, and needs but the eyes to see, the mood to understand.

Sonnets from the Portuguese

ELIZABETH BARRETT BROWNING

I

I thought once how Theocritus had
sung
Of the sweet years, the dear and wished-
for years,
Who each one in a gracious hand
appears
To bear a gift for mortals, old or young:
And, as I mused it in his antique
tongue,
I saw, in gradual vision through my
tears,
The sweet, sad years, the melancholy
years,
Those of my own life, who by turns
had flung
A shadow across me. Straightway I was
'ware,
So weeping, how a mystic Shape did
move
Behind me, and drew me backward by
the hair;
And a voice said in mastery, while I
strove,—
"Guess now who holds thee?" —
"Death," I said. But, there,
The silver answer rang,—"Not Death,
but Love."

II

But only three in all God's universe
Have heard this word thou hast said,—
Himself, beside
Thee speaking, and me listening! and
replied
One of us . . . *that* was God, . . . and
laid the curse
So darkly on my eyelids, as to amerce
My sight from seeing thee,—that if I
had died,
The deadweights, placed there, would
have signified
Less absolute exclusion. "Nay" is worse
From God than from all others, O my
friend!
Men could not part us with their
worldly jars,
Nor the seas change us, nor the tempests
bend;
Our hands would touch for all the
mountain-bars:
And, heaven being rolled between us at
the end,
We should but vow the faster for the
stars.

III

Unlike are we, unlike, O princely
Heart!
Unlike our uses and our destinies.
Our ministering two angels look sur-
prise
On one another, as they strike athwart
Their wings in passing. Thou, bethink
thee, art
A guest for queens to social pageantries,
With gages from a hundred brighter
eyes
Than tears even can make mine, to play
thy part
Of chief musician. What hast *thou* to do
With looking from the lattice-lights at
me,
A poor, tired, wandering singer, singing
through
The dark, and leaning up a cypress
tree?
The chrism is on thine head,—on mine,
the dew,—
And Death must dig the level where
these agree..

IV

Thou hast thy calling to some palace
floor,

Most gracious singer of high poems! where
The dancers will break footing from the care
Of watching up thy pregnant lips for more.
And dost thou lift this house's latch too poor
For hand of thine? and canst thou think and bear
To let thy music drop here unaware
In folds of golden fulness at my door?
Look up and see the casement broken in,
The bats and owlets builders in the roof!
My cricket chirps against thy mandolin.
Hush, call no echo up in further proof
Of desolation! there's a voice within
That weeps . . as thou must sing . . alone, aloof.

V

I lift my heavy heart up solemnly,
As once Electra her sepulchral urn,
And, looking in thine eyes, I overturn
The ashes at thy feet. Behold and see
What a great heap of grief lay hid in me
And how the red wild sparkles dimly burn
Through the ashen greyness. If thy foot in scorn
Could tread them out to darkness utterly,
It might be well perhaps. But if instead
Thou wait beside me for the wind to blow
The grey dust up, . . . those laurels on thine head,
O my Belovèd, will not shield thee so,
That none of all the fires shall scorch and shred
The hair beneath. Stand further off then! go.

VI

Go from me. Yet I feel that I shall stand
Henceforward in thy shadow. Nevermore

Alone upon the threshold of my door
Of individual life, I shall command
The uses of my soul, nor lift my hand
Serenely in the sunshine as before,
Without the sense of that which I forbore—
Thy touch upon the palm. The widest land
Doom takes to part us, leaves thy heart in mine
With pulses that beat double. What I do
And what I dream include thee, as the wine
Must taste of its own grapes. And when I sue
God for myself, He hears that name of thine,
And sees within my eyes the tears of two.

VII

The face of all the world is changed, I think,
Since first I heard the footsteps of thy soul
Move still, oh, still, beside me, as they stole
Betwixt me and the dreadful outer brink
Of obvious death, where I, who thought to sink,
Was caught up into love, and taught the whole
Of life in a new rhythm. The cup of dole
God gave for baptism I am fain to drink,
And praise its sweetness, Sweet, with thee anear.
The names of country, heaven, are changed away
For where thou art or shalt be, there or here;
And this . . this lute and song . . loved yesterday,
(The singing angels know) are only dear
Because thy name moves right in what they say.

VIII

What can I give thee back, O liberal
And princely giver, who hast brought
the gold
And purple of thine heart, unstained,
untold,
And laid them on the outside of the
wall
For such as I to take or leave withal,
In unexpected largesse? am I cold,
Ungrateful, that for these most mani-
fold
High gifts, I render nothing back at all?
Not so; not cold,—but very poor instead.
Ask God who knows. For frequent
tears have run
The colours from my life, and left so
dead
And pale a stuff, it were not fitly done
To give the same pillow to thy head.
Go farther! let it serve to trample on.

IX

Can it be right to give what I can give?
To let thee sit beneath the fall of tears
As salt as mine, and hear the sighing
years
Re-sighing on my lips renunciative
Through those infrequent smiles which
fail to live
For all thy adjurations? O my fears,
That this can scarce be right! We are
not peers,
So to be lovers; and I own, and grieve,
That givers of such gifts as mine are,
must
Be counted with the ungenerous. Out,
alas!
I will not soil thy purple with my dust,
Nor breathe my poison on thy Venice-
glass,
Nor give thee any love—which were un-
just.
Beloved, I only love thee! let it pass.

X

Yet, love, mere love, is beautiful indeed

And worthy of acceptation. Fire is
bright,
Let temple burn, or flax; an equal light
Leaps in the flame from cedar-plank or
weed:
And love is fire. And when I say at need
I love thee . . mark! . . *I love thee*—
in thy sight
I stand transfigured, glorified aright,
With conscience of the new rays that
proceed
Out of my face toward thine. There's
nothing low
In love, when love the lowest: meanest
creatures
Who love God, God accepts while lov-
ing so.
And what I *feel*, across the inferior fea-
tures
Of what I *am*, doth flash itself, and
show
How that great work of Love enhances
Nature's.

XI

And therefore if to love can be desert,
I am not all unworthy. Cheeks as pale
As these you see, and trembling knees
that fail
To bear the burden of a heavy heart,—
This weary minstrel-life that once was
girt
To climb Aornus, and can scarce avail
To pipe now 'gainst the valley nightin-
gale
A melancholy music,—why advert
To these things? O Belovèd, it is plain
I am not of thy worth nor for thy place!
And yet, because I love thee, I obtain
From that same love this vindicating
grace,
To live on still in love, and yet in
vain,—
To bless thee, yet renounce thee to thy
face.

XII

Indeed this very love which is my boast,

And which, when rising up from breast to brow,
Doth crown me with a ruby large enow
To draw men's eyes and prove the inner cost,—
This love even, all my worth, to the uttermost,
I should not love withal, unless that thou
Hadst set me an example, shown me how,
When first thine earnest eyes with mine were crossed,
And love called love. And thus, I cannot speak
Of love even, as a good thing of my own:
Thy soul hath snatched up mine all faint and weak,
And placed it by thee on a golden throne,—
And that I love (O soul, we must be meek!)
Is by thee only, whom I love alone.

XIII

And wilt thou have me fashion into speech
The love I bear thee, finding words enough,
And hold the torch out, while the winds are rough,
Between our faces, to cast light on each?—
I drop it at thy feet. I cannot teach
My hand to hold my spirit so far off
From myself—me—that I should bring thee proof
In words, of love hid in me out of reach.
Nay, let the silence of my womanhood
Commend my woman-love to thy belief,—
Seeing that I stand unwon, however wooed,
And rend the garment of my life, in brief,
By a most dauntless, voiceless fortitude,
Lest one touch of this heart convey its grief.

XIV

If thou must love me, let it be for nought
Except for love's sake only. Do not say
"I love her for her smile—her look—her way
Of speaking gently,—for a trick of thought
That falls in well with mine, and certes brought
A sense of pleasant ease on such a day"—
For these things in themselves, Belovèd, may
Be changed, or change for thee,—and love, so wrought,
May be unwrought so. Neither love me for
Thine own dear pity's wiping my cheeks dry,—
A creature might forget to weep, who bore
Thy comfort long, and lose thy love thereby!
But love me for love's sake, that evermore
Thou mayst love on, through love's eternity.

XV

Accuse me not, beseech thee, that I wear
Too calm and sad a face in front of thine;
For we two look two ways, and cannot shine
With the same sunlight on our brow and hair.
On me thou lookest with no doubting care,
As on a bee shut in a crystalline;
Since sorrow hath shut me safe in love's divine,
And to spread wing and fly in the outer air
Were most impossible failure, if I strove
To fail so. But I look on thee—on thee—
Beholding, besides love, the end of love,
Hearing oblivion beyond memory;
As on who sits and gazes from above,
Over the rivers to the bitter sea.

XVI

And yet, because thou overcomest so,
Because thou art more noble and like a
king,
Thou canst prevail against my fears and
fling
Thy purple round me, till my heart
shall grow
Too close against thine heart hence-
forth to know
How it shook when alone. Why, con-
quering
May prove as lordly and complete a
thing
In lifting upward, as in crushing low!
And as a vanquished soldier yields his
sword
To one who lifts him from the bloody
earth,
Even so, Belovèd, I at last record,
Here ends my strife. If *thou* invite me
forth,
I rise above abasement at the word.
Make thy love larger to enlarge my
worth.

XVII

My poet, thou canst touch on all the
notes
God set between His After and Before,
And strike up and strike off the general
roar
Of the rushing worlds a melody that
floats
In a serene air purely. Antidotes
Of medicated music, answering for
Mankind's forlornest uses, thou canst
pour
From thence into their ears. God's will
devotes
Thine to such ends, and mine to wait
on thine.
How, Dearest, wilt thou have me for
most use?
A hope, to sing by gladly? or a fine
Sad memory, with thy songs to inter-
fuse?

A shade, in which to sing—of palm or
pine?
A grave, on which to rest from singing?
Choose.

XVIII

I never gave a lock of hair away
To a man, Dearest, except this to thee,
Which now upon my fingers thought-
fully,
I ring out to the full brown length and
say
"Take it." My day of youth went yes-
terday;
My hair no longer bounds to my foot's
glee,
Nor plant I it from rose or myrtle-tree,
As girls do, any more; it only may
Now shade on two pale cheeks the mark
of tears,
Taught drooping from the head that
hangs aside
Through sorrow's trick. I thought the
funeral-shears
Would take this first, but Love is justi-
fied,—
Take it thou,—finding pure, from all
those years,
The kiss my mother left here when she
died.

XIX

The soul's Rialto hath its merchandise;
I barter curl for curl upon that mart,
And from my poet's forehead to my
heart
Receive this lock which outweighs argo-
sies,—
As purply black, as erst to Pindar's
eyes
The dim purpureal tresses gloomed
athwart
The nine white Muse-brows. For this
counterpart, . .
The bay-crown's shade, Belovèd, I sur-
mise,
Still lingers on thy curl, it is so black!

Thus, with a fillet of smooth-kissing breath,
I tie the shadows safe from gliding back,
And lay the gift where nothing hinder-
eth;
Here on my heart, as on thy brow, to
lack
No natural heat till mine grows cold in
death.

XX

Belovèd, my Belovèd, when I think
That thou wast in the world a year ago,
What time I sat alone here in the snow
And saw no footprint, heard the silence
sink
No moment at thy voice, but, link by
link,
Went counting all my chains as if that so
They never could fall off at any blow
Struck by thy possible hand,—why, thus
I drink
Of life's great cup of wonder! Won-
derful,
Never to feel thee thrill the day or night
With personal act or speech,—nor ever
cull
Some prescience of thee with the blos-
soms white
Thou sawest growing! Atheists are as
dull,
Who cannot guess God's presence out
of sight.

XXI

Say over again, and yet once over again,
That thou dost love me. Though the
word repeated
Should seem "a cuckoo-song," as thou
dost treat it.
Remember, never to the hill or plain,
Valley and wood, without her cuckoo-
strain
Comes the fresh Spring in all her green
completed.
Belovèd, I, amid the darkness greeted
By a doubtful spirit-voice, in that
doubt's pain

Cry, "Speak once more—thou lovest!"
Who can fear
Too many stars, though each in heaven
shall roll,
Too many flowers, though each shall
crown the year?
Say thou dost love me, love me, love me
—toll
The silver iterance!—only minding,
Dear,
To love me also in silence with thy soul.

XXII

When our two souls stand up erect and
strong,
Face to face, silent, drawing nigh and
nigher,
Until the lengthening wings break into
fire
At either curvèd point,—what bitter
wrong
Can the earth do to us, that we should
not long
Be here contented? Think. In mount-
ing higher,
The angels would press on us and aspire
To drop some golden orb of perfect
song
Into our deep, dear silence. Let us stay
Rather on earth, Belovèd—where the
unfit
Contrarious moods of men recoil away
And isolate pure spirits, and permit
A place to stand and love in for a day,
With darkness and the death-hour
rounding it.

XXIII

Is it indeed so? If I lay here dead,
Wouldst thou miss any life in losing
mine?
And would the sun for these more cold-
ly shine
Because of grave-damps falling round
my head?
I marvelled, my Belovèd, when I read
Thy thought so in the letter. I am
thine—

But . . . *so* much to thee? Can I pour thy wine
While my hands tremble? Then my soul, instead
Of dreams of death, resumes life's lower range.
Then, love me, Love! look on me—breathe on me!
As brighter ladies do not count it strange,
For love, to give up acres and degree,
I yield the grave for thy sake, and exchange
My near sweet view of Heaven, for earth with thee!

By a beating heart at dance-time. Hopes apace
Were changed to long despairs, till God's own grace
Could scarcely lift above the world forlorn
My heavy heart. Then *thou* didst bid me bring
And let it drop adown thy calmly great
Deep being! Fast it sinketh, as a thing
Which its own nature doth precipitate,
While thine doth close above it, mediating
Betwixt the stars and the unaccomplished fate.

XXIV

Let the world's sharpness, like a clasping knife,
Shut in upon itself and do no harm
In this close hand of Love, now soft and warm,
And let us hear no sound of human strife
After the click of the shutting. Life to life—
I lean upon thee, Dear, without alarm,
And feel as safe as guarded by a charm
Against the stab of worldlings, who if rife
Are weak to injure. Very whitely still
The lilies of our lives may reassure
Their blossoms from their roots, accessible
Alone to heavenly dews that drop not fewer
Growing straight, out of man's reach, on the hill.
God only, who made us rich, can make us poor.

XXV

A heavy heart, Belovèd, have I borne
From year to year until I saw thy face,
And sorrow after sorrow took the place
Of all those natural joys as lightly worn
As the stringed pearls, each lifted in its turn

XXVI

I lived with visions for my company
Instead of men and women, years ago,
And found them gentle mates, nor thought to know
A sweeter music than they played to me.
But soon their trailing purple was not free
Of this world's dust, their lutes did silent grow,
And I myself grew faint and blind below
Their vanishing eyes. Then THOU didst come—to be,
Belovèd, what they seemed. Their shining fronts,
Their songs, their splendours (better, yet the same,
As river-water hallowed into fonts),
Met in thee, and from out thee overcame
My soul with satisfaction of all wants:
Because God's gifts put man's best dreams to shame.

XXVII

My own Belovèd, who hast lifted me
From this drear flat of earth where I was thrown,
And, in betwixt the languid ringlets, blown
A life-breath, till the forehead hopefully

Shines out again, as all the angels see,
Before thy saving kiss! My own, my
    own,
Who camest to me when the world was
    gone,
And I who looked for only God, found
    thee!
I find thee; I am safe, and strong, and
    glad.
As one who stands in dewless asphodel
Looks backward on the tedious time he
    had
In the upper life,—so, I with bosom-
    swell,
Make witness, here, between the good
    and bad,
That Love, as strong as Death, retrieves
    as well.

XXVIII

My letters! all dead paper, mute and
    white!
And yet they seem alive and quivering
Against my tremulous hands which
    loose the string
And let them drop down on my knee
    tonight.
This said,—he wished to have me in his
    sight
Once, as a friend: this fixed a day in
    spring
To come and touch my hand . . . a sim-
    ple thing,
Yet I wept for it!—this, . . . the paper's
    light . . .
Said, *Dear, I love thee;* and I sank and
    quailed
As if God's future thundered on my
    past.
This said, *I am thine*—and so its ink
    has paled
With lying at my heart that beat too
    fast.
And this . . . O Love, thy words have
    ill availed
If, what this said, I dared repeat at
    last!

XXIX

I think of thee!—my thoughts do twine
    and bud
About thee, as wild vines, about a tree,
Put out broad leaves, and soon there's
    nought to see
Except the straggling green which hides
    the wood.
Yet, O my palm-tree, be it understood
I will not have my thoughts instead of
    thee
Who art dearer, better! Rather, in-
    stantly
Renew thy presence; as a strong tree
    should,
Rustle thy boughs and set thy trunk all
    bare,
And let these bands of greenery which
    insphere thee
Drop heavily down,—burst, shattered,
    everywhere!
Because, in this deep joy to see and
    hear thee
And breathe within thy shadow a new
    air,
I do not think of thee—I am too near
    thee.

XXX

I see thine image through my tears to-
    night,
And yet to-day I saw thee smiling. How
Refer the cause?—Belovèd, is it thou
Or I, who makes me sad? The acolyte
Amid the chanted joy and thankful rite
May so fall flat, with pale insensate
    brow,
On the altar-stair. I hear thy voice and
    vow,
Perplexed, uncertain, since thou art out
    of sight,
As he, in his swooning ears, the choir's
    Amen.
Belovèd, dost thou love? or did I see all
The glory as I dreamed, and fainted
    when

Too vehement light dilated my ideal,
For my soul's eyes? Will that light come
    again,
As now these tears come—falling hot
    and real?

XXXI

Thou comest! all is said without a word,
I sit beneath thy looks, as children do
In the noon-sun, with souls that tremble
    through
Their happy eyelids from an unaverred
Yet prodigal inward joy. Behold, I
    erred
In that last doubt! and yet I cannot rue
The sin most, but the occasion—that we
    two
Should for a moment stand unminis-
    tered
By a mutual presence. Ah, keep near
    and close,
Thou dovelike help! and, when my
    fears would rise,
With thy broad heart serenely inter-
    pose:
Brood down with thy divine sufficiencies
These thoughts which tremble when
    bereft of those,
Like callow birds left desert to the skies.

XXXII

The first time that the sun rose on thine
    oath
To love me, I looked forward to the
    moon
To slacken all those bonds which
    seemed too soon
And quickly tied to make a lasting
    troth.
Quick-loving hearts, I thought, may
    quickly loathe;
And, looking on myself, I seemed not
    one
For such a man's love!—more like an
    out-of-tune
Worn viol, a good singer would be
    wroth
To spoil his song with, and which,
    snatched in haste,
Is laid down at the first ill-sounding
    note.
I did not wrong myself so, but I placed
A wrong on *thee*. For perfect strains
    may float
'Neath master-hands, from instruments
    defaced,—
And great souls, at one stroke, may do
    and doat.

XXXIII

Yes, call me by my pet-name! let me
    hear
The name I used to run at, when a
    child,
From innocent play, and leave the cow-
    slips piled,
To glance up in some face that proved
    me dear
With the look of its eyes. I miss the
    clear
Fond voices which, being drawn and
    reconciled
Into the music of Heaven's undefiled,
Call me no longer. Silence on the bier,
While I call God—call God!—So let thy
    mouth
Be heir to those who are now exanimate.
Gather the north flowers to complete
    the south,
And catch the early love up in the late.
Yes, call me by that name,—and I, in
    truth,
With the same heart, will answer and
    not wait.

XXXIV

With the same heart, I said, I'll answer
    thee
As those, when thou shalt call me by
    my name—
Lo, the vain promise! is the same, the
    same,
Perplexed and ruffled by life's strategy?
When called before, I told how hastily
I dropped my flowers or brake off from
    a game,

To run and answer with the smile that
    came
At play last moment, and went on with
    me
Through my obedience. When I an-
    swer now,
I drop a grave thought, break from soli-
    tude;
Yet still my heart goes to thee—ponder
    how—
Not as to a single good, but all my good!
Lay thy hand on it, best one, and allow
That no child's foot could run fast as
    this blood.

XXXV

If I leave all for thee, wilt thou ex-
    change
And be all to me? Shall I never miss
Home-talk and blessing and the com-
    mon kiss
That comes to each in turn, nor count
    it strange,
When I look up, to drop on a new range
Of walls and floors, another home than
    this?
Nay, wilt thou fill that place by me
    which is
Filled by dead eyes too tender to know
    change?
That's hardest. If to conquer love, has
    tried,
To conquer grief, tries more, as all
    things prove;
For grief indeed is love and grief beside.
Alas, I have grieved so I am hard to
    love.
Yet love me—wilt thou? Open thine
    heart wide,
And fold within the wet wings of thy
    dove.

XXXVI

When we met first and loved, I did not
    build
Upon the event with marble. Could it
    mean

To last, a love set pendulous between
Sorrow and sorrow? Nay, I rather
    thrilled,
Distrusting every light that seemed to
    gild
The onward path, and feared to over-
    lean
A finger even. And, though I have
    grown serene
And strong since then, I think that God
    has willed
A still renewable fear . . . O love, O
    troth . . .
Lest these enclaspèd hands should nev-
    er hold,
This mutual kiss drop down between us
    both
As an unowned thing, once the lips
    being cold.
And Love, be false! if *he,* to keep one
    oath,
Must lose one joy, by his life's star
    foretold.

XXXVII

Pardon, oh, pardon, that my soul should
    make,
Of all that strong divineness which I
    know
For thine and thee, an image only so
Formed of the sand, and fit to shift and
    break.
It is that distant years which did not
    take
Thy sovranty, recoiling with a blow,
Have forced my swimming brain to un-
    dergo
Their doubt and dread, and blindly to
    forsake
Thy purity of likeness and distort
Thy worthiest love to a worthless coun-
    terfeit:
As if a shipwrecked Pagan, safe in port,
His guardian sea-god to commemorate,
Should set a sculptured porpoise, gills
    a-snort
And vibrant tail, within the temple-
    gate.

XXXVIII

First time he kissed me, he but only
    kissed
The fingers of this hand wherewith I
    write;
And ever since, it grew more clean and
    white,
Slow to world-greetings, quick with its
    "Oh, list,"
When the angels speak. A ring of ame-
    thyst
I could not wear here, plainer to my
    sight,
Than that first kiss. The second passed
    in height
The first, and sought the forehead, and
    half missed,
Half falling on the hair. O beyond
    meed!
That was the chrism of love, which
    love's own crown,
With sanctifying sweetness, did pre-
    cede.
The third upon my lips was folded
    down
In perfect, purple state; since when,
    indeed,
I have been proud and said, "My love,
    my own."

XXXIX

Because thou hast the power and own'st
    the grace
To look through and behind this mask
    of me
(Against which years have beat thus
    blanchingly
With their rains), and behold my soul's
    true face,
The dim and weary witness of life's
    race,—
Because thou hast the faith and love
    to see,
Through that same soul's distracting
    lethargy,
The patient angel waiting for a place
In the new Heavens,—because nor sin
    nor woe,

Nor God's infliction, nor death's neigh-
    bourhood,
Nor all which others viewing, turn to
    go,
Nor all which makes me tired of all,
    self-viewed,—
Nothing repels thee, . . . Dearest, teach
    me so
To pour out gratitude, as thou dost,
    good!

XL

Oh, yes, they love through all this world
    of ours!
I will not gainsay love, called love for-
    sooth.
I have heard love talked in my early
    youth,
And since, not so long back but that
    the flowers
Then gathered, smelt still. Musselmans
    and Giaours
Throw kerchiefs at a smile, and have no
    ruth
For any weeping. Polypheme's white
    tooth
Slips on the nut if, after frequent
    showers,
The shell is over-smooth,—and not so
    much
Will turn the thing called love, aside
    to hate
Or else to oblivion. But thou art not
    such
A lover, my Belovèd! Thou canst wait
Through sorrow and sickness, to bring
    souls to touch,
And think it soon when others cry "Too
    late."

XLI

I thank all who have loved me in their
    hearts,
With thanks and love from mine. Deep
    thanks to all
Who paused a little near the prison-
    wall
To hear my music in its louder parts

Ere they went onward, each one to the mart's
Or temple's occupation, beyond call.
But thou, who, in my voice's sink and fall
When the sob took it, thy divinest Art's
Own instrument didst drop down at thy foot
To hearken what I said between my tears, . . .
Instruct me how to thank thee! Oh, to shoot
My soul's full meaning into future years,
That *they* should lend it utterance, and salute
Love that endures, from Life that disappears!

XLII

"My future will not copy fair my past"—
I wrote that once; and thinking at my side
My ministering life-angel justified
The word by his appealing look upcast
To the white throne of God, I turned at last,
And there, instead, saw thee, not unallied
To angels in thy soul! Then I, long tried
By natural ills, received the comfort fast,
While budding, at thy sight, my pilgrim's staff
Gave out green leaves with morning dews impearled.
I seek no copy now of life's first half:
Leave here the pages with long musing curled,
And write me new my future's epigraph,
New angel mine, unhoped for in the world!

XLIII

How do I love thee? Let me count the ways.
I love thee to the depth and breadth and height

My soul can reach, when feeling out of sight
For the ends of Being and ideal Grace.
I love thee to the level of everyday's
Most quiet need, by sun and candlelight.
I love thee freely, as men strive for Right;
I love thee purely, as they turn from Praise.
I love thee with the passion put to use
In my old griefs, and with my childhood's faith.
I love thee with a love I seemed to lose
With my lost saints,—I love thee with the breath,
Smiles, tears, of all my life!—and, if God choose,
I shall but love thee better after death.

XLIV

Belovèd, thou hast brought me many flowers
Plucked in the garden, all the summer through
And winter, and it seemed as if they grew
In this close room, nor missed the sun and showers.
So, in the like name of that love of ours,
Take back these thoughts which here unfolded too,
And which on warm and cold days I withdrew
From my heart's ground. Indeed, those beds and bowers
Be overgrown with bitter weeds and rue,
And wait thy weeding; yet here's eglantine,
Here's ivy!—take them, as I used to do
Thy flowers, and keep them where they shall not pine.
Instruct thine eyes to keep their colours true,
And tell thy soul their roots are left in mine.

Riders to the Sea
By JOHN MILLINGTON SYNGE

CHARACTERS
MAURYA, an Old Woman; BARTLEY, her son;
CATHLEEN, her daughter; NORA, a younger daughter;
MEN and WOMEN

* * *

SCENE
An island off the west of Ireland.

Cottage kitchen, with nets, oilskins, spinning wheel, some new boards standing by the wall, etc. CATHLEEN, *a girl of about twenty, finishes kneading cake, and puts it down in the pot-oven by the fire; then wipes her hands, and begins to spin at the wheel.* NORA, *a young girl, puts her head in at the door.*

NORA *(in a low voice).* Where is she?

CATHLEEN. She's lying down, God help her, and may be sleeping, if she's able. (NORA *comes in softly, and takes a bundle from under her shawl).*

CATHLEEN *(spinning the wheel rapidly).* What is it you have?

NORA. The young priest is after bringing them. It's a shirt and a plain stocking were got off a drowned man in Donegal. (CATHLEEN *stops her wheel with a sudden movement, and leans out to listen.)*

NORA. We're to find out if it's Michael's they are, some time herself will be down looking by the sea.

CATHLEEN. How would they be Michael's Nora? How would he go the length of that way to the far north?

NORA. The young priest says he's known the like of it. "If it's Michael's they are," says he, "you can tell herself he's got a clean burial by the grace of God, and if they're not his, let no one say a word about them, for she'll be getting her death," says he, "with crying and lamenting." (*The door which* NORA *half closed is blown open by a gust of wind.)*

CATHLEEN *(looking out anxiously).* Did you ask him would he stop Bartley going this day with the horses to the Galway fair?

NORA. "I won't stop him," says he, "but let you not be afraid. Herself does be saying prayers half through the night, and the Almighty God won't leave her destitute," says he, "with no son living."

CATHLEEN. Is the sea bad by the white rocks, Nora?

NORA. Middling bad, God help us. There's a great roaring in the west, and it's worse it'll be getting when the tide's turned to the wind. (*She goes over to the table with the bundle.)* Shall I open it now?

CATHLEEN. Maybe she'd wake up on us, and come in before we'd done. (*Coming to the table*)—It's a long time we'll be, and the two of us crying.

NORA *(goes to the inner door and listens).* She's moving about on the bed. She'll be coming in a minute.

CATHLEEN. Give me the ladder, and I'll put them up in the turf-loft, the way she won't know of them at all, and maybe when the tide turns she'll be going down to see would he be floating from the east. (*They put the ladder against the gable of the chimney;* CATHLEEN *goes up a few steps and hides the bundle in the turf-loft.* MAURYA *comes from the inner room.)*

MAURYA (*looking up at* CATHLEEN *and speaking querulously*). Isn't it turf enough you have for this day and evening?

CATHLEEN. There's a cake baking at the fire for a short space (*throwing down the turf*) and Bartley will want it when the tide turns if he goes to Connemara. (NORA *picks up the turf and puts it round the pot-oven.*)

MAURYA (*sitting down on a stool at the fire*). He won't go this day with the wind rising from the south and west. He won't go this day, for the young priest will stop him surely.

NORA. He'll not stop him, mother, and I heard Hamon Simon and Stephen Pheety and Colum Shawn saying he would go.

MAURYA. Where is he itself?

NORA. He went down to see would there be another boat sailing in the week, and I'm thinking it won't be long till he's here now, for the tide's turning at the green head, and the hooker's tacking from the east.

CATHLEEN. I hear someone passing the big stones.

NORA (*looking out*). He's coming now, and he in a hurry.

BARTLEY (*comes in and looks round the room. Speaking sadly and quietly*). Where is the bit of new rope, Cathleen, was bought in Connemara?

CATHLEEN (*coming down*). Give it to him, Nora; it's on a nail by the white boards. I hung it up this morning, for the pig with the black feet was eating it.

NORA (*giving him a rope*). Is that it, Bartley?

MAURYA. You'd do right to leave that rope, Bartley, hanging by the boards. (BARTLEY *takes the rope.*) It will be wanting in this place, I'm telling you, if Michael is washed up tomorrow morning, or the next morning, or any morning in the week, for it's a deep grave we'll make him by the grace of God.

BARTLEY (*beginning to work with the rope*). I've no halter the way I can ride down on the mare, and I must go now quickly. This is the one boat going for two weeks or beyond it, and the fair will be a good fair for horses I heard them saying below.

MAURYA. It't a hard thing they'll be saying below if the body is washed up and there's no man in it to make the coffin, and I after giving a big price for the finest white boards you'd find in Connemara. (*She looks round at the boards.*)

BARTLEY. How would it be washed up, and we after looking each day for nine days, and a strong wind blowing a while back from the west and south?

MAURYA. If it wasn't found itself, that wind is raising the sea, and there was a star up against the moon, and it rising in the night. If it was a hundred horses, or a thousand horses you had itself, what is the price of a thousand horses against a son where there is one son only?

BARTLEY (*working at the halter, to* CATHLEEN). Let you go down each day, and see the sheep aren't jumping in on the rye, and if the jobber comes you can sell the pig with the black feet if there is a good price going.

MAURYA. How would the like of her get a good price for a pig?

BARTLEY (*to* CATHLEEN). If the west wind holds with the last bit of the moon let you and Nora get up weed enough for another cock for the keep. It's hard set we'll be from this day with no one in it but one man to work.

MAURYA. It's hard set we'll be surely the day you're drownd'd with the rest. What way will I live and the girls with me, and I an old woman looking for the grave? (BARTLEY *lays down the halter, takes off his old coat, and puts on a newer one of the*

239

same flannel.)

BARTLEY (*to* NORA). Is she coming to the pier?

NORA (*looking out*). She's passing the green head and letting fall her sails.

BARTLEY (*getting his purse and tobacco*). I'll have half an hour to go down, and you'll see me coming again in two days, or in three days, or maybe in four days if the wind is bad.

MAURYA (*turning round to the fire, and putting her shawl over her head*). Isn't it a hard and cruel man won't hear a word from an old woman, and she holding him from the sea?

CATHLEEN. It's the life of a young man to be going on the sea, and who would listen to an old woman with one thing and she saying it over?

BARTLEY (*taking the halter*). I must go now quickly. I'll ride down on the red mare, and the gray pony'll run behind me. . . . The blessing of God on you. (*He goes out.*)

MAURYA (*crying out as he is in the door*). He's gone now, God spare us, and we'll not see him again. He's gone now, and when the black night is falling I'll have no son left me in the world.

CATHLEEN. Why wouldn't you give him your blessing and he looking round in the door? Isn't it sorrow enough is on everyone in this house without your sending him out with an unlucky word behind him, and a hard word in his ear? (MAURYA *takes up the tongs and begins raking the fire aimlessly without looking round.*)

NORA (*turning towards her*). You're taking away the turf from the cake.

CATHLEEN (*crying out*). The Son of God forgive us, Nora, we're after forgetting his bit of bread. (*She comes over to the fire.*)

NORA. And it's destroyed he'll be going till dark night, and he after eating nothing since the sun went up.

CATHLEEN (*turning the cake out of the oven*). It's destroyed he'll be, surely. There's no sense left on any person in a house where an old woman will be talking forever. (MAURYA *sways herself on her stool.*)

CATHLEEN (*cutting off some of the bread and rolling it in a cloth; to* MAURYA). Let you go down now to the spring well and give him this and he passing. You'll see him then and the dark word will be broken, and you can say "God speed you," the way he'll be easy in his mind.

MAURYA (*taking the bread*). Will I be in it as soon as himself?

CATHLEEN. If you go now quickly.

MAURYA (*standing up unsteadily*). It's hard set I am to walk.

CATHLEEN (*looking at her anxiously*). Give her the stick, Nora, or maybe she'll slip on the big stones.

NORA. What stick?

CATHLEEN. The stick Michael brought from Connemara.

MAURYA (*taking a stick* NORA *gives her*). In the big world the old people do be leaving things after them for their sons and children, but in this place it is the young men do be leaving things behind for them that do be old. (*She goes out slowly.* NORA *goes over to the ladder.*)

CATHLEEN. Wait, Nora, maybe she'd turn back quickly. She's that sorry, God help her, you wouldn't know the thing she'd do.

NORA. Is she gone round by the bush?

CATHLEEN (*looking out*). She's gone now. Throw it down quickly for the Lord knows when she'll be out of it again.

NORA (*getting the bundle from the loft*). The young priest said he'd be passing tomorrow, and we might go down and speak to him below if it's Michael's they are surely.

CATHLEEN (*taking the bundle*). Did he say what way they were found?

NORA (*coming down*). "There were

two men," says he, "and they rowing round with poteen before the cocks crowed, and the oar of one of them caught the body, and they passing the black cliffs of the north."

CATHLEEN (*trying to open the bundle*). Give me a knife, Nora, the string's perished with the salt water, and there's a black knot on it you wouldn't loosen in a week.

NORA (*giving her a knife*). I've heard tell it was a long way to Donegal.

CATHLEEN (*cutting the string*). It is surely. There was a man in here a while ago—the man sold us that knife —and he said if you set off walking from the rocks beyond, it would be seven days you'd be in Donegal.

NORA. And what time would a man take, and he floating? (CATHLEEN *opens the bundle and takes out a bit of stocking. They look at them eagerly.*)

CATHLEEN (*in a low voice*). The Lord spare us, Nora! Isn't it a queer hard thing to say if it's his they are surely?

NORA. I'll get his shirt off the hook the way we can put the one flannel on the other. (*She looks through some clothes hanging in the corner.*) It's not with them, Cathleen, and where will it be?

CATHLEEN. I'm thinking Bartley put it on him in the morning, for his own shirt was heavy with the salt in it. (*Pointing to the corner.*) There's a bit of a sleeve; was of the same stuff. Give me that and it will do. (NORA *brings it to her and they compare the flannel.*)

CATHLEEN. It's the same stuff, Nora; but if it is itself aren't there great rolls of it in the shops of Galway, and isn't it many another man may have a shirt of it as well as Michael himself?

NORA (*who has taken up the stocking and counted the stitches, crying out*). It's Michael, Cathleen, it's Michael; God spare his soul, and what will

herself say when she hears this story, and Bartley on the sea?

CATHLEEN (*taking the stocking*). It's a plain stocking.

NORA. It's the second one of the third pair I knitted, and I put up three score stitches, and I dropped four of them.

CATHLEEN (*counts the stitches*). It's that number is in it. (*Crying out.*) Ah, Nora, isn't it a bitter thing to think of him floating that way to the far north, and no one to keen him but the black hags that do be flying on the sea?

NORA (*swinging herself round, and throwing out her arms on the clothes*). And isn't it a pitiful thing when there is nothing left of a man who was a great rower and fisher, but a bit of an old shirt and a plain stocking?

CATHLEEN (*after an instant*). Tell me is herself coming, Nora? I hear a little sound on the path.

NORA (*looking out*). She is, Cathleen. She's coming up to the door.

CATHLEEN. Put these things away before she'll come in. Maybe it's easier she'll be after giving her blessing to Bartley, and we won't let on we've heard anything the time he's on the sea.

NORA (*helping* CATHLEEN *to close the bundle*). We'll put them here in the corner. (*They put them into a hole in the chimney corner.* CATHLEEN *goes back to the spinning-wheel.*)

NORA. Will she see it was crying I was?

CATHLEEN. Keep your back to the door the way the light'll not be on you. (NORA *sits down at the chimney corner, with her back to the door.* MAURYA *comes in very slowly, without looking at the girls, and goes over to her stool at the other side of the fire. The cloth with the bread is still in her hand. The girls look at each other, and* NORA *points to the bundle of bread.*)

241

CATHLEEN (*after spinning for a moment*). You didn't give him his bit of bread? (MAURYA *begins to keen softly, without turning around.*)

CATHLEEN. Did you see him riding down? (MAURYA *goes on keening.*)

CATHLEEN (*a little impatiently*). God forgive you; isn't it a better thing to raise your voice and tell what you seen, than to be making lamentation for a thing that's done? Did you see Bartley, I'm saying to you?

MAURYA (*with a weak voice*). My heart's broken from this day.

CATHLEEN (*as before*). Did you see Bartley?

MAURYA. I seen the fearfulest thing.

CATHLEEN (*leaves her wheel and looks out*). God forgive you; he's riding the mare now over the green head, and the gray pony behind him.

MAURYA (*starts, so that her shawl falls back from her head and shows her white tossed hair. With a frightened voice*). The gray pony behind him.

CATHLEEN (*coming to the fire*). What is it ails you, at all?

MAURYA (*speaking very slowly*). I've seen the fearfulest thing any person has seen, since the day Bride Dara seen the dead man with the child in his arms.

CATHLEEN and NORA. Uah. (*They crouch down in front of the old woman at the fire.*)

NORA. Tell us what it is you seen.

MAURYA. I went down to the spring well, and I stood there saying a prayer to myself. Then Bartley came along, and he riding on the red mare with the gray pony behind him. (*She puts up her hands, as if to hide something from her eyes.*) The Son of God spare us, Nora!

CATHLEEN. What is it you seen?

MAURYA. I seen Michael himself.

CATHLEEN (*speaking softly*). You did not, mother; it wasn't Michael you seen, for his body is after being found in the far north, and he's got a clean burial by the grace of God.

MAURYA (*a little defiantly*). I'm after seeing him this day, and he riding and galloping. Bartley came first on the red mare; and I tried to say "God speed you," but something choked the words in my throat. He went by quickly; and "The blessing of God on you," says he, and I could say nothing. I looked up then, and I crying, at the gray pony, and there was Michael upon it—with fine clothes on him, and new shoes on his feet.

CATHLEEN (*begins to keen*). It's destroyed we are from this day. It's destroyed, surely.

NORA. Didn't the young priest say the Almighty God wouldn't leave her destitute with no son living?

MAURYA (*in a low voice, but clearly*). It's little the like of him knows of the sea. . . . Bartley will be lost now, and let you call in Eamon and make me a good coffin out of the white boards, for I won't live after them. I've had a husband, and a husband's father, and six sons in this house— six fine men, though it was a hard birth I had with every one of them and they coming to the world—and some of them were found and some of them were not found, but they're gone now the lot of them. . . . There were Stephen and Shawn were lost in the great wind, and found after in the Bay of Gregory of the Golden Mouth and carried up the two of them on the one plank, and in by that door. (*She pauses for a moment, the girls start as if they heard something through the door that is half open behind them.*)

NORA (*in a whisper*). Did you hear that, Cathleen? Did you hear a noise in the northeast?

CATHLEEN (*in a whisper*). There's someone after crying out by the seashore.

MAURYA (*continues without hearing

anything). There was Sheamus and his father, and his own father again, were lost in a dark night, and not a stick or sign was seen of them when the sun went up. There was Patch after was drowned out of a curagh that turned over. I was sitting here with Bartley, and he a baby, lying on my two knees, and I seen two women, and three women, and four women coming in, and they crossing themselves, and not saying a word. I looked out then, and there were men coming after them, and they holding a thing in the half of a red sail, and water dripping out of it—it was a dry day, Nora—and leaving a track to the door. (*She pauses again with her hand stretched out towards the door. It opens softly and old women begin to come in, crossing themselves on the threshold, and kneeling down in front of the stage with red petticoats over their heads.*)

MAURYA (*half in a dream, to* CATHLEEN). Is it Patch, or Michael, or what is it at all?

CATHLEEN. Michael is after being found in the far north, and when he is found there how could he be here in this place?

MAURYA. There does be a power of young men floating round in the sea, and what way would they know if it was Michael they had, or another man like him, for when a man is nine days in the sea, and the wind blowing, it's hard set his own mother would be to say what man was it.

CATHLEEN. It's Michael, God spare him, for they're after sending us a bit of his clothes from the far north. (*She reaches out and hands* MAURYA *the clothes that belonged to Michael.* MAURYA *stands up slowly, and takes them in her hands.* NORA *looks out.*)

NORA. They're carrying a thing among them and there's water dripping out of it and leaving a track by the big stones.

CATHLEEN (*in a whisper to the women who have come in*). Is it Bartley, it is?

ONE OF THE WOMEN. It is surely, God rest his soul! (*Two younger women come in and pull out the table. Then men carry in the body of* BARTLEY, *laid on a plank, with a bit of a sail over it, and lay it on the table.*)

CATHLEEN (*to the women, as they are doing so*). What way was he drowned?

ONE OF THE WOMEN. The gray pony knocked him into the sea, and he was washed out where there is a great surf on the white rocks. (*MAURYA has gone over and knelt down at the head of the table. The women are keening softly and swaying themselves with a slow movement.* CATHLEEN *and* NORA *kneel at the other end of the table. The men kneel near the door.*)

MAURYA (*raising her head and speaking as if she did not see the people around her*). They're all gone now, and there isn't anything more the sea can do to me. . . . I'll have no call now to be up crying and praying when the wind breaks from the south, and you can hear the surf is in the east, and the surf is in the west, making a great stir with the two noises, and they hitting one on the other. I'll have no call now to be going down and getting Holy Water in the dark nights after Samhain, and I won't care what way the sea is when the other women will be keening. (*To* NORA.) Give me the Holy Water, Nora, there's a small cup still on the dresser. (NORA *gives it to her.*)

MAURYA (*drops* MICHAEL's *c l o t h e s across* BARTLEY's *feet, and sprinkles the Holy Water over him*). It isn't that I haven't prayed for you, Bartley, to the Almighty God. It isn't that I haven't said prayers in the dark night till you wouldn't know what I'd be saying; but it's a great

rest I'll have now, and it's time surely. It's a great rest I'll have now, and
great sleeping in the long nights
after Samhain, if it's only a bit of
wet flour we do have to eat, and maybe a fish that would be stinking.
(*She kneels down again, crossing herself, and saying prayers under her
breath.*)

CATHLEEN (*to an old man*). Maybe
yourself and Eamon would make a
coffin when the sun rises. We have
fine white boards herself bought,
God help her, thinking Michael
would be found, and I have a new
cake you can eat while you'll be
working.

THE OLD MAN (*looking at the boards*).
Are there nails with them?

CATHLEEN. There are not, Colum; we
didn't think of the nails.

ANOTHER MAN. It's a great wonder she
wouldn't think of the nails, and all
the coffins she's seen made already.

CATHLEEN. It's getting old she is, and
broken. (MAURYA *stands up again
very slowly and spreads out the pieces
of* MICHAEL's *clothes beside the body,
sprinkling them with the last of the
Holy Water.*)

NORA (*in a whisper to* CATHLEEN).
She's quiet now and easy; but the
day Michael was drowned you could
hear her crying out from this to the
spring well. It's fonder she was of
Michael, and would anyone have
thought that?

CATHLEEN (*slowly and clearly*). An old
woman will be soon tired with anything she will do, and isn't it nine
days herself is after crying and keening, and making great sorrow in the
house?

MAURYA (*puts the empty cup mouth
downwards on the table, and lays her
hands together on* BARTLEY's *feet*).
They're all together this time, and
the end is come. May the Almighty
God have mercy on Bartley's soul,
and on Michael's soul, and on the
souls of Sheamus and Patch, and
Stephen and Shawn (*bending her
head*); and may He have mercy on
my soul, Nora, and on the soul of
everyone is left living in the world.
(*She pauses, and the keen rises a little
more loudly from the women, then
sinks away.*)

MAURYA (*continuing*). Michael has a
clean burial in the far north, by the
grace of the Almighty God. Bartley
will have a fine coffin out of the
white boards, and a deep grave surely. What more can we want than
that? No man at all can be living
forever, and we must be satisfied.
(*She kneels down again and the curtain falls slowly.*)

❦   ❦   ❦

THERE IS NO FRIGATE LIKE A BOOK

EMILY DICKINSON

There is no frigate like a book
　To take us lands away,
Nor any coursers like a page
　Of prancing poetry.

This traverse may the poorest take
　Without oppress of toil;
How frugal is the chariot
　That bears a human soul!

A SONG OF THE LILAC

LOUISE IMOGEN GUINEY

Above the wall that's broken,
　And from the coppice thinned,
So sacred and so sweet,
　The lilac in the wind!

And every night the May wind blows
　The lilac blooms apart,
The memory of his first love
　Is shaken on his heart.

244

WHERE THE FOREST MURMURS
By FIONA MACLEOD

IT IS when the trees are leafless, or when the last withered leaves rustle in the wintry air, creeping along the bare boughs like tremulous mice, or fluttering from the branches like the tired and starving swallows left behind in the ebbing tides of migration, that the secret of the forest is mostly likely to be surprised. Mystery is always there. Silence and whispers, still glooms, sudden radiances, the passage of winds and idle airs, all these inhabit the forest at every season. But it is not in their amplitude that great woodlands reveal their secret life. In the first vernal weeks the wave of green creates a mist or shimmering veil of delicate beauty, through which the missel-thrush calls, and the loud screech of the jay is heard like a savage trumpet-cry. The woods then are full of a virginal beauty. There is intoxication in the light air. The cold azure among the beech-spaces or where the tall elms sway in the east wind, is, like the sea, exquisitely desirable, exquisitely unfamiliar, inhuman, of another world. Then follow the days when the violets creep through the mosses at the base of great oaks, when the dust of snowbloom on the blackthorn gives way to the trailing dog-rose, when myriads of bees among the chestnut-blossoms fill the air with a continuous drowsy unnrest, when the cushat calls from the heart of the fir, when beyond the green billowy roof of elm and hornbeam, of oak and beech, of sycamore and lime and tardy ash, the mysterious bells of the South fall through leagues of warm air, as the unseen cuckoo sails on the long tides of the wind. Then, in truth, is there magic in the woods. The forest is alive in its divine youth. Every bough is a vast plume of joy: on every branch a sunray falls, or a thrush sways in song, or the gauzy ephemeridae dance in rising and falling aerial cones. The wind moves with the feet of a fawn, with the wings of a dove, with the passing breath of a white owl at dusk. There is not a spot where is neither fragrance nor beauty nor life. From the tiniest arch of grass and twig the shrew-mouse will peep: above the shallowest rain-pool the dragon-fly will hang in miraculous suspense, like one of the faery javelins of Midir which in a moment could be withheld in mid-flight. The squirrel swings from branch to branch: the leveret shakes the dew from the shadowed grass: the rabbits flitter to and fro like brown beams of life: the robin, the chaffinch, the ousel, call through the warm green-glooms: on the bramble-spray and from the fern-garth the yellow-hammer reiterates his gladsome single song: in the cloudless blue fields of the sky the swifts weave a maze of shadow, the rooks rise and fall in giddy ascents and descents like black galleys surmounting measureless waves and sinking into incalculable gulfs.

* * *

❧ WHATSOEVER THINGS are true, whatsoever things are honest, whatsoever things are just, whatsoever things are pure, whatsoever things are lovely, whatsoever things are of good report; if there be any virtue, and if there be any praise, think on these things. —*The Bible*

❧ WE ARE all parts of an infinite plan which is wholly wise and good.—*Bucke*

WE VALUE great men by their virtue and not success.—*Nepos*

GOOD, the more communicated, more abundant grows.—*Milton*

SELF-REVERENCE, self-knowledge, self-control, these three alone lead life to sovereign power.—*Tennyson*

THERE is no beautifier of complexion, or form, or behavior, like the wish to scatter joy and not pain around us.—*Virgil*

VIRTUE AND LEARNING, like gold, have their intrinsic value: but if they are not polished, they certainly lose a great deal of their luster; and even polished brass will pass upon more people than rough gold.—*Lord Chesterfield*

EVERY MAN has within himself a continent of undiscovered character. Happy is he who proves the Columbus of his soul.—*Goethe*

WHY SHOULD WE BE in such desperate haste to succeed and in such desperate enterprises? If a man does not keep pace with his companions, perhaps it is because he hears a different drummer. Let him step to the music which he hears, however measured or far away.—*Thoreau*

ALL WHO HAVE meditated on the art of governing mankind have been convinced that the fate of empires depends on the education of youth.
—*Aristotle*

WE LEARN wisdom from failure much more than from success.—*Smiles*

IF ANY MAN seeks for greatness, let him forget greatness and ask for truth, and he will find both.—*Horace Mann*

TO BE WHAT WE ARE, and to become what we are capable of becoming, is the only end of life.—*Spinoza*

EVERY MOUNTAIN means at least two valleys.—*Anonymous*

OF TRUTH

LOYALTY is the greatest good in the human heart.—*Latin Proverb*

THE WISE MAN becomes full of good, even if he gathers it little by little.
—*Buddha*

TRUE BRAVERY is shown by performing without witness what one might be capable of doing before all the world.—*La Rochefoucauld*

LITTLE MINDS are tamed and subdued by misfortune, but great minds rise above it.—*Irving*

THE MATTER of simplicity, then, comes into literary style, into building, into dress, into life, individualized always by one's personality. In each we aim at the expression of the best that is in us, not at imitation or ostentation.
—*Charles Dudley Warner*

ART comes to you proposing frankly to give nothing but the highest quality to your moments as they pass.—*Pater*

A FREE MIND is a great thing no doubt, but loftiness of heart, belief in goodness, capacity for enthusiasm and devotion, the thirst after perfection and holiness, are greater things still.—*Amiel*

THE RICHES of scholarship, the benignities of literature, defy fortune and outlive calamity.—*Lowell*

THE PLEASURES of the senses pass quickly; those of the heart become sorrow; but those of the mind are with us even to the end of our journey.
—*Spanish Proverb*

CHARACTER is like a tree and reputation like its shadow. The shadow is what we think of it; the tree is the real thing.—*Lincoln*

A MAN'S FORTUNES are the fruit of his character.—*Emerson*

A THOUGHT once awakened does not slumber.—*Carlyle*

A SONG

HERBERT HORNE

Be not too quick to carve our rhyme
And hearts, upon the tree of Time;
Lest one swift year prove, in its run,
They were but lines, and poorly done.
That longest lives, which longest grows
In stillness, and by sure degrees:
  So rest you, Sweet;
That, going hence with calmer feet,
We may be friends, when friends are
    foes,
And old days merely histories.

THE WAY THROUGH THE WOODS

RUDYARD KIPLING

They shut the road through the woods
Seventy years ago.
Weather and rain have undone it again,
And now you would never know
There was once a road through the
    woods
Before they planted the trees.
It is underneath the coppice and heath,
And the thin anemones.
Only the keeper sees
That, where the ring-dove broods,
And the badger rolls at ease,
There was once a way through the
    woods.

Yet, if you enter the woods
Of a summer evening late,
When the night air cools on the trout-
    ringed pools
Where the otter whistles his mate,
(They fear not men in the woods,
Because they see so few)
You will hear the beat of a horse's feet,
And the swish of a skirt in the dew,
Steadily cantering through
The misty solitudes,
As though they perfectly knew
The old lost road through the
    wood. . . .
But there is no road through the woods!

From SNOW-BOUND

JOHN GREENLEAF WHITTIER

The moon above the eastern wood
Shone at its full; the hill-range stood
Transfigured in the silver flood,
Its blown snows flashing cold and keen,
Dead white, save where some sharp
    ravine
Took shadow, or the sombre green
Of hemlocks turned to pitchy black
Against the whiteness at their back.
For such a world and such a night
Most fitting that unwarming light,
Which only seemed wherever it fell
To make the coldness visible.

From THE SENSITIVE PLANT

PERCY BYSSHE SHELLEY

The plumed insects swift and free,
Like golden boats on a sunny sea,
Laden with light and odour, which pass
Over the gleam of the living grass;

The unseen clouds of the dew, which lie
Like fire in the flowers till the sun rides
    high,
Then wander like spirits among the
    spheres,
Each cloud faint with the fragrance it
    bears;

The quivering vapours of dim noontide
Which like a sea o'er the warm earth
    glide,
In which every sound, and odour, and
    beam
Move as reeds in a single stream;

Each and all like ministering angels
    were,
For the Sensitive Plant sweet joy to
    bear,
While the lagging hours of the day went
    by
Like windless clouds o'er a tender sky.

248

From *REVERIE TO ASOLANDO*
Robert Browning

Then life is—to wake, not sleep.
  Rise and not rest, but press
From earth's level where blindy creep
  Things perfected, more or less,
To the heaven's height, far and steep.

BREAK OF DAY
John Donne

Stay, O sweet, and do not rise;
The light that shines comes from thine
    eyes;
The day breaks not, it is my heart,
Because that you and I must part.
  Stay, or else my joys will die
  And perish in their infancy.

AFFLATUS
Anthony Lane

The wind,
with a breath for beauty,
blew my song away from me
and let it soar . . .

From *THE TWO POETS OF CROISIC*
Robert Browning

PROLOGUE

Such a starved bank of moss
  Till, that May-morn,
Blue ran the flash across:
  Violets were born!

Sky—what a scowl of cloud
  Till, near and far,
Ray on ray split the shroud:
  Splendid, a star!

World—how it walled about
  Life with disgrace
Till God's own smile came out:
  That was thy face!

THE NEW YEAR
Horatio Nelson Powers

A flower unblown; a book unread;
A tree with fruit unharvested;
A path untrod; a house whose rooms
Lack yet the heart's divine perfumes;
A landscape whose wide border lies
In silent shade beneath the skies;
A wondrous fountain yet unsealed;
A casket with its gifts concealed—
This is the Year that for you waits
Beyond tomorrow's mystic gates.

THE THREE CHERRY TREES
Walter de la Mare

There were three cherry trees once,
  Grew in a garden all shady;
And there for delight of so gladsome
    a sight,
  Walked a most beautiful lady,
  Dreamed a most beautiful lady.

Birds in those branches did sing,
  Blackbird and throstle and linnet,
But she walking there was by far the
    most fair—
  Lovelier than all else within it,
  Blackbird and throstle and linnet.

But blossoms to berries do come,
  All hanging on stalks light and
    slender,
And one long summer's day charmed
    that lady away,
  With vows sweet and merry and
    tender;
  A lover with voice low and tender.

Moss and lichen the green branches
    deck;
  Weeds nod in its paths green and
    shady:
Yet a light footstep seems there to
    wander in dreams,
  The ghost of that beautiful lady,
  That happy and beautiful lady.

The Happy Prince

By OSCAR WILDE

*H*IGH ABOVE THE CITY, on a tall column, stood the statue of the Happy Prince. He was gilded all over with thin leaves of fine gold, for eyes he had two bright sapphires, and a large red ruby glowed on his sword-hilt.

He was very much admired indeed. "He is as beautiful as a weathercock," remarked one of the Town Councillors who wished to gain a reputation for having artistic tastes; "only not quite so useful," he added, fearing lest people should think him unpractical, which he really was not.

"Why can't you be like the Happy Prince?" asked a sensible mother of her little boy who was crying for the Moon. "The Happy Prince never dreams of crying for anything."

"I am glad there is some one in the world who is quite happy," muttered a disappointed man as he gazed at the wonderful statue.

"He looks just like an angel," said the Charity Children as they came out of the cathedral in their bright scarlet cloaks and their clean white pinafores.

"How do you know?" said the Mathematical Master, "you have never seen one."

"Ah! but we have, in our dreams," answered the children; and the Mathematical Master frowned and looked very severe, for he did not approve of children dreaming.

One night there flew over the city a little Swallow. His friends had gone away to Egypt six weeks before, but he had stayed behind, for he was in love with the most beautiful Reed. He had met her early in the spring as he was flying down the river after a big yellow moth, and had been so attracted by her slender waist that he had stopped to talk to her.

"Shall I love you?" said the Swallow, who liked to come to the point at once, and the Reed made him a low bow. So he flew round and round her, touching the water with his wings, and making silver ripples. This was his courtship, and it lasted all through the summer.

"It is a ridiculous attachment," twittered the other Swallows; "she has no money, and far too many relations;" and indeed the river was quite full of Reeds. Then, when the autumn came, they all flew away.

After they had gone he felt lonely, and began to tire of his lady-love. "She has no conversation," he said, "and I am afraid that she is a coquette, for she is always flirting with the wind." And certainly, whenever the wind blew, the Reed made the most graceful curtseys. "I admit that she is domestic," he continued, "but I love traveling, and my wife, consequently, should love traveling also."

"Will you come away with me?" he said finally to her; but the Reed shook her head, she was so attached to her home.

"You have been trifling with me," he cried. "I am off to the Pyramids. Goodbye!" and he flew away.

All day long he flew, and at nighttime he arrived at the city. "Where shall I put up?" he said; "I hope the town has made preparations."

Then he saw the statue on the tall column.

"I will put up there," he cried; "it is a fine position with plenty of fresh air."

So he alighted just between the feet of the Happy Prince.

"I have a golden bedroom," he said softly to himself as he looked round, and he prepared to go to sleep; but just as he was putting his head under his wing a large drop of water fell on him. "What a curious thing!" he cried; "there is not a single cloud in the sky, the stars are quite clear and bright, and yet it is raining. The climate in the north of Europe is really dreadful. The Reed used to like the rain, but that was merely her selfishness."

Then another drop fell.

"What is the use of a statue if it cannot keep the rain off?" he said; "I must look for a good chimney-pot," and he determined to fly away.

But before he had opened his wings, a third drop fell, and he looked up, and saw——Ah! what did he see?

The eyes of the Happy Prince were filled with tears, and tears were running down his golden cheeks. His face was so beautiful in the moonlight that the little Swallow was filled with pity.

"Who are you?" he said.

"I am the Happy Prince."

"Why are you weeping then?" asked the Swallow; "you have quite drenched me."

"When I was alive and had a human heart," answered the statue, "I did not know what tears were, for I lived in the Palace of Sans-Souci, where sorrow is not allowed to enter. In the daytime I played with my companions in the garden, and in the evening I led the dance in the Great Hall. Round the garden ran a very lofty wall, but I never cared to ask what lay beyond it, everything about me was so beautiful. My courtiers called me the Happy Prince, and happy indeed I was, if pleasure be happiness. So I lived, and so I died. And now that I am dead they have set me up here so high that I can see all the ugliness and all the misery of my city, and though my heart is made of lead yet I cannot choose but weep."

"What! is he not solid gold?" said the Swallow to himself. He was too polite to make any personal remarks out loud.

"Far away," continued the statue in a low musical voice, "far away in a little street there is a poor house. One of the windows is open, and through it I can see a woman seated at a table. Her face is thin and worn, and she has coarse, red hands, all pricked by the needle, for she is a seamstress. She is embroidering passion-flowers on a satin gown for the loveliest of the Queen's maids-of-honour to wear at the next Court-ball. In a bed in the corner of the room her little boy is lying ill. He has a fever, and is asking for oranges. His mother has nothing to give him but river water, so he is crying. Swallow, Swallow, little Swallow, will you not bring her the ruby out of my sword-hilt? My feet are fastened to this pedestal and I cannot move."

"I am waited for in Egypt," said the Swallow. "My friends are flying up and down the Nile, and talking to the large lotus-flowers. Soon they will go to sleep in the tomb of the great King. The King is there himself in his painted coffin. He is wrapped in yellow linen, and embalmed with spices. Round his neck is a chain of pale green jade, and his hands are like withered leaves."

"Swallow, Swallow, little Swallow," said the Prince, "will you not stay with me for one night, and be my messenger? The boy is so thirsty, and the mother so sad."

"I don't think I like boys," answered the Swallow. "Last summer, when I was staying on the river, there were two rude boys, the miller's sons, who were always throwing stones at me. They never hit me, of course; we swallows fly far too well for that, and besides, I come of a family famous for its agility; but still, it was a mark of disrespect."

But the Happy Prince looked so sad

that the little Swallow was sorry. "It is very cold here," he said; "but I will stay with you for one night, and be your messenger."

"Thank you, little swallow," said the Prince.

So the Swallow picked out the great ruby from the Prince's sword, and flew away with it in his beak over the roofs of the town.

He passed by the cathedral tower, where the white marble angels were sculptured. He passed by the palace and heard the sound of dancing. A beautiful girl came out on the balcony with her lover. "How wonderful the stars are," he said to her, "and how wonderful is the power of love!"

"I hope my dress will be ready in time for the State-ball," she answered; "I have ordered passion-flowers to be embroidered on it; but the seamstresses are so lazy."

He passed over the river, and saw the lanterns hanging to the masts of the ships. He passed over the Ghetto, and saw the old Jews bargaining with each other, and weighing out money in copper scales. At last he came to the poor house and looked in. The boy was tossing feverishly on his bed, and the mother had fallen asleep, she was so tired. In he hopped, and laid the great ruby on the table beside the woman's thimble. Then he flew gently round the bed, fanning the boy's forehead with his wings. "How cool I feel," said the boy, "I must be getting better;" and he sank into a delicious slumber.

Then the Swallow flew back to the Happy Prince, and told him what he had done. "It is curious," he remarked, "but I feel quite warm now, although it is so cold."

"That is because you have done a good action," said the Prince. And the little Swallow began to think, and then he fell asleep. Thinking always made him sleepy.

When day broke he flew down to the river and had a bath. "What a remarkable phenomenon," said the Professor of Ornithology as he was passing over the bridge. "A swallow in winter!" And he wrote a long letter about it to the local newspaper. Every one quoted it, it was full of so many words that they could not understand.

"Tonight I go to Egypt," said the Swallow, and he was in high spirits at the prospect. He visited all the public monuments, and sat a long time on top of the church steeple. Wherever he went the Sparrows chirruped, and said to each other: "What a distinguished stranger!" so he enjoyed himself very much.

When the moon rose he flew back to the Happy Prince. "Have you any commissions for Egypt?" he cried; "I am just starting."

"Swallow, Swallow, little Swallow," said the Prince, "will you not stay with me one night longer?"

"I am waited for in Egypt," answered the Swallow. "Tomorrow my friends will fly up to the Second Cataract. The river-horse couches there among the bulrushes, and on a great granite throne sits the God Memnon. All night long he watches the stars, and when the morning star shines he utters one cry of joy, and then he is silent. At noon the yellow lions come down to the water's edge to drink. They have eyes like green beryls, and their roar is louder than the roar of the cataract."

"Swallow, Swallow, little Swallow," said the Prince, "far away across the city I see a young man in a garret. He is leaning over a desk covered with papers, and in a tumbler by his side there is a bunch of withered violets. His hair is brown and crisp, and his lips are red as a pomegranate, and he has large and dreamy eyes. He is trying to finish a play for the Director of the Theatre, but he is too cold to write any more. There is no fire in the grate, and hunger has made him faint."

"I will wait with you one night longer," said the Swallow, who really had a good heart. "Shall I take him another ruby?"

"Alas! I have no ruby now," said the Prince; "my eyes are all that I have left. They are made of rare sapphires, which were brought out of India a thousand years ago. Pluck out one of them and take it to him. He will sell it to the jeweller, and buy food and firewood, and finish his play."

"Dear Prince," said the Swallow, "I cannot do that"; and he began to weep.

"Swallow, Swallow, little Swallow," said the Prince, "do as I command you."

So the Swallow plucked out the Prince's eye, and flew away to the student's garret. It was easy enough to get in, as there was a hole in the roof. Through this he darted, and came into the room. The young man had his head buried in his hands, so he did not hear the flutter of the bird's wings, and when he looked up he found the beautiful sapphire lying on the withered violets.

"I am beginning to be appreciated," he cried; "this is from some great admirer. Now I can finish my play," and he looked quite happy.

The next day the Swallow flew down to the harbour. He sat on the mast of a large vessel and watched the sailors hauling big chests out of the hold with ropes. "Heave a-hoy!" they shouted as each chest came up. "I am going to Egypt," cried the Swallow, but nobody minded, and when the Moon rose he flew back to the Happy Prince.

"I am come to bid you good-bye," he cried.

"Swallow, Swallow, little Swallow," said the Prince, "will you not stay with me one night longer?"

"It is winter," answered the Swallow, "and the chill snow will soon be here. In Egypt the sun is warm on the green palm-trees, and the crocodiles lie in the mud and look lazily about them. My companions are building a nest in the Temple of Baalbec, and the pink and white doves are watching them, and cooing to each other. Dear Prince, I must leave you, but I will never forget you, and next spring I will bring you back two beautiful jewels in place of those you have given away. The ruby shall be redder than a red rose, and the sapphire shall be as blue as the great sea."

"In the square below," said the Happy Prince, "there stands a little match-girl. She has let her matches fall in the gutter, and they are all spoiled. Her father will beat her if she does not bring home some money, and she is crying. She has no shoes or stockings, and her little head is bare. Pluck out my other eye, and give it to her, and her father will not beat her."

"I will stay with you one night longer," said the Swallow, " but I cannot pluck out your eye. You would be quite blind then."

"Swallow, Swallow, little Swallow," said the Prince, "do as I command you."

So he plucked out the Prince's other eye, and darted down with it. He swooped past the match-girl, and slipped the jewel into the palm of her hand. "What a lovely bit of glass," cried the little girl; and she ran home, laughing.

Then the Swallow came back to the Prince. "You are blind now," he said, "so I will stay with you always."

"No, little Swallow," said the poor Prince, "you must go away to Egypt."

"I will stay with you always," said the Swallow, and he slept at the Prince's feet.

All the next day he sat on the Prince's shoulder, and told him stories of what he had seen in strange lands. He told him of the red ibises, who stand in long rows on the banks of the Nile, and catch goldfish in their beaks; of the Sphinx, who is as old as the world itself, and lives in the desert, and knows everything; of the merchants, who walk slowly by the side of their camels, and carry amber beads in their hand; of the King of the Mountains of the Moon, who is as black as ebony, and worships a large crystal; of the great green snake that sleeps in a palm-tree, and has twenty priests to feed it with honey-cakes; and of the pygmies who sail over a big lake on large flat leaves, and are always at war with the butterflies.

"Dear little Swallow," said the Prince "you tell me of marvelous things, but more marvellous than anything is the suffering of men and of women. There is no Mystery so great as Misery. Fly over my city, little Swallow, and tell me what you see there."

So the Swallow flew over the great city, and saw the rich making merry in their beautiful houses, while the beggars were sitting at the gates. He flew into dark lanes, and saw the white faces of starving children looking out listlessly at the black streets. Under the archway of a bridge two little boys were lying in one another's arms to try and keep themselves warm. "How hungry we are!" they said. "You must not lie here," shouted the Watchman, and they wandered out into the rain.

Then he flew back and told the Prince what he had seen.

"I am covered with fine gold," said the Prince, "you must take it off, leaf by leaf, and give it to my poor; the living always think that gold can make them happy."

Leaf after leaf of the fine gold the Swallow picked off, till the Happy Prince looked quite dull and grey. Leaf after leaf of the fine gold he brought to the poor, and the children's faces grew rosier, and they laughed and played games in the street. "We have bread now!" they cried.

Then the snow came, and after the snow came the frost. The streets looked as if they were made of silver, they were so bright and glistening; long icicles like crystal daggers hung down from the eaves of the houses, everybody went about in furs, and the little boys wore scarlet caps and skated on the ice.

The poor little Swallow grew colder and colder, but he would not leave the Prince, he loved him too well. He picked up crumbs outside the baker's door when the baker was not looking, and tried to keep himself warm by flapping his wings.

But at last he knew that he was going to die. He had just strength to fly up to the Prince's shoulder once more. "Good-bye, dear Prince!" he murmured, "will you let me kiss your hand?"

"I am glad that you are going to Egypt at last, little Swallow," said the Prince, "you have stayed too long here; but you must kiss me on the lips, for I love you."

"It is not to Egypt that I am going," said the Swallow. "I am going to the House of Death. Death is the brother of Sleep, is he not?"

And he kissed the Happy Prince on the lips, and fell down dead at his feet.

At that moment a curious crack sounded inside the statue, as if something had broken. The fact is that the leaden heart had snapped right in two. It certainly was a dreadfully hard frost.

Early the next morning the Mayor was walking in the square below in company with the Town Councillors. As they passed the column he looked up at the statue: "Dear me! how shabby the Happy Prince looks!" he said.

"How shabby indeed!" cried the Town Councillors, who always agreed with the Mayor; and they went up to look at it.

"The ruby has fallen out of his sword, his eyes are gone, and he is golden no longer," said the Mayor; "in fact, he is little better than a beggar!"

"Little better than a beggar," said the

Town Councillors.

"And here is actually a dead bird at his feet!" continued the Mayor. "We must really issue a proclamation that birds are not to be allowed to die here." And the Town Clerk made a note of the suggestion.

So they pulled down the statue of the Happy Prince. "As he is no longer beautiful he is no longer useful," said the Art Professor at the University.

Then they melted the statue in a furnace, and the Mayor held a meeting of the Corporation to decide what was to be done with the metal. "We must have another statue, of course," he said, "and it shall be a statue of myself."

"Of myself," said each of the Town Councillors, and they quarrelled. When I last heard of them they were quarrelling still.

"What a strange thing!" said the overseer of the workmen at the foundry. "This broken lead heart will not melt in the furnace. We must throw it away." So they threw it on a dust-heap where the dead Swallow was also lying.

"Bring me the two most precious things in the city," said God to one of His Angels; and the Angel brought Him the leaden heart and the dead bird.

"You have rightly chosen," said God, "for in my garden of Paradise this little bird shall sing for evermore, and in my city of gold the Happy Prince shall praise me."

UP-HILL
Christina Georgina Rossetti

Does the road wind up-hill all the way?
  Yes, to the very end.
Will the day's-journey take the whole
    long day?
  From morn to night, my friend.

But is there for the night a resting-
    place?
  A roof for when the slow dark hours
    begin?
May not the darkness hide it from my
    face?
  You cannot miss that inn.

Shall I meet other wayfarers at night?
  Those who have gone before.
Then must I knock, or call when just
    in sight?
  *They will not keep you waiting at
    that door.*

Shall I find comfort, travel-sore and
    weak?
  Of labor you shall find the sum.
Will there be beds for me and all who
    seek?
  Yea, beds for all who come.

NOD
Walter de la Mare

Softly along the road of evening,
  In a twilight dim with rose,
Wrinkled with age, and drenched with
    dew
  Old Nod, the shepherd, goes.

His drowsy flock streams on before him,
  Their fleeces charged with gold,
To where the sun's last beam leans low
  On Nod the shepherd's fold.

The hedge is quick and green with
    briar,
  From their sand the conies creep;
And all the birds that fly in heaven
  Flock singing home to sleep.

His lambs outnumber a noon's roses,
  Yet, when night's shadows fall,
His blind old sheep-dog Slumber-soon,
  Misses not one of all.

His are the quiet steps of dreamland,
  The waters of no-more-pain,
His ram's bell rings 'neath an arch of
    stars,
  'Rest, rest, and rest again.'

* * *

❧ All who joy would win must share it. Happiness was born a twin.—*Byron*

WALK SLOWLY
ADELAIDE LOVE

If you should go before me, dear, walk slowly
Down the ways of death, well worn and wide,
For I would want to overtake you quickly
And seek the journey's ending by your side.

I would be so forlorn not to descry you
Down some shining highroad when I came;
Walk slowly, dear, and often look behind you,
And pause to hear if someone calls your name.

❧ ❧ ❧

NOTHING GOLD CAN STAY
ROBERT FROST

Nature's first green is gold,
Her hardest hue to hold.
Her early leaf's a flower;
But only so an hour.
Then leaf subsides to leaf.
So Eden sank to grief,
So dawn goes down to day.
Nothing gold can stay.

SONG
CHRISTINA GEORGINA ROSSETTI

When I am dead, my dearest,
  Sing no sad songs for me;
Plant thou no roses at my head,
  Nor shady cypress-tree:
Be the green grass above me
  With showers and dew drops wet;
And if thou wilt, remember,
  And if thou wilt, forget.

I shall not see the shadows,
  I shall not feel the rain;
I shall not hear the nightingale
  Sing on, as if in pain:
And dreaming through the twilight
  That doth not rise nor set,
Haply I may remember
  And haply may forget.

TO ONE IN PARADISE
EDGAR ALLAN POE

Thou wast that all to me, love,
  For which my soul did pine—
A green isle in the sea, love,
  A fountain and a shrine,
All wreathed with fairy fruits and
      flowers,
  And all the flowers were mine.

Ah, dream too bright to last!
  Ah, starry Hope! that didst arise
But to be overcast!
  A voice from out the Future cries,
"On! on!"—but o'er the Past
  (Dim gulf!) my spirit hovering lies
Mute, motionless, aghast!

For, alas! alas! with me
  The light of Life is o'er!
"No more—no more—no more—"
  (Such language holds the solemn sea
  To the sands upon the shore)
Shall bloom the thunder-blasted tree,
  Or the stricken eagle soar!

And all my days are trances,
  And all my nightly dreams
Are where thy dark eye glances,
  And where thy footstep gleams—
In what ethereal dances,
  By what eternal streams.

THE HILL
RUPERT BROOKE

Breathless, we flung us on the windy hill,
　　Laughed in the sun, and kissed the lovely grass.
　　You said, "Through glory and ecstasy we pass;
Wind, sun, and earth remain, the birds sing still,
When we are old, are old. . . ." "And when we die
　　All's over that is ours; and life burns on
Through other lovers, other lips," said I,
　　—"Heart of my heart, our heaven is now, is won!"
"We are Earth's best, that learnt her lesson here.
　　Life is our cry. We have kept the faith!" we said;
　　"We shall go down with unreluctant tread
Rose-crowned into the darkness!" . . . Proud we were,
And laughed, that had such brave true things to say.
—And then you suddenly cried, and turned away.

LET NOT MY DEATH BE LONG*
LEONORA SPEYER

Let not my death be long,
But light
As a bird's swinging;
Happy decision in the height
Of song—
Then flight
From off the ultimate bough!
And let my wing be strong,
And my last note the first
Of another's singing.
See to it, Thou!

JOY, SHIPMATE, JOY!
WALT WHITMAN

Joy, shipmate, joy!
(Pleased to my soul at death I cry,)
Our life is closed, our life begins,
The long, long anchorage we leave,
The ship is clear at last, she leaps!
She swiftly courses from the shore,
Joy, shipmate, joy!

IN MEMORIAM
MILDRED BOWERS ARMSTRONG

I ask of life this last request:
That word of mine may share
With all who read that loveliness—
The halo of the hair,
The softest voice, the busy hands,
The gentleness and grace—
The logic of the mind—the light
That brightened up a face.

TO————
PERCY BYSSHE SHELLEY

Music, when soft voices die,
Vibrates in the memory—
Odors, when sweet violets sicken,
Live within the sense they quicken,

Rose leaves, when the rose is dead,
Are heaped for the beloved's bed;
And so thy thoughts, when thou art
　　gone
Love itself shall slumber on.

*Reprinted from *Fiddler's Farewell* by Leonora Speyer, by permission of ALFRED A. KNOPF, INC. Copyight 1926 by Alfred A. Knopf, Inc.

From *ADONAIS*

PERCY BYSSHE SHELLEY

He has outsoared the shadow of our
night;
Envy and calumny and hate and pain,
And that unrest which men miscall
delight,
Can touch him not and torture not
again;
From the contagion of the world's
slow stain
He is secure, and now can never
mourn
A heart grown cold, a head grown
gray in vain;
Nor, when the spirit's self has ceased
to burn,
With sparkless ashes load an unlament-
ed urn.

He lives, he wakes—'tis Death is dead,
not he;
Mourn not for Adonais.—Thou
young Dawn,
Turn all thy dew to splendour, for
from thee
The spirit thou lamentest is not gone;
Ye caverns and ye forests, cease to
moan!
Cease, ye faint flowers and fountains,
and thou Air,
Which like a mourning veil thy scarf
hadst thrown
O'er the abandoned Earth, now leave
it bare
Even to the joyous stars which smile on
its despair!

He is made one with Nature: there is
heard
His voice in all her music, from the
moan
Of thunder, to the song of night's
sweet bird;
He is a presence to be felt and known
In darkness and in light, from herb
and stone,
Spreading itself where'er that Power
may move

Which has withdrawn his being to its
own;
Which wields the world with never-
wearied love,
Sustains it from beneath, and kindles it
above.

He is a portion of the loveliness
Which once he made more lovely: he
doth bear
His part, while the one Spirit's plastic
stress
Sweeps through the dull dense world,
compelling there,
All new successions to the forms they
wear;
Torturing th' unwilling dross that
checks its flight
To its own likeness, as each mass may
bear;
And bursting in its beauty and its
might
From trees and beasts and men into the
Heaven's light.

That Light whose smile kindles the
Universe,
That Beauty in which all things work
and move,
That Benediction which the eclipsing
Curse
Of birth can quench not, that sustain-
ing Love
Which through the web of being
blindly wove
By man and beast and earth and air
and sea,
Burns bright or dim, as each are
mirrors of
The fire for which all thirst; now
beams on me,
Consuming the last clouds of cold
mortality.

The breath whose might I have invoked in song
Descends on me; my spirit's bark is

driven,
Far from the shore, far from the
  trembling throng
Whose sails were never to the tempest
  given;
The massy earth and sphered skies are
  riven!

I am borne darkly, fearfully, afar;
Whilst, burning through the inmost
  veil of Heaven,
The soul of Adonais, like a star,
Beacons from the abode where the
  Eternal are.

❧ ❧ ❧

From *ODE TO THE WEST WIND*
PERCY BYSSHE SHELLEY

Make me thy lyre, even as the forest is:
What if my leaves are falling like its own!
The tumult of thy mighty harmonies

Will take from both a deep, autumnal tone,
Sweet though in sadness. Be thou, Spirit fierce,
My spirit! Be thou me, impetuous one!

Drive my dead thoughts over the universe
Like withered leaves to quicken a new birth!
And, by the incantation of this verse,

Scatter, as from an unextinguished hearth
Ashes and sparks, my words among mankind!
Be through my lips to unawakened earth

The trumpet of a prophecy! O, Wind,
If Winter comes, can Spring be far behind?

❧ ❧ ❧

LOVE'S PHILOSOPHY
PERCY BYSSHE SHELLEY

The Fountains mingle with the River
  And the Rivers with the Ocean,
The winds of Heaven mix for ever
  With a sweet emotion;
Nothing in the world is single;
  All things by a law divine
In one spirit meet and mingle.
  Why not I with thine?—

See the mountains kiss high Heaven
  And the waves clasp one another;
No sister-flower would be forgiven
  If it disdained its brother,
And the sunlight clasps the earth
  And the moonbeams kiss the sea:
What are all these kissings worth
  If thou kiss not me?

WHAT IS THE SPIRIT OF LIBERTY?

By Judge Learned Hand

WE HAVE gathered here to affirm a faith, a faith in a common purpose, a common conviction, a common devotion. Some of us have chosen America as the land of our adoption; the rest have come from those who did the same. For this reason we have some right to consider ourselves a picked group, a group of those who had the courage to break from the past and brave the dangers and the loneliness of a strange land.

What was the object that nerved us, or those who went before us, to this choice? We sought liberty; freedom from oppression, freedom from want, freedom to be ourselves. This we then sought. This we now believe that we are by way of winning.

What do we mean when we say that first of all we seek liberty? I often wonder whether we do not rest our hopes too much upon constitutions, upon laws and upon courts. These are false hopes; believe me, these are false hopes. Liberty lies in the hearts of men and women. When it dies there, no constitution, no law, no court can save it. No constitution, no law, no court can even do much to help it. While it lies there, it needs no constitution, no law, no court to save it.

And what is this liberty which must lie in the hearts of men and women? It is not the ruthless, the unbridled will. It is not freedom to do as one likes. That is the denial of liberty, and leads straight to its overthrow. A society in which men recognize no check upon their freedom soon becomes a society where freedom is the possession of only a savage few; as we have learned to our sorrow.

What then is the spirit of liberty? I cannot define it; I can only tell you my own faith. The spirit of liberty is the spirit which is not too sure that it is right. The spirit of liberty is the spirit which seeks to understand the minds of other men and women. The spirit of liberty is the spirit which weighs their interests alongside its own without bias. The spirit of liberty remembers that not even a sparrow falls to earth unheeded. The spirit of liberty is the spirit of Him who, near two thousand years ago, taught mankind that lesson it has never learned, but has never quite forgotten: that there may be a kingdom where the least shall be heard and considered side by side with the greatest.

And now in that spirit, that spirit of an America which has never been, and which may never be; nay, which never will be, except as the conscience and the courage of Americans create it; yet in the spirit of that America which lies hidden in some form in the aspirations of us all; in the spirit of that America for which our young men are at this moment fighting and dying; in that spirit of liberty and of America I ask you to rise and with me to pledge our faith in the glorious *destiny* of our beloved country—with liberty and justice for all.

* * *

✦ IF WE WORK upon marble, it will perish; if on brass, time will efface it; if we rear temples, they will crumble into dust; but if we work upon immortal minds, and imbue them with principles, with the just fear of God and love of our fellow men, we engrave on those tablets something that will brighten to all eternity　　　　　　　　　　　　　　　　　　　　—*Webster*

PATRIOTISM

By FISHER AMES (1798)

WHAT IS patriotism? Is it a narrow affection for the spot where a man was born? Are the very clods where we tread entitled to this ardent preference because they are greener? No, sir, this is not the character of the virtue, and it soars higher for its object. It is an extended self-love, mingling with all the enjoyments of life, and twisting itself with the minutest filaments of the heart. It is thus we obey the laws of society, because they are the laws of virtue. In their authority we see not the array of force and terror, but the venerable image of our country's honor. Every good citizen makes that honor his own and cherishes it not only as precious, but as sacred. He is willing to risk his life in its defense, and is conscious that he gains protection while he gives it.

OUR AMERICAN DREAM

By JAMES TRUSLOW ADAMS

WE HAVE a long and arduous road to travel if we are to realize our American dream in the life of our nation, but if we fail, there is nothing left but the old eternal round. The alternative is the failure of self-government, the failure of the common man to rise to full stature, the failure of all that the American dream has held of hope and promise for mankind.

That dream was not the product of a solitary thinker. It evolved from the hearts and burdened souls of many millions, who have come to us from all nations. If some of them appear to us to have too great faith, we know not yet to what faith may attain, and may hearken to the words of one of them, Mary Antin, a young immigrant girl who came to us from Russia, a child out of "the Middle Ages," as she says, into our twentieth century. Sitting on the steps of the Boston Public Library, where the treasures of the whole of human thought had been opened to her, she wrote, "This is my latest home, and it invites me to a glad new life. The endless ages have indeed throbbed through my blood, but a new rhythm dances in my veins. My spirit is not tied to the monumental past, any more than my feet were bound to my grandfather's house below the hill. The past was only my cradle, and now it cannot hold me, because I am grown too big; just as the little house in Polotzk, once my home has now become a toy of memory, as I move about at will in the wide spaces of this splendid palace, whose shadow covers acres. No! It is not I that belong to the past, but the past that belongs to me. America is the youngest of the nations, and inherits all that went before in history. And I am the youngest of America's children, and into my hands is given all her priceless heritage, to the last white star espied through the telescope, to the last great thought of the philosopher. Mine is the whole majestic past, and mine the shining future."

* * *

❧ MY MESSAGE TO YOU is simply "Look and Listen," that is, cultivate the habit of attention and try to gain opportunities to hear wise men and women talk. Indifference and inattention are the two most dangerous monsters that you will ever meet. Interest and attention will insure to you an education. —Robert A. Millikan

I BELIEVE
By JOHN D. ROCKEFELLER, JR.

I BELIEVE in the dignity of labor, whether with head or hand; that the world owes no man a living but that it owes every man an opportunity to make a living.

I believe in the supreme worth of the individual and in his right to life, liberty, and the pursuit of happiness.

I believe that truth and justice are fundamental to an enduring social order.

I believe in the sacredness of a promise, that a man's word should be as good as his bond; that character—not wealth or power or position—is of supreme worth.

I believe that every right implies a responsibility; every opportunity, an obligation; every possession, a duty.

I believe that law was made for man and not man for the law; that government is the servant of the people and not their master.

I believe that thrift is essential to well-ordered living and that economy is a prime requisite of a sound financial structure, whether in government, business or personal affairs.

I believe that the rendering of useful service is the common duty of mankind and that only in the purifying fire of sacrifice is the dross of selfishness consumed and the greatness of the human soul set free.

I believe in an all-wise and all-loving God, named by whatever name, and that the individual's highest fulfillment, greatest happiness, and widest usefulness are to be found in living in harmony with His will.

I believe that love is the greatest thing in the world; that it alone can overcome haste; that right can and will triumph over might.

ON IDEALS
By HENRI FRÉDÉRIC AMIEL

A WALK. The atmosphere incredibly pure—a warm, caressing gentleness in the sunshine—joy in one's whole being. . . . Every way I was happy—as idler, as painter, as poet. Forgotten impressions of childhood and youth came back to me—all those indescribable effects wrought by colour, shadow, sunlight, green hedges, and songs of birds, upon the soul just opening to poetry. I became again young, wondering, and simple, as candour and ignorance are simple. I abandoned myself to life and to nature, and they cradled me with an infinite gentleness. To open one's heart in purity to this ever pure nature, to allow this immortal life of things to penetrate into one's soul, is at the same time to listen to the voice of God.

From A WAYSIDE INN
HENRY WADSWORTH LONGFELLOW

Ships that pass in the night, and speak each other in passing,
Only a signal shown, and a distant voice in the darkness.
So on the ocean of life we pass and speak one another,
Only a look and a voice, then darkness again and a silence.

TO THE LITTLE PARLIAMENT
By OLIVER CROMWELL

HAVE a care of the whole flock. Love the sheep. Love the lambs. Love all; tend all; cherish and countenance all in all things that are good. And if the poorest Christian, the most mistaken Christian, shall desire to live peaceably and quietly under you: I say if any desire but to live a life of godliness and honesty, let him be protected.

⚜ CAST ALL your cares on God; that anchor holds.—*Tennyson*

MIRACLE
LIZETTE WOODWORTH REESE

Who is in love with loveliness,
  Need not shake with cold;
For he may tear a star in two,
  And frock himself in gold.

Who holds her first within his heart,
  In certain favor goes;
If his roof tumbles, he may find
  Harbor in a rose.

MOUNTAIN AIR
JOHN GALSWORTHY

Tell me of Progress if you will
But give me sunshine on a hill—
The grey rocks aspiring to the blue,
The scent of larches, pinks and dew,
And summer sighing in the trees,
And snowy breath on every breeze.
Take towns and all that you find
  there,
And leave me sun and mountain air!

BEFORE THE RAIN
THOMAS BAILEY ALDRICH

We knew it would rain, for all the morn
  A spirit on slender ropes of mist
Was lowering its golden buckets down
  Into the vapory amethyst

Of marshes and swamps and dismal
  fens—
  Scooping the dew that lay in the
  flowers,
Dipping the jewels out of the sea,
  To sprinkle them over the land in
  showers.

We knew it would rain, for the poplars
  showed
  The white of their leaves, the amber
  grain
Shrunk in the wind—and the lightning
  now
  Is tangled in tremulous skeins of rain.

THE COIN
SARA TEASDALE

Into my heart's treasury
  I slipped a coin
That time cannot take
  Nor a thief purloin,—
Oh, better than the minting
  Of a gold-crowned king
Is the safe-kept memory
  Of a lovely thing.

AUTUMN
EMILY DICKINSON

The morns are meeker than they were,
The nuts are getting brown;
The berry's cheek is plumper,
The rose is out of town.

The maple wears a gayer scarf,
The field a scarlet gown.
Lest I should be old-fashioned,
I'll put a trinket on.

NATURE
HENRY WADSWORTH LONGFELLOW

As a fond mother, when the day is o'er,
  Leads by the hand her little child to
  bed,
  Half willing, half reluctant to be led,
  And leave his broken playthings on
  the floor,
Still gazing at them through the open
  door,
  Nor wholly reassured and comforted
  By promises of others in their stead,
  Which, though more splendid, may
  not please him more;
So Nature deals with us, and takes away
  Our playthings one by one, and by
  the hand
  Leads us to rest so gently, that we go
Scarce knowing if we wish to go or stay,
  Being too full of sleep to understand
  How far the unknown transcends the
  what we know.

DEFENSE OF HOFER, THE TYROLESE PATRIOT

By Andreas Hofer

HOFER, *a Tyrolese patriot, was captured and executed by Napoleon. At his trial he spoke as follows:*

You ask what I have to say in my defense?—you, who glory in the name of France, who wander through the world to exalt the land of your birth. You demand how I could dare to arm myself against the invaders of my native rocks! Do you confine the love of home to yourselves? Do you punish in others the actions which you dignify among yourselves? Those stars which glitter on your breasts, are they the recompense of servitude?

I see the smile of contempt which curls your lips. You say: "This brute! he is a ruffian, a beggar!" "That patched jacket! that ragged cap! that rusty belt! Shall barbarians such as he close the pass against us, shower rocks on our heads, and single out our leaders with unfailing aim? We must subdue these groveling mountaineers, who know not the joys and brilliance of life, creeping amidst eternal snows, and snatching with greedy hand their stinted ear of corn."

Yet, poor as we are, we never envied our neighbors their smiling sun, their gilded palaces. We never strayed from our peaceful huts to blast the happiness of those who had not injured us. The traveler who visited our valleys met every hand outstretched to welcome him. For him every hearth blazed. Too happy for ambition, we were not jealous of his wealth, and listened with delight to his tale of distant lands.

Frenchmen, you have wives and children. When you return to your beautiful cities, amidst the roar of trumpets, the smiles of the lovely and the shouts of the multitude, they will ask:

"Where have you roamed? What have you achieved? What have you brought back to us?"

When laughing children climb your knees, will you tell them:

"We have pierced the barren crags; we have entered the naked cottage and leveled it to the ground; we found no treasures but honest hearts, and we broke them because they throbbed with love for their wild homes. Clasp this old firelock in your little hands. It was snatched from a peasant of Tyrol, who died in a vain effort to stem our torrent of invasion!"

Oh, Frenchmen! seated by your firesides, will you boast to generous and happy wives that you extinguished the last ember that lighted our gloom?

What is death to me? I have not reveled in pleasures wrung from innocence or want. Rough and discolored as these hands are, they are pure. We have rushed to the sacrifice, and the offering has been in vain for us. But our children will burst these fetters. The blood of virtue was never shed in vain, and Freedom can *never* die. I have heard that you killed your King once because he enslaved you; yet now you crouch before a single man, who bids you trample on all who abjure his yoke; and who shoots you if you have courage to disobey. Do you think that, when I am dead, no other Hofer shall breathe? Dream you that, if today you prostrate Hofer in the dust, tomorrow Hofer is no more?

In the distance I see Liberty which I shall not taste. Behind, I see my slaughtered countrymen, my orphans, my desolate fields. But a star rises before my aching sight, which points to Justice that shall come.

* * *

✤ No MAN is free who is not master of himself.—*Epictetus*

DRIFTING

Thomas Buchanan Read

My soul today
Is far away,
Sailing The Vesuvian Bay;
My winged boat,
A bird afloat,
Swims round the purple peaks remote:—

Round purple peaks
It sails, and seeks
Blue inlets and their crystal creeks,
Where high rocks throw,
Through deeps below,
A duplicated golden glow.

Far, vague, and dim
The mountains swim;
While on Vesuvius' misty brim,
With outstretched hands,
The gray smoke stands
Overlooking the volcanic lands.

Here Ischia smiles
Over liquid miles;
And yonder, bluest of the isles,
Calm Capri waits,
Her sapphire gates
Beguiling to her bright estates.

I heed not, if
My rippling skiff
Float swift or slow from cliff to cliff;—
With dreamed eyes
My spirit lies
Under the walls of Paradise.

Under the walls
Where swells and falls
The Bay's deep breast at intervals
At peace I lie,
Blown softly by,
A cloud upon this liquid sky.

The day, so mild,
Is Heaven's own child.
With Earth and Ocean reconciled;—

The airs I feel
Around me steal
Are murmuring to the murmuring keel.

Over the rail
My hand I trail
Within the shadow of the sail,
A joy intense,
The cooling sense
Glides down my drowsy indolence.

Here children, hid
The cliffs amid,
Are gambolling with the gambolling kid;
Or down the walls,
With tipsy calls,
Laugh on the rocks like waterfalls.

The fisher's child
With tresses wild,
Unto the smooth, bright and beguiled,
With glowing lips
Sings as she skips,
Or gazes at the far-off ships.

Yon deep bark goes
Where Traffic blows,
From lands of sun to lands of snows;—
This happier one,
Its course is run
From lands of snow to lands of sun.

O happy ship,
To rise and dip,
With the blue crystal at your lip!
O happy crew,
My heart with you
Sails, and sails, and sings anew!

No more, no more
The worldly shore
Upbraids me with its loud uproar!
With dreamful eyes
My spirit lies
Under the walls of Paradise!

265

A VAGABOND SONG

BLISS CARMAN

There is something in the autumn that
    is native to my blood—
Touch of manner, hint of mood;
And my heart is like a rhyme,
With the yellow and the purple and the
    crimson keeping time.

The scarlet of the maples can shake me
    like a cry
Of bugles going by.
And my lonely spirit thrills
To see the frosty asters like a smoke
    upon the hills.

There is something in October sets the
    gipsy blood astir;
We must rise and follow her,
When from every hill of flame
She calls and calls each vagabond
    by name.

From *UNDER A THATCHED ROOF*

By JAMES NORMAN HALL

WHO INVENTED the whistles for American locomotive engines? Perhaps there were many collaborators who perfected them over a long period of years. Others besides myself must think often of those anonymous benefactors of boyhood, and thank them for their labour of love. For it must have been that. Engineers are often poets at heart, and these must have said, or thought:

'The horns of Elfland shall not be sweeter to the ear than the varying tones of our whistles, heard in the wide air of the prairie country on drowsy summer afternoons, or coming from afar across the plains of Kansas, the deserts of Arizona or New Mexico, or reverberating among the rocky fastnesses of the Continental Divide. They shall be in keeping with the spirit of a great continent. They shall give voice to its vastness and beauty, to the promise of its future, if not to the memories of its past. Some shall be single in tone, some double, the notes harmoniously blended to float over corn lands, and fields of wind-rippled oats and wheat and rye, and meadows where the cattle are browsing knee-deep in clover. They shall make midsummer peace the deeper, and midwinter loneliness on remote farms and in little towns less hard to bear. And they shall all mean this to the ears and hearts of boyhood: "Over the hills and far away." '

Such was their meaning to me on golden autumn afternoons, but I heard them then without longing, with no wish ever to see a different world from that I knew, for now, after the red haws and mulberries and wild grapes, came the nutting season, with the hickory, walnut, and butternut trees raining down blessings after the first heavy frosts. On winter nights I would hear the whistles for all the howling of the north wind that shook and buffeted our old house on its exposed hilltop. Number 6, the eastbound evening passenger train, had a whistle that sounds as clearly in memory now as ever it echoed among the wooded hills along the river. It was a through train and stopped at Prairie Hills only to take on passengers for Chicago or beyond. Usually it thundered down the five-mile Middleton grade at tremendous speed, whistling repeatedly, and it passed through town in a flash of time, the pitch of the whistle dropping by quarter-tones as the distance increased. The whistle of the Rocky Mountain Limited—'the Midnight Flier,' we called it—I heard rarely, for boyhood slumbers are deep; but sometimes I would be brought to my knees in bed, gooseflesh tingling all over me. Midnight—that fabulous hour to a boy's fancy. The whistle of the Midnight Flier set its enchantment to music, growing fainter and fainter, till at last I heard it, the very ghost of sound, far out on the prairies to the westward.

THE VAGABOND
[To an Air by Schubert]
ROBERT LOUIS STEVENSON

Give to me the life I love,
  Let the lave go by me,
Give the jolly heaven above
  And the byway nigh me.
Bed in the bush with stars to see,
  Bread I dip in the river—
There's the life for a man like me,
  There's the life forever.

Let the blow fall soon or late,
  Let what will be o'er me;
Give the face of earth around
  And the road before me.
Wealth I seek not, hope nor love,
  Nor a friend to know me;
All I seek the heaven above
  And the road below me.

Or let autumn fall on me
  Where afield I linger,
Silencing the bird on tree,
  Biting the blue finger;
White as meal the frosty field—
  Warm the fireside haven—
Not to autumn will I yield,
  Not to winter even!

Let the blow fall soon or late,
  Let what will be o'er me;
Give the face of earth around,
  And the road before me.
Wealth I ask not, hope nor love,
  Nor a friend to know me.
All I ask the heaven above,
  And the road below me.

A SHIP, AN ISLE, A SICKLE MOON
JAMES ELROY FLECKER

A ship, an isle, a sickle moon—
With few but with how splendid stars
The mirrors of the sea are strewn
Between their silver bars!

. . . .

An isle beside an isle she lay,
The pale ship anchored in the bay,
While in the young moon's port of gold
A star-ship—as the mirrors told—
Put forth its great and lonely light
To the unreflecting Ocean, Night.
And still, a ship upon her seas,
The isle and the island cypresses
Went sail on without the gale:
And still there moved the moon so pale,
A crescent ship without a sail!

* * *

'Tis heaven alone that is given away;
'Tis only **God** may be had for the
  asking.

—*Lowell*

THE MAGIC MOMENT
By H. M. TOMLINSON

I MYSELF learned that the treasures found in travel, the chance rewards of travel which make it worth while, cannot be accounted for beforehand, and seldom are matters a listener would care to hear about afterward; for they have no substance. They are no matter. They are untranslatable from their time and place; and like the man who unwittingly lies down to sleep in the tumulus where the little people dance on midsummer night, and dreams that in the place where man has never been his pockets were filled with fairy gold, waking to find pebbles there instead, so the traveler cannot prove the dreams he had, showing us only pebbles when he tries. Such fair things cannot be taken from the magic moment. They are but filmy, high in the ceiling of your thoughts for so brief a while, rosy and sunlit by the chance of the light, transtory, melting as you watch.

from Moby Dick

By HERMAN MELVILLE

*L*IKE NOISELESS NAUTILUS SHELLS, their light prows sped through the sea; but only slowly they neared the foe. As they neared him, the ocean grew still more smooth; seemed drawing a carpet over its waves; seemed a noon-meadow, so serenely it spread. At length the breathless hunter came so nigh his seemingly unsuspecting prey, that his entire dazzling hump was distinctly visible, sliding along the sea as if an isolated thing, and continually set in a revolving ring of finest, fleecy, greenish foam. He saw the vast, involved wrinkles of the slightly projecting head beyond. Before it, far out on the soft Turkish-rugged waters, went the glistening white shadow from his broad, milky forehead, a musical rippling playfully accompanying the shade; and behind, the blue waters interchangeably flowed over into the moving valley of his steady wake; and on either hand bright bubbles arose and danced by his side. But these were broken again by the light toes of hundreds of gay fowls softly feathering the sea, alternate with their fitful flight; and like to some flagstaff rising from the painted hull of an argosy, the tall but shattered pole of a recent lance projected from the white whale's back; and at intervals one of the cloud of soft-toed fowls hovering, and to and fro skimming like a canopy over the fish, silently perched and rocked on this pole, the long tail feathers streaming like pennons.

A gentle joyousness—a mighty mildness of repose in swiftness, invested the gliding whale. Not the white bull Jupiter swimming away with ravished Europa clinging to his graceful horns; his lovely, leering eyes sideways intent upon the maid; with smooth bewitching fleetness, rippling straight for the nuptial bower in Crete; not Jove, not that great majesty Supreme! did surpass the glorified White Whale as he so divinely swam.

On each soft side—coincident with the parted swell, that but once leaving him, then flowed so wide away—on each bright side, the whale shed off enticings. No wonder there had been some among the hunters who namelessly transported and allured by all this serenity, had ventured to assail it; but had fatally found that quietude but the vesture of tornadoes. Yet calm, enticing, calm, oh, whale! thou glidest on, to all who for the first time eye thee, no matter how many in that same way thou may'st have bejuggled and destroyed before.

And thus, through the serene tranquilities of the tropical sea, among waves whose hand-clappings were suspended by exceeding rapture, Moby Dick moved on, still withholding from sight the full terrors of his submerged trunk, entirely hiding the wrenched hideousness of his jaw. But soon the fore part of him slowly rose from the water; for an instant his whole marbleized body formed a high arch, like Virginia's Natural Bridge, and warningly waving his bannered flukes in the air, the grand god revealed himself, sounded and went out of sight. Hoveringly halting, and dipping on the wing, the white sea-fowls longingly lingered over the agitated pool that he left.

With oars apeak, and paddles down, the sheets of their sails adrift, the three boats now stilly floated, awaiting Moby Dick's reappearance.

'An hour,' said Ahab, standing rooted

in his boat's stern; and he gazed beyond the whale's place, towards the dim blue spaces and wide wooing vacancies to leeward. It was only an instant; for again his eyes seemed whirling round in his head as he swept the watery circle. The breeze now freshened; the sea began to swell.

'The birds!—the birds!' cried Tashtego.

In long Indian file, as when herons take wing, the white birds were now all flying towards Ahab's boat; and when within a few yards began fluttering over the water there, wheeling round and round, with joyous, expectant cries. Their vision was keener than man's; Ahab could discover no sign in the sea. But suddenly as he peered down and down into its depths, he profoundly saw a white living spot no bigger than a white weasel, with wonderful celerity uprising, and magnifying as it rose, till it turned, and then there were plainly revealed two long crooked rows of white glistening teeth, floating up from the undiscoverable bottom. It was Moby Dick's open mouth and scrolled jaw; his vast, shadowed bulk still half blending with the blue of the sea. The glittering mouth yawned beneath the boat like an open-doored marble tomb; and giving one side-long sweep with his steering oar, Ahab whirled the craft aside from this tremendous apparition. Then, calling upon Fedallah to change places with him, went forward to the bows, and seizing Perth's harpoon, commanded his crew to grasp their oars and stand by to stern.

Now, by reason of this timely spinning round the boat upon its axis, its bow, by anticipation, was made to face the whale's head while yet under water. But as if perceiving this startagem, Moby Dick, with that malicious intelligence ascribed to him, sidelingly transplanted himself, as it were, in an instant, shooting his pleated head lengthwise beneath the boat.

Through and through; through every plank and each rib, it thrilled for an instant, the whale obliquely lying on his back, in the manner of a biting shark, slowly and feelingly taking its bows full within his mouth, so that the long, narrow, scrolled lower jaw curled high up into the open air, and one of the teeth caught in a row-lock. The bluish pearl-white of the inside of the jaw was within six inches of Ahab's head, and reached higher than that. In this attitude the White Whale now shook the slight cedar as a mildly cruel cat her mouse. With unastonished eyes Fedallah gazed, and crossed his arms; but the tiger-yellow crew were tumbling over each other's heads to gain the uttermost stern.

And now, while both elastic gunwales were springing in and out, as the whale dallied with the doomed craft in this devilish way; and from his body being submerged beneath the boat, he could not be darted at from the bows, for the bows were almost inside of him, as it were; and while the other boats involuntarily paused, as before a quick crisis impossible to withstand, then it was that monomaniac Ahab, furious with this tantalizing vicinity of his foe, which placed him all alive and helpless in the very jaws he hated; frenzied with all this, he seized the long bone with his naked hands, and wildly strove to wrench it from its gripe. As now he thus vainly strove, the jaw slipped from him; the frail gunwales bent in, collapsed, and snapped, as both jaws, like an enormous shears, sliding further aft, bit the craft completely in twain and locked themselves fast again in the sea, midway between the two floating wrecks. These floated aside, the broken ends drooping, the crew at the stern-wreck clinging to the gunwales, and striving to hold fast to the oars to lash them across.

At that preluding moment, ere the boat was yet snapped, Ahab, the first to perceive the whale's intent, by the crafty upraising of his head, a movement that loosed his hold for the time; at that moment his hand had made one final effort to push the boat out of the bite. But only slipping further into the whale's mouth, and tilting over sideways as it slipped, the boat had shaken off his hold on the jaw; spilled him out of it, as he leaned to the push; and so he fell flat-faced upon the sea.

Ripplingly withdrawing from his prey, Moby Dick now lay at a little distance, vertically thrusting his oblong white head up and down in the billows; and at the same time slowly revolving his whole spindled body; so that when his vast wrinkled forehead rose—some twenty or more feet out of the water—the now rising swells, with all their confluent waves, dazzlingly broke against it; vindictively tossing their shivered spray still higher into the air. So, in a gale, the but half baffled Channel billows only recoil from the base of the Eddystone, triumphantly to overleap its summit with their scud.

But soon resuming his horizontal attitude, Moby Dick swam swiftly round and round the wrecked crew; sideways churning the water in his vengeful wake, as if lashing himself up to still another and more deadly assault. The sight of the splintered boat seemed to madden him, as the blood of grapes and mulberries cast before Antiochus's elephants in the book of Maccabees. Meanwhile Ahab half smothered in the foam of the whale's insolent tail, and too much of a cripple to swim,—though he could still keep afloat, even in the heart of such a whirlpool as that; helpless Ahab's head was seen, like a tossed bubble which the least chance shock might burst. From the boat's fragmentary stern, Fedallah incuriously and mildly eyed him; the clinging crew, at the other drifting end, could not succor him; more than enough was it for them

to look to themselves. For so revolvingly appalling was the White Whale's aspect, and so planetarily swift the ever-contracting circles he made, that he seemed horizontally swooping upon them. And though the other boats, unharmed, still hovered hard by; still they dared not pull into the eddy to strike, lest that should be the signal for the instant destruction of the jeopardized castaways, Ahab and all; nor in that case could they themselves hope to escape. With straining eyes, then, they remained on the outer edge of the direful zone, whose centre had now become the old man's head.

Meantime, from the beginning all this had been descried from the ship's mast heads; and squaring her yards, she had borne down upon the scene; and was now so nigh, that Ahab in the water hailed her;—'Sail on the'—but that moment a breaking sea dashed on him from Moby Dick, and whelmed him for the time. But struggling out of it again, and chancing to rise on a towering crest, he shouted,—'Sail on the whale!—Drive him off!'

The Pequod's prows were pointed; and breaking up the charmed circle, she effectually parted the white whale from his victim. As he sullenly swam off, the boats flew to the rescue.

Dragged into Stubb's boat with blood-shot, blinded eyes, the white brine caking in his wrinkles; the long tension of Ahab's bodily strength did crack, and helplessly he yielded to his body's doom for a time, lying all crushed in the bottom of Stubb's boat, like one trodden under foot of herds of elephants. Far inland, nameless wails came from him, as desolate sounds from out ravines.

But this intensity of his physical prostration did but so much the more abbreviate it. In an instant's compass, great hearts sometimes condense to one deep pang, the sum total of those shallow pains kindly diffused through feebler men's whole lives. And so, such hearts, though summary in each one suffering; still, if the gods decree it, in their life-time aggregate a whole age of woe, wholly made up of instantaneous intensities; for even in their pointless centres, those noble natures contain the entire circumferences of inferior souls.

'The harpoon,' said Ahab, half way rising, and draggingly leaning on one bended arm—'is it safe?'

'Aye, sir, for it was not darted; this is it,' said Stubb, showing it.

'Lay it before me;—any missing men?'

'One, two, three, four, five;—there were five oars, sir, and here are five men.'

'That's good.—Help me, man; I wish to stand. So, so, I see him! there! there! going to leeward still; what a leaping spout!—Hands off from me! The eternal sap runs up in Ahab's bones again! Set the sail; out oars; the helm!'

It is often the case that when a boat is stove, its crew, being picked up by another boat, help to work that second boat; and the chase is thus continued with what is called double-banked oars. It was thus now. But the added power of the boat did not equal the added power of the whale, for he seemed to have treble-banked his every fin; swimming with a velocity which plainly showed, that if now, under these circumstances, pushed on, the chase would prove an indefinitely prolonged, if not a hopeless one; nor could any crew endure for so long a period, such an unintermitted, intense straining at the oar; a thing barely tolerable only in some one brief vicissitude. The ship itself, then, as it sometimes happens, offered the most promising intermediate means of overtaking the chase. Accordingly, the boats now made for her, and were soon swayed up to their cranes—the two parts of the wrecked boats having been previously secured by her—and then hoisting everything to her side, and

stacking her canvas high up, and sideways outstretching it with stun-sails, like the double-pointed wings of an albatross; the Pequod bore down in the leeward wake of Moby Dick. At the well known, methodic intervals, the whale's glittering spout was regularly announced from the manned mastheads; and when he would be reported as just gone down, Ahab would take the time, and then pacing the deck, binnacle-watch in hand, so soon as the last second of the allotted hour expired, his voice was heard.—'Whose is the doubloon now? D'ye see him?' and if the reply was No, sir! straightway he commanded them to lift him to his perch. In this way the day wore on; Ahab, now aloft and motionless; anon, unrestingly pacing the planks.

As he was thus walking, uttering no sound, except to hail the men aloft, or to bid them hoist a sail still higher, or to spread one to a still greater breadth—thus to and fro pacing, beneath his slouched hat, at every turn he passed his own wrecked boat, which had been dropped upon the quarter-deck, and lay there reversed; broken bow to shattered stern. At last he paused before it; and as in an already over-clouded sky fresh troops of clouds will sometimes sail across, so over the old man's face there now stole some such added gloom as this.

Stubb saw him pause; and perhaps intending, not vainly, though, to evince his own unabated fortitude, and thus keep up a valiant place in his Captain's mind, he advanced, and eyeing the wreck exclaimed—'The thistle the ass refused; it pricked his mouth too keenly, sir, ha! ha!'

'What soulless thing is this that laughs before a wreck? Man, man! did I not know thee brave as fearless fire (and as mechanical) I could swear thou wert a poltroon. Groan nor laugh should be heard before a wreck.'

'Aye, sir,' said Starbuck drawing near, ''tis a solemn sight; an omen, and an ill one.'

'Omen? omen?—the dictionary! If the gods think to speak outright to man, they will honorably speak outright; not shake their heads, and give an old wives' darkling hint.—Begone! Ye two are the opposite poles of one thing; Starbuck is Stubb reversed, and Stubb is Starbuck; and ye two are all mankind; and Ahab stands alone among the millions of the peopled earth, nor gods nor men his neighbors! Cold, cold—I shiver!—How now? Aloft there! D'ye see him? Sing out for every spout, though he spout ten times a second!'

The day was nearly done; only the hem of his golden robe was rustling. Soon it was almost dark, but the look-out men still remained unset.

'Can't see the spout now, sir;—too dark'—cried a voice from the air.

'How heading when last seen?'

'As before, sir,—straight to leeward.'

'Good! he will travel slower now 'tis night. Down royals and top-gallant stun-sails, Mr. Starbuck. We must not run over him before morning; he's making a passage now, and may heave-to a while. Helm there! keep her full before the wind!—Aloft! come down!—Mr. Stubb, send a fresh hand to the fore-mast head, and see it manned till morning.'—Then advancing towards the dou-bloon in the main-mast—'Men, this gold is mine, for I earned it; but I shall let it abide here till the White Whale is dead; and then, whosoever of ye first raises him, upon the day he shall be killed, this gold is that man's; and if on that day I shall again raise him, then, ten times of its sum shall be divided among all of ye! Away now! the deck is thine, sir.'

And so saying, he placed himself half way within the scuttle, and slouching his hat, stood there till dawn, except when at intervals rousing himself to see how the night wore on.

MORNING AT SEA
By Pierre Loti

The morning light, the real light, had finally come, and as in Genesis, it was "divided from the darkness," which seemed to be heaped up over the horizon and to rest there heavily in shadowy masses; and now that one could see so clearly one could easily tell that night had been left behind and that that former radiance had been as strange and vague as the light of a dream.

Here and there in the thick and over-hanging sky there were rents like windows in a dome, through which great shafts of golden, rosy light shot down.

The lower clouds lay in a band of deep shadow all about the horizon, in-folding the ocean distances in dim obscurity, producing the illusion of enclosed space; they were like curtains drawn over the infinite, like veils let down to conceal mysteries too gigantic for the imagination of men. This morning, around the little craft . . . the changing world had taken on the look of a vast cloister,—a sanctuary, where the rays of light which came through the rifts in the temple's dome fell in long reflected rays upon the motionless water, as on a pavement of marble. And then, little by little, in the growing light another vision appeared from afar, —a towering promontory of gloomy Iceland cut out like a rosy cameo against the dull gray sky.

* * *

❧ Ideals are like the stars—we never reach them, but like the mariners on the sea, we chart our course by them.

—*Carl Schurz*

SEAL LULLABY
RUDYARD KIPLING

Oh! hush thee, my baby, the night is behind us,
 And black are the waters that sparkled so green.
The moon, o'er the combers, looks downward to find us
 At rest in the hollows that rustle between.
Where billow meets billow, there soft be thy pillow;
 Ah, weary wee flipperling, curl at thy ease!
The storm shall not wake thee, nor shark overtake thee,
 Asleep in the arms of the slow-swinging seas.

A SEA SONG
ALLAN CUNNINGHAM

A wet sheet and a flowing sea;
 A wind that follows fast,
And fills the white and rustling sail
 And bends the gallant mast;
And bends the gallant mast, my boys,
 While like the eagle free,
Away the good ship flies, and leaves
 Old England on the lee.

O for a soft and gentle wind!
 I heard a fair one cry;
But give to me the snoring breeze
 And white waves heaving high;
And white waves heaving high, my lads,
 The good ship light and free—
The world of waters is our home,
 And merry men are we.

There's tempest in yon horned moon,
 And lightning in yon cloud;
But hark the music, mariners!
 The wind is piping loud;
The wind is piping loud, my boys,
 The lightning flashes free—
While the hollow oak our palace is,
 Our heritage the sea.

IF ONCE YOU HAVE SLEPT ON AN ISLAND
RACHEL FIELD

If once you have slept on an island
 You'll never be quite the same;
You may look as you looked the day
 before
And go by the same old name,

You may bustle about in street and
 shop;
 You may sit at home and sew,
But you'll see blue water and wheeling
 gulls
Wherever your feet may go.

You may chat with the neighbors of
 this and that
 And close to your fire keep,
But you'll hear ship whistle and light-
 house bell
 And tides beat through your sleep.

Oh, you won't know why, and you can't
 say how
Such change upon you came,
But—once you have slept on an island
 You'll never be quite the same!

* * *

☘ OF JOURNEYING the benefits are many; for seeing and hearing marvelous things, beholding strange cities, meeting new friends,—these things bring freshness to the heart.
    —Sadi the Gulistan

273

Greater Love Hath No Man

By IAN MACLAREN

SURELY NO FUNERAL is like unto that of a doctor for pathos, and a peculiar sadness fell on that company as his body was carried out who for nearly half a century had been their help in sickness, and had beaten back death time after time from their door. Death after all was victor, for the man that saved them had not been able to save himself.

As the coffin passed the stable door a horse neighed within, and every man looked at his neighbour. It was his old mare crying for her master.

Jamie slipped into the stable, and went up into the stall.

"Puir lass, ye're no gaein wi' him the day, an' ye 'ill never see him again; ye've hed yir last ride thegither, an' ye were true tae the end."

After the funeral Drumsheugh came himself for Jess, and took her to his farm. Saunders made a bed for her with soft, dry straw, and prepared for her supper such things as horses love. Jess would neither take food nor rest, but moved uneasily in her stall, and seemed to be waiting for someone that never came. No man knows what a horse or a dog undertsands and feels, for God hath not given them our speech. If any footstep was heard in the courtyard, she began to neigh, and was always looking round as the door opened. But nothing would tempt her to eat, and in the nighttime Drumsheugh heard her crying as if she expected to be taken out for sudden journey. The Kildrummie veterinary came to see her, and said that nothing could be done when it happened after this fashion with an old horse.

"A've seen it aince afore," he said. "Gin she were a Christian instead o' a horse, ye micht say she wes dying o' a broken hert."

He recommended that she should be shot to end her misery, but no man could be found in the Glen to do the deed, and Jess relieved them of the trouble. When Drumsheugh went to the stable on Monday morning, a week after Dr. MacLure fell on sleep, Jess was resting at last, but her eyes were open and her face turned to the door.

"She wes a' the wife he hed," said Jamie, as he rejoined the procession, "an' they luved ane anither weel."

The black thread wound itself along the whiteness of the Glen, the coffin first, with his lordship and Drumsheugh behind, and the others as they pleased, but in closer ranks than usual, because the snow on either side was deep, and because this was not as other funerals. They could see the women standing at the door of every house on the hillside, and weeping, for each family had some good reason in forty years to remember MacLure. When Bell Baxter saw Saunders alive and the coffin of the doctor that saved him on her man's shoulder, she bowed her head on the dyke, and the bairns in the village made such a wail for him they loved that the men nearly disgraced themselves.

"A'm gled we're through that, at ony rate," said Hillocks; "he wes awfu' taen up wi' the bairns, conseederin' he hed nane o' his ain."

There was only one drift on the road between his cottage and the kirkyard, and it had been cut early that morning. Before daybreak Saunders had roused the lads in the bothy, and they had set to work by the light of lanterns with such good will that, when Drumsheugh came down to engineer a circuit for the funeral, there was a fair passage, with walls of snow twelve feet high on either side.

"Man, Sounders," he said, "this wes a kind thocht, and rael weel dune."

But Saunders' only reply was this:

"Mony a time he's hed tae gang roond; he micht as weel hae an open road for his last traivel."

When the coffin was laid down at the mouth of the grave, the only blackness in the white kirkyard, Tammas Mitchell did the most beautiful thing in all his life. He knelt down and carefully wiped off the snow the wind had blown upon the coffin, and which had covered the name, and when he had done this he disappeared behind the others, so that Drumsheugh could hardly find him to take a cord. For these were the eight that buried Dr. MacLure—Lord Kilspindie at the head as landlord and Drumsheugh at the feet as his friend; the two ministers of the parish came first on the right and left; then Burnbrae and Hillocks of the farmers, and Saunders and Tammas for the ploughmen. So the Glen he loved laid him to rest.

When the bedrel had finished his work and the turf had been spread, Lord Kilspindie spoke:

"Friends of Drumtochty, it would not be right that we should part in silence and no man say what is in every heart. We have buried the remains of one that served this Glen with a devotion that has known no reserve, and a kindliness that never failed, for more than forty years. I have seen many brave men in my day, but no man in the trenches of Sebastopol carried himself more knightly than William MacLure. You will never have heard from his lips what I may tell you today, that my father secured for him a valuable post in his younger days, and he preferred to work among his own people; and I wished to do many things for him when he was old, but he would have nothing for himself. He will never be forgotten while one of us lives, and I pray that all doctors everywhere may share his spirit. If it be your pleasure, I shall erect a cross above his grave, and shall ask my old friend and companion Dr. Davidson, your minister, to choose the text to be inscribed."

"We thank you, Lord Kilspindie," said the doctor, "for your presence with us in our sorrow and your tribute to the memory of William MacLure, and I choose this for his text:

"'Greater love hath no man than this, that a man lay down his life for his friends.'"

Milton was, at that time, held in the bonds of a very bitter theology, and his indignation was stirred by this unqualified eulogium.

"No doubt Dr. MacLure hed mony natural virtues, an' he did his wark weel, but it wes a petty he didna mak mair profession o' religion."

"When William MacLure appears before the Judge, Milton," said Lachlan Campbell, who that day spoke his last words in public, and they were in defence of charity, "He will not be asking him about his professions, for the doctor's judgment hass been ready long ago; and it iss a good judgment, and you and I will be happy men if we get the like of it.

"It iss written in the Gospel, but it iss William MacLure that will not be expecting it."

"What is't, Lachlan?" asked Jamie Souiar, eagerly.

The old man, now very feeble, stood in the middle of the road, and his face, once so hard, was softened into a winsome tenderness.

"'Come, ye blessed of My Father . . . I was sick, and ye visited Me.'"

—From *Beside the Bonnie Briar Bush*

From *THE DEVIL AND DANIEL WEBSTER*

By Stephen Vincent Benet

*The great Dan'l Webster defends Jabez Stone, who
has sold his soul to the Devil. Here is the trial scene
from a celebrated short story.*

THEN the trial began, and, as you must expect, it didn't look anyways good for the defence. And Jabez Stone didn't make much of a witness in his own behalf. He took one look at Simon Girty and screeched, and they had to put him back in his corner, in a kind of swoon.

It didn't halt the trial, though—the trial went on, as trials do. Dan'l Webster had faced some hard juries and hanging judges in his time—but this was the hardest he'd ever faced, and he knew it. They sat there, with a kind of glitter in their eyes, and the stranger's smooth voice went on and on. Every time he'd raise an objection, it'd be, "Objection sustained," but whenever Dan'l objected, it'd be, "Objection denied." Well, you couldn't expect fair play from a fellow like this Mr. Scratch.

It got to Dan'l in the end, and he began to heat, like iron in the forge. When he got up to speak, he was going to flay that stranger with every trick known to the law, and the judge and jury, too. He didn't care if it was contempt of court or what would happen to him for it. He didn't care any more what happened to Jabez Stone. He just got madder and madder, thinking of what he'd say. And yet, curiously enough, the more he thought about it, the less he was able to arrange his speech in his mind.

Till, finally, it was time for him to get up on his feet, and he did so—all ready to bust out with lightnings and denunciations. But before he started he looked over the judge and jury for a moment, such being his custom. And he noticed the glitter in their eyes was twice as strong as before, and they all leaned forward. Like hounds just before they get the fox, they looked—and the blue mist of evil in the room thickened as he watched them. Then he saw what he'd been about to do—and he wiped his forehead, as a man might who's just escaped falling into a pit in the dark.

For it was him they'd come for—not only Jabez Stone. He read it in the glitter of their eyes and in the way the stranger hid his mouth with one hand. And, if he fought them with their own weapons, he'd fall into their power—he knew that, though he couldn't have told you how. It was his own anger and horror that burned in their eyes—and he'd have to wipe that out or the case was lost. He stood there for a moment, his black eyes burning like anthracite. And then he began to speak. He started off in a low voice, though you could hear every word. They say he could call on the harps of the blessed when he chose. And this was just as simple and easy as a man could talk. But he didn't start out by condemning or reviling. He was talking about the things that make a country a country, and a man a man.

And he begun with the simple things that everybody's known and felt—the freshness of a fine morning, when you're young and the taste of food when you're hungry and the new day that's every day when you're a child. He took them up and he turned them in his hands. They were good things for any man. But, without freedom, they sickened. And when he talked of

276

those enslaved, and the sorrows of slavery, his voice got like a big bell. He talked of the early days of America and the men who had made those days. It wasn't a spread-eagle speech but he made you see it. He admitted all the wrong that had ever been done. But he showed how, out of the wrong and the right, the suffering and the starvations, something new had come. And everybody had played a part in it, even the traitors.

Then he turned to Jabez Stone and showed him as he was—an ordinary man who'd had hard luck and wanted to change it. And, because he'd wanted to change it, now he was going to be punished for all eternity. And yet there was good in Jabez Stone—and he showed that good. He was hard and mean, in some ways—but he was a man. There was sadness in being a man but it was a proud thing, too. And he showed what the pride of it was till you couldn't help feeling it. Yes, even in hell, if a man was a man, you'd know it. And he wasn't pleading for any one person any more—though his voice rang like an organ. He was telling the story and the failures and the endless journey of mankind. They got tricked and trapped and bamboozled, but it was a great journey. And no demon that was ever foaled could know the inwardness of it—it took a man to do that.

The fire began to die on the hearth and the wind before morning to blow. The light was getting grey in the room when Dan'l Webster finished. And his words come back at the end to New Hampshire ground—and the one spot of land that each man loves and clings to. He painted a picture of that—and, to each one of that jury he spoke of things long-forgotten. For his voice could search the heart, and that was his gift and his strength. And to one his voice was like the forest and its secrecy, and to another like the sea and the storms of the sea; and one heard the cry of his lost nation in it, and another saw a little harmless scene he hadn't remembered for years. But each saw something. And, when Dan'l Webster finished, he didn't know whether or not he'd saved Jabez Stone. But he knew he'd done a miracle. For the glitter was gone from the eyes of judge and jury, and, for the moment, they were men again, and knew they were men.

"The defense rests," said Dan'l Webster, and stood there like a mountain . . .

❦ ❦ ❦

ON LIVING

THE RIDERS in a race do not stop short when they reach the goal. There is a little finishing canter before coming to a standstill. There is time to hear the kind voice of friends and to say to one's self: "The work is done." But just as one says that, the answer comes: "The race is over, but the work never is done while the power to work remains." The canter that brings you to a standstill need not be only coming to rest. It cannot be, while you still live. For to live is to function. That is all there is in living. —*Oliver Wendell Holmes, Jr.*

THE JOY OF WORK

GIVE US, oh, give us, the man who sings at his work! He will do more in the same time,—he will do it better,—he will persevere longer. One is scarcely sensible of fatigue whilst he marches to music. The very stars are said to make harmony as they revolve in their spheres. Wondrous is the strength of cheerfulness, altogether past calculation in its powers of endurance. Efforts, to be permanently useful, must be uniformly joyous, a spirit all sunshine, graceful from very gladness, beautiful because bright. —*Carlyle*

277

THEY that work not cannot pray.—*Dwight*

IT'S NOT what man does which exalts him, but what
man would do.—*Browning*

THE GLORY is not in never failing, but in rising every time
you fail.—*Chinese Proverb*

I AM CONVINCED, both by faith and experience, that to maintain one's self
on this earth is not a hardship but a pastime, if we live simply and wisely.
... While I enjoy the friendship of the seasons, I trust that nothing can
make life a burden to me.—*Thoreau*

BEHAVE toward every one as if receiving a great guest.—*Confucius*

A SYMPHONY ORCHESTRA shows the culture of a community, not opera. The
man who does not know Shakespeare is to be pitied; and the man who does
not understand Beethoven and has not been under his spell has not half lived
his life.—*Theodore Thomas*

LIFE IS MADE UP, not of great sacrifices or duties, but of little things, in
which smiles and kindnesses and small obligations, given habitually, are what
win and preserve the heart and secure comfort.—*Sir Humphry Davy*

AGE APPEARS to be best in four things,—old wood best to burn, old wine to
drink, old friends to trust, and old authors to read.—*Bacon*

IT IS IN YOUR POWER to withdraw into yourself whenever you desire. Perfect
tranquility within consists in the good ordering of the mind,—the realm of
your own.—*Marcus Aurelius*

A MAN should never be ashamed to say he has been in the wrong,
which is but saying in other words that he is wiser today than he was
yesterday.—*Pope*

I HAVE NEVER had a policy. I have simply tried to do what seemed
best each day, as each day came.—*Lincoln*

278

BY WISE MEN

I LOVE tranquil solitude and such society
as is quiet, wise and good.—*Shelley*

ONE SHOULD take good care not to grow too wise for so great a
pleasure of life as laughter.—*Addison*

IS IT so small a thing to have enjoyed the sun, to have lived light in the
spring, to have loved, to have thought, to have done?—*Arnold*

OUR THOUGHT is the key which unlocks the doors of the world. There is
something in us which corresponds to that which is around us, beneath us,
and above us.—*Samuel McChord Crothers*

THE GREATEST PLEASURE I know is to do a good action by stealth,
and to have it found out by accident.—*Charles Lamb*

TAKE LIFE too seriously, and what is it worth? If the morning wake us to
no new joys, if the evening bring us not the hope of new pleasures, is it
worth while to dress and undress? Does the sun shine on me today that I
may reflect on yesterday? That I may endeavor to foresee and to control what
can neither be foreseen nor controlled—the destiny of tomorrow?—*Goethe*

THIS LEARNED I from the shadow of a tree, that to and fro did
sway against a wall, our shadow selves, our influence, may fall
where we can never be.—*Anonymous*

REMEMBER THIS, and also be persuaded of its truth—the future is not in the
hands of fate, but in ourselves.—*Jules Jusserand*

ALL THE ARTS are brothers; each one is a light to the others.—*Voltaire*

RESOLVE to be thyself: and know, that he who finds
himself, loses his misery.—*Arnold*

OUR TODAYS and yesterdays are the blocks with which
we build.—*Longfellow*

The Bishop's Candlesticks

By VICTOR HUGO

*A*N HOUR BEFORE SUNSET, on an October evening in 1815, a man travelling afoot entered the village of D———. A few people saw him walk into the town and looked at him with suspicion. His sun-tanned face was half hidden by a leather cap, and was dripping with sweat. His shaggy breast could be seen through a coarse yellow shirt; his tie was twisted like a rope; his worn blue trousers were shabby, with holes in the knees; and he wore a ragged grey blouse, roughly patched with green cloth sewed with twine. On his back was a strongly buckled knapsack, well-filled and quite new; in his hand was a heavy knotted stick; his stockingless feet were in hobnailed shoes; his hair was cropped close, and his beard was long.

The sweat, the heat, and the dust from his long journey added greatly to the wretchedness of his appearance.

The same evening, after a stroll through the town, the Bishop of D——— stayed quite late in his room, working on his great treatise on Duty. At eight o'clock, knowing that the table was laid for supper, and that his sister, Mlle. Baptistine, was waiting, he left his work and went into the dining room.

The housekeeper, Mme. Magloire, was setting the plates for the brother and sister, when there was a loud knocking at the door.

"Come in!" said the bishop.

The door opened, and the traveller entered, knapsack on his back, stick in his hand, and a weary but hard and fierce look in his eyes. Mme. Magloire stood trembling, her mouth open as though she would scream with fright. Mlle. Baptistine started up, at first alarmed; then, slowly turning, she looked at her brother and her face resumed its usual calm.

The bishop looked at the man with a tranquil eye, and started to speak, to ask the stranger what he wanted; but the man, without waiting for the bishop to begin, said in a loud voice:

"My name is Jean Valjean. I am a convict; I have spent nineteen years in the galleys. Four days ago I was set free, and in those four days I have walked from Toulon. Today I walked twelve leagues. When I reached this town tonight, I went to an inn, and they would not take me in because of my yellow passport, which I had to show at the mayor's office. I went to another inn; no one would have me. I went to the prison, and the jailer would not let me in. I crept into a kennel, and the dog bit me and drove me away; you would have said he knew who I was. I went into a field to sleep beneath the stars, but there were no stars, and I thought it would rain, so I came back to the town to find shelter in some doorway. There in the square I lay down upon the stone; a good woman showed me your house and said, 'Knock there.' I have knocked. What is this place? Are you an inn? I have money: one hundred and nine francs and fifteen sous, my savings from what I earned in the galleys in those nineteen years. Can I stay?"

"Mme. Magloire," said the bishop, "put on another plate."

The man came near the table.

"Stop," he exclaimed, "didn't you understand me? I am a galley-slave—a convict—I have just left the galleys." He drew from his pocket a large sheet of yellow paper. "See, here is what they have put in the passport: 'Jean Valjean, a liberated convict, native of ———, nineteen years in the galleys. This man is very dangerous.'"

"Mme. Magloire," said the bishop, "put some sheets on the bed in the alcove."

Mme. Magloire went out to fulfill her orders, and the bishop turned to the man:

"Monsieur, sit down and warm yourself; we are going to take supper presently, and your bed will be made ready while you sup."

Now the man understood; his face, which had been gloomy and hard, expressed stupefaction and joy, and he began to stutter like a madman.

"Is it true? You will keep me, a convict? You call me 'Monsieur' and don't say 'Get out, dog!' like every one else! I shall have a supper! a bed like other people, with a mattress and sheets! Why, it is nineteen years since I slept in a bed. You are really willing for me to stay? You are good people! And I have money; I will pay well. I beg your pardon, Monsieur Innkeeper, but what is your name?"

"I am a priest who lives here," said the bishop.

"A priest!" said the man. "Oh, noble priest! Then you do not ask any money?"

"No," said the bishop, "keep your money."

Mme. Magloire brought in a plate and put it on the table.

"Mme. Magloire," said the bishop, "put this man's place near the fire." Then, turning to his guest, he added: "The night wind is raw in the Alps, Monsieur; you must be cold."

"Mme. Magloire," said the bishop, "this lamp gives a very poor light."

Mme. Magloire understood, and taking the two silver candlesticks from the mantle, she lighted the candles and placed them on the table.

"Monsieur le Curé," said the man, "you are very good. You take me into your house and light your candles for me. I haven't hid from you what I am, and yet you do not despise me."

The bishop touched his hand and said: "This is not my house, it is the house of Christ. It does not ask any comer what he is, but whether he has an affliction. You are suffering; you are cold and hungry; be welcome. And do not thank me or tell me that I have taken you into my house; for this is the home of on man, except him who needs a refuge. You, who are a traveller, are more at home here than I; whatever is here is yours."

"Stop, monsieur le Curé," exclaimed the man. "I was cold and hungry when I came in, but you are so kind that now I don't know what I am. All that is gone."

The bishop looked at him again and said, "You have seen much suffering?"

"Yes," said the man. "The ball and chain, the plank to sleep on, the heat, the cold, the lash, the double chain for nothing, the dungeon for a word,—even when sick, the chain. The dogs are happier! Nineteen years, and I am forty-six and have a yellow passport and that is all."

"Yes," said the bishop, "you have left a place of great suffering. But listen, there will be more joy in heaven over the tears of one repentant sinner than over the salvation of a hundred good men. If you leave that place with hate and anger against men, you are worthy of compassion; if you leave it with good will and gentleness, you are better than any of us."

Mme. Magloire had served up supper, which consisted of soup, a scrap of pork, a bit of mutton, figs, cheese, and a loaf of bread; and she had added without asking a bottle of fine old wine. "To supper," the bishop said briskly, and he seated the man at his right, while Mlle. Baptistine took her place at his left. The bishop said the blessing, and served the soup himself; the stranger ate greedily, like a starving man, and paid attention to no one.

After supper, the bishop said goodnight to his sister, took one of the silver candlesticks from the table, handed the other to his guest, and said to him, "Monsieur, I will show you to your room."

The alcove where the man was to sleep could be reached only by passing through the bishop's bed chamber, and just as they were passing through this room, Mme. Magloire was putting away the silver in the cupboard at the head of the bed, as was her nightly custom. The bishop left his guest in the alcove, where there was a clean white bed.

"A good night's rest to you," said the bishop, "and tomorrow morning before you go, you shall have a cup of warm milk from our cows."

As the cathedral clock struck two, Jean Valjean awoke. What awakened him was that it was too good a bed. For nineteen years he had not slept in a bed, and his sleep was unquiet.

Many thoughts came to him as he lay there, but one repeated itself and drove away all others. For he remembered the six silver plates and the large silver ladle that he had seen Mme. Magloire putting away in the cupboard, and the thought of them took possession of him. There they were, a few steps away. They were solid, and old silver; they would bring at least two hundred francs, double what he had earned in those long years of imprisonment.

His mind struggled with this thought for an hour, when the clock struck three. He opened his eyes, thrust out his legs, placed his feet on the ground, and sat on the edge of the bed, lost in thought. He might have remained there until daybreak, if the clock had not struck the quarter-hour. It seemed to say to him, "Come along!"

He rose to his feet, hesitated for a moment, and listened. All was still. He walked cautiously toward the window; it had no bars, opened into the garden, and was unfastened. The garden was enclosed with a low white wall, that he could easily scale.

He turned quickly, like a man with mind made up, went to the alcove. where he took his haversack, put his shoes into a pocket, swung his bundle upon his shoulders, put on his cap and pulled it down over his eyes. Holding his breath, he moved toward the door of the bishop's room with stealthy steps. There was not a sound.

Jean Valjean pushed open the door.

A deep calm filled the chamber. At the further end of the room he could hear the quiet breathing of the sleeping bishop. A ray of moonlight, coming through the high window, suddenly lighted up the bishop's pale face. He slept tranquilly. His head had fallen on the pillow in an attitude of untroubled slumber; over the side of the bed hung his hand, ornamented with the pastoral ring. His countenance was lit with an expression of hope and happiness.

For a moment Jean Valjean did not remove his eyes from the face of the old man. Then he walked quickly along the bed straight to the cupboard at its head; the key was in it; he opened it and took the basket of silver, crossed the room with hasty stride, stepped out the window, put the silver in his knapsack, threw away the basket, ran across the garden, leaped over the wall like a tiger, and fled.

The next day at sunrise, the bishop was walking in the garden, when Mme. Magloire came running out of the house quite beside herself.

"Monseigneur, monseigneur," s h e cried. "Does your excellency know where the basket of silver is?"

"Yes," said the bishop.

"God be praised," she said. "I did not know what had become of it."

The bishop had just found the basket in a flower-bed. He handed it to Mme. Magloire and said, "Here it is."

"But . . . there is nothing in it!" she exclaimed. "Where is the silver?"

"Ah!" said the bishop, "it is the silver then that troubles you. I do not know where that is."

"Good heavens! It is stolen! That man who came last night must have taken it!"

The bishop was silent for a moment, then raising his serious eyes, he said quietly to Mme. Magloire:

"Now, first, did this silver belong to us?"

Mme. Magloire did not answer, and the bishop continued:

"Mme. Magloire, for a long time I have wrongfully withheld this silver; it belonged to the poor. Who was that man? A poor man, evidently."

In a few minutes he was breakfasting with his sister at the same table where Jean Valjean had sat the night before.

Just as the bishop and Mlle. Baptistine were rising from the table, there was a knock at the door.

"Come in," said the bishop.

The door opened. A strange, unruly group appeared on the threshold; three gendarmes were holding Jean Valjean by the collar. A brigadier of gendarmes appeared to head the group, and advanced toward the bishop, giving a military salute.

"Monseigneur," he said. . . .

At this, Jean Valjean raised his head with a stupefied air.

"Monseigneur!" he m u r m u r e d. "Then it is not the curé!"

"Silence!" and the brigadier. "It is monseigneur, the bishop."

The bishop had risen and walked toward the group.

"Ah, there you are!" he said, looking toward Jean Valjean. "I am glad to see you. But . . . I gave you the candlesticks also, which are silver like the rest, and would bring another two hundred francs. Why did you not take them along with your plates?"

Jean Valjean looked at the bishop amazedly.

"Monseigneur," said the brigadier, "then what this man said was true? He was hurrying like a man who was running away, and we arrested him in order to see. In his knapsack he had this silver."

"And he told you," said the bishop, with a smile, "that it had been given him by a good priest with whom he had passed the night. I see it all. And you brought him back here? That was a mistake."

"If that is so," said the brigadier, "we can let him go."

"Certainly," replied the bishop.

The gendarmes released Jean Valjean, who shrank away from them.

"Is it true that they have let me go?" he asked, in a voice almost inaudible.

"Yes, you can go," said a gendarme. "Don't you understand?"

"My friend," said the bishop, "before you leave, here are your candlesticks. Take them."

He went to the mantelpiece, took the two candlesticks, and handed them to Jean Valjean. The two women beheld the action without a word or gesture that might disturb the bishop.

Jean Valjean was trembling. He took the two candlesticks mechanically.

"Now," said the bishop, "go in peace. And, friend, when you come again, you need not come through the garden; you can always come in and go out by the front door, for it is closed only with a latch, day or night."

Then, turning to the gendarmes, he said:

"Messieurs, you may retire."

The men withdrew.

Jean Valjean looked like a man about to faint. The bishop approached him, and said in a low voice:

"Forget not, never forget that you have promised me to use this silver to become an honest man."

Jean Valjean, who had no recollection of such a promise, stood confused.

The bishop had laid much stress upon these words as he uttered them, and he continued solemnly:

"Jean Valjean, my brother; you belong no longer to evil, but to good. It is your soul that I am buying for you. I withdraw it from dark thoughts and from the spirit of perdition, and I give it to God!"

—From *Les Misérables*

※　※　※

THE HAPPY MAN
By W. Beran Wolfe

IF YOU observe a really happy man you will find him building a boat, writing a symphony, educating his son, growing double dahlias in his garden, or looking for dinosaur eggs in the Gobi desert. He will not be searching for happiness as if it were a collar button that has rolled under the radiator. He will not be striving for it as if it were a goal in itself, nor will he be seeking for it among the nebulous wastes of metaphysics.

To find happiness we must seek for it in a focus outside ourselves.

From *PROMETHEUS UNBOUND*
Percy Bysshe Shelley

To suffer woes which Hope thinks infinite;
To forgive wrongs darker than death or night;
To defy Power, which seems omnipotent;
To love, and bear; to hope till Hope creates
From its own wreck the thing it contemplates;
Neither to change, nor falter, nor repent;
This, like thy glory, Titan, is to be
Good, great and joyous, beautiful and free;
This is alone Life, Joy, Empire, and Victory.

From *HONEST MAN'S FORTUNE*
Beaumont and Fletcher

Man is his own star; and the soul that can
Render an honest and a perfect man
Commands all light, all influence, all fate;
Nothing to him falls early or too late.
Our acts our angels are, or good or ill,
Our fatal shadows that walk by us still.

From *IN HIS STEPS*
By Charles M. Sheldon

IT IS THE personal element that Christian discipleship needs to emphasize. "The gift, without the giver, is bare." The Christianity that attempts to suffer by proxy is not the Christianity of Christ. Each individual Christian, business man, citizen, needs to follow in His steps along the path of personal sacrifice for Him. There is not a different path to-day from that of Jesus' own times. It is the same path. The call of this century . . . is a call for a discipleship, a new following of Jesus, more like the early, simple, apostolic Christianity when the disciples left all and literally followed the Master. Nothing but a discipleship of this kind can face the destructive selfishness of the age, with any hope of overcoming it. There is a great quantity of nominal Christianity to-day. There is a need of more of the real kind. We need a revival of the Christianity of Christ.

JULY

Elizabeth Barrett Browning

The little cares that fretted me,
  I lost them yesterday
Among the fields above the sea,
  Among the winds at play;
Among the lowing of the herds,
  The rustling of the trees,
Among the singing of the birds,
  The humming of the bees.

The foolish fears of what may happen—
  I cast them all away
Among the clover-scented grass,
  Among the new-mown hay;
Among the husking of the corn
  Where drowsy poppies nod,
Where ill thoughts die and good are
  born,
  Out in the fields with God.

THE FOUNTAIN

James Russell Lowell

Into the sunshine,
  Full of the light,
Leaping and flashing
Morning and night.

Into the moonlight,
  Whiter than snow,
Waving so flower-like
  When the winds blow;

Into the starlight
  Rushing in spray,
Happy at midnight
  Happy by day;

Even in motion
  Blithesome and cheery,
Still climbing heavenward,
  Never aweary;

Glorious fountain,
  Let my heart be
Fresh, changeful, constant,
  Upward, like thee!

FLOWER IN THE CRANNIED WALL

Alfred, Lord Tennyson

Flower in the crannied wall,
I pluck you out of the crannies,
I hold you here, root and all, in my
  hand,
Little flower—but *if* I could understand
What you are, root and all, and all in
  all,
I should know what God and man is.

WHO LOVES THE RAIN

Frances Shaw

Who loves the rain
  And loves his home,
And looks on life with quiet eyes,
  Him will I follow through the storm;
  And at his hearth-fire keep me warm;
Nor hell nor heaven shall that soul
  surprise,
  Who loves the rain,
  And loves his home,
And looks on life with quiet eyes.

RAIN IN SUMMER

Henry Wadsworth Longfellow

How beautiful is the rain!
After the dust and heat,
In the broad and fiery street,
In the narrow lane,
How beautiful is the rain!

How it clatters along the roofs,
Like the tramp of hoofs!
How it gushes and struggles out
From the throat of the overflowing
  spout!

Across the windowpane
It pours and pours;
And swift and wide,
With a muddy tide,
Like a river down the gutter roars
The rain, the welcome rain!

TRIBUTE TO THE FLAG

By SENATOR GEORGE F. HOAR

I HAVE seen the glories of art and architecture and of river and mountain. I have seen the sun set on the Jungfrau and the moon rise over Mont Blanc. But the fairest vision on which these eyes ever rested was the flag of my country in a foreign port. Beautiful as a flower to those who love it, terrible as a meteor to those who hate it, it is the symbol of the power and the glory and the honor of millions of Americans.

THE GOOD JOAN

LIZETTE WOODWORTH REESE

Along the thousand roads of France,
Now there, now here, swift as a glance,
A cloud, a mist blown down the sky,
Good Joan of Arc goes riding by.

In Domremy at candlelight,
The orchards blowing rose and white
About the shadowy houses lie;
And Joan of Arc goes riding by.

On Avignon there falls a hush,
Brief as the singing of a thrush
Across old gardens April-high;
And Joan of Arc goes riding by.

The women bring the apples in,
Round Arles when the long gusts begin,
Then sit them down to sob and cry;
And Joan of Arc goes riding by.

Dim fall of hoofs round old Calais;
In Tours a flash of silver-gray,
Like flair of rain in a clear sky;
And Joan of Arc goes riding by.

Who saith that ancient France shall fail,
A rotting leaf driven down the gale?
Then her sons know not how to die;
*Then good God dwells no more on
 high.*

Tours, Arles, and Domremy reply!
For Joan of Arc goes riding by.

THE FLAG

ARTHUR MACY

Here comes The Flag.
Hail it!
Who dares to drag
Or trail it?
Give it hurrahs,—
Three for the stars
Three for the bars.
Uncover your head to it!
The soldiers who tread to it
Shout at the sight of it,
The justice and right of it,
The unsullied white of it,
The blue and the red of it,
And tyranny's dread of it!
Here comes The Flag!
Cheer it!
Valley and crag
Shall hear it.
Fathers shall bless it,
Children caress it.
All maintain it,
No one shall stain it,
Cheers for the sailors that fought on the
 wave for it,
Cheers for the soldiers that always were
 brave for it,
Tears for the men that went down to
 the grave for it.
Here comes The Flag!

PRAYER USED BY ADMIRAL HART

DEAR GOD, give us strength to accept with serenity the things that cannot be changed. Give us courage to change the things that can and should be changed. And give us wisdom to distinguish one from the other.

WALT WHITMAN ON AMERICA

HERE at last is something in the doings of man that corresponds with the broadcast doings of the day and night. Here is not merely a nation but a teeming nation of nations.

INSCRIPTION ON PLYMOUTH ROCK MONUMENT, MASSACHUSETTS

THIS MONUMENT marks the first burying ground in Plymouth of the passengers of the Mayflower. Here, under cover of darkness, the fast dwindling company laid their dead, leveling the earth above them lest the Indians should learn how many were the graves. History records no nobler venture for faith and freedom than of this Pilgrim band. In weariness and painfulness, in watching often in hunger and cold, they laid the foundation of a state wherein every man through countless ages should have liberty to worship God in his own way. May their example inspire thee to do thy part in perpetuating and spreading the lofty ideals of our republic throughout the world.

They laid the foundation of a state wherein every man through countless ages should have liberty.

LORD BYRON'S INSCRIPTION ON THE MONUMENT OF A NEW-FOUNDLAND DOG

NEAR this spot are deposited the remains of one who possessed Beauty without Vanity, Strength without Insolence, Courage without Ferocity, and all the Virtues of Man, without his Vices. This Praise, which would be unmeaning Flattery if inscribed over human ashes is but a just tribute to the Memory of Boatswain, a Dog.

EXAMPLE
JOHANN WOLFGANG VON GOETHE

Like the star
Shining afar
Slowly now
And without rest,
Let each man turn, with steady sway,
Round the task that rules the day
And do his best.

DREAM
EDGAR ALLAN POE

All that we see or seem
Is but a dream within a dream.

O MASTER, LET ME WALK WITH THEE
WASHINGTON GLADDEN

O Master, let me walk with Thee
In lowly paths of service free;
Tell me Thy secret; help me bear
The strain of toil, the fret of care.

Teach me Thy patience; still with
Thee
In closer, dearer company,
In work that keeps faith sweet and
strong,
In trust that triumphs over wrong.

COME, THOU ALMIGHTY KING
CHARLES WESLEY

Come, Thou almighty King,
Help us Thy name to sing,
Help us to praise:
Father All-glorious,
Over all victorious,
Come, and reign over us,
Ancient of Days.

Come, Thou incarnate Word,
Gird on Thy mighty sword,
Our prayer attend:
Come, and Thy people bless,
And give Thy word success:
Spirit of holiness,
On us descend.

Come, holy Comforter
Thy sacred witness bear
In this glad hour:
Thou who almighty art,
Now rule in every heart,
And never from us depart,
Spirit of power.

AMONG THE ROCKS
ROBERT BROWNING

Oh, good gigantic smile of the brown old earth.
   This autumn morning! How he sets his bones
To bask in the sun, and thrusts out knees and feet
For the ripple to run over in its mirth;
   Listening the while, where on the heap of stones
The white breast of the sea-lark twitters sweet.

That is the doctrine, simple, ancient, true;
   Such is life's trial, as old earth smiles and knows.
If you loved only what were worth your love,
Love were clear gain, and wholly well for you:
Make the low nature better by your throes!
Give earth yourself, go up for gain above!

SUMMER
By GEORGE GISSING

TODAY, as I was reading in the garden, a waft of summer perfume—some hidden link of association in what I read—I know now what it may have been—took me back to schoolboy holidays; I recovered with strange intensity that lightsome mood of long release from tasks, of going away to the seaside, which is one of childhood's blessings. I was in the train; no rushing express, such as bears you great distances; the sober train which goes to no place of importance, which lets you see the white steam of the engine float and fall upon a meadow ere you pass. Thanks to a good and wise father, we youngsters saw nothing of seaside places where crowds assemble; I am speaking, too, of a time more than forty years ago, when it was still possible to find on the coasts of northern England, east or west, spots known only to those who loved the shore for its beauty and its solitude. At every station the train stopped; little stations, decked with beds of flowers, smelling warm in the sunshine where country folk got in with baskets, and talked in an unfamiliar dialect an English which to us sounded almost like a foreign tongue. Then the first glimpse of the sea; the excitement of noting whether the tide was high or low—stretches of sand and weedy pools, or halcyon wavelets frothing at their furthest reach, under the sea-banks starred with convolvulus. Of a sudden, *our* station!

Ah, that taste of the brine on a child's lips! Nowadays, I can take holiday when I will, and go whithersoever it pleases me; but that salt kiss of the sea air I shall never know again. My senses are dulled; I cannot get so near to Nature; I have a sorry dread of her clouds, her winds, and must walk with tedious circumspection where once I ran and leapt exultingly. Were it possible, but for one half-hour, to plunge and bask in the sunny surf, to roll on the silvery sand hills, to leap from rock to rock on shining sea-ferns, laughing if I slipped into the shallows among starfish and anemones!

—From *The Private Papers of Henry Ryecroft*

From *MARE NOSTRUM*

By Vicente Blasco Ibanez

ALL THAT MANKIND had ever written or dreamed about the Mediterranean, the doctor had in his library and could repeat to his eager little listener. In Ferragut's estimation the *mare nostrum* was a species of blue beast, powerful and of great intelligence—a sacred animal like the dragons and serpents that certain religions adored, believing them to be the source of life. The rivers that threw themselves impetuously into its bosom in order to renew it were few and scanty. The Rhone and the Nile appeared to be pitiful little rivulets compared with the river courses of other continents that empty into the oceans.

Losing by evaporation three times more liquid than the rivers bring to it, this sunburnt sea would soon have been converted into a great salt desert were not the Atlantic sending it a rapid current of renewal that was precipitated through the Straits of Gibraltar. Under this superficial current existed still another, flowing in an opposite direction, that returned a part of the Mediterranean to the ocean, because the Mediterranean waters were more salt and dense than those of the Atlantic. The tide scarcely made itself felt on its strands. Its basin was mined by subterranean fires that were always seeking extraordinary outlets through Vesuvius and Aetna, and breathed continually through the mouth of Stromboli. Sometimes these Plutonic ebulli-

tions would come to the surface, making new islands rise up upon the waters like tumors of lava.

In its bosom exist still double the quantity of animal species that abound in other seas, although less numerous. The tunny fish, playful lambs of the blue pasture lands, were gamboling over its surface or passing in schools under the furrows of the waves. Men were setting netted traps for them along the coasts of Spain and France, in Sardinia, the Straits of Messina and the waters of the Adriatic. But this wholesale slaughter scarcely lessened the compact, fishy squadrons. After wandering through the windings of the Grecian Archipelago, they passed the Dardanelles and the Bosphorus, stirring the two narrow passageways with the violence of their invisible gallopade and making a turn at the bowl of the Black Sea, swimming back, decimated but impetuous, to the depths of the Mediterranean.

Red coral was forming immovable groves on the substrata of the Balearic Islands, and on the coasts of Naples and Africa. Ambergris was constantly being found on the steep shores of Sicily. Sponges were growing in the tranquil waters in the shadow of the great rocks of Mallorca and the Isles of Greece. Naked men without any equipment whatever, holding their breath, were still descending to the bottom as in primitive times, in order to snatch these treasures away.

* * *

❧ MORTAL THOUGH I BE, yea ephemeral, if but a moment I gaze up to the night's starry domain of heaven, then no longer on earth I stand; I touch the Creator, and my lively spirit drinketh immortality.

—Ptolemy the Astronomer

❧ TOO LOW they build who build beneath the stars.—*Young*

My Heroine

By JAMES M. BARRIE

*W*HEN IT WAS KNOWN that I had begun another story my mother might ask what it was to be about this time.

'Fine we can guess who it is about,' my sister would say pointedly.

'Maybe you can guess, but it is beyond me,' says my mother, with the meekness of one who knows that she is a dull person.

My sister scorned her at such times. 'What woman is in all his books?' she would demand.

'I'm sure I canna say,' replies my mother determinedly. 'I thought the women were different every time.'

'Mother, I wonder you can be so audacious! Fine you know what woman I mean.'

'How can I know? What woman is it? You should bear in mind that I hinna your cleverness' (they were constantly giving each other little knocks).

'I won't give you the satisfaction of saying her name. But this I will say, it is high time he was keeping her out of his books.'

And then as usual my mother would give herself away unconsciously. 'That is what I tell him,' she says chuckling, 'and he tries to keep me out, but he canna; it's more than he can do!'

On an evening after my mother had gone to bed, the first chapter would be brought upstairs, and I read, sitting at the foot of the bed, while my sister watched to make my mother behave herself, and my father cried H'sh! when there were interruptions. All would go well at the start, the reflections were accepted with a little nod of the head, the descriptions of scenery as ruts on the road that must be got over at a walking pace (my mother did not care for scenery, and that is why there is so little of it in my books). But now I am reading too quickly, a little apprehensively, because I know that the next paragraph begins with—let us say with, 'Along this path came a woman: I had intended to rush on here in a loud bullying voice, but 'Along this path came a woman' I read; and stop. Did I hear a faint sound from the other end of the bed? Perhaps I did not; I may only have been listening for it, but I falter and look up. My sister and I look sternly at my mother. She bites her under-lip and clutches the bed with both hands, really she is doing her best for me, but first comes a smothered gurgling sound, then her hold on herself relaxes and she shakes with mirth.

'That's a way to behave!' cries my sister.

'I canna help it,' my mother gasps.

'And there's nothing to laugh at.'

'It's that woman,' my mother explains unnecessarily.

'Maybe she's not the woman you think her,' I say, crushed.

'Maybe not,' says my mother doubtfully. 'What was her name?'

'Her name,' I answer with triumph, 'was not Margaret'; but this makes her ripple again. 'I have so many names nowadays,' she mutters.

'H'sh!' says my father, and the reading is resumed.

Perhaps the woman who came along the path was of tall and majestic figure, which should have shown my mother that I had contrived to start my train without her this time. But it did not.

'What are you laughing at now?' says my sister severely. 'Do you not hear that she was a tall, majestic woman?'

'It's the first time I ever heard it said of her,' replies my mother.

'But she is.'

'Ke fy, havers!'

'The book says it.'

'There will be a many queer things in the book. What was she wearing?'

'I have not described her clothes.'

'That's a mistake,' says my mother. 'When I come upon a woman in a book, the first thing I want to know about her is whether she was good-looking, and the second, how she was put on.'

The woman on the path was eighteen years of age, and of remarkable beauty.

'That settles you,' says my sister.

'I was no beauty at eighteen,' my mother admits, but here my father interferes unexpectedly. 'There wasna your like in this countryside at eighteen,' says he stoutly.

'Pooh!' says she, well-pleased.

'Were you plain, then?' we ask.

'Sal,' she replies briskly, 'I was far from plain.'

'H'sh!'

Perhaps in the next chapter this lady (or another) appears in a carriage.

'I assure you we're mounting in the world,' I hear my mother murmur, but I hurry on without looking up. The lady lives in a house where there are footmen—but the footmen have come on the scene too hurriedly. 'This is more than I can stand,' gasps my mother, and just as she is getting the better of a fit of laughter, 'Footman, give me a drink of water,' she cries, and this sets her off again. Often the readings had to end abruptly because her mirth brought on violent fits of coughing.

Sometimes I read to my sister alone, and she assured me that she could not see my mother among the women this time. This she said to humour me. Presently she would slip upstairs to announce triumphantly, 'You are in again!'

Or in the small hours I might make a confidant to my father, and when I had finished reading he would say thoughtfully, 'That lassie is very natural. Some of the ways you say she had—your mother had them just the same. Did you ever notice what an extraordinary woman your mother is?'

Then would I seek my mother for comfort. She was the more ready to give it because of her profound conviction that if I was found out—that is, if readers discovered how frequently and in how many guises she appeared in my books—the affair would become a public scandal.

'You see Jess is not really you,' I begin inquiringly.

'Oh, no, she is another kind of woman altogether,' my mother says, and then spoils the compliment by adding naively, 'She had but two rooms and I have six.'

I sigh. 'Without counting the pantry, and it's a great big pantry,' she mutters.

This was not the sort of difference I could greatly plume myself upon, and honesty would force me to say, 'As far as that goes, there was a time when you had but two rooms yourself—'

'That's long since,' she breaks in. 'I began with an up-the-stair, but I always had it in my mind—I never mentioned it, but there it was—to have the down-the-stair as well. Ay, and I've had it this many a year.'

'Still, there is no denying that Jess had the same ambition.'

'She had, but to her two-roomed house she had to stick all her born days. Was that like me?'

'No, but she wanted—'

'She wanted, and I wanted, but I got and she didna. That's the difference betwixt her and me.'

'If that is all the difference, it is little credit I can claim for having created her.'

My mother sees that I need soothing. 'That is far from being all the difference,' she would say eagerly. 'There's my silk, for instance. Though I say it myself, there's not a better silk in the valley of Strathmore. Had Jess a silk of any kind—not to speak of a silk like that?'

'Well, she had no silk, but you remember how she got that cloak with beads.'

'An eleven and a bit! Hoots, what was that to boast of! I tell you, every single yard of my silk cost—'

'Mother, that is the very way Jess spoke about her cloak!'

She lets this pass, perhaps without hearing it, for solicitude about her silk had hurried her to the wardrobe where it hangs.

'Ah, Mother, I am afraid that was very like Jess!'

'How could it be like her when she didna even have a wardrobe? I tell you what, if there had been a real Jess and she had boasted to me about her cloak with beads, I would have said to her in a careless sort of voice, "Step across with me, Jess, and I'll let you see something that is hanging in my wardrobe." That would have lowered her pride!'

'I don't believe that is what you would have done, Mother.'

Then a sweeter expression would come into her face. 'No,' she would say reflectively, 'it's not.'

'What would you have done? I think I know.'

'You cannot know. But I'm thinking I would have called to mind that she was a poor woman, and ailing, and terrible windy about her cloak, and I would just have said it was a beauty and that I wished I had one like it.'

'Yes, I am certain that is what you would have done. But oh, Mother, that is just how Jess would have acted if some poorer woman than she had shown her a new shawl.'

'Maybe, but though I hadna boasted about my silk I would have wanted to do it.'

'Just as Jess would have been fidget-

ing to show off her eleven and a bit!'

It seems advisable to jump to another book; not to my first, because—well, as it was my first there would naturally be something of my mother in it, and not to the second, as it was my first novel and not much esteemed even in our family. (But the little touches of my mother in it are not so bad.) Let us try the story about the minister.

My mother's first remark is decidedly damping. 'Many a time in my young days,' she says, 'I played about the Auld Licht manse, but I little thought I should live to be the mistress of it!'

'But Margaret is not you.'

'N—no, oh no. She had a very different life from mine. I never let on to a soul that she is me!'

'She was not meant to be you when I began. Mother, what a way you have of coming creeping in!'

'You should keep better watch on yourself.'

'Perhaps if I had called Margaret by some other name—'

'I should have seen through her just the same. As soon as I heard she was the mother I began to laugh. In some ways, though, she's not so very like me. She was long in finding out about Babbie. I'se uphaud I should have been quicker.'

'Babbie, you see, kept close to the garden-wall.'

'It's not the wall up at the manse that would have hidden her from me.'

'She came out in the dark.'

'I'm thinking she would have found me looking for her with a candle.'

'And Gavin was secretive.'

'That would have put me on my mettle.'

'She never suspected anything.'

'I wonder at her.'

But my new heroine is to be a child. What has madam to say to that?

A child! Yes, she has something to say even to that. 'This beats all!' are the words.

'Come, come, Mother, I see what you are thinking, but I assure you that this time—'

'Of course not,' she said soothingly, 'oh, no, she canna be me'; but anon her real thoughts, are revealed by the artless remark, 'I doubt, though, this is a tough job you have on hand—it is so long since I was a bairn.'

We came very close to each other in those talks. 'It is a queer thing,' she would say softly, 'that near everything you write is about this bit place. You little expected that when you began. I mind well the time when it never entered your head, any more than mine, that you could write a page about our squares and wynds. I wonder how it has come about?'

There was a time when I could not have answered that question, but that time had long passed. 'I suppose, Mother, it was because you were most at home in your own town, and there was never much pleasure to me in writing of you, nor of squares and wynds you never passed through, nor of a countryside of people who could not have known where you never carried your father's dinner in a flaggon. There is scarce a house in all my books where I have not seemed to see you a thousand times, bending over the fireplace or winding up the clock.'

'And yet you used to be in such a quandary because you knew nobody you could make your women-folk out of! Do you mind that, and how we both laughed at the notion of your having to make them out of me?'

'I remember.'

'And now you've gone back to my father's time. It's more than sixty years since I carried his dinner in a flaggon through the long parks of Kinnordy.'

'I often go into the long parks, Mother, and sit on the stile at the edge of the wood till I fancy I see a little girl coming toward me with a flaggon in her hand.'

'Jumping the burn (I was once so proud of my jumps!) and swinging the flaggon round so quick that what was inside hadna time to fall out. I used to wear a magenta frock and a white pinafore. Did I ever tell you that?'

'Mother, the little girl in my story wears a magenta frock and a white pinafore.'

'You minded that! But I'm thinking it wasna a lassie in a pinafore you saw in the long parks of Kinnordy, it was just a gey done auld woman.'

'It was a lassie in a pinafore, Mother, when she was far away, but when she came near it was a gey done auld woman.'

'And a fell ugly one!'

'The most beautiful one I shall ever see.'

'I wonder to hear you say it. Look at my wrinkled auld face.'

'It is the sweetest face in all the world.'

'See how the rings drop off my poor wasted finger.'

'There will always be some one nigh, Mother, to put them on again.'

'Ay, will there! Well I know it. Do you mind how when you were but a bairn you used to say, "Wait till I'm a man, and you'll never have a reason for greeting again?"'

I remembered.

'You used to come running into the house to say, "There's a proud dame going down the Marywellbrae in a cloak that is black on one side and white on the other; wait till I'm a man, and you'll have one the very same." And when I lay on gey hard beds you said, "When I'm a man you'll lie on feathers." You saw nothing bonny, you never heard of my setting my heart on anything, but what you flung up your head and cried, "Wait till I'm a man." You fair shamed me before the neighbours, and yet I was windy, too. And now it has all come true like a dream. I can call to mind not one little thing I ettled for in my lusty days that hasna been put into my hands in my auld age; I sit here useless, surrounded by the gratification of all my wishes and all my ambitions, and at times I'm near terrified, for it's as if God had mista'en me for some other woman.'

'Your hopes and ambitions were so simple,' I would say, but she did not like that. 'They werna that simple,' she would answer, flushing.

I am reluctant to leave those happy days, but the end must be faced, and as I write I seem to see my mother growing smaller and her face more wistful, and still she lingers with us, as if God had said, 'Child of mine, your time has come, be not afraid,' and she was not afraid, but still she lingered, and He waited, smiling. I never read any of that last book to her; when it was finished she was too heavy with years to follow a story. To me this was as if my book must go out cold into the world (like all that may come after it from me), and my sister, who took more thought for others and less for herself than any other human being I have known, saw this, and by some means unfathomable to a man coaxed my mother into being once again the woman she had been. On a day but three weeks before she died my father and I were called softly upstairs. My mother was sitting bolt upright, as she loved to sit, in her old chair by the window, with a manuscript in her hands. But she was looking about her without much understanding. 'Just to please him,' my sister whispered, and then in a low, trembling voice my mother began to read. I looked at my sister. Tears of woe were stealing down her face. Soon the reading became very slow and stopped. After a pause, 'There was something you were to say to him,' my sister reminded her. 'Luck,' muttered a voice as from the dead, 'luck.' And then the old smile came running to her face like a lamplighter, and she said to me, 'I am ower far gone to read, but I'm thinking I am in it again!' My father put her Testament in her hands, and it fell open—as it always does—at the Fourteenth of John. She made an effort to read but could not. Suddenly she stooped and kissed the broad page. 'Will that do instead?' she asked.

—From *Margaret Ogilvy*

❧   ❧   ❧

UNFAILING
FRANCES SHAW

When, like a flower, your loved one lies
   Beneath the grasses
   Sleeping the great sleep,
Go out unlonely to the folding hills—
   They will not let you weep.

When one by one your dreams have stolen by,
   And blackness fills the night,
   And pain and care,
Reach up for comfort to the leaning sky—
   The coming of the dawn is still a prayer.

MY HEART'S IN THE HIGHLANDS
ROBERT BURNS

My heart's in the Highlands, my heart
    is not here;
My heart's in the Highlands a-chasing
    the deer;
Chasing the wild deer, and following
    the roe,
My heart's in the Highlands wherever
    I go.
Farewell to the Highlands, farewell to
    the North,
The birthplace of valor, the country of
    worth;
Wherever I wander, wherever I rove,
The hills of the Highlands forever I
    love.

Farewell to the mountains high
    covered with snow;
Farewell to the straths and green valleys
    below;
Farewell to the forests and wild-hanging
    woods;
Farewell to the torrents and loud-
    pouring floods.
My heart's in the Highlands, my heart
    is not here;
My heart's in the Highlands a-chasing
    the deer;
Chasing the wild deer, and following
    the roe,
My heart's in the Highlands wherever
    I go.

OF A' THE AIRTS THE WIND CAN BLAW
ROBERT BURNS

Of a' the airts the wind can blaw,
    I dearly like the west;
For there the bonnie lassie lives,
    The lassie I lo'e best.
There wild woods grow, and rivers row,
    And monie a hill's between;
But day and night my fancy's flight
    Is ever wi' my Jean.

I see her in the dewy flowers,
    I see her sweet and fair;
I hear her in the tunefu' birds,
    I hear her charm the air;
There's not a bonnie flower that springs
    By fountain, shaw, or green,—
There's not a bonnie bird that sings,
    But minds me of my Jean.

JOHN ANDERSON MY JO
ROBERT BURNS

John Anderson my jo, John,
    When we were first acquent,
Your locks were like the raven,
    Your bonnie brow was brent;
But now your brow is beld, John,
    Your locks are like the snaw,
But blessing on your frosty pow,
    John Anderson my jo!

John Anderson my jo, John,
    We clamb the hill thegither,
And monie a cantie day, John,
    We've had wi ane anither;
Now we maun totter down, John,
    And hand in hand we'll go,
And sleep thegither at the foot,
    John Anderson my jo!

* * *

THE GREAT CHARM of Scottish poetry consists in its simplicity and genuine, unaffected sympathy with the common joys and sorrows of daily life. It is a home-taught, household melody. It calls to mind the pastoral bleat on the hillsides, the kirk-bells of a summer Sabbath, the song of the lark in the sunrise. —*Whittier*

HOME
By JOHN RUSKIN

THIS IS the true nature of home—it is the place of Peace; the shelter, not only from all injury, but from all terror, doubt, and division. In so far as it is not this, it is not home: so far as the anxieties of the outer life penetrate into it, and the inconsistently-minded, unknown, unloved, or hostile society of the outer world is allowed by either husband or wife to cross the threshold, it ceases to be home; it is then only a part of that outer world which you have roofed over, and lighted fire in. But so far as it is a sacred place, a vestal temple, a temple of the hearth watched over by Household Gods, before whose faces none may come but those whom they can receive with love,—so far as it is this, and roof and fire are types only of a nobler shade and light,—shade as of the rock in a weary land, and light as of the Pharos in the stormy sea,—so far it vindicates the name, and fulfills the praise, of home.

And wherever a true wife comes, this home is always round her. The stars only may be over her head; the glow-worm in the night-cold grass may be the only fire at her foot; but home is yet wherever she is; and for a noble woman it stretches far round her, better than ceiled with cedar, or painted with vermilion, shedding its quiet light far, for those whose else were homeless.

BED IS TOO SMALL
ELIZABETH COATSWORTH

Bed is too small to rest my tiredness,
I'll take a hill for pillow, soft with trees.
Now draw the clouds up tight beneath my chin.
God, blow the moon out, please.

ASLEEP
DOROTHY ALDIS

When he's asleep
He never knows
If it rains
Or if is snows;

If the stars
Are in the sky,
Or if a wind
Is hurrying by.

His little room
Is cool and dim:
He does not feel
Her kissing him.

WISH
MILDRED BOWERS ARMSTRONG

I am not dainty as a flower,
Magnificent as the sea,
Or full of carols as a bird;
But I should like to be.

FOR A CHILD
FANNY STEARNS DAVIS

Your friends shall be the tall wind,
The river and the tree;
The sun that laughs and marches,
The swallow and the sea.

Your prayers shall be the murmur
Of grasses in the rain;
The song of wildwood thrushes
That makes God glad again.

And you shall run and wander
And you shall dream and sing
Of brave things and bright things
Beyond the swallow's wing.

And you shall envy no man,
Nor hurt your heart with sighs,
For I will keep you simple
That God may make you wise.

OF A SMALL DAUGHTER WALKING OUTDOORS

Frances M. Frost

Easy, wind!
Go softly here!
She is small
And very dear.

She is young
And cannot say
Words to chase
The wind away.

She is new
To walking, so
Wind, be kind
And gently blow

On her ruffled head,
On grass and clover.
Easy, wind . . .
She'll tumble over!

TRACINGS

Bernard Raymund

Finger prints on the window,
The smear of a dog's wet nose,
Thousands of marks on the stairway
Of clattering heels and toes,
A headlong path through the garden
To a low place in the wall,
Beyond to a ring of ashes
By the boulder. That is all,
All they have left behind them—
You may search the whole place
    through,
Never know what the children looked
    like
Nor the tricks their dog could do.

GENTLE JESUS, MEEK AND MILD

Charles Wesley

Gentle Jesus, meek and mild,
Look upon a little child,
Pity my simplicity,
Suffer to come to Thee!

WISDOM AND BEAUTY
By Donn Byrne

"My dear son, God has put wisdom in my head and beauty into yours. Wisdom is needed for the governance of this world, but beauty is needed for its existence. In arid deserts there is no life. Birds do not sing in the dark of night. Show me a waste country, and I'll show you a brutal people. No faith can live that is not beautiful. . .

"The beauty God has put in your heart, child, you must always keep. . . I will not keep you any longer. Only to say this, and this is the chiefest thing: never let your dream be taken from you. Keep it unspotted from the world. In darkness and in tribulation it will go with you as a friend; but in wealth and power hold fast to it, for then is danger. Let not the mists of the world, the gay diversions, the little trifles, draw you from glory.

"Remember!" —From *Messer Marco Polo*

KNOW YOU WHAT IT IS TO BE A CHILD?

By Francis Thompson

Know you what it is to be a child? It is to be something very different from the man of today.

It is to have a spirit yet streaming from the waters of baptism, it is to believe in love, to believe in loveliness, to believe in belief. It is to be so little that the elves can reach to whisper in your ear. It is to turn pumpkins into coaches, and mice into horses, lowness into loftiness and nothing into everything—for each child has his fairy godmother in his own soul. It is to live in a nutshell and count yourself king of the infinite space; it is

To see a world in a grain of sand,
    Heaven in a wild flower,
To hold infinity in the palm of your
    hand,
    And Eternity in an hour.

I LOVE OLD THINGS

Wilson MacDonald

I love old things:
Streets of old cities
Crowded with ghosts
And banked with oranges,
Gay scarfs and shawls
That flow like red water.

I love old abbeys
With high, carved portals
And dim, cool corners
Where tired hearts pray:
I join them in the silence
And repair my soul.

I love old inns
Where floors creak eerily
And doors blow open
On windless nights,
Where heavy curtains
Dance a slow waltz.

I love old trees
That lift up their voices
High above the grasses.
They do not sing
At the light wind's bidding:
They chant alone to storms.

I love old china,
Knowing well the flavour
Of great, strong men
And fair, sweet women
Lurks at the rim
Of each deep brown bowl.

I love old books
Frayed from the searching
Of truth-hungry fingers:
Their warm, soft vellum
Leads me up through sorrow
Like a dear friend's hand.

I love old men
And old, dear women
Who keep red cheeks
As the snows of winter
Keep the round red berry
Of the winter-green.

(This verse to be chanted)
I love old things:
Weather-beaten, worn things,
Cracked, broken, torn things,
The old sun, the old moon,
The old earth's face,
Old wine in dim flagons,
Old ships and old wagons—
OLD SHIPS AND OLD WAGONS—
    (This line softly)
Old coin and old lace,
Rare old lace.

TUSCAN OLIVES

A. Mary F. Robinson

The colour of the olives who shall say?
    In winter on the yellow ground
    they're blue,
A wind can change the green to white
    or grey,
    But they are olives still in every hue;

But they are olives always, green or
    white,
As love is love in torment or delight;
But they are olives, ruffled or at rest,
As love is always love in tears or jest.

MY STAR

Robert Browning

All that I know
    Of a certain star
Is, it can throw
    (Like the angled spar)
Now a dart of red,
    Now a dart of blue;
Till my friends have said
    They would fain see, too,
My star that dartles the red and the
    blue!
Then it stops like a bird; like a flower,
    hangs furled:
They must solace themselves with the
    Saturn above it.
What matter to me if their star is a
    world?
Mine has opened its soul to me; there-
    fore I love it.

298

A LITTLE SCOTCH GIRL *made a list of*
"My Twelve Loveliest Things, People
Not Counted." They were:

The scrunch of dry leaves as you walk
    through them
The feel of clean clothes
Water running into bath
The cold of ice cream
Cool wind on a hot day
Climbing up and looking back
Honey in your mouth
Smell of a drugstore
Hot-water bottle in bed
Babies smiling
The feeling inside when you sing
Baby kittens

—Dr. Douglas Horton

A GOODLY LIFE

By ROBERT LOUIS STEVENSON

To BE honest, to be kind—to earn a
little and to spend a little less, to make,
upon the whole, a family happier for
his presence—to keep a few friends.

MARGARITAE SORORI

WILLIAM ERNEST HENLEY

A late lark twitters from the quiet skies;
And from the west,
Where the sun, his day's work ended,
Lingers as in content,
There falls on the old grey city
An influence luminous and serene,
A shining peace.

The smoke ascends
In a rosy-and-golden haze. The spires
Shine, and are changed. In the valley
Shadows rise. The lark sings on. The
    sun,
Closing his benediction,
Sinks, and the darkening air
Thrills with a sense of the triumphing
    night—
Night with her train of stars
And her great gift of sleep.

STANZAS FOR MUSIC

LORD BYRON

There be none of Beauty's daughters
With a magic like thee;
And like music on the waters
Is thy sweet voice to me:
When, as if its sound were causing
The charmed ocean's pausing,
The waves lie still and gleaming,
And the lulled winds seem dreaming;

And the midnight moon is weaving
Her bright chain o'er the deep;
Whose breast is gently heaving,
As an infant's asleep:
So the spirit bows before thee,
To listen and adore thee;
With a full but soft emotion,
Like the swell of Summer's ocean.

THE LADIES OF ST. JAMES'S!

AUSTIN DOBSON

The ladies of St. James's!
    They are so fine and fair,
You'd think a box of essences
    Was broken in the air:
But Phyllida, my Phyllida!
    The breath of heath and furze
When breezes blow at morning
    Is not so fresh as hers.

The ladies of St. James's!
    They're painted to the eyes.
Their white it stays for ever,
    Their red it never dies:
But Phyllida, my Phyllida!
    Her colour comes and goes.
It trembles to a lily—
    It wavers to a rose.

The ladies of St. James's!
    You scarce can understand
The half of all their speeches,
    Their phrases are so grand:
But Phyllida, my Phyllida!
    Her shy and simple words
Are clear as after rain-drops
    The music of the birds.

From *MIDSTREAM*
By HELEN KELLER

It is through her great faith that the world has been illumined for Miss Keller. In Midstream she has stated her creed as follows:

I believe that we can live on earth according to the teachings of Jesus, and that the greatest happiness will come to the world when man obeys His commandment "Love ye one another."

I believe that every question between man and man is a religious question, and that every social wrong is a moral wrong.

I believe that we can live on earth according to the fulfilment of God's will, and that when the will of God is done on earth as it is done in heaven, every man will love his fellow men, and act towards them as he desires they should act towards him. I believe that the welfare of each is bound up in the welfare of all.

I believe that life is given us so we may grow in love, and I believe that God is in me as the sun is in the colour and fragrance of a flower—the Light in my darkness, the Voice in my silence.

I believe that only in broken gleams has the Sun of Truth yet shone upon men. I believe that love will finally establish the Kingdom of God on earth, and that the Cornerstones of that Kingdom will be Liberty, Truth, Brotherhood, and Service.

I believe that no good shall be lost, and that all man has willed or hoped or dreamed of good shall exist forever.

I believe in the immortality of the soul because I have within me immortal longings. I believe that the state we enter after death is wrought of our own motives, thoughts, and deeds. I believe that in the life to come I shall have the senses I have not had here, and that my home there will be beautiful with colour, music, and speech of flowers and faces I love.

Without this faith there would be little meaning in my life. I should be "a mere pillar of darkness in the dark." Observers in the full enjoyment of their bodily senses pity me, but it is because they do not see the golden chamber in my life where I dwell delighted; for, dark as my path may seem to them, I carry a magic light in my heart. Faith, the spiritual strong searchlight, illumines the way, and although sinister doubts lurk in the shadow, I walk unafraid towards the Enchanted Wood where the foliage is always green, where joy abides, where nightingales nest and sing, and where life and death are one in the Presence of the Lord.

HOW HELEN KELLER SEES COLOR
By NELLA BRADDY

IT IS ANNOYING to a certain type of mind to have Miss Keller describe something she obviously cannot know through direct sensation. The annoyance is mutual. These sensations, whatever expert opinion on them may be, are as real to her as any others. Her idea of colour, to take only one instance, is built up through association and analogy. Pink is "like a baby's cheek or a soft Southern breeze." Gray is "like a soft shawl around the shoulders." Yellow is "like the sun. It means life and is rich in promise." There are two kinds of brown. "One is "warm and friendly like leaf mould." The other is "like the trunks of aged trees with worm holes in them, or like withered hands." Lilac, which is her Teacher's favourite colour, "makes her think of faces she has loved and kissed." The warm sun brings out odours that make her think of red. Coolness brings out odours that make her think of green. A sparkling colour brings to mind soap bubbles quivering under her hand.

—From the Preface of *Midstream*

DREAMERS

By Herbert Kaufman

DREAMERS are the architects of greatness. Their brains have wrought all human miracles. In lace of stone their spires stab the Old World's skies and with their golden crosses kiss the sun. The belted wheel, the trail of steel, the churning screw, are shuttles in the loom on which they weave their magic tapestries. A flash out in the night leaps leagues of snarling seas and cries to shore for help, which, but for one man's dream, would never come. Their tunnels plow the river bed and chain islands to the Motherland. Their wings of canvas beat the air and add the highways of the eagle to the human paths. A Godhewn voice swells from a disc of glue and wells out through a throat of brass, caught sweet and whole, to last beyond the maker of the song, because a dreamer dreamt. Your homes are set upon a land a dreamer found. The pictures on its walls are visions from a dreamer's soul. A dreamer's pain wails from your violin. They are the chosen few—the Blazers of the Way—who never wear Doubt's bandage on their eyes—who starve and chill and hurt, but hold to courage and to hope, because they know that there is always proof of truth for them who try—that only cowardice and lack of faith can keep the seeker from his chosen goal; but if his heart be strong and if he dream enough and dream it hard enough, he can attain, no matter where men failed before.

Walls crumble and empires fall. The tidal wave sweeps from the sea and tears a fortress from its rocks. The rotting nations drop off Time's bough, and only things the dreamers make live on.

ON THE JOY OF LIVING

A MORNING of intoxicating beauty, fresh as the feelings of sixteen, and crowned with flowers like a bride. The poetry of youth, of innocence, and of love, overflowed my soul. Even to the light mist hovering over the bosom of the plain—image of that tender modesty which veils the features and shrouds in mystery the inmost thoughts of the maiden—everything that I saw delighted my eyes and spoke to my imagination. It was a sacred, a nuptial day! and the matin bells ringing in some distant village harmonized marvelously with the hymn of nature. "Pray," they said, "and love! Adore a fatherly and beneficent God. They recalled to me the accent of Haydn; there was in them and in the landscape a childlike joyousness, a naive gratitude, a radiant heavenly joy innocent of pain and sin, like the sacred simple-hearted ravishment of Eve on the first day of her awakening in the new world.—How good a thing is feeling,—admiration! It is the bread of angels, the eternal food of cherubim and seraphim.

I have not yet felt the air so pure, so life-giving, so ethereal, during the five days that I have been here. To breathe is a beatitude. One understands the delights of a bird's existence—that emancipation from all encumbering weight—that luminous and empyrean life, floating in blue space, and passing from one horizon to another with a stroke of the wing. One must have a great deal of air below one before one can be conscious of such inner freedom as this, such lightness of the whole being. Every element has its poetry, but the poetry of air is liberty. —*Amiel*

Twenty Minutes of Reality

By M. P. MONTAGUE

As A CHILD I WAS AFRAID of world without end, of life everlasting. The thought of it used to clutch me at times with a crushing sense of the inevitable, and make me long to run away. But where could one run? If never-ending life were true, then I was already caught fast in it, and it would never end. Perhaps it had never had a beginning. Life everlasting, eternity, forever and ever: these are tremendous words for even a grown person to face; and for a child—if he grasp their significance at all—they may be hardly short of appalling. The picture that Heaven presented to my mind was of myself, a desperate little atom, dancing in a streak of light around and around and around forever and ever. I do not know what could have suggested such an idea; I only knew that I could not think of myself caught there in eternity like a chip in a whirlpool, or say 'round again, and round again, and round again' for more than a minute, without hypnotizing myself into a state of sheer terror. Of course, as I grew older I threw off this truly awful conception; yet shorn of its crudeness and looked at with grown-up eyes, there were moments when, much as I believed in, and desired, eternal life, that old feeling of 'round again, and round again' would swoop back upon me with all its unutterable weariness, and no state of bliss that I could imagine seemed to me proof forever against boredom. Nevertheless, I still had faith to believe that eternity and enjoyment of life could in some way be squared, though I did not see how it was to be done. I am glad that I had, for I came at last to a time when faith was justified by sight, and it is of that time that I wish to write here.

If this paper ever chances to be printed, it will be read, I think, by two sets of persons. There will be those who will wonder if I speak of something that is really there, or who will be quite sure that I do not—that I either imagined or made up the whole thing, or else that it was entirely due to the physical condition of convalescence. Others there will be, who will believe that I am speaking of the truth that is there, because they, too, have seen it. These last will think that it was not because I was returning to health that I imagined all life as beautiful, but that with the cleared vision that sometimes attends convalescence I 'saw into reality,' and felt the ecstasy which is always there, but which we are enabled to perceive only on very rare and fleeting occasions.

It is these last for whom I wish to write. If this clearing of the vision is an occasional occurrence of convalescence, then what I saw is of far more value than it would be had my experience been unique.

I do not really know how long the insight lasted. I have said, at a rough guess, twenty minutes. It may have been a little shorter time, it may have been a little longer. But at best it was very transitory.

It happened to me about two years ago, on the day when my bed was first pushed out of doors to the open gallery of the hospital. I was recovering from a surgical operation. I had undergone a certain amount of physical pain, and had suffered for a short time the most acute mental depression which it has ever been my misfortune to encounter. I suppose that this depression was due to physical causes, but at the time it seemed to me that somewhere down there under the anaesthetic, in the black abyss of unconsciousness, I had discovered a terrible secret, and the secret was that there was no God; or if there was one, He was indifferent to all human suffering.

Though I had hardly re-established my normal state of faith, still the first acuteness of that depression had faded, and only a scar of fear was left when, several days later, my bed was first wheeled out to the porch. There other patients took their airing and received their visitors; busy internes and nurses came and went, and one could get a glimpse of the sky, with bare gray branches against it, and of the ground, with here and there a patch of melting snow.

It was an ordinary cloudy March day. I am glad to think that it was. I am glad to remember that there was nothing extraordinary about the weather, nor any unusualness of setting—no flush of spring or beauty of scenery—to induce what I saw. It was, on the contrary, almost a dingy day. The branches were bare and colorless, and the occasional half-melted piles of snow were a forlorn gray rather than white. Colorless little city sparrows flew and chirped in the trees, while human beings, in no way remarkable, passed along the porch.

There was, however, a wind blowing, and if any outside thing intensified the experience, it was the blowing of that wind. In every other respect it was an ordinary commonplace day. Yet here, in this everyday setting, and entirely unexpectedly (for I had never dreamed of such a thing), my eyes were opened, and for the first time in all my life I caught a glimpse of the ecstatic beauty of reality.

I cannot now recall whether the revelation came suddenly or gradually; I only remember finding myself in the very midst of those wonderful moments, beholding life for the first time in all its young intoxication of loveliness, in its unspeakable joy, beauty, and importance. I cannot say exactly what the mysterious change was. I saw no new thing, but I saw all the usual things in a miraculous new light—in what I believe is their true light. I saw for the first time how wildly beautiful and joyous, beyond any words of mine to describe, is the whole of life. Every human being moving across that porch, every sparrow that flew, every branch tossing in the wind, was caught in and was a part of the whole mad ecstasy of loveliness, of joy, of importance, of intoxication of life.

It was not that for a few keyed-up moments I *imagined* all existence as beautiful, but that my inner vision was cleared to the truth so that I *saw* the actual loveliness which is always there, but which we so rarely perceive; and I knew that every man, woman, bird, and tree, every living thing before me, was extravagantly beautiful, and extravagantly important. And as I beheld, my heart melted out of me in a rapture of love and delight. A nurse was walking past; the wind caught a strand of her hair and blew it out in a momentary gleam of sunshine, and never in my life before had I seen how beautiful beyond all belief is a woman's hair. Nor had I ever guessed how marvelous it is for a human being to walk. As for the internes in their white suits, I had never realized before the whiteness of white linen; but much more than that, I had never so much as dreamed of the mad beauty of young manhood. A little sparrow chirped and flew to a nearby branch, and I honestly believe that only 'the morning stars singing together, and the sons of God shouting for joy' can in the least express the ecstasy of a bird's flight. I cannot express it, but I have seen it.

Once out of all the gray days of my life I have looked into the heart of reality; I have witnessed the truth; I have seen life as it really is—ravishingly ecstatically, madly beautiful, and filled to overflowing with a wild joy, and a value unspeakable. For those glorified moments I was in love with every living thing before me—the trees in the wind, the little birds flying, the nurses, the internes, the people who came and went. There was nothing that was alive that was not a miracle. Just to be alive was in itself a miracle. My very soul flowed out of me in a great joy.

No one can be as happy as I was and not have it show in some way. A stranger passing paused by my bed and said, 'What are you lying here all alone looking so happy about?' I made some inadequate response as to the pleasure of being out-of-doors and of getting well. How could I explain all the beauty that I was seeing? How could I say that the gray curtain of unreality had swirled away and that I was seeing into the heart of life? It was not an experience for words. It was an emotion, a rapture of the heart.

Besides all the joy and beauty and that curious sense of importance, there was a wonderful feeling of rhythm as well, only it was somehow just beyond the grasp of my mind. I heard no music, yet there was an exquisite sense of time, as though all life went by to a vast, unseen melody. Everything that moved wove out a little thread of rhythm in this tremendous whole. When a bird flew, it did so because somewhere a note had been struck for it to fly on; or else its flying struck the note; or else again the great Will that is Melody willed that it should fly. When people walked, somewhere they beat out a bit of rhythm that was in harmony with the whole great theme. Then, the extraordinary importance of everything! Every living creature was intensely alive and intensely beautiful, but it was as well of a marvelous value.

Whether this value was in itself or a part of the whole, I could not see; but it seemed as though before my very eyes I actually beheld the truth of Christ's saying that not even a sparrow falls to the ground without the knowledge of the Father in Heaven. Yet *what* the importance was, I did not grasp. If my heart could have seen just a little further I should have understood. Even now the tips of my thoughts are forever on the verge of grasping it, forever just missing it. I have a curious half-feeling that somewhere, deep inside of myself, I know very well what this importance is, and have always known; but I cannot get it from the depth of myself into my mind, and thence into words. But whatever it is, the importance seemed to be nearer to beauty and joy than to an anxious morality. I had a feeling that it was in some way different from the importance I had usually attached to life.

It was perhaps as though that great value in every living thing was not so much here and now in ourselves as somewhere else. There is a great significance in every created thing, but the significance is beyond our present grasp. I do not know what it is; I only know that it is there, and that all life is far more valuable than we ever dream of its being. Perhaps the following quotation from Milton may be what I was conscious of:—

What if earth
Be but the shadow of Heaven, and things therein
Each to each other like, more than on earth is thought.

What if here we are only symbols of ourselves, and our real being is somewhere else,—perhaps in the heart of God? Certainly that unspeakable importance had to do with our relationship to the great Whole; but what the relationship was, I could not tell. Was it a relationship of love toward us, or only the delight in creation? But it is hardly likely that a glimpse of a cold Creator would have filled me with such an extravagant joy, or so melted the heart within me. For those fleeting, lovely moments I did indeed, and in truth, love my neighbor as myself. Nay, more; of myself I was hardly conscious, while with my neighbor in every form, from wind-tossed branches and little sparrows flying, up to human beings, I was madly in love. Is it likely that I could have experienced such love if there were not some such emotion at the heart of Reality? If I did not actually see it, it was not that it was not there, but that I did not see quite far enough.

Perhaps this was because I was still somewhat in the grip of that black doubt which I had experienced, and of which I have spoken. I think it was owing to this doubt also that afterwards I had a certain feeling of distrust. I was afraid that all that beauty might be an uncaring joy. As if, though we were indeed intensely important in some unguessed way to the great Reality, our own small individual sorrows were perhaps not of much moment. I am not sure that I actually had this feeling, as it is very difficult, after a lapse of almost two years, to recapture in memory all the emotions of so fleeting and so unusual an experience. If I did, however, I comfort myself, as I have said, with the thought of the intense joy that I experienced. The vision of an uncaring Reality would hardly have melted me to such happiness. That the Creator is a loving Creator I believe with all my heart; but this is belief, not sight. What I saw that day was an unspeakable joy and loveliness, and a value to all life beyond anything that we have knowledge of; while in myself I knew a wilder happiness than I have ever before or since experienced.

Moreover, though there was nothing exactly religious in what I saw, the accounts given by people who have passed through religious conversion or illumination come nearer to describing my emotions than anything else that I have come across.

These testimonies I read almost a year after my hospital episode. I came upon them by chance, and was astonished to find that they were describing very much what I had passed through. I think if I had had nothing to match them in my own experience I should almost certainly have felt sure that these people, because of the emotional excitement within themselves, imagined all the beauties that they described. Now I believe that they are describing what is actually there. Nor are poets making up—as the average mind believes, and as I think I always believed — the extravagant beauty of which they sing. They are telling us of the truth that is there, and that they are occasionally enabled to see.

Here are some of the testimonies offered by people who have experienced illumination in one form or another. 'Natural objects were glorified,' one person affirms. 'My spiritual vision was so clarified that I saw beauty in every natural object in the universe.' Another says, 'When I went into the field to work, the glory of God appeared in all His visible creation. I well remember we reaped oats, and how every straw and beard of the oats seemed, as it were, arrayed in a kind of rainbow glory, or to glow, if I may so express it, in the glory of God.' The father of Rabindranath Tagore thus describes his illumination: 'I felt a serenity and joy which I had never experienced before ... the joy I felt ... that day overflowed my soul. . . . I could not sleep that night. The reason of my sleeplessness

305

was the ecstasy of soul; as if moonlight had spread itself over my mind for the whole of that night.' And when Tagore speaks of his own illumination he says, 'It was morning; I was watching the sunrise in Free School Street. A veil was suddenly drawn and everything I saw became luminous. The whole scene was one perfect music; one marvelous rhythm.' (Note his sense of rhythm, of which I also was conscious.) 'The houses in the street, the children playing, all seemed part of one luminous whole — inexpressibly glorified.' (Perhaps the significance of that tremendous importance which I felt, but failed to grasp, was that we are all parts of a wonderful whole.) 'I was full of gladness, full of love for every tiniest thing.'

And this was what—in a smaller degree—I, too, saw for those fleeting moments out there upon the hospital porch. Mine was, I think, a sort of accidental clearing of the vision by the rebirth of returning health. I believe that a good many people have experienced the same thing during convalescence. Perhaps this is the way in which we should all view life if we were born into it grown up. As it was, when we first arrive we are so engaged in the tremendous business of cutting teeth, saying words, and taking steps, that we have no time for, and little consciousness of, outside wonders; and by the time we have the leisure for admiration life has lost for us its first freshness. Convalescence is a sort of grown-up rebirth, enabling us to see life with a fresh eye.

Doubtless almost any intense emotion may open our 'inward eye' to the beauty of reality. Falling in love appears to do it for some people. The beauties of nature or the exhilaration of artistic creation does it for others. Probably any high experience may momentarily stretch our souls up on tiptoe, so that we catch a glimpse of that marvelous beauty which is always

there, but which we are not often tall enough to perceive.

Emerson says, 'We are immersed in beauty, but our eyes have no clear vision.' I believe that religious conversion more often clears the eyes to this beauty of truth than any other experience; and it is possible that had I not still been somewhat under that black cloud of doubt, I should have seen further than I did. Yet what I did see was very good indeed.

The following quotation from Canon Inge may not be entirely out of place in this connection: 'Incidentally I may say that the peculiar happiness which accompanies every glimpse of insight into truth and reality, whether in the scientific, aesthetic, or emotional sphere, seems to me to have a greater apologetic value than has been generally recognized. It is the clearest possible indication that the truth is for us the good, and forms the ground of a reasonable faith that all things, if we could see them as they are, would be found to work together for good to those who love God.'

In what I saw there was nothing seemingly of an ethical nature. There were no new rules of conduct revealed by those twenty minutes. Indeed, it seemed as though beauty and joy were more at the heart of Reality than an over-anxious morality. It was a little as though (to transpose the quotation),

I had slept and dreamed that life was duty,
But waked to find that life was beauty.

Perhaps at such times of illumination there is no need to worry over sin, for one is so transported by the beauty of humanity and so poured out in love toward every human being, that sin becomes almost impossible.

Perhaps duty may merely point the way. When one arrives at one's destination it would be absurd to go back and reconsult the guide-post. Blindness of heart may be the real sin, and if we could only purify our hearts to behold the beauty that is all about us, sin would vanish away. When Christ says, 'Seek ye the Kingdom of God; and all these things shall be added unto you,' He may mean by 'all these things' spiritual virtues even more than things temporal, such as what we shall eat, and wherewithal we shall be clothed. It may be that He stood forever conscious of a transcendent beauty, and joy, and love, and that what grieved Him most was mankind's inability to behold what was there before their very eyes.

Perhaps, too, this may be the great difference between the saints and the Puritans. Both are agreed that goodness is the means to the end, but the saints have passed on to the end and entered into the realization, and are happy. (One of the most endearing attributes of saints of a certain type was —or rather is, for one refuses to believe that saints are all of the past—their childlike gayety, which can proceed only from a happy and trustful heart.) The Puritan, on the other hand, has stuck fast in the means—is still worrying over the guide-posts, and is distrustful and over-anxious.

It is like walking and dancing. One could never dance unless he had first learned to walk, or continue to dance unless walking were always possible; yet if one is too intent upon the fact of walking, dancing becomes impossible. The Puritan walks in a worried morality; the saint dances in the vision of God's love; and doubtless both are right dear in the sight of the Lord, but the saint is the happiest.

Father Tyrrel says, 'For Jesus the moral is not the highest life, but its condition.'

Some may object that I preach a dangerous doctrine; others, that I am trying to whip a mad moment of Pagan beauty into line with Christian thought. Possibly I am; yet I am trying not to do the one or the other. I am merely wondering, and endeavoring to get at the truth of something that I saw.

And all the beauty is forever there before us, forever piping to us, and we are forever failing to dance. We could not help but dance if we could see things as they really are. Then we should kiss both hands to Fate and fling our bodies, hearts, minds, and souls into life with a glorious abandonment, and extravagant, delighted loyalty, knowing that our wildest enthusiasm cannot more than brush the hem of the real beauty and joy and wonder that is always there.

This is how, for me, all fear of eternity has been wiped away. I have had a little taste of bliss, and if Heaven can offer this, no eternity will be too long to enjoy the miracle of existence. But that was not the greatest thing that those twenty minutes revealed, and that did most to end all dread of life everlasting. The great thing was the realization that weariness, and boredom, and questions as to the use of it all, belong entirely to unreality. When once we wake to Reality—whether we do so here or have to wait for the next life for it,—we shall never be bored, for in Reality there is no such thing.

Chesterton has pointed out the power for endless enjoyment of the same thing which most children possess, and suggested that this is a God-like capacity; that perhaps to God His creation always presents itself with a freshness of delight; that perhaps the rising of the sun this morning was for Him the same ecstatic event that it was upon the first day of its creation. I think it was the truth of this suggestion that I perceived in those twenty minutes of cleared vision, and realized that in the youth of eternity we shall recapture that God-like and child-like attribute which the old age and unreality of

Time have temporarily snatched from us.

No; I shall have no more fear of eternity. And even if there were no other life, this life here and now, if we could but open our dull eyes to see it in its truth, is lovely enough to require no far-off Heaven for its justification. Heaven, in all its spring-tide of beauty, is here and now, before our very eyes, surging up to our very feet, lapping against our hearts; but we, alas, know not how to let it in!

Once again, when I was almost recovered, I had another fleeting visitation of this extreme beauty. A friend came into my room dressed for the opera. I had seen her thus a great number of times before, but for a moment I saw her clothed in all that wild beauty of Reality, and, as before, my heart melted with joy at the sight. But this second occasion was even more transitory than the first, and since then I have had no return. Tagore's illumination, he says, lasted for seven or eight days, and Jacob Boehme knew a 'Sabbath calm of the soul that lasted for seven days,' during which he was, as it were, inwardly surrounded by a divine light. 'The triumph that was then in my soul,' he says, 'I can neither tell nor describe; I can only liken it to a resurrection from the dead.'

And this miraculous time was with him for a whole week, while I have only tasted it for those few short minutes! But he was a saint, and had really ascended to the holy hill of the Lord through clean hands and a pure heart, while I was swept there momentarily, and, as it were, by accident, through the rebirth of returning health. But when the inspired ones testify to a great joy and a great beauty I too can cry, 'Yes, I have seen it also! Yes, O Beauty, O Reality, O Mad Joy! I too have seen you face to face!' And though I have never again touched the fullness of that ecstatic vision, I know all created things to be of a beauty and value unspeakable, and I shall not fail to pay homage to all the loveliness with which existence overflows. Nor shall I fear to accord to all of life's experiences, whether sad or gay, as high, as extravagant, and as undismayed a tribute of enthusiasm as I am capable of.

Perhaps some day I shall meet it face to face again. Again the gray veil of unreality will be swirled aside; once more I shall see into Reality. Sometimes still, when the wind is blowing through trees, or flowers, I have an eery sense that I am almost in touch with it. The veil was very thin in my garden one day last summer. The wind was blowing there, and I knew that all that beauty and wild young ecstasy at the heart of life was rioting with it through the tossing larkspurs and rose-pink canterbury bells, and bowing with the foxgloves; only I just could not see it. But it is there—it is always there—and some day I shall meet it again. The vision will clear, the inner eye open, and again all that mad joy will be upon me. Some day—not yet perhaps—but some day!

THE SHEPHERD
William Blake

How sweet is the shepherd's sweet lot;
  From the morn to the evening he
    strays;
He shall follow his sheep all the day,
  And his tongue shall be filled with
    praise.

For he hears the lamb's innocent
  call,
  And he hears the ewes' tender reply;
He is watchful while they are in peace,
  For they know when their shepherd
    is nigh.

From *ON A DISTANT PROSPECT OF ETON COLLEGE*
THOMAS GRAY

Ye distant spires, ye antique towers,
  That crown the watery glade,
Where grateful Science still adores
  Her Henry's holy shade;
And ye, that from the stately brow
Of Windsor's heights the expanse below
  Of grove, of lawn, of mead survey,
Whose turf, whose shade, whose flowers
    among
Wanders the hoary Thames along
  His silver-winding way:

Ah, happy hills! ah, pleasing shade!
  Ah, fields beloved in vain!
Where once my careless childhood
    strayed,
  A stranger yet to pain!
I feel the gales that from ye blow
A momentary bliss bestow,
  As waving fresh their gladsome wing,
My weary soul they seem to soothe,
And, redolent of joy and youth,
  To breathe a second spring.

TO THE FRINGED GENTIAN
WILLIAM CULLEN BRYANT

Thou blossom bright with autumn dew,
And colored with the heaven's own
    blue,
That openest when the quiet light
Succeeds the keen and frosty night,

Thou comest not when violets lean
O'er wandering brooks and spring un-
    seen,
Or columbines, in purple dressed,
Nod o'er the ground-bird's hidden nest.

Thou waitest late and com'st alone,
When woods are bare and birds are
    flown,
And frost and shortening days portend
The aged year is near his end.

Then doth thy sweet and quiet eye
Look through its fringes to the sky,
Blue—blue—as if that sky let fall
A flower from its cerulean wall.

I would that thus, when I shall see
The hour of death draw near to me,
Hope, blossoming within my heart,
May look to heaven as I depart.

CRADLE HYMN
MARTIN LUTHER

Away in a manger, no crib for a bed,
The little Lord Jesus laid down his
    sweet head.
The stars in the bright sky looked
    down where he lay—
The little Lord Jesus asleep on the hay.

The cattle are lowing, the baby awakes,
But little Lord Jesus no crying he
    makes.
I love thee, Lord Jesus! look down from
    the sky,
And stay by my cradle till morning is
    nigh.

SONG
WILLIAM BLAKE

Memory, hither come,
  And tune your merry notes:
And, while upon the wind
  Your music floats,
I'll pore upon the stream
Where sighing lovers dream,
And fish for fancies as they pass
Within the watery glass.

* * *

  ❧ NEXT TO acquiring good friends, the best acquisition is that of a good
book.
      —*Colton*

Walking Tours

By ROBERT LOUIS STEVENSON

*I*T MUST NOT be imagined that a walking tour, as some would have us fancy, is merely a better or worse way of seeing the country. There are many ways of seeing landscape quite as good; and none more vivid, in spite of canting dilettantes, than from a railway train. But landscape on a walking tour is quite accessory. He who is indeed of the brotherhood does not voyage in quest of the picturesque, but of certain jolly humours—of the hope and spirit with which the march begins at morning, and the peace and spiritual repletion of the evening's rest. He cannot tell whether he puts his knapsack on, or takes it off, with more delight. The excitement of the departure puts him in key for that of the arrival. Whatever he does is not only a reward in itself, but will be further rewarded in the sequel; and so pleasure leads on to pleasure in an endless chain. It is this that so few can understand; they will either be always lounging or always at five miles an hour; they do not play off the one against the other, prepare all day for the evening, and all evening for the next day. And, above all, it is here that your overwalker fails of comprehension. His heart rises against those who drink their curaoca in liqueur glasses, when he himself can swill it in a brown john. He will not believe that the flavour is more delicate in the smaller dose. He will not believe that to walk this unconscionable distance is merely to stupefy and brutalize himself, and come to his inn, at night, with a sort of frost on his five wits, and a starless night of darkness in his spirit. Not for him the mild luminous evening of the temperate walker! He has nothing left of man but a physical need for bedtime and a double nightcap; and even his pipe, if he be a smoker, will be savourless and disenchanted. It is the fate of such an one to take twice as much trouble as is needed to obtain happiness, and miss the happiness in the end; he is the man of the proverb, in short, who goes further and fares worse.

Now, to be properly enjoyed, a walking tour should be gone upon alone. If you go in a company, or even in pairs, it is no longer a walking tour in anything but name; it is something else and more in the nature of a picnic. A walking tour should be gone upon alone, because freedom is of the essence; because you should be able to stop and go on, and follow this way or that, as the freak takes you; and because you must have your own pace, and neither trot alongside a champion walker, nor mince in time with a girl. And then you must be open to all impressions and let your thoughts take colour from what you see. You should be as a pipe for any wind to play upon. "I cannot see the wit," says Hazlitt, "of walking and talking at the same time. When I am in the country I wish to vegetate like the country,"—which is the gist of all that can be said upon the matter. There should be no cackle of voices at your elbow, to jar on the meditative silence of the morning. And so long as a man is reasoning he cannot surrender himself to that fine intoxication that comes of much motion in the open air, that begins in a sort of dazzle and sluggishness of the brain, and ends in a peace that passes comprehension.

During the first day or so of any tour

there are moments of bitterness, when the traveller feels more than coldly towards his knapsack, when he is half in a mind to throw it bodily over the hedge and, like Christian on a similar occasion, "give three leaps and go on singing." And yet it soon acquires a property of easiness. It becomes magnetic; the spirit of the journey enters into it. And no sooner have you passed the straps over your shoulder than the lees of sleep are cleared from you, you pull yourself together with a shake, and fall at once into your stride. And surely, of all possible moods, this, in which a man takes the road, is the best. Of course, if he *will* keep thinking of his anxieties, if he *will* open the merchant Abudah's chest and walk arm-in-arm with the hag—why, wherever he is, and whether he walk fast or slow, the chances are that he will not be happy. And so much the more shame to himself! There are perhaps thirty men setting forth at that same hour, and I would lay a large wager there is not another dull face among the thirty. It would be a fine thing to follow, in a coat of darkness, one after another of these wayfarers, some summer morning, for the first few miles upon the road. This one, who walks fast, with a keen look in his eyes, is all concentrated in his own mind; he is up at his loom, weaving and weaving, to set the landscape to words. This one peers about, as he goes, among the grasses; he waits by the canal to watch the dragon-flies; he leans on the gate of the pasture, and cannot look enough upon the complacent kine. And here comes another, talking, laughing, and gesticulating to himself. His face changes from time to time, as indignation flashes from his eyes or anger clouds his forehead. He is composing articles, delivering orations, and conducting the most impassioned interviews, by the way. A little farther on, and it is as like as not he will begin to sing. And

well for him, supposing him to be no great master in that art, if he stumble across no stolid peasant at a corner; for on such an occasion, I scarcely know which is the more troubled, or whether it is worse to suffer the confusion of your troubadour, or the unfeigned alarm of your clown. A sedentary population, accustomed, besides, to the strange mechanical bearing of the common tramp, can in no wise explain to itself the gaiety of these passers-by. I knew one man who was arrested as a runaway lunatic, because, although a full-grown person with a red beard, he skipped as he went like a child. And you would be astonished if I were to tell you all the grave and learned heads who have confessed to me that, when on walking tours, they sang—and sang very ill—and had a pair of red ears when, as described above, the inauspicious peasant plumped into their arms from round a corner. And here, lest you should think I am exaggerating, is Hazlitt's own confession, from his essay *On Going a Journey*, which is so good that there should be a tax levied on all who have not read it:

"Give me the clear blue sky over my head," says he, "and the green turf beneath my feet, a winding road before me, and a three hours' march to dinner —and then to thinking! It is hard if I cannot start some game on these lone heaths. I laugh, I run, I leap, I sing for joy."

Bravo! After that adventure of my friend with the policeman, you would not have cared, would you, to publish that in the first person? But we have no bravery nowadays, and, even in books, must all pretend to be as dull and foolish as our neighbours. It was not so with Hazlitt. And notice how learned he is (as, indeed, throughout the essay) in the theory of walking tours. He is none of your athletic men in purple stockings, who walk their fifty miles a day: three hours' march is his ideal. And then he must have a winding road, the epicure!

Yet there is one thing I object to in these words of his, one thing in the great master's practice that seems to me not wholly wise. I do not approve of that leaping and running. Both of these hurry the respiration; they both shake up the brain out of its glorious open-air confusion; and they both break the pace. Uneven walking is not so agreeable to the body, and it distracts and irritates the mind. Whereas, when once you have fallen into an equable stride, it requires no conscious thought from you to keep it up, and yet it prevents you from thinking earnestly of anything else. Like knitting, like the work of a copying clerk, it gradually neutralizes and sets to sleep the serious activity of the mind. We can think of this or that, lightly and laughingly, as a child thinks, or as we think in a morning doze; we can make puns or puzzle out acrostics, and trifle in a thousand ways with words and rhymes; but when it comes to honest work, when we come to gather ourselves together for an effort, we may sound the trumpet as loud and long as we please; the great barons of the mind will not rally to the standard, but sit, each one, at home, warming his hands over his own fire and brooding on his own private thought!

In the course of a day's walk, you see, there is much variance in the mood. From the exhilaration of the start, to the happy phlegm of the arrival, the change is certainly great. As the day goes on, the traveller moves from the one extreme towards the other. He becomes more and more incorporated with the material landscape, and the open-air drunkenness grows upon him with great strides, until he posts along the road, and sees everything about him, as in a cheerful dream. The first is certainly brighter, but the second stage is the more peaceful. A man does not make so many articles towards the end, nor does he laugh aloud; but the purely animal pleasures, the sense of physical wellbeing, the delight of every inhalation, of every time the muscles tighten down the thigh, console him for the absence of the others, and bring him to his destination still content.

Nor must I forget to say a word on bivouacs. You come to a milestone on a hill, or some place where deep ways meet under trees; and off goes the knapsack, and down you sit to smoke a pipe in the shade. You sink into yourself, and the birds come round and look at you; and your smoke dissipates upon the afternoon under the blue dome of heaven; and the sun lies warm upon your feet, and the cool air visits your neck and turns aside your open shirt. If you are not happy, you must have an evil conscience. You may dally as long as you like by the roadside. It is almost as if the millennium were arrived, when we shall throw our clocks and watches over the housetop, and remember time and seasons no more. Not to keep hours for a lifetime is, I was going to say, to live for ever. You have no idea, unless you have tried it, how endlessly long is a summer's day, that you measure out only by hunger, and bring to an end only when you are drowsy. I know a village where there are hardly any clocks, where no one knows more of the days of the week than by a sort of instinct for the fête on Sundays, and where only one person can tell you the day of the month, and she is generally wrong; and if people were aware how slow Time journied in that village, and what armfuls of spare hours he gives, over and above the bargain, to its wise inhabitants, I believe there would be a stampede out of London, Liverpool, Paris, and a variety of large towns, where the clocks lose their heads, and shake the hours out each one faster than the other, as though they were all in a wager. And all these foolish pilgrims would each bring his own misery along with him, in a watch-pocket! It is to be noticed, there were no clocks and watches in the much-vaunted days before the flood. It follows, of course, there were no appointments, and punctuality was not yet thought upon. "Though ye take from a covetous man all his treasure," says Milton, "he has yet one jewel left; ye cannot deprive him of his covetousness." And so I would say of a modern man of business, you may do what you will for him, put him in Eden, give him the elixir of life—he has still a flaw at heart, he still has his business habits. Now, there is no time when business habits are more mitigated than on a walking tour. And so during these halts, as I say, you will feel almost free.

But it is at night, and after dinner, that the best hour comes. There are no such pipes to be smoked as those that follow a good day's march; the flavour of the tobacco is a thing to be remembered, it is so dry and aromatic, so full and so fine. If you wind up the evening with grog, you will own there was never such grog; at every sip a jocund tranquility spreads about your limbs, and sits easily in your heart. If you read a book—and you will never do so save by fits and starts—you find the language strangely racy and harmonious; words take a new meaning; single sentences possess the ear for half an hour together; and the writer endears himself to you, at every page, by the nicest coincidence of sentiment. It seems as if it were a book you had written yourself in a dream. To all we have read on such occasions we look back with special favour. "It was on the 10th of April, 1798," says Hazlitt, with amorous precision, "that I sat down to a volume of the new *Héloïse*, at the Inn at Llangollen, over a bottle of sherry

and a cold chicken." I should wish to quote more, for though we are mighty fine fellows nowadays, we cannot write like Hazlitt. And, talking of that, a volume of Hazlitt's essays would be a capital pocket-book on such a journey; so would a volume of Heine's songs; and for *Tristram Shandy* I can pledge a fair experience.

If the evening be fine and warm, there is nothing better in life than to lounge before the inn door in the sunset, or lean over the parapet of the bridge, to watch the weeds and the quick fishes. It is then, if ever, that you taste Joviality to the full significance of that audacious word. Your muscles are so agreeably slack, you feel so clean and so strong and so idle, that whether you move or sit still, whatever you do is done with pride and a kingly sort of pleasure. You fall in talk with any one, wise or foolish, drunk or sober. And it seems as if a hot walk purged you, more than of anything else, of all narrowness and pride, and left curiosity to play its part freely, as in a child or a man of science. You lay aside all your own hobbies, to watch provincial humours develop themselves before you, now as a laughable farce, and now grave and beautiful like an old tale.

Or perhaps you are left to your own company for the night, and surly weather imprisons you by the fire. You may remember how Burns, numbering past pleasures, dwells upon the hours when he has been "happy thinking." It is a phrase that may well perplex a poor modern, girt about on every side by clocks and chimes, and haunted, even at night, by flaming dial-plates. For we are all so busy, and have so many far-off projects to realise, and castles in the fire to turn into solid habitable mansions on a gravel soil, that we can find no time for pleasure trips into the Land of Thought and among the Hills of Vanity. Changed times, indeed, when we must sit all night, beside the fire, with folded hands; and a changed world for most of us, when we find we can pass the hours without discontent, and be happy thinking. We are in such haste to be doing, to be writing, to be gathering gear, to make our voice audible a moment in the derisive silence of eternity, that we forget that one thing, of which these are but the parts—namely, to live. We fall in love, we drink hard, we run to and fro upon the earth like frightened sheep. And now you are to ask yourself if, when all is done, you would not have been better to sit by the fire at home, and be happy thinking. To sit still and contemplate,—to remember the faces of women without desire, to be pleased by the great deeds of men without envy, to be everything and everywhere in sympathy, and yet content to remain where and what you are—is not this to know both wisdom and virtue, and to dwell with happiness? After all, it is not they who carry flags, but they who look upon it from a private chamber, who have the fun of the procession. And once you are at that, you are in the very humour of all social heresy. It is no time for shuffling, or for big, empty words. If

you ask yourself what you mean by fame, riches, or learning, the answer is far to seek; and you go back into that kingdom of light imaginations, which seem so vain in the eyes of Philistines perspiring after wealth, and so momentous to those who are stricken with the disproportions of the world, and, in the face of the gigantic stars, cannot stop to split differences between two degrees of the infinitesimally small, such as a tobacco pipe or the Roman Empire, a million of money or a fiddlestick's end.

You lean from the window, your last pipe reeking whitely into the darkness, your body full of delicious pains, your mind enthroned in the seventh circle of content; when suddenly the mood changes, the weathercock goes about, and you ask yourself one question more: whether, for the interval, you have been the wisest philosopher or the most egregious of donkeys? Human experience is not yet able to reply; but at least you have had a fine moment, and looked down upon all the kingdoms of the earth. And whether it was wise or foolish, tomorrow's travel will carry you, body and mind, into some different parish of the infinite.

❦   ❦   ❦

THE MARSHES OF GLYNN
SIDNEY LANIER

Glooms of the live-oaks, beautiful-braided and woven
With intricate shades of the vines that myriad-cloven
  Clamber the forks of the multiform boughs,—
    Emerald twilights,—
    Virginal shy lights,
Wrought of the leaves to allure to the whisper of vows,
When lovers pace timidly down through the green colonnades
Of the dim sweet woods, of the dear

dark woods,
  Of the heavenly woods and glades,
That run to the radiant marginal sand-beach within
  The wide sea-marshes of Glynn;—

Beautiful glooms, soft dusks in the noon-day fire,—
Wildwood privacies, closets of lone desire,
Chamber from chamber parted with wavering arras of leaves,—
Cells for the passionate pleasure of

314

prayer to the soul that grieves,
Pure with a sense of the passing of
saints through the wood,
Cool for the dutiful weighing of ill
with good;—

O braided dusks of the oak and woven
shades of the vine,
While the riotous noon-day sun of the
June-day long did shine
Ye held me fast in your heart and I
held you fast in mine;
But now when the noon is no more,
and riot is rest,
And the sun is a-wait at the ponderous
gate of the West,
And the slant yellow beam down the
wood-aisle doth seem
Like a lane into heaven that leads from
a dream,—
Ay, now, when my soul all day hath
drunken the soul of the oak,
And my heart is at ease from men, and
the wearisome sound of the stroke
Of the scythe of time and the trowel
of trade is low,
And belief overmasters doubt, and
I know that I know,
And my spirit is grown to a lordly
great compass within,
That the length and the breadth and
the sweep of the marshes of Glynn
Will work me no fear like the fear they
have wrought me of yore
When length was fatigue, and when
breadth was but bitterness sore,
And when terror and shrinking and
dreary unnamable pain
Drew over me out of the merciless miles
of the plain,—

Oh, now, unafraid, I am fain to face
The vast sweet visage of space.
To the edge of the wood I am drawn,
I am drawn,
Where the gray beach glimmering runs,
as a belt of the dawn,
For a mete and a mark
To the forest-dark:—
So:

Affable live-oak, leaning low,—
Thus—with your favor—soft, with a
reverent hand,
(Not lightly touching your person,
Lord of the land!)
Bending your beauty aside, with a step
I stand
On the firm-packed sand,
Free
By a world of marsh that borders a
world of sea.
Sinuous southward and sinuous
northward the shimmering band
Of the sand-beach fastens the fringe
of the marsh to the folds of the
land.
Inward and outward to northward and
southward the beach-lines linger
and curl
As a silver-wrought garment that clings
to and follows the firm sweet limbs
of a girl.
Vanishing, swerving, evermore curv-
ing again into sight,
Softly the sand-beach wavers away to
a dim gray looping of light.
And what if behind me to westward
the wall of the woods stands high?
The world lies east: how ample, the
marsh and the sea and the sky!
A league and a league of marsh-grass,
waist-high, broad in the blade,
Green, and all of a height, and un-
flecked with a light or a shade,
Stretch leisurely off, in a pleasant plain,
To the terminal blue of the main.

Oh, what is abroad in the marsh and
the terminal sea?
Somehow my soul seems suddenly
free
From the weighing of fate and the sad
discussion of sin,
By the length and the breadth and the
sweep of the marshes of Glynn.

Ye marshes, how candid and simple
and nothing withholding and free
Ye publish yourselves to the sky and
offer yourselves to the sea!

Tolerant plains, that suffer the sea and
the rains and the sun,
Ye spread and span like the catholic
man who hath mightily won
God out of knowledge and good out
of infinite pain
And sight out of blindness and purity
out of a stain.

As the marsh-hen secretly builds on
the watery sod,
Behold I will build me a nest on the
greatness of God:
I will fly in the greatness of God as the
marsh-hen flies
In the freedom that fills all the space
'twixt the marsh and the skies:
By so many roots as the marsh-grass
sends in the sod
I will heartily lay me a-hold on the
greatness of God:
Oh, like to the greatness of God is the
greatness within
The range of the marshes, the liberal
marshes of Glynn.

And the sea lends large, as the marsh:
lo, out of his plenty the sea
Pours fast: full soon the time of the
flood tide must be:
Look how the grace of the sea doth go
About and about through the intricate
channels that flow
Here and there,
Everywhere,

Till his waters have flooded the utter-
most creeks and the low-lying lanes,
And the marsh is meshed with a million
veins,
That like as with rosy and silvery
essences flow
In the rose-and-silver evening glow.
Farewell, my lord Sun!
The creeks overflow: a thousand rivu-
lets run
'Twixt the roots of the sod; the blades
of the marsh-grass stir;
Passeth a hurrying sound of wings that
westward whirr;
Passeth, and all is still; and the currents
cease to run;
And the sea and the marsh are one.

How still the plains of the waters be!
The tide is in his ecstasy.
The tide is at his highest height:
And it is night.

And now from the Vast of the Lord will
the waters of sleep
Roll in on the souls of men,
But who will reveal to our waking ken
The forms that swim and the shapes
that creep
Under the waters of sleep?
And I would I could know what swim-
meth below when the tide comes in
On the length and the breadth of the
marvellous marshes of Glynn.

❧ ❧ ❧

WAS THIS THE FACE?
CHRISTOPHER MARLOWE

Was this the face that launched a thousand ships
And burned the topless towers of Ilium?
Sweet Helen, make me immortal with a kiss!
Her lips suck forth my soul—see where it flies.
Come, Helen, come give me my soul again;
Here will I dwell, for heaven is in these lips,
And all is dross that is not Helena. . . .
O thou art fairer than the evening air,
Clad in the beauty of a thousand stars!

TO THE ROSE
ROBERT HERRICK

Go, happy Rose! and, interwove
With other flowers, bind my love!
  Tell her, too, she must not be
  Longer flowing, longer free,
  That so oft hath fettered me.

Say, if she's fretful, I have bands
Of pearl and gold to bind her hands;
  Tell her, if she struggle still,
  I have myrtle rods at will,
  For to tame, though not to kill.

Take then my blessing thus, and go,
And tell her this,—but do not so!
  Lest a handsome anger fly,
  Like a lightning from her eye,
  And burn thee up, as well as I.

THE NYMPH'S REPLY
SIR WALTER RALEIGH

If all the world and love were young,
And truth in every shepherd's tongue,
These pretty pleasures might me move
To live with them, and be thy Love.

But Time drives flocks from field to
  fold;
When rivers rage and rocks grow cold;
And Philomel becometh dumb;
The rest complains of cares to come.

The flowers do fade, and wanton fields
To wayward Winter reckoning yields:
A honey tongue, a heart of gall,
Is Fancy's spring, but Sorrow's fall.
. . . .

But could youth last, and love still
  breed,
Had joys no date, nor age no need,
Then these delights my mind might
  move
To live with thee and be thy Love.

O FAIR! O SWEET!
SIR PHILIP SIDNEY

O fair! O sweet! when I do look on
  thee,
  In whom all joys so well agree,
  Heart and soul do sing in me,
  Just accord all music makes;
In thee just accord excelleth,
Where each part in such peace
  dwelleth,
  One of other beauty takes,
Since, then, truth to all minds telleth
  That in thee lives harmony,
  Heart and soul do sing in me.

THE SONG OF LOVE
DANTE GABRIEL ROSSETTI

Your hands lie open in the long fresh
  grass,—
The finger-points look through like
  rosy blooms:
Your eyes smile peace. The pasture
  gleams and glooms
'Neath billowing skies that scatter and
  amass.
All round our nest, far as the eye can
  pass,
Are golden kingcup-fields with silver
  edge
Where the cow-parsley skirts the haw-
  thorn-hedge.
'Tis visible silence, still as the hour-
  glass.
Deep in the sun-searched growths the
  dragon-fly
Hangs like a blue thread loosened from
  the sky:—
So this winged hour is dropped to us
  from above.
Oh! clasp we to our hearts, for deathless dower,
This close-companioned inarticulate
  hour
When twofold silence was the song of
  love.

* * *

❦ GOD is the silent partner in all great enterprises.—*Lincoln*

317

FAIRY SONG
JOHN KEATS

Shed no tear! O, shed no tear!
The flower will bloom another year.
Weep no more! O, weep no more!
Young buds sleep in the root's white
    core.
Dry your eyes! O, dry your eyes!
For I was taught in Paradise
To ease my breast of melodies,—
       Shed no tear.

Overhead! look overhead!
'Mong the blossoms white and red,—
Look up, look up! I flutter now
On this fresh pomegranate bough,
See me! 'tis this silvery bill
Ever cures the good man's ill,
Shed no tear! O, shed no tear!
The flower will bloom another year.
Adieu, adieu—I fly—adieu!
      Adieu, adieu!

SONG
EDMUND WALLER

Go, lovely Rose!
Tell her, that wastes her time and me,
  That now she knows,
When I resemble her to thee,
How sweet, and fair, she seems to be.

Tell her that's young,
And shuns to have her graces spy'd,
  That had'st thou sprung
In deserts where no men abide,
Thou must have uncommended dy'd.

Small is the worth
Of beauty from the light retir'd;
  Bid her come forth,
Suffer herself to be desir'd,
And not blush so to be admir'd.

Then die! that she
The common fate of all things rare
  May read in thee;
How small a part of time they share
That are so wondrous sweet and fair!

REST
JOHANN WOLFGANG VON GOETHE

Rest is not quitting the busy career;
Rest is the fitting of self to one's
  sphere;
It's loving and serving the highest and
  best;
It's onward, unswerving; and this is
  true rest.

THE POET'S REWARD
JOHN GREENLEAF WHITTIER

Thanks untraced to lips unknown
Shall greet me like the odors blown
From unseen meadows newly mown,
Or lilies floating in some pond,
Wood-fringed, the wayside gaze beyond;
The traveller owns the grateful sense
Of sweetness near, he knows not
  whence,
And, pausing, takes with forehead bare
The benediction of the air.
          —From *Snow-Bound*

SONG
HENRY WADSWORTH LONGFELLOW

Stay, stay at home, my heart and rest;
Home-keeping hearts are happiest,
For those that wander they know not
  where
Are full of trouble and full of care;
    To stay at home is best.

Weary and homesick and distressed,
They wander east, they wander west,
And are baffled and beaten and blown
  about
By the winds of the wilderness of doubt;
    To stay at home is best.

Then stay at home, my heart, and rest;
The bird is safest in its nest,
Over all that flutter their wings and fly
A hawk is hovering in the sky;
    To stay at home is best.

DAY
James Thomson ("B.V.")

Waking one morning
In a pleasant land,
By a river flowing
Over golden sand:—

Whence flow ye, waters,
O'er your golden sand?
We come flowing
From the Silent Land.

Whither flow ye, waters,
O'er your golden sand?
We go flowing
To the Silent Land.

And what is this fair realm?
A grain of golden sand
In the great darkness
Of the Silent Land.

THE SONNET
Richard Watson Gilder

What is a sonnet? It's the pearly shell
That murmurs of the far-off murmuring
  sea;
A precious jewel carved most curiously;
It is a little picture painted well.
What is a sonnet? It's the tear that fell
From a great poet's hidden ecstasy;
A two-edged sword, a star, a song—ah
  me!
Sometimes a heavy-tolling funeral bell.

This was the flame that shook with
  Dante's breath;
The solemn organ whereon Milton
  played,
And the clear glass where Shakespeare's
  shadow falls;
A sea this is—beware who ventureth!
For like a fjord the narrow floor is laid
Mid-ocean deep to the sheer mountain
  walls.

THE TILLED LANDS
By Jean François Millet

The most joyful thing I know is the peace, the silence, that one enjoys in the woods or on the tilled lands. One sees a poor, heavily laden creature with a bundle of faggots advancing from a narrow path in the fields. The manner in which this figure comes suddenly before one is a momentary reminder of the fundamental condition of human life, toil. On the tilled land around, one watches figures hoeing and digging. One sees how this or that one rises and wipes away the sweat with the back of his hand. "In the sweat of thy face shalt thou eat bread." Is that merry, enlivening work? And yet it is here that I find the true humanity, the great poetry.

WORLD FOREVER NEW
By Ralph Waldo Emerson

Consider that the perpetual admonition of Nature to us is, The world is new, untried. Do not believe in the past. I give you the universe new and unhandled every hour. You think in your idle hours that there is literature, history, science behind you so accumulated as to exhaust thought and prescribe your own future and the future. In your sane hour you shall see that not a line has yet been written; that for all the poetry that is in the world your first sensation on entering a wood or standing on the shore of a lake has not been chanted yet. It remains for you, so does all thought, all object, all life remain unwritten still.

WINTER ANIMALS
By Henry David Thoreau

When the ponds were firmly frozen, they afforded not only new and shorter routes to many points, but new views from their surfaces of the familiar landscape around them. When I crossed Flint's Pond, after it was covered with snow, though I had often paddled about and skated over it, it was so unexpectedly wide and so strange that I could think of nothing but Baffin's Bay. The Lincoln hills rose up around me at the extremity of a snowy plain, in which I did not remember to have stood before; and the fishermen, at an indeterminable distance over the ice, moving slowly about with their wolfish dogs, passed for sealers or Esquimaux, or in misty weather loomed like fabulous creatures, and I did not know whether they were giants or pygmies. I took this course when I went to lecture in Lincoln in the evening, travelling in no road and passing no house between my own hut and the lecture room. In Goose Pond, which lay in my way, a colony of muskrats dwelt, and raised their cabins high above the ice, though none could be seen abroad when I crossed it. Walden, being like the rest usually bare of snow, or with only shallow and interrupted drifts on it, was my yard where I could walk freely when the snow was nearly two feet deep on a level elsewhere and the villagers were confined to their streets. There, far from the village street, and except at very long intervals, from the jingle of sleigh-bells, I slid and skated, as in a vast moose-yard well trodden, overhung by oak woods and solemn pines bent down with snow or bristling with icicles.

For sounds in winter nights, and often in winter days, I heard the forlorn but melodious note of a hooting owl indefinitely far; such a sound as the frozen earth would yield if struck with a suitable plectrum, the very *lingua ver-* *nacula* of Walden Wood, and quite familiar to me at last, though I never saw the bird while it was making it. I seldom opened my door in a winter evening without hearing it; *Hoo hoo hoo, hoorer hoo,* sounded sonorously, and the first three syllables accented somewhat like *how der do;* or sometimes *hoo hoo* only. One night in the beginning of winter, before the pond froze over, about nine o'clock, I was startled by the loud honking of a goose, and, stepping to the door, heard the sound of their wings like a tempest in the woods as they flew low over my house. They passed over the pond toward Fair Haven, seemingly deterred from settling by my light, their commodore honking all the while with a regular beat. Suddenly an unmistakable cat-owl from very near me, with the most harsh and tremendous voice I ever heard from any inhabitant of the woods, responded at regular intervals to the goose, as if determined to expose and disgrace this intruder from Hudson's Bay by exhibiting a greater compass and volume of voice in a native, and *boo-hoo* him out of Concord horizon. What do you mean by alarming the citadel at this time of night consecrated to me? Do you think I am ever caught napping at such an hour, and that I have not got lungs and a larynx, as well as yourself? Boo-hoo, boo-hoo, boo-hoo! It was one of the most thrilling discords I ever heard. And yet, if you had a discriminating ear, there were in it the elements of a concord such as these plains never saw nor heard.

I also heard the whooping of the ice in the pond, my great bedfellow in that part of Concord, as if it were restless in its bed and would fain turn over, were troubled with flatulency and bad dreams; or I was waked by the cracking of the ground by the frost, as if some one had driven a team against my door, and in the morning would find a crack in the earth a quarter of a mile long and a third of an inch wide.

Sometimes I heard the foxes as they ranged over the snow crust, in moonlight nights, in search of a partridge or other game, barking raggedly and demoniacally like forest dogs, as if laboring with some anxiety, or seeking expression, struggling for light and to be dogs outright and run freely in the streets; for if we take the ages into our account, may there not be a civilization going on among brutes as well as men? They seemed to me to be rudimental, burrowing men, still standing on their defence, awaiting their transformation. Sometimes one came near to my window, attracted by my light, barked a vulpine curse at me, and then retreated.

Usually the red squirrel (*Sciurus Hudsonius*) waked me in the dawn, coursing over the roof and up and down the sides of the house, as if sent out of the woods for this purpose. In the course of the winter I threw out half a bushel of ears of sweetcorn, which had not got ripe, on to the snow crust by my door, and was amused by watching the motions of the various animals which were baited by it. In the twilight and the night the rabbits came regularly and made a hearty meal. All day long the red squirrels came and went, and afforded me much entertainment by their manoeuvres. One would approach at first warily through the shrub-oaks, running over the snow crust by fits and starts like a leaf blown by the wind, now a few paces this way, with wonderful speed and waste of energy, making inconceivable haste with his "trotters," as if it were for a wager, and now as many paces that way, but never getting on more than half a rod at a time; and then suddenly pausing with a ludicrous expression and a gratuitous somerset, as if all the eyes in the universe were fixed on him,—for all the motions of a squirrel, even in the most solitary recesses of the forest, imply spectators as much as those of a dancing girl,—wasting more time in delay and circumspection than would have sufficed to walk the whole distance, —I never saw one walk, —and then suddenly, before you could say Jack Robinson, he would be in the top of a young pitch-pine, winding up his clock and chiding all imaginary spectators, soliloquizing and talking to all the universe at the same time, —for no reason that I could ever detect, or he himself was aware of, I suspect. At length he would reach the corn, and selecting a suitable ear, frisk about in the same uncertain trigonometrical way to the top-most stick of my wood-pile, before my window, where he looked me in the face, and there sit for hours, supplying himself with a new ear from time to time, nibbling at first voraciously and throwing the half-naked cobs about; till at length he grew more dainty still and played with his food, tasting only the inside of the kernel, and the ear, which was held balanced over the stick by one paw, slipped from his careless grasp and fell to the ground, when he would look over at it with a ludicrous expression of uncertainty, as if suspecting that it had life, with a mind not made up whether to get it again, or a new one, or be off; now thinking of corn, then listening to hear what was in the wind. So the little impudent fellow would waste many an ear in a forenoon; till at last, seizing some longer and plumper one, considerably bigger than himself, and skillfully balancing it, he would set out with it to the woods, like a tiger with a buffalo, by the same zigzag course and frequent pauses, scratching along with it as if it were too heavy for him and falling all the while, making its fall a diagonal between a perpendicular and horizontal, being determined to put it through at any rate; —a singularly frivolous and whimsical fellow;—and so he would get off with it to where he lived, perhaps carry it to the top of a pine-tree forty or fifty rods distant, and I would afterwards find the cobs strewn about the woods in various directions.

At length the jays arrive, whose discordants screams were heard long before, as they were warily making their approach an eighth of a mile off, and in a stealthy and sneaking manner they flit from tree to tree, nearer and nearer, and pick up the kernels which the squirrels have dropped. Then, sitting on a pitch-pine bough, they attempt to swallow in their haste a kernel which is too big for their throats and chokes them; and after great labor they disgorge it, and spend an hour in the endeavor to crack it by repeated blows with their bills. They were manifestly thieves, and I had not much respect for them; but the squirrels, though at first shy, went to work as if they were taking what was their own.

Meanwhile also came the chickadees in flocks, which, picking up the crumbs the squirrels had dropped, flew to the nearest twig, and, placing them under their claws, hammered away at them with their little bills, as if it were an insect in the bark, till they were sufficiently reduced for their slender throats. A little flock of these tit-mice came daily to pick a dinner out of my wood-pile, or the crumbs at my door, with faint flitting lisping notes, like the tinkling of icicles in the grass, or else with sprightly *day day day,* or more rarely, in spring-like days, a wiry summery *phe-be* from the wood-side. They were so familiar that at length one alighted on an armful of wood which I was carrying in, and pecked at the sticks without fear. I once had a sparrow alight upon my shoulder for a moment while I was hoeing in a village garden, and I felt that I was more distinguished by that circumstance than I should have been by any epaulet I could have worn. The squirrels also grew at last to be quite familiar, and occasionally stepped upon my shoe, when that was the nearest way.

When the ground was not yet quite covered, and again near the end of winter, when the snow was melted on my south hill-side and about my wood-pile, the partridges came out of the woods morning and evening to feed there. Whichever side you walk in the woods the partridge bursts away on whirring wings, jarring the snow from the dry leaves and twigs on high, which comes sifting down in the sunbeams like golden dust, for this brave bird is not to be scared by winter. It is frequently covered up by drifts, and, it is said, "sometimes plunges from on wing into the soft snow, where it remains concealed for a day or two." I used to start them in the open land also, where they had come out of the woods at sunset to "bud" the wild apple-trees. They will come regularly every evening to particular trees, where the cunning sportsman lies in wait for them, and the distant orchards next the woods suffer thus not a little. I am glad that the partridge gets fed, at any rate. It is Nature's own bird which lives on buds and diet-drink.

In dark winter mornings, or in short winter afternoons, I sometimes heard a pack of hounds threading all the woods with hounding cry and yelp, unable to resist the instinct of the chase, and the note of the hunting horn at intervals, proving that man was in the rear. The woods ring again, and yet no fox bursts forth on to the open level of the pond, nor following pack pursuing their Actaeon. And perhaps at evening I see the hunters returning with a single brush trailing from their sleigh for a trophy, seeking their inn. They tell me that if the fox would remain in the bosom of the frozen earth he would be safe, or if he would run in a straight line away no fox-hound could overtake him; but, having left his pursuers far behind, he stops to rest and listen till they come up, and when he runs he circles round to his old haunts, where the hunters await him. Sometimes, however, he will run upon a wall many rods, and then leap off far to one side, and he appears to know that water will not retain his scent. A hunter told me that he once saw a fox pursued by hounds burst out on to Walden when the ice was covered with shallow puddles, run part way across, and then return to the same shore. Ere long the hounds arrived, but there they lost the scent. Sometimes a pack hunting by themselves would pass my door, and circle round my house, and yelp and hound without regarding me, as if afflicted by a species of madness, so that nothing could divert them from the pursuit. Thus they circle until they fall upon the recent trail of a fox, for a wise hound will forsake everything else for this. One day a man came to my hut from Lexington to inquire after his hound that made a large track, and had been hunting for a week by himself. But I fear that he was not the wiser for all I told him, for every time I attempted to answer his questions he interrupted me by asking, "What do you do here?" He had lost a dog, but found a man.

One old hunter who has a dry tongue, who used to come to bathe in Walden once every year when the water was warmest, and at such times looked in upon me, told me that many years ago he took his gun one afternoon and went out for a cruise in Walden Wood; and as he walked the Wayland road he heard the cry of hounds approaching, and ere long a fox leaped the wall into the road, and as quick as thought leaped the other wall out of the road, and his swift bullet had not touched him. Some way behind came an old hound and her three pups in full pursuit, hunting on their own account, and disappeared again in the woods. Late in the afternoon, as he was resting in the thick woods south of Walden, he heard the voice of the hounds far over toward Fair Haven still pursuing the fox; and on they came, their hounding cry which made all the woods ring sounding nearer and nearer, now from Well-Meadow, now from the Baker Farm. For a long time he stood still and listened to their music, so sweet to a hunter's ear, when suddenly the fox appeared, threading the solemn aisles with an easy coursing pace, whose sound was concealed by a sympathetic rustle of the leaves, swift and still, keeping the ground; leaving his pursuers far behind; and, leaping upon a rock amid the woods, he sat erect and listening, with his back to the hunter. For a moment compassion restrained the latter's arm; but that was a short-lived mood, and as quick as thought can follow thought his piece was levelled, and *whang!*—the fox rolling over the rock lay dead on the ground. The hunter still kept his place and listened to the hounds. Still on they came, and now the near woods resounded through all their aisles with their demoniac cry. At length the old hound burst into view with muzzle to the ground, and snapping the air as if possessed, and ran directly to the rock; but spying the dead fox she suddenly ceased her hounding, as if struck dumb with amazement, and walked round and round him in silence; and one by one her pups arrived, and, like their mother, were sobered into silence by the mystery. Then the hunter came forward and stood in their midst, and the mystery was solved. They waited in silence while he skinned the fox, then followed the brush a while, and at length turned off into the woods again. That evening a Weston Squire came to the Concord hunter's cottage to inquire for his hounds, and told how for a week they had been hunting on their own account from Weston woods. The Concord hunter told him what he knew and offered him the skin; but the other declined it and departed. He did not find his hounds that night, but the next day learned that they had crossed the river and put up at a farmhouse for the night, whence, having been well fed, they took their departure early in the morning.

The hunter who told me this could remember one Sam Nutting, who used to hunt bears on Fair Haven Lodges, and exchange their skins for rum in Concord village; who told him, even, that he had seen a moose there. Nutting had a famous fox-hound named Burgoyne,—he pronounced it Bugine, —which my informant used to borrow. In the "Wast Book" of an old trader of this town, who was also a captain, town-clerk, and representative, I find the following entry. Jan. 18th, 1742-3, "John Melvin Cr. by 1 Grey Fox 0 - 2 - 3;" they are not now found here; and in his ledger, Feb. 7th, 1743, Hezekiah Stratton has credit "by ½ a Catt skin 0 - 1 - 4½;" of course, a wildcat, for Stratton was a sergeant in the old French war, and would not have got credit for hunting less noble game. Credit is given for deer skins also, and they were daily sold. One man still preserves the horns of the last deer that was killed in this vicinity, and another has told me the particulars of the hunt in which his uncle was engaged. The hunters were formerly a numerous and merry crew here. I remember well one gaunt Nimrod who would catch up a leaf by the road-side and play a strain on it wilder and more melodious, if my memory serves me, than any hunting horn.

At midnight, when there was a moon, I sometimes met with hounds in my path prowling about the woods, which would skulk out of my way, as if afraid, and stand silent amid the bushes till I had passed.

Squirrels and wild mice disputed for my store of nuts. There were scores of pitch-pines around my house, from one to four inches in diameter, which had been gnawed by mice the previous winter,—a Norwegian winter for them, for the snow lay long and deep, and they were obliged to mix a large proportion of pine bark with their other diet. These trees were alive and apparently flourishing at midsummer, and many of them had grown a foot, though completely girdled; but after another winter such were without exception dead. It is remarkable that a single mouse should thus be allowed a whole pine-tree for its dinner, gnawing round instead of up and down it; but perhaps it is necessary in order to thin these trees, which are wont to grow up densely.

The hares (*Lepus Americanus*) were very familiar. One had her form under my house all winter, separated from me only by the flooring, and she startled me each morning by her hasty departure when I began to stir, —thump, thump, thump, striking her head against the floor timbers in her hurry. They used to come round my door at dusk to nibble the potato parings which I had thrown out, and were so nearly the color of the ground that they could hardly be distinguished when still. Sometimes in the twilight I alternately lost and recovered sight of one sitting motionless under my window. When I opened my door in the evening, off they would go with a squeak and a bounce. Near at hand they only excited my pity. One evening one sat by my door two paces from me, at first trembling with fear, yet unwilling to move; a poor wee thing, lean and bony, with ragged ears and sharp nose, scant tail and slender paws. It looked as if Nature no longer contained the breed of nobler bloods, but stood on her last toes. Its large eyes appeared young and unhealthy, almost dropsical. I took a step, and lo, away it scud with an elastic spring over the snow crust, straightening its body and its limbs into graceful length, and soon put the forest between me and itself, —the wild free venison, asserting its vigor and the dignity of Nature. Not without reason was its slenderness. Such then was its nature. (*Lepus, levipes,* light-foot, some think.)

What is a country without rabbits and partridges? They are among the most simple and indigenous animal products; ancient and venerable families known to antiquity as to modern times; of the very hue and substance of Nature, nearest allied to leaves and to the ground, —and to one another; it is either winged or it is legged. It is hardly as if you had seen a wild creature when a rabbit or a partridge bursts away, only a natural one, as much to be expected as rustling leaves. The partridge and the rabbit are still sure to thrive, like true natives of the soil, whatever revolutions occur. If the forest is cut off, the sprouts and bushes which spring up afford them concealment, and they become more numerous than ever. That must be a poor country indeed that does not support a hare. Our woods teem with them both, and around every swamp may be seen the partridge or rabbit walk, beset with twiggy fences and horse-hair snares, which some cowboy tends.

—From *Walden*

❦ ❦ ❦

PEACE
SARA TEASDALE

Peace flows into me
  As the tide to the pool by the shore;
  It is mine forevermore,
It will not ebb like the sea.

I am the pool of blue
  That worships the vivid sky;

My hopes were heaven-high,
They are all fulfilled in you.

I am the pool of gold
  When sunset burns and dies—
  You are my deepening skies;
Give me your stars to hold.

FRIENDSHIP
By SIR THOMAS BROWNE

. . .I HAVE LOVED my friend as I do virtue, my soul, my God. From hence methinks I do conceive how God loves men, what happiness there is in the love of God. . . . There are wonders in true affection; . . .United souls are not satisfied with embraces, but desire to be truly each other; which being impossible, their desires are infinite, and must proceed without a possibility of satisfaction. Another misery there is in affection, that whom we truly love like our own, we forget their looks, nor can our memory retain the Idea of their faces; and it is no wonder, for they are our selves, and our affection makes their looks our own.

HARMONY
By SIR THOMAS BROWNE

IT IS MY TEMPER . . . to affect all harmony: and sure there is music even in the beauty and the silent note which Cupid strikes, far sweeter than the sound of an instrument: for there is music wherever there is harmony, order, or proportion; and thus far we may maintain the *music of the spheres;* for these well-ordered motions, and regular paces, though they give no sound to the ear, yet to the understanding they strike a note most full of harmony. . . . It is a . . . shadowed lesson of the whole world, and creatures of God; such a melody to the ear, as the whole world, well understood, would afford the understanding. . . .

SOMETHING TOLD THE WILD GEESE
RACHEL FIELD

Something told the wild geese
　It was time to go.
Though the fields lay golden
　Something whispered,—"Snow."
Leaves were green and stirring,
　Berries, luster-glossed,
But beneath warm feathers
　Something cautioned,—"Frost."

All the sagging orchards
　Steamed with amber spice,
But each wild breast stiffened
　At remembered ice.
Something told the wild geese
　It was time to fly,—
Summer sun was on their wings,
　Winter in their cry.

THE PURPLE GRASSES
By HENRY DAVID THOREAU

BY THE twentieth of August, every-where in woods and swamps we are re-minded of the fall. The purple grass is now in the height of its beauty. I re-member still when I first noticed this grass particularly. Standing on the hill-side near our river, I saw, thirty or forty rods off, a stripe of purple half a dozen rods long, under the edge of a wood, where the ground sloped toward a meadow. It was as high-colored and in-teresting, though not quite so bright, as the patches of rhexia, being a darker purple, like a berry's stain laid on close and thick. On going to and examining it, I found it to be a kind of grass in bloom, hardly a foot high, with but a few green blades, and a fine spreading panicle of purple flowers, a shallow, pur-plish mist trembling around me. Close at hand it appeared but a dull purple, and made little impression on the eye; it was even difficult to detect; and if you plucked a single plant, you were sur-prised to find how thin it was, and how little color it had. But viewed at a dis-tance in a favorable light, it was a fine lively purple, flower-like, enriching the earth. Such puny causes combine to pro-duce these decided effects. I was the more surprised and charmed because grass is commonly of a sober and hum-ble color

With its beautiful purplish blush it reminds me, and supplies the place, of the rhexia, which is now leaving off, and is one of the most interesting phenom-ena of August. The finest patches of it grow on waste strips or selvages of land at the base of dry hills, just above the edge of the meadows, where the greedy mower does not deign to swing his scythe; for this is a thin and poor grass, beneath his notice. Or, it may be, be-cause it is so beautiful and he does not know that it exists; for the same eye does not see this and timothy. He care-fully gets the meadow hay and the more nutritious grasses which grow next to that, but he leaves the fine purple mist for the walker's harvest—fodder for his fancy's stock. Higher up the hill, per-chance, grow also blackberries, John's-wort, and neglected and withered, the wiry June-grass. How fortunate that it grows in such places, and not in the midst of the rank grasses which are an-nually cut! Nature thus keeps use and beauty distinct. I know of many such localities, where it does not fail to pre-sent itself annually, and paint the earth with its blush. It grows on the gentle slopes, either in a continuous patch or in scattered and rounded tufts a foot in diameter, and it lasts until it is killed by the first smart frosts.

RONDEL FOR SEPTEMBER
KARLE WILSON BAKER

You thought it was a falling leaf we heard;
I knew it was the Summer's gypsy feet,
A sound so reticent it scarcely stirred
The ear so still a message to repeat,—
"I go, and lo, I make my going sweet."
What wonder you should miss so soft a word?
You thought it was a falling leaf we heard;
I knew it was the Summer's gypsy feet.

With slender torches for her service meet
The golden-rod is coming; softer slurred
Midsummer noises take a note replete
With hint of change; who told the mocking bird?
I knew it was the Summer's gypsy feet—
You thought it was a falling leaf we heard.

DIRT FARMER
ARDEN ANTONY

He finds beauty among these simple things;
The path a plow makes in the rich, red loam,
Gay sun-gold in ripe wheat—a plover's wings—
A cow-bell, tinkling as the herd comes home.

He treads the soil, with earth-love in his heart;
Watches the young crops spring from fertile ground,
Loves the warm rain that makes the peach buds start,
Land—and a man—in close communion bound!

INDIAN SUMMER
By HENRY WADSWORTH LONGFELLOW

IT IS the Indian summer. The rising sun blazes throught the misty air like a conflagration. A yellowish, smoky haze fills the atmosphere, and a filmy mist lies like a silver lining on the sky. The wind is soft and low. It wafts to us the odor of forest leaves, that hang wilted on the dripping branches, or drop into the stream. Their gorgeous tints are gone, as if the autumnal rains had washed them out. Orange, yellow and scarlet, all are changed to one melancholy russet hue. The birds, too, have taken wing, and have left their roofless dwellings. Not the whistle of a robin, not the twitter of an eavesdropping swallow, not the carol of one sweet, familiar voice. All gone. Only the dismal cawing of a crow, as he sits and curses that the harvest is over; or the chit-chat of an idle squirrel, the noisy denizen of a hollow tree, the mendicant friar of a large parish, the absolute monarch of a dozen acorns.

LIFE! I KNOW NOT WHAT THOU ART
ANNA L. BARBAULD

Life! I know not what thou art,
But know that thou and I must part;
And when, or how, or where we met
I own to me's a secret yet.

Life! we've been long together
Through pleasant and through cloudy
    weather.

It's hard to part when friends are
    dear,—
Perhaps it will cost a sigh, a tear;
—Then steal away, give little warning,
Choose thine own time: Say not good-
    night—
But—some brighter time
Bid me good morning.

THE SONG OF THE UNGIRT RUNNERS
CHARLES HAMILTON SORLEY

We swing ungirded hips,
  And lightened are our eyes,
The rain is on our lips,
  We do not run for prize.
We know not whom we trust
  Nor whitherward we fare,
But we run because we must
  Through the great wide air.

The waters of the seas
  Are troubled as by storm.
The tempest strips the trees
  And does not leave them warm.

Does the tearing tempest pause?
  Do the tree-tops ask it why?
So we run without a cause
  'Neath the big bare sky.

The rain is on our lips,
  We do not run for prize.
But the storm the water whips
  And the wave howls to the skies.
The winds arise and strike it
  And scatter it like sand,
And we run because we like it
  Through the broad bright land.

MONTANA WIVES
GWENDOLEN HASTE

I had to laugh,
For when she said it we were sitting by
    the door,
And straight down was the Fork
Twisting and turning and gleaming in
    the sun.
And then your eyes carried across to the
    purple bench beyond the river
With the Beartooth Mountains fairly
    screaming with light and blue and
    snow
And fold and turn of rimrock and
    prairie as far as your eye could go.
And she says: "Dear Laura, sometimes
    I feel so sorry for you,
Shut away from everything—eating out
    your heart with loneliness.

When I think of my own full life I wish
    that I could share it.
Just pray for happier days to come, and
    bear it."
She goes back to Billings to her white
    stucco house,
And looks through net curtains at
    another white stucco house,
And a brick house,
And a yellow frame house,
And six trimmed poplar trees,
And little squares of shaved grass.

Oh, dear, she stared at me like I was
    daft.
I couldn't help it! I just laughed and
    laughed.

THE MIST AND ALL
DIXIE WILLSON

I like the fall,
The mist and all.
I like the night owl's
Lonely call—
And wailing sound
Of wind around.

I like the gray
November day,
And bare, dead boughs
That coldly sway
Against my pane.
I like the rain.

I like to sit
And laugh at it—
And tend
My cozy fire a bit.
I like the fall—
The mist and all—

DREAM-PEDLARY
THOMAS LOVELL BEDDOES

If there were dreams to sell,
  What would you buy?
Some cost a passing bell;
  Some a light sigh,
That shakes from Life's fresh crown
Only a rose-leaf down.
If there were dreams to sell,
Merry and sad to tell,
And the crier rang the bell,
  What would you buy?

A cottage lone and still,
  With bowers nigh,
Shadowy, my woes to still,
  Until I die.
Such pearl from Life's fresh crown
Fain would I shake me down.
Were dreams to have at will,
This would best heal my ill,
  This would I buy.

SONNET
CHRISTINA GEORGINA ROSSETTI

I wish I could remember that first day,
First hour, first moment of your meet-
    ing me,
If bright or dim the season, it might be
Summer or Winter for aught I can say;
So unrecorded did it slip away,
So blind was I to see and to foresee,
So dull to mark the budding of my tree
That would not blossom yet for many
    a May.
If only I could recollect it, such
A day of days! I let it come and go
As traceless as a thaw of bygone snow;
It seemed to mean so little, meant so
    much;
If only now I could recall that touch
First touch of hand in hand—did one
    but know!

RETURN
MILDRED BOWERS ARMSTRONG

When other hearts are tuned
To a glad singing
In the spring, ever new,
Ever song-bringing;
When other hearts are feeling
The joy I knew,
Let me come back again,
Singing, too.

I shall know
When the pale petals blow
And spring comes flashing back
Another year.
You must not search and call.
When the first petals fall
I shall be here.

If you cannot see
The hands and eyes of me
When petals fill the air
You will hear a song
The wind blows along—
I shall be there.

EVENING IN PARADISE
JOHN MILTON

Now came still evening on, and twilight gray
Had in her sober livery all things clad;
Silence accompanied; for beast and bird,
They to their grassy couch, these to their nests,
Were slunk, all but the wakeful nightingale;
She all night long her amorous descant sung.
Silence was pleased: now glowed the firmament
With living sapphires; Herperus, that led
The starry host, rode brightest, till the moon,
Rising in clouded majesty, at length
Apparent queen, unveiled her peerless light,
And o'er the dark her silver mantle threw.

From *RESOLUTION AND INDEPENDENCE*
WILLIAM WORDSWORTH

There was a roaring in the wind all night;
The rain came heavily and fell in floods;
But now the sun is rising calm and bright;
The birds are singing in the distant woods;
Over his own sweet voice the Stock-dove broods;
The Jay makes answer as the Magpie chatters;
And all the air is filled with pleasant noise of waters.

All things that love the sun are out of doors;
The sky rejoices in the morning's birth;
The grass is bright with rain-drops;—on the moors
The hare is running races in her mirth;
And with her feet she from the plashy earth
Raises a mist, that, glittering in the sun,
Runs with her all the way, wherever she doth run.

* * *

❧ WHEREVER SNOW FALLS, or water flows, or birds fly, wherever day and night meet in twilight, wherever the blue heaven is hung by clouds, or sown with stars, wherever are forms with transparent boundaries, wherever are outlets into celestial space, wherever is danger, and awe, and love, there is beauty, plenteous as rain, shed for thee, and though thou shouldst walk the world over, thou shalt not be able to find a condition inopportune or ignoble.

—Emerson

ISLANDERS
Harold Vinal

Those who are born on islands know the sound
Of spindrift breaking and the drift of foam,
The sight of white-keeled luggers sailing home,
The cry of gulls at daybreak ocean bound.
Always a wind is singing in their ears,
Always they lean to catch a drift of spray,
Or reef-blown water tossing in a bay,
Or drift of ebb tide around salty piers.
Those who are born on islands must remain
Aware of ships and anchors and tall spars,
Of schooners sailing by beneath the stars,
Of buoys sounding in the dripping rain;
Their thoughts are not of city streets or walls,
But how the full tide lifts and how it falls.

WIND IN THE PINE
Lew Sarett

Oh, I can hear you, God, above the cry
  Of tossing trees—
Rolling your windy tides across the sky,
  And splashing your silver seas
    Over the pine,
    To the water line
    Of the moon.
Oh, I can hear you, God,
Above the wail of the lonely loon—
When the pine tops pitch and nod—
  Chanting your melodies
Of ghostly waterfalls and avalanches,
Swashing your wind among the branches
  To make them pure and white.

Wash over me, God, with your piney breeze,
  And your moon's wet silver pool;
Wash over me, God, with your wind and night
  And leave me clean and cool.

* * *

❦ Great art is an instant arrested in eternity.—*Huneker*

331

ROMANCE
ANDREW LANG

My Love dwelt in a northern land.
  A grey tower in a forest green
Was hers, and far on either hand
  The long wash of the waves was seen,
And leagues on leagues of yellow sand,
  The woven forest boughs between!

And through the silver Northern night
  The sunset slowly died away,
And herds of strange deer, lily-white,
  Stole forth among the branches grey;
About the coming of the light,
  They fled like ghosts before the day!

I know not if the forest green
  Still girdles round that castle grey;
I know not if the boughs between
  The white deer vanish ere the day;
Above my Love the grass is green,
  My heart is colder than the clay!

REQUIESCAT
MATTHEW ARNOLD

Strew on her roses, roses,
  And never a spray of yew.
In quiet she reposes—
  Ah! would that I did too!

Her mirth the world required,
  She bathed it in smiles of glee.
But her heart was tired, tired,
  And now they let her be.

Her life was turning, turning
  In mazes of heat and sound.
But for peace her soul was yearning
  And now peace laps her round.

Her cabined, ample spirit,
  It fluttered and failed for breath.
Tonight it doth inherit
  The vasty hall of death.

UNDERSTANDING
By ROBERT LOUIS STEVENSON

"IT TAKES," says Thoreau, in the noblest and most useful passage I remember to have read in any modern author, "two to speak truth—one to speak and another to hear." He must be very little experienced, or have no great zeal for truth, who does not recognize the fact. . . . With our chosen friends, . . . and still more between lovers (for mutual understanding is love's essence), the truth is easily indicated by the one and aptly comprehended by the other. A hint taken, a look understood, conveys the gist of long and delicate explanations; and where the life is known even *yea* and *nay* become luminous. In the closest of all relations—that of a love well founded and equally shared—speech is half discarded, like a roundabout, infantile process or a ceremony of formal etiquette; and the two communicate directly by their presences, and with few looks and fewer words contrive to share their good and evil and uphold each other's hearts in joy. For love rests upon a physical basis; it is a familiarity of nature's making and apart from voluntary choice. Understanding has in some sort outrun knowledge, for the affection perhaps began with the acquaintance; and as it was not made like other relations, so it is not, like them, to be perturbed or clouded. Each knows more than can be uttered; each lives by faith, and believes by a natural compulsion; and between man and wife the language of the body is largely developed and grown strangely eloquent. The thought that prompted and was conveyed in a caress would only lose to be set down in words—ay, although Shakespeare himself should be the scribe.

O NIGHTINGALE THAT ON YON BLOOMY SPRAY
JOHN MILTON

O nightingale, that on yon bloomy spray
Warblest at eve, when all the woods are still,
Thou with fresh hope the lover's heart dost fill,
While the jolly hours lead on propitious May.

Thy liquid notes that close the eye of day,
First heard before the swallow cuckoo's bill,
Portend success in love—oh, if Jove's will
Have linked that amorous power to thy soft lay,

Now timely sing, ere the rude bird of hate
Foretell my hopeless doom in some grove nigh:
As thou from year to year hast sung too late
For my relief, yet hadst no reason why,
Whether the Muse or Love call thee his mate,
Both them I serve, and of their train am I.

A BALLAD OF TREES AND THE MASTER
SIDNEY LANIER

Into the woods my Master went,
Clean forspent, forspent.
Into the woods my Master came,
Forspent with love and shame.
But the olives they were not blind to Him;
The little gray leaves were kind to Him;
The thorn-tree had a mind to Him
When into the woods He came.

Out of the woods my Master went,
And He was well content.
Out of the woods my Master came,
Content with death and shame.
When Death and Shame would woo Him last,
From under the trees they drew Him last:
'Twas on a tree they slew Him—last
When out of the woods He came.

From *ALL FOR LOVE*
JOHN DRYDEN

How I loved
Witness, ye days and nights, and all ye hours,
That danced away with down upon your feet,
As all your business were to count my passion!
One day passed by, and nothing saw but love;
Another came, and still 'twas only love:
The suns were wearied out with looking on,
And I untired with loving.
I saw you every day, and all the day;
And every day was still but as the first,
So eager was I still to see you more. . . .

* * *

Be noble! and the nobleness that lies
In other men, sleeping but never dead,
Will rise in majesty to meet thine own.
                                        —*Lowell.*

Our Lady's Juggler

By ANATOLE FRANCE

*I*N THE DAYS of King Louis there was a poor juggler in France, a native of Compiègne, Barnaby by name, who went about from town to town performing feats of skill and strength.

On fair days he would unfold an old worn-out carpet in the public square, and when by means of a jovial address, which he had learned of a very ancient juggler, and which he never varied in the least, he had drawn together the children and loafers, he assumed extraordinary attitudes, and balanced a tin plate on the tip of his nose. At first the crowd would feign indifference.

But when, supporting himself on his hands face downwards, he threw into the air six copper balls, which glittered in the sunshine, and caught them again with his feet; or when throwing himself backwards until his heels and the nape of the neck met, giving his body the form of a perfect wheel, he would juggle in this posture with a dozen knives, a murmur of admiration would escape the spectators, and pieces of money would rain down upon the carpet.

Nevertheless, like the majority of those who live by their wits, Barnaby of Compiègne had a great struggle to make a living.

Earning his bread in the sweat of his brow, he bore rather more than his share of the penalties consequent upon the misdoings of our father Adam.

Again, he was unable to work as constantly as he would have been willing to do. The warmth of the sun and the broad daylight were as necessary to enable him to display his brilliant parts as to the trees if flower and fruit should be expected of them. In winter time he was nothing more than a tree stripped of its leaves, and as it were dead. The frozen ground was hard to the juggler, and, like the grasshopper of which Marie de France tells us, the inclement season caused him to suffer both cold and hunger. But as he was simple-natured he bore his ills patiently.

He had never meditated on the origin of wealth, nor upon the inequality of human conditions. He believed firmly that if this life should prove hard, the life to come could not fail to redress the balance, and this hope upheld him. He did not resemble those thievish and miscreant Merry Andrews who sell their souls to the devil. He never blasphemed God's name; he lived uprightly, and although he had no wife of his own, he did not covet his neighbour's, since woman is ever the enemy of the strong man, as it appears by the history of Samson recorded in the Scriptures.

In truth, his was not a nature much disposed to carnal delights, and it was a greater deprivation to him to forsake the tankard than the Hebe who bore it. For whilst not wanting in sobriety, he was fond of a drink when the weather waxed hot. He was a worthy man who feared God, and was very devoted to the Blessed Virgin.

Never did he fail on entering a church to fall upon his knees before the image of the Mother of God, and offer up this prayer to her:

"Blessed Lady, keep watch over my life until it shall please God that I die, and when I am dead, ensure to me the possession of the joys of paradise."

Now on a certain evening after a dreary wet day, as Barnaby pursued his road, sad and bent, carrying under his arm his balls and knives wrapped up in his old carpet, on the watch for some barn where, though he might not sup, he might sleep, he perceived on the road, going in the same direction as himself, a monk, whom he saluted courteously. And as they walked at the same rate they fell into conversation with one another.

"Fellow traveller," said the monk, "how comes it about that you are clothed all in green? Is it perhaps in order to take the part of a jester in some mystery play?"

"Not at all, good father," replied Barnaby. "Such as you see me, I am called Barnaby, and for my calling I am a juggler. There would be no pleasanter calling in the world if it would always provide one with daily bread."

"Friend Barnaby," returned the monk, "be careful what you say. There is no calling more pleasant than the monastic life. Those who lead it are occupied with the praises of God, the Blessed Virgin, and the saints; and, indeed, the religious life is one ceaseless hymn to the Lord."

Barnaby replied—

"Good father, I own that I spoke like an ignorant man. Your calling cannot be in any respect compared to mine, and although there may be some merit in dancing with a penny balanced on a stick on the tip of one's nose, it is not a merit which comes within hail of your own. Gladly would I, like you, good father, sing my office day by day, and especially, the office of the most Holy Virgin, to whom I have vowed a singular devotion. In order to embrace the monastic life I would willingly abandon the art by which from Soissons to Beauvais I am well known in upwards of six hundred towns and villages."

The monk was touched by the juggler's simplicity, and as he was not lacking in discernment, he at once recognized in Barnaby one of those men of whom it is said in the Scriptures: Peace on earth to men of good will. And for this reason he replied—

"Friend Barnaby, come with me, and I will have you admitted into the monastery of which I am Prior. He who guided St. Mary of Egypt in the desert set me upon your path to lead you into the way of salvation."

It was in this manner, then, that Barnaby became a monk. In the monastery into which he was received the religious vied with one another in the worship of the Blessed Virgin, and in her honour each employed all the knowledge and all the skill which God had given him.

The prior on his part wrote books dealing according to the rules of scholarship with the virtues of the Mother of God.

Brother Maurice with a deft hand copied out these treaties upon sheets of vellum.

Brother Alexander adorned the leaves with delicate miniature paintings. Here were displayed the Queen of Heaven seated upon Solomon's throne, and while four lions were on guard at her feet, around the nimbus which encircled her head hovered seven doves, which are the seven gifts of the Holy Spirit, the gifts, namely, of Fear, Piety, Knowledge, Strength, Counsel, Understanding, and Wisdom. For her companions she had six virgins with hair of gold, namely, Humility, Prudence, Seclusion, Submission, Virginity, and Obedience.

At her feet were two little naked figures, perfectly white, in an attitude of supplication. These were souls imploring her all-powerful intercession for their soul's health, and we may be sure not imploring in vain.

Upon another page facing this, Brother Alexander represented Eve, so that the Fall and the Redemption could be perceived at one and the same time —Eve the Wife abased, and Mary the Virgin exalted.

Furthermore, to the marvel of the beholder, this book contained presentments of The Well of Living Waters, the Fountain, the Lily, the Moon, the Sun, and the Garden enclosed of which the Song of Songs tells us, the Gate of Heaven and the City of God, and all these things were symbols of the Blessed Virgin.

Brother Marbode was likewise one of the most loving children of Mary.

He spent all his days carving images in stone, so that his beard, his eyebrows, and his hair were white with dust, and his eyes continually swollen and weeping; but his strength and cheerfulness were not diminished, although he was now well gone in years, and it was clear that the Queen of Paradise still cherished her servant in his old age. Marbode represented her seated upon a throne, her brow encircled with an orb-shaped nimbus set with pearls. And he took care that the folds of her dress should cover the feet of her, concerning whom the prophet declared: My beloved is as a garden enclosed.

Sometimes, too, he depicted her in the semblance of a child full of grace, and appearing to say, "Thou art my God, even from my mother's womb."

In the priory, moreover, were poets who composed hymns in Latin, both in prose and verse, in honour of the Blessed Virgin Mary, and amongst the company was even a brother from Picardy who sang the miracles of Our Lady in rhymed verse and in the vulgar tongue.

III

Being a witness of this emulation in praise and the glorious harvest of their labours, Barnaby mourned his own ignorance and simplicity.

"Alas!" he sighed, as he took his solitary walk in the little shelterless garden of the monastery, "wretched wight that I am, to be unable, like my brother, worthily to praise the Holy Mother of God, to whom I have vowed my whole heart's affection. Alas! alas! I am but a rough man and unskilled in the arts, and I can render you in service, blessed Lady, neither edifying sermons, nor treatises set out in order according to rule, nor ingenious paintings, nor statues truthfully sculptured, nor verses whose march is measured to the beat of feet. No gift have I, alas!"

After this fashion he groaned and gave himself up to sorrow. But one evening, when the monks were spending their hour of liberty in conversation, he heard one of them tell the tale of a religious man who could repeat nothing other than the Ave Maria. This poor man was despised for his ignorance; but after his death there issued forth from his mouth five roses in honour of the five letters of the name Mary (Marie), and thus his sanctity was made manifest.

Whilst he listened to this narrative Barnaby marvelled yet once again at the loving kindness of the Virgin; but the lesson of that blessed death did not avail to console him, for his heart overflowed with zeal, and he longed to advance the glory of his Lady, who is in heaven.

How to compass this he sought but could find no way, and day by day he became the more cast down, when one morning he awakened filled full with joy, hastened to the chapel, and remained there alone for more than an hour. After dinner he returned to the chapel once more.

And, starting from that moment, he repaired daily to the chapel at such hours as it was deserted, and spent within it a good part of the time which the other monks devoted to the liberal and mechanical arts. His sadness vanished, nor did he any longer groan.

A demeanor so strange awakened the curiosity of the monks.

These began to ask one another for what purpose Brother Barnaby could be indulging so persistently in retreat.

The prior, whose duty it is to let nothing escape him in the behaviour of his children in religion, resolved to keep a watch over Barnaby during his withdrawals to the chapel. One day, then, when he was shut up there after his custom, the prior, accompanied by two of the older monks, went to discover through the chinks in the door what was going on within the chapel.

They saw Barnaby before the altar of the Blessed Virgin, head downwards, with his feet in the air, and he was juggling with six balls of copper and a dozen knives. In honour of the Holy Mother of God he was performing those feats, which aforetime had won him most renown. Not recognizing that the simple fellow was thus placing at the service of the Blessed Virgin his knowledge and skill, the two old monks exclaimed against the sacrilege.

The prior was aware how stainless was Barnaby's soul, but he concluded that he had been seized with madness. They were all three preparing to lead him swiftly from the chapel, when they saw the Blessed Virgin descend the steps of the altar and advance to wipe away with a fold of her azure robe the sweat which was dropping from her juggler's forehead.

Then the prior, falling upon his face upon the pavement, uttered these words—

"Blessed are the simple-hearted, for they shall see God."

"Amen!" responded the old brethren, and kissed the ground.

—*Translated by Frederic Chapman*

SONNET

Edna St. Vincent Millay

Here is a wound that never will heal, I know,
Being wrought not of a dearness and a death,
But of a love turned ashes and the breath
Gone out of beauty; never again will grow
The grass on that scarred acre, though I sow
Young seed there yearly and the sky bequeath
Its friendly weathers down, far underneath
Shall be such bitterness of an old woe.
That April should be shattered by a gust,
That August should be levelled by a rain,
I can endure, and that the lifted dust
Of man should settle to the earth again;
But that a dream can die, will be a thrust
Between my ribs forever of hot pain.

THE LOST MASTER
ROBERT SERVICE

"And when I come to die," he said,
"Ye shall not lay me out in state,
Nor leave your laurels at my head,
Nor cause your men of speech orate;
No monument your gift shall be,
No column in the Hall of Fame;
But just this line ye grave for me:
    "He played the game."

So when his glorious task was done,
It was not of his fame we thought;
It was not of his battles won,
But of the pride with which he fought;
But of his zest, his ringing laugh,
His trenchant scorn of praise or blame:
And so we graved his epitaph,
    "He played the game."

And so we, too, in humbler ways
Went forth to fight the fight anew,
And heeding neither blame nor praise,
We held the course he set us true,
And we, too, find the fighting sweet;
And we, too, fight for fighting's sake;
And though we go down in defeat,
And though our stormy hearts may
    break,
We will not do our Master shame:
We'll play the game, please God,
    We'll play the game.

WHAT IS LOVE?
BY GUY DE MAUPASSANT

To LOVE very much is to love inade-
quately; we love—that is all. Love cannot be modified without being nullified.
Love is a short word but it contains
everything. Love means the body, the
soul, the life, the entire being. We feel
love as we feel the warmth of our blood,
we breathe love as we breathe the air,
we hold it in ourselves as we hold our
thoughts. Nothing more exists for us.
Love is not a word; it is a wordless state
indicated by four letters. . .

ON THE HEIGHT
EUNICE TIETJENS

The foothills called us, green and
    sweet;
  We dallied, but we might not stay,
And all day long we set our feet
  In the wind's way.

We climbed with him the wandering
    trail
  Up to the last keen, lonely height—
Where snow-peaks clustered, sharp and
    frail,
  Swimming in light.

Sheer on the edge of heaven we dwelt
  And laughed above the blue abyss,
While on my happy lips I felt
  Your windy kiss.

You were the spirit of the height,
  The breath of sun and air.
A bird dipped wing, and, swift and
    white,
Peace brooded there.

EASTER
JOYCE KILMER

The air is like a butterfly
  With frail blue wings.
The happy earth looks at the sky
  And sings.

WHAT IS POETRY?
BY WILLIAM HAZLITT

POETRY is the universal language
which the heart holds with nature and
itself. He who has a contempt for poetry
cannot have much respect for himself
or for anything else . . . for all that is
worth remembering in life is the poetry
of it. Fear is poetry, hope is poetry, love
is poetry, hatred is poetry; contempt,
jealousy, remorse, admiration, wonder,
pity, despair, or madness are all poetry.

WHITE BUTTERFLIES
ALGERNON CHARLES SWINBURNE

Fly, white butterflies, out to sea,
Frail, pale wings for the wind to try,
Small white wings that we scarce can see,
    Fly!
Some fly light as a laugh of glee,
Some fly soft as a long, low sigh;
All to the haven where each would be,
    Fly!

PROSPICE
ROBERT BROWNING

Fear death?—to feel the fog in my throat,
  The mist in my face,
When the snows begin, and the blasts denote
  I am nearing the place,
The power of the night, the press of the storm,
  The post of the foe;
Where he stands, the Arch Fear in a visible form,
  Yet the strong man must go;
For the journey is done and the summit attained,
  And the barriers fall,
Though a battle's to fight ere the guerdon be gained,
  The reward of it all.
I was ever a fighter, so—one fight more,
  The best and the last!
I would hate that death bandaged my eyes, and forbore,
  And bade me creep past.
No! let me taste the whole of it, fare like my peers,
  The heroes of old,
Bear the brunt, in a minute pay glad life's arrears
  Of pain, darkness, and cold.
For sudden the worst turns the best to the brave,
  The black minute's at end,
And the elements that rage, the fiend-voices that rave:
  Shall dwindle, shall blend,
Shall change, shall become first a peace out of pain,
  Then a light, then thy breast,
O thou soul of my soul! I shall clasp thee again,
  And with God be the rest!

From CHILDE HAROLD
Lord Byron

The moon is up, and yet it is not night;
Sunset divides the sky with her; a sea
Of glory streams along the Alpine
    height
Of blue Fruili's mountains; Heaven is
    free
From clouds, but of all colors seems to
    be,—
Melted to one vast Iris of the West,—
Where the Day joins the past Eternity,
While, on the other hand, meek Dian's
    crest
Floats through the azure air—an island
    of the blest!

A single star is at her side, and reigns
With her over half the lovely heaven;
    but still
Yon sunny sea heaves brightly, and
    remains
Rolled over the peak of the far Phae-
    tian hill,
As Day and Night contending were,
    until
Nature reclaimed her order;—gently
    flows
The deep-dyed Brenta, where their
    hues instill
The odorous purple of a new-born rose,
Which streams upon her stream, and
    glassed within it glows.

Filled with the face of heaven, which,
    from afar,
Comes down upon the waters; all its
    hues,
From the rich sunset to the rising star,
Their magical variety diffuse:
And now they change; a paler shadow
    strews
Its mantle over the mountains; parting
    day
Dies like the dolphin, whom each pang
    imbues
With a new color as it gasps away,
The last still loveliest,—till—it's gone—
    and all is gray.

HIE AWAY, HIE AWAY
Sir Walter Scott

Hie away, hie away,
Over bank and over brae,
Where the copsewood is the greenest,
Where the fountains glisten sheenest,
Where the lady-fern grows strongest,
Where the morning dew lies longest,
Where the black-cock sweetest sips it,
Where the fairy latest trips it:
Hie to haunts right seldom seen,
Lovely, lonesome, cool and green,
Over bank and over brae,
Hie away, hie away.

WHO HAS SEEN THE WIND?
Christina Georgina Rossetti

Who has seen the wind?
    Neither I nor you:
But when the leaves hang trembling,
    The wind is passing through.

Who has seen the wind?
    Neither you nor I:
But when the trees bow down their
    heads,
    The wind is passing by.

YE STARS
Lord Byron

Ye stars! which are the poetry of heaven!
If in your bright leaves we would read
    the fate
Of men and empires,—'tis to be
    forgiven,
That in our aspirations to be great,
Our destinies o'erleap their mortal
    state,
And claim a kindred with you; for ye
    are
A beauty and a mystery, and create
In us such love and reverence from afar,
That fortune, fame, power, life, have
    named themselves a star.

TO NIGHT
PERCY BYSSHE SHELLEY

Swiftly walk over the western wave,
  Spirit of Night!
Out of thy misty eastern cave,
Where all the long and lone daylight
Thou wovest dreams of joy and fear,
Which make thee terrible and dear,—
  Swift be thy flight!

Wrap thy form in a mantle gray,
  Star-inwrought!
Blind with thine hair the eyes of Day;
Kiss her until she be wearied out,
Then wander o'er city, and sea, and
  land,
Touching all with thine opiate wand—
  Come, long sought!

When I arose and saw the dawn,
  I sighed for thee;
When light rode high, and the dew was
  gone,
And noon lay heavy on flower and tree,
And the weary Day turned to his rest,
Lingering like an unloved guest,
  I sighed for thee.

Thy brother Death came, and cried,
  Wouldst thou me?
Thy sweet child Sleep, the filmy-eyed,
Murmured like a noontide bee,
Shall I nestle near thy side?
Wouldst thou me?—And I replied,
  No, not thee!

Death will come when thou art dead,
  Soon, too soon—
Sleep will come when thou are fled;
Of neither would I ask the boon
I ask of thee, beloved Night—
Swift be thine approaching flight,
  Come soon, soon!

    *   *   *

Let others crowd the giddy Court
  Of mirth and revelry,
The simple joys that Nature yields
Are dearer far to me.
        —*Robert Tannahill*

From *THE WORLD*
HENRY VAUGHAN

I saw Eternity the other night,
Like a great ring of pure and endless
  light,
All calm, as it was bright;
And round beneath it Time in hours,
  days, years,
Driven by the spheres
Like a cast shadow moved; in which the
  world
And all her train were hurled.

THE SEA
BARRY CORNWALL

The sea, the sea, the open sea,
The blue, the fresh, the ever free;
Without a mark, without a bound,
It runneth the earth's wide regions
  round,
It plays with the clouds, it mocks the
  skies,
Or like a cradled creature lies.
I'm on the sea, I'm on the sea,
I am where I would ever be,
With the blue above and the blue
  below,
And silence wheresoever I go.
If a storm should come and awake the
  deep,
What matter? I shall ride and sleep.

I love, oh! how I love to ride
On the fierce, foaming, bursting tide,
Where every mad wave drowns the
  moon,
And whistles aloft its tempest tune,
And tells how goeth the world below,
And why the southwest wind doth
  blow!
I never was on the dull, tame shore
But I loved the great sea more and
  more,
And backward flew to her billowy
  breast,
Like a bird that seeketh her mother's
  nest,—
And a mother she was and is to me,
For I was born on the open sea.

A CHRISTMAS CAROL

JOSIAH GILBERT HOLLAND

There's a song in the air!
There's a star in the sky!
There's a mother's deep prayer
And a baby's low cry!
And the star rains its fire while the Beautiful sing,
For the manger of Bethlehem cradles a king.

There's a tumult of joy
O'er the wonderful birth,
For the virgin's sweet boy
Is the Lord of the earth.
Ay! the star rains its fire and the Beautiful sing,
For the manger of Bethlehem cradles a king.

In the light of that star
Lie the Ages impearled,
And that song from afar
Has swept over the world.
Every hearth is aflame, and the Beautiful sing,
In the homes of the nations that Jesus is King.

We rejoice in the light,
And we echo the song
That comes down through the night
From the heavenly throng.
Ay! we shout to the lovely evangel they bring,
And we greet in his cradle our Savior and King.

❧ ❧ ❧

SLEEP, BABY, SLEEP

[From The German]

Sleep, baby, sleep!
Thy father watches the sheep;
Thy mother is shaking the dreamland tree
And down comes a little dream on thee.
Sleep, baby, sleep!

Sleep, baby, sleep!
The large stars are the sheep;

The little stars are the lambs, I guess;
And the gentle moon is the shepherdess.
Sleep, baby, sleep!

Sleep, baby, sleep!
Our Savior loves His sheep;
He is the Lamb of God on high
Who for our sakes come down to die.
Sleep, baby, sleep!

A nation's growth from sea to sea
Stirs in his heart who plants a tree.
—*Bunner*

❧ ❧

Over the winter glaciers I see the summer glow,
And through the wide-piled snowdrift
the warm rosebuds below.
—*Emerson*

❧ ❧

Heaven and earth help him who plants
a tree,
And his work its own reward shall be.
—*Larcom*

❧ ❧

So here hath been dawning
Another blue day;
Think, wilt thou let it
Slip useless away?
—*Carlyle*

❧ ❧

Great truths are portions of the soul of
man;
Great souls are portions of eternity.
—*Lowell*

❧ ❧

Love, like a bird, hath perch'd upon a
spray
For thee and me to hearken what he
sings.
Contented, he forgets to fly away;
But hush! . . . remind not Eros of his
wings.
—*Sir William Watson*

❧ ❧

Faith of our fathers, we will love
Both friend and foe in all our strife,
And preach Thee, too, as love knows
how
By kindly words and virtuous life.
—*Faber*

For whatever men say in their blindness,
And spite of the fancies of youth,
There's nothing so kingly as kindness,
And nothing so royal as truth.
—*Cary*

❧ ❧

True worth is in *being*, not *seeming*,—
In doing, each day that goes by,
Some little good—not in dreaming
Of great things to do by and by.
—*Cary*

❧ ❧

Hast thou named all the birds without
a gun?
Loved the wood-rose, and left it on its
stalk?
—*Emerson*

❧ ❧

Silence is deep as Eternity,
Speech is shallow as Time.
—*Carlyle*

❧ ❧

I would that the loving were loved, and
I would that the weary should sleep,
And that man should hearken to man,
And that he that soweth should reap.
—*William Morris*

❧ ❧

Minds that have nothing to confer
Find little to perceive.
—*Wordsworth*

❧ ❧

Time has no flight,—'tis we who speed
along.
The days and nights are but the same
as when
The earth awoke with the first rush of
song,
And felt the swiftly passing feet of men.
—*Thomas S. Collier*

from Cavalcade

By NOEL COWARD

SCENE

The deck of an Atlantic liner. This is quite a small inset scene. The rail of the Promenade Deck faces the audience. Behind it can be seen the lighted windows of the lounge. Above can be seen vaguely the Boat Deck, with ventilators and a funnel silhouetted against the stars.

TIME: *About 7 p. m. Sunday, April 14, 1912.*

EDWARD and EDITH, *he in dinner-jacket, she in evening dress, are leaning on the rail.*

EDITH. It's too big, the Atlantic, isn't it?

EDWARD. Far too big.

EDITH. And too deep.

EDWARD. Much, much too deep.

EDITH. I don't care a bit, do you?

EDWARD. Not a scrap.

EDITH. Wouldn't it be awful if a magician came to us and said: "Unless you count accurately every single fish in the Atlantic you die to-night?"

EDWARD. We should die to-night.

EDITH. How much would you mind—dying, I mean?

EDWARD. I don't know really—a good deal, I expect.

EDITH. I don't believe I should mind so very much now. You see, we could never in our whole lives be happier than we are now, could we?

EDWARD. Darling, there *are* different sorts of happiness.

EDITH. This is the best sort.

EDWARD (*kissing her*). Sweetheart!

EDITH. Don't darling, we don't want any more of the stewards to know we're on our honeymoon.

EDWARD. Why not? It gives them so much vicarious pleasure. Most of them have forgotten what it was like.

EDITH. Are all honeymoons like this?

EDWARD (*firmly*). Exactly.

EDITH. Oh, Edward—that's rather disheartening, isn't it? I do so want this to be unique.

EDWARD. It is, for us.

EDITH. Did you ever think when we were children, going to the pantomime, and going to the Zoo, and playing soldiers, that we should ever be married?

EDWARD. Of course I didn't.

EDITH. Was I nice as a child?

EDWARD. Horrible!

EDITH. So were you, and so was Joe—vile. You always used to take sides against me.

EDWARD. And yet we liked one another really.

EDITH. I think I liked Joe better than you, but then he was younger and easier to manage. Dear Joe, he was awfully funny at the wedding, wasn't he?

EDWARD. Ribald little beast!

EDITH. He has no reverence, I'm afraid.

EDWARD. Absolutely none.

EDITH. He's passing gallantly through the chorus-girl phase now, isn't he?

EDWARD. Gallantly but not quickly.

EDITH. Well, darling, you took your time over it.

EDWARD. Now then, Edith—

EDITH. You had several affairs before you married me, didn't you?

EDWARD. Light of my life, shut up!

EDITH. You'd be awfully cross if *I* had, wouldn't you?

EDWARD. Had what!

EDITH. Affairs—love affairs—before you.

EDWARD. Did you?

EDITH. Hundreds.

EDWARD. Liar!

EDITH. I rather wish I had, really. Perhaps I should have learnt some tricks

344

to hold you with when you begin to get tired of me.

EDWARD. I never shall, tricks or no tricks.

EDITH. Yes, you will one day. You're bound to; people always do. This complete loveliness that we feel together now will fade, so many years and the gilt wears off the gingerbread, and just the same as the stewards, we shall have forgotten what it was like.

EDWARD (seriously). Answer me one thing, truly, dearest. Have you ever seen gingerbread with gilt on it?

EDITH. Never!

EDWARD. Then the whole argument is disposed of. Anyhow, look at father and mother; they're perfectly happy and devoted, and they always have been.

EDITH. They had a better chance at the beginning. Things weren't changing so swiftly; life wasn't so restless.

EDWARD. How long do you give us?

EDITH. I don't know—and Edward— (she turns to him) I don't care. This is our moment—complete and heavenly. I'm not afraid of anything. This is our own, for ever. EDWARD takes EDITH in his arms; kisses her.

EDWARD. Do you think a nice warming glass of sherry would make it any more heavenly?

EDITH. You have no soul, darling, but I'm very attached to you. Come on— EDITH takes up her cloak which has been hanging over the rail, and they walk away. The cloak has been covering a life-belt, and when it is withdrawn the words "S. S. Titanic" can be seen in black letters on the white.

The lights fade into complete darkness, but the letters remain glowing as The orchestra plays very softly and tragically "Nearer My God to Thee."

❧ ❧ ❧

SHIPS THAT LIFT TALL SPIRES OF CANVAS
By RALPH D. PAINE

STEAM has not banished from the deep sea the ships that lift tall spires of canvas to win their way from port to port. The gleam of their topsails recalls the centuries in which men wrought with stubborn courage to fashion fabrics of wood and cordage that would survive the enmity of the implacable ocean and make the winds obedient. Their genius was unsung, their hard toil forgotten, but with each generation the sailing ship became nobler and more enduring, until it was a perfect thing. Its great days live in memory with a peculiar atmosphere of romance. Its humming shrouds were vibrant with the eternal call of the sea, and in a phantom fleet pass the towering East Indiaman, the hard driven Atlantic packet and the gracious clipper that fled before the Southern trades.

A hundred years ago every bay and inlet of the New England coast were building ships that fared bravely forth to the West Indies, to the roadsteads of Europe, to the mysterious havens of the Far East. They sailed in peril of pirate and privateer, and fought these rascals as sturdily as they battled with wicked weather. Coasts were unlighted, the seas uncharted, and navigation was mostly guesswork, but these seamen were the flower of an American merchant marine whose deeds are heroic in the nation's story. Great hearts in little ships, they dared and suffered with simple, uncomplaining fortitude. Shipwreck was an incident, and to be adrift in lonely seas or cast upon a barbarous shore was sadly commonplace. They lived the stuff that made fiction after they were gone.

GROWING OLD
KARLE WILSON BAKER

Let me grow lovely, growing old—
  So many fine things do;
Laces and ivory, and gold,
  And silks need not be new;

And there is healing in old trees,
  Old streets a glamour hold;
Why may not I, as well as these,
  Grow lovely, growing old?

From *FREE LANCE*
By E. ALEXANDER POWELL

PERHAPS I am more susceptible than most to the effect of perfumes . . . I do not know. But the scent of roses brings back with overwhelming vividness the loveliness of an Indian rose-garden where I wandered with Her in the fragrance and the moonlight, long, oh, long ago. The redolence of cedar and I see in my mind's eye a carpenter's shop which I passed daily when I lived in Syria, with the white-turbaned patriarch working at his bench amid a litter of shavings, while camels, laden with logs from the Cedars of Lebanon, knelt patiently at the door. Ylang-ylang translates me to a mission-station in Madagascar and I hear the sonorous chanting of the Pères Blancs in their snowy robes. Sandalwood conjures up a vision of Eastern temples, with shafts of sunlight striking through the murky interiors to be reflected by brazen Buddhas; of twilight on the Ganges at Benares; of the pink palaces and towers of Jaipur. Geranium, heliotrope, lemon verbena, lavender—these show me again the stately, white-pillared house in which I was born, with my grandmother bending lovingly over the flowers in her old-fashioned garden, the stretches of close-cropped greensward, the leaves of the venerable elms whispering in the summer breeze. . . .

NIGHT
SARA TEASDALE

Stars over snow,
  And in the west a planet
Swinging below a star—
  Look for a lovely thing and you will
    find it,
It is not far—
It never will be far.

WHAT I WOULD DO

IF I WERE as young in years again as I still am inside, I should make me a list of a few things to do before I die:

To go at least once clear around this jolly world.

To live with savages and in jungles now and then and learn how splendid they are.

To ride and read and shoot and play and study and think and be silent with such enthusiasm that every moment of unnecessary sleep would be a crime.

To live so fully that most people would seem dead on their feet.

To own a magnificent telescope and by frequent use never to forget the humor of my size and place and ambitions in the universe.

Finally, do the things all over again, for I have done them and am still at it, and I know.

For just this once I have broken my motto of "Don't tell." And now forget everything that I have said and live your own life.

—Will Beebe

A PRAYER
ANONYMOUS

LORD, support us all the day long of this troublous life, until the shadows lengthen and the evening comes and the busy world is hushed and the fever of life is over and our work is done. Then, of Thy great mercy grant us a safe lodging, and holy rest, and peace at the last, through Jesus Christ. Amen.

ET IN ARCADIA EGO*

By KATHERINE MANSFIELD

To SIT in front of the little wood fire, your hands crossed in your lap and your eyes closed—to fancy you see again upon your eyelids all the dancing beauty of the day, to feel the flame on your throat as you used to imagine you felt the spot of yellow when Bogey held a buttercup under your chin . . . when breathing is such delight that you are almost afraid to breathe—as though a butterfly fanned its wings upon your breast. Still to taste the warm sunlight that melted in your mouth; still to smell the white waxy scent that lay upon the jonquil fields and the wild spicy scent of the rosemary growing in little tufts among the red rocks close to the brim of the sea. . . .

The moon is rising but the reluctant day lingers upon the sea and sky. The sea is dabbled with a pink the colour of unripe cherries, and in the sky there is a flying yellow light like the wings of canaries. Very stubborn and solid are the trunks of the palm trees. Springing from their tops the stiff green bouquets seem to cut into the evening air and among them, the blue gum trees, tall and slender with sickle-shaped leaves and drooping branches half blue, half violet. The moon is just over the mountain behind the village. The dogs know she is there; already they begin to howl and bark. The fishermen are shouting and whistling to one another as they bring in their boats, some young boys are singing in half-broken voices down by the shore, and there is a noise of children crying, little children with burnt cheeks and sand between their toes being carried to bed. . . .

I am tired, blissfully tired. Do you suppose that daisies feel blissfully tired when they shut for the night and the dews descend upon them?

THE GREAT UNIVERSE

By EDWIN B. FROST

DO YOU know that your bodies are made of some of the same substances that are found in the sun and the other stars? You are a sample of the great Universe. So do not let little things trouble you but think and act as if you were a part of a bigger world than the little earth upon which you live.

I LOVE ALL BEAUTEOUS THINGS

ROBERT BRIDGES

I love all beauteous things,
  I seek and adore them;
God hath no better praise,
And man in his hasty days
  Is honoured for them.

I too will something make
  And joy in the making;
Although to-morrow it seem
Like the empty words of a dream
  Remembered on waking.

I LOVE YOU

I LOVE YOU for what you are, but I love you yet more for what you are going to be.

I love you not so much for your realities as for your ideals. I pray for your desires that they may be great, rather than for your satisfactions, which may be so hazardously little.

A satisfied flower is one whose petals are about to fall. The most beautiful rose is one hardly more than a bud wherein the pangs and ecstacies of desire are working for larger and finer growth.

Not always shall you be what you are now.

You are going forward toward something great. I am on the way with you and therefore I love you.

—Carl Sandburg

*Reprinted from the *Journal of Katherine Mansfield* by Katherine Mansfield, by permission of ALFRED A. KNOPF, INC. Copyright 1927 by Alfred A. Knopf, Inc.

From *NOTES ON BERMUDA*

By Christopher Morley

WHEN Will Beebe drops the ladder over the launch's side and puts a diver's helmet on you, his only instruction is, "Keep your head upright." He adds casually, "Oh, the sharks round here won't bother you." It suddenly occurs to you that there are several questions you want to ask, but now the helmet is on and it is too heavy to lift off yourself. They are leaning over the boat's side and practically shoving you down. You descend, surprised at yourself; the weight of the helmet on your shoulders vanishes like magic. Through the glass window you see the dark bottom of the launch poised above you in a great glow of pale water. This new world is so fascinating there isn't the slightest sense of anxiety. But you are under water and unconsciously you are holding your breath. You hear the pump clicking evenly and suddenly you realize the air in the helmet is getting tight. So you take your breath in sudden gulps and swallows, when you happen to remember it. Each time you exhale there is a delicious gargling sound, and you feel a big clot of air slide over your shoulder and go bubbling upward. It is somehow reassuring.

Now you are on the clean sandy floor. The little striped fish they call sergeant-majors are shoaling about; you see the black line of your air-pipe reaching up to the ceiling of this great cloudy hall. And the immediate surprise is that you cannot move. In that warm, heavy element you are like a fly in syrup. Your feet seem glued to the bottom. At first you proceed by swimming motions with the arms. Then gradually you learn the trick of bending forward until the weight of the helmet overbalances you and your feet follow. So you walk as though leaning against heavy wind.

The launch is moored to the projecting sternpost of an old sunken wreck. Her hull is crusted thick with corals and waving growths, all in a shimmer of amber and pale lime-green. Fish twirl about you like birds; clumsily you try to catch one in your hand, they vanish and return again. Above you a jellyfish is floating, and inside his transparent cavity a small fish is luxuriously loitering, like a goldfish in a private travelling bowl. At your feet a magenta fan-coral sways softly in the tide. You stoop to pick it: the helmet tilts on your shoulders and a rush of water pours in around your face. This is the end, you think; but even as you think it you have straightened up again and the water recedes. The armored headpiece is not sealed around your shoulders: only the air pressure keeps the water out. Groping in the tangle of stony growths on the wreck, little hands and twigs of brown coral, you realize with amazement that you are perfectly comfortable. You would gladly spend an hour. But another guest is also waiting for his first descent. Reluctantly you follow your hose back to the ladder. Most pleasing of all is to walk about on the white floor in a glimmer of sandy and pearly colors—very like the lighting effect of a New York railway station at night—and see overhead the dark shape of the boat, like a small whale.

* * *

Even more thrilling, now that the first trial had enlarged confidence, was to go down again at the Bermuda Aquarium. . . . Here the rocks slope inward under water, there is a coral cavern of jagged ledges and crevices and a whole jungle of marine underbrush. When you gain the shadow of the cave the sunlight outside is like a golden curtain wavering in the glassy flow. Colors and graces the eye almost refuses to credit are thick about you: anemones and lichens, queer flowers of rubbery substance, some as blue as bunches of violets. It is like a liquid greenhouse of plants cut out of sponge and spaghetti. Pink, orange, salmon, lilac, they sway in the eddy; when you touch them, a whole foliage of tubes and blossoms suddenly retracts or snaps shut. These flowers are alert with crude and stinging life. A passion of unbelief fills the immigrant behind his glass window: he wants to reach and touch, sprawls on his knees over misjudged ledges, knifes his fingers breaking off twigs and fringes of coral. The cavern, looming up like a rock-garden, deepens into dark liquid fissures of terrifying loveliness. . . .

There is no thrill like it, and it is completely indescribable. . . .

It is the greatest adventure Bermuda offers: an entree to the most authentic Garden of Eden any of us is likely to see. . . .

❧ ❧ ❧

AS DOWN IN THE SUNLESS RETREATS
THOMAS MOORE

As down in the sunless retreats of the ocean
    Sweet flowers are springing no mortal can see,
So deep in my soul the still prayer of devotion,
    Unheard by the world, rises silent to Thee.

As still to the star of its worship, though clouded,
    The needle points faithfully o'er the dim sea,
So dark when I roam in this wintry world shrouded,
    The hope of my spirit turns trembling to Thee.

PSALM 46—THE BIBLE

GOD IS our refuge and strength, a very present help in trouble.

Therefore will not we fear, though the earth be removed, and though the mountains be carried into the midst of the sea;

Though the waters thereof roar and be troubled, though the mountains shake with the swelling thereof. Selah.

There is a river, the streams whereof shall make glad the city of God, the holy place of the tabernacles of the most High.

God is in the midst of her; she shall not be moved: God shall help her, and that right early.

The heathen raged, the kingdoms were moved: he uttered his voice, the earth melted.

The Lord of hosts is with us; the God of Jacob is our refuge.

Come, behold the works of the Lord, what desolations he hath made in the earth.

He maketh wars to cease unto the end of the earth; he breaketh the bow, and cutteth the spear in sunder; he burneth the chariot in the fire.

Be still, and know that I am God: I will be exalted among the heathen, I will be exalted in the earth.

The Lord of hosts is with us; the God of Jacob is our refuge.

HE IS TRUE to God who's true to man.—*Lowell*

ONLY ONE THING is necessary; to possess God.—*Amiel*

LIVE PURE, speak true, right the wrong, follow the King—else
wherefore born?—*Tennyson*

I REMEMBER my mother's prayers and they have always followed me.
They have clung to me all my life.—*Lincoln*

FEAR knocked at the door. Faith answered. No one was there.
—*Old English Legend*

PRAYER FOR worldly goods is worse than fruitless, but prayer for strength of
soul is that passion of the soul which catches the gift it seeks.—*Meredith*

CONVICTION BRINGS a silent, indefinable beauty into faces made of the com-
monest human clay; the devout worshiper at any shrine reflects something of
its golden glow, even as the glory of a noble love shines like a sort of light
from a woman's face.—*Balzac*

SUCH was the rule of life! I worked my best, subject to ultimate judgment,
God's, not man's.—*Browning*

THE ONLY RELIGION that will do anything toward enriching your life is the
religion which inspires you to do something toward enriching the life of
others.—*Anonymous*

WHAT WE MUST DO, let us love to do. Never lose an opportunity to
see anything beautiful. Beauty is God's handwriting.—*Kingsley*

IN THE FACES of men and women I see God.—*Whitman*

ONE LIFE,—a little gleam of time between two
Eternities.—*Carlyle*

MIND OF MAN

ALL SERVICE ranks the same with God.—*Browning*

SURELY God endures forever.—*Lowell*

ART IS the gift of God, and must be used unto His glory. That in art is highest which aims at this.—*Michelangelo*

THESE BE OUR PRAYERS—more strength, more light, more constancy, more progress.—*Phillips Brooks*

IF YOU MEAN to act nobly and seek to know the best things God has put within reach of men, you must learn to fix your mind on that end, and not on what will happen to you because of it.—*George Eliot*

AND LET EACH TRY, by great thoughts and good deeds to show the most of Heaven he hath in him.—*Bailey*

ALTHOUGH THOU ART not able to see the mind of man as thou seest not God, yet, so thou recognizist God from his works, so thou must acknowledge the divine power of the mind from its powers of invention, and the desire it has for the beautiful.—*Cicero*

WHILE RIVERS RUN into the sea, while on the mountains shadows move over the slopes, while heaven feeds the stars, ever shall thy honour, thy name, and thy praises endure.—*Virgil*

GOD REVEALS Himself unfailingly to the thoughtful seeker.—*Balzac*

WHATEVER makes men good Christians, makes them good citizens.—*Webster*

ALL GREAT ART is the expression of man's delight in God's work, not his own.—*Ruskin*

351

* * *

From *THE CHOIR INVISIBLE*
GEORGE ELIOT

O may I join the choir invisible
Of those immortal dead who live again
In minds made better by their presence: live
In pulses stirred to generosity,
In deeds of daring rectitude, in scorn
For miserable aims that end with self,
In thoughts sublime that pierce the night like stars,
And with their mild persistence urge man's search
To vaster issues.

So to live is Heaven;
To make undying music in the world!

From *THE INDIAN SUMMER OF A FORSYTE*
[On the Death of an Old Man]
By JOHN GALSWORTHY

IT WAS quite shady under the tree; the sun could not get at him, only make the rest of the world bright so that he could see the Grand Stand at Epsom away out there, very far, and the cows cropping the clover in the field and swishing at the flies with their tails. He smelled the scent of limes, and lavender. Ah! that was why there was such a racket of bees. They were excited—busy, as his heart was busy and excited. Drowsy, too, drowsy and drugged on honey and happiness; as his heart was drugged and drowsy. Summer —summer—they seemed saying; great bees and little bees, and the flies too!

The stable clock struck four; in half an hour she would be here. He would have just one tiny nap, because he had had so little sleep of late; and then he would be fresh for her, fresh for youth and beauty, coming towards him across the sunlit lawn—lady in grey! And settling back in his chair he closed his eyes. Some thistledown came on what little air there was, and pitched on his moustache more white than itself. He did not know; but his breathing stirred it, caught there. A ray of sunlight struck through and lodged on his boot. A bumble-bee alighted and strolled on the crown of his Panama hat. And the delicious surge of slumber reached the brain beneath that hat, and the head swayed forward and rested on his breast. Summer—summer! So went the hum.

The stable clock struck the quarter past. The dog Balthasar stretched and looked up at his master. The thistledown no longer moved. The dog placed his chin over the sunlit foot. It did not stir. The dog withdrew his chin, quickly, rose, and leaped on old Jolyon's lap, looked in his face, whined; then, leaping down, sat on his haunches, gazing up. And suddenly he uttered a long, long howl.

But the thistledown was still as death, and the face of his old master.

Summer — summer — summer! The soundless footsteps on the grass!

* * *

LE SPECTRE DE LA ROSE
[The Story of the Ballet]
By Cyril W. Beaumont

Scene. *A young girl's bedroom. The room, octagonal in shape, is pure white, except where the walls are covered with a deep blue paper on which stands out, in sharp relief, a simple floral design, also in white. Between the two windows is placed a sofa covered in blue and white chintz, at the side of which is a round table, on which stands a bowl of roses. To the right, situated in an alcove, is a small wooden bed, the sheets of which are thrown back as if awaiting to enfold their dainty mistress. At the foot is a comfortable leather armchair and her sketching easel. On the left side is her dressing-table with looking-glass and powder-puff carefully arranged. Everything indicates the neatness and simplicity of the owner. In the left and right back corners are tall French windows thrown wide open to reveal a garden with high clusters of rosebushes almost covered with pink and red blossoms. Overhead can be seen the warm blue sky of a summer's evening, and through the open window streams the moonlight, flecking the floor with bright patches of green and yellow.*

From the garden comes a gentle breeze laden with the fragrance of roses, and into the room steps a young girl, sweet and demure in her high-cut ball-dress of creamy white, over which is lightly fastened a little cloak. In her hand she gently holds a rose, fearful lest her tiny fingers should crumple its fragile beauty. She raises it to her lips and imprints on it a loving kiss. What tender secrets does it hold, this lover's gift? She gazes upon it with downcast eyes. Surely it is not wrong to be loved? Her lips quiver and seem to murmur his name. She glances around the room, so friendly, so dear to her, with all its innocent treasures. Now that her face is upraised how tired she looks. Perhaps, little accustomed to wordly pleasures, the excitement of the ball has proved too great for her. She throws off her wrap and walks slowly to her arm-chair. She sinks into it with a sigh of content, her eyes close and in a few moments she is fast asleep. Her limp hands fall and through her fingers the rose slips, caresses her dress, and glides to the floor.

The music quickens to a rapturous movement and through the open window alights the object of her dream, the spirit of the rose. With what joy, with what abandon, does he dance, blown hither and thither like a rose petal in the wind.

At his magic touch she is spirited out of her chair to join him in the ever-quickening, soothing melody of the waltz. How high she leaps, yet so gracefully that it seems as if she, too, had forsaken her mortal body. Together they float through the still air, impelled everywhere by the fairy-like touch of his hand. Then the music slowly dies away and ceases. A moment and she is again in her chair, her features still calm in repose, unruffled, as if what has just transpired was but an elfin touch of our imagination. Bending over her for a brief instant, the rose-coloured sprite disappears through the open window just as the first rays of dawn trace curious shadows on the wall.

The maiden stirs, and, smoothing her sleep-laden eyes, looks about her as if what was in truth but a dream were reality. The room is empty. Still doubting, she bends and picks up her precious rose. Then she remembers, her face lights up in a sad half-smile, and as she presses the rose to her bosom the curtain falls.

THE CAVE OF SLEEP
EDMUND SPENSER

He, making speedy way through
    spersed ayre,
And through the world of waters wide
    and deepe,
To Morpheus house doth hastily
    repaire,
Amid the bowels of the earth full
    steepe,
And low, where dawning day doth
    never peepe,
His dwelling is; there Tethys his wet
    bed
Doth ever wash, and Cynthia still
    doth steepe
In silver deaw, his ever-drouping
    head,
Whiles sad Night over him her mantle
    black doth spread.

And, more, to lulle him in his
    slumber soft,
A tricking streame from high rock
    tumbling downe,
And ever-drizling raine upon the loft,
Mixt with a murmuring winde, much
    like the sowne
Of swarming bees, did cast him in a
    swone.
No other noyse, nor peoples troublous
    cryes,
As still are wont t'annoy the walled
    towne,
Might there be heard; but carelesse
    Quiet lyes
Wrapt in eternale silence, farre from
    enimyes.
—From *The Faerie Queene*

AD DOMNULAM SUAM
ERNEST DOWSON

Little lady of my heart!
    Just a little longer,
Love me: we will pass and part,
    Ere this love grow stronger.

I have loved thee, Child! too well,
    To do aught but leave thee:
Nay! my lips should never tell
    Any tale, to grieve thee.

Little lady of my heart!
    Just a little longer,
I may love thee: we will part,
    Ere my love grow stronger.

Soon thou leavest fairy-land;
    Darker grow thy tresses:
Soon no more of hand in hand;
    Soon no more caresses!

Little lady of my heart!
    Just a little longer,
Be a child: then, we will part,
    Ere this love grow stronger.

THE RIVER, ON . . .
ROBERT LOUIS STEVENSON

The river, on from mill to mill,
Flows past our childhood's garden still:
But, ah! we children never more
Shall watch it from the water-door!
Below the yew it still is there—
Our phantom voices haunt the air
As we were still at play,
And I can hear them call and say:
    "How far is it to Babylon?"

Ah, far enough, my dear,
Far, far enough from here—
Yet you have farther gone!
    "Can I get there by candlelight?"
So goes the old refrain.
I do not know—perchance you might—
But only children hear it right.
Ah! never to return again!
The eternal dawn beyond a doubt,
Shall break on hill and plain,
And put all stars and candles out,
Ere we be young again.

ORPHEUS WITH HIS LUTE

WILLIAM SHAKESPEARE

Orpheus with his lute made trees,
And the mountain tops that freeze,
  Bow themselves when he did sing:
To his music, plants and flowers
Ever sprung; as sun and showers
  There had made a lasting spring.

Everything that heard him play,
Even the billows of the sea,
  Hung their heads, and then lay by.
In sweet music is such art,
Killing care and grief of heart
  Fall asleep, or, hearing, die.

THE VILLAGE DANCE

[*Translated from Medieval Students' Songs*]

JOHN ADDINGTON SYMONDS

Wide the lime-tree to the air
Spreads her boughs and foliage fair;
  Thyme beneath is growing
On the verdant meadow where
  Dancers' feet are going.

Through the grass a little spring
Runs with jocund murmuring;
  All the place rejoices;
Cooling zephyrs breathe and sing
  With their summer voices.

INVITATION TO THE DANCE

[*Translated from
Medieval Latin Students' Songs*]

JOHN ADDINGTON SYMONDS

Cast aside dull books and thought;
  Sweet is folly, sweet is play:
Take the pleasure Spring hath brought
  In youth's opening holiday!
Right it is old age should ponder
  On grave matters fraught with care;
Tender youth is free to wander,
  Free to frolic light as air.
    Like a dream our prime is flown,
    Prisoned in a study:
    Sport and folly are youth's own,
    Tender youth and ruddy.

Lo, the Spring of life slips by,
  Frozen Winter comes apace;
Strength is 'minished silently,
  Care writes wrinkles on our face:
Blood dries up and courage fails us,
  Pleasures dwindle, joys decrease,
Till old age at length assails us
  With his troop of illnesses.
    Like a dream our prime is flown,
    Prisoned in a study;
    Sport and folly are youth's own,
    Tender youth and ruddy.

Live we like the gods above:
  This is wisdom, this is truth:
Chase the joys of tender love
  In the leisure of our youth!
Keep the vows we swore together,
  Lads, obey that ordinance;
Seek the fields in sunny weather,
  Where the laughing maidens dance,
    Like a dream our prime is flown,
    Prisoned in a study;
    Sport and folly are youth's own,
    Tender youth and ruddy.

There the lad who lists may see
  Which among the maids is kind:
There young limbs deliciously
  Flashing through the dances wind:
While the girls their arms are raising,
  Moving, winding over the lea,
Still I stand and gaze, and gazing
  They have stolen the soul of me!
    Like a dream our prime is flown,
    Prisoned in a study;
    Sport and folly are youth's own,
    Tender youth and ruddy.

ROBERT LOUIS STEVENSON GIVES AWAY
HIS BIRTHDAY

A little girl who regretted that her birthday came on Christmas Day received word from a friend that he would give her his birthday, which occurred in November. Her friend was Robert Louis Stevenson, and these were the documents in the case.

I, Robert Louis Stevenson, Advocate of the Scots Bar, author of *The Master of Ballantrae* and *Moral Emblems*, stuck civil engineer, sole owner and patentee of the Palace and Plantation known as Vailima in the island of Upolu, Samoa, a British Subject, being in sound mind, and pretty well, I thank you, in body:

In consideration that Miss Annie H. Ide, daughter of H. C. Ide, in the town of Saint Johnsbury, in the county of Caledonia, in the State of Vermont, United States of America, was born, out of all reason, upon Christmas Day, and is therefore out of all justice denied the consolation and profit of a proper birthday;

And considering that I, the said Robert Louis Stevenson, have attained an age when we never mention it, and that I have now no further use for a birthday of any description;

And in consideration that I have met H. C. Ide, the father of the said Annie H. Ide, and found him about as white a land commissioner as I require:

Have transferred, and *do hereby transfer,* to the said Annie H. Ide, *all and whole* my rights and privileges in the thirteenth day of November, formerly my birthday, now, hereby, and henceforth, the birthday of the said Annie H. Ide, to have, hold, exercise, and enjoy the same in the customary manner, by the sporting of fine raiment, eating of rich meals, and receipt of gifts, compliments, and copies of verse, according to the manner of our ancestors;

And I direct the said Annie H. Ide to add to the said name of Annie H. Ide the name Louisa—at least in private; and I charge her to use my said birthday with moderation and humanity, *et tamquam bona filia familiae,* the said birthday not being so young as it once was, and having carried me in a very satisfactory manner since I can remember;

And in case the said Annie H. Ide shall neglect or contravene either of the above conditions, I hereby revoke the donation and transfer my rights in the said birthday to the President of the United States of America for the time being:

In witness whereof I have set my hand and seal this nineteenth day of June in the year of grace eighteen hundred and ninety-one.

          Robert Louis Stevenson
   (Seal)
Witness, Lloyd Osbourne
Witness, Harold Watts

Several months passed before a reply from the little girl reached him at his South Seas home. He wrote back:

Vailima, Samoa, November 1891
My dear Louisa,—

Your picture of the church, the photograph of yourself and your sister, and your very witty and pleasing letter, came all in a bundle, and made me feel I had my money's worth for that birthday. I am now, I must be, one of your nearest relatives; exactly what we are to each other, I do not know; I doubt if the case has ever happened before—your papa ought to know, and I don't believe he does; but I think I ought to call you in the meanwhile, and until we get the advice of counsel learned in the law, my name-daughter. Well, I was extremely pleased to see by the

356

church that my name-daughter could draw; by the letter, that she was no fool; and by the photograph, that she was a pretty girl, which hurts nothing. See how virtues are rewarded; My first idea of adopting you was entirely charitable; and here I find that I am quite proud of it, and of you, and that I chose just the kind of name-daughter I wanted. For I can draw too, or rather I mean to say I could before I forgot how; and I am very far from being a fool myself, however much I may look it; and I am as beautiful as the day, or at least I once hoped that perhaps I might be going to be. And so I might. So that you see we are well met, and peers on these important points. I am very glad, also, that you are older than your sister; so should I have been, if I had had one. So that the number of points and virtues which you have inherited from your name-father is already surprising.

I wish you would tell your father—not that I like to encourage my rival—that we have had a wonderful time here of late, and that they are having a cold day on Mulinuu, and the consuls are writing reports, and I am writing to the *Times,* and if we don't get rid of our friends this time I shall begin to despair of everything but my name-daughter.

You are quite wrong as to the effect of the birthday on your age. From the moment the deed was registered (as it was in the public press, with every solemnity), the 13th of November became your own *and only* birthday, and you ceased to have been born on Christmas Day. Ask your father; I am sure he will tell you this is sound law. You are thus become a month and twelve days younger than you were, but will go on growing older for the future in the regular and human manner, from one 13th November to the next. The effect on me is more doubtful; I may, as you suggest, live forever; I might, on the other hand, come to pieces, like the one-horse shay, at a moment's notice; doubtless the step was risky, but I do not the least regret that which enables me to sign myself your revered and delighted name-father,   Robert Louis Stevenson

NOVEMBER NIGHT*
ADELAIDE CRAPSEY

Listen. . . .
With faint dry sound
Like steps of passing ghosts,
The leaves, frost-crisped, break from
    the trees
And fall.

GROW OLD ALONG WITH ME!
ROBERT BROWNING

Grow old along with me!
The best is yet to be;
The last of life, for which the first was
    made;
Our times are in his hand who saith,
    "A whole I planned,
Youth shows but half; trust God: See
    all, nor be afraid!"
—From *Rabbi Ben Ezra*

EVENSONG
ROBERT LOUIS STEVENSON

The embers of the day are red
Beyond the murky hill.
The kitchen smokes; the bed
In the darkling house is spread:
The great sky darkens overhead,
And the great woods are shrill.
So far have I been lead,
Lord, by Thy will:
So far I have followed, Lord, and won-
    dered still.
The breeze from the embalmed land
Blows sudden towards the shore,
And claps my cottage door.
I hear the signal, Lord—I understand.
The night at Thy command
Comes. I will eat and sleep and will not
    question more.

*Reprinted from *Verse* by Adelaide Crapsey, by permission of ALFRED A. KNOPF, INC. Copyright 1915, 1922, by Algernon S. Crapsey.

AUTUMN

By Roger Wray

Spring is a serenade, but autumn is a nocturne. In the waning of the year, the world is full of sombre solemnity and a pathetic sense of old age. I have gleaned this information by reading poems on the subject.

The melancholy days are come, the saddest of the year,
Of wailing winds, and naked woods, and meadows brown and sere.

So begins the dirge of William Cullen Bryant.

Yes, the year is growing old,
And his eye is pale and bleared.

This is from Longfellow, and the poet proceeds to compare autumn to the insane old King Lear. Wordsworth speaks of the "pensive" beauty of autumn, but to Shelley—

The year
On the earth, her deathbed, in a shroud of leaves dead
Is lying.

And Hood's admirable little poem ends—

But here the autumn melancholy dwells,
And sighs her tearful spells,
Among the sunless shadows of the plain.

All of which is most impressive; and reading it to an accompaniment of minor music, rendered by wind-demons in the key-hole, it convinced me absolutely. Accordingly, when I went a long ramble through the countryside this morning I was fully prepared to observe the sad tokens of Nature's senility and decay.

But a glorious surprise met me at the outset, and changed my mood from lamentation to exultation. I passed from the dismal poetic fiction to the actual glowing fact; from mournful reverie to mighty revelry. And all the predictions of the gloomy poets were scattered like the autumn leaves. For who can look at the blaze of autumn colors and declare them solemn? Who can drink deep draughts of the autumn gales and talk about senility?

Autumn is youthful, mirthful, frolicsome—the child of summer's joy—and on every side there are suggestions of juvenility and mischief. While spring is a careful artist who paints each flower with delicate workmanship, autumn flings whole pots of paint about in wildest carelessness. The crimson and scarlet colours reserved for roses and tulips are splashed on the brambles till every bush is aflame, and the old creeper-covered house blushes like a sunset.

The violet paint is smeared grotesquely on the riotous foliage; daffodil and crocus dyes are emptied over limes and chestnuts. Our eyes surfeit themselves on the gorgeous feast of colours—purple, mauve, vermilion, saffron, russet, silver, copper, bronze, and old gold. The leaves are dipped and soaked in fiery hues, and the mischievous 'artist' will never rest till he has used up every drop. Yet Shelley gazed at the pantomime-woods and declared (amid all the pomp and pageantry) that the year was on her deathbed, and this was her shroud!

Why do the poets feel that autumn is ancient? He romps over the earth, chasing the puppy-like gales, making them scamper over the mirrored pools, and ruffling their surface till the water-reeds hiss him away. He revels in boisterous gaiety, playing pranks like a schoolboy on the first day of his holidays. He turns on the raintaps to try the effect; he daubs a few toadstools blood-red; he switches on summer sunshine for an hour, and then lets loose a tempest. He torments the stately trees, tears their foliage off in handfuls, rocks them backwards and forwards till they groan, and then scampers away for a brief interval leaving heavenly peace behind him. The fallen leaves are set racing down the lane. With madcap destructiveness he wastes his own handiwork, stripping the finery from the woods and forests. The bare trees sigh and shiver, but he mocks them with howls and caterwaulings. Then he sets the bracken afire and pauses to admire the October tints. Finally, with deceptive golden sunshine, he tempts the sage out of doors, suddenly drenches him, and drives him home saturated to the skin. The sage thereupon changes his raiment, and murmurs about the solemnity of the dying year and the pensive beauties of autumn!

The whole spirit of autumn is frolicsome and changeful as that of an eager child. The 'solemn tints' are the grotesque hues of the harlequin, and the 'mournful winds' are suggestive of young giants playing leapfrog over the tree-tops. The lengthening period of darkness is a reminder of the long sleep of a healthy child, and when the sun awakes each autumn morning he rubs his misty eyes and wonders what antics he will see before bed-time.

Spring is a lovely maiden; Summer a radiant bride; but Autumn is a tomboy whose occasional quietness is more alarming than his noisiest escapades.

WHAT IS A MAN PROFITED?
By WILLIAM ALLEN WHITE

THE OTHER DAY in Emporia, the longest funeral procession that has formed in ten years followed the Rev. John Jones three long miles in the hot July sun out to Dry Creek Cemetery. Now, a funeral procession may mean little or much. When a rich and powerful man dies, the people play politics and attend his funeral for various reasons. But here was the body of a meek, gentle little old man—a man "without purse or scrip." It won't take twenty minutes to settle his estate in probate court. He was a preacher of the gospel—but preachers have been buried before this in Emporia without much show of sorrow.

The reason so many people lined up behind the hearse that held the kind old man's mortality was simple: they loved him. He devoted his life to helping people. In a very simple way, without money or worldly power, he gave of the gentleness of his heart to all around him. We are apt to say that money talks, but it speaks a broken, poverty-stricken language. Hearts talk better, clearer, and with a wider intelligence. This old man with the soft voice and the kindly manners knew the language of the heart and he spoke it where it would give zest to joy. He worked manfully and with a will in his section of the vineyard, and against odds and discouragements he won time and again. He was infinitely patient and brave. He held a simple, old-fashioned faith in God and his loving kindness.

When others gave money—which was of their store—he gave prayers and hard work and an inspiring courage. He helped. In his sphere he was a power. And so when he lay down to sleep hundreds of friends trudged out to bid him good-by with moist eyes and with cramped throats to wish him slumber.

And then they turned back to the world to make money—to make money —what a hollow impotent thing! What is a man profited if he gain the whole world and lose his own soul?

YOUTH, DAY, OLD AGE AND NIGHT
WALT WHITMAN

Youth, large, lusty, loving—youth full of grace,
    force, fascination,
Do you know that Old Age may come after you with
    equal grace, force, fascination?

Day full-blown and splendid—day of the immense
    sun, action, ambition, laughter,
The Night follows close with millions of suns, and
    sleep and restoring darkness.

❦   ❦   ❦

Small service is true service while it lasts.
Of humblest friends, bright creature! scorn not one:
The daisy, by the shadow that it casts,
Protects the lingering dewdrop from the sun.

—Wordsworth

❦   ❦   ❦

SCOOP
By BEN HECHT

A SNOWSTORM came to town the other day and shouldered its way onto the front pages alongside the Greeks, the English, and the Rumanians. Now, it takes a powerful piece of local news to pry into the Medusa-headed company of page 1 these days. Yet there this snowstorm stood—smiling amiably away in printer's ink with no more to recommend it as journalism than that it was very white and fluttering and would call for some shoveling.

Certain of the gazettes tried to inject a bit of false excitement into this most innocuous of events by referring to it as a blizzard. There appeared in several of the reports a sort of bravado that reminded me of the editor in the Bret Harte story. This editor ran a newspaper in one of the boom towns of the old West. During a flood that threatened to wipe his Leadville off the map, he announced in his columns with pensive pride that "an area greater than the State of Rhode Island is now under water."

In the case of our snowstorm the bravado was a little feigned. It was no blizzard and was never going to be; it froze nobody, wrecked nothing, inconvenienced only a few drunks and old ladies, and fluttered to a close as harmlessly as a white fan in a damsel's hand.

Yet it was news. A sort of cryptic and tongue-tied account of Nature's visit appeared under headlines almost as bold as those that revealed the massacres in Bucharest. The fact was that, though the editors of the town gave it plenty of space, they were too shy to tell the truth about it.

Even *PM*, my own fearless and bellicose alma mater, side-stepped the significance of the snowstorm. No more than any of the others did it report what 3,000,000 readers (not all its own) were thinking: that everybody (except a few preoccupied criminals and bankrupts) was looking at the falling snow full of a sense that something beautiful was happening.

You can't blame the press for this, for there is such a thing as journalistic tradition. As well expect the British Admiralty to describe a sunrise over Valona as to expect a story of our snowstorm to begin:

"The soul of New York was thrilled today by a lovely and capering snowfall that painted ghostly summer on the trees of Central Park and brought to the harried citizens of the town a few hours of aesthetic exaltation superior to anything the stage or screen has offered this season."

Yet this is why the snow was news. This is actually what happened. The town looked up and saw Pavlova in the air, saw Cellini at work, and consorted with seraphs. A literary shyness kept the reportorial pens scratching away at weather bureau statistics, and half-hearted hints of troubles here and there.

Yes, I am sure countless readers looked in vain for the truth of what they had seen and experienced—the white capes on the electric signs, the busy snow-covered streets become suddenly haunted with long-ago village memories, the familiar and the commonplace taking on rakish fairy-tale contours.

Perhaps the memories were the real news. For of all pleasant events of the past, a snowstorm is about the only thing that hasn't changed. No new meanings have come into the flakes. They have not been harnessed for progress or conquest. They have remained an unaltered souvenir of happier days. And so when the snow came down, people drifted with it into the past, smelled again the freshness of young and untroubled times.

There were also the policemen in their rubber Invernesses looking like child drawings, and the buildings swaying behind white veils like a flock of Albertina Rasch girls. There were Moorish roof-tops where only factory chimneys had been before, and there were muted avenues, muted avenues that seemed to be sleep-walking and full of dreams.

And the readers themselves, walking behind the quick and disappearing spaces of the snow, had a look like those jerky figures in the old silent films, and seemed launched on equally dramatic errands. The poor looked full of a poetry usually missing from their poverty, and the rich acquired a carnival air that seldom attaches to their mink coats and dashing fedoras.

Unfortunately it was not a big enough snowstorm. It was only a sonnet of a snowfall. I am sure our readers hoped for more, and dreamed of impassable roads, of gas buggies reduced to impotence, of inaccessible offices and desks, of an hour of childhood the storm would bring them if it lasted long enough to blot out the face of the boss and the war.

Come to think of it, the press was not entirely remiss in its coverage. To some extent the camera boys told the story that the editors blushed to put into type. The readers were treated to a sort of art exhibit view of the town. Photographs of snow scenes, of rows of white-haloed lampposts, of bushes looking like lace fountains, of children on sleds, of snowmen, and even of Jack Frost himself, filled the columns.

Perhaps the next time it snows Mr. Roosevelt will lend our old poet laureate, Archibald MacLeish, to the Associated Press to cover it, and our 3,000,000 readers will not have to rely on this sort of unmetrical account of what happened.

THE WORTH OF BEAUTY
By JAMES C. DERIEUX

THERE IS NOT anywhere, so far as I can learn, a monument to the Rev. John Grimké-Drayton. Yet Mr. Drayton did one of the remarkable bits of work that has been done in this world. About his country home, Magnolia Gardens, near Charleston, S. C., he brought into being such beauty as perhaps no other individual in America has been able to achieve.

Each spring thousands of persons travel hundreds of miles to see the work of this modest clergyman. In a prewar edition of his famous travel guide, Baedeker marked but three places in the United States with the double star: the Grand Canyon, Niagara Falls and Mr. Drayton's garden.

Said John Galsworthy: "Nothing so lovely and wistful, nothing so richly colored, yet so ghostlike, exists, planted by the sons of men. Beyond anything I have ever seen, it is other-worldly. To this day I have seen no garden so beautiful as Magnolia Gardens."

I shall not even attempt to tell of the millions of azalea blooms of many hues; of the stately camellias, a single bush yielding blooms of many colors; of the white and bluish wisteria climbing to the very tops of mighty trees; the roses; the *Magnolia grandiflora;* the live oaks with their eerie draperies of gray moss; the mirroring pools. Acre after acre of rapturous beauty, changing from hour to hour as the sun's angle alters, from week to week as the season advances. There seems no end to the clergyman's desire to make manifest here on earth some hint of the heavenly glimpses that came to his heart.

Last summer an elderly woman leaving Magnolia Gardens said, "This is my fortieth visit here. I come each spring to South Carolina to see Magnolia. It restores my soul."

Another woman said to Mr. C. Norwood Hastie, present owner of the garden and grandson of Mr. Drayton: "My husband, a clergyman, was on the edge of losing his reason when he first came here. Day after day he returned. In the end, his faith returned to him, and his poise. This garden saved him, made it possible for him to continue in his pastorate."

Innumerable persons, afflicted with grief too heavy for them, go to Magnolia to find peace. A man stood looking across one of the small lakes at banks of color, at the clear reflections of that color beneath water. Softly he spoke to the woman with him.

"I know now what Heaven is like, and I am content for my child to be there."

There is no record of any person's ever having been ejected from the garden for misconduct. Rarely does one hear loud talking or noisy laughter—no more than in a cathedral. As many as 12,000 persons have entered the garden within a single day—and when night came on, no flowers were missing, no damage of any kind had been done, no litter left. Yet there never are guards on duty.

One day Mr. Hastie himself went out to gather flowers. Twenty persons started toward him. "Stop that!" they demanded. Now when he wishes flowers for his own use, he gathers them before the gates have been opened.

Many a garden within 50 miles of Magnolia has been despoiled by visitors, but there is something about Magnolia that puts thievery and all other low conduct out of one's mind. "Dis gyrden ain't fo' sin," is the way an old Negro explains it. "Gawd, He done walk here."

In the heart of every imaginative person resides a desire to be of lasting worth. But what can he do that will

362

survive him? If he has access to a bit of earth, this he can make lovely, and so add immensely to his own satisfaction with life and to the joy of others.

The village in which I live, Summerville, S. C., is one of several established by the rice planters of the early 19th century. Most of these settlements have pined away, some have disappeared, but Summerville is living merrily, though it has no industry to speak of, and is not a trading center. Why did Summerville survive? Because many years ago it had intelligence enough to prohibit the cutting of trees, and its home owners esthetic sense enough to plant wisteria, roses, tea olives, magnolias, azaleas, camellias, and innumerable other flowering trees, vines and bushes. To this day one may not cut a tree in Summerville, though it is in his own yard, without permission of the town authorities. Now the huge wisteria vines spread over the tops of tall trees, roofing the village with heavenly blueness, while the floor of the forest flames in many flower colors.

It is beauty that sustains the community, that brings to it annually hundreds of winter residents, some of whom, having traveled widely, declare it to be America's loveliest forest village.

In a Carolina valley an old woman lives in a small, unpainted house. There is no sign to tell passers-by that here he can buy eggs, butter, milk and vegetables, yet the old woman rarely can supply the demand for them.

"How do people know you have them for sale?" I asked her.

"Well, sir, mostly they don't know right off. But when they're drivin' by, they sees my flowers, and they stop. Then they come in to ask questions, and I tell 'em what I've got."

And so, with the most remarkable front yard within 20 miles as her advertisement, the old woman gets along. The beauty she developed by transplanting flowers from the mountainsides and glens and by obtaining cuttings and bulbs from friends is her sales agent. More, her yard is a contagious beauty spot. Other women are getting flowers from her, and inspiration. Her presence is transforming that whole valley into a more pleasing, more civilized place.

If we ever should attain to universal enthusiasm for beauty, many of our sorest economic problems would dissolve. We then would find more of the satisfaction in activities that are not costly. We would have a standard of living, as distinguished from the standard of spending. And that may be what we must have before we can climb toward the heights of satisfying life. On those heights dwells serenity, and serenity and beauty are sisters.

STARRY NIGHT

LOUISE AYRES GARNETT

Like snowflakes on a windowpane
the stars lie scattered on the dome,
and Mary and her child look down
at the shining speck that was their
    home.

Sweet Mary and her child look down
through a silver casement in the night.
Remembering tears are in her eyes,
he reaches out with young delight.

She leans and whispers in his ear:
"I see the town of Bethlehem,
the shepherds on the very hills
you traveled to Jerusalem.

Our God is good to let me hold
my baby still against my breast.
Oh, time is everywhere at once:
I choose the moment I love best."

The stars no longer seem like flakes:
the sky's a patterned coverlet
to tuck about the little feet
of him who is her baby yet.

TO AUTUMN
John Keats

Season of mists and mellow fruitfulness!
  Close bosom-friend of the maturing sun;
Conspiring with him how to load and bless
  With fruit the vines that round the thatch-eaves run.
To bend with apples the moss'd cottage-trees,
  And fill all fruit with ripeness to the core;
    To swell the gourd, and plump the hazel shells
With a sweet kernel; to set budding more,
And still more, later flowers for the bees,
Until they think warm days will never cease,
    For Summer has o'er-brimm'd their clammy cells.

Who hath not seen thee oft amid thy store?
  Sometimes whoever seeks abroad may find
Thee sitting careless on a granary floor,
  Thy hair soft-lifted by the winnowing wind;
Or on a half-reap'd furrow sound asleep,
  Drowsed with the fumes of poppies, while thy hook
    Spares the next swath and all its twined flowers:
And sometimes like a gleaner thou dost keep
  Steady thy laden head across a brook;
  Or by a cider-press, with patient look,
    Thou watchest the last oozings, hours by hours.

Where are the songs of Spring? Ay, where are they?
  Think not of them, thou hast thy music too,
    While barred clouds bloom the soft-dying day.
And touch the stubble-plains with rosy hue;
  Then in a wailful choir the small gnats mourn
  Among the river sallows, borne aloft
    Or sinking as the light wind lives or dies;
And full-grown lambs loud bleat from hilly bourn;
  Hedge-crickets sing; and now with treble soft
  The redbreast whistles from a garden-croft,
    And gathering swallows twitter in the skies.

* * *

❧ LET MYSTERY have its place in you; do not be always turning up your whole soil with the ploughshare of self-examination, but leave a little fallow corner in your heart ready for any seed the winds may bring, and reserve a nook of shadow for the passing bird; keep a place in your heart for the unexpected guest, an altar for the unknown God.   —*Amiel*

DOVER BEACH
MATTHEW ARNOLD

The sea is calm to-night.
The tide is full, the moon lies fair
Upon the straits;—on the French coast the light
Gleams and is gone; the cliffs of England stand,
Glimmering and vast, out in the tranquil bay.
Come to the window, sweet is the night-air!
Only, from the long line of spray
Where the sea meets the moon-blanch'd land,
Listen! you hear the grating roar
Of pebbles which the waves draw back, and fling,
At their return, up the high strand,
Begin, and cease, and then again begin,
With tremulous cadence slow, and bring
The eternal note of sadness in.

Sophocles long ago
Heard it on the Ægean, and it brought
Into his mind the turbid ebb and flow
Of human misery; we
Find also in the sound a thought,
Hearing it by this distant northern sea.

The Sea of Faith
Was once, too, at the full, and round earth's shore
Lay like the folds of a bright girdle furl'd.
But now I only hear
Its melancholy, long, withdrawing roar,
Retreating, to the breath
Of the night-wind, down the vast edges drear
And naked shingles of the world.

Ah, love, let us be true
To one another; for the world, which seems
To lie before us like a land of dreams,
So various, so beautiful, so new,
Hath really neither joy, nor love, nor light,
Nor certitude, nor peace, nor help for pain;
And we are here as on a darkling plain
Swept with confused alarms of struggle and flight,
Where ignorant armies clash by night.

VAGABOND'S HOUSE
Don Blanding

When I have a house . . . as I sometime may . . .
I'll suit my fancy in every way.
I'll fill it with things that have caught my eye
In drifting from Iceland to Molokai.
It won't be correct or in period style
But . . . oh, I've thought for a long, long while
Of all the corners and all the nooks,
Of all the bookshelves and all the books,
The great big table, the deep soft chairs
And the Chinese rug at the foot of the stairs,
(it's an old, old rug from far Chow Wan
that a Chinese princess once walked on).

My house will stand on the side of a hill
By a slow broad river, deep and still,
With a tall lone pine on guard nearby
Where the birds can sing and storm winds cry.
A flagstone walk with lazy curves
Will lead to the door where a Pan's head serves
As a knocker there like a vibrant drum
To let me know that a friend has come,
And the door will squeak as I swing it wide
To welcome you to the cheer inside.

For I'll have good friends who can sit and chat
Or simply sit, when it comes to that,
By the fireplace where the fir logs blaze
And the smoke rolls up a weaving haze.
I'll want a wood-box, scarred and rough,
For leaves and bark and odorous stuff
Like resinous knots and cones and gums
To chuck on the flames when winter comes.
And I hope a cricket will stay around
For I love its creaky lonesome sound.

There'll be driftwood powder to burn on logs
And a shaggy rug for a couple of dogs,
Boreas, winner of prize and cup,
And Micky, a loveable gutter-pup.

366

Thoroughbreds, both of them, right from the start,
One by breeding, the other by heart.

There are times when only a dog will do
For a friend . . . when you're beaten, sick and blue
And the world's all wrong, for he won't care
If you break and cry, or grouch and swear,
For he'll let you know as he licks your hands
That he's downright sorry . . . and understands.

I'll have on a bench a box inlaid
With dragon-plaques of milk-white jade
To hold my own particular brand
Of cigarettes brought from the Pharoah's land
With a cloisonne bowl on a lizard's skin
To flick my cigarette ashes in.
And a squat blue jar for a certain blend
Of pipe tobacco. I'll have to send
To a quaint old chap I chanced to meet
In his fusty shop on a London street.

A long low shelf of teak will hold
My best-loved books in leather and gold
While magazines lie on a bowlegged stand
In a polyglot mixture close at hand.
I'll have on a table a rich brocade
That I think the pyxies must have made
For the dull gold thread on blues and grays
Weaves the pattern of Puck . . the Magic Maze.
On the mantelpiece I'll have a place
For a little mud god with a painted face
That was given to me . . . oh, long ago
By a Philippine maid in Olongapo.
Then . . . just in range of a lazy reach . . .
A bulging bowl of Indian beech
Will brim with things that are good to munch,
Hickory nuts to crack and crunch,
Big fat raisins and sun-dried dates
And curious fruits from the Malay Straits,
Maple sugar and cookies brown
With good hard cider to wash them down,
Wine-sap apples, pick of the crop,

And ears of corn to shell and pop
With plenty of butter and lots of salt . . .
If you don't get filled it's not my fault.

And there where the shadows fall I've planned
To have a magnificent Concert-Grand
With polished wood and ivory keys
For wild discordant rhapsodies,
For wailing minor Hindu songs,
For Chinese chants with clanging gongs,
For flippant jazz and for lullabies
And moody things that I'll improvise
To play the long gray dusk away
And bid good-bye to another day.
Pictures . . . I think I'll have but three;
One, in oil, of a wind-swept sea
With the flying scud and the waves whipped white . . .
(I know the chap who can paint it right)
In lapis blue and a deep jade green . . .
A great big smashing fine marine
That'll make you feel the spray in your face.
I'll hang it over my fireplace. . . .
The picture I love the best of all
Will hang alone on my study wall
Where the sunset's glow and the moon's cold gleam
Will fall on the face and make it seem
That the eyes in the picture are meeting mine,
That the lips are curved in the fine sweet line
Of that wistful, tender, provocative smile
That has stirred my heart for a wondrous while.
It's a sketch of the girl who loved too well
To tie me down to that bit of Hell
That a drifter knows when he finds he's held
By the soft strong chains that passions weld.

It was best for her and for me, I know,
That she measured my love and bade me go
For we both have our great illusion yet
Unsoiled, unspoiled by a vain regret.
I won't deny that it makes me sad
To know that I've missed what I might have had.
It's a clean sweet memory, quite apart,

368

And I've been faithful . . . in my heart.
All these things I will have about,
Not a one could I do without;
Cedar and sandalwood chips to burn
In the tarnished bowl of a copper urn,
A paperweight of meteorite
That seared and scorched the sky one night,
A Moro kris . . . my paperknife . . .
Once slit the throat of a Rajah's wife.

The beams of my house will be fragrant wood
That once in a teeming jungle stood
As a proud tall tree where the leopards couched
And the parrot screamed and the black men crouched.
The roof must have a rakish dip
To shadowy eaves where the rain can drip
In a damp, persistent tuneful way;
It's a cheerful sound on a gloomy day.
And I want a shingle loose somewhere
To wail like a banshee in despair
When the wind is high and the storm-gods race
And I am snug by my fireplace.

I hope a couple of birds will nest
Around the house. I'll do my best
To make them happy, so every year
They'll raise their brood of fledglings here.
When I have my house I will suit myself
And have what I'll call my "Condiment Shelf"
Filled with all manner of herbs and spice,
Curry and chutney for meats and rice,
Pots and bottles of extracts rare . . .
Onions and garlic will both be there. . . .
And soyo and saffron and savory-goo
And stuff that I'll buy from an old Hindu,
Ginger with syrup in quaint stone jars,
Almonds and figs in tinselled bars,
Astrakhan caviar, highly prized,
And citron and orange peel crystallized,
Anchovy paste and poha jam,
Basil and chili and marjoram,
Pickles and cheeses from every land

And flavors that come from Samarkand.
And, hung with a string from a handy hook,
Will be a dog-eared, well-thumbed book
That is pasted full of recipes
From France and Spain and the Caribbees,
Roots and leaves and herbs to use
For curious soups and odd ragouts.

I'll have a cook that I'll name Oh Joy,
A sleek, fat, yellow-faced China boy
Who can roast a pig or mix a drink,
 (you can't improve on a slant-eyed Chink).
On the gray-stone hearth there'll be a mat
For a scrappy, swaggering yellow cat
With a war-scarred face from a hundred fights
With neighbors' cats on moonlight nights.
A wise old Tom who can hold his own
And make my dogs let him alone.

I'll have a window-seat broad and deep
Where I can sprawl to read or sleep,
With windows placed so I can turn
And watch the sunsets blaze and burn
Beyond high peaks that scar the sky
Like bare white wolf-fangs that defy
The very gods. I'll have a nook
For a savage idol that I took
From a ruined temple in Peru,
A demon-chaser named Mang-Chu
To guard my house by night and day
And keep all evil things away.

Pewter and bronze and hammered brass,
Old carved wood and gleaming glass,
Candles in polychrome candlesticks
And peasant lamps in floating wicks,
Dragons in silk on a Mandarin suit
In a chest that is filled with vagabond-loot.
All of the beautiful useless things
That a vagabond's aimless drifting brings.
. . . Then when my house is all complete
I'll stretch me out on the window seat

With a favorite book and a cigarette
And a long cool drink that Oh Joy will get
And I'll look about at my bachelor-nest
While the sun goes zooming down the west
And the hot gold light will fall on my face
And make me think of some heathen place
That I've failed to see ... that I've missed some way ...
A place that I'd planned to find some day,
And I'll feel the lure of it drawing me.
Oh damn! I know what the end will be.
I'll go. And my house will fall away
While the mice by night and the moths by day
Will nibble the covers off all my books
And the spiders weave in the shadowed nooks
And my dogs ... I'll see that they have a home
While I follow the sun, while I drift and roam
To the ends of the earth like a chip on the stream,
Like a straw on the wind, like a vagrant dream,
And the thought will strike with a swift sharp pain
That I probably never will build again
This house that I'll have in some far day.
Well ... it's just a dream-house anyway.

HYMN TO THE NIGHT
HENRY WADSWORTH LONGFELLOW

I heard the trailing garments of the
   Night
   Sweep through her marble halls!
I saw her sable skirts all fringed with
   light
   From the celestial walls!

I felt her presence, by its spell of might,
   Stoop over me from above;
The calm, majestic presence of the
   Night,
   As of the one I love.

I heard the sounds of sorrow and
   delight,
   The manifold, soft chimes,
That fill the haunted chambers of the
   Night,
   Like some old poet's rhymes.

From the cool cisterns of the midnight
   air
   My spirit drank repose;
The fountain of perpetual peace flows
   there,—
   From those deep cisterns flows.

O holy Night! from thee I learn to bear
   What man has borne before!
Thou layest thy finger on the lips of
   Care,
   And they complain no more.

Peace! Peace! Orestes-like I breathe
   this prayer!
   Descend with broad-winged flight,
The welcome, the thrice-prayed for, the
   most fair,
   The best-beloved Night!

From *A SLICE OF SUNLIGHT**
By CHRISTOPHER MORLEY

IN EVERY MAN'S HEART there is a secret nerve that answers to the vibration of beauty. I can imagine no more fascinating privilege than to be allowed to ransack the desks of a thousand American business men, men supposed to be hardheaded, absorbed in brisk commerce. Somewhere in each desk one would find some hidden betrayal of that man's private worship. It might be some old newspaper clipping, perhaps a poem that had once touched him, for even the humblest poets are stout partisans of reality. It might be a photograph of children playing in the surf, or a little box of fishhooks, or a soiled old timetable of some queer backwoods railroad or primitive steamer service that had once carried him into his land of heart's desire.

I remember a friend of mine, a man much perplexed by the cares of earth, but slow to give utterance to his inner and tenderer impulses, telling me how he first grasped the meaning and value of these inscrutable powers of virtue that hurl the whole universe daily around our heads in an unerring orbit. For some reason or other—he was writing a book, I think, and sought a place of quiet—he had drifted for some winter weeks to the shore of a southern bay, down in Florida. When he came back he told me about it. It was several years ago, but I remember the odd look in his eyes as he tried to describe his experience. "I never knew until now," he said, "what sunshine and sky meant. I had always taken them for granted before." He told me of the strange sensation of lightness and quiet smiling that had flooded through him in that land where Nature writes her benignant lessons so plainly that all must draw their own conclusions. He told me of sunset flushes over long, purple waters, and of lying on sand beaches wrapped in sunshine, all the problems of human intercourse soothed away in a naked and unquestioning content. What he said was very little, but watching his eyes I could guess what had happened. He had found more than sunshine and colour and an arc of violet sea. He had found a new philosophy, a new strength and realization of the worthiness of life. He had travelled far to find it: it might just as well be learned in Independence Square any sunny day when the golden light falls upon springing grass.

It is strange that men should have to be reminded of these things! How patiently, how persistently, with what dogged and misdirected pluck, they have taught themselves to ignore the elemental blessings of mankind, subsisting instead on pale and wizened and ingenious substitutes. It is like a man who should shoulder for a place at a quick lunch counter when a broad and leisurely banquet table was spread free just around the corner. The days tick by, as busy, as fleeting, as full of empty gestures as a moving picture film. We crowd old age upon ourselves and run out to embrace it, for age is not measured by number of days but by the exhaustion of each day. Twenty days lived at slow pulse, in harmony with earth's loveliness, are longer than two hundred crowded with feverish appointments and disappointments. Many a man has lived fifty or sixty hectic years and never yet learned the unreckonable endlessness of one day's loitering, measured only by the gracious turning of earth and sun. Someone often asks me, "Why don't you wind the clocks?" But in those rare moments when I am sane clocks do not interest me.

Something of these thoughts flashes into my mind as I see that beam of pale and narrow sunlight fallen upon the roof of that bank building. How strange it is, when life is bursting with light and strength, renewing itself every day in colour and freshness, that we should sunder ourselves from these great sources of power. With all the treasures of earth at hand, we coop ourselves in narrow causeways where even a sudden knife-edge of brightness is a matter for joyful surprise. As Stevenson once said, it is all very well to believe in immortality, but one must first believe in life. Why do we grudge ourselves the embraces of "Our brother and good friend the Sun"?

꙰ ꙰ ꙰

INDIAN SUMMER
JOHN GREENLEAF WHITTIER

From gold to gray
Our mild sweet day
Of Indian summer fades too soon;
But tenderly
Above the sea
Hangs, white and calm, the hunter's moon.

In its pale fire,
The village spire
Shows like the zodiac's spectral lance;
The painted walls
Whereon it falls
Transfigured stand in marble trance!

AFTER THE RAIN
THOMAS BAILEY ALDRICH

The rain has ceased, and in my room
The sunshine pours an airy flood;
And on the church's dizzy vane
The ancient cross is bathed in blood.

From out the dripping ivy leaves,
Antiquely carven, gray and high,
A dormer, facing westward, looks
Upon the village like an eye.

And now it glimmers in the sun,
A globe of gold, a disk, a speck;
And in the belfry sits a dove
With purple ripples on her neck.

THE HOUSE BEAUTIFUL
ROBERT LOUIS STEVENSON

A naked house, a naked moor,
A shivering pool before the door,
A garden bare of flowers and fruit,
And poplars at the garden foot,—
Such is the place that I live in,
Bleak without and bare within.

Yet shall your ragged moor receive
The incomparable pomp of eve,
And the cold glories of the dawn
Behind your shivering trees be drawn;
And when the wind from place to place
Doth the unmoored cloud-galleons chase,
Your garden gloom and gleam again,
With leaping sun, with dancing rain.
Here shall the wizard moon ascend
The heavens, in the crimson end
Of day's declining splendor; here

The army of the stars appear.
The neighbor hollows dry or wet,
Spring shall with tender flowers beset;
And oft the morning muser see
Larks rising from the broomy lea,
And every fairy wheel and thread
Of cobweb dew-bediamonded.
When daisies go, shall winter time
Silver the simple grass with rime,
Autumnal frosts enchant the pool
And make the cart-ruts beautiful.
And when snow-bright the moor expands,
How shall your children clap their hands!
To make this earth, our hermitage,
A cheerful and a pleasant page,
God's bright and intricate device
Of days and seasons doth suffice.

SEPTEMBER IN THE FIELDS*

By Dorothy Easton

SOMETIMES, walking through a meadow that one has crossed a hundred times before, one will suddenly feel to be seeing "hedges," and "grass," for the first time.

On such a day in September, I left the sea and strolled inland.

A new keenness in the wind made me breathe deep, though there was not a cloud in the sky and the sun burnt my face.

Blue downs stretched in the distance; hazy, unreal, a vision seen by flat fields.

Berries were ripe; withered hawthorns flamed scarlet and crimson. It was that mingling of blue and red—gold on the straw ricks, yellow on the stubble —that made my heart glad, with a sense of fulness.

Those bushes had a dusky bloom of defiance; hips and haws were brave, like a sunset in the morning.

I sat on the bank of a slow tidal river that cut my path; mounds of grass in shadow were grey with dew; fields beyond—yellow with warmth and sunlight.

Spikes of dead grass, dried a light string colour, waved and bent a foot above the green; purple brambles clung to low branches of the thorn trees; cows in the field seemed to dream and doze like the sky.

One yellow leaf fluttered down. . . .

The river, muddy-brown, held a reflection of sky on its ripples; swallows and martins swooped over the water. A kingfisher came out from the shadows of a side-stream; it seemed to wear on its wings the green of rushes, the blue of the sky; for an instant it flashed gold, and a glint of scarlet—then it was gone.

"The most perfect day in the year! I must go blackberrying."

With my baby sister I set out to gather something of the ripeness of the fields—but more to recapture my vision.

All the time we walked, I wanted still to go farther—to push off the yellow haze on the stubble, to shake the hedges into flame.

Presently the joy of picking possessed us. Baby, with her pinafore, caught on the brambles; myself, astride a ditch, straining after the impossible one. The hedges were bound with convolvulus chains—white, trumpet-shaped flowers that died as we plucked them; gold leaves and stems, and clusters of poisonous berries. There were hops, dried thistles, sloes, and blackberry blossom; and sometimes a concealed ditch, choked with summer growth of weeds, bleached and withered, a matted tangle of dry sticks and grass.

The brambles above were thick with red, unripe berries—crisp, and acid to the taste; big purple ones clustered on the far side; pin-pricks of white light reflected on each round, black seed; and a strong autumn flavour of sun and damp and wine.

Village children scoured hedgerows in the distance; boys with schoolbags, little girls with baskets and limp sunbonnets, to hold the blackberries in; a scarlet hat hung on the neck of one.

Baby was very serious, absorbed in the joy of "hunting"; anticipating, too, the pudding we were going to make.

The air was faintly sweet with a smell of clover, full of rustling from the stubble under our feet. I felt I might chase along the hedges forever—I should never catch what I was seeking.

We lay on the landward side of the tamarisk—sorrel, and the last dandelions, the last meadow-sweet, high as a forest in front of our eyes. Through a break in the hedge I could see a line of blue water; the sound of the sea, unhurried, unchanging, was like wind in a wood far away.

The earth stretched flat to the Downs, and the sky was flat—the sea. Peace had

*Reprinted from *The Golden Bird* by Dorothy Easton, by permission of ALFRED A. KNOPF, INC. Copyright 1920 by Alfred A. Knopf, Inc.

rolled over them. Thin, shining spiderwebs waved all across from spike to spike of withered blossom; a brown bee booming over the clover was an event.

The lark's song came to one through a veil of silence; when a covey of partridges started up, their rustling was caught and hushed by the grass.

Baby came to me; hot, tired, blackberry-stained; all her little feeling for the hour expressed itself in blowing a silver thistleball, and lying with her head on my chest, watching it sail up into the blue.

Idly we dipped our hands in the basket. The berries had a warm, wildgrape flavour in the sun. Baby talked about our pudding, then sucked clover petals, and twined hops round her head. She asked me why "today" couldn't be always—with just this much blue and gold—and then she bit a sloe, and I had to comfort her.

We sat up, a little breeze stirred and shook the feathery tamarisk.

"Today will come again!" I told her —but still longed to seize and hold that pleasant dream which lay on the fields —that something unnamable which had burnished the trees, and touched all the stubble land; which had made that soft belt round the sky, and caused my heart to leap.

"Oh, look! They're gone!" cried Baby's shrill voice. The blackberry basket was empty.

"Never mind! We've eaten them all! There are lots more!"

"But you'll never come again! There'll be clouds tomorrow or somethin'—"

She was right; we didn't come; we couldn't recapture the spirit of that day —those sweet, half-conscious moments lying in the grass, with the scent of wood-smoke, and the fluttering of a crimson leaf.

It is sweet to watch a flame while it burns.

NOVEMBER THIRTEENTH
By Donald Culross Peattie

No SMELL so sweet as the reek of wood fires. And more than sweet—exciting, quietly, some depths of my feelings where I am not easily stirred. I am speaking of that sense of Nature that is enjoyed in human fraternity, in the pleasurable sensations that always accompany simple obedience to our own instincts. Nor do I suppose that only men enjoy gregariousness. The swallow must feel it when he joins in the autumn flocks, and the bee dies of loneliness when isolated.

The evocative djinni of this emotion for me is the smell of wood smoke, blowing on the air, stealing out of the home chimneys, curling up to a bedroom while the evening is yet young, from a just left hearth below, whispering across twilit miles of tranquil villages and old farm houses warmly inhabited. Even a miserable hut, a black man's cabin, or a gypsy's bivouac stirs me to a blind emotion, half wistful and half lusty. I have descended at nightfall on a hamlet in a strange mountain valley, or entered an old city standing in a long silver rain, and caught a whiff of men's hearths that has stirred up in me the loud call of, Brother! For it speaks of hospitality, of women, of children like apples good enough to eat, and, perhaps, of music, wine, and books—all those aspects of greater Nature that are particular to human nature.

—From *An Almanac for Moderns*

ONE GREAT POET is a masterpiece of nature.—*Shelley*

NO ONE is useless in this world who lightens the burden of
it to anyone else.—*Dickens*

A FORGIVENESS ought to be like a cancelled note, torn in two and burned
up, so that it never can be shown against the man.—*Beecher*

NO MAN can afford to invest his being in anything lower than faith, hope,
love—these three, the greatest of which is love.—*Beecher*

THE COUNTRY is both the philosopher's garden and library, in which he reads
and contemplates the power, wisdom, and goodness of God.—*Penn*

WORDS ARE INSTRUMENTS of music: an ignorant man uses them for jargon; but
when a master touches them they have unexpected life and soul. Some words
sound out like drums; some breathe memories sweet as flutes; some call like a
clarionet; some show a charge like trumpets; some are sweet as children's talk;
others rich as a mother's answering back.—*Anonymous*

BEAUTY does not lie in the face. It lies in the harmony between man and his
industry. Beauty is expression. When I paint a mother I try to render her
beautiful by the mere look she gives her child.—*Millet*

WHAT PLACE is so rugged and so homely that there is no beauty,
if you only have a feeling for beauty?—*Beecher*

DOST THOU love life? Then do not squander time, for that
is the stuff life is made of.—*Franklin*

THE MORNING WIND forever blows, the poem of creation is
uninterrupted; but few are the ears that hear. Olympus is but
the outside of the earth everywhere.—*Thoreau*

IF THERE IS a saving virtue, it is the loving service
of mankind.—*The Talmud*

AND NATURE

EACH man reaps on his own farm.—*Plautus*

HE WHO IS plenteously provided for from within needs but little from without.—*Goethe*

BUT THERE'S NOTHING half so sweet in life as love's young dream.—*Moore*

LIKE A GREAT POET, nature produces the greatest results with the simplest means. There are simply a sun, flowers, water, and love.—*Heine*

THE MEN whom I have seen succeed have always been cheerful and hopeful, who went about their business with a smile on their faces, and took the changes and chances of this mortal life like men.—*Kingsley*

AT THE PORTIÈRES of that silent Faubourg St. Germain, there is but brief question, "Do you deserve to enter? Pass. Do you ask to be the companion of nobles? Make yourself noble, and you shall be. Do you long for the conversation of the wise? Learn to understand it, and you shall hear it. But on other terms?—no. If you will not rise to us, we cannot stoop to you."—*Ruskin*

WE REQUIRE from buildings, as from men, two kinds of goodness: first, the doing their practical duty well: then that they be graceful and pleasing in doing it; which last is itself another form of duty.—*Ruskin*

AWAKE, O NORTH WIND; and come, thou south; blow upon my garden, that the spices thereof may flow out. Let my beloved come into his garden, and eat his pleasant fruits.—*Song of Solomon*

NOT TILL THE FIRE is dying in the grate, look we for any kinship with the stars.—*Meredith*

IT IS NOT ENOUGH merely to possess virtue, as if it were an art; it should be practised.—*Cicero*

NO PLEASURE is comparable to the standing upon the vantage-ground of truth.—*Bacon*

A WINTER RIDE
AMY LOWELL

Who shall declare the joy of the running!
　　Who shall tell of the pleasures of flight!
Springing and spurning the tufts of wild heather,
　　Sweeping, wide-winged, through the blue dome of light.
Everything mortal has moments immortal,
　　Swift and God-gifted, immeasurably bright.
So with the stretch of the white road before me
　　Shining snow crystals rainbowed by the sun,
Fields that are white, stained with long, cool, blue shadows,
　　Strong with the strength of my horse as we run.
Joy in the touch of the wind and the sunlight!
　　Joy! With the vigorous earth I am one.

A BOY, A LAKE, A SUN
ROBERT P. TRISTRAM COFFIN

My little boy, the vast, still lake,
　　And the big low sun
Keep each other company,
　　Now the day is done.

The child is quiet, and his curls
　　Are full of evening light,
He sits in utter confidence
　　On the edge of night.

A little golden bubble cast
　　Up from eternity,

The sun is just as much his friend
　　As the evening bee.

He does not know that he is small
　　Or different or apart,
The sun is not a grander thing
　　Than a daisy's heart.

But he is pleased to have me come
　　And moves to let me sit
Beside him and the setting sun,
　　And I am proud of it.

From LEAF AND TENDRIL
By JOHN BURROUGHS

NEARLY every season I note what I call the bridal day of summer—a white, lucid, shining day, with a delicate veil of mist softening all outlines. How the river dances and sparkles; how the new leaves of all the trees shine under the sun; the air has a soft lustre; there is a haze, it is not blue, but a kind of shining, diffused nimbus. No clouds, the sky a bluish white, very soft and delicate. It is the nuptial day of the season; the sun fairly takes the earth to be his own, for better or for worse, on such a day, and what marriages there are going on all about us: the marriages of the flowers, of the bees, of the birds. Everything suggests life, love, fruition. These bridal days are often repeated; the serenity and equipoise of the elements combine. They were such days as these that the poet Lowell had in mind when he wrote, "What is so rare as a day in June?"

378

MIRACLES

Walt Whitman

Why, who makes much of a miracle?
As to me I know of nothing else but miracles,
Whether I walk the streets of Manhattan,
  Or dart my sight over the roofs of houses toward the sky,
  Or wade with naked feet along the beach just in the edge of the water,
Or stand under trees in the woods,
Or talk by day with any one I love, or sleep in the bed at night
    with any one I love,
Or sit at table at dinner with the rest,
Or look at strangers opposite me riding in the car,
Or watch honey-bees busy around the hive of a summer forenoon,
Or animals feeding in the fields,
Or birds, or the wonderfulness of insects in the air,
Or the wonderfulness of the sundown, or of stars shining
    so quiet and bright,
Or the exquisite delicate thin curve of the new moon in spring;
These with the rest, one and all, are to me miracles,
The whole referring, yet each distinct in its place.

To me every hour of the light and dark is a miracle,
Every cubic inch of space is a miracle,
Every square yard of the surface of the earth is spread with the same,
Every foot of the interior swarms with the same.
To me the sea is a continual miracle,
The fishes that swim—the rocks—the motion of the waves—
    the ships with men in them.
What stranger miracles are there?

SUNDOWN

By Walt Whitman

Sundown is the hour for many strange effects in light and shade—enough to make the colorist go delirious—long spokes of molten silver sent horizontally through the trees (now in their brightest, tenderest green), each leaf and branch of endless foliage a lit-up miracle, then lying all prone on the youthful-ripe, interminable grass, and giving the blades not only aggregate but individual splendor, in ways unknown to any other hour.

I have particular spots where I get these effects in their perfection. One broad splash lies on the water, with many a ripping twinkle, offset by the rapidly deepening black-green murky-transparent shadows behind, and at intervals all along the banks. These, with great shafts of horizontal fire thrown among the trees and along the grass as the sun lowers, give effects more peculiar, more and more superb, unearthly, rich and dazzling.

The Apple Tree

By JOHN GALSWORTHY

"The Apple tree, the singing, and the gold." Murray's Hippolytus of Euripides

*O*N THEIR SILVER-WEDDING DAY Ashurst and his wife were motoring along the outskirts of the moor, intending to crown the festival by stopping the night at Torquay, where they had first met. This was the idea of Stella Ashurst, whose character contained a streak of sentiment. If she had long lost the blue-eyed flower-like charm, the cool slim purity of face and form, the apple-blossom colouring, which had so swiftly and so oddly affected Ashurst twenty-six years ago, she was still at forty-three a comely and faithful companion, whose cheeks were faintly mottled, and whose grey-blue eyes had acquired a certain fullness.

It was she who had stopped the car where the common rose steeply to the left, and a narrow strip of larch and beech, with here and there a pine, stretched out towards the valley between the road and the first long high hill of the full moor. She was looking for a place where they might lunch, for Ashurst never looked for anything; and this, between the golden furze and the feathery green larches smelling of lemons in the last sun of April—this, with a view into the deep valley and up to the long moor heights, seemed fitting to the decisive nature of one who sketched in water-colours, and loved romantic spots. Grasping her paint box, she got out.

"Won't this do, Frank?"

Ashurst, rather like a bearded Schiller, grey in the wings, tall, long-legged, with large remote grey eyes which sometimes filled with meaning and became almost beautiful, with nose a little to one side, and bearded lips just open— Ashurst, forty-eight, and silent, grasped the luncheon basket, and got out too.

"Oh! Look, Frank! A grave!"

By the side of the road, where the track from the top of the common crossed it at right angles and ran through a gate past the narrow wood, was a thin mound of turf, six feet by one, with a moorstone to the west, and on it someone had thrown a blackthorn spray and a handful of bluebells. Ashurst looked, and the poet in him moved. At cross-roads—a suicide's grave! Poor mortals with their superstitions! Whoever lay there, though, had the best of it—no clammy sepulcher among other hideous graves carved with futilities— just a rough stone, the wide sky, and wayside blessings! And, without comment, for he had learned not to be a philosopher in the bosom of his family, he strode away up on to the common, dropped the luncheon basket under a wall, spread a rug for his wife to sit on —she would turn up from her sketching when she was hungry—and took from his pocket Murray's translation of the "Hippolytus." He had soon finished reading of "The Cyprian" and her revenge, and looked at the sky instead. And watching the white clouds so bright against the intense blue, Ashurst, on his silver-wedding day, longed for—he knew not what. Maladjusted to life—man's organism! One's mode of life might be high and scrupulous, but there was always an undercurrent of greediness, a hankering, and sense of waste. Did women have it too? Who could tell? And yet, men who gave vent to their appetites for novelty, their riotous longings for new adventures, new risks, new pleasures, these suffered, no doubt, from the reverse side of starvation, from surfeit. No getting out of it—a mal-adjusted animal, civilized man! There could be no garden of his choosing, of "the Apple-tree, the singing, and the gold," in the words of that lovely Greek chorus, no achievable elysium in life, or lasting haven of happiness for any man with a sense of beauty—nothing which could compare with the captured loveliness in a work of art, set down for ever, so that to look on it or read was always to have the same precious sense of exaltation and restful inebriety. Life no doubt had moments with that quality of beauty, of unbidden flying rapture, but the trouble was, they lasted no longer than the span of a cloud's flight over the sun; impossible to keep them with you, as Art caught beauty and held it fast. They were fleeting as one of the glimmering or golden visions one had of the soul in nature, glimpses of its remote and brooding spirit. Here, with the sun hot on his face, a cuckoo calling from a thorn tree, and in the air the honey savour of gorse—here among the little fronds of the young fern, the starry blackthorn, while the bright clouds drifted by high above the hills and dreamy valleys—here and now was such a glimpse. But in a moment it would pass—as the face of Pan, which looks round the corner of a rock, vanishes at your stare. And suddenly he sat up. Surely there was something familiar about this view, this bit of common, that ribbon of road, the old wall behind him. While they were driving he had not been taking notice—n e v e r d i d; thinking of far things or of nothing—but now he saw! Twenty-six years ago, just at this time of year, from the farmhouse within half a mile of this very spot he had started for that day in Tor-

quay whence it might be said he had never returned. And a sudden ache beset his heart; he had stumbled on just one of those past moments in his life, whose beauty and rapture he had failed to arrest, whose wings had fluttered away into the unknown; he had stumbled on a buried memory, a wild sweet time, swiftly choked and ended. And, turning on his face, he rested his chin on his hands, and stared at the short grass where the little blue milkwort was growing. . . .

And this is what he remembered.

On the first of May, after their last year together at college, Frank Ashurst and his friend Robert Garton were on a tramp. They had walked that day from Brent, intending to make Chagford, but Ashurst's football knee had given out, and according to their map they had still some seven miles to go. They were sitting on a bank beside the road, where a track crossed alongside a wood, resting the knee and talking of the universe, as young men will. Both were over six feet, and thin as rails; Ashurst pale, idealistic, full of absence; Garton queer, round-the-corner, knotted, curly, like some primeval beast. Both had a literary bent; neither wore a hat. Ashurst's hair was smooth, pale, wavy, and had a way of rising on either side of his brow, as if always being flung back; Garton's was a kind of dark unfathomed mop. They had not met a soul for miles.

"My dear fellow," Garton was saying, "pity's only an effect of self-consciousness; it's a disease of the last five thousand years. The world was happier without."

Ashurst, following the clouds with his eyes, answered:

"It's the pearl in the oyster, anyway."

"My dear chap, all our modern unhappiness comes from pity. Look at animals, and Red Indians, limited to feeling their own occasional misfortunes; then look at ourselves—never free from feeling the toothaches of others. Let's get back to feeling for nobody, and have a better time."

"You'll never practise that."

Garton pensively stirred the hotch-potch of his hair.

"To attain full growth, one mustn't be squeamish. To starve oneself emotionally's a mistake. All emotion is to the good—enriches life."

"Yes, and when it runs up against chivalry?"

"Ah! That's so English! If you speak of emotion the English always think you want something physical, and are shocked. They're afraid of passion but not of lust—oh, no!—so long as they can keep it secret."

Ashurst did not answer; he had plucked a blue floweret, and was twiddling it against the sky. A cuckoo began calling from a thorn tree. The sky, the flowers, the songs of birds! Robert was talking through his hat! And he said:

"Well, let's go on, and find some farm where we can put up." In uttering those words, he was conscious of a girl coming down from the common just above them. She was outlined against the sky, carrying a basket, and you could see that sky through the crook of her arm. And Ashurst, who saw beauty without wondering how it could advantage him, thought: 'How pretty!' The wind, blowing her dark frieze skirt against her legs, lifted her battered p e a c o c k tam-o'-shanter; her greyish blouse was worn and old, her shoes were split, her little hands rough and red, her neck browned. Her dark hair waved untidy across her broad forehead, her face was short, her upper lip short, showing a glint of teeth, her brows were straight and dark, her lashes long and dark, her nose straight; but her grey eyes were the wonder—dewy as if opened for the first time that day. She looked at Ashurst—perhaps he struck her as strange, limping along without a

hat, with his large eyes on her, and his hair flung back. He could not take off what was not on his head, but put up his hand in a salute, and said:

"Can you tell us if there's a farm near here where we could stay the night? I've gone lame."

"There's only our farm near, sir." She spoke without shyness, in a pretty, soft, crisp voice.

"And where is that?"

"Down here, sir."

"Would you put us up?"

"Oh! I think we would."

"Will you show us the way?"

"Yes, sir."

He limped on, silent, and Garton took up the catechism.

"Are you a Devonshire girl?"

"No, sir."

"What then?"

"From Wales."

"Ah! I *thought* you were a Celt; so it's not your farm?"

"My aunt's, sir."

"And your uncle's?"

"He is dead."

"Who farms it, then?"

"My aunt, and my three cousins."

"But your uncle was a Devonshire man?"

"Yes, sir."

"Have you lived here long?"

"Seven years."

"And how'd you like it after Wales?"

"I don't know, sir."

"I suppose you don't remember?"

"Oh, yes! But it is different."

"I believe you!"

Ashurst broke in suddenly:

"How old are you?"

"Seventeen, sir."

"And what's your name?"

"Megan David."

"This is Robert Garton, and I am Frank Ashurst. We wanted to get on to Chagford."

"It is a pity your leg is hurting you."

Ashurst smiled, and when he smiled his face was rather beautiful.

Descending past the narrow wood, they came on the farm suddenly—a long, low, stone-built dwelling with casement windows, in a farmyard where pigs and fowls and an old mare were straying. A short steep-up grass hill behind was crowned with a few Scotch firs, and in front, an old orchard of apple-trees, just breaking into flower, stretched down to a stream and a long wild meadow. A little boy with oblique dark eyes was shepherding a pig, and by the house door stood a woman, who came towards them. The girl said:

"It is Mrs. Narracombe, my aunt."

"Mrs. Narracombe, my aunt," had a quick, dark eye, like a mother wild-duck's, and something of the same snaky turn about her neck.

"We met your niece on the road," said Ashurst; "she thought you might perhaps put us up for the night."

Mrs. Narracombe, taking them in from head to heel, answered:

"Well, I can, if you don't mind one room. Megan, get the spare room ready, and a bowl of cream. You'll be wanting tea, I suppose."

Passing through a sort of porch made by two yew trees and some flowering-currant bushes, the girl disappeared into the house, her peacock tam-o'-shanter bright athwart that rosy-pink and the dark green of the yews.

'Will you come into the parlour and rest your leg? You'll be from college, perhaps?"

"We were, but we've gone down now."

Mrs. Narracombe nodded sagely.

The parlour, brick-floored, with bare table and shiny chairs and sofa stuffed with horsehair, seemed never to have been used, it was so terribly clean. Ashurst sat down at once on the sofa, holding his lame knee between his hands, and Mrs. Narracombe gazed at him. He was the only son of a late professor of chemistry, but people found a certain lordliness in one who was often so

sublimely unconscious of them.

"Is there a stream where we could bathe?"

"There's the stream at the bottom of the orchard, but sittin' down you'll not be covered!"

"How deep?"

"Well, 'tis about a foot and a half, maybe."

"Oh! That'll do fine. Which way?"

"Down the lane, through the second gate on the right, an' the pool's by the big apple tree that stands by itself. There's trout there, if you can tickle them."

"They're more likely to tickle us!"

Mrs. Narracombe smiled. "There'll be the tea ready when you come back."

The pool, formed by the damming of a rock, had a sandy bottom; and the big apple tree, lowest in the orchard, grew so close that its boughs almost overhung the water; it was in leaf, and all but in flower—its crimson buds just bursting. There was not room for more than one at a time in that narrow bath, and Ashurst waited his turn, rubbing his knee and gazing at the wild meadow, all rocks and thorn trees and field flowers, with a grove of beeches beyond, raised up on a flat mound. Every bough was swinging in the wind, every spring bird calling, and a slanting sunlight dappled the grass. He thought of Theocritus, and the river Cherwell, of the moon, and the maiden with the dewy eyes; of so many things that he seemed to think of nothing; and he felt absurdly happy.

During a late and sumptuous tea with eggs to it, cream and jam, and thin, fresh cakes touched with saffron, Garton descanted on the Celts. It was about the period of the Celtic awakening, and the discovery that there was Celtic blood about this family had excited one who believed that he was a Celt himself. Sprawling on a horsehair chair, with a hand-made cigarette dribbling from the corner of his curly lips, he had been plunging his cold pin-points of eyes into Ashurst's and praising the refinement of the Welsh. To come out of Wales into England was like the change from china to earthenware! Frank, as a d——d Englishman, had not of course perceived the exquisite refinement and emotional capacity of that Welsh girl! And, delicately stirring in the dark mat of his still wet hair, he explained how exactly she illustrated the writings of the Welsh bard Morgan-ap-Something in the twelfth century.

Ashurst, full length on the horsehair sofa, and jutting far beyond its end, smoked a deeply-coloured pipe, and did not listen, thinking of the girl's face when she brought in a relay of cakes. It had been exactly like looking at a flower, or some other pretty sight in Nature —till, with a funny little shiver, she had lowered her glance and gone out, quiet as a mouse.

"Let's go to the kitchen," said Garton, "and see some more of her."

The kitchen was a white-washed room with rafters, to which were attached smoked hams; there were flowerpots on the window-sill, and guns hanging on nails, queer mugs, china and pewter, and portraits of Queen Victoria. A long, narrow table of plain wood was set with bowls and spoons, under a string of high-hung onions; two sheepdogs and three cats lay here and there. On one side of the recessed fireplace sat two small boys, idle, and good as gold; on the other sat a stout, light-eyed, red-faced youth with hair and lashes the colour of the tow he was running through the barrel of a gun; between them Mrs. Narracombe dreamily stirred some savoury-scented stew in a large pot. Two other youths, oblique-eyed, dark-haired, rather sly-faced, like the two little boys, were talking together and lolling against the wall; and a short, elderly, clean-shaven man in corduroys, seated in the window, was conning a battered journal. The girl Megan seemed the only active creature—drawing cider and passing with the jugs from cask to table. Seeing them thus about to eat, Garton said:

"Ah! If you'll let us, we'll come back when supper's over," and without waiting for an answer they withdrew again to the parlour. But the colour in the kitchen, the warmth, the scents, and all those faces, heightened the bleakness of their shiny room, and they resumed their seats moodily.

"Regular gipsy type, those boys. There was only one Saxon—the fellow cleaning the gun. That girl is a very subtle study psychologically."

Ashurst's lips twitched. Garton seemed to him an ass just then. Subtle study! She was a wild flower. A creature it did you good to look at. Study!

Garton went on:

"Emotionally she would be wonderful. She wants awakening."

"Are you going to awaken her?"

Garton looked at him and smiled. 'How coarse and English you are!' that curly smile seemed saying.

And Ashurst puffed his pipe. Awaken her! This fool had the best opinion of himself! He threw up the window and leaned out. Dusk had gathered thick. The farm buildings and the wheel-house were all dim and bluish, the apple trees but a blurred wilderness; the air smelled of wood smoke from the kitchen fire. One bird going to bed later than the others was uttering a half-hearted twitter, as though surprised at the darkness. From the stable came the snuffle and stamp of a feeding horse. And away over there was the loom of the moor, and away and away the shy stars which had not as yet full light, pricking white through the deep blue heavens. A quavering owl hooted. Ashurst drew a deep breath. What a night to wander out in! A padding of unshod hoofs came up the lane, and three dim, dark shapes passed— ponies on an evening march. Their heads, black and fuzzy, showed above the gate. At the tap of his pipe, and a shower of little sparks, they shied round and scampered. A bat went fluttering past, uttering its almost inaudible "chip, chip." Ashurst held out his hand; on the upturned palm he could feel the dew. Suddenly from overhead he heard little burring boys' voices, little thumps of boots thrown down, and another voice, crisp and soft—the girl's putting them to bed, no doubt; and nine clear words: "No, Rick, you can't have the cat in bed"; then came a skirmish of giggles and gurgles, a soft slap, a laugh so low and pretty that it made him shiver a little. A blowing sound, and the glim of the candle which was fingering the dusk above, went out; silence reigned. Ashurst withdrew into the room and sat down; his knee pained him, and his soul felt gloomy.

"You go to the kitchen," he said; "I'm going to bed."

For Ashurst the wheel of slumber was wont to turn noiseless and slick and swift, but though he seemed sunk in sleep when his companion came up, he was really wide awake; and long after Garton, smothered in the other bed of that low-roofed room, was worshipping darkness with his upturned nose, he heard the owls. Barring the discomfort of his knee, it was not unpleasant—the cares of life did not loom large in night watches for this young man. In fact he had none; just enrolled a barrister, with literary aspirations, the world before him, no father or mother, and four hundred a year of his own. Did it matter where he went, what he did, or when he did it? His bed, too, was hard, and this preserved him from fever. He lay, sniffing the scent of the night which drifted into the low room through the open casement close to his head. Except for a definite irritation with his friend, nat-

ural when you have tramped with a man for three days, Ashurst's memories and visions that sleepless night were kindly and wistful and exciting. One vision, specially clear and unreasonable, for he had not even been conscious of noting it, was the face of the youth cleaning the gun; its intent, stolid, yet startled uplook at the kitchen doorway, quickly shifted to the girl carrying the cider jug. This red, blue-eyed, light-lashed, tow-haired face stuck as firmly in his memory as the girl's own face, so dewy and simple. But at last, in the square of darkness through the uncurtained casement, he saw day coming, and heard one hoarse and sleepy caw. Then followed silence, dead as ever, till the song of a blackbird, not properly awake, adventured into the hush. And, from staring at the framed brightening light, Ashurst fell asleep.

Next day his knee was badly swollen; the walking tour was obviously over. Garton, due back in London on the morrow, departed at midday with an ironical smile which left a scar of irritation—healed the moment his loping figure vanished round the corner of the steep lane. All day Ashurst rested his knee, in a green-painted wooden chair on the patch of grass by the yew-tree porch, where the sunlight distilled the scent of stocks and gillyflowers, and a ghost of scent from the flowering-currant bushes. Beatifically he smoked, dreamed, watched.

A farm in spring is all birth—young things coming out of bud and shell, and human beings watching over the process with faint excitement feeding and tending what has been born. So still the young man sat, that a mother-goose, with stately cross-footed waddle, brought her six yellow-necked grey-backed goslings to strop their little beaks against the grass blades at his feet. Now and again Mrs. Narracombe or the girl Megan would come and ask if he wanted anything, and he would smile and say: "Nothing, thanks. It's splendid here." Towards tea-time they came out together, bearing a long poultice of some dark stuff in a bowl, and after a long and solemn scrutiny of his swollen knee, bound it on. When they were gone, he thought of the girl's soft "Oh!"—of her pitying eyes, and the little wrinkle in her brow. And again he felt that unreasoning irritation against his departed friend, who had talked such rot about her. When she brought out his tea, he said:

"How did you like my friend, Megan?"

She forced down her upper lip, as if afraid that to smile was not polite. "He was a funny gentleman; he made us laugh. I think he is very clever."

"What did he say to make you laugh?"

"He said I was a daughter of the bards. What are they?"

"Welsh poets, who lived hundreds of years ago."

"Why am I their daughter, please?"

"He meant that you were the sort of girl they sang about."

She wrinkled her brows. "I think he likes to joke. Am I?"

"Would you believe me, if I told you?"

"Oh, yes."

"Well, I think he was right."

She smiled.

And Ashurst thought: 'You *are* a pretty thing!'

"He said, too, that Joe was a Saxon type. What would that be?"

"Which is Joe? With the blue eyes and red face?"

"Yes. He's uncle's nephew."

"Not your cousin, then?"

"No."

"Well, he meant that Joe was like the men who came over to England about fourteen hundred years ago, and conquered it."

"Oh! I know about them; but is he?"

"Garton's crazy about that sort of thing; but I must say Joe does look a bit Early Saxon."

"Yes."

That "Yes" tickled Ashurst. It was so crisp and graceful, so conclusive, and politely acquiescent in what was evidently Greek to her.

"He said that all the other boys were regular gipsies. He should not have said that. My aunt laughed, but she didn't like it, of course, and my cousins were angry. Uncle was a farmer—farmers are not gipsies. It is wrong to hurt people."

Ashurst wanted to take her hand and give it a squeeze, but he only answered:

"Quite right, Megan. By the way, I heard you putting the little ones to bed last night."

She flushed a little. "Please to drink your tea—it is getting cold. Shall I get you some fresh?"

"Do you ever have time to do anything for yourself?"

"Oh, yes."

"I've been watching, but I haven't seen it yet."

She wrinkled her brows in a puzzled frown, and her colour deepened.

When she was gone, Ashurst thought: 'Did she think I was chaffing her? I wouldn't for the world!' He was at that age when to some men "Beauty's a flower," as the poet says, and inspires in them the thoughts of chivalry. Never very conscious of his surroundings, it was some time before he was aware that the youth whom Garton had called "a Saxon type" was standing outside the stable door; and a fine bit of colour he made in his soiled brown velvetcords, muddy gaiters, and blue shirt; redarmed, red-faced, the sun turning his hair from tow to flax; immovably stolid, persistent, unsmiling he stood. Then, seeing Ashurst looking at him, he crossed the yard at that gait of the young countryman always ashamed not to be slow and heavy-dwelling on each leg, and disappeared round the end of the house towards the kitchen entrance. A chill came over Ashurst's mood. Clods! With all the good will in the world, how impossible to get on terms with them! And yet—see that girl! Her shoes were split, her hands rough; but—what was it? Was it really her Celtic blood, as Garton had said?—she was a lady born, a jewel, though probably she could do no more than just read and write!

The elderly, clean-shaven man he had seen last night in the kitchen had come into the yard with a dog, driving the cows to their milking. Ashurst saw that he was lame.

"You've got some good ones there!"

The lame man's face brightened. He had the upward look in his eyes which prolonged suffering often brings.

"Yeas; they'm praaper buties; gude milkers tu."

"I bet they are."

"'Ope as yure leg's better, zurr."

"Thank you, it's getting on."

The lame man touched his own: "I know what 'tes, meself; 'tes a main worritin' thing, the knee. I've a 'ad mine bad this ten year."

Ashurst made the sound of sympathy that comes so readily from those who have an independent income, and the lame man smiled again.

"Mustn't complain, though—they mighty near 'ad it off."

"Ho!"

"Yeas; an' compared with what 'twas, 'tes almost so gude as nu."

"They've put a bandage of splendid stuff on mine."

"The maid she picks et. She'm a gude maid wi' the flowers. There's folks zeem to know the healin' in things. My mother was a rare one for that. 'Ope yu'll zune be better, zurr. Goo ahn, therr!"

Ashurst smiled. "Wi' the flowers!" A flower herself.

That evening, after his supper of cold duck, junket, and cider, the girl came in.

"Please, auntie says—will you try a piece of our Mayday cake?"

"If I may come to the kitchen for it."

"Oh, yes! You'll be missing your friend."

"Not I. But are you sure no one minds?"

"Who would mind? We shall be very pleased."

Ashurst rose too suddenly for his stiff knee, staggered, and subsided. The girl gave a little gasp, and held out her hands. Ashurst took them, small, rough, brown; checked his impulse to put them to his lips, and let her pull him up. She came close beside him, offering her shoulder. And leaning on her he walked across the room. That shoulder seemed quite the pleasantest thing he had ever touched. But he had presence of mind enough to catch his stick out of the rack, and withdraw his hand before arriving at the kitchen.

That night he slept like a top, and woke with his knee of almost normal size. He again spent the morning in his chair on the grass patch, scribbling down verses; but in the afternoon he wandered about with the two little boys Nick and Rick. It was Saturday, so they were early home from school; quick, shy, dark little rascals of seven and six, soon talkative, for Ashurst had a way with children. By four o'clock they had shown him all their methods of destroying life, except the tickling of trout; and with breeches tucked up, lay on their stomachs over the trout stream, pretending they had this accomplishment also. They tickled nothing, of course, for their giggling and shouting scared every spotted thing away. Ashurst, on a rock at the edge of the beech clump, watched them, and listened to the cuckoos, till Nick, the elder and less persevering, came up and stood beside him.

"The gipsy bogle zets on that stone," he said.

"What gipsy bogle?"

"Dunno; never zeen 'e. Megan zays 'e zets there; an' old Jim zeed 'e once. 'E was zettin' there naight afore our pony kicked-in father's 'ead. 'E plays the viddle."

"What tune does he play?"

"Dunno."

"What's he like?"

" 'E's black. Old Jim zays 'e's all over 'air. 'E's a praaper bogle. 'E don' come only at naight." The little boy's oblique dark eyes slid round. "D'yu think 'e might want to take me away? Megan's feared of 'e."

"Has she seen him?"

"No. She's not afeared o' yu."

"I should think not. Why should she be?"

"She zays a prayer for yu."

"How do you know that, you little rascal?"

"When I was asleep, she said: 'God bless us all, an' Mr. Ashes.' I yeard 'er whisperin'."

"You're a little ruffian to tell what you hear when you're not meant to hear it!"

The little boy was silent. Then he said aggressively:

"I can skin rabbets. Megan, she can't bear skinnin' 'em. I like blood."

"Oh! you do; you little monster!"

"What's that?"

"A creature that likes hurting others."

The little boy scowled. "They'm only dead rabbets, what us eats."

"Quite right, Nick. I beg your pardon."

"I can skin frogs, tu."

But Ashurst had become absent. "God bless us all, and Mr. Ashes!" And puzzled by that sudden inaccessibility, Nick ran back to the stream where the giggling and shouts again uprose at once.

When Megan brought his tea, he said:

"What's the gipsy bogle, Megan?"

She looked up, startled.

"He brings bad things."

"Surely you don't believe in gnosts?"

"I hope I will never see him."

"Of course you won't. There aren't such things. What old Jim saw was a pony."

"No! There are bogles in the rocks; they are the men who lived long ago."

"They aren't gipsies, anyway; those old men were dead long before gipsies came."

She said simply: "They are all bad."

"Why? If there are any, they're only wild, like the rabbits. The flowers aren't bad for being wild; the thorn trees were never planted—and you don't mind them. I shall go down at night and look for your bogle, and have a talk with him."

"Oh, no! Oh, no!"

"Oh, yes! I shall go and sit on his rock."

She clasped her hands together: "Oh, please!"

"Why! What does it matter if anything happens to me?"

She did not answer; and in a sort of pet he added:

"Well, I daresay I shan't see him, because I suppose I must be off soon."

"Soon?"

"Your aunt won't want to keep me here."

"Oh, yes! We always let lodgings in summer."

Fixing his eyes on her face, he asked:

"Would you like me to stay?"

"Yes."

"I'm going to say a prayer for *you* tonight!"

She flushed crimson, frowned, and went out of the room. He sat cursing himself, till his tea was stewed. It was as if he had hacked with his thick boots at a clump of bluebells. Why had he said such a silly thing? Was he just a towny college ass like Robert Garton, as far from understanding this girl?

Ashurst spent the next week confirming the restoration of his leg, by exploration of the country within easy reach. Spring was a revelation to him this year. In a kind of intoxication he would watch the pink-white buds of some backward beech tree sprayed up in the sunlight against the deep blue sky, or the trunks and limbs of the few Scotch firs, tawny in violent light, or again on the moor, the gale-bent larches which had such a look of life when the wind streamed in their young green, above the rusty black underboughs. Or he would lie on the banks, gazing at the clusters of dog-violets, or up in the dead bracken, fingering the pink, transparent buds of the dewberry, while the cuckoos called and yaffes laughed, or a lark, from very high, dripped its beads of song. It was certainly different from any spring he had ever known, for spring was within him, not without.

In the day time he hardly saw the family; and when Megan brought in his meals she always seemed too busy in the house or among the young things in the yard to stay talking long. But in the evenings he installed himself in the window seat in the kitchen, smoking and chatting with the lame man Jim, or Mrs. Narracombe, while the girl sewed, or moved about, clearing the supper things away. And sometimes with the sensation a cat must feel when it purrs, he would become conscious that Megan's eyes—those dew-grey eyes —were fixed on him with a sort of lingering soft look which was strangely flattering.

It was on Sunday week in the evening, when he was lying in the orchard listening to a blackbird and composing a love poem, that he heard the gate swing to, and saw the girl come running among the trees, with the red-cheeked, stolid Joe in swift pursuit. About twenty yards away the chase ended, and the two stood fronting each other, not noticing the stranger in the grass—the boy pressing on, the girl fending him off.

Ashurst could see her face, angry, disturbed; and the youth's—who would have thought that red-faced yokel could look so distraught! And painfully affected by that sight, he jumped up. They saw him then. Megan dropped her hands, and shrank behind a treetrunk; the boy gave an angry grunt, rushed at the bank, scrambled over and vanished. Ashurst went slowly up to her. She was standing quite still, biting her lip—very pretty, with her fine, dark hair blown loose about her face, and her eyes cast down.

"I beg your pardon," he said.

She gave him one upward look, from eyes much dilated; then, catching her breath, turned away. Ashurst followed.

"Megan!"

But she went on; and taking hold of her arm, he turned her gently round to him.

"Stop and speak to me."

"Why do you beg my pardon? It is not to me you should do that."

"Well, then, to Joe."

"How dare he come after me?"

"In love with you, I suppose."

She stamped her foot.

Ashurst uttered a short laugh. "Would you like me to punch his head?"

She cried with sudden passion:

"You laugh at me—you laugh at us!"

He caught hold of her hands, but she shrank back, till her passionate little face and loose dark hair were caught among the pink clusters of the apple blossom. Ashurst raised one of her imprisoned hands and put his lips to it. He felt how chivalrous he was, and superior to that clod Joe—just brushing that small, rough hand with his mouth! Her shrinking ceased suddenly; she seemed to tremble towards him. A sweet warmth overtook Ashurst from top to toe. This slim maiden, so simple and fine and pretty, was pleased, then, at the touch of his lips! And, yielding to a swift impulse, he put his arms round her, pressed her to him, and kissed her forehead. Then he was frightened—she went so pale, closing her eyes, so that the long, dark lashes lay on her pale cheeks; her hands, too, lay inert at her sides. The touch of her breast sent a shiver through him. "Megan" he sighed out, and let her go. In the utter silence a blackbird shouted. Then the girl seized his hand, put it to her cheek, her heart, her lips, kissed it passionately, and fled away among the mossy trunks of the apple trees, till they hid her from him.

Ashurst sat down on a twisted old tree growing almost along the ground, and, all throbbing and bewildered, gazed vacantly at the blossom which had crowned her hair—those pink buds with one white open apple star. What had he done? How had he let himself be thus stampeded by beauty—or—just the spring! He felt curiously happy, all the same; happy and triumphant, with shivers running through his limbs, and a vague alarm. This was the beginning of—what? The midges bit him, the dancing gnats tried to fly into his mouth, and all the spring around him seemed to grow more lovely and alive; the songs of the cuckoos and the blackbirds, the laughter of the yaffles, the level-slanting sunlight, the apple blossom which had crowned her head——! He got up from the old trunk and strode out of the orchard, wanting space, an open sky, to get on terms with these new sensations. He made for the moor, and from an ash tree in the hedge a magpie flew out to herald him.

Of man—at any age from five years on—who can say he has never been in love? Ashurst had loved his partners at his dancing class; loved his nursery governess; girls in school-holidays; perhaps never been quite out of love, cherishing always some more or less remote admiration. But this was different, not remote at all. Quite a new sensation; terribly delightful, bringing a sense of completed manhood. To be holding in his fingers such a wild flower, to be able to put it to his lips, and feel it tremble with delight against them! What intoxication, and—embarrassment! What to do with it—how to meet her next time? His first caress had been cool, pitiful; but the next could not be, now that, by her burning little kiss on his hand, by her pressure of it to her heart, he knew that she loved him. Some natures are coarsened by love bestowed on them; others, like Ashurst's, are swayed and drawn, warmed and softened, almost exalted, by what they feel to be a sort of miracle.

And up there among the tors he was racked between the passionate desire to revel in this new sensation of spring fulfilled within him, and a vague but very real uneasiness. At one moment he gave himself up completely to his pride at having captured this pretty, trustful, dewy-eyed thing! At the next he thought with factitious solemnity: 'Yes, my boy! But look out what you're doing! You know what comes of it!'

Dusk dropped down without his noticing—dusk on the carved, Assyrian-looking masses of the rocks. And the voice of Nature said: "This is a new world for you" As when a man gets up at four o'clock and goes out into a summer morning, and beasts, birds, trees stare at him and he feels as if all had been made new.

He stayed up there for hours, till it grew cold, then groped his way down the stones and heather roots to the road, back into the lane, and came again past the wild meadow to the orchard. There he struck a match and looked at his watch. Nearly twelve! It was black and unstirring in there now, very different from the lingering, bird-befriended brightness of six hours ago! And suddenly he saw this idyll of his with the eyes of the outer world—had mental vision of Mrs. Narracombe's snake-like neck turned, her quick dark glance taking it all in, her shrewd face hardening; saw the gipsy-like cousins coarsely mocking and distrustful; Joe stolid and furious; only the lame man, Jim, with the suffering eyes, seemed tolerable to his mind. And the village pub!—the gossiping matrons he passed on his walks; and then—his own friends—Robert Garton's smile when he went off that morning ten days ago; so ironical and knowing! Disgusting! For a minute he literally hated this earthly, cynical world to which one belonged, willy-nilly. The gate where he was leaning grew grey, a sort of shimmer passed before him and spread into the bluish darkness. The moon! He could just see it over the bank behind; red, nearly round—a strange moon! And turning away, he went up the lane which smelled of the night and cow-dung and young leaves. In the straw-yard he could see the dark shapes of cattle, broken by the pale sickles of their horns, like so many thin moons, fallen ends-up. He unlatched the farm gate stealthily. All was dark in the house. Muffling his footsteps, he gained the porch, and, blotted against one of the yew trees, looked up at Megan's window. It was open. Was she sleeping, or lying awake perhaps disturbed—unhappy at his absence? An owl hooted while he stood there peering up, and the sound seemed to fill the whole night, so quiet was all else, save for the never-ending murmur of the stream running below the orchard. The cuckoos by day, and now the owls—how wonderfully they voiced this troubled ecstasy within him! And suddenly he saw her at her window, looking out. He moved a little from the yew tree, and whispered: "Megan!" She drew back, vanished, reappeared, leaning far down. He stole forward on the grass patch, hit his shin against the green-painted chair, and held his breath at the sound. The pale blur of her stretched-down arm and face did not stir; he moved the chair, and noiselessly

mounted it. By stretching up his arm he could just reach. Her hand held the huge key of the front door, and he clasped that burning hand with the cold key in it. He could just see her face, the glint of teeth between her lips, her tumbled hair. She was still dressed— poor child, sitting up for him, no doubt! "Pretty Megan!" Her hot, roughened fingers clung to his; her face had a strange, lost look. To have been able to reach it—even with his hand! The owl hooted, a scent of sweetbriar crept into his nostrils. Then one of the farm dogs barked; her grasp relaxed, she shrank back.

"Good night, Megan!"

"Good night, sir!" She was gone! With a sigh he dropped back to earth, and sitting on that chair, took off his boots. Nothing for it but to creep in and go to bed; yet for a long while he sat unmoving, his feet chilly in the dew, drunk on the memory of her lost, half-smiling face, and the clinging grip of her burning fingers, pressing the cold key into his hand.

He awoke feeling as if he had eaten heavily overnight, instead of having eaten nothing. And far off, unreal, seemed yesterday's romance! Yet it was a golden morning. Full spring had burst at last—in one night the "goldie-cups," as the little boys called them, seemed to have made the field their own, and from his window he could see apple blossoms covering the orchard as with a rose and white quilt. He went down almost dreading to see Megan; and yet, when not she but Mrs. Narra-combe brought in his breakfast, he felt vexed and disappointed. The woman's quick eye and snaky neck seemed to have a new alacrity this morning. Had she noticed?

"So you an' the moon went walkin' last night, Mr. Ashurst! Did ye have your supper anywheres?"

Ashurst shook his head.

"We kept it for you, but I suppose you was too busy in your brain to think o' such a thing as that?"

Was she mocking him, in that voice of hers, which still kept some Welsh crispness against the invading burr of the West Country? If she knew! And at that moment he thought: 'No, no; I'll clear out. I won't put myself in such a beastly false position.'

But, after breakfast, the longing to see Megan began and increased with every minute, together with fear lest something should have been said to her which had spoiled everything. Sinister that she had not appeared, not given him even a glimpse of her! And the love poem, whose manufacture had been so important and absorbing yesterday afternoon under the apple trees, now seemed so paltry that he tore it up and rolled it into pipe spills. What had he known of love, till she seized his hand and kissed it! And now—what did he not know? But to write of it seemed mere insipidity! He went up to his bedroom to get a book, and his heart began to beat violently, for she was in there making the bed. He stood in the doorway watching; and suddenly, with turbulent joy, he saw her stoop and kiss his pillow, just at the hollow made by his head last night. How let her know he had seen that pretty act of devotion? And yet if she heard him stealing away, it would be even worse. She took the pillow up, holding it as if reluctant to shake out the impress of his cheek, dropped it, and turned round.

"Megan!"

She put her hands up to her cheeks, but her eyes seemed to look right into him. He had never before realized the depth and purity and touching faithfulness in those dew-bright eyes, and he stammered:

"It was sweet of you to wait up for me last night."

She still said nothing, and he stammered on:

"I was wandering about on the moor; it was such a jolly night. I—I've just come up for a book."

Then, the kiss he had seen her give the pillow afflicted him with sudden headiness, and he went up to her. Touching her eyes with his lips, he thought with queer excitement: 'I've done it! Yesterday all was sudden—anyhow; but now—I've done it!' The girl let her forehead rest against his lips, which moved downwards till they reached hers. That first real lover's kiss —strange, wonderful, still almost innocent—in which heart did it make the most disturbance?

"Come to the big apple tree tonight, after they've gone to bed. Megan—promise!"

She whispered back: " I promise!"

Then, scared at her white face, scared at everything, he let her go, and went downstairs again. Yes! he had done it now! Accepted her love, declared his own! He went out to the green chair as devoid of a book as ever; and there he sat staring vacantly before him, triumphant and remorseful, while under his nose and behind his back the work of the farm went on. How long he had been sitting in that curious state of vacancy he had no notion when he saw Joe standing a little behind him to the right. The youth had evidently come from hard work in the fields, and stood shifting his feet, breathing loudly, his face coloured like a setting sun, and his arms, below the rolled-up sleeves of his blue shirt, showing the hue and furry sheen of ripe peaches. His red lips were open, his blue eyes with their flaxen lashes stared fixedly at Ashurst, who said ironically:

"Well, Joe, anything I can do for you?"

"Yeas."

"What, then?"

"Yu can goo away from yere. Us don' want yu."

Ashurst's face, never too humble, assumed its most lordly look.

"Very good of you, but, do you know, I prefer the others should speak for themselves."

The youth moved a pace or two nearer, and the scent of his honest heat afflicted Ashurst's nostrils.

"What d'yu stay yere for?"

"Because it pleases me."

" 'Twon't please yu when I've bashed yure head in!"

"Indeed! When would you like to begin that?"

Joe answered only with the loudness of his breathing, but his eyes looked like those of a young and angry bull. Then a sort of spasm seemed to convulse his face.

"Megan don' want yu."

A rush of jealousy, of contempt, and anger with this thick, loud-breathing rustic got the better of Ashurst's self-possession; he jumped up and pushed back his chair.

"You can go to the devil!"

And as he said those simple words, he saw Megan in the doorway with a tiny brown spaniel puppy in her arms. She came up to him quickly:

"Its eyes are blue!" she said.

Joe turned away; the back of his neck was literally crimson.

Ashurst put his finger to the mouth of the tiny brown bull-frog of a creature in her arms. How cosy it looked against her!

"It's fond of you already. Ah! Megan, everything is fond of *you.*"

"What was Joe saying to you, please?"

"Telling me to go away, because you didn't want me here."

She stamped her foot; then looked up at Ashurst. At that adoring look he felt his nerves quiver, just as if he had seen a moth scorching its wings.

"Tonight!" he said. "Don't forget!"

"No." And smothering her face against the puppy's little fat, brown body, she slipped back into the house.

Ashurst wandered down the lane. At the gate of the wild meadow he came on the lame man and his cows.

"Beautiful day, Jim!"

"Ah! 'Tes brave weather for the grass. The ashes be later than th' oaks this year. 'When th' oak before th' ash—' "

Ashurst said idly: "Where were you standing when you saw the gipsy bogle, Jim?"

"It might be under that big apple tree, as you might say."

"And you really do think it was there?"

The lame man answered cautiously:

"I shouldn't like to say rightly that 't *was* there. 'Twas in my mind as 'twas there."

"What do you make of it?"

The lame man lowered his voice.

"They du zay old master, Mist' Narracombe, come o' gipsy stock. But that's tellin'. They'm a wonderful people, yu know, for claimin' their own. Maybe they knu 'e was goin', an' sent this feller along for company. That's what I've a-thought about it."

"What was he like?"

" 'E 'ad 'air all over 'is face, an' goin' like this, he was, zame as if 'e 'ad a viddle. They zay there's no such thing as bogles, but I've a-zeen the 'air on this dog standin' up of a dark naight, when I couldn' zee nothin', meself."

"Was there a moon?"

"Yeas, very near full, but 'twas on'y just risen, gold-like be'ind them trees."

"And you think a ghost means trouble, do you?"

The lame man pushed his hat up; his aspiring eyes looked at Ashurst more earnestly than ever.

" 'Tes' not for me to zay that—but 'tes they bein' so unrestin'-like. There's things us don' understand, that's zartin, fore zure. There's people that zee things, tu, an' others that don' never zee nothin'. Now, our Joe—yu might putt anything under 'is eyes an' 'e'd never zee it; and them other boys, tu, they'm rattlin' fellers. But yu take an' putt our

Megan where there's suthin', she'll zee it, an' more tu, or I'm mistaken."

"She's sensitive, that's why."

"What's that?"

"I mean, she feels everything."

"Ah! She'm very lovin'-'earted."

Ashurst, who felt colour coming into his cheeks, held out his tobacco pouch.

"Have a fill, Jim?"

"Thank 'ee, sir. She'm one in an 'underd, I think."

"I expect so," said Ashurst shortly, and folding up his pouch, walked on. "Lovin'-'earted!" Yes! And what was he doing? What were his intentions—as they say—towards this loving-hearted girl? The thought dogged him, wandering through fields bright with buttercups, where the little red calves were feeding, and the swallows flying high. Yes, the oaks were before the ashes, brown-gold already; every tree in different stage and hue. The cuckoos and a thousand birds were singing; the little streams were very bright. The ancients believed in a golden age, in the garden of the Hesperides! . . . A queen wasp settled on his sleeve. Each queen wasp killed meant two thousand fewer wasps to thieve the apples which would grow from that blossom in the orchard; but who, with love in his heart, could kill anything on a day like this? He entered a field where a young red bull was feeding. It seemed to Ashurst that he looked like Joe. But the young bull took no notice of this visitor, a little drunk himself, perhaps, on the singing and the glamour of the golden pasture, under his short legs. Ashurst crossed out unchallenged to the hillside above the stream. From that slop a tor mounted to its crown of rocks. The ground there was covered with a mist of bluebells, and nearly a score of crab-apple trees were in full bloom. He threw himself down on the grass. The change from the buttercup glory and oak-golden glamour of the fields to this ethereal beauty under the grey tor filled him with a sort of wonder; nothing the same, save the sound of running water and the songs of the cuckoos. He lay there a long time, watching the sunlight wheel till the crab-trees threw shadows over the bluebells, his only companions a few wild bees. He was not quite sane, thinking of that morning's kiss, and of tonight under the apple tree. In such a spot as this, fauns and dryads surely lived; nymphs, white as the crab-appleblossom, retired within those trees; fauns, brown as the dead bracken, with pointed ears, lay in wait for them. The cuckoos were still calling when he woke, there was the sound of running water; but the sun had couched behind the tor, the hillside was cool, and some rabbits had come out. 'Tonight!' he thought. Just as from the earth everything was pushing up unfolding under the soft insistent fingers of an unseen hand, so were his heart and senses being pushed, unfolded. He got up and broke off a spray from a crab-apple tree. The buds were like Megan—shell-like, rose-pink, wild, and fresh; and so, too, the opening flowers, white, and wild, and touching. He put the spray into his coat. And all the rush of the spring within him escaped in a triumphant sigh. But the rabbits scurried away.

It was nearly eleven that night when Ashurst put down the pocket *Odyssey* which for half an hour he had held in his hands without reading, and slipped through the yard down to the orchard. The moon had just risen, very golden, over the hill, and like a bright powerful, watching spirit peered through the bars of an ash tree's half-naked boughs. In among the apple trees it was still dark, and he stood making sure of his direction, feeling the rough grass with his feet. A black mass close behind him stirred with a heavy grunting sound, and three large pigs settled down again close to each other, under the wall. He listened. There was no wind, but the stream's burbling whispering chuckle had gained twice its daytime strength. One bird, he could not tell what, cried "Pip—pip," "Pip—pip," with perfect monotony; he could hear a night-jar spinning very far off; an owl hooting. Ashurst moved a step or two, and again halted, aware of a dim living whiteness all round his head. On the dark unstirring trees innumerable flowers and buds all soft and blurred were being bewitched to life by the creeping moonlight. He had the oddest feeling of actual companionship, as if a million white moths or spirits had floated in and settled between dark sky and darker ground, and were opening and shutting their wings on a level with his eyes. In the bewildering, still, scentless beauty of that moment he almost lost memory of why he had come to the orchard. The flying glamour which had clothed the earth all day had not gone now that night had fallen, but only changed into this new form. He moved on through the thicket of stems and boughs covered with that live powdering whiteness, till he reached the big apple tree. No mistaking that, even in the dark, nearly twice the height and size of any other, and leaning out towards the open meadows and the stream. Under the thick branches he stood still again, to listen. The same sounds exactly, and a faint grunting from the sleepy pigs. He put his hands on the dry, almost warm tree trunk, whose rough mossy surface gave forth a peaty scent at his touch. Would she come—would she? And among these quivering, haunting, moon-witched trees he was seized with doubts of everything! All was unearthly here, fit for no earthly lovers; fit only for god and goddess, faun and nymph—not for him and his little country girl. Would it not be almost a relief if she did not come? But all the time he was listening. And still that unknown bird went "Pip—pip," "Pip—pip," and there rose the busy chatter of the little trout stream, whereon the moon was flinging glances through the bars of her tree-prison. The blossom on a level with his eyes seemed to grow more living every moment, seemed with its mysterious white beauty more and more a part of his suspense. He plucked a fragment and held it close —three blossoms. Sacrilege to pluck fruit-tree blossom—soft, sacred, young blossom—and throw it away! Then suddenly he heard the gate close, the pigs stirring again and grunting; and leaning against the trunk, he pressed his hands to its mossy sides behind him, and held his breath. She might have been a spirit threading the trees, for all the noise she made! Then he saw her quite close—her dark form part of a little tree, her white face part of its blossoms; so still, and peering towards him. He whispered: "Megan!" and held out his hands. She ran forward, straight to his breast. When he felt her heart beating against him, Ashurst knew to the full the sensations of chivalry and passion. Because she was not of his world, because she was so simple and young and headlong, adoring and defenceless, how could he be other than her protector, in the dark! Because she was all simple Nature and beauty, as much a part of this spring night as was the living blossom, how should he not take all that she would give him—how not fulfil the spring in her heart and his! And torn between these two emotions he clasped her close, and kissed her hair. How long they stood there without speaking he knew not. The stream went on chattering, the owls hooting, the moon kept stealing up and growing whiter; the blossoms all round them and above brightened in suspense of living beauty. Their lips had sought each other's, and they did not speak. The moment speech began all would be unreal! Spring has no speech, nothing but rustling and whispering. Spring has so much more than speech in its unfolding flowers and leaves, and the coursing of its streams, and in its sweet restless seeking! And sometimes spring will come alive, and, like a mysterious Presence, stand, encircling lovers with its arms, laying on them the fingers of enchantment, so that, standing lips to lips, they forget everything but just a kiss. While her heart beat against him, and her lips quivered on his, Ashurst felt nothing but simple rapture—Destiny meant her for his arms, Love could not be flouted! But when their lips parted for breath, division began again at once. Only, passion now was so much the stronger, and he sighed:

"Oh! Megan! Why did you come?"

She looked up, hurt, amazed.

"Sir, you asked me to."

"Don't call me 'sir,' my pretty sweet."

"What should I be callin' you?"

"Frank."

"I could not. Oh, no!'

"But you love me—don't you?"

"I could not help lovin' you. I want to be with you—that's all."

"All!"

So faint that he hardly heard, she whispered:

"I shall die if I can't be with you."

Ashurst took a mighty breath.

"Come and be with me, then!"

"Oh!"

Intoxicated by the awe and rapture in that "Oh!" he went on, whispering:

"We'll go to London. I'll show you the world. And I *will* take care of you, I promise, Megan. I'll never be a brute to you!"

"If I can be with you—that is all."

He stroked her hair, and whispered on:

"Tomorrow I'll go to Torquay and get some money, and get you some clothes that won't be noticed, and then we'll steal away. And when we get to London, soon perhaps, if you love me well enough, we'll be married."

He could feel her hair shiver with the shake of her head.

"Oh, no! I could not. I only want to be with you!"

Drunk on his own chivalry, Ashurst went on murmuring:

"It's I who am not good enough for you. Oh! Megan, when did you begin to love me?"

"When I saw you in the road, and you looked at me. The first night I loved you; but I never thought you would want me."

She slipped down suddenly to her knees, trying to kiss his feet.

A shiver of horror went through Ashurst; he lifted her up bodily and held her fast—too upset to speak.

She whispered: "Why won't you let me?"

"It's I who will kiss your feet!"

Her smile brought tears into his eyes. The whiteness of her moonlit face so close to his, the faint pink of her opened lips, had the living unearthly beauty of the apple blossom.

And then, suddenly her eyes widened and stared past him painfully: she writhed out of his arms, and whispered: "Look!"

Ashurst saw nothing but the brightened stream, the furze faintly gilded, the beech trees glistening, and behind them all the wide loom of the moonlit hill. Behind him came her frozen whisper: "The gypsy bogle!"

"Where?"

"There — by the stone — under the trees!'

Exasperated, he leaped the stream, and strode towards the beech clump. Prank of the moonlight! Nothing! In and out of the boulders and thorn trees, muttering and cursing, yet with a kind of terror, he rushed and stumbled. Absurd! Silly! Then he went back to the apple-tree. But she was gone; he could hear a rustle, the grunting of the pigs, the sound of a gate closing. Instead of her, only this old apple-tree! He flung his arms round the trunk. What a substitute for her soft body; the rough moss against his face—what a substitute for her soft cheek; only the scent, as of the woods, a little the same! And above him, and around, the blossoms, more living, more moonlit than ever, seemed to glow and breathe.

Descending from the train at Torquay station, Ashurst wandered uncertainly along the front, for he did not know this particular queen of English watering places. Having little sense of what he had on, he was quite unconscious of being remarkable among its inhabitants, and strode along in his rough Norfolk jacket, dusty boots, and battered hat, without observing that people gazed at him rather blankly. He was seeking a branch of his London bank, and having found one, found also the first obstacle to his mood. Did he know anyone in Torquay? No. In that case, if he would wire to his bank in London, they would be happy to oblige him on receipt of the reply. That suspicious breath from the matter-of-fact world somewhat tarnished the brightness of his visions. But he sent the telegram.

Nearly opposite to the post office he saw a shop full of ladies' garments, and examined the window with strange sensations. To have to undertake the clothing of his rustic love was more than a little disturbing. He went in. A young woman came forward; she had blue eyes and a faintly puzzled forehead. Ashurst stared at her in silence.

"Yes, sir?"

"I want a dress for a young lady."

The young woman smiled. Ashurst frowned—the peculiarity of his request struck him with sudden force.

The young woman added hastily:

"What style would you like—something modish?"

"No. Simple."

"What figure would the young lady be?"

"I don't know; about two inches

shorter than you, I should say."

"Could you give me her waist measurement?"

Megan's waist!

"Oh! Anything usual!"

"Quite!"

While she was gone he stood disconsolately eyeing the models in the windows, and suddenly it seemed to him incredible that Megan—his Megan—could ever be dressed save in the rough tweed skirt, coarse blouse, and tam-o'-shanter cap he was wont to see her in. The young woman had come back with several dresses in her arms, and Ashurst eyed her laying them against her own modish figure. There was one whose color he liked, a dove-grey, but to imagine Megan clothed in it was beyond him. The young woman went away, and brought some more. But on Ashurst there had now come a feeling of paralysis. How choose? She would want a hat too, and shoes, and gloves; and, suppose, when he had got them all, they commonised her, as Sunday clothes always commonised village folk Why should she not travel as she was? Ah! but conspicuousness would matter; this was a serious elopement. And, staring at the young woman, he thought: 'I wonder if she guesses, and thinks me a blackguard?'

"Do you mind putting aside that grey one for me?" he said desperately at last. "I can't decide now; I'll come in again this afternoon."

The young woman sighed.

"Oh! certainly. It's a very tasteful costume. I don't think you'll get anything that will suit your purpose better."

"I expect not," Ashurst murmured, and went out.

Freed again from the suspicious matter-of-factness of the world, he took a long breath, and went back to visions. In fancy he saw the trustful, pretty creature who was going to join her life to his; saw himself and her stealing forth at night, walking over the moor under the moon, he with his arm round her, and carrying her new garments, till, in some far-off wood, when dawn was coming, she would slip off her old things and put on these, and an early train at a distant station would bear them away on their honeymoon journey, till London swallowed them up, and the dreams of love came true.

"Frank Ashurst! Haven't seen you since Rugby, old chap!"

Ashurst's frown dissolved; the face, close to his own, was blue-eyed, suffused with sun—one of those faces where sun from within and without join in a sort of lustre. And he answered:

"Phil Halliday, by Jove!"

"What are you doing here?"

"Oh! nothing. Just looking around, and getting some money. I'm staying on the moor."

"Are you lunching anywhere? Come and lunch with us; I'm here with my young sisters. They've had measles."

Hooked in by that friendly arm Ashurst went along, up a hill, down a hill, away out of the town, while the voice of Halliday, redolent of optimism as his face was of sun, explained how "in this mouldy place the only decent things were the bathing and boating," and so on, till presently they came to a crescent of houses a little above and back from the sea, and into the centre one—an hotel—made their way.

"Come up to my room and have a wash. Lunch'll be ready in a jiffy."

Ashurst contemplated his visage in a looking-glass. After his farmhouse bedroom, the comb and one spare shirt *régime* of the last fortnight, this room littered with clothes and brushes was a sort of Capua; and he thought: 'Queer—one doesn't realize——' But what—he did not quite know.

When he followed Halliday into the sitting-room for lunch, three faces, very fair and blue-eyed, were turned suddenly at the words: "This is Frank Ashurst —my young sisters."

Two were indeed young, about eleven and ten. The third was perhaps seventeen, tall and fair-haired too, with pink-and-white cheeks just touched by the sun, and eyebrows, rather darker than the hair, running a little upwards from her nose to their outer points. The voices of all three were like Halliday's, high and cheerful; they stood up straight, shook hands with a quick movement, looked at Ashurst critically, away again at once, and began to talk of what they were going to do in the afternoon. A regular Diana and attendant nymphs! After the farm this crisp, slangy, eager talk, this cool, clean, off-hand refinement, was queer at first, and then so natural that what he had come from became suddenly remote. The names of the two little ones seemed to be Sabina and Freda; of the eldest, Stella.

Presently the one called Sabina turned to him and said:

"I say, will you come shrimping with us?—it's awful fun!"

Surprised by this unexpected friendliness, Ashurst murmured:

"I'm afraid I've got to get back this afternoon."

"Oh!"

"Can't you put it off?"

Ashurst turned to the new speaker, Stella, shook his head, and smiled. She was very pretty! Sabina said regretfully: "You might!" Then the talk switched off to caves and swimming.

"Can you swim far?"

"About two miles."

"Oh!"

"I say!"

"How jolly!"

The three pairs of blue eyes, fixed on him, made him conscious of his new importance. The sensation was agreeable. Halliday said:

"I say, you simply must stop and have a bathe. You'd better stay the night."

398

"Yes, do!"

But again Ashurst smiled and shook his head. Then suddenly he found himself being catechised about his physical achievements. He had rowed—it seemed—in his college boat, played in his college football team, won his college mile and he rose from table a sort of hero. The two little girls insisted that he must see "their" cave, and they set forth chattering like magpies, Ashurst between them, Stella and her brother a little behind. In the cave, damp and darkish like any other cave, the great feature was a pool with possibility of creatures which might be caught and put into bottles. Sabina and Freda, who wore no stockings on their shapely brown legs, exhorted Ashurst to join them in the middle of it, and help sieve the water. He too was soon bootless and sockless. Time goes fast for one who has a sense of beauty, when there are pretty children in a pool and a young Diana on the edge, to receive with wonder anything you can catch! Ashurst never had much sense of time. It was a shock when, pulling out his watch, he saw it was well past three. No cashing his check today—the bank would be closed before he could get there. Watching his expression, the little girls cried out at once:

"Hurrah! Now you'll have to stay!"

Ashurst did not answer. He was seeing again Megan's face, when at breakfast he had whispered: "I'm going to Torquay, darling, to get everything; I shall be back this evening. If it's fine we can go tonight. Be ready." He was seeing again how she quivered and hung on his words. What would she think? Then he pulled himself together, conscious suddenly of the calm scrutiny of this other young girl, so tall and fair and Diana-like, at the edge of the pool, of her wondering blue eyes under those brows which slanted up a little. If they knew what was in his mind—if they knew that this very night he had

meant——! Well, there would be a little sound of disgust, and he would be alone in the cave. And with a curious mixture of anger, chagrin, and shame, he put his watch back into his pocket and said abruptly:

"Yes; I'm dished for today."

"Hurrah! Now you can bathe with us."

It was impossible not to succumb a little to the contentment of these pretty children, to the smile on Stella's lips, to Halliday's "Ripping, old chap! I can lend you things for the night!" But again a spasm of longing and remorse throbbed through Ashurst, and he said moodily:

"I must send a wire!"

The attractions of the pool palling, they went back to the hotel. Ashurst sent his wire, addressing it to Mrs. Narracombe: "Sorry, detained for the night, back tomorrow." Surely Megan would undertsand that he had too much to do; and his heart grew lighter. It was a lovely afternoon, warm, the sea calm and blue, and swimming his great passion; the favour of these pretty children flattered him, the pleasure of looking at them, at Stella, at Halliday's sunny face; the slight unreality, yet extreme naturalness of it all—as of a last peep at normality before he took this plunge with Megan! He got his borrowed bathing dress, and they all set forth. Halliday and he undressed behind one rock, the three girls behind another. He was first into the sea, and at once swam out with the bravado of justifying his self-given reputation. When he turned he could see Halliday swimming along shore, and the girls flopping and dipping, and riding the little waves, in the way he was accustomed to despise, but now thought pretty and sensible, since it gave him the distinction of the only deep-water fish. But drawing near, he wondered if they would like him, a stranger, to come into their splashing group; he felt shy, approaching that slim nymph. Then Sabina summoned him to teach her to float, and between them the little girls kept him so busy that he had no time even to notice whether Stella was accustomed to his presence, till suddenly he heard a startled sound from her. She was standing submerged to the waist, leaning a little forward, her slim white arms stretched out and pointing, her wet face puckered by the sun and an expression of fear.

"Look at Phil! Is he all right? Oh, look!"

Ashurst saw at once that Phil was not all right. He was splashing and struggling out of his depth, perhaps a hundred yards away; suddenly he gave a cry, threw up his arms, and went down. Ashurst saw the girl launch herself towards him, and crying out: "Go back, Stella! Go back!" he dashed out. He had never swun so fast, and reached Halliday just as he was coming up a second time. It was a case of cramp, but to get him in was not difficult, for he did not struggle. The girl, who had stopped where Ashurst told her to, helped as soon as he was in his depth, and once on the beach they sat down one on each side of him to rub his limbs, while the little ones stood by with scared faces. Halliday was soon smiling. It was—he said—rotten of him, absolutely rotten! If Frank would give him an arm, he could get to his clothes all right now. Ashurst gave him the arm, and as he did so caught sight of Stella's face, wet and flushed and tearful, all broken up out of its calm; and he thought: 'I called her Stella! Wonder if she minded?'

While they were dressing, Halliday said quietly:

"You saved my life, old chap!"

"Rot!"

Clothed, but not quite in their right minds, they went up all together to the hotel and sat down to tea, except Halliday who was lying down in his room. After some slices of bread and jam, Sabina said:

"I say, you know, you *are* a brick!"
And Freda chimed in:

"Rather!"

Ashurst saw Stella looking down; he got up in confusion, and went to the window. From there he heard Sabina mutter: "I say, let's swear blood bond. Where's your knife, Freda?" and out of the corner of his eye could see each of them solemnly prick herself, squeeze out a drop of blood and dabble on a bit of paper. He turned and made for the door.

"Don't be a stoat! Come back!" His arms were seized; imprisoned between the little girls he was brought back to the table. On it lay a piece of paper with an effigy drawn in blood, and the three names Stella Halliday, Sabina Halliday, Freda Halliday—also in blood, running towards it like the rays of a star. Sabina said:

"That's you. We shall have to kiss you, you know."

And Freda echoed:

"Oh! Blow—Yes!"

Before Ashurst could escape, some wettish hair dangled against his face, something like a bite descended on his nose, he felt his left arm pinched, and other teeth softly searching his cheek. Then he was released, and Freda said:

"Now, Stella."

Ashurst, red and rigid, looked across the table at a red and rigid Stella. Sabina giggled; Freda cried:

"Buck up—it spoils everything!"

A queer, ashamed eagerness shot through Ashurst: then he said quietly:

"Shut up, you little demons!"

Again Sabina giggled.

"Well, then, she can kiss her hand, and you can put it against your nose. It *is* on one side!"

To his amazement the girl did kiss her hand and stretch it out. Solemnly he took that cool, slim hand and laid it to his cheek. The two little girls broke into clapping, and Freda said:

"Now then, we shall have to save your life at any time; that's settled. Can I have another cup, Stella, not so beastly weak?"

Tea was resumed, and Ashurst, folding up the paper, put it in his pocket. The talk turned on the advantages of measles, tangerine oranges, honey in a spoon, no lessons; and so forth. Ashurst listened, silent, exchanging friendly looks with Stella, whose face was again of its normal sun-touched pink and white. It was soothing to be so taken to the heart of this jolly family, fascinating to watch their faces. And after tea, while the two little girls pressed seaweed, he talked to Stella in the window seat and looked at her water-colour sketches. The whole thing was like a pleasurable dream; time and incident hung up, importance and reality suspended. Tomorrow he would go back to Megan, with nothing of all this left save the paper with the blood of these children, in his pocket. Children! Stella was not quite that—as old as Megan! Her talk—quick, rather hard and shy, yet friendly—seemed to flourish on his silences, and about her there was something cool and virginal—a maiden in a bower. At dinner, to which Halliday, who had swallowed too much sea-water, did not come, Sabina said:

"I'm going to call you Frank."

Freda echoed:

"Frank, Frank, Franky."

Ashurst grinned and bowed.

"Every time Stella calls you Mr. Ashurst, she's got to pay a forfeit. It's ridiculous."

Ashurst looked at Stella, who grew slowly red. Sabina giggled; Freda cried:

"She's 'smoking'—'smoking!'—Yah!"

Ashurst reached out to right and left, and grasped some fair hair in each hand.

"Look here," he said, "you two! Leave Stella alone, or I'll tie you together!"

Freda gurgled:

"Ouch! You *are* a beast!"

Sabina murmured cautiously:

"*You* call *her* Stella, you see!"

"Why shouldn't I? It's a jolly name!"

"All right; we give you leave to!"

Ashurst released the hair. Stella! What would she call him—after this? But she called him nothing; till at bedtime he said, deliberately:

"Good night, Stella!"

"Good night, Mr. —— Good night, Frank! It *was* jolly of you, you know!"

"Oh—that! Bosh!"

Her quick, straight handshake tightened suddenly, and as suddenly, became slack.

Ashurst stood motionless in the empty sitting-room. Only last night, under the apple tree and the living blossom, he had held Megan to him, kissing her eyes and lips. And he gasped, swept by that rush of remembrance. Tonight it should have begun—his life with her who only wanted to be with him. And now, twenty-four hours and more must pass, because—of not looking at his watch! Why had he made friends with this family of innocents just when he was saying good-bye to innocence, and all the rest of it? 'But I mean to marry her,' he thought; 'I told her so!'

He took a candle, lighted it, and went to his bedroom, which was next to Halliday's. His friend's voice called as he was passing:

"Is that you, old chap? I say, come in."

He was sitting up in bed, smoking a pipe and reading.

"Sit down a bit."

Ashurst sat down by the open window.

"I've been thinking about this afternoon, you know," said Halliday rather suddenly. "They say you go through all your past. I didn't. I suppose I wasn't far enough gone."

"What did you think of?"

Halliday was silent for a little, then said quietly:

"Well, I did think of one thing—

401

rather odd—of a girl at Cambridge that I might have—you know; I was glad I hadn't got her on my mind. Anyhow, old chap, I owe it to you that I'm here; I should have been in the big dark by now. No more bed, no baccy; no more anything. I say, what d'you suppose happens to us?"

Ashurst murmured:

"Go out like flames, I expect."

"Phew!"

"We may flicker, and cling about a bit, perhaps."

"H'm! I think that's rather gloomy. I say, I hope my young sisters have been decent to you?"

"Awfully decent."

Halliday put his pipe down, crossed his hands behind his neck, and turned his face towards the window.

"They're not bad kids!" he said.

Watching his friend, lying there, with that smile, and the candle-light on his face, Ashurst shuddered. Quite true! He might have been lying there with no smile, with all that sunny look gone out for ever! He might not have been lying there at all, but "sanded" at the bottom of the sea, waiting for resurrection on the—ninth day, was it? And that smile of Halliday's seemed to him suddenly something wonderful, as if in it were all the difference between life and death— the little flame—the all! He got up, and said softly:

"Well, you ought to sleep, I expect. Shall I blow out?"

Halliday caught his hand.

"I can't say it, you know; but it must be rotten to be dead. Good-night, old boy!"

Stirred and moved, Ashurst squeezed the hand, and went downstairs. The hall door was still open, and he passed out on to the lawn before the Crescent. The stars were bright in a very dark blue sky, and by their light some lilacs had that mysterious color of flowers by night which no one can describe. Ashurst pressed his face against a spray;

and before his closed eyes Megan started up, with the tiny brown spaniel pup against her breast. "I thought of a girl that I might have—you know. I was glad I hadn't got her on my mind!" He jerked his head away from the lilac, and began pacing up and down over the grass, a gray phantom coming to substance for a moment in the light from the lamp at either end. He was with her again under the living, breathing whiteness of the blossom, the stream chattering by, the moon glinting steel-blue on the bathing-pool; back in the rapture of his kisses on her upturned face of innocence and humble passion, back in the suspense and beauty of that pagan night. He stood still once more in the shadow of the lilacs. Here the sea, not the stream, was Night's voice; the sea with its sigh and rustle; no little bird, no owl, no nightjar called or spun; but a piano tinkled, and the white houses cut the sky with solid curve, and the scent from the lilacs filled the air.

A window of the hotel, high up, was lighted; he saw a shadow move across the blind. And most queer sensations stirred within him, a sort of churning, and twining, and turning of a single emotion on itself, as though spring and love, bewildered and confused, seeking the way, were baffled. This girl, who had called him Frank, whose hand had given his that sudden little clutch, this girl so cool and pure—what would *she* think of such wild, unlawful loving? He sank down on the grass, setting there cross-legged, with his back to the house, motionless as some carved Buddha. Was he really going to break through innocence, and steal? Sniff the scent out of a wild flower, and—perhaps—throw it away? "Of a girl at Cambridge that I might have—you know!" He put his hands to the grass, one on each side, palms downward, and pressed; it was just warm still—the grass, barely moist, soft and firm and friendly. 'What am I going to do?' he thought. Perhaps

Megan was at her window, looking out at the blossom, thinking of him! Poor little Megan! 'Why not?' he thought. 'I love her! But do I—really love her? or do I only want her because she is so pretty, and loves me? What am I going to do?' The piano tinkled on, the stars winked; and Ashurst gazed out before him at the dark sea, as if spell-bound. He got up at last, cramped and rather chilly. There was no longer light in any window. And he went in to bed.

Out of a deep and dreamless sleep he was awakened by the sound of thumping on the door. A shrill voice called:
"Hi! Breakfast's ready."
He jumped up. Where was he——? Ah!
He found them already eating marmalade, and sat down in the empty place between Stella and Sabina, who, after watching him a little, said:
"I say, do buck up; we're going to start at half-past nine."
"We're going to Berry Head, old chap; you *must* come!"
Ashurst thought: 'Come! Impossible. I shall be getting things and going back.' He looked at Stella. She said quickly:
"Do come!"
Sabina chimed in:
"It'll be no fun without you."
Freda got up and stood behind his chair.
"You've got to come, or else I'll pull your hair!"
Ashurst thought: 'Well—one day more—to think it over! One day more!' And he said:
"All right! You needn't tweak my mane!"
"Hurrah!"
At the station he wrote a second telegram to the farm, and then—tore it up; he could not have explained why. From Brixham they drove in a very little wagonette. There, squeezed between Sabina and Freda, with his knees touching

Stella's, they played "Up Jenkins"; and the gloom he was feeling gave way to frolic. In this one day more to think it over, he did not want to think! They ran races, wrestled, paddled—for today nobody wanted to bathe—they sang catches, played games, and ate all they had brought. The little girls fell asleep against him on the way back, and his knees still touched Stella's in the wagonette. It seemed incredible that thirty hours ago he had never set eyes on any of those three flaxen heads. In the train he talked to Stella of poetry, discovering her favourites, and telling her his own with a pleasing sense of superiority; till suddenly she said, rather low:
"Phil says you don't believe in a future life, Frank. I think that's dreadful."
Disconcerted, Ashurst muttered:
"I don't either believe or not believe —I simply don't know."
She said quickly:
"I couldn't bear that. What would be the use of living?"
Watching the frown of those pretty oblique brows, Ashurst answered:
"I don't believe in believing things because one wants to."
"But why should one *wish* to live again, if one isn't going to?"
And she looked full at him.
He did not want to hurt her, but an itch to dominate pushed him on to say:
"While one's alive one naturally wants to go on living for ever; that's part of being alive. But it probably isn't anything more."
"Don't you believe in the Bible at all, then?"
Ashurst thought: 'Now I shall really hurt her!'
"I believe in the sermon on the Mount, because it's beautiful and good for all time."
"But don't you believe Christ was divine?"
He shook his head.
She turned her face quickly to the

window, and there sprang into his mind Megan's prayer, repeated by little Nick: "God bless us all, and Mr. Ashes!" Who else would ever say a prayer for him, like her who at this moment must be waiting—waiting to see him come down the lane? And he thought suddenly: 'What a scoundrel I am!'

All that evening this thought kept coming back; but, as is not unusual, each time with less poignancy, till it seemed almost a matter of course to be a scoundrel. And—strange!—he did not know whether he was a scoundrel if he meant to go back to Megan, or if he did not mean to go back to her.

They played cards till the children were sent off to bed; then Stella went to the piano. From over on the window seat, where it was nearly dark, Ashurst watched her between the candles—that fair head on the long, white neck bending to the movement of her hands. She played fluently, without much expression; but what a picture she made, the faint golden radiance, a sort of angelic atmosphere—hovering about her! Who could have passionate thoughts or wild desires in the presence of that swaying, white-clothed girl with the seraphic head? She played a thing of Schumann's called *"Warum?"* Then Halliday brought out a flute, and the spell was broken. After this they made Ashurst sing, Stella playing him accompaniments from a book of Schumann songs, till, in the middle of *"Ich grolle nicht,"* two small figures clad in blue dressing gowns crept in and tried to conceal themselves beneath the piano. The evening broke up in confusion, and what Sabina called "a splendid rag."

That night Ashurst hardly slept at all. He was thinking, tossing and turning. The intense domestic intimacy of these last two days, the strength of this Halliday atmosphere, seemed to ring him around, and make the farm and Megan—even Megan—seem unreal. Had he really made love to her—really promised to take her away to live with him? He must have been bewitched by the spring, the night, the apple blossom! The notion that he was going to make her his mistress—that simple child not yet eighteen—now filled him with a sort of horror, even while it still stung and whipped his blood. He muttered to himself: "It's awful, what I've done—awful!" And the sound of Schumann's music throbbed and mingled with his fevered thoughts, and he saw again Stella's cool, white, fair-haired figure and bending neck, the queer, angelic radiance about her. 'I must have been—I must be—mad!' he thought. 'What came into me? Poor little Megan!'

"God bless us all, and Mr. Ashes!" "I want to be with you—only to be with you!" And burying his face in his pillow, he smothered down a fit of sobbing. Not to go back was awful! To go back—more awful still.

Emotion, when you are young, and give real vent to it, loses its power of torture. And he fell asleep, thinking: 'What was it—a few kisses—all forgotten in a month!'

Next morning he got his check cashed, but avoided the shop of the dove-grey dress like the plague; and, instead, bought himself some necessaries. He spent the whole day in a queer mood, cherishing a kind of sullenness against himself. Instead of the hankering of the last two days, he felt nothing but a blank—all passionate longing gone, as if quenched in that outburst of tears. After tea Stella put a book down beside him, and said shyly:

"Have you read that, Frank?"

It was Farrar's *Life of Christ*. Ashurst smiled. Her anxiety about his beliefs seemed to him comic, but touching. Infectious, too, perhaps, for he began to have an itch to justify himself, if not to convert her. And in the evening, when the children and Halliday were mending their shrimping nets, he said:

"At the back of orthodox religion, so far as I can see, there's always the idea of reward—what you can get for being good; a kind of begging for favours. I think it all starts in fear."

She was sitting on the sofa making reefer knots with a bit of string. She looked up quickly:

"I think it's much deeper than that." Ashurst felt again that wish to dominate.

"You think so," he said; "but wanting the *'quid pro quo'* is about the deepest thing in all of us! It's jolly hard to get to the bottom of it!"

She wrinkled her brows in a puzzled frown.

"I don't think I understand."

He went on obstinately:

"Well, think, and see if the most religious people aren't those who feel that this life doesn't give them all they want. I believe in being good because to be good is good in itself."

"Then you do believe in being good?"

How pretty she looked now—it was easy to be good with her! He nodded and said:

"I say, show me how to make that knot!"

With her fingers touching his, in manœuvering the bit of string he felt soothed and happy. And when he went to bed he willfully kept his thoughts on her, wrapping himself in her fair, cool sisterly radiance, as in some garment of protection.

Next day he found they had arranged to go by train to Totnes, and picnic at Berry Pomeroy Castle. Still in that resolute oblivion of the past, he took his place with them in the landau beside Halliday, back to the horses. And, then, along the sea front, nearly at the turning to the railway station, his heart almost leaped into his mouth. Megan—Megan herself!—was walking on the far pathway, in her old skirt and jacket and her tam-o'-shanter, looking up into the faces of the passers-by. Instinctively

he threw his hand up for cover, then made a feint of clearing dust out of his eyes; but between his fingers he could see her still, moving, not with her free country step, but wavering, lost-looking, pitiful—like some little dog which has missed its master and does not know whether to run on, or run back—where to run. How had she come like this?—what excuse had she found to get away? —what did she hope for? But with every turn of the wheels bearing him away from her, his heart revolted and cried to him to stop them, to get out, and go to her! When the landau turned the corner to the station he could stand no more, and opening the carriage door, muttered: "I've forgotten something! Go on—don't wait for me! I'll join you at the castle by the next train!" He jumped, stumbled, spun around, recovered his balance, and walked forward, while the carriage with the astonished Hallidays rolled on.

From the corner he could only just see Megan, a long way ahead now. He ran a few steps, checked himself, and dropped into a walk. With each step nearer to her, further from the Hallidays, he walked more and more slowly. How did it alter anything—this sight of her? How make the going to her, and that which must come of it, less ugly? For there was no hiding it—since he had met the Hallidays he had become gradually sure that he would not marry Megan. It would only be a wild lovetime, a troubled, remorseful, difficult time—and then—well, then he would get tired, just because she gave him everything, was so simple, and so trustful, so dewy. And dew—wears off! The little spot of faded colour, her tam-o'-shanter cap, wavered on far in front of him, she was looking up into every face, and at the house windows. Had any man ever such a cruel moment to go through? Whatever he did, he felt he would be a beast. And he uttered a groan which made a nurse-maid turn and stare. He saw Megan stop and lean against the sea-wall, looking at the sea; and he too stopped. Quite likely she had never seen the sea before, and even in her distress could not resist that sight. 'Yes—she's seen nothing,' he thought; 'everything's before her. And just for a few weeks' passion, I shall be cutting her life to ribbons. I'd better go and hang myself rather than do it!' And suddenly he seemed to see Stella's calm eyes looking into his, the wave of fluffy hair on her forehead stirred by the wind. Ah! it would be madness, would mean giving up all that he respected, and his own self-respect. He turned and walked quickly back towards the station. But memory of that poor, bewildered little figure, those anxious eyes searching the passers-by, smote him too hard again, and once more he turned towards the sea. The cap was no longer visible; that little spot of colour had vanished in the stream of the noon promenaders. And impelled by the passion of longing, the dearth which comes on one when life seems to be whiling something out of reach, he hurried forward. She was nowhere to be seen; for half an hour he looked for her; then on the beach flung himself face downward in the sand. To find her again he knew he had only to go to the station and wait till she returned from her fruitless quest, to take her train home; or to take train himself and go back to the farm, so that she found him there when she returned. But he lay inert in the sand, among the indifferent groups of children with their spades and buckets. Pity at her little figure wandering, seeking, was well-nigh merged in the spring-running of his blood; for it was all wild feeling now— the chivalrous part, what there had been of it, was gone. He wanted her again, wanted her kisses, her soft, little body, her abandonment, all her quick, warm, pagan emotion; wanted the wonderful feeling of that night under the moonlit apple boughs; wanted it all with a horrible intensity, as the faun wants the nymph. The quick chatter of the little bright trout-stream, the dazzle of the buttercups, the rocks of the old "wild men"; the calling of the cuckoos and yaffles, the hooting of the owls; and the red moon peeping out of the velvet dark at the living whiteness of the blossom; and her face just out of reach at the window, lost in its love-look; and her heart against his, her lips answering his, under the apple tree— all this besieged him. Yet he lay inert. What was it which struggled against pity and this feverish longing, and kept him there paralyzed in the warm sand? Three flaxen heads—a fair face with friendly blue-grey eyes, a slim hand pressing his, a quick voice speaking his name—"So you do believe in being good?" Yes, and a sort of atmosphere as of some old walled-in English garden, with pinks, and corn-flowers, and roses, and scents of lavender and lilac—cool and fair, untouched, almost holy—all that he had been brought up to feel was clean and good. And suddenly he thought: 'She might come along the front again and see me!' and he got up and made his way to the rock at the far end of the beach. There, with the spray biting into his face, he could think more coolly. To go back to the farm and love Megan out in the woods, among the rocks, with everything around wild and fitting—that, he knew, was impossible, utterly. To transplant her to a great town, to keep, in some little flat or rooms, one who belonged so wholly to Nature—the poet in him shrank from it. His passion would be a mere sensuous revel, soon gone; in London, her very simplicity, her lack of all intellectual quality, would make her his secret plaything—nothing else. The longer he sat on the rock, with his feet dangling over a greenish pool from which the sea was ebbing, the more clearly he saw this; but it was as if her arms and all of her were slipping slowly, slowly down from him, into the pool, to be carried away out to sea; and her face looking up, her lost face with beseeching eyes, and dark, wet hair—possessed, haunted, tortured him! He got up at last, scaled the low rock-cliff, and made his way down into a sheltered cove. Perhaps in the sea he could get back his control—lose this fever! And stripping off his clothes, he swam out. He wanted to tire himself so that nothing mattered, and swam recklessly, fast and far; then suddenly, for no reason, felt afraid. Suppose he could not reach shore again—suppose the current set him out—or he got cramp, like Halliday! He turned to swim in. The red cliffs looked a long way off. If he were drowned they would find his clothes. The Hallidays would know; but Megan perhaps never—they took no newspaper at the farm. And Phil Halliday's words came back to him again: "A girl at Cambridge I might have—Glad I haven't got her on my mind!" And in that moment of unreasoning fear he vowed he would not have her on his mind. Then his fear left him; he swam in easily enough, dried himself in the sun, and put on his clothes. His heart felt sore, but no longer ached; his body cool and refreshed.

When one is as young as Ashurst, pity is not a violent emotion. And, back in the Hallidays' sitting-room, eating a ravenous tea, he felt much like a man recovered from fever. Everything seemed new and clear; the tea, the buttered toast and jam tasted absurdly good; tobacco had never smelt so nice. And walking up and down the empty room, he stopped here and there to touch or look. He took up Stella's work-basket, fingered the cotton reels and a gaily-coloured plait of sewing silks, smelt at the little bag filled with woodroffe she kept among them. He sat down at the piano, playing tunes with one finger, thinking; 'Tonight she'll play; I shall watch her while she's playing; it does me good to watch her.' He took up the book, which still lay where she had placed it beside him, and tried to read. But Megan's little, sad figure began to come back at once, and he got up and leaned in the window, listening to the thrushes in the Crescent gardens, gazing at the sea, dreamy and blue below the trees. A servant came in and cleared the tea away, and he still stood, inhaling the evening air, trying not to think. Then he saw the Hallidays coming through the gate of the Crescent, Stella a little in front of Phil and the children, with their baskets, and instinctively he drew back. His heart, too sore and discomfited, shrank from this encounter, yet wanted its friendly solace —bore a grudge against this influence, yet craved its cool innocence, and the pleasure of watching Stella's face. From against the wall behind the piano he saw her come in and stand looking a little blank as though disappointed; then she saw him and smiled, a swift, brilliant smile which warmed yet irritated Ashurst.

"You never came after us, Frank."

"No; I found I couldn't."

"Look! We picked such lovely late violets!" She held out a bunch. Ashurst put his nose to them, and there stirred within him vague longings, chilled instantly by a vision of Megan's anxious face lifted to the faces of the passers-by.

He said shortly: "How jolly!" and turned away. He went up to his room, and, avoiding the children, who were coming up the stairs, threw himself on his bed, and lay there with his arms crossed over his face. Now that he felt the die really cast, and Megan given up, he hated himself, and almost hated the Hallidays and their atmosphere of healthy, happy English homes. Why should they have chanced here, to drive away first love—to show him that he was going to be no better than a common seducer? What right had Stella, with her fair, shy beauty, to make him know for certain that he would never marry Megan; and, tarnishing it all, bring him such bitterness of regretful longing and such pity? Megan would be back by now, worn out by her miserable seeking—poor little thing!—expecting, perhaps, to find him there when she reached home. Ashurst bit at his sleeve, to stifle a groan of remorseful longing. He went to dinner glum and silent, and his mood threw a dinge even over the children. It was a melancholy, rather ill-tempered evening, for they were all tired; several times he caught Stella looking at him with a hurt, puzzled expression, and this pleased his evil mood. He slept miserably; got up quite early, and wandered out. He went down to the beach. Alone there with the serene, the blue, the sunlit sea, his heart relaxed a little. Conceited fool—to think that Megan would take it so hard! In a week or two she would almost have forgotten! And he—well, he would have the reward of virtue! A good young man! If Stella knew, she would give him her blessing for resisting that devil she believed in; and he uttered a hard laugh. But slowly the peace and beauty of sea and sky, the flight of the lonely seagulls, made him feel ashamed. He bathed, and turned homeward.

In the Crescent gardens Stella herself was sitting on a camp stool, sketching. He stole up close behind. How fair and pretty she was, bent diligently, holding up her brush, measuring, wrinkling her brows.

He said gently:

"Sorry I was such a beast last night, Stella."

She turned round, startled, flushed very pink, and said in her quick way:

"It's all right. I knew there was something. Between friends it doesn't matter, does it?"

Ashurst answered:

"Between friends—and we are, aren't we?"

She looked up at him, nodded vehe-mently, and her upper teeth gleamed again it that swift, brilliant smile.

Three days later he went back to London, traveling with the Hallidays. He had not written to the farm. What was there he could say?

On the last day of April in the following year he and Stella were married. . . .

Such were Ashurst's memories, sitting against the wall among the gorse, on his silver-wedding day. At this very spot, where he had laid out the lunch, Megan must have stood outlined against the sky when he had first caught sight of her. Of all queer coincidences! And there moved in him a longing to go down and see again the farm and the orchard, and the meadow of the gipsy bogle. It would not take long; Stella would be an hour yet, perhaps.

How well he remembered it all—the little crowning group of pine trees, the steep-out grass hill behind! He paused at the farm gate. The low stone house, the yew-tree porch, the flowering currants—not changed a bit; even the old green chair was out there on the grass under the window, where he had reached up to her that night to take the key. Then he turned down the lane, and stood leaning on the orchard gate—grey skeleton of a gate, as then. A black pig even was wandering in there among the trees. Was it true that twenty-six years had passed, or had he dreamed and awakened to find Megan waiting for him by the big apple tree? Unconsciously he put up his hand to his grizzled beard and brought himself back to reality. Opening the gate, he made his way down through the docks and nettles till he came to the edge and the old apple tree itself. Unchanged! A little more of the grey-green lichen, a dead branch or two, and for the rest it might have been only last night that he had embraced that mossy trunk after Megan's flight and inhaled its woody savour, while above his head the moonlit

408

blossom had seemed to breathe and live. In that early spring a few buds were showing already; the blackbirds shouting their songs, a cuckoo calling, the sunlight bright and warm. Incredibly the same—the chattering trout-stream, the narrow pool he had lain in every morning, splashing the water over his flanks and chest; and out there in the wild meadow the beech clump and the stone where the gipsy bogle was supposed to sit. And an ache for lost youth, a hankering, a sense of wasted love and sweetness, gripped Ashurst by the throat. Surely, on this earth of such wild beauty, one was meant to hold rapture to one's heart, as this earth and sky held it! And yet, one could not!

He went to the edge of the stream, and looking down at the little pool, thought: 'Youth and spring! What has become of them all, I wonder?' And then, in sudden fear of having this memory jarred by human encounter, he went back to the lane, and pensively retraced his steps to the cross-roads.

Beside the car an old, grey-bearded labourer was leaning on a stick, talking to the chauffeur. He broke off at once, as though guilty of disrespect, and touching his hat, prepared to limp on down the lane.

Ashurst pointed to the narrow green mound. "Can you tell me what this is?"

The old fellow stopped; on his face had come a look as though he were thinking: 'You've come to the right shop, mister!'

" 'Tes a grave," he said.

"But why out here?"

The old man smiled. "That's a tale, as yu may say. An' not the first time as I've a-told et—there's plenty folks asks 'bout that bit o' turf. 'Maid's Grave' us calls et, 'ereabouts."

Ashurst held out his pouch. "Have a fill?"

The old man touched his hat again, and slowly filled an old clay pipe. His eyes, looking upward out of a mass of wrinkles and hair, were still quite bright.

"If yu don' mind, zurr, I'll zet down—my leg's 'urtin' a bit today." And he sat down on the mound of turf.

"There's always a vlower on this grave. An' 'tain't so very lonesome, neither; brave lot o' folks goes by now, in they new motor cars an' things—not as 'twas in th' old days. She've a-got company up 'ere. 'Twas a poor soul killed 'erself."

"I see!" said Ashurst. "Cross-roads burial. I didn't know that custom was kept up."

"Ah! but 'twas a main long time ago. Us 'ad a parson as was very God-fearin' then. Let me see, I've a 'ad my pension six year come Michaelmas, an' I were just on fifty when t'appened. There's none livin' knows more about et than what I du. She belonged close 'ere; same farm as where I used to work along o' Mrs. Narracombe—'tes Nick Narracombe's now; I dus a bit for 'im still, odd times."

Ashurst, who was leaning against the gate, lighting his pipe, left his curved hands before his face for long after the flame of the match had gone out.

"Yes?" he said, and to himself his voice sounded hoarse and queer.

"She was one in an 'underd, poor maid! I putts a vlower 'ere every time I passes. Pretty maid an' gude maid she was, though they wouldn't burry 'er up tu th' church, nor where she wanted to be buried neither." The old labourer paused, and put his hairy, twisted hand flat down on the turf beside the blue-bells.

"Yes?" said Ashurst.

"In a manner of speakin'," the old man went on, "I think as 'twas a love-story—though there's no one never knu for zartin. Yu can't tell what's in a maid's 'ead—but that's wot I think about it." He drew his hand along the turf. "I was fond o' that maid—don' know as there was anyone as wasn' fond

409

of 'er. But she was tu lovin'-'earted—that's where 'twas, I think." He looked up. And Ashurst, whose lips were trembling in the cover of his beard, murmured again: "Yes?"

"'Twas in the spring, 'bout now as 't might be, or a little later—blossom time—an' we 'ad one o' they young college gentlemen stayin' at the farm—nice feller tu, with 'is 'ead in the air. I liked 'e very well, an' I never see nothin' between 'em, but to my thinkin' 'e turned the maid's fancy." The old man took the pipe out of his mouth, spat, and went on:

"Yu see, 'e went away sudden one day, an' never come back. They got 'is knapsack and bits o' things down there still. That's what stuck in my mind—'is never sendin' for 'em. 'Is name was Ashes, or somethin' like that."

"Yes?" said Ashurst once more.

The old man licked his lips.

"'Er never said nothin', but from that day 'er went kind of dazed lukin'; didn't seem rightly therr at all. I never knu a 'uman creature so changed in me life—never. There was another young feller at the farm—Joe Biddaford 'is name wer', that was praaperly sweet on 'er, tu; I guess 'e used to plague 'er wi' 'is attentions. She got to luke quite wild. I'd zee her sometimes of an avenin' when I was bringin' up the calves; ther' she'd stand in th' orchard, under the big apple tree, lukin' straight before 'er. 'Well,' I used t' think, 'I dunno what 'tes that's the matter wi' yu, but yu'm lukin' pitiful, that yu be!'"

The old man relit his pipe, and sucked at it reflectively.

"Yes?" said Ashurst.

"I remembers one day I said to 'er; 'What's the matter, Megan?'—'er name was Megan David, she come from Wales same as 'er aunt, ol' Missis Narracombe. 'Yu'm frettin' about somethin',' I says. 'No, Jim,' she says, 'I'm not frettin'.' 'Yes, yu be!' I says. 'No,' she says, and tu tears cam' rollin' out. 'Yu'm cryin'—what's that, then?' I says. She putts 'er 'and over 'er 'eart: 'It 'urts me,' she says; 'but 'twill sune be better,' she says. 'But if anything shude 'appen to me, Jim, I wants to be burried under this 'ere apple tree.' I laughed. 'What's goin' to 'appen to yu?' I says: 'don't 'ee be fulish.' 'No,' she says, 'I won't be fulish.' Well, I know what maids are, an' I never thought no more about et, till tu days arter that, 'bout six in the avenin' I was comin' up wi' the calves, when I see somethin' dark lyin' in the strame, close to that big apple tree. I says to meself: 'Is that a pig—funny place for a pig to get to!' an' I goes up to et, an' I see what 'twas."

The old man stopped: his eyes, turned upward, had a bright, suffering look.

"'Twas the maid, in a little narrer pool ther' that's made by the stoppin' of a rock—where I see the young gentleman bathin' once or twice. 'Er was lyin' on 'er face in the watter. There was a plant o' goldie-cups growin' out o' the stone just above 'er 'ead. An' when I come to luke at 'er face, 'twas luvly, butiful, so calm's a baby's—wonderful butiful et was. When the doctor saw 'er, 'e said: 'Er culdn' never a'done it in that little bit o' watter ef 'er 'adn't a-been in an extarsy.' Ah! an' judgin' from 'er face, that was just 'ow she was. Et made me cry praaper—butiful et was! 'Twas June then, but she'd a-found a little bit of apple-blossom left over somewheres, and stuck et in 'er 'air. That's why I thinks 'er must a-been in an extarsy, to go to et gay, like that. Why! there wasn't more than a fute and 'arf o' watter. But I tell 'ee one thing—that meadder's 'arnted; I knu et, an' she knu et; an' no one'll persuade me as 'tesn't. I told 'em what she said to me 'bout bein' burried under th' apple tree. But I think that turned 'em—made et luke tu much 's ef she'd 'ad it in 'er mind deliberate; an' so they burried 'er up 'ere. Parson we 'ad then was very particular, 'e was."

Again the old man drew his hand over the turf.

" 'Tes wonderful, et seems," he added slowly, "what maids'll du for love. She 'ad a lovin' 'eart; I guess 'twas broken. But us never *knu* nothin'!"

He looked up as if for approval of his story, but Ashurst had walked past him as if he were not there.

Up on the top of the hill, beyond where he had spread the lunch, over, out of sight, he lay down on his face. So had his virtue been rewarded, and "The Cyprian," goddess of love, taken her revenge! And before his eyes, dim with tears, came Megan's face with the sprig of apple blossoms in her dark, wet hair. 'What did I do that was wrong?' he thought. 'What did I do?' But he could not answer. Spring, with its rush of passion, its flowers and song—the spring in his heart and Megan's! Was it just Love seeking a victim! The Greek was right, then—the words of the "Hippolytus" as true today!

"For mad is the heart of Love,
And gold the gleam of his wing;
And all to the spell thereof
Bend when he makes his spring.
All life that is wild and young
In mountain and wave and stream,
All that of earth is sprung,
Or breathes in the red sunbeam;
Yea, and Mankind. O'er all a royal throne
Cyprian, Cyprian, is thine alone!"

The Greek was right! Megan! Poor little Megan—coming over the hill! Megan under the old apple tree waiting and looking! Megan dead, with beauty printed on her! . . .

A voice said:

"Oh, there you are! Look."

Ashurst rose, took his wife's sketch, and stared at it in silence.

"Is the foreground right, Frank?"

"Yes."

"But there's something wanting, isn't there?"

Ashurst nodded. Wanting? The apple tree, the singing, and the gold!

❧ ❧ ❧

SHALL I COMPARE THEE TO A SUMMER'S DAY?
WILLIAM SHAKESPEARE

Shall I compare thee to a summer's day?
Thou art more lovely and more temperate:
Rough winds do shake the darling buds of May,
And summer's lease hath all too short a date:
Sometime too hot the eye of heaven shines,
And often is his gold complexion dimm'd;
And every fair from fair sometime declines,
By change or nature's changing course untrimm'd;
But thy eternal summer shall not fade
Nor lose possession of that fair thou owest;
Nor shall Death brag thou wander'st in his shade,
When in eternal lines to time thou growest;
    So long as men can breathe or eyes can see,
    So long lives this and this gives life to thee.

THE ORNAMENTS of our house are the friends
that frequent it.—*Emerson*

HAPPY is the house that shelters a friend!—*Emerson*

I AM CERTAIN of nothing but of the holiness of the heart's affections,
and the truth of Imagination. What the Imagination seizes as Beauty
must be Truth.—*Keats*

DO GOOD to thy friend to keep him, to thy enemy to gain him.—*Franklin*

OH, THE COMFORT, the inexpressible comfort of feeling safe with a person,
having neither to weigh thoughts nor measure words, but pouring them all
right out, just as they are, chaff and grain together; certain that a faithful
hand will take and sift them, keep what is worth keeping, and then with the
breath of kindness blow the rest away.—*Dinah Maria Mulock Craik*

BE COURTEOUS to all, but intimate with few, and let those few be well tried
before you give them your confidence. True friendship is a plant of slow
growth, and must undergo and withstand the shocks of adversity before it is
entitled to the appellation.—*George Washington*

WE MUST TAKE care to indulge only in such generosity as will help
our friends and hurt no one—for nothing is generous, if it is not at the
same time just.—*Cicero*

WE CAN NEVER replace a friend. When a man is fortunate enough to have
several, he finds they are all different. No one has a double in friendship.
—*Schiller*

NOTHING is there more friendly to a man than a friend in need.—*Plautus*

WHEN you leave a country, you leave behind something of
your heart.—*Belgian Proverb*

A TRUE FRIEND is forever a friend.—*MacDonald*

ON FRIENDSHIP

I WOULD NOT live without the love of my friends.—*Keats*

GOOD WORDS shall gain you honour in the market-place;
but good deeds shall gain you friends among men.—*Lao-tse*

WE MUST be as courteous to a man as to a picture which we are
willing to give the benefit of a good light.—*Emerson*

A FRIEND is a person with whom I may be sincere. Before him, I may
think aloud.—*Emerson*

LET US, then, be what we are, and speak what we think, and in all things keep
ourselves loyal to truth and the sacred professions of friendship.—*Longfellow*

DO NOT KEEP the alabaster boxes of your love and tenderness sealed up until
your friends are dead. Fill their lives with sweetness. Speak approving, cheering words while their ears can hear them, and while their hearts can be
thrilled and made happier by them.—*George William Childs*

IF INSTEAD of a gem, or even a flower, we should cast the gift of a loving
thought into the heart of a friend, that would be giving as the angels give.
—*George MacDonald*

WE MAY BUILD more splendid habitations, fill our rooms with paintings and
with sculptures. But we cannot buy with gold the old associations.
—*Longfellow*

"WHAT IS THE SECRET of your life?" asked Mrs. Browning of Charles
Kingsley. "Tell me, that I may make mine beautiful, too." He replied: "I had a friend."—*Related by William Channing Gannett*

WE SHOULD RENDER a service to a friend to bind him closer to us,
and to an enemy to make a friend of him.—*Cleobulus*

LOVE HAS POWER to give in a moment what toil can
scarcely reach in an age.—*Goethe*

Christmas in the Heart

By RACHEL FIELD

*Y*EARS AGO AND YEARS AGO two little girls trudged up a long hill in the twilight of late December. They carried a basket between them, and one was I, and one was Helga Swanson. The smell of warm coffeecake and braided cinnamon bread and little brown twists like deer horns comes back to me now from that remembered basket. Sweeter than all the perfumes of Arabia that fragrance reached our half-frozen noses, yet we never lifted the folded napkin, for we took our responsibility hard. Helga's mother and grandmother had spent the better part of three days over that Christmas baking, and we had been chosen to deliver it and help trim the tree at the Lutheran Home on the hill above Fallen Leaf Lake.

"We must hurry," Helga said. "They've lighted the parlors already."

Four squares of brightness drew us like magnets up that steep hill. Our feet went crunching through the icy road ruts as we kept step together except when we stopped to change hands with the basket.

I could hardly see Helga's face for the darkness, but I felt her warm, vigorous presence beside me in her tightly buttoned coat and knitted tam that half covered her fair braids. I would be seven in another month and she had been eight last March when we had moved from the state of Maine to Minnesota. It had seemed strange and a little frightening to me then to hear so many people speaking to one another in words I couldn't understand. Helga, herself, could drop into Swedish if it seemed worth her while to join in such conversations.

"It's nothing. I'll teach you," she had promised. But her enthusiasm had waned after a few attempts. So Helga became my interpreter as well as my most intimate friend. Without her I should never have known the old men and women in the red brick house who were our hosts that night. I should never have seen Pastor Hanson bending over the melodeon or heard old Christine Berglund tell about the star.

Until we came to live at Fallen Leaf Lake I had never seen so many old people together under one roof. There were rosy, fat old men and women; others frail and shrunken, and some with the limp look of tallow candles in hot weather.

It wasn't long before I knew them all by name. The spryer old men worked in the vegetable garden in summer, where Helga and I sometimes helped them pick berries or tomatoes until we were no longer hungry. Often we sat on the shady back porch and helped the old women shell peas, and then we would be rewarded by cookies or a tune from an old music box.

One tune in particular always made me feel sad and happy in an altogether satisfying way. *Butterflies at Haga,* they called it, and whether there happened to be two or a dozen listeners, old voices would chirp along with the music like crickets clinging fast to summer on a frosty night. Helga would join in, too, for she had learned it from her grandmother.

She tried to tell me what the words meant—something about a butterfly at a place called Haga, a butterfly hunting for a shelter from frost. Helga assured me that the butterfly didn't die; that it found a flowery parlor deep in some

414

blossoms. She couldn't explain the rest of the song, but she thought the one who wrote it was homesick for the flowers and streams and woods of that place. I thought that must be true, because the old people openly wiped their glasses after the music box stopped playing, or sat very still, with that look which meant they might be sitting close beside you but they were somewhere else in their minds.

"Now," Helga whispered when we reached the yard; "let's set the basket on the steps and get as close to the windows as we can."

The shades were not drawn. We could see those grouped about the polished nickel stove with rosy windows of isinglass, and others busy about the long table in the dining-room. But they could not see us, creeping close, for we belonged to the darkness and the wind that worried the branches of two big hemlocks by the gate. We sang our carol, and it was like a play to watch the heads lift and the old faces come close to the windowpanes, with potted geraniums and begonias bright between us and them.

> "Shine out, O Blessed Star,
> Promise of the dawn;
> Glad tidings send afar,
> Christ the Lord is born."

Helga's voice soared so high it seemed to mount straight and unhindered as smoke from chimneys on winter mornings. My own voice took on unexpected power as I stood beside her singing.

"Merry Christmas!" we called even before the door was thrown open and the spiciness of cooking food came out to us as from the gates of heaven.

"Merry Christmas! God Jul!" Old voices hailed us, and hands drew us across the threshold into a world that had been transplanted across miles of salt sea and rolling, plowed land.

"Come; supper is ready." Pastor Hanson's chubby wife came bustling from the kitchen to take the basket we had brought.

Captain Christiansen took me by the hand, and I felt proud, because he looked so handsome in his blue coat with the brass buttons that he used to wear when he had his freight boat on Lake Superior.

There were sixteen of us, counting Helga and me, round that table with its white cloth, and its soup tureen at one end and round yellow cheese at the other. We all stood at our places while Pastor Hanson said a blessing in Swedish.

"There is a church in every man's heart," I remember he said in English at the end of his prayer, "but let us be sure that it is always God who preaches the sermon."

The smell from those bowls of pea soup stays with me yet! Golden and smooth and rich to the last spoonful, we ate it with slices of fresh rye bread and home-churned butter. Pastor Hanson, himself, sliced the cheese with a knife that shaved it into one yellow curl after another. Cinnamon and coffee and hot bread and molasses mingled in one delicious scent as dishes and cups and plates passed from hand to hand.

At last we gathered in the parlor and another scuttle of coal went into the big stove. The time had come for decorating the tree, and everyone took a hand in it except old Mrs. Berglund, who stayed in a wheel chair because of her rheumatism. But even she gave advice about where more strings of popcorn were needed and if the candles were placed where they would show best among the green branches. Mr. Johnson had made birds out of pine cones, and there were cranberries in long strings as red as the popcorn was white. There were hearts and crescents of tinfoil and balls made out of bright bits of worsted. But there was no star anywhere and I wondered about that, for no Christmas tree could be complete without a star to light its tip. But I need not have been troubled about that, as it turned out.

The clock with the rising sun painted on its face struck eight and the last candle was in its place. Pastor Hanson went over to the melodeon against the wall and began to play a Christmas carol. His plump fingers ran over the keys like pink mice, and he bent so lovingly to the music that there wasn't a single wrinkle in his neat black coat. He sang first in his deep, strong voice, and all the other voices came in on the chorus. I sang, too, English words along with their Swedish and Norwegian.

When we had finished, someone went over and whispered to old Mrs. Berglund in her wheel chair. From under her shawl she took out a small box that she held fast in her hands, which were thin and crooked as apple twigs. It was very still in the room for a moment, the kind of stillness that makes you know something exceedingly important is going to happen.

"Well, Pastor Hanson," she said, and held out the little box, "I did not think God would spare me for another year, but here I am, and here is the Christmas star."

"You must tell the children," he said. "It is right that they should hear before we hang it on the tree."

Helga and I pressed closer to the wheel chair. Her eyes were on our faces, yet they looked past us, as if she were summoning her own youth back from across the sea. The room was warm with the fire and our own breath. Even the tree standing in its load of loveliness gave out a woody fragrance, as if it, too, were breathing and listening with us.

"Yust like tonight it vas," Christine Berglund began, and I felt grateful that she was telling it so for my sake, even though her j's and y's and v's and w's had a way of changing places as she said them. "I vere eleven year old then and

sick in my heart because Christmas is coming and I am so far from my mother and my brothers and sisters—"

I could see that big country estate as she told us about it—the stone walls and courtyard, the park with its thick woods; the tiled floors and great fireplaces; the heavy, carved furniture, the enormous beds that would have held her whole family of brothers and sisters. She was young to be sent away into service, and everything and everyone in that house was old, from the mistress to the servants who had tended her for many years.

"They had need of my young knees and quick fingers," she explained, "for they had grown too stiff to bend and dust under all the tables and chairs."

Christine had not minded the hard work. It was the stillness that made her sad. Some of those old servants were deaf, and those who were not had taken on the habit of silence from their mistress.

Sometimes she went with one of the servants to a certain room that was always kept locked. It was a beautiful room with painted furniture and gay pictures and books. The bedspread was embroidered with spring flowers, but you could tell no one had slept there for years. Gilded cages hung empty, with no sweet-singing birds on their perches. The porcelain clock on the mantel was silent, as if time had stopped forever in that room. Whenever she went there with her dustcloths and brushes Christine wondered who had slept in that bed and fed the birds that once had sung in the cages. She could get no answer from the servants, but at last she found out from Pastor Lange.

He came once each month to hold service in the stone chapel, because his parish church was too far away for the servants to attend. Pastor Lange was a very kind old man, and Christine did not feel so lonely on the days when he came. He always spent the night there and, though the mistress of the house never went into the chapel, after the service was over she sent for him and they ate supper together and talked before the fire until bedtime. Christine knew this because once she was sent with a tray from the kitchen to set before them.

"God bless you, my child," Pastor Lange had said. "May you rest well."

But the old lady had kept her lips shut in a thin line and she would not let her eyes rest on her young serving maid. It was the next morning that Pastor Lange answered Christine's questions. Their mistress had hardened her heart against every living thing because years ago she had lost her only child, a daughter as good as she was gay and beautiful. When death had taken her child the mother had turned as cold and gray as a boulder. She had ordered the girl's room closed and the birds let out of their cages. She had had a cloth hung over her portrait and every reminder of her presence taken from each nook and corner. Worst of all, she had summoned Pastor Lange and told him that she would live if she must, but he need never look for her in the family pew again. God had forsaken her, and Sunday and Easter and Christmas would be for her as any other days.

And she had kept her vow, though Pastor Lange had never ceased to pray that a miracle might turn her bitterness into faith once more.

"And did it?" Helga and I interrupted in our impatience.

But the story could not be hurried.

"Christmas it is the vorst," old Christine went on, "for in that big house there is not one cake baked or one bit of green hung on any door. At home ve are poor, but ve put out grain for the birds and have our candles to light and our songs to sing."

Each night she cried as the holiday drew near. She thought of her mother and brothers and sisters all together in a house that was small but savory with holiday cooking. She thought also of the little church on Christmas Eve, with its lighted windows, and the graves outside, each with a torch set there to burn through the long hours till Christmas morning. It was right, her mother had told her, that even the dead should join with the living on that Holy Night. And there was nothing that Christine could do, a half-grown girl in that house of silence and old, old people, to show that Christmas was in her heart.

But once she had noticed near the chapel some tilted gravestones and among them one not so old and gray as the others. Lichens covered the letters cut upon it. She was afraid to scrape away the moss to read the name, but there could be no harm, she thought, in putting a branch of green upon it. Perhaps she might even take her own candle out there to burn and say a prayer and sing a carol. The thought of that made her feel less lonely. She hummed a Christmas hymn as she went back to her work, and it was as she crossed the courtyard that something bright caught her eye in a crack between two flagstones. She bent to pick it up and there, half hidden by moss, was a pin, star-shaped and shining and giving out jets of color as she turned it in the sun.

"Like the Star of Bethlehem," she thought, and her heart beat fast under the apron she wore, for surely it seemed like a sign to comfort her.

She pinned it where no one would see it under her dress, and all day she felt it close to her heart as she went about her duties. That night she slept with it beneath her pillow, and she thought of the Wise Men of old who had seen that other star in the East and followed it to Bethlehem.

Next day she slipped out and stopped by the gravestones. On the smallest stone she set a green branch of fir with cones. It stood straight and fine—almost,

Christine Berglund told us, like the Christmas tree we had just trimmed.

"That night is Christmas Eve," she went on, "and I think there can be no harm if I go out after it is dark and light my candle and set the star there to keep vatch till it is morning."

But, as the afternoon passed and twilight came, Christine did not feel so happy. The hidden star pricked her with its points, almost as if it were her own conscience telling her that stars were not meant to be hidden, that what we pick up is not ours merely for the finding. She tried to tell herself that it would be different if she had found her treasure in the house, not out there between the stones of the courtyard.

So darkness fell and it was Christmas Eve. Some of the old servants remembered and spoke of other times when there had been laughter and festivity in those rooms, and the chapel bell ringing to call them to midnight service. Christine sat quiet until she could slip away to her little room. It was chill there in the darkness because she dared not waste her candle.

At last the fires were banked and the house grew silent. Then Christine put on her cloak and crept down the stairs. She let herself into the courtyard, where nothing stirred but the shadows of trees beyond the walls. The moon was high above the stone turrets. She and it seemed to be the only things which moved in that world of winter quiet. She passed the chapel where no bells pealed from the dark belfry. There were the old tilted gravestones and the one with the bit of green to mark it. Her fingers shook as she set her candle on the headstone and tried to light it. Twice it went out before the small flame shone clear. Her hands still trembled as she took out the star and pinned it among the green needles of the fir bough.

"And then I get down on my knees and first I say 'Our Father.' Then I

make another one that is mine, so God shall know that I do not forget the night of our Saviour's birth. It is hard for me to find the words for my prayer and my teeth are chattering like little hammers, so I don't hear someone come tap-tapping on the stones—"

"Oh!" Helga and I drew sharp breaths. "Who was it?"

But old Christine must tell the story in her own way.

"There I am on my knees," she repeated, "praying to God, and my candle is still burning. Yes, that is how she found me."

We dared not interrupt her again, but our eyes never left her face.

"'Mistress,' I said," she went on, "'forgive me.' But she don't answer me; she yust stand there and look at the stone and the candle."

"And then what?" We whispered the question.

"Oh, I am so afraid I cry, and I give her back the pin, and she yust stand there and turn it in her hands, and she act like she is seeing a ghost."

They must have stood so a long time. The candle burned out on the headstone before the old mistress took Christine back to the house. She did not speak until they reached the great hall, though tears ran down her cheeks at each step they took. Her hands reached for the bell rope and the house echoed to her frantic ringing. Christine could hear the servants hurrying to and fro upstairs in answer to the summons.

"I think she send for them because I have done a bad thing," old Christine told us, "so I stand and shiver there and don't know what is going to happen to me. And then they come down, all so sleepy they forget to make their curtsies. And Mistress point to me, and I cry so I don't see her face any more. But she say to them, 'Go; make a fire in the locked room. Spread linen and blankets on the bed and warm it, and bring food, that this child may eat and be comforted.'

"I think I don't hear her right, but they take me there, and I see the fire lighted and the bed vaiting, so I don't try to think any more. I yust lie down with the flowers spread over me, and I sleep and sleep. And there is no one to come and shake me at sunrise to help in the kitchen. I vake, and it is Christmas morning and bells are ringing so sveet I think I dream them from home. But they are ringing in the chapel. Then the maids come and bring me a beautiful warm dress that smells of cloves and lavender. And they dress me in it, and I ask them the meaning of all this; but they yust smile and say, 'Pastor Lange, he vill tell you.' "

And, sure enough, Pastor Lange and the old mistress came from the chapel. He had driven since sunrise in the carriage she had sent to bring him there.

"You shall see for yourself, Pastor," the old coachman had said, "that the day of miracles is not past."

So Christine went down to meet them in the dress that was heavy with gold embroidery and slippers so soft she seemed to be walking on snow. These rooms were no longer gray and gloomy but warm with leaping fires. The covers were gone from the portrait of a laughing girl no older than she. Her dress was the same that Christine wore, and the star showed plainly on the painted folds. Christine marveled at each change she saw about her, most of all at her mistress's face, which was still sad, but no longer set like stone.

Then Pastor Lange put his hand on Christine's head and blessed her in God's name. But to the old woman he said, "Blessed are they that mourn, for they shall be comforted."

And Christine sat between them at dinner, and felt strange that she should now be served who had so lately carried in the dishes.

"And after dinner is over Pastor Lange he tells me that it is indeed a miracle God has vorked through me to bring faith to our mistress. I don't understand how that can be, for it was not right that I keep the pin and tell no one. But Pastor Lange does not know how to explain that to me. So he says, 'Christine, it must have been that God vas in your heart to do this thing.' 'No, Pastor,' I tell him the truth; 'it was Christmas in my heart.' And Pastor Lange he don't scold me, he yust say maybe that is the same thing."

Old Christine was growing tired. Her voice had dwindled to a thin thread of sound by the time she had answered our questions. . . . Yes, the pin had belonged to her mistress's daughter. She had lost it one winter day and grown so chill hunting for it in the courtyard that she had fallen ill and died. It was her gravestone by the chapel that Christine had chosen to light and decorate with green. So great had been that mother's grief that it was more than thirty years since she had spoken her daughter's name or let anything be a reminder. But Christine's candle shining on Christmas Eve had been like a sign sent from her dead child by a living one on that most happy night of the year.

So Christine no longer served as a maid in that great house. She lived as the old woman's daughter, and in winter the rooms were warm and bright with fires and laughter, and in summer sweet with flowers and the singing of birds.

"And see, here is the star to hang on the tree."

"The same one? The very same?"

"Yes, the same. It goes with me always since that night."

We touched the five shining points with wonder in our finger tips before Christine's old fingers lifted it from the bed of cotton.

"Real diamonds and not one missing," she said proudly as she handed it to Captain Christiansen, because he was tall enough to set it on the topmost tip.

"But I never think it vould come all the way to America. I never think I come all that vay myself."

We watched it send out little jets of brightness when the candles were lighted below and all the old faces shining in loveliest of light. We sang another carol all together, and then it was time to go home with Helga's father, who had come for us.

"Good night." Their voices followed us to the door. "*God Jul!* Merry Christmas!"

"Merry Christmas!" Helga and I called back before we turned to follow her father's lantern into the wintry dark.

❧ ❧ ❧

A CHRISTMAS CAROL
JAMES RUSSELL LOWELL

"What means this glory round our feet,"
  The Magi mused, "more bright than
    morn?"
And voices chanted clear and sweet,
  "Today the Prince of Peace is born!"

"What means that star," the Shepherds said,
  "That brightens through the rocky
    glen?"
And angels, answering overhead,
  Sang, "Peace on earth, good-will to
    men!"

It's eighteen hundred years and more
  Since those sweet oracles were dumb;
We wait for Him, like them of yore;
  Alas, He seems so slow to come!

But it was said, in words of gold

No time or sorrow ever shall dim,
That little children might be bold
  In perfect trust to come to Him.

All round about our feet shall shine
  A light like that the Wise Men saw,
If we our loving wills incline
  To that sweet Life which is the Law.

So shall we learn to understand
  The simple faith of shepherds then,
And, clasping kindly hand in hand,
  Sing, "Peace on earth, good-will to
    men!"

And they who do their souls no wrong,
  But keep at eve the faith of morn,
Shall daily hear the angel-song,
  "Today the Prince of Peace is born!"

IT CAME UPON THE MIDNIGHT CLEAR
EDMUND HAMILTON SEARS

It came upon the midnight clear,
  That glorious song of old,
From angels bending near the earth
  To touch their harps of gold:
"Peace on the earth, good will to men
  From heaven's all-gracious King"—
The world in solemn stillness lay
  To hear the angels sing.

For lo! the days are hastening on
  By prophet bards foretold,
When with the ever circling years
  Comes round the age of gold;
When Peace shall over all the earth
  In ancient splendors fling,
And the whole world give back the song
  Which now the angels sing.

SKYLINER AT NIGHT
John Ritchey

The great wing tips, the motors roar
their wealth of sound
across the wide sky's floor.

In the long canyons of the night,
with fiery sweep,
this creature climbed the trail of Flight
and now sinks—half asleep.

While on the ground
the beacons flash, the searchlights arc
their grinding beam.

*From the country of the dark
descends a silver dream.*

LANTERN IN THE SNOW
Robert P. Tristram Coffin

This thing is beautiful, I know,
A lantern burning in the snow,
Which diggers left so men might see
Their hole beneath my lilac tree.

The lantern makes a spot of gold,
Alien to the dark and cold,
Burning steady as it can,
As if a warm, good part of man
Were left outside there in the night
To go on working, giving light.
The glow strikes down and shows the
    ground
A single solitary mound
Of whiteness set in vacant space,
The light strikes up and shows the grace
Of the lilac's limbs and bark,
An open fan against the dark.
The snow falls round the common
    thing
And makes a dim, mysterious ring
Of flaky flame that wheels and turns
As the lonely lantern burns.

There are only four or five
Such sights for any man alive
In all the years he has to go
Like this lantern in the snow.

VELVET SHOES*
Elinor Wylie

Let us walk in the white snow
    In a soundless space;
With footsteps quiet and slow,
    At a tranquil pace,
    Under veils of white lace.

I shall go shod in silk,
    And you in wool,
White as a white cow's milk,
    More beautiful
    Than the breast of a gull.

We shall walk through the still town
    In a windless peace;
We shall step upon white down,
    Upon silver fleece,
    Upon softer than these.

We shall walk in velvet shoes;
    Wherever we go
Silence will fall like dews
    On white silence below.
    We shall walk in the snow.

STOPPING BY WOODS ON A
SNOWY EVENING
Robert Frost

Whose woods these are I think I know.
His house is in the village though;
He will not see me stopping here
To watch his woods fill up with snow.

My little horse must think it queer
To stop without a farmhouse near
Between the woods and frozen lake
The darkest evening of the year.

He gives his harness bells a shake
To ask if there is some mistake.
The only other sound's the sweep
Of easy wind and downy flake.

The woods are lovely, dark and deep,
But I have promises to keep,
And miles to go before I sleep,
And miles to go before I sleep.

THE CHRISTMAS STORY
THE BIBLE

AND it came to pass in those days, that there went out a decree from Caesar Augustus, that all the world should be taxed.

(*And* this taxing was first made when Cyrenius was governor of Syria.)

And all went to be taxed, every one into his own city.

And Joseph also went up from Galilee, out of the city of Nazareth, into Judaea, unto the city of David, which is called Bethlehem; (because he was of the house and lineage of David:)

To be taxed with Mary his espoused wife, being great with child.

And so it was, that, while they were there, the days were accomplished that she should be delivered.

And she brought forth her firstborn son, and wrapped him in swaddling clothes, and laid him in a manger; because there was no room for them in the inn.

And there were in the same country shepherds abiding in the field, keeping watch over their flock by night.

And, lo, the angel of the Lord came upon them, and the glory of the Lord shone round about them: and they were sore afraid.

And the angel said unto them, Fear not: for, behold, I bring you good tidings of great joy, which shall be to all people.

For unto you is born this day in the city of David a Saviour, which is Christ the Lord.

And this *shall be* a sign unto you; Ye shall find the babe wrapped in swaddling clothes, lying in a manger.

And suddenly there was with the angel a multitude of the heavenly host praising God, and saying,

Glory to God in the highest, and on earth peace, good will toward men.

THE BALLAD OF THE CHRISTMAS STAR
FRANCES M. FROST

Above the mountain's crest,
The star against the blue
Blossomed; and on the breast
Of darkness, hemlocks knew
The gentle weight of whiteness,
The easy wind's soft sound
That sifted the silver lightness
Across the drifted ground.

Huddled within the grey
Barn's warm and weathered walls,
The calves were restless; hay
Was sweet in the bedded stalls,
But the horses whinnied, shaking
Their halters, seeing the star
Through the small window, breaking
Over the mountain's bar.

Like an opening flower, gold
Upon the heaven's deep
Clear cobalt, as of old.
The drowsy mother-sheep,
Her lamb nuzzling her side,
Lay in the dusky straw;
The lamb tottered and cried
Toward the window, when it saw
The great star lifting slowly
Over the snowy sod,
Over all creatures lowly,
As over the lamb of God
It burned once on a blowing
Night . . .and the lamb was still,
Watching that brilliance growing
Over the wintry hill.

CHRISTMAS MORNING

Elizabeth Madox Roberts

If Bethlehem were here today,
  Or this were very long ago,
There wouldn't be a winter time
  Nor any cold or snow.

I'd run out through the garden gate,
  And down along the pasture walk;
And off beside the cattle barns
  I'd hear a kind of gentle talk.

I'd move the heavy iron chain
  And pull away the wooden pin;
I'd push the door a little bit
  And tiptoe very softly in.

The pigeons and the yellow hens
  And all the cows would stand away;
Their eyes would open wide to see
  A lady in the manger hay,
If this were very long ago
  And Bethlehem were here today.

And Mother held my hand and smiled—
  I mean the lady would—and she

Would take the woolly blankets off
  Her little boy so I could see.

His shut-up eyes would be asleep,
  And he would look just like our John,
And he would be all crumpled too,
  And have a pinkish color on.

I'd watch his breath go in and out.
  His little clothes would all be white.
I'd slip my finger in his hand
  To feel how he could hold it tight.

And she would smile and say, "Take
    care,"
  The mother, Mary, would, "Take
    care;"
And I would kiss his little hand
  And touch his hair.

While Mary put the blankets back,
  The gentle talk would soon begin.
And when I'd tiptoe softly out
  I'd meet the wise men going in.

THE MEANING OF CHRISTMAS

By Francis Cardinal Spellman
Archbishop of New York

HOLIDAY and Holy Day, Christmas is more than a yule log, holly or tree. It is more than natural good cheer and the giving of gifts. Christmas is even more than the feast of the home and of children, the feast of love and friendship. It is more than all of these together. Christmas is Christ, the Christ of justice and charity, of freedom and peace.

The joy of Christmas is a joy that war cannot kill, for it is the joy of the soul and the soul cannot die. Poverty cannot prevent the joy of Christmas, for it is a joy no earthly wealth can give. Time cannot wither Christmas, for it belongs to eternity. The world cannot shatter it, for it is union with Him who has overcome the world.

The leaders and peoples of nations must understand these fundamental truths if we are ever to have freedom and peace. Unless charters and pacts have a divine sanction, unless "God is the Paramount Ruler of the world," then again and again, as the waves upon the shore, must catastrophe follow catastrophe. Not until men lay aside greed, hatred, pride and the tyranny of evil passions, to travel the road that began at Bethlehem, will the Star of Christmas peace illuminate the world. Christmas is the Birthday of freedom, for it is only the following of Christ that makes men free.

GREATER THAN KINGS AND PARLIAMENTS
ANONYMOUS

HERE IS a man who was born in an obscure village, the child of a peasant woman. He grew up in another obscure village. He worked in a carpenter shop until He was thirty, and then for three years He was an itinerant preacher. He never wrote a book. He never held an office. He never owned a home. He never had a family. He never went to college. He never put His foot inside a big city. He never traveled two hundred miles from the place where He was born. He never did one of the things that usually accompany greatness. He had no credentials but Himself. He had nothing to do with this world except the naked power of His divine manhood. While still a young man, the tide of popular opinion turned against Him. His friends ran away. One of them denied Him. He was turned over to His enemies. He went through the mockery of a trial. He was nailed upon a cross between two thieves. His executioners gambled for the only piece of property He had on earth while He was dying—and that was His coat. When He was dead He was taken down and laid in a borrowed grave through the pity of a friend.

Nineteen wide centuries have come and gone and today He is the centerpiece of the human race and the leader of . . . progress.

I am far within the mark when I say that all the armies that ever marched, and all the navies that ever were built, and all the parliaments that ever sat, and all the kings that ever reigned, put together, have not affected the life of man upon this earth as powerfully as has this One solitary life.

From THE CROWN OF WILD OLIVE
BY JOHN RUSKIN

NO PROUD ONE! no jewelled circlet flaming through Heaven above the height of the unmerited throne, only some few leaves of wild olive, cool to the tired brow, through a few years of peace. It should have been of gold, they thought; but Jupiter was poor; this was the best the god could give them. Seeking a greater than this, they had known it a mockery. Not in war, not in wealth, not in tyranny, was there any happiness to be found for them—only in kindly peace, fruitful and free. The wreath was to be of *wild* olive, mark you—the tree that grows carelessly, tufting the rocks with no vivid bloom, no verdure of branch; only with soft snow of blossom, and scarcely fulfilled fruit, mixed with grey leaf and thorn-set stem; no fastening of diadem for you but with such sharp embroidery! But this, such as it is, you may win while yet you live; type of grey honour, and sweet rest. Free-heartedness, and graciousness, and undisturbed trust and requited love, and the sight of the peace of others, and the ministry of their pain—these, and the blue sky above you, and the sweet waters and flowers of the earth beneath; and mysteries and presences, innumerable, of living things—these may yet be here your riches; untormenting and divine; serviceable for the life that now is; nor, it may be, without promise of that which is to come.

WHO WALKS WITH BEAUTY
DAVID MORTON

Who walks with Beauty has no need of fear:
The sun and moon and stars keep pace with him;
Invisible hands restore the ruined year,
And time itself grows beautifully dim.
One hill will keep the footprints of the moon
That came and went a hushed and secret hour;
One star at dusk will yield the lasting boon:
Remembered beauty's white, immortal flower.
Who takes of Beauty wine and daily bread,
Will know no lack when bitter years are lean;
The brimming cup is by, the feast is spread;
The sun and moon and stars his eyes have seen,
Are for his hunger and the thirst he slakes:
The wine of Beauty and the bread he breaks.

PRAYER FOR THE UNITED STATES OF AMERICA
By GEORGE WASHINGTON

ALMIGHTY God; we make our earnest prayer that Thou wilt keep the United States in Thy holy protection; that Thou wilt incline the hearts of the citizens to cultivate a spirit of subordination and obedience to government. . . . And finally that Thou wilt most graciously be pleased to dispose us all to do justice, to love mercy and to demean ourselves with that charity, humility and pacific temper of mind which were the characteristics of the Divine Author of our blessed religion, and without a humble imitation of whose example in these things we can never hope to be a happy nation. Grant our supplication, we beseech Thee, through Jesus Christ our Lord. Amen.

A SIOUX PRAYER

GRANDFATHER, Great Spirit, you have been always, and before you nothing has been. There is no one to pray to but you. The star nations all over the heavens are yours, and yours are the grasses of the earth. You are older than all need, older than all pain and prayer.

Grandfather, Great Spirit, all over the world the faces of living ones are alike. With tenderness they have come up out of the ground. Look upon your children, with children in their arms, that they may face the winds and walk the good road to the day of quiet.

Grandfather, Great Spirit, fill us with the light. Give us the strength to understand and the eyes to see. Teach us to walk the soft earth as relatives to all that live.

Help us, for without you we are nothing.

From *TRISTRAM*

Edwin Arlington Robinson

I am not one
Who must have everything; yet I must have
My dreams if I must live, for they are mine.
Wisdom is not one word and then another,
Till words are like dry leaves under a tree;
Wisdom is like a dawn that comes up slowly
Out of an unknown ocean.

ELAINE

Edna St. Vincent Millay

Oh, come again to Astolat!
I will not ask you to be kind.
And you may go when you will go,
And I will stay behind.

I will not say how dear you are,
Or ask you if you hold me dear,
Or trouble you with things for you
The way I did last year.

So still the orchard, Lancelot,
So very still the lake shall be,
You could not guess—though you should guess—
What is become of me.

So wide shall be the garden-walk,
The garden-seat so very wide,
You needs must think—if you should think—
The lily maid had died.

Save that, a little way away,
I'd watch you for a little while,
To see you speak, the way you speak,
And smile—if you should smile.

IDYLL

Siegfried Sassoon

In the grey summer garden I shall find you
With day-break and the morning hills behind you.
There will be rain-wet roses; stir of wings;
And down the wood a thrush that wakes and sings.
Not from the past you'll come, but from that deep
Where beauty murmurs to the soul asleep:
And I shall know the sense of life re-born
From dreams into the mystery of morn
Where gloom and brightness meet. And standing there
Till that calm song is done, at last we'll share
The league-spread quiring symphonies that are
Joy in the world, and peace, and dawn's one star.

426

MUSIC I HEARD

CONRAD AIKEN

Music I heard with you was more than music,
And bread I broke with you was more than bread;
Now that I am without you, all is desolate;
All that was once so beautiful is dead.

Your hands once touched this table and this silver,
And I have seen your fingers hold this glass.
These things do not remember you, beloved,—
And yet your touch upon them will not pass.

For it was in my heart you moved among them,
And blessed them with your hands and with your eyes;
And in my heart they will remember always,—
They knew you once, O beautiful and wise.

ISOLT OF THE WHITE HANDS

EDWIN ARLINGTON ROBINSON

        Yet there she gazed
Across the water, over the white waves,
Upon a castle that she had never seen,
And could not see, save as a phantom shape
Against a phantom sky.

        He had been all,
And would be always all there was for her,
And he had not come back to her alive,
Not even to go again. It was like that
For women, sometimes, and might be so too often
For women like her. She hoped there were not many
Of them, or many of them to be, now knowing
More about that than about waves and foam,
And white birds everywhere, flying and flying;
Alone, with her white face and her gray eyes,
She watched them there till even her thoughts were white,
And there was nothing alive but white birds flying,
Flying, and always flying, and still flying,
And the white sunlight flashing on the sea.

—From *Tristram*

427

ON GROWING OLD
JOHN MASEFIELD

Be with me, Beauty, for the fire is dying,
My dog and I are old, too old for roving,
Man, whose young passion sets the spindrift flying
Is soon too lame to march, too cold for loving.

I take the book and gather to the fire,
Turning old yellow leaves; minute by minute,
The clock ticks to my heart; a withered wire
Moves a thin ghost of music in the spinet.

I cannot sail your seas, I cannot wander
Your cornland, nor your hill-land nor your valleys,
Ever again, nor share the battle yonder
Where the young knight the broken squadron rallies.

Only stay quiet while my mind remembers
The beauty of fire from the beauty of embers.

Beauty, have pity, for the strong have power,
The rich their wealth, the beautiful their grace,
Summer of man its sunlight and its flower,
Spring time of man all April in a face.

Only, as in the jostling in the Strand,
Where the mob thrusts or loiters or is loud
The beggar with the saucer in his hand
Asks only a penny from the passing crowd,

So, from this glittering world with all its fashion,
Its fire and play of men, its stir, its march,
Let me have wisdom, Beauty, wisdom and passion,
Bread to the soul, rain where the summers parch.

Give me but these, and though the darkness close,
Even the night will blossom as the rose.

EVERYONE SANG
SIEGFRIED SASSOON

Everyone suddenly burst out singing;
And I was filled with such delight
As prisoned birds must find in freedom,
Winging wildly across the white
Orchards and dark green fields; on, on, and out of sight.

Everyone's voice was suddenly lifted,
And beauty came like the setting sun.
My heart was shaken with tears, and horror
Drifted away . . . O but everyone
Was a bird; and the song was wordless; the singing will never be done.

IN THE COOL OF THE EVENING*
ALFRED NOYES

In the cool of the evening, when the low sweet whispers waken,
    When the labourers turn them homeward, and the weary have their will,
When the censers of the roses o'er the forest-aisles are shaken,
    Is it but the wind that cometh o'er the far green hill?

For they say 'tis but the sunset winds that wander through the heather,
    Rustle all the meadow-grass and bend the dewy fern;
They say 'tis but the winds that bow the reeds in prayer together,
    And fill the shaken pools with fire along the shadowy burn.

In the beauty of the twilight, in the Garden that He loveth,
    They have veiled His lovely vesture with the darkness of a name!
Thro' His Garden, thro' His Garden it is but the wind that moveth,
    No more; but O, the miracle, the miracle is the same!

In the cool of the evening, when the sky is an old story
    Slowly dying, but remembered, ay, and loved with passion still,
Hush! . . . the fringes of His garment, in the fading golden glory,
    Softly rustling as He cometh o'er the far green hill.

*Reprinted by permission of the publishers, J. B. Lippincott Company, from *Collected Poems, Volume I,* by Alfred Noyes. Copyright, 1906, by Alfred Noyes.

429

Subject Index

LOVE

NATURE

THE WORLD OF NATURE

SUBJECT INDEX

PATRIOTISM AND PEACE

RELIGION

SPIRIT OF ADVENTURE

WISDOM OF THE AGES

YOUTH AND OLD AGE

438

Author Index

440

448

MOST OF THE SELECTIONS are held in copyright. Permissions have been obtained for their inclusion in this book. A list of acknowledgments and original copyright notices is as follows:

OUR AMERICAN DREAM, from *The Epic of America*, by James Truslow Adams, reprinted by permission of Little, Brown & Company and Atlantic Monthly Press: THE UNKNOWN GOD, from *Collected Poems*, by "A.E.," reprinted by permission of The Macmillan Company, publishers: MUSIC I HEARD, from *Selected Poems*, by Conrad Aiken, reprinted by permission of Charles Scribner's Sons: ASLEEP and WORDS, from *Every Spring*, by Dorothy Aldis. Copyright, 1933, by Dorothy Aldis. Courtesy of G. P. Putnam's Sons: (AFTER THE RAIN, BEFORE THE RAIN, and MEMORY, by Thomas Bailey Aldrich, originally published by Houghton Mifflin Company.): DIRT FARMER, by Arden Antony, reprinted by permission of *The Christian Science Monitor*: I HOPE, IN JUDEA, RETURN, STRANGE, TO YOUR LITTLE HOUSE, and WISH, from *Twist O' Smoke* by Mildred Bowers, reprinted by permission of Yale University Press: DAYS and RONDEL FOR SEPTEMBER, from *Blue Smoke*, by Karle Wilson Baker, reprinted by permission of Yale University Press: GOOD COMPANY, from *Dreamers on Horseback*, by Karle Wilson Baker, reprinted by permission of Southwest Press: POLO PONIES, by Eleanor Baldwin, reprinted by permission of *Forum*: MY HEROINE, from *Margaret Ogilvy*, by James M. Barrie, reprinted by permission of Charles Scribner's Sons: LE SPECTRE DE LA ROSE, by Cyril W. Beaumont, from *Complete Book of Ballets*, copyright, 1938 by Cyril W. Beaumont. Courtesy of G. P. Putnam's Sons: From THE DEVIL AND DANIEL WEBSTER, by Stephen Vincent Benét, published by Rinehart & Co. Copyright, 1936, by Stephen Vincent Benét: From FREEDOM FROM FEAR, by Stephen Vincent Benét, published by *The Saturday Evening Post*. Copyright, 1943, by Curtis Publishing Company. Copyright, 1943, by Rosemary Carr Benét: BEAUTY, from *From a College Window*, by A. C. Benson. Courtesy of G. P. Putnam's Sons: FOR THE FALLEN, by Laurence Binyon, reprinted by permission of the Society of Authors as the Literary Representative of Mrs. Binyon: VAGABOND'S HOUSE, from *Vagabond's House*, by Don Blanding, reprinted by permission of Dodd, Mead & Company. Copyright, 1928, by Don Blanding: From MARE NOSTRUM, by Vicente Blasco Ibanez, translated by Charlotte Brewster Jordan, published and copyrighted by E. P. Dutton & Co., Inc., New York. Copyright 1919. Renewed 1947: How HELEN KELLER SEES COLOR, by Nella Braddy, from *Midstream*, by Helen Keller, copyright 1929 by Helen Keller, reprinted by permission of Doubleday & Company, Inc.: THE HILL, from *The Collected Poems of Rupert Brooke*, reprinted by permission of Dodd, Mead & Company, Inc.: Quotation, from *Poems*, by H. C. Bunner, reprinted by permission of Charles Scribner's Sons: (From LEAF AND TENDRIL, by John Burroughs, originally published by Houghton Mifflin Company.): WISDOM AND BEAUTY, by Donn Byrne, from *Messer Marco Polo*, reprinted by permission of D. Appleton-Century Company, Inc.: A VAGABOND SONG and VESTIGIA, from *Poems*, by Bliss Carman, reprinted by permission of Dodd, Mead & Company, Inc.: PRAYER IS POWER, by Alexis Carrel, M. D., reprinted by permission of *The Reader's Digest*: SONG OF THE RABBITS OUTSIDE THE TAVERN and SWIFT THINGS ARE BEAUTIFUL, from *Away Goes Sally*, by Elizabeth Coatsworth, reprinted by permission of The Macmillan Company, publishers: A BOY, A LAKE, A SUN, from *Strange Holiness*, by Robert P. Tristram Coffin, reprinted by permission of The Macmillan Company, publishers: EYES ARE LIT UP, LANTERN IN THE SNOW, THE ROCKER, and WILD GEESE, from *Collected Poems*, by Robert P. Tristram Coffin, reprinted by permission of The Macmillan Company, publishers: Quotation, by Colton, from *Goodly Company*, by Jessie E. Logan, published by Beckley-Cardy Company: AN OLD WOMAN OF THE ROADS, from *Wild Earth*, by Padraic Colum, reprinted by permission of The Macmillan Company, publishers: From LORD JIM, by Joseph Conrad, copyright 1899, 1900, by Doubleday & Company, Inc.: ANN RUTLEDGE, from *Thirteen by Corwin*, by Norman Corwin, by permission of the publishers, Henry Holt and Company, Inc. Copyright, 1942, by Norman Corwin: From CAVALCADE (Part II, Scene 5), by Noel Coward, copyright 1931, 1932, reprinted by permission of Doubleday & Company, Inc.: IN HEAVEN SOME LITTLE BLADES OF GRASS, reprinted from *The Collected Poems of Stephen Crane*, by permission of Alfred A. Knopf, Inc. Copyright 1922 by William H. Crane. Copyright 1895, 1899, 1926, 1929, 1930, by Alfred A. Knopf, Inc.: ADVENTURE and NOVEMBER NIGHT, reprinted from *Verse* by Adelaide Crapsey, by permission of Alfred A. Knopf, Inc. Copyright 1915, 1922, by Algernon S. Crapsey: (Quotation by Samuel McChord Crothers, originally published by Houghton Mifflin Company.): THE MUSTANG, from *This Golden Summit*, by Grace Noll Crowell, published by Harper & Brothers. Copyright, 1937, by Harper & Brothers: LEISURE, from *Collected Poems*, by W. H. Davies, reprinted by permission of Jonathan Cape Ltd.: LETTER TO SAINT PETER, by Elma Dean, reprinted by permission of *The American Mercury*: DREAM-SONG, from *Peacock Pie* included in *Collected Poems* by Walter de la Mare, Book II. Copyright, 1920, by Henry Holt and Company: THE LINNET, from *Motley* included in *Collected Poems* by Walter de la Mare, Book I. Copyright, 1920, by Henry Holt and Company: NOD and THE THREE CHERRY TREES, from *The Listeners* included in *Collected Poems* by Walter de la Mare, Book I. Copyright, 1920, by Henry Holt and Company: THE WORTH OF BEAUTY, by James C. Derieux, as condensed in *The Reader's Digest*, originally published in *Good Housekeeping*: AUTUMN and THERE IS NO FRIGATE LIKE A BOOK, from *The Poems of Emily Dickinson*, edited by Martha Dickinson Bianchi and Alfred Leete Hampson. Reprinted by permission of Little, Brown & Company: SONG WITHOUT WORDS and AD DOMNULAM SUAM, by Ernest Dowson, reprinted by permission of Dodd, Mead & Company, Inc.: RECIPROCITY, from *Poems* by John Drinkwater, reprinted by permission of Houghton Mifflin Company: Quotation from DON RODRIGUEZ, by Lord Dunsany, courtesy of G. P. Putnam's Sons: SEPTEMBER IN THE FIELDS and WAVES, reprinted from *The Golden Bird*, by Dorothy Easton, by permission of Alfred A. Knopf, Inc.:

449

ARCADIA EGO, reprinted from *Journal of Katherine Mansfield*, by permission of Alfred A. Knopf, Inc. Copyright 1927 by Alfred A. Knopf, Inc.: EARTH IS ENOUGH, by Edwin Markham, reprinted by permission: LAUGH AND BE MERRY, ON GROWING OLD, TEWKESBURY ROAD, and THE WANDERER'S SONG, from *Poems*, by John Masefield, reprinted by permission of The Macmillan Company, publishers: AUTUMN CHANT and SONNET, from *The Harp-Weaver and Other Poems*, by Edna St. Vincent Millay, published by Harper & Brothers. Copyright, 1920, 1921, 1922, 1923, by Edna St. Vincent Millay: ELAINE, from *Second April*, by Edna St. Vincent Millay, published by Harper & Brothers. Copyright, 1918, 1920, 1921, by Edna St. Vincent Millay: GOD'S WORLD, reprinted from *Renascence*, by Edna St. Vincent Millay, published by Harper & Brothers. Copyright, 1917, by Edna St. Vincent Millay: THE PRINCESS MARRIES THE PAGE, by Edna St. Vincent Millay, published by Harper & Brothers. Copyright, 1932, by Edna St. Vincent Millay: TWENTY MINUTES OF REALITY, by M. P. Montague, reprinted from *The Atlantic Monthly*, by permission of the author: From NOTES ON BERMUDA, by Christopher Morley, reprinted by permission of Essential Books: A SLICE OF SUNLIGHT, from *Essays*, by Christopher Morley. Copyright, 1928, by Christopher Morley, published by J. B. Lippincott Co.: OLD SHIPS, SYMBOL and WHO WALKS WITH BEAUTY, from *Ships in Harbour*, by David Morton, reprinted by permission of the author. Courtesy G. P. Putnam's Sons: THE HIGHWAY MAN and IN THE COOL OF THE EVENING, reprinted by permission of the publishers, J. B. Lippincott Company, from *Collected Poems, Volume I*, by Alfred Noyes. Copyright, 1906, by Alfred Noyes: SO LONG !, by Howard Vincent O'Brien, courtesy of *The Chicago Daily News*: From THE HAIRY APE, by Eugene O'Neill. Copyright, 1926, by Eugene O'Neill. Reprinted by permission of Random House, Inc.: HE WHOM A DREAM HATH POSSESSED, by Shaemus O'Sheel, by permission: SHIPS THAT LIFT TALL SPIRES OF CANVAS, from *Lost Ships and Lonely Seas*, by Ralph D. Paine, reprinted by permission of D. Appleton-Century Company, Inc.: LOUIS PASTEUR ADDRESSES THE FRENCH ACADEMY, from the Warner Brothers' production, *The Story of Louis Pasteur*: JULY TWENTY-THIRD and NOVEMBER THIRTEENTH, from *Almanac for Moderns*, by Donald Culross Peattie. Courtesy of G. P. Putnam's Sons: TREES, by Donald Culross Peattie, from the *North American Review*, reprinted by permission of George T. Bye: From FREE LANCE, by E. Alexander Powell. Copyright, 1937, by Harcourt, Brace and Company, Inc.: (From THE MEANING OF CULTURE, by John Powys, originally published by W. W. Norton & Company, Inc.): From BRAVE MEN, by Ernie Pyle, by permission of Henry Holt and Company: From CROSS CREEK, by Marjorie Kinnan Rawlings, reprinted by permission of Charles Scribner's Sons: TRACINGS, from *Hidden Waters*, by Bernard Raymund, reprinted by permission of Yale University Press: THE GOOD JOAN, A LITTLE SONG OF LIFE, and MIRACLE, from *A Wayside Lute*, by Lizette Woodworth Reese, reprinted by permission of The Mosher Press: Quotation from *The Influence of Men— Incurable*, by Eudora Ramsay Richardson. Copyright 1936. Used by special permission of the Publishers, The Bobbs-Merrill Company: AWAY, from *Rhymes of Childhood*, by James Whitcomb Riley, reprinted by permission of The Bobbs-Merrill Company: DEAR LORD, KIND LORD, from *Afterwhiles*, by James Whitcomb Riley, reprinted by permission of The Bobbs-Merrill Company: SKYLINER AT NIGHT, by John Ritchey, reprinted by permission of the author and *The Christian Science Monitor*: CHRISTMAS MORNING, from *Under the Tree*, by Elizabeth Madox Roberts. Copyright 1922 by B. W. Huebsch, Inc., 1930 by The Viking Press, Inc., New York: From TRISTRAM and ISOLT OF THE WHITE HANDS, from *Tristram*, by Edwin Arlington Robinson, reprinted by permission of The Macmillan Company, publishers: THE MASTER, from *The Town Down the River*, by Edwin Arlington Robinson, reprinted by permission of Charles Scribner's Sons: From DEDICATION OF THE CLOISTERS, NEW YORK, and I BELIEVE, by John D. Rockefeller, Jr., reprinted by permission: A KISS and ROXANNE, from *Cyrano de Bergerac*, by Edmond Rostand. Copyright, 1923, by Henry Holt and Company: I GOT A GLORY, from *It Will Be Daybreak Soon*, by Archibald Rutledge, reprinted by permission of Fleming H. Revell Company: From WIND, SAND AND STARS, by Antoine de Saint Exupéry, reprinted by permission of Reynal & Hitchcock, Inc., New York: THE TWO LEAVES, from *Bambi*, by Felix Salten, copyright, 1929, by Simon and Schuster, Inc.: INVENTORY AT DAWN, by Eleanor Saltzman, reprinted from *Household* by permission: THE ROAD AND THE END and UNDER THE HARVEST MOON, from *Chicago Poems*, by Carl Sandburg. Copyright, 1916, by Henry Holt and Company. Copyright, 1943, by Carl Sandburg: THE UNKNOWABLE, from *Obiter Scripta*, by George Santayana, reprinted by permission of Charles Scribner's Sons: FOUR LITTLE FOXES, from *Slow Smoke*, by Lew Sarett. Copyright, 1925, by Henry Holt and Company: THE GREAT DIVIDE, from *Many Many Moons*, by Lew Sarett. Copyright, 1920, by Henry Holt and Company: WIND IN THE PINE, from *Box of God*, by Lew Sarett. Copyright, 1922, by Henry Holt and Company: EVERYONE SANG and IDYLL, from *Picture Show*, by Siegfried Sassoon. Copyright, 1920, by E. P. Dutton: THE LOST MASTER, from *Rhymes of a Rolling Stone*, by Robert Service. Copyright, 1912, 1939, by Robert Service. Reprinted by permission of Dodd, Mead & Company, Inc.: UNFAILING and WHO LOVES THE RAIN, by Frances Shaw, reprinted by permission: THE SONG OF THE UNGIRT RUNNERS, from *Marlborough and Other Poems*, by Charles Hamilton Sorley, reprinted by permission of the Cambridge University Press: THE MEANING OF CHRISTMAS, by Francis Cardinal Spellman, reprinted by permission of *The Reader's Digest*: LET NOT MY DEATH BE LONG, reprinted from *Fiddler's Farewell*, by Leonora Speyer, by permission of Alfred A. Knopf, Inc. Copyright, 1926, by Alfred A. Knopf, Inc: WHITE FIELDS, from *Collected Poems*, by James Stephens, reprinted by permission of The Macmillan Company, publishers: (THE CELESTIAL SURGEON, EVENSONG, ENVOY, A GOODLY LIFE, THE HOUSE BEAUTIFUL, LAST PRAYER, A MORNING PRAYER, QUOTATIONS, THE RIVER ON . . . , ROBERT LOUIS STEVENSON GIVES AWAY HIS BIRTHDAY, ROMANCE, UNDERSTANDING, THE VAGABOND, A VISIT FROM THE SEA, and WALKING TOURS, by Robert Louis Stevenson, originally published by Charles Scribner's Sons.):(THE GARDEN OF PROSERPINE, by Algernon Charles Swinburne, originally published by Harper & Brothers.): TO NIGHT, by Arthur Symonds, reprinted by permission of Dodd, Mead & Company, Inc.: BEAUTY, by J. M. T., from *Creative Writing for College Students*, by Babcock, Horn and English, reprinted by permission of American Book Company: JUNE IN NEW ENGLAND, from *Diary of Domesticity*, by Gladys Taber, reprinted by special permission from the *Ladies' Home Journal*. Copyright, 1945, by The Curtis Publishing Co.: Quotation by Lorado Taft, reprinted by permission: THIS IS MY PRAYER and WHERE THE MIND IS WITHOUT FEAR, from *Gitanjali*, by Rabindranath Tagore, reprinted by permission of The Macmillan Company, publishers: HE KNEW LINCOLN, from *He Knew Lincoln and Other Stories*, by Ida M. Tarbell, reprinted by permission of The MacMillan Company, publishers: ON A FINAL DAY, from *The Lost Woods*, by Edwin Way Teale. Copyright, 1945, by Edwin Way Teale. Reprinted by permission of Dodd, Mead & Company, Inc.: BARTER, I SHALL NOT CARE, and PEACE, from *Love Songs*, by Sara Teasdale, reprinted by permission of The Macmillan Company, publishers: THE COIN, NIGHT, and TO ARCTURUS RETURNING, from *Stars Tonight*, by Sara Teasdale, reprinted by permission of The Macmillan Company. publishers: ON THE HEIGHT, from *Poems for Every Mood*, by Eunice Tietjens, published by Alfred A. Knopf, reprinted by permission: (ROAD SONG, by W. G. Tinckom-Fernandez, originally published by Houghton Mifflin Company.): THE MAGIC MOMENT, reprinted from *The Sea and the Jungle*, by H. M. Tomlinson, by permission of Harper & Brothers: CALIBAN IN THE COAL MINES, from *Challenge*, by Louis Untermeyer, copyright, 1914, by Harcourt, Brace and Company, Inc.: PRAYER, reprinted from *Selected Poems and Parodies of Louis Untermeyer*, by permission of Harcourt, Brace and Company, Inc. Copyright, 1914: (THE FOOT-PATH TO PEACE, THESE ARE THE GIFTS I ASK, and TIME IS, by Henry van Dyke, originally published by Charles Scribner's Sons.): AMERICA FOR ME, from *The Poems of Henry van Dyke*, and PEACE, from *The Builders and Other Poems*, by Henry van Dyke, reprinted by permission of Charles Scribner's Sons: THE STORY OF THE OTHER WISE MAN, by Henry van Dyke, published by Harper & Brothers. Copyright, 1895, by Harper & Brothers. Copyright, 1923, by Henry van Dyke: Quotation by Hendrik Willem van Loon, reprinted by permission: ISLANDERS, by Harold Vinal, reprinted by permission of the author and *The Christian Science Monitor*: Quotation from *Up from Slavery*, by Booker T. Washington, copyright 1900, 1901, reprinted by permission of Doubleday & Company, Inc.: WHAT IS A MAN PROFITED?, by William Allen White, reprinted from *The Emporia Gazette* by permission: ALL MEN ARE PIONEERS and THIS MOUNTAIN IS MY PROPERTY ALONE, from *Landscape with Figures*, by Lionel Wiggam. Copyright 1936 by Lionel Wiggam. By permission of The Viking Press, Inc., New York: From THE BRIDGE OF SAN LUIS REY, by Thornton Wilder, reprinted by permission of Albert & Charles Boni, Inc.: Quotation from *The New Freedom*, by Woodrow Wilson, copyright 1913 by Doubleday & Company, Inc.: AMERICAN LANDSCAPE, from *Of Time and the River*, by Thomas Wolfe, reprinted by permission of Charles Scribner's Sons: THE HAPPY MAN, from *How To Be Happy Though Human*, by W. Beran Wolfe. Copyright 1931 by W. Beran Wolfe and reprinted by permission of Rinehart & Company, Inc., publishers: VELVET SHOES, reprinted from *Collected Poems*, by Elinor Wylie, by permission of Alfred A. Knopf, Inc. Copyright, 1921: DOWN BY THE SALLEY GARDENS, from *Later Poems*, by William Butler Yeats, reprinted by permission of The Macmillan Company, publishers: TAWNY LIONESS, from *Flowering Dusk*, by Ella Young, reprinted by permission of Longmans, Green and Co.

PERMISSIONS TO REPRINT other selections have been obtained from the following authors and agents: Mildred Bowers Armstrong, Karle Wilson Baker, Will Beebe, Elizabeth Coatsworth, Fanny Stearns Davis, Glenn Ward Dresbach, Frances M. Frost, Hildegarde Hawthorne, Helen Hoyt, Mary West Jorgensen, Anthony Lane, Noel Lane, Edgar Lee Masters, Robert A. Millikan, Marco Morrow, Bernard Raymund, Kenneth Allan Robinson, Carl Sandburg, T. V. Smith, Vincent Starrett, Charles Hanson Towne, Nancy Byrd Turner, Henry Wellington Wack, Dixie Willson, Roger Wray, Ella Young, The Argus Book Shop, Brandt & Brandt, Curtis Brown, Ltd., Sally Harrison, and A. P. Watt & Son.

THE EDITOR WISHES TO THANK the many publishers, authors' agents, and authors who have allowed these selections to be reprinted in this book. Great pains have been taken to obtain permission from the owners to reprint material which is in copyright. Any errors that may possibly have been made are unintentional and will gladly be corrected in future printings if notification is sent to Consolidated Book Publishers.

The editor is deeply grateful for the help she has received from her assistant editors: Mathilda Schirmer, Audrey Morris, Betty Stone, Jane McHenry, George Eaton, and Arthur Cummings. For the typographical design of the book she also wishes to express her thanks to Edward Fitzgerald, and for other helpful suggestions she thanks Henriette Mertz, Cara Verson, Barbara Clyne, Katherine Frost, Mabel B. Gorder, Mary West Jorgensen, Florence Penfold, Herbert H. Hewitt, and Rollo Fogarty.